Phil Edmonston
LEMON-AID
2007
SUVs, VANS, and TRUCKS

Copyright © 2006 Les Editions Edmonston

Published in Canada by Fitzhenry and Whiteside Limited, 195 Allstate Parkway, Markham, Ontario L3R 4T8

www.fitzhenry.ca godwit@fitzhenry.ca

1 3 5 7 9 10 8 6 4 2

Library and Archives Canada has catalogued this publication as follows:

Edmonston, Louis-Philippe, 1944-
Lemon-aid SUVs, vans and trucks / Phil Edmonston.

Annual.
2002-
Imprint varies.
Formed by the union of: Lemon-aid new 4x4s, vans and trucks, ISSN 1485-5682
and Lemon-aid used 4x4s, vans and trucks, ISSN 1487-041X.
ISSN 1701-1884
ISBN-13: 978-1-55455-014-2 (2007 edition)
ISBN-10: 1-55455-014-9 (2007 edition)

1. Sport utility vehicles—Purchasing—Periodicals. 2. Vans—Purchasing—
Periodicals. 3. Trucks—Purchasing—Periodicals. I. Title.

TL162.E33955   629.223'029'6   C2001-904274-4

Fitzhenry & Whiteside acknowledges with thanks the Canada Council for the Arts, and the Ontario Arts Council for their support of our publishing program. We acknowledge the financial support of the Government of Canada through the Book Publishing Industry Development Program (BPIDP) for our publishing activities.

Printed in Canada by Webcom
Packaged by Colborne Communications, Toronto
Publications manager: Greg Ioannou
Project co-ordinator: Andrea Battiston
Layout and production: Rachel Rosen
Editing: Heather Ball, Andrea Battiston, Andrea Douglas,
Greg Ioannou, Leslie Mutic
Illustrations: Rachel Rosen
Design: Ingrid Paulson

CONTENTS

Part Four

VEHICLE RATINGS: THE GOOD, THE BAD, AND THE UGLY 212

Appendix I

Appendix II

Appendix III

LEMON-PROOFING BEFORE YOU BUY.......... 641

Appendix IV

LEGAL TOOLS: FORD AND GM ENGINE GASKETS 647

KEY DOCUMENTS

Lemon-Aid is a feisty owner's manual that has no equal anywhere. We don't want you stuck with a lemon, or to wind up paying for repairs that are the automaker's fault and are covered by secret "goodwill" warranties. That's why we are the only book that includes many hard-to-find, confidential, and little-known documents that automakers don't want you to see.

In short, we know you can't win what you can't prove.

The following charts, documents, and service bulletins are included in this index so that you can stand your ground and be treated fairly. Photocopy and circulate whichever document will prove helpful in your dealings with automakers, dealers, service managers, insurance companies, or government agencies. Remember, most of the hundreds of summarized service bulletins outline repairs or replacements that should be done for free.

Part Two   ## USED, NOT ABUSED

Part Three   ## FIGHTING BACK!

Part Four   ## VEHICLE RATINGS: THE GOOD, THE BAD, AND THE UGLY

Minivans and Vans

Pickup Trucks

Appendix IV

Introduction

DOING MORE WITH LESS

Moonshine Motoring: A Blow to Shell and Seagrams?

An upstart Tennessee business is marketing stills that can be set up as private distilleries making ethanol—190-proof grain alcohol—out of fermented starchy crops such as corn, apples or sugar cane. The company claims the still's output can reduce fuel costs by nearly a third from the pump price of gasoline.

Buyers of stills need a federal permit to make ethanol on private property. In what amounts to an honor system, they are to add a poison to their homemade alcohol so it isn't "white lightning."

ASSOCIATED PRESS
MAY 17, 2006

Modest Changes on the Way

Despite what we have read in the media, don't expect major changes in the auto industry for at least another decade. For example, ethanol will take at least 15 years to work its way into the fuel distribution system, as was the case with unleaded gas decades ago. Furthermore, some things are likely to change very little, or change for the worse: Fuel prices will eventually climb higher, with "unreal" fuel economy figures being the norm; many SUVs, trucks, and minivans will be downsized—with unrealistic upscale prices; poor-quality Detroit products will still be a hard sell; and women will continue to be treated as dummies when they enter many automobile showrooms.

In these days of political and corporate scams and skullduggery, *Lemon-Aid* stands out as an honest guide that can't be bought or intimidated. Since we don't accept ads, we're free to tell the truth—as we've been doing for more than 35 years. Sure, we're a pain in the backsides of automakers and dealers alike, but the facts we unearth can save you big bucks in buying and servicing costs.

And we don't play favourites, as Honda and Nissan will confirm: Three decades ago, their $5-million lawsuit against *Lemon-Aid* was unsuccessful. Even venerable Toyota has been on the receiving end of our criticism when we said the company's Access Toyota pricing scheme was price-fixing, warned consumers that many Toyota and Lexus engines had sludge problems and that the 2004 revised Sienna and Camry were seriously glitch-prone, and called for an engineering fix for dangerous engine and transmission hesitation when accelerating.

All of the above-mentioned firms have used many of *Lemon-Aid*'s laments to improve their product lineup and better serve their customers.

It's fair to say that the *Lemon-Aid* series has also enraged some automakers with its tough-customer buying tips (singling out Ford's Explorer as a "roll-me-over-in-the-clover" SUV), pro-consumer jurisprudence (such as DaimlerChrysler Canada's recent Supreme Court drubbing over its fire-prone Ram), and realistic car, truck, SUV, minivan, and van ratings for both new and used vehicles.

Lemon-Aid SUVs, Vans, and Trucks 2007 is different from the other books in the series: It's a comprehensive consumer guide that rates both new *and* used SUVs, vans, and trucks sold during the past three decades. It has recently been restyled to include more data on 1997–2007 models and to make information more accessible and easier to read. Readers will also find the book longer, larger, and cheaper than it used to be. It has more content to help you decide whether you should buy, sell, or hold your present vehicle; determine which makes are luxury lemons; find vehicles that are both fuel-efficient *and* reliable; and get your money back when things go wrong.

We give you reliability information early. To this end, we have expanded our regional field reports to expose "secret" warranties and sales and service scams, list "real" prices, and publicize little-known pro-consumer court decisions rendered from the small claims court level up to the Supreme Court of Canada.

Of course, all of this data means *Lemon-Aid* has grown to over 650 pages, with more current information, such as:

- How to get dealer bids by fax or email (including a sample letter)
- How to use the dealer markup to trim your offer for each model
- Which fuel economy ratings are pure fiction
- Which safety features may actually be unsafe, and why
- Which 2006 model year vehicles may be better buys than the 2007 models
- Why 2007 is not the time to buy a diesel model
- Why some optional features are a waste of money
- Why every vehicle has a legal guarantee, even if sold "as is"
- How to write a dealer/automaker complaint letter that works

The 2007 edition tackles new issues, including:

- The best and worst diesel engines, and key confidential service bulletins, like the three that follow, exposing GM diesel-engine factory goofs covered by secret warranties:

GM SPECIAL POLICY—INJECTORS—REPLACE

BULLETIN NO.: 04039   **DATE: MAY 26, 2004**

2001–2002 Chevrolet Silverado
2001–2002 GMC Sierra
Equipped with 6.6L Duramax Diesel (RPO LB7 – VIN Code 1) Engine

CONDITION: Some customers of 2001–02 model year Chevrolet Silverado and GMC Sierra vehicles, equipped with a 6.6L Duramax Diesel (RPO LB7 – VIN Code 1) engine, may experience vehicle service engine soon (SES) light illumination, low engine power, hard start, and/or fuel in crankcase, requiring injector replacement, as a result of high fuel return rates due to fuel injector body cracks or ball seat erosion.

SPECIAL POLICY ADJUSTMENT: This special policy covers the condition described above for a period of 7 years or 200,000 miles (320,000 km), whichever occurs first, from the date the vehicle was originally placed in service, regardless of ownership. The repairs will be made at no charge to the customer.

GM DIESEL ENGINE—COOLANT LOSS WITH NO VISIBLE LEAKS

BULLETIN NO.: 03-06-02-005B

DATE: NOVEMBER 18, 2004

ENGINE COOLANT LOSS WITH NO VISIBLE LEAKS (RESEAL INJECTOR SLEEVE)

2001–2004 Chevrolet Silverado; GMC Sierra

2003–2004 Chevrolet and GMC C4500/5500 Models with 6.6L Diesel Engine

CONDITION: Some owners may comment on engine coolant loss with no visible leaks. Excessive white smoke or a coolant type odor coming from the exhaust pipe, along with low coolant levels, may indicate coolant in the combustion chamber.

GM SPECIAL POLICY ADJUSTMENT—ELECTRONIC DIESEL FUEL INJECTION PUMP FAILURE— REPAIR/REPLACE

BULLETIN NO.: 00064F

DATE: SEPTEMBER 2004

1994–2002 Chevrolet and GMC C/K, G and P model trucks; and 1997–98 B7 school bus chassis, equipped with a 6.5L diesel engine

CONDITION: Some customers of 1994–2002 Chevrolet and GMC C/K, G, and P model trucks; and 1997–98 B7 school bus chassis, equipped with a 6.5 liter diesel engine (RPO L49 – VIN Code P; RPO L56 – VIN Code S; or RPO L55 – VIN Code F), may experience a failure of the electronic diesel fuel injection pump.

SPECIAL POLICY ADJUSTMENT: This special policy covers the condition described above for a period of eleven (11) years or 120,000 miles (193,000 km), whichever occurs first, from the date the vehicle was originally placed in service, regardless of ownership. Damage from poor quality or incorrect grade diesel fuel, and gasoline or water contamination, is not covered under the terms of the 6.5L diesel warranty or this Special Policy.

GM's engine problems may end up bankrupting the company.

- Troubleshooting rotten-egg exhaust odours and poor fuel economy
- New secret warranties and bulletins covering Ford and GM engine manifold and tranny failures
- Dodge Dakota and Durango, GM Silverado and Sierra, Mazda MPV, Nissan Quest, Lexus SUV, and Toyota Sienna quality downgrades
- Canadian court decisions allowing claimants to receive up to $25,000 in punitive damages from automakers

The 2007 model year will see many new models introduced and, consequently, many new claims made by automakers. Use *Lemon-Aid SUVs, Vans, and Trucks 2007* to separate the steak from the sizzle.

Phil Edmonston
September 2006

Part One
DEALS ON WHEELS

A Quick Fix for the Gas Addicts

The sooner General Motors gets taken over by Toyota, the better off our country will be.... First GM offers a gasoline subsidy so more Americans can get hooked on nine-mile-per-gallon [26 L/100 km] Hummers, and then it offers a discount to the soldiers who have to protect the oil lines to keep GM's gas guzzlers guzzling. Here's a rule of thumb: The more Hummers we have on the road in America, the more military Humvees we will need in the Middle East.

You want to do something patriotic, GM, Ford and Daimler-Chrysler? Why don't you stop using your diminishing pools of cash to buy votes so Congress will never impose improved mileage standards? That kind of strategy is why Toyota today is worth $198.9 billion and GM $15.8 billion. GM is worth just slightly more than Harley-Davidson, the motorcycle company ($13.6 billion)...

THOMAS L. FRIEDMAN
THE NEW YORK TIMES
MAY 31, 2006

Why a New SUV, Truck, or Van?

Even though you'll save much more money buying used (see Part Two), buying new isn't a bad idea if you can put off your purchase until the late winter or early spring of 2007, keep your new vehicle 8–10 years to amortize depreciation, and resist the lure of problem-prone 2007 diesel powerplants. This is especially true if you want performance or safety features not found with earlier models. Although you'll likely spend more than you expect for a new truck, sport-utility, or van, you won't lose much money through depreciation, unless you go for the largest models—and even they will be carrying price tags already cut by about 20 percent.

Downsized

Canadians are reacting to high fuel and finance charges by downsizing their purchases. In fact, auto industry consultant Dennis DesRosiers points out that 9 of the 10 bestselling cars and 3 of the 10 bestselling light trucks are compacts or subcompacts. He feels the smaller SUVs and trucks are "cannibalizing" the larger versions of the same vehicles:

> Compact sport-utility sales are up 23.0 percent on the month of May 2006 and 23.1 percent on the year, while the most likely competitive segment (intermediate sport-utility) is down 26.2 percent on the month and 29.7 percent on the year through May. This is not a coincidence. It is obvious that the compact SUV is cannibalizing intermediate SUVs....

> Well over half the market is now entry-level vehicles. Large sport utilities now represent only 1 percent of the market, although luxury sport utilities have grown to about 3 percent of the market. Still, together the least fuel-efficient vehicles only account for about 4 percent of the market. To put this in perspective, in the U.S. they still account for about 15 percent of the market.

The phenomenal popularity of downsized models—such as the Jeep Liberty, Mazda5, Honda CR-V, Nissan X-Trail, Hyundai Tucson, and Toyota RAV4 and Tacoma—is due to a number of factors. They can do almost everything that their big brothers are capable of doing; they are more practical, safer, more fuel efficient, and more reliable than larger versions; and rebates or discounts more than compensate for increased fuel, insurance, and financing costs. Plus, depreciation is practically non-existent—good news for purchasers of new models. Patient used-vehicle buyers, however, can get a substantial depreciation payoff by getting a 4- or 5-year-old model that hasn't changed much over the years.

SUVs, trucks, and vans can easily be converted to suit anyone's needs or tastes. Most owners also feel safer driving them, especially since they now offer many standard safety features, such as multiple airbags, electronic stability-control, and adjustable pedals. And improved crashworthiness, larger passenger- and cargo-carrying capacities, extra weight, all-wheel-drive (AWD) capability, and better-than-average forward and rear visibility further enhance driver confidence.

The cheaper, hard-riding, truck-based SUVs, vans, and AWD–equipped models will generally use more fuel than vehicles set on an extended car platform; however, they are said to offer better side-impact protection and are more durable and easier to repair. Still, if you want to save fuel, maximize on-road performance, and have a comfortable ride, you should consider a small model built on a car platform, without the AWD option.

2007 Prices: Excessive but Temporary

Approximately 1.3 million Canadians buy a new car or truck in a given year, excluding fleet sales, and this year consumers are truly in the driver's seat. It's been a brutal sales year for Detroit automakers; they've suffered a sharp decline in sales and profits caused by high fuel prices, Asian competition, and the higher cost of borrowing. And Detroit Big Three auto sales are getting worse, not better.

Full-sized truck sales have slowed to a crawl as inventory piles up on dealers' lots and finance costs eat into profits. Hurting more than most, DaimlerChrysler set off a late summer price war in order to clear out its 125-day supply of full-sized Ram pickups (a 60-day supply is considered ideal). Chrysler's offering of employee-level pricing to any car buyer, plus money-back guarantees, launched late last summer, forced both Ford and GM to match the lower prices through their own sales incentives and rebates. Ford has a 104-day supply of its F-Series, and General Motors is loaded with a 90-day supply of Silverados and Sierras. By mid-winter, all three automakers will be in a bruising battle waged with zero percent financing and unbelievable discounting that will drop prices by $10,000 or more. Nissan, overstocked with 100 days' worth of Titans, will likely follow suit.

GM's reworking of the 2007 Escalade, Tahoe (above), and Yukon has forced them to offer sizeable rebates on their unsold 2006 versions. Leftover 2006 GM Silverados and Sierras, Nissan Titans, and Toyota Tundras will likely be similarly discounted after the new year.

So here's how you take advantage of this price war: If you *must* buy a new sport-utility, truck, or van this year, seriously consider buying a discounted 2006 model, particularly if the 2007 version has been upgraded and you want to avoid the inflated prices and first-year glitches that almost always accompany model improvements. Be wary of 2007 reworked diesel engines. They will require much more maintenance and will be especially failure-prone because both the fuel formulation and fuel systems will be radically changed. Finally, both GM and Toyota will launch reworked 2007 full-sized pickups, which will dramatically lower the cost of the carried-over 2006 models.

REBATE SUMMARY FOR 2006 MODELS

MODEL	REBATE
DaimlerChrysler	
Chrysler Pacifica, Town & Country	$3,000
Chrysler PT Cruiser	$2,500
Dodge Caravan, Durango, Grand Caravan, Ram 1500 (excluding Mega Cab)	$3,000–$5,000
Dodge Dakota, Ram 1500 Mega Cab, Ram 2500/3500 (excluding Mega Cab)	$2,500
Dodge Ram 2500/3500 Mega Cab	$2,500
Jeep Grand Cherokee, Liberty (excluding diesel)	$2,500
Jeep Liberty diesel	$1,500
Jeep Commander	$1,000
Jeep Wrangler	$500
Ford	
Expedition	$4,000
Freestar	$3,000
F-Series	$2,500
Explorer, Escape, Ranger	$2,000
E-Series Van	$1,000
Lincoln LS, Mark LT	$3,000
Lincoln Navigator	$2,500
General Motors	
Buick Terraza, Rainier, Rendezvous	$1,000
Cadillac Escalade ESV, EXT	$6,000
Chevrolet Suburban, Tahoe	$5,500
Chevrolet Avalanche	$4,000
Chevrolet Silverado 1500	$2,500
Chevrolet Silverado 2500/3500 (excluding LBZ)	$1,500
Chevrolet Uplander, Colorado, TrailBlazer	$1,000
GMC Yukon (all)	$5,500
GMC Sierra 1500	$2,500
GMC Canyon, Envoy, Yukon Denali (all)	$1,000
GMC Savana, Sierra 2500/3500	$500
Pontiac Montana	$1,000
Honda	
Ridgeline	$1,000
Hyundai	
Santa Fe, Tucson	$500

MODEL	REBATE
Mazda	
MPV	$1,500
Mitsubishi	
Montero, Raider	$1,500–$3,000
Nissan	
Titan	$2,500–$3,000
Armada	$2,000
Maxima, Quest	$1,500
Frontier	$1,000
Xterra, Pathfinder	$500
Suzuki	
XL-7	$750
Grand Vitara	$500

Many of the above rebates can be combined with dealer incentive programs that can cut thousands of dollars more off the selling price. Incidentally, the rebate leader as of July 2006 is the 2006 Mercedes' S-Class with its $7,000 to $12,000 rebate.

Automakers say that they intend to raise prices by only a moderate 2 percent on most 2007 model year vehicles. What you are not told, however, is that Canadian starting prices have been inflated on many popular makes by over $10,000 more than what currency differences should allow. This scam is particularly evident with most of the crossover models found in the chart on page pages 11–12.

The 2006 Torrent SUV is way overpriced, but its price will likely be substantially lowered through discounts and zero percent financing. Its 185-hp engine can't compete with Toyota's all-new RAV4, with 268 hp and three rows of seats; Ford's Escape, with up to 200 hp and a hybrid powertrain; Jeep's Liberty, with classic four-wheel drive capability and an optional diesel engine (dropped for 2007); and Hyundai's Santa Fe and Tucson, two top-quality SUVs offered with comprehensive warranties and a bevy of airbags.

"Crossover" Price-Gouging

Detroit's latest marketing ploy is to sell feature-laden tall-wagon versions of existing models as "crossovers"—vehicles that are built off of a car platform and combine the attributes of more than one vehicle category. For example, the PT Cruiser is classified as a truck for emissions purposes, but it's actually a wagon model of the Dodge Neon.

As smaller SUVs, trucks, and vans gain added features usually seen in cars, many crossovers are morphing into vans sans the long hood (think of the Mazda5 or the long-gone Nissan Axxess), rather than becoming a brand new category of vehicle. Usually, crossovers provide a more comfortable ride, better handling, and higher fuel economy than the truck-based versions they replace. Audi, Ford, Jeep, and Lincoln are all launching new car-based sport-utilities for 2007.

Automakers are also overcharging on the suggested retail prices of their vehicles. According to DesRosiers automotive consultants, a typical new vehicle now costs 17 percent more in Canada than in the United States because automakers have not adjusted their prices to reflect the Canadian dollar's new-found strength.

Although DesRosiers says the difference represents only $5,842 (CDN) for a typical vehicle, a comparison of American and Canadian retail prices shows clearly that Canadians may pay tens of thousands of dollars more than Americans do for the same vehicle (and *Lemon-Aid* readers agree).

2006–07 "CROSSOVER" MODELS (BASE PRICES)

MODEL	U.S.	CANADIAN
SUVs		
2007 Acura MDX	$37,125	$51,600
2007 Audi Q7	$49,900	$69,600
2007 BMW X3	$36,800	$44,900
2006 Ford Escape	$19,165	$23,002
2006 Ford Escape Hybrid	$25,600	$33,599
2007 GM Buick Rendezvous	$24,780	$28,610
2006 GM Cadillac SRX	$36,270	$48,775
2006 GM Chevrolet Equinox	$21,400	$25,375
2007 GM Pontiac Torrent	$21,400	$26,585
2006 Honda CR-V	$20,395	$29,300
2006 Honda Element	$17,750	$24,200
2006 Honda Pilot	$26,995	$39,400
2006 Infiniti FX35	$37,800	$54,500
2006 Infiniti FX45	$49,750	$61,100

MODEL	U.S.	CANADIAN
SUVs (continued)		
2006 Lexus RX 330	$36,370	$50,500
2007 Lexus RX 350	$37,400	$51,550
2006 Lexus RX 400h	$44,660	$62,200
2007 Mazda CX-7	$23,750	$31,995
2006 Mazda Tribute	$20,115	$24,595
2006 Mitsubishi Endeavor	$26,599	$34,998
2006 Mitsubishi Outlander	$18,499	$23,998
2006 Nissan Murano	$27,600	$38,798
2006 Porsche Cayenne	$42,200	$60,100
2007 Saturn Vue	$17,370	$22,995
2006 Subaru B9 Tribeca	$30,695	$41,995
2006 Toyota Highlander	$24,530	$37,855
2006 Toyota Highlander Hybrid	$33,030	$44,205
2006 Toyota RAV4	$20,300	$28,700
2006 Volkswagen Touareg	$37,410	$50,790
2006 Volvo XC90	$36,075	$49,995
Trucks		
2007 GM Cadillac Escalade EXT	$53,335	$71,800
2006 GM Chevrolet Avalanche 1500	$33,910	$40,480
2006 GM Hummer H2 SUT	$53,035	$67,085
2006 Subaru Baja	$22,495	$29,995
Wagons and Vans		
2006 Chrysler Pacifica	$25,415	$37,050
2006 Ford Freestyle	$25,545	$33,499
2006 Mazda5	$17,435	$19,995
2006 Mercedes-Benz R-Class	$48,000	$64,400
2006 Subaru Forester	$21,795	$27,995
2006 Subaru Impreza	$18,295	$23,495
2006 Subaru Outback	$24,795	$32,995
2006 Volvo XC70	$36,135	$47,121

Cut the dealer's price to somewhere between the above American and Canadian figures, minus whatever rebates and dealer sales incentives may apply. Be wary of dealers trying to "option-pack" or make backdoor profits from high delivery and administration fees.

Focus on Real Costs (and Don't Go Alone)

There are over 19 million vehicles on Canada's roads, and about 4,000 dealerships wanting to sell you a new one—at almost $32,000 for the average vehicle, and lots more for fully equipped sport-utilities, trucks, and vans. This means that you have to figure out a realistic budget for a vehicle that suits your needs—spending no more than 20 percent of your take-home pay on auto payments. So, if you're bringing home $2,000 a month in paycheques, no more than $400 of it should go toward car payments.

According to the Canadian Automobile Association (CAA), the average household owns two vehicles, which are each driven about 20,000 km annually. Based on an average mileage of 18,000 kilometres, a 2005 Chevrolet Z24 will cost 2.48 cents per kilometre for maintenance and $1,777 for insurance. A 2005 Chrysler Caravan will cost an average of 2.87 cents per kilometre and $1,652 for insurance. The CAA also estimates in its 2005 "Driving Costs" study (available at *www.caa.ca/PDF/3708-EN-2005.pdf*) that the per-kilometre cost of driving a 2005 Caravan minivan 24,000 kilometres would be 49.2 cents, or $11,808 per year. Amazingly, a 2005 Chevrolet Cavalier Z24 compact wouldn't offer that much savings, costing 45.3 cents/km, or $10,872 for the year. Remember, these estimates were made in December 2004, before fuel prices were increased by almost 30 percent, so driving costs will likely be a bit more today.

Keep in mind that it's practically impossible to buy a bare-bones SUV, truck, or van, because automakers cram them with costly, non-essential performance and convenience features in order to maximize their profits. Nevertheless, you can pass on money-wasting gadgets like electronic navigation and sophisticated entertainment systems with little impact on safety or convenience.

Before paying big bucks, you should know what your real needs are and how much you can afford to spend. Don't confuse *needs* with *style*, or *trendy* with *essential*. Visiting the showroom with your spouse or a level-headed relative or friend will help you steer a course through all the non-essential options you'll be offered.

Automakers market sport-utilities and pickups to appeal to the macho crowd (look at the ads) by emphasizing luxury, power, adventure, and ruggedness. This is quite a marketing coup when you consider that *Popular Mechanics* estimates that 95 percent of all sport-utilities are driven on paved roads 95 percent of the time—that is, they aren't purchased for off-road use—and that *Consumer Reports* doesn't consider sport-utilities all that rugged or dependable, anyway.

Consider All the Choices

Determine how much money you can spend and then decide which vehicles in that price range interest you. Have several models in mind so that the overpriced one won't tempt you. As your benchmarks, use the ratings, alternative models, estimated purchase-cost, and residual value figures shown in Part Four of this guide. Remember, logic and prudence are the first casualties of showroom hype, so carefully consider your actual requirements and how much you can budget to meet them before comparing models and prices at a dealership. Write down your first, second, and third choices relative to each model and list the equipment offered. Browse automakers' websites and *www.carcostcanada.com* for manufacturers' suggested retail prices (MSRP), pre-delivery and freight fees, package discounts, promotions, and the most popular options.

Look for special low prices that may only apply to Internet-generated referrals, or $500–$1,000 rebates given to recent school graduates. Be leery of these graduate rebates, however. Sometimes, they're used as bait to sell overpriced vehicles to new drivers, as the following British Columbia *Lemon-Aid* reader recounts:

> I live in Nanaimo BC. I am a recent grad of the University of Victoria.
>
> In early March I began looking for another car for myself. I called all of the Pontiac dealers in Nanaimo and Duncan to get information about some used/newer Sunfires. I was given similar prices from everyone and all of them suggested that as a new grad I should buy a new car and take part in GM Canada's New Grad program. This entitled me to $1,000 off the purchase price.

I decided on a new (2005) 2-door Sunfire from the Nanaimo Pontiac lot. The people there were quite helpful. However, the salesman went to check on whether the discount was before or after taxes, when he returned he said they no longer offered the program.

He gave me the number for the GM help/info line. The women I spoke to was unhelpful and almost rude. They offered to cover the first payment if I wanted to lease or finance the car. The catch: The purchase price went up $5,000.

Hearing one thing from multiple salespeople, the GM website, and a lot of the literature on the new vehicles and then another thing when you actually decide to buy a car is definitely getting close to fraudulent practices.

Once you get a good idea of the price variations, use your fax machine or PC at home or work to make offers and get the dealers bidding against each other (see pages 95–96). Then, to be assured of getting a sales agent's complete attention, call the lowest-bidding dealership and ask for an appointment. Take along the downloaded info from the automaker's website to avoid arguments.

You Can Get More for Less

Sure, sometimes a cheaper twin will fill the bill. Twins are those nameplates made by different auto manufacturers, or different divisions of the same company, that are virtually identical in body design and mechanical components. Examples are GM's Escalade, Tahoe, and Yukon SUVs; Ford's Escape and Mazda's Tribute pickups; or Chrysler's Caravan and Voyager minivans.

But this often works in reverse, as well, where you frequently get less when paying more. For example, a perfectly acceptable 2003 Grand Caravan that originally listed for $29,300 is now worth about $13,000. An upscale 2003 Chrysler Town & Country that performs similarly to the Grand Caravan, with just a few additional gizmos, first sold for $42,700 and is now worth about $18,000. Where once $13,400 separated the two minivans, the price difference is now only $5,000—and you can expect the gap to close to almost nil over the next few years. Did the little extras really justify the Town & Country's higher price? Obviously, the market-place thinks not.

American manufacturers are a wily bunch. While beating their chests and shouting about the need to "Buy American!" they have joined Asian automakers in co-ventures where they know they can't compete on their own. This has resulted in models whose parentage is impossible to nail down but that incorporate a high degree of quality control. Suzuki built a fairly reliable Chevrolet Tracker (formerly known as the Geo) 4×4 in Ontario, and Ford and Mazda churn out identical Rangers and B Series pickups in the United States, though for some strange reason the Tribute has posted better quality ratings than the Escape.

Chrysler's Town & Country isn't worth the $13,000 premium. Choose the Grand Caravan, instead.

Sometimes choosing a higher trim line that packages many options as standard features will cost you less when you take all the standard features into account. It's hard to compare these bundled prices with the manufacturer's base price and added options, though. All of the separate prices are inflated and must be negotiated downward individually, while fully equipped vehicles don't allow for options to be deleted or priced separately. Furthermore, many of the bundled options are superfluous, and you probably wouldn't have chosen them to begin with.

There are other ways to reduce the selling price. Minivans, for example, often come in two versions: a base commercial, or cargo, version and a more luxurious model for private use. The commercial version doesn't have as many bells and whistles, but it's more likely to be in stock and will probably cost much less. And if you're planning to convert it, there's a wide choice of independent customizers that will likely do a better—and less expensive—job than the dealer. Of course, you will want a written guarantee from the dealer or customizer, or sometimes both, that no changes will invalidate the manufacturer's warranty. Also, look on the lot for a low-mileage (less than 5,000 km) current-year demonstrator that is carried over unchanged as a 2007 version. You will get an end-of-model-year rebate, a lower price for the extra mileage, and sundry other sales incentives that apply. Remember, if the vehicle has been registered to another company or individual, it is *not* a demo and should be considered used and be discounted accordingly (by at least 25 percent). You will also want to carry out a CarProof search and have a complete printout of the vehicle's service history.

Look Before You Lease

Why Leasing May Cost More

There are many reasons why leasing is a bad idea. It's often touted as an alternative used to make high-cost vehicles more affordable, but for most people, it's really more expensive than buying outright. Lessees usually pay the full MSRP on a vehicle loaded with costly options, plus hidden fees and interest charges that wouldn't be included if the vehicle were purchased, instead of leased. Researchers have found that some fully loaded entry-level cars *leased* with high interest rates and deceptive "special fees" could cost more than what some luxury models would cost to *buy*. A useful website that takes the mystery out of leasing is at *www.federalreserve.gov/pubs/leasing* (*Keys to Vehicle Leasing*), run by the U.S. Federal Reserve Board. It goes into incredible detail, comparing leasing versus buying, and has a handy dictionary of the terms you're most likely to encounter.

Decoding Leasing Ads

Take a close look at the small print found in most leasing ads. Pay particular attention to words relating to the model year, condition of the vehicle (demonstration or used), equipment, warranty, interest rate, buy-back amount, down payment, security payment, monthly payment, transportation and preparation charges, administration fees ("acquisition" and "disposal" fees), insurance premiums, number of free kilometres, and excess kilometre charges.

Leased or Fleeced?

Leasing in Canada makes up almost 35 percent of all motor vehicle sales transactions because of rising interest rates and prices. This has led to 40-month leases being stretched to 60 months (Hyundai, Kia, and Toyota) and a proliferation of entry-level models that are now being leased in addition to the traditional "luxe" toys. Nevertheless, insiders say that almost 95 percent of all vehicles costing $60,000 or more are leased vehicles.

Experts agree: If you must lease, keep your costs to a minimum by leasing for the shortest time possible, by assuming the unexpired portion of an existing lease (see "Leasebusters," later in this section), and by making sure that the lease is close-ended (meaning that you walk away from the vehicle when the lease period ends)—an option used by 75 percent of lessees, according to the CAA.

Leasing does have a few advantages, though. First, it saves some of your capital, which you can invest to get a return greater than the leasing interest charges. Second, if you are taking a chance on a new model that hasn't been proven, you know that yours can be dumped at the dealer when the lease expires. But that raises more questions: What are you doing choosing such a risky venture in the first place? Will you have the patience to wait in the service bay while your luxury lemon is being repaired for the umpteenth time? Finally, do you want to be saddled with a 4-year contract where the dealer is the judge and jury as to whether you go carless or not?

 Instead of leasing, consider purchasing used. Look for a 3- to 5-year-old off-lease vehicle with 60,000–100,000 km on the clock and some of the original warranty left. Such a vehicle will be just as reliable for less than half the cost of one bought new or leased. Parts will be easier to find, independent servicing should be a breeze, insurance premiums will come down from the stratosphere, and your financial risk will be lessened considerably if you end up with a lemon.

On both new and used purchases, be wary of unjustified hidden costs, like a $495 "administrative" or "disposal" fee, an "acquisition" charge, or boosted transport and freight costs that can collectively add several thousand dollars to the retail price. Also, look at the lease transfer fee charged by the leasing company or dealer or both. This can vary considerably. For example, Ford Credit, GMAC Financial Services, and BMW Financial Services charge $175, $450, and $1,500, respectively. Ford and BMW dealers can also impose a transfer fee.

Getting Out of a Lease

Not an easy thing to do, and you may wind up paying $3,000 to $8,000 in cancellation fees.

The last thing you want to do is stop your payments: The dealer can easily sue you for the remaining money owed, and you will have to pay the legal fees for both sides. You won't be able to prove the vehicle was defective or unreliable because it would have been seized after the lease payments stopped. So, there you are without the vehicle to make your proof and on the receiving end of a costly lawsuit.

Lawyers advise three ways of breaking a lease. First, you can ask for free Canadian Motor Vehicle Arbitration Plan (CAMVAP) arbitration (see page 182). A second recourse, if there's a huge debt remaining, is to send a lawyer's letter cancelling the contract by putting the leasing agency and automaker on notice that the vehicle is unacceptable. This should lead to some negotiation. If this fails, inspect the vehicle, have it legally tendered back to the dealer, and then sue for what you owe plus inconvenience and assorted sundry expenses. You can use the small claims court on your own if the amount in litigation is less than the court's claim limit.

The third way is to legally transfer the lease using a firm like Leasebusters (*www. leasebusters.com*).

Leasebusters

Leasebusters is a Canadian company, affiliated with Car Cost Canada, that puts you in touch with people willing to take over your lease. Before listing your vehicle, the company will evaluate your present lease obligations online and free of charge to determine if a lease transfer is a wise idea.

Leasebusters has been in business for almost a decade and says about 80 percent of the leased vehicles they offer are disposed of within 60 days. For $295 plus GST ($240 in Western Canada and $205 in Newfoundland and the Maritimes),

Leasebusters provides a how-to-exit-a-car-lease guide, a large display ad, and an aggressive advertising campaign to shop your lease around.

Here is how the process works through Leasebusters: All lease transfers are credit-approved legal transfers sanctioned by the lessor. Typically, the original selling dealership must participate in the transfer because they are the selling agent for the lessor and, in many cases, own the leasing agency. The order of operations for the person accepting the lease is as follows:

- Go see the vehicle (inspect, test-drive, and discuss the vehicle with the original lessee).
- Make a deal-in-principal with the original lessee (including who pays for transfer fees, inspections, security deposits, cash incentives, and/or down payments). The deal is subject to credit approval.
- Complete a credit application and submit it to the original selling dealership.
- Wait for a credit decision after the dealership submits the deal to the lessor.
- Coordinate a delivery and signing date with the dealership and the original lessee upon receipt of credit approval.
- Pay the fee that will be charged for the transfer by either or both the dealer and the lessor.

Assuming an existing lease from another driver has many advantages and a few pitfalls. First, you get a vehicle that may be depreciated by almost 40 percent of its original value, and you don't have to pay for freight, pre-delivery inspection (PDI), air tax, gas tax, etc.—increasing your savings even more. And of course, you reduce PST and GST and get the balance of all factory warranties. Secondly, you can have a short-term fling with an exotic vehicle without risking a long-term commitment. This is especially advantageous when leasing imports and "luxe" toys where servicing and performance aren't up to the advertised hype.

On the downside, you may be asked to assume the obligation to pay for a lease that was a bad deal in the first place. However, if you can get the previous lessee to put additional money up front as compensation, the deal may be acceptable. Furthermore, servicing by the dealer will likely be obligatory in order to maintain the warranty, which will add to overall maintenance costs.

The leasing agency or dealer may claim extra money when the lease expires, because the vehicle might miss some original equipment or show "unreasonable" wear and tear (dings, paint problems, and excessive tire wear are the most common reasons for extra charges). Prevent this from happening by having the vehicle inspected prior to the lease takeover. Remember, some leasing companies will hold the original lessee liable for the lease until the end of the term; once a buyer is approved to take over the lease, the next lessee will be added on to the original contract, making the current lessee like a co-signer on the lease.

Deciding to Buy

Know Your Driving Needs

Our driving needs are influenced by where we live, our lifestyles, and our ages. In the city, a small wagon or hatchback is more practical and less expensive to drive than a minivan. However, if you're going to be doing a lot of highway driving, transporting small groups of people (especially kids), or loading up on accessories, a small minivan like the Mazda5 or a compact SUV such as a Honda CR-V could be a more logical choice for price, comfort, and reliability.

Don't let the recent surge in fuel prices stampede you into buying a vehicle unsuitable to your driving needs. Most families who travel less than 20,000 km per year should avoid the smallest and largest engines available with a given model. The smallest engines usually come with bare-bones models, where fuel economy trumps high-speed merging into traffic and driving comfort isn't important. Try a model with a small engine (not necessarily the smallest one) that offers economy, performance, and a comfortable ride and interior. Conversely, driving more than 20,000 km a year means spending a lot more time in a larger vehicle, requiring more reserve power for better performance and handling, and accommodating the energy drain from additional safety, comfort, and convenience accessories. If you spend lots of time on the road or plan to buy a minivan or van, you'll definitely need a large 6- or 8-cylinder powerplant to handle the air conditioning (AC) and other power-hungry accessories essential to your driving comfort and convenience. Fuel savings will be the last thing on your mind if you buy an underpowered truck or van, such as Honda's early Odyssey minivans and GM's Canyon or Colorado small pickups.

If you must have a larger engine but wish to protect the environment and your wallet, take advantage of the many bargains available on used SUVs and trucks with large engines. You score in three ways:

1. You'll save thousands of dollars, which will buy more fuel than you would ever conserve with an econobox.
2. You're recycling what's out there and not adding to the car population.
3. You'll save energy and resources because there will be one less vehicle built.

Pushrod or overhead cam?

Most North American automakers prefer overhead valve engines (or pushrods) because they cost about $800 less, provide better low-end power, use fewer parts, and weigh less than the overhead cam (multi-valve) engines favoured by automakers globally. Still, the more popular overhead cam configuration is used extensively by Japanese manufacturers because it offers more power at higher rpm and uses variable valve timing for a better torque range, smoother idling, increased fuel economy, and cleaner emissions.

GM's popular Silverado/Sierra full-sized trucks use pushrod V8s, while Ford's F-150 pickups sport overhead cam V8s. Dodge has it both ways: Its Ram pickup comes with an overhead cam V8 as well as an optional 5.7L Hemi pushrod V8.

From a quality and performance perspective, cheaper pushrods are low-tech and outdated. Recent versions haven't been particularly reliable, and maintenance costs are about the same as with multi-valve engines.

Be especially wary of the towing-capability claims bandied about by automakers. They routinely exaggerate towing capability and seldom mention the need for expensive optional equipment or that the maximum safe towing speed may be only 72 km/h (45 mph), as is the case with some Japanese minivans and trucks. Chrysler, for example, bought back many 1997–99 Ram pickups because they would only tow 900 kg (2,000 lb.), not the 2,700 kg (6,000 lb.) advertised. GM pickups and vans have been the objects of similar complaints.

Finally, remember that crew cab pickups sacrifice some utility with a shorter bed but provide a much roomier interior—essential for carrying rear passengers in greater comfort, or for keeping some cargo out of the weather.

Are you choosing a comfortable, safe vehicle?

The advantages of many sport-utilities, pickups, and vans quickly pale in direct proportion to your tolerance for nuisances such as these: a harsh ride, excessive interior noise when driving with the roof hatch or windows open, a high step-up, a cold interior, lots of buffeting from wind and passing trucks, and rear visibility that's blocked by the spare tire hanging on the rear tailgate.

Take the following simple tests: Check to see if the vehicle's interior is user-friendly. Can you sit a foot away from the steering wheel and still reach the accelerator and brake pedals? Can you reach the sound system and AC controls without straining or taking your eyes off the road? Are the controls just as easy to operate by feel as by sight? When you look out the windshield and use the rear- and side-view mirrors, do you detect any serious blind spots? Are you sure that optional mirrors will give you an unobstructed view? What about dash glare on the front windshield? Does the seat feel comfortable enough for long trips, and do rear-seat passengers have to be contortionists to enter or exit? Is there a head restraint to protect you from hitting the rear windshield in a collision? And, finally, do all rear seating positions have head restraints?

To answer these questions, you need to drive the vehicle over a period of time to test how well your driving needs are met by your choice—without having some impatient sales agent yapping in your ear. And, speaking of your ears, be sure to carry out a "howling" and "harmonic vibration" test by driving between 50 and 120 km/h with one or more windows lowered or with the sunroof open. This test often produces a painful noise described as a howl or roar, which is associated especially with SUVs and trucks.

Do you have the required driving skills?

Maybe not. You will have to drive more conservatively than you would in a car when you're behind the wheel of an SUV, truck, or van to avoid rolling over or losing control. Front-drive braking (especially with anti-lock brakes) is quite different from braking with a rear-drive. Rear-drive minivans handle like trucks, and full-sized vans tend to scrub the right rear tire during sharp right-hand turns until you get the hang of making wider turns. Limited rear visibility is another problem with larger sport-utilities and vans, forcing drivers to carefully survey side and rear traffic before changing lanes or merging. Also, be wary of mirrors. Side-view mirrors are notorious for showing vehicles to be much farther away than they actually are. In fact, they often show a 3-metre distance when there is only a 1-metre separation. You will have to trust your centre-mounted rear-view mirror more.

Which safety features are unsafe?

Some safety innovations, like anti-lock brakes and adaptive cruise control, don't deliver the safety payoffs promised by automakers and may create additional dangers. Yet there are more effective safety features that do quite well. Many vehicles offer superior front, side, and offset crash protection; high resistance to rollovers; head-protecting side and de-powered airbags; electronic stability-control; adjustable brake and accelerator pedals; standard integrated child safety seats; seat belt pretensioners; innovative head restraints; and sophisticated communication systems.

Size Doesn't Always Matter

Statistics show that if two vehicles with the same National Highway Traffic Safety Administration (NHTSA) full-frontal rating crash into each other head on, but one vehicle weighs twice as much as the other, the occupants of the lighter vehicle (909 kg/2,000 lb.) are eight times more likely to be killed than the occupants of the heavier one (1,818 kg/4,000 lb.). However, vehicle weight offers no safety advantage or disadvantage in single-vehicle crashes.

In March 2005, the Insurance Institute for Highway Safety (IIHS), a Washington-based safety research group, published a status report titled "The Risk of Dying in One Vehicle Versus Another" (*www.hwysafety.org*). The IIHS study concluded that the death rate in some larger vehicles was two to three times higher than in others—a contradiction of what the safety establishment has said for decades about large size enhancing safety.

In a two-vehicle crash with a smaller car, occupants of SUVs and trucks are more likely to be killed than are the people in the car, according to the IIHS report, which is based on a 2002–03 study of U.S. highway traffic fatalities involving vehicles made from 1999 through 2002.

In the two-vehicle crashes studied, 7 percent of the people in the cars were killed versus 10 percent of the people in the SUVs and trucks. Some reasons given for the higher death rate are that SUV and truck drivers are more aggressive and push the vehicles beyond their rollover tolerances, seat belts aren't used often enough, and these vehicles are often overloaded with cargo and passengers.

IIHS SAFETY REPORT RESULTS

LOWEST DRIVER DEATH RATES	HIGHEST DRIVER DEATH RATES
Mercedes E-Class	Chevrolet Blazer (two door)
Toyota 4Runner	Mitsubishi Mirage
Volkswagen Passat	Pontiac Firebird
Lexus RX 300	Kia Rio
Toyota RAV4	Kia Sportage 4X2 (four door)
Honda Odyssey	Chevrolet Blazer (four door)
Mercury Villager	Ford Explorer (two door)
Mercedes S-Class	Chevrolet Camaro
Nissan Pathfinder	Mazda B Series
Cadillac DeVille	Chevrolet Tracker
Nissan Quest	Chevrolet S10
Toyota Camry Solara	Chevrolet Cavalier (two door)
Cadillac Eldorado	Kia Sportage 4X4 (four door)

More Safety Considerations

There are no more cheap or easy safety solutions; most all of the low-hanging fruit has been picked. Except for increasing roof and side crashworthiness, changing driver behaviour (increased seat belt use and more severe DUI enforcement), and requiring young people up to the age of 14 (up from 12) to sit in the rear seat, there aren't any more feasible safety innovations.

According to NHTSA, 59 percent of the vehicle occupants who died in 2002 weren't wearing seat belts, and 42 percent of the highway deaths occurred in alcohol-related crashes. Although figures show a dramatic reduction in fatalities and injuries over the past three decades, safety experts agree that more built-in safety features will henceforth pay small dividends.

NHTSA says 76 percent of the almost 7 million annual crashes on North American highways are caused by driver error. This means safety programs that concentrate primarily upon motor vehicle standards won't be as effective as measures that target the driver, like stricter licence requirements and law enforcement.

Incidentally, police studies have shown an important side benefit to arresting traffic scofflaws: They often net dangerous career criminals and seriously impaired drivers before they harm others. Apparently, sociopaths and substance abusers don't care which laws they break.

Active Safety

Advocates of active safety stress that accidents are caused by the proverbial "nut behind the wheel" and believe that safe driving is best taught through schools or private driving courses. Active safety components are generally those mechanical systems—such as anti-lock brake systems (ABS), high-performance tires, and traction control—that may help to avoid accidents if the driver is skillful and mature.

The theory of active safety has several drawbacks. First, drivers who are under the influence of alcohol or drugs cause about 40 percent of all fatal accidents. All the high-performance options and specialized driving courses in the world will not provide much protection from impaired drivers who draw a bead on your vehicle. And because active safety components get a lot of use—you're likely to need anti-lock brakes 99 times more often than you'll need an airbag—they have to be well designed and well maintained to remain effective. Finally, consider that independent studies show that safe driving taught to young drivers doesn't necessarily reduce the number of driving-related deaths and injuries (*Lancet,* July 2001; 1978 DeKalb County, Georgia, study):

> In 1980, the U.S. Department of Transportation conducted a study designed to prove the value of driver education in the nation's high schools. It's commonly referred to as the DeKalb Study, from the county in Georgia where the research took place. The DeKalb Study compared the accident records of 9,000 teens that had taken driver education in the county's high schools with 9,000 teens that had no formal driver training. The final results showed no significant difference between the two groups. In other words, DeKalb County, Georgia, paid a large amount of money for absolutely no value.

Passive Safety

Passive safety assumes that you will be involved in life-threatening situations and should be warned in time to avoid a collision, or automatically protected from collision forces when they occur. Daytime running lights, a centre-mounted third brake light, and head-protecting airbags are three passive safety features that have paid off handsomely in reducing injuries and saving lives. Stability-control features have potential, but their long-term effectiveness is still unproven.

Passive safety features also assume that some accidents aren't avoidable and that, when an accident occurs, the vehicle should provide as much protection as possible to the driver, the vehicle's other occupants, and other people who may be struck by the vehicle—without depending on the driver's reactions. Passive safety components that have consistently proven to reduce vehicular deaths and injuries are seat belts, vehicle structures that enhance crashworthiness by absorbing or deflecting crash forces away from the vehicle's occupants, and electronic stability-control.

All the above factors have led researchers to the conclusion that *what* you drive can kill you because of poor crashworthiness. Large SUVs and trucks usually show very low death-rate figures, while models with the highest rates are mostly small cars and small to mid-sized SUVs. For example, the two-door, front-drive 1999–2002 Chevrolet Blazer has had three times the driver death rate of any passenger vehicle on the road in both single- and multiple-vehicle accidents, according to IIHS.

Rollovers

When you buy a pickup, van, or SUV, you should be concerned about the vehicle rolling over when cornering or changing lanes. Although rollovers represent only 3 percent of crashes (out of 10,000 annual U.S. road accidents), they cause one-third of all traffic deaths. And these crashes aren't with other vehicles. Most rollover deaths occur in single-vehicle accidents, representing nearly 40 percent of the fatal accidents that involved SUVs. While additional passengers make low-riding sedans more stable, additional passengers make high-riding SUVs more unstable, says Consumers Union, publisher of *Consumer Reports* magazine.

Ford's Explorer Sport Trac 4×2 posted the single worst rating for rollover propensity among all 2004 vehicles analyzed—including cars, vans, and SUVs. Its two-star rating indicated a nearly 35 percent chance of tipping over. In the NHTSA's August 2004 rankings of one to five stars, the Explorer Sport Trac 4×4, the Explorer four-door 4×2, and the Mountaineer four-door 4×2 were in the bottom six of the SUV class, which as a group posted the lowest three-star scores.

These results give a black eye to Ford and add credibility to Firestone's claims that previous Explorer rollover accident deaths and injuries were caused by the Explorer's design rather than by faulty tires. Bridgestone/Firestone raised the design argument at hearings in 2001 where the tiremaker disclosed that independent tests showed conclusively that the Explorer would roll over when equipped with competitors' tires. Ford claimed the tests were rigged.

When asked to comment upon the poor NHTSA crash protection scores, Ford spokesperson Kristen Kinley dropped the "rigged" excuse and gave the following lame statement:

> While we believe the NHTSA rating system has some value, we don't believe it's a good indicator of how a vehicle performs in the real world...

For the first time, NHTSA's 2004 results included dynamic tests that simulate real-world performance instead of the previously used mathematical formula. This has led to striking differences in results. For example, Saturn's Vue SUV received three stars in the earlier test. However, when two models were tested dynamically, the rear wheels collapsed. GM voluntarily recalled all 2002–04 models. Fortunately, other vehicles that are based on the Vue platform, like the Chevrolet Equinox, have posted excellent crashworthiness scores. All of the results for 2007 and prior years and models can be found in Part Four, or at *www.nhtsa.dot.gov/ncap*.

 ## Crashworthiness

A vehicle with a high crash protection rating is a lifesaver. In fact, crashworthiness is the one safety improvement over the past 30 years that everyone agrees has paid off handsomely without presenting any additional risks to drivers or passengers. By surrounding occupants in a protective cocoon and deflecting crash forces away from the interior, auto engineers have successfully created safer vehicles without increasing size or cost. And purchasing a vehicle with the idea that you'll be involved in an accident at some point is not unreasonable. According to IIHS, the average car will likely have two accidents before ending up as scrap, and it's twice as likely to be in a severe front-impact crash as a side-impact crash.

Side Impacts: A New Challenge

Although side-impact collisions occur less frequently than frontal collisions, they often happen to seniors turning at intersections. Without full-torso side curtain airbags, an occupant's head will bounce off the side window or pillar, which is only approximately 7.5 cm away from the occupant sitting on the side that's struck by the other vehicle. Furthermore, there are no bumpers or designed-in "crumple zones" on the sides of vehicles to help absorb and deflect the energy of the impact.

Among five 2005 mid-sized sedans tested by IIHS, the Audi A4 with standard side airbags and the Chevrolet Malibu equipped with optional side airbags earned good ratings. They also scored the "best pick" designation in side-impact crash tests recently conducted by the same organization.

Interestingly, Volvo's much-vaunted safety reputation took a major hit: Its S60 earned only an "acceptable" rating. The Nissan Maxima and Suzuki Verona got "marginal" scores.

There are other elements that may affect crashworthiness, like a vehicle's size and heft. Nevertheless, smart engineering can make small models just as safe as larger ones. And a large vehicle will likely roll over more easily. Therefore, look for something that gives you the best protection from frontal, frontal offset, and side collisions while keeping rollover potential to a minimum.

For example, in identical crash tests, the 2003 Ford Windstar performed much better than the regular-sized 2003 Chrysler Caravan minivan. However, side-impact protection was increased by adding full-torso side airbags and by extending the Chrysler's length.

Don't get taken in by the five-star crash rating hoopla touted by automakers, either. There isn't any one vehicle that can claim a prize for being the safest. Vehicles that do well in NHTSA side and front crash tests may not do very well in IIHS offset crash tests, or may have poorly designed head restraints that would increase the severity of neck injuries. Or a vehicle may have a high number of airbag failures. Before making a final decision on the vehicle you want, look up its crashworthiness and overall safety profile in Part Four.

 Two Washington-based agencies monitor how vehicle design affects crash safety: NHTSA and IIHS. Crash information from these two groups doesn't always correspond because, while IIHS's results incorporate all kinds of accidents, including offset crashes and bumper damage sustained from low-speed collisions, NHTSA's figures relate only to 56 km/h (35 mph) frontal collisions and some side collisions. The frontal tests are equivalent to two vehicles of equal weight hitting each other head-on while travelling at 56 km/h, or to a car slamming into a parked car at 114 km/h (70 mph). Bear in mind that a vehicle providing good injury protection may also cost more to repair because its structure, not the occupant, absorbs most of the collision force. That's why safer vehicles don't always have lower insurance rates.

Cars Versus Trucks (When Size Does Matter)

Occupants of large vehicles have fewer severe injury claims than do occupants of small vehicles. This was proven conclusively in a 1996 NHTSA study that showed collisions between light trucks or vans and small cars resulted in an 81 percent higher fatality rate for the occupants of the small cars than for the occupants of the light trucks or vans. Interestingly, NHTSA's study contradicts the 2002–03

IIHS study mentioned earlier, which shows a higher level of fatalities and injuries for SUV and truck drivers. Apparently, the IIHS considered factors beyond crash-worthiness (such as driver attitude, single-vehicle crashes, and rollovers) and concluded that a larger size may be detrimental to safety.

Vehicle weight offers the most protection in two-vehicle crashes. In a head-on crash, for example, the heavier vehicle drives the lighter one backward, which decreases force inside the heavy vehicle and increases force in the lighter one. All heavy vehicles, even poorly designed ones, offer this advantage in two-vehicle collisions. However, they may not offer good protection in single-vehicle crashes.

Crash test figures show that SUVs, vans, and trucks also offer more protection to adult occupants than passenger cars in most crashes because their higher set-up allows them to ride over other vehicles (Ford's 2002 4×4 Explorer lowered its bumper height to prevent this hazard). Conversely, because of their high centre of gravity, easily overloaded tires, and unforgiving suspensions, these vehicles have a disproportionate number of single-vehicle rollovers, which are far deadlier than frontal or side collisions. In the case of the early Ford Explorer, Bridgestone/Firestone CEO John Lampe testified in August 2001 that 42 of 43 rollovers involving Ford Explorers in Venezuela were on competitor's tires—shifting the rollover blame to the Explorer's design and crashworthiness.

IIHS figures show that for every 450 kg (1,000 lb.) added to a vehicle's mass, the risk of injury to an unrestrained driver is lowered by 34 percent and the risk of injury to a restrained driver is lowered by 25 percent. GM's series of two-car crash tests carried out a decade ago dramatically confirm this fact. Its engineers concluded that if two cars collide and one weighs half as much as the other, the driver in the lighter car is 10 times more likely to be killed than the driver in the heavier one. This held true no matter how many stars the smaller car was awarded in government crash tests.

Interestingly, a vehicle's size or past crashworthiness rating doesn't always guarantee that you won't be injured. For example, a 2004 Honda Civic earned five stars for front collision protection and four stars in side-impact tests. However, four years earlier, the 2000 Civic garnered only four stars in frontal crashes and two stars in side-impact crashes. GM's 2004 Extended Cab Silverado pickup earned four stars for the driver and three for the passenger in similar frontal crash tests.

Unsafe Designs

Although it sounds hard to believe, automakers *will* deliberately manufacture a vehicle that will kill or maim simply because, in the long run, it costs less to stonewall complaints and pay off victims than to make a safer vehicle. I learned this lesson after listening to the court testimony of GM engineers—who deliberately placed fire-prone "sidesaddle" gas tanks in millions of pickups to save $3 per vehicle—and after reading the court transcripts of *Grimshaw v. Ford* (fire-prone Pintos). Reporter Anthony Prince wrote the following assessment of Ford's indifference in an article titled "Lessons of the Ford/Firestone scandal: Profit motive turns consumers into road kill," *People's Tribune* (Online Edition); Vol. 26, No. 11, November 2000; (*www.lrna.org*):

> Rejecting safety designs costing between only $1.80 and $15.30 per Pinto, Ford had calculated the damages it would likely pay in wrongful death and injury cases and pocketed the difference. In a cold and calculating "costs/benefits" analysis, Ford projected that the Pinto would probably cause 180 burn deaths, 180 serious burn injuries, 2,100 burned vehicles each year. Also, Ford estimated civil suits of $200,000 per death, $67,000 per injury, $700 per vehicle for a grand total of $49.5 million. The costs for installing safety features would cost approximately $137 million per year. As a result, the Pinto became a moving target, its unguarded fuel tank subject to rupture by exposed differential bolts shoved into it by rear-end collisions at speeds of as little as 21 miles per hour [34 km/h]. Spewing gasoline into the passenger compartment, the car and its passengers became engulfed in a raging inferno.

And here are more recent examples of corporate greed triumphing over public safety: Pre-1997 airbag designs that maim or kill women, children, and seniors; anti-lock brake systems that don't brake (a major problem with some GM minivans, trucks, and sport-utilities and Chrysler sport-utilities and minivans); flimsy front seats and seatbacks; the absence of rear head restraints; and fire-prone GM pickup fuel tanks and Ford truck, van, and SUV cruise-control deactivation switches. Three other examples of hazardous engineering designs that put profit ahead of safety are failure-prone Chrysler, Ford, and GM minivan sliding doors; automatic transmissions that suddenly shift into Neutral, allow the vehicle to roll away when parked on an incline, or break down in traffic; and rear pickup seats that injure children.

Children in the rear jump seats of compact extended-cab pickup trucks run a higher risk of becoming injured in an accident than children riding in other vehicles because they are more likely to hit something in the confined space, according to a University of Pennsylvania School of Medicine study, published in the April 2002 *Journal of the American Medical Association*:

> Children in rear side-facing, fold-down or jump seats of compact pickup trucks are at substantially increased risk of injury compared with children in the rear seats of other vehicles. This increase in risk appears to be caused at least in part by contact with the interior of the vehicle at impact.

Flaming Fords

Over 16 million Fords may have a defective cruise-control deactivation switch that can cause the vehicle to catch fire—even when the engine is shut off and the key is taken from the ignition. Over 559 spontaneous fires have been reported to NHTSA (almost half involving vehicles never recalled), and one wrongful death lawsuit has been filed.

The $20 switch was used from 1992–2003 to shut off the cruise control when the brakes are applied. The switch, also known as a "brake pressure switch," is attached to the brake master cylinder and cruise control. Electrical current passes through the switch continuously, causing ignition even if the vehicle is shut down.

Ford has already recalled more than 1 million vehicles to replace the switch (1992 and 1993 Crown Victoria, Grand Marquis, and Lincoln Town Car; 2000 F-150 pickup, Expedition, and Navigator; and 2001 F-Series SuperCrew). In its recall notice, Ford cautions owners: The "switch may overheat, smoke or burn which could result in an underhood fire," it said. "This condition may occur either when the vehicle is parked or when it is being operated, even if the speed control is not in use…"

CRUISE-CONTROL FIRE DANGER

The following signs could indicate that you have a problem with your cruise-control switch: The cruise control is not working properly; brake fluid is leaking around the switch; fuses are blown near the switch; or the fuse for the speed control cannot be opened.

Until the above-named vehicles have been recalled or declared safe, owners would be wise to consider the following steps:
- Do not park your vehicle in an enclosed garage; many incidents involve homes destroyed when the fire ignited while the vehicle was parked in a garage.
- Disconnect the switch (Ford dealers will do this free of charge for owners of vehicles with recalled switches that are waiting for replacement parts).
- Replace the old switch with a 2004 improved version.
- If the vehicle has caught fire, do not tow it to the dealer. Instead, ask your insurance provider to hire an accident reconstruction expert who can prove if Ford is at fault.

Ford admits that its lawyers have settled "a number" of fire claims linked to the cruise-control switch out of court. Its own internal documents show that the same switch is used on 16 million cars, SUVs, trucks, minivans, and vans.

Those vehicles include:

- Taurus/Sable and Taurus SHO 2.3 L, 1993–95
- Ranger, 1995–2003
- F-Series, 1993–2003
- Windstar, 1994–2003

- Econoline, 1992–2003
- Explorer without IVD, 1995–2003
- Explorer Sport/Sport Trac, 2002–03
- Expedition, 1997–2003
- Mark VII/VIII, 1994–98

In March 2005, NHTSA opened an expanded investigation into 3.7 million F-150 pickups from the 1995–99 and 2001–02 model years and Ford Expeditions and Lincoln Navigators from the 1997–99 and 2001–02 model years—far fewer than the 16 million vehicles that owners claim are fire-prone.

Flying Seats and Seatbacks

Seat anchorages have to conform to government load regulations, but the regulations are so minimal that seats can easily collapse or tear loose from their anchorages, leaving drivers and passengers vulnerable in accidents. NHTSA's complaint database is replete with instances where occupants report severe injuries caused by collapsing seatbacks that have injured front-seat occupants or crushed children in safety seats placed in the rear seat.

Driver and passenger seatbacks frequently collapse in rear-end collisions. In one Illinois Appeal Court decision (*Carillo v. Ford*, Cook County Circuit Court), a $14.5-million jury verdict was levied against Ford after a driver's 1991 Explorer seatback failed, leaving the driver paralyzed from the chest down.

Experts testified that the seatback design was unreasonably dangerous in high-speed rear-impact collisions. Ford's experts countered that the "yielding seats" were reasonably safe and met the NHTSA safety standard for seatback strength established in 1971, based on a 1963 recommendation by the Society of Automotive Engineers. This standard requires a seat to withstand 90–136 kg (200–300 lb.) of force. However, in a typical rear-impact crash, seats are subjected to four or five times that much force, according to Kenneth Saczalski, an engineering consultant who specializes in seat design. The Appeal Court rejected Ford's plea.

Safety Features That Kill

In the late '60s, Washington forced automakers to include essential safety features like collapsing steering columns and safety windshields in their cars but exempted trucks and vans and, later, SUVs and minivans. As the years passed, the number of mandatory safety features increased to include seat belts, airbags, and crashworthy construction, and fewer vehicles were exempted. These improvements met with public approval until quite recently, when reports of deaths and injuries caused by anti-lock brake systems (ABS) and airbag failures showed that defective components and poor engineering negated the potential life-saving benefits associated with these devices.

For example, one out of every five ongoing NHTSA defect investigations concerns inadvertent airbag deployment, failure of the airbag to deploy, or injuries suffered when the bag did go off. In fact, airbags are the agency's single largest cause of current investigations, exceeding even the full range of brake problems, which runs second.

Transport Canada allows car owners to have a mechanic disengage airbags for several reasons: having to sit fewer than 25 cm from the steering wheel, having to put children in the front seat, or having adult passengers with medical conditions that may intensify airbag injuries. Motorists are required by regulation to submit the forms, but Transport Canada does not verify the accuracy of the information. People can have the work done without waiting for a response from the government, and the department does not track people who disconnect their bags without going through the official route.

Anti-lock brake systems (ABS)

I am not a fan of ABS brakes. They are often ineffective, failure-prone, and expensive to service.

Essentially, ABS prevents a vehicle's wheels from locking when the brakes are applied in an emergency situation, thus reducing skidding and the loss of directional control. When braking on wet or dry roads, your stopping distance will be about the same as with conventional braking systems. But in gravel, slush, or snow, your stopping distance will be greater.

The most important feature of ABS is that it preserves steering control. As you brake in an emergency, ABS will release the brakes if it senses wheel lock-up. Braking distances will lengthen accordingly, but at least you'll have some steering control. However, if you start sliding on glare ice, don't expect ABS to help you out very much. The laws of physics (no friction, no stopping!) still apply on ABS–equipped vehicles. You can decrease the stopping distance, however, by removing your all-season tires and installing four snow tires that are of the same make and size.

Transport Canada studies show ABS effectiveness is highly overrated. IIHS—an American insurance research group that collects and analyzes insurance-claims data—says that cars with ABS brakes are actually more likely to be in crashes where no other car is involved but a passenger is killed. Other insurance-claim statistics show that ABS brakes aren't producing the overall safety benefits that were predicted by the government and automakers. One IIHS study found that a passenger has a 45 percent greater chance of dying in a single-vehicle crash in a car with anti-lock brakes than in the same car with traditional brakes. On wet pavement, where ABS supposedly excels, that figure rises to a 65 percent greater chance of being killed. In multi-vehicle crashes, ABS–equipped vehicles have a passenger death rate 6 percent higher than vehicles not equipped with ABS.

The high cost of ABS maintenance is one disadvantage that few safety advocates mention, but consider the following: Original parts can cost five times more than regular braking components, and many dealers prefer to replace the entire ABS unit rather than troubleshoot a very complex system.

Keep in mind that anti-lock brakes are notoriously unreliable on all makes and models. They often fail completely, resulting in no braking whatsoever, or they may extend stopping distances by 30 percent. This phenomenon is amply documented throughout NHTSA's complaint database.

Airbag dangers (unsafe at any speed?)

First, the good news. It is estimated that airbags have reduced head-on crash fatalities by up to 30 percent and moderate-to-severe injuries by 25–29 percent. Injury claims at hospitals resulting from traffic crashes have dropped 24 percent as a result of airbag use.

Now for the bad news. To begin with, no airbag is safe, although some model years are safer than others. Pre-1997 airbags explode too forcefully and can seriously injure or kill small-statured or older occupants. Later de-powered "smart" devices are less hazardous, but they're not that smart. Many systems will disable the airbag even though a normal-sized adult occupies the passenger seat, as may be the case with Nissan's Quest minivan and Titan pickup, Hyundai's Elantra, and Jaguar, Jeep, Lexus, and Toyota models.

Inadvertent airbag deployment

Airbags frequently go off for no apparent reason, usually because of faulty sensors. Causes of sudden deployment include passing over a bump in the road; slamming the car door; having wet carpets; or, in some Chrysler minivans, simply putting the key into the ignition.

This happens more often than you might imagine, judging by the frequent recalls and thousands of complaints recorded on NHTSA's website at *www-odi.nhtsa.dot. gov/cars/problems/complain*. Incidentally, dealers and manufacturers routinely ask owners to pay for the interior damage caused by exploding airbags, denying claims by alleging that airbags don't go off without a collision. They usually pay the claim if the insured has proof the airbag went off for no reason.

> On June 17, 2004, after dropping my son off for baseball practice in Toronto, I decided to run a couple of errands. Upon returning to the ball field, I put my 1998 Dodge Grand Caravan in park and turned off the ignition. Immediately thereafter, my air bag deployed. I was struck on the left side of my face and neck and my left ear received some trauma. The BANG from the air bag deploying was so loud that people from 3 surrounding ball fields heard the blast...

•

Our airbags on our 2003 Volkswagen Jetta TDI deployed for no reason on a smooth surface [on] July 3, 2004. We were denied warranty [coverage] because the Calgary Volkswagen field technician found two small dents on the bottom of the car. We met another Volkswagen Jetta TDI driver who experienced basically the same as us on July 1, 2004, and was also denied warranty. An employee at the dealership stated that another customer had an airbag deploy on a Jetta one month earlier, causing $5,600 in damage.... The deployment of our airbag tore open the ceiling along the passenger side of the car, ruptured the seat, damaged the panel beside the passenger seat, and immobilized the front passenger seatbelt.... These airbags, instead of bringing safety, are more of a danger. If we had been aware of this or the way Volkswagen would respond to this problem, we never would have bought from them...

Airbags, except for full-powered, pre-1997 systems, shouldn't be disabled; their benefits generally outweigh their shortcomings. If you feel vulnerable, you'll want to choose a vehicle with adjustable brake and accelerator pedals or an adjustable seat that can travel backward far enough to keep you at a safe distance (over 25 cm, or 1 ft.) from the front airbag's explosive force. You can assure children's safety by getting a vehicle with an airbag shut-off switch, or by having the children sit in the rear middle-seat position, away from front seatbacks that frequently collapse in rear-enders.

Nevertheless, airbags are still dangerous, even when they work properly. In fender-benders, for example, where no one would have been hurt if the airbag hadn't deployed, early, full-power airbag systems can kill women, seniors, and children— or leave them horribly scarred or deaf.

If you are hit from the rear and thrown within 25 cm of the steering wheel as the airbag deploys, you risk severe head, neck, or chest trauma, or even death. If you are making a turn with your arms crossing in front of the steering wheel, you are out of position and risk fractures to both arms. If you drive with your thumbs extended a bit into the steering hub area, as I often do, you risk losing both thumbs when the housing cover explodes.

Sometimes, just being female is enough to get you killed.

Two startling Transport Canada studies were uncovered in October 1999 as part of a CBC *Marketplace* investigation into airbag safety. The consumer TV show unearthed government-financed research that showed airbags reduce the risk of injury by *only* 2 percent for adults who wear seat belts. Even more incredible, the studies confirm that airbags actually *increase* the risk of injury to women by 9 percent and the risk of death for children by 21 percent.

The research was conducted in 1996 and 1998 on early, full-powered airbags. Fearing the public disclosure of the findings, it took Transport Canada four months to release the studies to *Marketplace*. American government officials have refused to comment on the Canadian research, despite the fact that it contradicts the basic premise of airbag use—that they are safe at any speed, regardless of gender.

In fact, the danger to women is so great that an earlier 1996 Transport Canada and George Washington University study of 445 drivers and passengers drew these frightening conclusions:

DANGER OF AIRBAGS TO WOMEN

While the initial findings of this study confirm that belted drivers are afforded added protection against head and facial injury in moderate to severe frontal collisions, the findings also suggest that these benefits are being negated by a high incidence of bag-induced injury. The incidence of bag-induced injury was greatest among female drivers. Furthermore, the intervention of the airbag can be expected to introduce a variety of new injury mechanisms such as facial injuries from "bag slap," upper extremity fractures, either directly from the deploying airbag module or from arm flailing, and thermal burns to the face and arms.

Side airbags—good and bad

In crashes with another passenger vehicle, 51 percent of driver deaths in contemporary model year cars during 2000–01 occurred in side impacts, up from 31 percent in 1980–81.

Side airbags and side curtains are included in about 80 percent of new cars and SUVs as standard or optional equipment, but in less than half of all pickups. The airbag deploys from the ceiling, the seat, or the door and is designed to protect drivers and passengers in rollovers and side-impact crashes, which are estimated to account for almost one-third of vehicle deaths. Studies show that torso-protecting side airbags reduce deaths by 26 percent. The fatality rate drops by 37 percent when head protection is included. Serious crash injuries are reduced by 45 percent with the head-protection feature, versus only 10 percent when the torso-protecting side airbag is employed.

Because side airbags aren't required by federal regulation in the States or in Canada, neither government has developed any tests to measure their safety for children and smaller adults. IIHS hopes its test results will goad government regulators and automakers into standardizing side airbag design and increasing their effectiveness and safety.

In the meantime, keep in mind that preliminary safety studies show side airbags may be deadly to children or to any occupant sitting too close to the airbag, resting his or her head on the side pillar, or holding onto the roof-mounted assist handle. Research carried out in 1998 by safety researchers (Anil Khadikar, Biodynamics Engineering, Inc., and Lonney Pauls, Springwater Micro Data Systems, "Assessment of Injury Protection Performance of Side Impact Airbags") shows that there are four hazards that vehicle occupants should consider:

1. Inadvertent airbag firing (due to a short circuit, or faulty hardware or software)
2. Unnecessary firing (sometimes the opposite side airbag will fire, or the airbag may deploy when a low-speed side-swipe wouldn't have endangered occupant safety)
3. Small children (a three-year-old, for example) restrained in booster seats can be seriously injured
4. Out-of-position restrained occupants can be seriously injured

The researchers conclude with the following observation: "Even properly restrained vehicle occupants can have their upper or lower extremities in harm's way in the path of an exploding [side] airbag."

The above study and dozens of other scientific papers confirm that small and tall restrained drivers face death or severe injury from frontal and side airbag deployments for one simple reason—they are outside of the norm of the 5′8″, 180-pound male test dummy.

These studies also debunk the safety merits of ABS brakes, so it's no surprise they go unheralded by Transport Canada and other government and private safety groups. With a bit of patience, however, you can find these studies and the results of other research—such as what percentage of airbag deployments cause eye injuries, the effectiveness of electronic stability devices, and the need for laminated glass in side windows to prevent occupants' partial ejection—at *www-nrd.nhtsa.dot. gov/departments/nrd-01/esv/esv.html* or *www.nhtsa.dot.gov/esv*.

In the meantime, don't forget the NHTSA's side airbag warning issued on October 14, 1999:

> Side impact airbags can provide significant supplemental safety benefits to adults in side impact crashes. However, children who are seated in close proximity to a side airbag may be at risk of serious or fatal injury, especially if the child's head, neck, or chest is in close proximity to the airbag at the time of deployment.

 ## Protect yourself and your passengers

Additionally, you should take the following steps to reduce the danger from airbag deployment:

- Don't buy a vehicle with side airbags unless it offers head protection and you are confident that all occupants will remain properly positioned and out of harm's way. This is another reason why children should sit in the middle of the back seat.
- Make sure that seat belts are buckled and that all head restraints are properly adjusted (to about ear level).

- Make sure the head restraints are rated "good" by IIHS (check Part Four).
- Insist that passengers who are frail or short, or who have recently had surgery, sit in the back.
- Make sure that the driver's seat can be adjusted for height and has tracks with sufficient rearward travel to allow short drivers to remain a safe distance (25 cm) away from the bag's deployment.
- If you are short-statured, consider buying aftermarket pedal extensions from auto parts retailers, or buying optional adjustable accelerator and brake pedals to keep you at a safe distance away from a deploying airbag.
- Buy a vehicle that comes with manual passenger-side airbag disablers.
- Buy a vehicle that uses sensors to detect the presence of an electronically tagged child safety seat in the passenger seat and then disables the airbag for that seat.

Top 20 Safety Defects

The U.S. federal government's online safety complaints database contains well over 100,000 entries, going back to vehicles made in the late '70s. Although the database was originally intended to record only incidents of component failures that relate to safety, you will find every problem imaginable dutifully recorded by clerks working for NHTSA.

A perusal of the listed complaints shows that some safety-related failures occur more frequently than others and often affect one manufacturer more than another. Here is a summary of some of the more commonly reported failures, in order of frequency:

1. Airbags not deploying when they should, or deploying when they shouldn't
2. ABS total brake failure; wheel lock-up
3. Tire-tread separation
4. Electrical or fuel-system fire
5. Sudden acceleration
6. Sudden stalling
7. Sudden electrical failure
8. Transmission failing to engage or suddenly disengaging
9. Transmission jumping from Park to Reverse or Neutral; vehicle rolling away when parked
10. Steering or suspension failure
11. Seat belt failure
12. Collapsing seatback
13. Defective sliding door, door locks, and latches
14. Poor headlight illumination
15. Dash reflecting onto windshield
16. Hood flying up
17. Wheel falling away
18. Steering wheel lifting off
19. Transmission lever pulling out
20. Exploding windshield

Senior Safety

According to the Canada Safety Council, almost 30 percent of Canada's population was over age 50 in 2002, and half of Canadians 65 and older living in private households drive motor vehicles—though most drive only a few times a week. Furthermore, drivers over 80 years old are the fastest-growing segment of the driving population. Husbands do the bulk of family driving, which usually involves short trips (11–17 km per day, on average) for medical appointments and visits to family, friends, and shopping malls. This puts older women, who tend to outlive their husbands, in a serious bind because of their lesser driving experience—particularly in rural areas, where driving is a necessity rather than a choice.

Safe, reliable choices

Older drivers, like most of us, want cars that are reliable, relatively inexpensive, and fuel-efficient. Additionally, they require vehicles that compensate for some of the physical challenges associated with aging and that provide protection for accidents more common to mature drivers (side-impacts, for example). Furthermore, as drivers get older, they find that the very act of getting into a car (sitting down while moving sideways without bumping their heads or twisting their necks) demands considerable acrobatic skill.

OLD FAVOURITES

New vehicles with the highest percentage of buyers over 70, first four months of 2006 (American data).

1.	Mercury Grand Marquis	55.4%
2.	Lincoln Town Car	52.4%
3.	Buick Lucerne	48.6%
4.	Cadillac DTS	46.6%
5.	Buick LaCrosse	46.5%
6.	Ford Crown Victoria	35.4%
7.	Mercury Monterey	30.9%
8.	Mercury Montego	28.0%
9.	Lincoln Zephyr	25.8%
10.	Lexus LS	24.2%

Vans, small SUVs set upon car platforms, and Cadillac SUVs such as the Escalade generally meet the above requirements and remain quite popular with senior drivers who have limited mobility. Nevertheless, seniors are sometimes reluctant to change their buying habits, so traditional full-sized cars still dominate the seniors' market, though more frugal and reliable Japanese luxury compacts are coming on strong.

Access and comfort

Drivers with arthritic hands may have to insert a pencil into their key ring to twist the key in the ignition. Make sure that your ignition lock doesn't require that much effort. Power locks and windows are a must, especially if the vehicle will be operated with hand controls. A remote keyless entry will allow entry without having to twist a key in the door lock. A vehicle equipped with a buttonless shifter will be less difficult to activate for arthritis sufferers and for drivers with limited upper-body mobility. Cruise control can be helpful for those with lower-body mobility challenges.

Get a vehicle that's easy to enter and exit. Check for door openings that are wide enough to get in and out of easily, both for you and for any wheelchairs or scooters that may need to be loaded. Make sure the door catches when opened on

An $8,600 option, this seat was introduced in October 2003 and is offered with most of GM's vans. 2001 model year and later GM minivans can also be retrofitted. The seat can support 136 kg (300 lbs.), includes a slide-out footrest, and can be lowered to approximately 42.5 cm (17 inches) from seat bottom to ground.

a slight incline so that it doesn't close as you are exiting. If necessary, your trunk or rear cargo area should have a low liftover and room to stow your wheelchair or scooter. Bench seats are preferable because they're roomier and easier to access; a power-adjustable driver seat with memory is also a good idea. Make sure the seat is comfortable and has plenty of side bolstering.

Forget minivans and large trucks unless you invest in a step-up, choose one with an easily reached inside grip handle, and don't mind bumping the left-side steering column stalk with your knee each time you slide into the driver's seat.

Drivers with limited mobility or those who are recovering from hip surgery give kudos to the Buick LeSabre, the Cadillac Escalade, and the GM Venture/Montana minivans; Toyota's Echo, Matrix, and Avalon; and small SUVs like the Honda CR-V, the Hyundai Tucson and Santa Fe, or the Toyota Matrix and RAV4.

Incidentally, General Motors' minivans offer a Sit-N-Lift option, which is a motorized, rotating lift-and-lower rear passenger seat that's accessed through the middle door and can be taken out when not needed.

Seeing, driving, and surviving

The driver's seat should be mounted high enough to give a commanding view of the road (with slower reaction times, seniors need earlier warnings). Driver's seats must offer enough rearward travel to attenuate the force of an exploding airbag, which can be particularly hazardous to older or small-statured occupants, children, or anyone recovering from surgery. Adjustable gas and brake pedals are a must for short-legged drivers.

And, while we're discussing airbags, remember that, prior to 1997, most airbags were full-force, making it especially important that you put at least 25 cm between your upper torso and the front airbag. As full-powered airbags deploy, they expand with an explosive force that is greatest in the first 8 cm of travel. Sit within this zone, and you are likely to be killed or seriously injured from the explosion. Tests have shown that short drivers tend to sit about 24 cm from the steering wheel (measured from the chest), in comparison to an average-sized male, who sits at a distance of about 39 cm. Moreover, pre-impact braking may throw you even closer to the airbag prior to its deployment, which certainly isn't a confidence-builder, is it?

Transport Canada recommends that adults sit more than 25 cm away from the airbag housing and that children sit in the rear of the vehicle. Also, since most intersection collisions involving mature drivers occur when drivers are making a turn into oncoming traffic, head-protecting side airbags are a must.

Look for handles near the door frame that can be gripped for support when entering or leaving the vehicle, bright dashboard gauges that can be seen in sunlight, and instruments with large-sized controls.

Remote-controlled mirrors are a must, along with adjustable, unobtrusive head restraints and a non-reflective front windshield (many drivers put a cloth on the dash top to cut the distraction). Make sure brake and accelerator pedals aren't mounted too closely together.

As far as safety features are concerned, a superior crashworthiness rating is essential, as well as torso- and head-protecting side airbags. The extra head protection can make a critical difference in side impacts. For example, Toyota's 2004 RAV4 with $680 head-protecting side airbags earned a "best pick" designation from IIHS. When tested without the head protection, it received a "poor" rating in the side test.

A SAFE CAR FOR SENIORS

Don't be overly impressed by anti-lock brakes, because their proper operation (no tapping on the brakes) runs counter to everything you have been taught and they aren't that reliable. Look for headlights that give you a comfortable view at night, as well as easily seen and heard dash-mounted turn signal indicators. Ensure that the vehicle's knobs and switches are large and easy to identify. An easily accessed, full-sized spare tire and user-friendly lug wrench and jack stand are also important.

Senior trip tips

Before you begin a—perhaps oxymoronic—driving vacation, make sure that the vehicle is properly serviced, that baggage and occupants don't exceed a safe limit, and that visibility is unobstructed. Above all, don't treat the trip as an endurance marathon. Plan your route with rest stops scheduled every two hours or 200 km, don't drive at night (even with glasses, your night vision can be poor) or during weekends (lots of impaired, crazy drivers), and if you fall behind schedule, call ahead to say you'll be a bit late.

Sooner or later, you'll find that everyone on the highway is going much faster than you are. Although the speed limit says 100 km/h, most drivers will speed by at 120 km/h. It will also seem as if every vehicle in your rear-view mirror is a huge commercial truck hugging your rear bumper. All the more reason to stay in the middle lane and to let the speeders pass you by. Why not simply stay all the way to the right, you ask? Because there are too many exits that cut off the right lane and too many merging cars entering the highway. Your slow speed will likely cause them to speed up and then cut you off as they dart from the far-right lane to the middle lane.

When to stop driving

Most older drivers know when it's time to stop driving, but many continue driving because they have to. The Ontario Ministry of Transportation lists the following five warning signs that tell you when to stop driving:

1. Frequent near collisions
2. Direct involvement in minor collisions
3. Difficulty seeing pedestrians, objects, and other vehicles
4. Difficulty coordinating hand and foot movements
5. Increased nervousness behind the wheel

Other Buying Considerations

When "New" Isn't New

There's no guarantee that what you buy is really new. The odometer may have been disconnected, or the vehicle could have been involved in an accident; both of these are common occurrences.

Even if the vehicle hasn't been used, it may have been left outdoors for a considerable length of time, causing the deterioration of rubber components, premature body and chassis rusting, or severe rusting of internal mechanical parts (leading to brake malfunction, fuel line contamination, hard starting, and stalling).

You can check a vehicle's age by looking at the date-of-manufacture plate found on the driver-side door pillar. If the date of manufacture reads "7/06," your vehicle was probably one of the last 2006 models made before the September changeover to the 2007s. Redesigned vehicles or those new to the market are exceptions to this rule. They may arrive at dealerships in early spring or mid-summer, but they're considered to be next year's models. They also depreciate more quickly, owing to their earlier launching, but this difference narrows over time.

Sometimes, a vehicle can be too new and end up costing you more in maintenance because redesign glitches haven't yet been worked out. As Honda's North American manufacturing chief, Koki Hirashima, so ably put it, carryover models generally have fewer problems than vehicles that have been significantly reworked or just introduced to the market. Newly redesigned vehicles get quality scores that are, on average, 2 percent worse than vehicles that have been around for a while, says J.D. Power and Associates. Some surprising poor performers are the 2002 Jaguar X-Type, 2002 Nissan Altima, 2002 Toyota Avalon and Camry, and 2001 Honda Civic. More recently, the 2004 Nissan Quest and Titan and the Toyota Sienna failed to live up to expectations.

Because they're the first off the assembly line for a model year, most vehicles assembled between September and February are called "first series" cars. "Second series" vehicles, made between March and August, incorporate more assembly-line fixes and are better built than the earlier models, which may depend on ineffective "field fixes" to mask problems until their warranties expire. Both vehicles will initially sell for the same price, but the post-February ones will be a far better buy because they benefit from more assembly-line upgrades and rebates. This is an important fact to remember if you are considering the purchase of a reworked 2007 GM Silverado or Sierra pickup, for example.

There's also the very real possibility that the new vehicle you've just purchased was damaged while being shipped to the dealer and was later fixed in the service bay during the pre-delivery inspection. It's estimated that this happens to about 10 percent of all new vehicles. Although there's no specific Canadian legislation allowing buyers of vehicles damaged in transit to cancel their contracts, B.C. legislation says that dealers must disclose damages of $2,000 or more. In a more general sense, Canadian common-law jurisprudence *does* allow for cancellation or compensation whenever the delivered product differs markedly from what the buyer expected to receive. Ontario's revised *Consumer Protection Act* is particularly hard-nosed in prohibiting this kind of misrepresentation.

Fuel Economy Fantasies

Oh, Canada!

The hidden expense of poor gas mileage is one of the top complaints among owners of new cars and mini-vans. Drivers say gas mileage is seldom as high as it's hyped to be; in fact, it's likely to be 10–20 percent *less* than advertised. (Fuel efficiency, measured in mpg, is the opposite of metric fuel consumption, measured in L/100 km. In other words, you want gas mileage to be high and consumption to be low.) *Consumer Reports* magazine estimates that 90 percent of vehicles sold don't get the gas mileage advertised, and their reporters target hybrids built by Honda and Toyota as the worst offenders.

This is not a new phenomenon. Environment Canada's independent research confirms that 2003–04 models were much less fuel efficient than vehicles built 15 years ago. At that time, cars and trucks averaged 10.5 L/100 km (22 mpg); now that figure is estimated by independent analysis to be 11.2 L/100 km (21 mpg), once all of the gas-guzzling SUVs and pickups are factored into the study. Even more astounding, a Ford Model T got 7.8–11.5 L/100 km (20–30 mpg) nearly a century ago. Today, the average Ford gets 12.5 L/100 km (19 mpg).

Oh, we wanted so badly to believe in the 1.2 L/100 km (200 mpg) Pogue carburetor invented in 1953 by Charles Nelson Pogue, a Montreal automotive engineer. As his 15 minutes of fame approached the 14-minute mark, Pogue recanted, saying that he had never claimed that his carburetor would get 200 miles per gallon, "or even half of that," declaring all such numbers were "violently distorted by newspapermen and magazine writers."

And who can forget '70s icon Liz Carmichael, a 6-foot, 200-pound transsexual born Jerry Dean Michael, who built a three-wheeled prototype car called the Dale that was to be powered by a 2-cylinder engine, get 3.4 L/100 km (70 mpg), and sell for under $2,000. Dealers bought franchises, but no cars were delivered, and Carmichael was hauled off to jail.

Now, after we've had our hopes dashed by Pogue and Carmichael, Transport Canada hoodwinks us with gas mileage figures that are impossible to achieve.

Gas mileage claims on individual models trumpeted by the manufacturers or Transport Canada aren't that reliable: They can be lower than "real-life" mileage by 40–45 percent for city driving and about 20–23 percent lower overall, says *Consumer Reports*. Additionally, the Union of Concerned Scientists levels some harsh criticism at government-sanctioned fuel consumption figures (*www.ucsusa. org/clean_vehicles/fuel_economy/fixing-the-epas-fuel-economy-tests.html*):

FUEL ECONOMY TEST CRITICISM

Because the Environmental Protection Agency's (EPA) fuel economy tests are 30 years old, they are out of step with current driving habits, traffic patterns, and vehicle technologies. The result is EPA's tests overstate fuel economy by as much as 30%... Despite EPA's attempt to band-aid over some of these problems, the fuel economy tests still suffer from several fundamental flaws, including:

- **Underestimating highway speeds**—The EPA highway cycle assumes an average speed of 48 mph [72 km/h] and a top speed of 60 mph [97 km/h]. Many state highway speed limits are set at or above 65 mph [105 km/h]. Government data indicates that fuel economy can drop by 17% for modern vehicles that drive at 70 mph [113 km/h] instead of 55 mph [89 km/h]. Even at 65 mph [105 km/h], fuel economy can drop by nearly 10% compared to driving at 55 mph [89 km/h].
- **Underestimating the severity of and amount of time spent in stop-and-go urban congestion**—Congestion is getting worse. In 1982, congestion added about 7 hours per year to the average person's annual travel, by 2001, congestion effects had nearly quadrupled to 26 hours per year. While EPA data shows that we spend about 62% of our time in urban driving, EPA still assumes only 55%.
- **Assuming very gentle acceleration and braking**—The maximum acceleration rate in the EPA test cycles is 3.3 mph [5.3 km/h] per second, about the same as going from zero to 60 mph [97 km/h] in about 18 seconds. The average new car or truck can accelerate nearly twice as fast. While most consumers don't use all the power in their vehicle, EPA data shows that people accelerate as fast as 15 mph [24 km/h] per second, nearly 5 times the EPA tests. In 1996 EPA established a new driving cycle (US06) that includes tougher acceleration and deceleration and higher speeds, but this cycle is not used for fuel economy purposes.
- **Neglecting the wide range of outdoor temperatures experienced in the real world**—The EPA tests are performed between 68 and 86 degrees Fahrenheit [20 and 30 degrees Celsius]. Most states frequently experience weather conditions outside this range and fuel economy can be significantly affected as a result.
- **Failing to reflect the use of air conditioning**—Fuel economy tests are run with the air conditioning off, while over 99% of all cars and trucks come with air conditioning. In 1996 EPA established a new driving cycle (SC03) that included air conditioning, but this cycle is not used for fuel economy purposes.

- **Overestimating trip lengths**—The EPA city test cycle is 7.5 miles [12 km] long. EPA's own data, however, indicate that average trip lengths may be only 5 miles [8 km] long, with typical trips as short as 2.5 miles [4 km]. Shorter trips often mean lower fuel economy because the engine does not have time to warm up and operate efficiently.
- **Ignoring advances in automotive technology**—Over the past 20–30 years, vehicle technology has changed significantly and new technologies are continuing to enter the market. Many of the factors listed above affect vehicles with new technologies differently than they affect today's conventional cars. Therefore, EPA's 30-year test procedures and the concept of a new set of "adjustments" are even more ineffective for new technologies. This will make it difficult for consumers to compare diesel, hybrid, alternative fuel, and conventional vehicles with each other.
- **Ignoring heavier vehicles**—Fuel economy information is not required for nearly 6 million light duty trucks on the road today. These are SUVs, pickups, and vans rated above 8,500 pounds [3,850 kg] gross vehicle weight. A recent J.D. Power survey found that the top complaint with the Hummer H2 was its poor fuel economy—consumers just did not know what they were getting in to. And if you are a farmer or small-business owner who needs a big pickup, you are left in the dark.

Another serious flaw in the testing procedures is that automakers submit their own test results to the American government after running the vehicles under optimum conditions, and Transport Canada then publishes these self-serving cooked figures as gospel truth. In fact, one Ford bulletin warns dealers:

> Very few people will drive in a way that is identical to the EPA [sanctioned] tests… These [fuel economy] numbers are the result of test procedures that were originally developed to test emissions, not fuel economy.

Stephen Akehurst, a senior manager at Natural Resources Canada, which tests vehicles and publishes the annual *Fuel Consumption Guide*, admits that his lab tests vehicles under ideal conditions. He says that actual driving may burn about 25 percent more fuel than what the government tests show. Too bad we never see this fact hyped in the automakers' fuel economy ads.

Some examples: One of the biggest gas-guzzlers tested, the Lincoln Aviator, burned 44 percent more than the *Fuel Consumption Guide*'s estimate. A Nissan Quest burned twice as much fuel as was advertised in the *Guide*. Only the Hyundai Elantra did well. It burned a full litre less than predicted by the guys in the white lab coats. It's not surprising, therefore, that J.D. Power and Associates' 2003 quality survey showed that poor gas mileage was one of the top complaints among owners of 2003 model cars and trucks.

The U.S. Environmental Protection Agency says it will share new fuel economy figures, based upon revised tests, with Transport Canada in 2007. These tests will give more accurate fuel economy ratings and, according to *Detroit News* columnist John McCormick ("The threat of realistic fuel economy numbers," February 1, 2006), are likely to cut truck and hybrid ratings dramatically:

> It's expected that fuel economy figures will drop by between five and 20 percent, perhaps more, depending on the testing cycle [to be adopted in 2007].... This issue is particularly pertinent to two vehicle types on the market today; full-size sport utilities/pick-ups and hybrids. It's a given that large SUVs are relatively heavy on fuel versus cars, but when the new EPA tests are conducted, full size SUVs are going to end up with composite mpg numbers in the low rather than the mid to high teens. For the really heavy metal, trucks with extra large V8 or V10 engines, the mpg numbers may plunge into the single digits.

 ## "Miracle" Fuels

The lure of cheap, "clean" fuel has never been stronger, and the misrepresentations as to the advantages of different fuels have never been greater. Take a look at the following list of flavour-of-the-month alternate fuels that have been proposed by politicians and businesses and consider that, except for diesel (an alleged carcinogen), *not a single other alternate fuel is economically viable.*

Ethanol and flex-fuel vehicles (FFVs)

The trendy fuel of the month for automakers, oil companies, and politicians who have their heads stuck up their tailpipes. All three groups recite the mantra that increased ethanol use will cut fuel costs, make us less dependent upon foreign oil sources (goodbye, Big Oil; hello, Big Corn), and create a cleaner environment. Unfortunately, this is simply not true—it's reminiscent of the misguided embrace of the 1997 Kyoto Accord by governments who promised they would be effective in cutting emissions that lead to global warming. Ironically, research now shows signatories to the Accord produce more emissions than non-signatories.

FFVs are all the rage with the Detroit Big Three and Nissan, and they're being promoted over hybrids and diesel engines because the switchover is less costly for them. Millions of their vehicles already on the market can run on a mixture of 85 percent ethanol and 15 percent gasoline (called E85). Oil companies have no problem with ethanol, either, since they can continue to charge high gasoline prices—governments won't pony up with the billions of dollars needed to construct new ethanol pipelines (at an estimated cost of $1.6 million per kilometre for 322,000 km) and to convert filling stations that would provide real competition for gas-selling stations ($240,000 for a new tank and pump). At the moment, most E85 FFVs are gasoline powered because ethanol retailers can't be found (only 608 out of 168,987 filling stations sell ethanol in the States; there are only a couple in Canada that do).

Brazil, a huge ethanol producer since the late '70s, doesn't need a pipeline because most of its sugar cane fields are located where they can be distilled and the resulting ethanol marketed—thereby forgoing expensive transportation costs. In North America, most of the corn and other ethanol-producing crops are found in the U.S. Midwest and Central and Western Canada, far away from major population areas.

Indeed, ethanol is smokeless, burns cleaner, and (theoretically) leads to less engine maintenance. Plus, you can drink it (diluted, or with a chaser).

But will the increased use of ethanol make North America much less dependent upon gasoline? No way, not if you do the math: About 4 billion gallons of ethanol is produced annually in the States, but they burn an average of 140 billion gallons of gasoline each year.

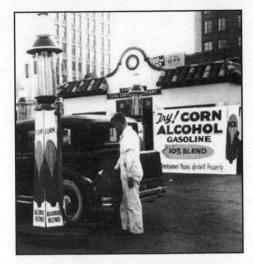

This photo, courtesy of Dogwood Energy, was taken in April 1933 and shows a Lincoln, Nebraska, gas station selling ethanol fuel. According to Dogwood, grain alcohol (ethanol) is a renewable fuel, and it's pretty much pollution free, since the by-products of combustion are only water and CO_2.

Dogwood Energy, of Tullahoma, Tennessee, sells recipes for 190-proof grain alcohol (ethanol) on its website, www.dogwoodenergy.com. For $1,600, you can buy a still like this one and legally brew up to 9.8 L (2.6 gallons) of ethanol in two and a half days at a cost of about 65 cents (U.S.) per gallon. For the average car, that's about a tank full of ethanol every two weeks. Home brewers are expected not to drink the stuff (Scout's honour).

Ethanol filling stations are practically non-existent, the fuel costs almost as much as gasoline in some places (unless you distill it yourself), gas mileage *drops* by up to 30 percent when ethanol is used, and the product is highly corrosive, with a particular fondness for plastic and rubber components.

Hybrids

You have to be quite stupid to plunk down about $30,000 for a hybrid vehicle in the hope of saving gas—or the environment.

Hybrids are a pie-in-the-sky alternative fuel system that uses expensive and complex electronic and mechanical components to achieve the same fuel economy that a bare-bones Honda Civic or Toyota Yaris can achieve at half the initial purchase price—and without polluting the environment with exotic toxic metals leeched from used battery packs. Once again, the Union of Concerned Scientists weighs in:

> The idea that hybrids will save their owners money is gradually being replaced by a realization that the payback period of these more expensive vehicles is to be measured in years. Furthermore the launch of more performance-oriented hybrids has confused environmentalists who thought the hybrid concept was purely aimed at saving fuel. But even more alarming to hybrid fans will be the impact of real world EPA mpg testing, especially on the city driving cycle. Because hybrids currently have such impressively high fuel economy numbers, their percentage drop will appear all the more dramatic.

Want the real-world hybrid fuel economy and cost-of-ownership numbers?

Consumer Reports tested six pairs of vehicles, with each pair including a conventional vehicle and the equivalent hybrid model, and published the astounding results in its April 2006 edition. *CR* found that in each category of car, truck, and SUV, the extra cost for the hybrid version was unacceptably *higher* than the same vehicle equipped with a conventional propulsion system.

ESTIMATED COSTS FOR 2006 GASOLINE-FUELED VEHICLES VS. HYBRIDS

Over a 5-year period, the smallest estimated U.S.–dollar operating cost difference was between the two Honda Civics ($3,700), followed by Toyota's Corolla and Prius ($5,250). The biggest gap between two similar models was registered by the gasoline-powered Toyota Highlander SUV and its hybrid version ($13,300 U.S.), with the Lexus RX330 and RX400h posting a $13,100 higher cost for the hybrid version. The first two figures are the manufacturers' suggested retail prices.

	GASOLINE	HYBRID	HIGHER OPERATING COST
Ford Escape SUV	$22,818	$29,140	$8,350
Honda Accord EX	$25,862	$31,540	$10,250
Honda Civic	$18,444	$22,400	$3,750
Lexus RX330/RX400h	$37,960	$46,755	$13,100
Toyota Highlander	$32,650	$39,835	$13,300
Toyota Corolla/Prius	$16,607	$22,305	$5,250

Source: *Consumer Reports*, April 2006

Other disadvantages of hybrids are their mechanical and electronic complexities, dependence upon specialized dealers for basic servicing, high depreciation rates and insurance costs, overblown fuel-efficiency numbers (owners report getting

40 percent less than promised), and $6,000 to $8,000 costs to replace their battery packs.

Hybrid reliability has been problematic, as well. For example, Honda's first hybrid, the Insight, won't return in 2007. This is a move that will further enrage unhappy owners who claim the car's a lemon, like this *Lemon-Aid* reader who drives a 2001 Insight and has the following complaints:

- Honda Insight hybrid MSRP: $26,000. The total cost of warranty, repair, recalls, and diagnosis as of Nov. 7, 2005 is approx. $14,119.94, which is 54.3% of the MSRP. Out of pocket expense Approx. $5,000.
- Random complete loss of the Integrated Motor Assist engine (Battery power) which I believe has put my life at risk.
- Honda's consistent inability to properly diagnose my Honda hybrid's problems without a "Check Engine Light"; this has lead to even MORE damage.
- Three catalytic converters within 155,000 km. Because of the complexity of this Honda hybrid there aren't any other options then to purchase the parts through Honda, at approximately $2,000. How can Honda allow the need for replacement every 60,000 km?
- Long waiting periods for almost every part I have ever needed for my Honda hybrid, which in turn has caused weeks, if not months of vehicle downtime and approx. 367 days of open work orders/un-resolved problems, 6 months of loss of use due to the IMA failure, 6 months of inconsistent/unreliable use due to IMA periodic failure, approx 4–5 months of loss of use due to other failures/matters.
- At 150,000 km I have a lifetime mpg of only 42.3 mpg [5.6 L/100 km], a large contrast from Honda's initially advertised 68 mpg [3.5 L/100 km].
- Strange, electric noises randomly coming from the IMA Battery Compartment.
- Water damaged $300+ speakers, carpet rot and interior rust probably due to a chronic drivers side window leak that they can't seem to permanently fix.
- Transmission failure, ABS Brake system failure, and AC failure.

In June 2006, Ford announced that it wouldn't launch many more hybrid models, despite a previous promise made a year earlier that its goal was for most of its production to change to hybrids. Instead, the company pledged to add ethanol flex-fuel vehicles to its model lineup.

Diesel

Of all the alternate fuels tested by independent researchers, diesel comes closest to the estimated fuel economy figures. It's also widely available and neither requires a steep learning curve in the service bay nor needs exotic replacement parts. Additionally, unlike hybrids, diesel-equipped vehicles are reasonably priced and hold their value quite well. Unfortunately, all this will change next year as diesel-fuel formulation is changed and the fuel delivery systems are radically revamped to reduce emissions. Already, DaimlerChrysler has thrown in the towel and announced that its best-selling diesel-equipped Jeep Liberty will be dropped in late 2006.

As with the changeover to unleaded gasoline two decades ago, owners of diesel-equipped vehicles can expect horrendously expensive maintenance costs, considerable repair downtime, and worsening of the diesel's poor reliability trend, which was seen over the past decade with Ford's Powerstroke and General Motors' Duramax.

Plus, there's always the pricing of diesel fuel, which already costs almost as much as regular gasoline, and a predicted shortage outlined by Michael Tusiani, a senior fellow at Columbia University's Center for Energy, Marine Transportation and Public Policy. In a research paper published in *The Washington Post* on August 8, 2005 (and reproduced on their website at *www.washingtonpost.com*), titled "Diesel Won't Solve Our Gasoline Woes," Tusiani issued the following warning:

> Automakers are eager to sell you a diesel-powered vehicle. One of their responses to the rising price of gasoline has been to tell American motorists they can keep their large, powerful vehicles and at the same time save on fuel by buying a car or truck that burns diesel instead of gasoline.... Diesel-fueled vehicles do afford somewhat better mileage and may not require as much maintenance as gasoline-burners. But now and for years to come, the U.S. refining industry simply cannot produce enough diesel fuel to accommodate a significant increase in the number of vehicles that burn it.... Diesel oil prices in Europe are soaring as demand pushes past the amount refiners can make.

Fuel economy misrepresentation

So, if you can't make a gas-saving product that pours into your fuel tank, or attaches to the fuel or air lines, you have to use that old standby and, well, lie. Hell, if automakers and government fuel efficiency advocates can do it, then why not dealers?

Fuel economy misrepresentation is actionable, and there is Canadian jurisprudence that allows for a contract's cancellation if the gas-mileage figures are false (see Appendix III). Most people, however, simply keep the car they bought and live with the fact that they were fooled.

There are a few new-car choices you can make that will lower fuel consumption. First off, choose a smaller version of the vehicle style you are interested in buying. Secondly, choose a manual transmission or an automatic with a fuel-saving Fifth gear. Thirdly, an engine with a cylinder deactivation feature or variable valve timing will increase fuel economy by 8 and 3 percent, respectively.

Although good fuel economy is important, it's hardly worth a harsh ride, excessive highway noise, side-wind buffeting, anemic acceleration, and a cramped interior. If you make your choice based entirely on fuel economy, you may end up with much worse gas mileage than advertised and a vehicle that's underpowered for your needs.

If you never quite got the hang of metric fuel economy measurements, use the fuel conversion table that follows to establish how many miles to a gallon of gas your vehicle provides.

FUEL ECONOMY CONVERSION TABLE

L/100 KM	MPG	L/100 KM	MPG	L/100 KM	MPG
5.0	56	7.4	38	12.5	23
5.2	54	7.6	37	13.0	22
5.4	52	7.8	36	13.5	21
5.6	50	8.0	35	14.0	20
5.8	48	8.5	33	15.0	19
6.0	47	9.0	31	15.0	18
6.2	46	9.5	30	17.0	17
6.4	44	10.0	28	18.0	16
6.7	43	10.5	27	19.0	15
6.8	42	11.0	26	20.0	14
7.0	40	11.5	25	21.0	13
7.2	39	12.0	24	23.0	12

Excessive Maintenance Fees

Maintenance inspections and parts costs represent hidden expenses that are usually exaggerated by dealers and automakers to increase their profits on vehicles that rarely require fixing or that are sold in insufficient numbers to support a service bay. Both Mazda and Honda owners suspect this to be the case, and a CBC *Marketplace* survey confirms the accusations against Mazda dealers.

In an investigative report shown on February 18, 2003, CBC TV's *Marketplace* surveyed 12 Mazda dealers across the country to determine how much they charged for a "regularly scheduled maintenance inspection," as listed in the owner's manual of a 2001 Mazda MPV with 48,000 km (*www.cbc.ca/consumers/market/files/cars/ mazda_warranty*). Even with different labour rates, Mazda says the check-up should not cost more than about $280 anywhere in Canada. Here are the prices they were quoted:

- $400 (Montreal)
- $546 (Burlington)
- $225 (Toronto)
- $300 (Toronto)
- $271 (Winnipeg)
- $700 (Winnipeg)
- $253 (Calgary)
- $340 (Calgary)
- $450 (Calgary)
- $350 (Vancouver)
- $500 (Vancouver)
- $525 (Vancouver)

The first quote for service in Winnipeg was $700. A service technician told *Marketplace*'s producer that the price varied between $400 and $500 and warned that the work was needed to maintain the warranty. However, a check of the owner's manual didn't show any connection between the service and keeping the warranty in place. Gregory Young, director of Corporate Public Relations for Mazda Canada, said, "There's nothing in the owner's manual that says if you don't have this work done in its entirety at a prescribed time that automatically your warranty is void."

Alan Gelman, a well-known Toronto garage owner and host of CFRB radio's *Car Talk*, warns drivers:

> There are actually two maintenance schedules handed out by car companies and dealers. The dealer inspection sheets often call for far more extensive and expensive routine maintenance checks than what's listed in the owner's manual. Most of those checks are padding; smart owners will stick with the essential checks listed in the manual and have them done by cheaper, independent garages.

Getting routine work done at independent facilities will cost about one-third to one-half the price usually charged by dealers. Just be sure to follow the automaker's suggested schedule so no warranty claim can be tied to botched servicing. Additionally, a $25 ALLDATA service bulletin subscription (see Appendix I) will keep you current as to your vehicle's factory defects, required check-ups, and recalls; will tell you what's covered by little-known "goodwill" warranties; and will save you valuable time and money when troubleshooting common problems (I just *hate* it when mechanics replace all of the good parts to get to that one defective component).

More Information Sources

The government lies to us about fuel economy and airbag dangers. Automakers lie to us about the reliability and "real" prices of their products. Car dealers routinely charge us for services covered by "goodwill" extended warranties and put pricing information in such small print in newspapers that no one can read it. And many car journalists lie to us when they say that they're unbiased, aren't intimidated by their editors and automaker reps, and can't be, ahem...bribed.

Most investigative stories done on the auto industry in Canada (such as exposés on secret car warranties, dangerous airbags, and car company shenanigans) have been written by business columnists, freelancers, or "action line" troubleshooters rather than by reporters on the auto beat. This is because most auto beat reporters are regularly beaten into submission by myopic editors and greedy publishers who don't give them the time or the encouragement to do hard-hitting investigative exposés. In fact, it's quite impressive that we do have a small cadre of reporters who won't be cowed. Links to some of the best Canadian and American websites on these subjects can be found at *www.lemonaidcars.com* or in this book's Appendix I. Here are some examples:

- The non-profit Automobile Protection Association (*www.apa.ca*) is a consumer-protection website. The group specializes in exposing unsafe and unreliable cars and trucks. Presently, it is in the middle of a campaign to get Ford Canada to recall 1997–2004 F-Series trucks with defective tie-rod ends that may suddenly throw the truck out of control. After almost two years of APA pressure, Ford's only response has been to send a service letter reminding owners to inspect or repair their trucks—at the owners' expense, of course.
- *Straight-six.com* is an independent, Ottawa-based car enthusiast website that offers a unique and entertaining voice to the dedicated car zealot. The editorial content, mostly written by publisher John LeBlanc, who also writes regularly for the *Ottawa Citizen*, focuses on topics right through the automotive enthusiast spectrum, from automaker marketing strategies to product and business trends. Readers of *straight-six.com* get unbiased, BS- and PR-free reviews and commentary on automotive issues related to the love of driving cars. LeBlanc is at his best when he gives no-nonsense reviews of high-performance vehicles and proves that dollar power doesn't always convert to performance power.
- Toronto-based Kurt Binnie's *OnTheHoist.com* is a well-written site replete with auto information from consumer advocacy and car enthusiast perspectives (not an easy balance). Binnie buttresses information files and frequent blog entries with URLs from around the world that run the gamut from the well known to the obscure. He is particularly effective as a price analyst who tracks down auto companies' suggested retail prices, customer and dealer rebates, and sales incentives and discount programs and then compares them on both sides of the border. His website is an essential free tool for effective price haggling.
- The *CanadianDriver* website (*www.canadiandriver.com*) offers a cornucopia of Canadian car critics who are relatively independent of industry influence.

Canada also has a number of media personalities who are not afraid to take on the auto industry and follow good stories, no matter where they lead. Here are some of my favourites:

- Jeremy Cato and Michael Vaughan, two of Canada's best-known business journalists, host *Car Business*, shown Friday, Saturday, and Sunday on *Report on Business Television (ROBTv)*. This duo epitomizes the best combination of auto journalism and business reporting by asking the tough questions automakers hate to answer.
- Mohamed Bouchama, president of Car Help Canada, shakes up the auto industry by rating new and used cars, providing legal advice, and teaching consumers the art of complaining on *AutoShop* every Sunday night at 4:00 p.m. EST on Toronto's CityPulse24.
- The *Vancouver Sun*'s Linda Bates does an outstanding job without compromising her integrity; she was the first to blow the whistle on "bad gas" in B.C.

- There's also the *Toronto Star*'s Ellen Roseman, one of Canada's foremost consumer advocates and business columnists. A few years ago, she skewered Mazda Canada over its $40,000 RX-8 sports cars that wouldn't start:

  > We did our own search and found many similar stories, including one from a female owner who gave the car a one-star rating (out of five) at *Consumer Reports* magazine's website. "A nightmare for any woman," she wrote. "Cannot move to wash, etc., or engine will flood."

  > Mazda subsequently put out a service bulletin, which can be found online, covering repair techniques for flooded 2004 and 2005 RX-8 models that have to be towed into dealerships. (The title: "Engine cranks, no start.")

  > *TORONTO STAR*
  > MAY 28, 2005

- Maryanna Lewyckyj is another crusading consumer advocate and journalist. She is a *Toronto Sun* business and consumer columnist who's more car-savvy than most automaker PR stuffed shirts. For example, Chrysler press honchos once had the Toronto motoring press fawning over their announcement that they were extending low-interest financing throughout Canada as a service to buyers everywhere. When Lewyckyj took a close look at the numbers, she came away unimpressed, and she effectively challenged Chrysler's pro-consumer pretensions.

- Phil Bailey is a Lachine, Quebec, garage owner with over four decades of experience with European, Japanese, and American cars. In his insightful comments on the car industry, he's as skillful with his pen as he is with a wrench, and he's got the everyday garage experience that make him and Toronto CFRB broadcaster Alan Gelman such unimpeachable auto industry critics. Bailey was particularly prophetic when he said this about hybrids, three years before *Consumer Reports* confirmed his findings (*www.baileycar.com/baileyblog.html*):

  > Everybody in the hybrid market is losing money. The current units, which are very complex, cost about $5,000 more than a normal IC engine. The buyer is paying about a $3,000 premium, which means the manufacturer is upside down for about $2,000. That, plus the fact that fuel economy gains are less than people think, what with winter when the heater and defroster are used and summer when the AC is in operation. Yes, there is a small improvement in city mpg, but it's negligible on the open road. Couple that with the still undetermined cost of maintenance of the Rube Goldberg power units and the unknown life cycle of the battery packs, and the economic advantages become hazy at best. A great deal depends on the future price of gasoline or if the government radically increases fuel mileage standards. But as it stands now, the average customer is going to stay with a conventional automobile because the mpg cost factor makes obvious economic sense. The price of fuel and lower cost technology will govern the market, and the role hybrids will play remains doubtful at best...

These reporters and consumer advocates are the exception, not the rule. Even the most ardent reporters frequently have to jump through hoops to get their stories out, simply because their editors or station managers have bought into many of the fraudulent practices so common to the auto industry. Haranguing staff for more "balance" is the pretext *du jour* for squelching hard-hitting stories that implicate dealers and automakers. News editors don't want truth; they want copy and comfort. They'll spend weeks sifting through Prime Minister Stephen Harper's or Belinda Stronach's trash cans looking for conflicts of interest or love letters while ignoring the auto industry scams threaded throughout their own advertisers' ads and commercials.

Want proof? Try to decipher the fine print in the *Globe and Mail's* or *Toronto Star's* leasing ads or, better yet, tell me what the fine print scrolled at breakneck speed on television commercials really says. Where is the investigative reporter who will submit these ads to an optometrists' group to confirm that the message is unreadable?

Think about this: Dealers selling used cars from residences, posing as private parties ("curbsiders"), are periodically exposed by dealer associations and "crusading" auto journalists. Yet these scam artists place dozens or more ads weekly in the classified sections of local newspapers that employ these muckraking reporters. The same phone numbers and billing addresses reappear, sometimes days after the scam has been featured in local news reports. The ad order-takers know who these crooks are. News editors know that their own papers are promoting these scammers. Why isn't there an exposé by reporters working for these papers? Why don't they publish the fact that it's mostly new-vehicle dealers who supply curbsiders with their cars? That's what I'd call balanced reporting. Although car columnists claim that their integrity is not for sale, there's no doubt that it can be rented. Travel junkets and public relations and advertising contracts all sweeten the pot for these pseudo-journalists.

Two of my favourite auto journalists, Dan Neil, automotive writer for the liberal *Los Angeles Times*, and Robert Farago, a long-time columnist, auto critic, and creator of *The Truth About Cars*, a British-based website, were both punished recently for writing the truth.

Neil's paper was hit with a $10-million (U.S.) loss after General Motors and its dealers pulled their ads in response to his sharp criticism of GM for a series of poor management decisions that lead to the flop of its 2005 G6 model:

> GM is a morass of a business case, but one thing seems clear enough, and Lutz's mistake was to state the obvious and then recant: The company's multiplicity of divisions and models is turning into a circular firing squad...someone's head ought to roll, and

the most likely candidate would be the luminous white noggin of Lutz...[the G6] is not an awful car. It's entirely adequate. But plainly, adequate is not nearly enough...

LOS ANGELES TIMES
APRIL 6, 2005

The *Times* stood by Neil, a Pulitzer Prize–winning automobile columnist. GM's ads eventually returned after a hiatus of several months.

Farago didn't fare as well. In late August 2005, he was canned and stayed canned. His column was permanently axed, without explanation, by the uber-liberal *San Francisco Chronicle* after his criticism of Subaru's Tribeca, an SUV wannabe that never will be:

> I'm not sure if the *Chronicle* removed my description of the SUV's front end as a "flying vagina" (the editors ignored my request for a copy of the published review), but even without it my analysis of the B9 was not bound to please its manufacturer....
>
> In fact, the Subaru B9 Tribeca is both subjectively (to the best of my knowledge and experience) and empirically a dreadful machine that besmirches the reputation of its manufacturer. Sure, the B9 handles well. The review pointed this out. But to suggest that it's an SUV worthy of its manufacturer's hype ("The end of the SUV as we know it" and "The ideal balance of power and refinement") is to become a co-conspirator in Subaru's attempts to mislead the public....
>
> And here's the thing: I believe the media in general, and newspapers in particular, have an obligation to tell the truth about cars. You know all those puff pieces that fill up the odd blank spot in every single automotive section in this great country of ours?... And that's why so many car enthusiasts have turned to the web. Other than Dan Neil at the *Los Angeles Times*, there are no print journalists ready, willing and able to directly challenge the auto manufacturers' influence with the plain, unvarnished truth (including the writers found in the happy clappy buff books). Car lovers yearn for the truth about cars. Sites like *www.jalopnik.com* are dedicated to providing it. And that's why the mainstream press' cozy little Boys' Club is doomed....

Steer Clear of the "Car of the Year"

Once you've established a budget and selected some vehicles that interest you, the next step is to ascertain which ones have high safety and reliability ratings. Be wary of the ratings announced by car journalist groups, magazines, and enthusiast websites; their supposedly independent tests are a lot of baloney (see "Keeping Ratings Honest and Fair" in Part Four).

In 1994, North American car journalists awarded the first annual North American Car of the Year at the Detroit Auto Show. They picked the Mercedes C-Class—an entry-level compact noted for its mediocre reliability and poor performance. The

Dodge Ram garnered the top truck award, while the Chevrolet S-10/GMC Sonoma and Land Rover Defender 90 (another sales and quality loser) were chosen as top contenders.

A year later, top honours went to the Chrysler Cirrus, Ford Contour, and Oldsmobile Aurora. Chevrolet's Blazer was named Truck of the Year, along with finalists Ford Explorer and Windstar.

All of these vehicles, except for the Explorer and Ram, are now extinct.

You want proof of how misleading the magazine ratings can be? Take *Car and Driver* as an example. It rated the Ford Focus as a "Best Buy" during its first three model years, while government and consumer groups decried the car's dozen or so recall campaigns and the huge number of owner safety and reliability complaints. *Consumer Reports* made the same mistake with the 2006 Focus and then recanted the following day.

Getting Reliable Info

Funny, as soon as people hear that you're shopping for a new vehicle, they all want to tell you what to buy. After a while, you'll get so many conflicting opinions that it'll seem as if any choice you make will be the wrong one. Before making your decision, remember that you should invest a couple of months in researching costs and models. The following sources provide a variety of useful information that will help you to ferret out what vehicle best suits your needs and budget.

There are hundreds of organizations and magazines that rate cars for everything from their overall reliability and frequency of repairs (J.D. Power and *Consumer Reports*) to their crashworthiness and appeal to owners (NHTSA, IIHS, and Strategic Vision's Total Quality Index, or TQI). These ratings don't always match. For instance, BMW's Mini ranked 25th out of 28 brands in J.D. Power's Initial Quality Survey (IQS). But the popular import ranks second out of 30 brands included in the TQI. And, as fuel prices hit record levels, Mini dealers are tacking on extra charges. Such is the popularity of their little car.

Auto shows

Auto shows are held from January through March throughout Canada, starting in Montreal and ending in Vancouver. Although you can't buy or drive a car at the show, you can easily compare prices and the interior/exterior styling of different vehicles. In fact, show officials estimate that about 20 percent of auto show visitors are actively seeking info for an upcoming new-car purchase. Interestingly, while the shows are open, dealer traffic nosedives, making for much more generous deals in showrooms. Business usually picks up following the show.

Online services

Anyone with access to the Internet can now obtain useful information relating to the auto industry in a matter of minutes at little or no cost. This is accomplished in two ways: subscribing to an online service, like America Online (AOL), that offers consumer forums and easy Internet access; or going directly to the Internet through a low-cost Canadian Internet service provider (ISP) and using a search engine like Google that helps you to find thousands of helpful sites. An extensive listing of informative and helpful sites can be found in Appendix I; however, I've listed a few of my favourite sites below. Many of them are a bit offbeat and highly critical of the auto industry:

American Car Fans
www.worldcarfans.com/country.cfm/country/acf

Autoblog
www.autoblog.com

Autoextremist
www.autoextremist.com

Automobile Magazine
www.automobilemag.com

AutoMuse
www.vehicleinfo.com/AutoMuse

AutoSpies
www.autospies.com

AutoWeek
www.autoweek.com

AutoWonder
www.autowonder.com

Cars! Cars! Cars!
www.carscarscars.blogs.com

Car Connection
www.thecarconnection.com

Car Design News
www.cardesignnews.com

Shopping on the Internet

The key word here is "shopping," because *Consumer Reports* magazine has found that barely 2 percent of Internet surfers actually buy a new or used car online. Yet over 80 percent of buyers admit to using the Internet to get prices and specifications before visiting the dealership. Apparently, few buyers want to purchase a new or used vehicle without seeing what's offered and knowing that all the money paid will be accounted for.

New-vehicle shopping through automaker and independent websites is a quick and easy way to compare prices and model specifications, but you will have to be careful. Many so-called independent sites are merely fronts for dealers and automakers, tailoring their information to steer you into their showroom or convince you to buy a certain brand of car. One independent Canadian site for real discounted prices is *OnTheHoist.com*.

Shoppers now have access to information they once were routinely denied or had trouble finding such as dealer price markups and incentive programs, the book value for trade-ins, and considerable safety data. Canadian shoppers can get invoice prices and specs by contacting the Automobile Protection Association (APA) by phone or fax, or by visiting *CarCostCanada.com*.

Other advantages to online shopping are as follows: Some dealers offer a lower price to online shoppers; the entire transaction, including financing, can be done on the Internet; and buyers don't have to haggle, they merely post their best offer electronically to a number of dealers in their area code (for more convenient servicing of the vehicle) and then await counteroffers. But here are three caveats: (1) You will have to go to a dealer to finalize the contract and be preyed upon by the financing and insurance (F&I) sales agents; (2) as far as bargains are concerned, *Consumer Reports* says its test shoppers obtained lower prices more frequently by visiting the dealer showroom and concluding the sale there; and (3) only one-third of online dealers respond to customer queries.

Auto Quality Rankings

There are two major surveyors of automobile quality: J.D. Power and Associates and Consumers Union, an American non-profit consumer organization that publishes *Consumer Reports*.

J.D. Power and Associates

Each year, J.D. Power and Associates publishes the results of two important surveys measuring vehicle quality (Vehicle Dependability Study, or VDS) and owners' customer service satisfaction (Customer Service Satisfaction Index Study, or CSI). Interestingly, these two polls often contradict each other. For example, the Dependability Index places Saturn near the bottom of the list; however, Saturn has placed sixth from the top in the Power Service Index. This leads one to conclude that the car isn't very reliable, but service comes with a smile!

J.D. Power does have influence in the auto industry. Its criticism of Nissan's 2004 Quest minivan had that company's engineers working overtime fixing or replacing faulty sliding doors, power window switches, interior reading lights, second-row seat levers, and airbag sensors after the group's 2004 Initial Quality Study rated the Quest last among minivans in consumer perceptions of quality during the first 100 days of ownership. Nissan's Titan full-sized pickup and Armada full-sized SUV also placed last in their segments for other problems. All three models continue to sell poorly, in part because of their poor-quality image and, secondarily, due to on-going mechanical and body deficiencies.

Another revealing, though lesser-known, report is J.D. Power's annual Customer Retention Study, which measures the percentage of owners who remain loyal to a particular automaker. Since poor build quality or inadequate servicing are factors that may lead to owners taking their business elsewhere, this study provides an early warning that an automaker is struggling to keep its customers.

Consumer Reports

Consumer groups and non-profit auto associations like the Automobile Protection Association and Car Help Canada (see Appendix I) are your best bets for the most unbiased auto ratings for Canadians. They're not perfect, though, so it's a good idea to consult both groups and look for ratings that match.

Consumer Reports (CR) is an American publication that once had a tenuous affiliation with the Consumers' Association of Canada. Its ratings, extrapolated from Consumers Union's annual U.S. member survey, don't quite mirror the Canadian experience. Components that are particularly vulnerable to our harsh climate usually don't perform as well as the *CR* reliability ratings indicate, and poor servicing caused by a weak dealer body in Canada can make some service-dependent vehicles a nightmare to own here, whereas the American experience may be less problematic.

Based on just over one million responses from subscribers to *Consumer Reports* and *ConsumerReports.org*, *CR's* annual auto reliability findings are impressively comprehensive, though they may not always be correct. Statisticians agree that *CR's* sampling method leaves some room for error, but, with a few notable exceptions, the ratings are fair, conservative, and consistent guidelines for buying a reliable vehicle.

My only criticisms of the ratings are that many Asian models, like Toyota and Honda, are not as harshly scrutinized as their American counterparts, yet service bulletins and extended "goodwill" warranties have shown for years that they also have serious engine, transmission, brake, and electrical problems. *Consumer Reports* confirms this anomaly in its April 2006 edition, where it admits that Asian vehicle quality improvement has "slowed" since 2002. Too bad the organization didn't consult the auto companies' own service bulletins four years earlier, as *Lemon-Aid* did when we downrated a slew of formerly sacrosanct Japanese models, like the Honda Odyssey, Nissan Quest, and Toyota Sienna minivans. Summaries of bulletins for the 2004 Quest and Sienna appear on pages 61–63.

Older vehicles (pre-1998) are excluded from *CR's* detailed ratings, just as statistics show that owners are keeping their vehicles for a decade or longer. Also, many of the ratings about the frequency of repairs of certain components aren't specific enough. For example, instead of just mentioning problems with the engine or the fuel or electrical system, ratings should be specific about which components are likely to fail. Is it the engine intake manifold and fuel pumps that are failure-prone, or is it the injectors that clog up, or the battery that suddenly dies?

2004 NISSAN QUEST BULLETINS: DISCLOSED PROBLEMS

NUMBER	DATE	TITLE
04-060	11/23/2005	Erratic/Harsh A/T Shifts
05-021A	10/26/2005	Rattle/Buzzing Noise on Acceleration
05-095	10/21/2005	Rattle on Acceleration
NHTSA05V474000	10/11/2005	Recall: Second-Row Seat
NHTSA05V480000	10/11/2005	Recall: Third-Row Seat
04-014A	09/21/2005	Skyview Roof Leaks
03-080A	09/21/2005	Side Door Squeaks/Rattles/Hard to Close
05-071	08/10/2005	Insufficient Cooling
SN050600-011	06/01/2005	Heater Blows Cold Air, AC Blows Warm Air
05-016	05/17/2005	Child Seat Anchor–Locating Button Missing
SN050508	05/01/2005	Catalytic Converter Noise
04-021	04/08/2005	Recall: Automatic Transmission
04-060	03/04/2005	Campaign: PCM Upgrade
SN050314	03/01/2005	A/T Banjo-Bolt Leaks
04-144A	02/07/2005	Low Power/Stays in Third Gear/DTC's
03-022	02/04/2005	Audio Controls Don't Work Properly
05-010	02/03/2005	Interior Power Seat Lifter Clicking/Popping Noises
05-003	01/12/2005	Tire Dressing Stains Paint
05-001	01/03/2005	Harsh 1–2 Shift
04-136	11/18/2004	Third-Row Seat Rattles
03-031B	11/11/2004	Vehicle No-Start
04-063	11/09/2004	Accelerator Pedal Hard to Press
04-090A	10/21/2004	MIL on/Misfire
04-123	10/14/2004	Airbag Lamp Flashing
01-005A	10/07/2004	Seat Belts Slow to Retract
04-111	10/06/2004	Engine No-Crank In Extreme Cold
04-049	09/30/2004	Recall: Fuel-Pump Connector Corrosion
04-110	09/21/2004	Running Board Lights Inoperative
04-087C	09/20/2004	Treble Fades In and Out
03-113B	09/15/2004	Static/Cuts Out on A/M Band
00-033B	08/30/2004	Brake Judder/Noise/Pedal Feel
NHTSA04V420000	08/25/2004	Recall: Fuel-Pump Replacement
04-096	08/24/2004	Exhaust Booming/Vibration at 2000 rpm
04-099	08/24/2004	Navigation System Inoperative
SN040813	08/01/2004	Thump When Accelerating or Braking
04-030	07/30/2004	Right A-Pillar Creaking
04-020B	07/20/2004	Warm Air Blows from the Floor Vents
SN040703	07/01/2004	Poor Cooling During Hard Acceleration
04-053	06/23/2004	Campaign: Vehicle Systems Upgrade
04-051	06/16/2004	Recall: Occupant Detection System
04-078	06/16/2004	Radio Cuts In and Out
04-052	06/16/2004	Recall: Power-Sliding Door
04-063	05/24/2004	Hard Start
SN040505	05/01/2004	Broken Alternator Bracket/Mounting Bolt

NUMBER	DATE	TITLE
04-021A	04/29/2004	Hard/No-Start after a Cold Soak
04-019A,	04/19/2004	Exhaust Ticking Noise
NHTSA04V186000	04/01/2004	Recall: Power-Sliding Door
NHTSA04V176000	04/01/2004	Recall: A/T Gear Failure
SN040414	04/01/2004	Roof Rack Wind Noise
04-019	03/23/2004	Rear Brake Clunk Sound
04-038	03/16/2004	Slow Tire Leak
04-035	03/10/2004	Abnormal Shifting
04-034	03/08/2004	DVD Player Inoperative
NHTSA04V103000	03/01/2004	Recall: Occupant Sensing System
SN040310	03/01/2004	ABS Grunts When Doing a Self-Check
SN040315	03/01/2004	Water Leak from Door
04-030	02/25/2004	Whistle from Door Mirror
04-029	02/24/2004	Sunroof Water Leaks
04-026	02/23/2004	Power-Sliding Door Malfunctions
04-018	02/06/2004	Cooling System Leaks/Overheating
03-115A	01/27/2004	Second-/Third-Row Seat Head-Restraint Holder Broken
SN040115	01/01/2004	Engine Cranks but Doesn't Start
SN040113	01/01/2004	Shift Lever Stuck In Park
SN031208	12/01/2003	Leak from A/T Cooler Line
SN031107	11/01/2003	Blower Motor Gets Hot/Blows a Fuse
SN031101	11/01/2003	Humming or Growling Wheel Bearings
SN031106	11/01/2003	Air Fresheners: Bad News for Paint or Plastic
03-085	09/18/2003	Interior Lights Inoperative
SN030915	09/01/2003	Drifting & Pulling at Highway Speeds
03-074	07/29/2003	Headlight Fogging
03-068	07/08/2003	Horn Chirp/Lamp Flash Error
00-033A	06/11/2003	Brake Judder/Vibration

2004 TOYOTA SIENNA BULLETINS: DISCLOSED PROBLEMS

NUMBER	DATE	TITLE
ST005R-01	10/21/2005	Vehicle Pulls to One Side, Manual Supplement
BO012-05	10/20/2005	Front-Seat Side Table Won't Lock in Position
EG043-05	09/28/2005	No-Start in Extreme Cold
AC006-05	09/16/2005	Blower Motor Squeal or Chirping Noise
AU001R-05	08/19/2005	Pop Noise When Turning Off Ignition
NHTSA05V327000	07/19/2005	Recall: Seat Belt Bezel
AC003-05	07/12/2005	AC Compressor Seized/Noisy
EG016R-05	06/28/2005	Fuel-Injector Ticking Noise
EL011-05	06/03/2005	Inoperative AC Light/Flashing
BO008-05	06/02/2005	Poor Rear Wiper Performance
TC007R-03	06/01/2005	A/T Downshift Lag/Gear Hunting
EL007-05	05/23/2005	Poor Rear-Seat Screen Visibility

NUMBER	DATE	TITLE
BR009R-04	05/13/2005	Premature Brake Pad Wear
EL003-05	03/29/2005	No Image Displayed from Back-Up Camera
EG011-05	03/11/2005	Squeak or Creak Noise While Driving
BR008R-04	02/23/2005	ABS/TCS Intermittent VSC Activation
AC005R-04	02/09/2005	Seat Heater Only Works on High Position
ST003R-04	11/18/2004	Steering-Column Squeak/Pop/Click Noise
BR002R-04	08/20/2004	Rear Disc Brake Groaning Noise
BO016-04	07/16/2004	Rear Seats Won't Lock
ST003R-04	04/29/2004	Steering-Shaft Noise on Turns
EL004-04	04/19/2004	Power-Sliding Door Inoperative
NV004-04	04/02/2004	Sliding Side-Door Rattles
BO006-04	03/30/2004	Rear-Quarter Window-Shade Clip Falls Off
BO003-04	03/09/2004	Back-Door Shudder/Water Leaks
BO017R-03	03/03/2004	Trim Panels Loose/Fit Poorly
TC010-04	12/12/2003	Hard Gear Selection
NV009R-03	10/03/2003	Front-Door Area Wind Noise

Lemon-Aid *versus* Consumer Reports

I have a lot of respect for *Consumer Reports,* having been an elected member of its Board almost 30 years ago. Therefore, it's not surprising that *CR* and *Lemon-Aid* ratings often agree. Where they differ is in *Lemon-Aid*'s greater reliance upon NHTSA safety complaints, service bulletin admissions of defects, and owner complaints received through the Internet (rather than from *CR*'s subscriber base, which may simply attract owners singing from the same hymnal).

In looking over *CR*'s best new- and used-vehicle picks for 2003, as published in its December 2002 edition, a number of recommended vehicles defy all logic. Foremost of these is the Ford Windstar and the Saturn Vue. It is inconceivable that *CR* isn't aware of the multiplicity of powertrain, body, and suspension failures affecting these vehicles. Then there's the assorted Chrysler lineup. Now, you'd have to live on another planet not to know that Chryslers are afflicted with chronic automatic transmission, ball joint, body, brake, and AC defects. And in fact *Consumer Reports*' "Frequency of Repair" tables give out plenty of black marks to the aforementioned models and components—in the very same edition where these vehicles are praised. I'll admit that car ratings are part science and part art, but in this case I'll have to assume that sloppy research and editing failed to pick up on these contradictions.

CR has done a better job with its 2005–06 ratings. But once again Ford trips them up. This time they gave a "Recommended" rating to the Focus, one of the worst Fords ever built. *CR* pulled its rating the very next day, as NHTSA government crash tests showed the Focus to be dangerously vulnerable to side impacts.

When and Where to Buy (New Vehicles)

When to Buy

A good time to buy a new sport-utility, van, or truck that hasn't been redesigned is between January and March, when you get the first series of rebates and dealer incentives and production quality begins to improve. Try not to buy when there's strike action—it will be especially tough to get a bargain because there's less product to sell and dealers have to make as much profit as possible on each vehicle remaining in their diminishing stock. Furthermore, work stoppages increase the chances that on-the-line defects will go uncorrected and the vehicle will be delivered, as is, to product-starved dealers.

Instead, lie low for a while and then return in the summer and early fall, when you can double-dip from additional automakers' dealer incentives and aggressive price-cutting, which can mean getting thousands of dollars in additional savings. Remember, too, that vehicles made between March and August offer the most factory upgrades, based on field complaints from those unfortunate fleet managers and rental car agencies who bought the vehicles when they first came out.

Allow yourself at least two weeks to finalize a deal if you're not trading in your vehicle and longer if you sell your vehicle privately. Visit the showroom at the end of the month, just before closing, when the salesperson will want to make that one last sale to meet their month's quota. If sales have been terrible, the sales manager may be willing to do some extra negotiating in order to boost sales staff morale.

Where to Buy

If all you care about is a low price, then shopping in auto-factory towns will get you the cheapest vehicles, as assembly-line workers "flip" their heavily discounted cars. Large towns have more of a selection and a variety of payment plans that will likely suit your budget. On the downside, servicing is likely to be hit or miss because of the transient nature of the customers and mechanics. And you can forget about individual service.

Good dealers aren't always the ones with the lowest prices, though. Buying from someone who you know gives honest and reliable service is just as important as getting a good price. Check a dealer's honesty and reliability by talking with motorists who drive vehicles purchased from that dealer (identified by the nameplate on the trunk). If these customers have been treated fairly, they'll be glad to recommend their dealer. You can also ascertain the quality of new-vehicle preparation and servicing by renting one of the dealer's minivans or pickups for a weekend, or by getting your trade-in serviced.

How can you tell which dealers are the most honest and competent? Well, judging from the thousands of reports I receive each year, dealerships in small suburban and rural communities are fairer than big-city dealers because they're more vulnerable to negative word-of-mouth advertising and to poor sales—when their vehicles aren't selling, good service takes up the slack. Their prices may also be more competitive, but don't count on it.

Dealers selling more than one manufacturer's product line (Chrysler and Mitsubishi; Mercedes-Benz and Smart) present special problems. Overhead can be quite high, and the cancellation of a dual dealership by an automaker in favour of an exclusive franchise elsewhere is an ever-present threat. Parts availability may also be a problem because a dealer with two separate vehicle lines must split the inventory and may, therefore, have an inadequate supply on hand.

The quality of new-vehicle service is directly linked to the number and competence of dealerships within the network. If the network is weak, parts are likely to be unavailable, repair costs can go through the roof, and the skill level of the mechanics may be questionable. Among foreign manufacturers, Asian automakers have the best overall dealer representation across Canada, except for Mitsubishi and Kia.

Kia's dealer network is very weak, having been left by its owner, Hyundai, to fend for itself for many years. The company's new Sportage SUV will decide the Kia's future. Mitsubishi is almost bankrupt, with a handful of its top executives headed for the slammer for concealing manufacturing defects that killed owners. Its Canadian dealers are piggybacked onto existing Chrysler franchises, who have their own sales problems, so don't expect the alliance to last for long.

BMW and Porsche are leading the European automakers in sales profits this year. Sure, their cars are highly dealer-dependent for parts and service, and they tend to be pricier than Japanese and American components, but their popularity continues to grow. Servicing by other European makes in Canada is still woefully inadequate, with VW's lack of a Canadian customer-assistance office making a bad situation even worse.

And, speaking of bad situations, Mercedes-Benz has gained a reputation for poor quality vehicles regarding its SUVs and C-Series and E-Series cars (complaints include engine sludge and electrical system problems).

Despite the above drawbacks, you can always get better treatment by patronizing dealerships that are accredited by auto clubs such as the CAA or consumer groups like the APA or Car Help Canada. Auto club accreditation is no ironclad guarantee of courteous, honest, or competent business practices; however, if you're insulted, cheated, or given bad service by one of their recommended garages (look for the accreditation symbol in their phone book ads or on their shop windows), the accrediting club is one more place to take your complaint and apply additional mediation pressure. And as you'll see under "Repairs" in Part Three, plaintiffs have won substantial refunds by pleading that the auto club is legally responsible for the actions of the garage it recommends.

Automobile Brokers and Vehicle-Buying Services

Brokers are independent agents who act as intermediaries to find the new or used vehicle you want at a price below what you'd normally pay. They have their Rolodex of contacts, speak the sales lingo, know all of the angles and scams, and can generally cut through the bull to find a fair price—usually within days. Their services may cost a few hundred dollars, but you may save a few thousand. Additionally, you save the stress and hassle associated with the dealership experience, which for many people is like a trip to the dentist.

Brokers get new vehicles through dealers, while used vehicles may come from dealers, auctions, private sellers, and leasing companies. The broker's job is to find a vehicle that meets a client's expressed needs and then to negotiate its purchase (or lease) on behalf of that client. The majority of brokers tend to deal exclusively in new vehicles, with a small percentage dealing in both new and used vehicles. Ancillary services vary among brokers and may include such things as comparative vehicle analysis and price research.

The cost of hiring a broker can be charged either as a flat fee of a few hundred dollars or as a percentage of the value of the vehicle (usually 1–2 percent). The flat fee is usually best because it encourages the broker to keep the selling price low. Reputable brokers are not beholden to any particular dealership or make, and they'll disclose their flat fee up front or tell you the percentage amount they'll charge on a specific vehicle.

 Finding the right broker

This is a tall order because good brokers are hard to find, particularly in Western Canada. Buyers who are looking for a broker should first ask friends and acquaintances if they could recommend one. Word-of-mouth referrals are often the best because people won't refer others to a service with which they were dissatisfied.

Your local credit union or the regional CAA office is a good place to get a broker referral. Toronto's Alterna Savings (formerly Metro Credit Union) has a vehicle counselling and purchasing service (Auto Advisory Services), where members can hire an expert "car shopper" who will do the legwork—including the tedious and frustrating dickering with sales staff—and save members time and hassle. This program can also get you a new or used vehicle at a reduced (fleet) rate, arrange top-dollar prices for trade-ins, provide independent advice on options like rust-proofing and extended warranties, carry out lien searches, and even negotiate the best settlement with insurance agents. The credit union holds regular car-buying seminars throughout the year in the Greater Toronto Area and maintains a CarFacts Centre, a free automotive information centre for members of Alterna Savings. The centre keeps an up-to-date library stocked with government publications, magazines such as *Consumer Reports* and *Consumer's Guide,* and, of course, copies of *Lemon-Aid* (Tel: 416-252-5621 or 1-877-560-0100; Website: *www.metrocu. com/Personal/Services/AutoAdvisoryServices*).

Finding a Reliable, Cheap Vehicle

The Death of Detroit

Of course we want to buy domestic, but what does that mean? DaimlerChrysler is a German automaker that was once allied with Hitler and used slave labour; most Asian cars are made in North America; Saab is being force-marched to GM's plant in Germany; and all of the top independent survey organizations put GM and Ford on the bottom rung of the quality ladder.

Today, Detroit's Big Three quality control is still way below average when compared with Japanese and South Korean automakers. Where the gap is particularly noticeable is in engine, automatic transmission, airbag, and anti-lock brake reliability as well as in fit and finish.

Do this simple test: Next time you're stuck in traffic, look closely at how the trunk and body panels are out of alignment on most Chrysler, Ford, and GM models. Notice the different-sized gaps on each side of the trunk lid and around the light assembly. Finally, ask yourself, "Who let these vehicles leave the factory uncorrected?"

Want more proof that not even your dealer's service manager can deny? Take a look at the Ford and GM internal service bulletins on the following page, which describe serious engine manifold failures. Note how the same defect has been carried over since 1997, with owners paying huge bills to fix the automakers' goof.

Don't get the impression that Chrysler, Ford, and GM can't make reasonably good vehicles. Chrysler's Sebring and PT Cruiser, Ford's Mustang, and GM's full-sized rear-drive vans are fairly reliable, but the Asian competition still makes better products. More about Chrysler's quality may be revealed, however, because its comprehensive 7-year powertrain warranty is no longer offered.

Ford's best vehicles are the Crown Victoria, the Mustang, and the Econoline full-sized van—all rear drives that have changed little over the past three decades.

GM HIGHER THAN EXPECTED OIL CONSUMPTION, BLUE SMOKE ON ACCELERATION

BULLETIN NO: 05-06-01-003   DATE: JANUARY 18, 2005

INSPECT INTAKE MANIFOLD AND/OR CAM COVER, REPLACE IF NECESSARY

2003–2004 Chevrolet Cavalier, Malibu

2004 Chevrolet Classic

2003–2004 Oldsmobile Alero

2003–2004 Pontiac Grand Am, Sunfire

with Ecotec 2.2L 4 Cylinder Engine (VIN F – RPO L61)

CONDITION: Some customers may comment on higher than expected oil consumption or blue smoke on acceleration. Oil consumption of more than one quart in 2000 miles (.94L in 3200 km) is considered higher than normal.

CAUSE: Incorrect sizing of the PCV office and/or misalignment of the oil baffle in the cam cover may allow higher than desired amounts of oil into the combustion chamber.

CORRECTION: Inspect the cam cover for heat skate marks and inspect the intake manifold for PCV orifice size. Replace either, as necessary, based on inspection.

FORD USE OF STAINLESS STEEL EXHAUST STUDS IN SERVICE FOR 5.4L 2V ENGINE

BULLETIN NO: 05-5-4

FORD:

1997–2004 Expedition, F-150

1999–2004 F-Super Duty

1999–2005 E-Series

LINCOLN:

1998–1999 Navigator

ISSUE: Some vehicles equipped with the 5.4L 2-valve (non supercharged) engine, may exhibit broken exhaust manifold studs.

ACTION: On the affected bank only, replace the exhaust manifold, manifold gasket(s), and install all new stainless steel exhaust manifold studs and nuts. Torque the studs in the cylinder head to 71–115 lb-in (8-13 N·m). Torque nuts on studs to 204–239 lb-in (23-27 N·m). Refer to Workshop Manual Section 313-01A for exhaust manifold removal and installation.

General Motors is more of a mixed bag. Its full-sized vans and SUVs, small cars, and joint ventures with Daewoo and Toyota have all performed well, but its trucks and newly released mid-sized family cars are mediocre at best—and its minivans are poison.

Most studies done by consumer groups and private firms show that, in spite of improvements attempted over the past two decades, vehicles made by DaimlerChrysler, Ford, and (to a lesser extent) GM still don't measure up to Japanese and some South Korean products, such as Hyundai, in terms of quality and technology. This is particularly evident in SUVs and minivans, where Honda, Nissan, and Toyota have long retained the highest reliability and dependability ratings, despite a handful of recent missteps with powertrain quality.

Whether you buy domestic or imported, overall vehicle safety and body fit and finish have improved among all automakers during the past three decades. On one hand, premature rusting is less of a problem and reliability is improving. On the other hand, repairs are outrageously expensive and complicated. Owners of cars and minivans made by GM, Ford, and Chrysler still report serious powertrain deficiencies, often within the vehicle's first year in service. These defects include electrical system failures caused by faulty computer modules; malfunctioning ABS systems, brake rotor warpage, and early pad wearout; failure-prone air conditioning and automatic transmissions; and defective engine head gaskets, intake manifolds, diesel fuel injectors and pumps, suspensions, steering, and paint.

Asian Automakers

Don't buy the myth that parts for imports are overpriced or hard to find. It's actually easier to find parts for Japanese vehicles than for domestic ones because of the large number of units produced, the presence of hundreds of independent suppliers, the ease with which relatively simple parts can be interchanged among different models, and the large reservoir of used parts stocked by junkyards. When a part is hard to find, the annual *Mitchell* manuals are useful guides to substitute parts that can be used for many different models. They're available in some libraries, most auto parts stores, and practically all junkyards.

Sadly, customer relations is the Japanese automakers' Achilles heel. Dealers are spoiled rotten by decades of easy sales and have developed a "take it or leave it" showroom attitude, often accompanied by a woeful ignorance of their own model lineup. This was once a frequent complaint of Honda and Toyota shoppers, though recent APA undercover surveys show a big improvement among Toyota dealers.

Where it has gotten worse is in the service bay, where periodic maintenance visits and warranty claims are like sessions with Liberal bagmen. Well-known factory-related defects (Honda engine oil leaks, Nissan exhaust manifolds, and Toyota engine and tranny problems) are corrected under extended warranties, but you always have the feeling you owe the "family."

There's no problem with discourteous or ill-informed South Korean automakers. Instead, poor quality has been their bugaboo. Yet, like Honda's and Toyota's recoveries following their own start-up quality glitches, Hyundai, South Korea's biggest automaker, has made considerable progress in bringing quality up almost to Toyota and Honda's level.

The same can't be said for Kia, a struggling, low-quality, small South Korean compact automaker bought by Hyundai in October 1998. Since then, Kia has languished under Hyundai's benign neglect, as Hyundai spent most of its resources on its more profitable middle-range and luxury models. Hyundai has said it will work hard to improve Kia quality and promised to show its commitment with the return of the Kia Sportage SUV in 2005 (it had been absent since 2002).

Up to the mid-'90s, South Korean vehicles were merely cheap, poor-quality knock-offs of their Japanese counterparts. They would start to fall apart after their third year because of subpar body construction and unreliable automatic transmission and electrical components as well as parts suppliers who put low prices ahead of reliability and durability. This was particularly evident with Hyundai's Pony, Stellar, Excel, and early Sonata models. During the past several years, though, Hyundai's product lineup has been extended and refined, and quality is no longer a worry. Hyundai's comprehensive base warranty protects owners from most of the more expensive breakdowns that may occur.

Hyundais are easily repaired in independent garages, and their rapid depreciation doesn't mean much. They cost little initially, and entry-level buyers are known to keep their cars longer than most, thereby easily amortizing the higher depreciation rate.

European Models

Lemon-Aid doesn't recommend any new or used European SUVs or minivans; there are way too many with serious and expensive quality and servicing problems. We all know the European automakers have fallen all over themselves trying to get a larger piece of the lucrative SUV and minivan markets—such is the pull of sky-high profits (a Lincoln Navigator may garner $15,000). But they haven't given us the same high-quality vehicles offered by many Asian automakers. Heck, even the Germans have abandoned their own products. For example, a 2002 J.D. Power survey of 15,000 German car owners found that German drivers are happiest at the wheel of a Lexus, a Toyota spin-off. This survey included compact and luxury cars as well as off-roaders. Toyota won first place on quality, reliability, and owner satisfaction, while Nissan's Maxima headed the luxury class standings.

Money-losing Land Rover, now owned by Ford, is still struggling since it moved into the North American market with its overpriced, quality-challenged, and under-serviced SUVs. But Land Rover of North America shrugs off its quality problems, and Ford isn't likely to improve things much while it struggles with its own mismanagement and poor-quality woes. For many years, Land Rovers got a free ride from fawning car columnists on this side of the Atlantic (British press criticism had been merciless about the vehicles' terrible quality control and marginal sales figures). A 2003 study of 34,000 car owners with vehicles up to eight years old published by Britain's Consumers' Association found that less than half of British owners would recommend a British-made Rover or Vauxhall to a friend. The most highly rated cars in the study were the Japanese Subaru, Isuzu, and Lexus: Over 85 percent of British drivers would recommend them.

Here's another surprise: Although it builds some fine vehicles, Mercedes-Benz's SUV quality control isn't equal to the company's pretensions. After stumbling badly when it first launched its rushed-to-production, American-made ML320 for the 1998 model year, the automaker has sent out many urgent service bulletins that seek to correct a surprisingly large number of production deficiencies. Judging by its own confidential bulletins, Mercedes' many factory-related defects have overwhelmed the company's resources at a critical time, when its redesigned 2006 SUVs hit the market this fall.

This year, the German automaker will revamp its entire line of M-Series SUVs to make them roomier, better-performing, and—dare we say it—more dependable. It will be a Herculean task, complicated by M-B's huge financial losses (its Smart Car division has lost billions and won't hit the States before 2008) and management chaos where the only secure jobs are with the Chrysler group.

Volkswagen's quality is just as bad as Mercedes', and its sales have been equally dismal. True, VW has always been early on the scene with great concepts, but they have also always been accompanied by poor execution and a weak servicing network. With its failure-prone and under-serviced EuroVan and Camper, the company hasn't been a serious minivan player since the late '60s, and VW's few sport-utility and pickup variants have been resounding duds. Even the company's forays into the luxury cruiser market have been met by underwhelming enthusiasm and general derision.

With European models, your service options are limited and customer-relations staffers can be particularly insensitive and arrogant. You can count on lots of aggravation and expense because of the unacceptably slow distribution of parts and their high markup. Because these companies have a quasi-monopoly on replacement parts, you can turn to few independent suppliers for help. And auto wreckers, the last-chance repository for inexpensive car parts, are unlikely to carry European parts for vehicles that are more than three years old or were manufactured in small numbers.

These vehicles also age badly. The weakest areas remain the drivetrains, electronic control modules, electrical and fuel systems, brakes, accessories (sound system, AC, etc.), and body components.

Watch the Warranty

There's a big difference between warranty promise and warranty performance. Most automakers offer bumper-to-bumper warranties, good for at least the first 3 years/60,000 km, and some problem-prone models and luxury makes get additional base coverage up to 5 years/100,000 km. DaimlerChrysler and South Korean automakers are also using more comprehensive 5- to 7-year warranties as important marketing tools to give their cars luxury cachet—or to allay buyers' fears of poor quality and reliability. It's also becoming an industry standard for car companies to pay for roadside assistance, a loaner car, or hotel accommodations if your vehicle breaks down while you're away from home and it's still under warranty. *Lemon-Aid* readers report few problems with these ancillary warranty benefits.

Warranty costs vary enormously among manufacturers and are often a good indication of how well the company stands behind its product. For example, Ford's automotive costs increased by $1.4 billion in the first half of 2005, with about $300 million coming from worse-than-expected warranty repairs for old models still under warranty.

Don't Buy More Warranty Than You Need

If you pick a vehicle rated recommended by *Lemon-Aid,* you don't need additional bumper-to-bumper protection and you can pocket the $2,000 an extra warranty would cost. However, you may get a good price on a vehicle known for some engine or transmission problems with past models. In that case, you may want a $1,000 extended powertrain warranty. If you are picking up an SUV or truck that has a sorry repair history, you will likely need a full $2,000 comprehensive warranty. But first, ask yourself this question: "Why am I buying a vehicle so poorly made that I need to spend several thousand dollars to protect myself until the warranty company gets tired of seeing my face?"

Just like the weight-loss ads you see on TV, what you see isn't always what you get with warranties. For example, bumper-to-bumper coverage usually excludes stereo components, brake pads, clutch plates, and many other expensive workings. Automakers will pull every trick in the book to make you pay for their factory screw-ups. This includes blaming your driving or poor maintenance, penalizing you for using an independent garage or the wrong fuel, or simply stating that the problem is "normal" and it's really you who's out of whack.

Part Three has all the answers to the above lame excuses. There you will find plenty of court decisions and sample claim letters that will make automakers and their dealers think twice about rejecting your claim.

Don't Pay for Repairs Covered by "Secret" Warranties

Automobile manufacturers are reluctant to publicize their secret warranty programs because they feel that such publicity would weaken consumer confidence in their products and increase their legal liability. The closest they come to an admission is to send out a "goodwill policy," "special policy," or "product update" service bulletin for dealers' eyes only. These bulletins admit liability and propose free repairs for defects that include faulty paint and engine and transmission failures on Chrysler, Ford, and GM vehicles (see Part Three).

If you're refused compensation, keep in mind that secret warranty extensions are, first and foremost, an admission of manufacturing negligence. You can usually find them in technical service bulletins (TSBs) that are sent daily to dealers by automakers. Your bottom-line position should be to accept a pro rata adjustment from the manufacturer, whereby you share one-third of the repair costs with the dealer and automaker. If polite negotiations fail, challenge the refusal in court on the grounds that you should not be penalized for failing to make a reimbursement claim under a secret warranty that you never even knew existed!

For example, the following list of bulletins hows a pattern of engine, transmission, and body failures that are Ford's responsibility. By brandishing these documents, you are proving the factory screwed up and must pay for the repair.

ALLDATA SERVICE BULLETIN SUMMARY (2001 FORD F-150 TRUCK)

NUMBER	DATE	TITLE
04-25-1	12/27/2004	Corrosion Service Tip
04-24-3	12/13/2004	Loose Steering Wheel
04-24-21	12/13/2004	Seat Belts Slow to Retract
04-18-11	09/20/2004	Corrosion at Bottom of Door or Tailgate
04-17-4	09/06/2004	MIL On/Lean DTC Service Tips
14L19	09/01/2004	Campaign: Tie-Rod Inspection
04-16-1	08/23/2004	Ignition System: Tips to Diagnose Engine Misfires
04-11-1	06/08/2004	MIL On/Driveability Issues
04-5-7	03/22/2004	Front Window(s) Pop/Thump Noise
04-2-2	02/09/2004	Back Glass Wind Noise/Water Leaks
04-1-6	01/26/2004	Clunking or Grunting Noise/Shudder
03-25-6	12/22/2003	Engine: Ticking When Idling
03-23-2	11/24/2003	Mirror Glass/Motor Service Tips
03-15-13	08/04/2003	Tie-Rod End Inspections
03-11-10	06/09/2003	Moon Roof Sticks or Leaks Water
03-6-2	03/31/2003	Oil Leak From R/H Cylinder Head Gasket
03-2-4	02/03/2003	Driver-Side Window Binds
02-22-1	11/11/2002	Engine Surge/Rolling Idle
02-21-1	10/28/2002	Dislodged Torque Converter Access Plug
02-21-4	10/28/2002	Roof Ditch Material Cracking
02-20-8	10/14/2002	AC Diagnosis and Service Tips
02-17-6	09/02/2002	Disabling an Inadvertent Shift Interlock
02-16-4	08/19/2002	Whining or Buzzing Noise from Speakers
02-12-1	06/24/2002	White Flakes Coming from AC Vents
02-3-5	02/18/2002	Tailgate: Squeaking/Binding
01-25-5	12/24/2001	Reduced Braking in Freezing Weather
01-24-8	12/10/2001	Seat Vibration at Idle
01-21-5	10/29/2001	High Idle/Sticking Throttle
01-21-13	10/29/2001	Ignition Switch: High Turning Effort
01-24-1	10/01/2001	Clutch Pedal Stays on Floor/Sticks
01-15-6	08/06/2001	Heater Core: Repeated Failure
01-14-1	07/23/2001	Transfer Case: Inadvertent Shifts
01-13-5	07/09/2001	Delayed or No Second Gear Shift

NUMBER	DATE	TITLE
01-13-7	07/09/2001	Clunk on Second to First Gear Shift
01-11-7	06/11/2001	Delayed Shift/No Forward Gears
01-11-12	06/11/2001	Tail Lamp: Moisture/Dirt Inside Lens
01-9-7	05/14/2001	Emissions: Driveability Diagnosis
01-7-3	04/16/2001	Radio Speaker Whine
01-5-8	03/19/2001	Ticking Noise in First Gear

Trim Insurance Costs

Insurance premiums can average between $900 and $2,000 per year, depending on the type of vehicle you own, your personal statistics and driving habits, and whether you can obtain coverage under your family policy. Small SUVs and pickups are charged huge insurance premiums because they are considered to be high risks.

There are some general rules to follow when looking for insurance savings. For example, vehicles older than five years don't necessarily need collision coverage, and you may not need loss-of-use coverage or a rental car. Here are some other factors that should be considered:

- A low damageability rating and an average theft history can reduce rates by 10–15 percent. These rankings can be checked at *www.ibc.ca/vehinfo_pub_ howcarsmeasureup.asp*. Don't be surprised, though, if there appears to be no rhyme or reason for the disparity in the ratings of similar vehicles. Insurance statistics aren't as scientific as insurers pretend—they often charge whatever the market will bear.
- When you phone for quotes, make sure you have your serial number in hand. Many factors—such as the make of the car, the number of doors, the inclusion of a sports package, and the insurer's experience with the car—can affect the quote. And be honest, or you'll find your claim denied, the policy cancelled, or your premium cost boosted.
- Where you live and work also determine how much you pay. Auto insurance rates are 25–40 percent lower in London, Ontario, than in downtown Toronto, for example, because there are fewer cars in the city and fewer kilometres to drive to work. Similar disparities are found in B.C. and Alberta.
- A driver-training course can save you thousands of premium dollars. For example, a policy on a '98 Honda Civic for a schooled driver under 25 years old may be $3,000 less than the regular premium price.
- You may be able to include your home or apartment insurance as part of a premium package that's eligible for additional discounts.

InsuranceHotline.com, based in Ontario but with quotes for other provinces, says that it pays to shop around for cheap auto insurance rates. In February 2003, the group discovered that the same insurance policy could vary in cost by a whopping 400 percent. For example, a 41-year-old married female driving a 2002 Honda Accord and a 41-year-old married male driving a 1998 Dodge Caravan, both with unblemished driving records, should pay no more than $1,880, but some companies surveyed asked as much as $7,515.

InsuranceHotline.com tells consumers which companies have the lowest car insurance rates. The service can be accessed only through the Internet, and there is a very reasonable fee charged for the service.

Other Money-Saving Ideas

Appreciating Depreciation

Depreciation is the biggest—and most often ignored—expense that you encounter when you trade in your vehicle, or when an accident forces you to buy another vehicle before the depreciated loss can be amortized. Most new cars depreciate a whopping 30–45 percent during the first two years of ownership. Fortunately, some average-sized minivans, vans, trucks, and sport-utilities don't lose that much of their value before their fourth year of use. The best way to use depreciation rates to your advantage is to choose a vehicle listed as being both reliable and economical to own and then keep it for five to 10 years. Generally, by choosing a lower-depreciating vehicle—such as one that keeps at least half its value over three years—you are storing up equity that will give you a bigger down payment and fewer loan costs with your next purchase.

More Dirt on Diesels

The only reasons to buy a diesel-equipped vehicle are for their potential to deliver outstanding fuel economy and for their much lower maintenance and repair costs when compared with similar-sized vehicles powered by gasoline engines. Unfortunately, independent data suggest that both claims by automakers may be false.

Let's examine the fuel-savings issue first. In theory, when compared with gasoline powerplants, diesel engines are up to 30 percent more efficient in a light vehicle and up to 70 percent cheaper to run in a heavy-duty towing and hauling truck or SUV. They become more efficient as the engine load increases, whereas gasoline engines become less so. This is the main reason diesels are best used where the driving cycle includes a lot of city driving—slow speeds, heavy loads, frequent stops, and long idling times. At full throttle, both engines are essentially equal from a fuel-efficiency standpoint. The gasoline engine, however, leaves the diesel in the dust when it comes to high-speed performance.

On the downside, fleet administrators and owners report that diesel fuel economy in real driving situations is much less than what's advertised—a complaint also voiced by owners of hybrids. Many owners say that their diesel-run rigs get about 30 percent less than what the manufacturer promised.

Also undercutting fuel savings claims is the fact that in some regions, the increased cost of diesel fuel—because of high taxes and oil company greed, some say—makes it more expensive than regular fuel.

The diesel engine's reputation for superior reliability may have been true in the past, but no longer. This fact is easily confirmed if you cross-reference owner complaints with confidential automaker service bulletins and independent industry polling results put out by J.D. Power and others, a task done for you in Part Four's pickup trucks section.

Many owners of diesel-equipped vehicles are frustrated by chronic breakdowns, excessive repair costs, and poor road performance. It's practically axiomatic that bad injectors have plagued Dodge Cummins, Ford Power Stroke, and GM Duramax engines.

Defective injectors were often replaced in the past at the owner's expense and at a cost of thousands of dollars. Now, GM and Ford are using special programs to cover the replacement cost long after the base warranty has expired. Chrysler has been more recalcitrant in making payouts, apparently because fewer vehicles may be involved and costs can be quite high (their lift pumps and injectors may be faulty).

And here are even more diesel-equipped-vehicle disadvantages: They use enough performance-robbing, poorly performing, and unreliable special components to fill a hardware store in order to meet emissions regulations that will get more stringent as cleaner fuel is introduced in North America in 2007. This new fuel requires major changes to the engine and additional expensive emissions hardware, as well as mechanics who know what they are doing when servicing these modified engines (an iffy proposition at best). Owners of diesel-equipped models made before 2007 also have to contend with some engine clatter; a smelly exhaust; high nitrous oxide emissions (a cause of acid rain); and excessive particulates (soot) that aggravate respiratory maladies.

Performance Should Be Tested

Take the phrase "carlike handling" with a large grain of salt. You are not buying a car. Since many rear-drive models are built on a modified truck chassis and use steering and suspension components from their truck divisions, they tend to handle more like trucks than cars, in spite of automakers' claims to the contrary. Also, what you see isn't necessarily what you get when you buy or lease a new sport-utility, van, or pickup, because these vehicles seldom come with enough standard features to fully exploit their versatility. Additional options are usually a prerequisite to make them safe and comfortable to drive. Consequently, the term "multipurpose" is a misnomer unless you are prepared to spend extra dollars to outfit your sport-utility, van, or pickup. Even fully equipped, these vehicles don't always provide the performance touted by automakers. And bear in mind that off-roading requires suspension, engine, and drivetrain packages as well as other components such as off-road tires and a skid plate that seldom come as standard equipment. Also be wary of ABS brakes when going off-road, as they can degrade handling considerably.

Front-drives handle better than rear-drives, but the size and weight of multipurpose vehicles still require a whole new set of driving skills when cornering at moderate speeds or when parking or turning. Sport-utilities and pickups are more likely to roll over than passenger cars, and it sometimes takes only a moment's inattention.

Four-Wheel Drive/All-Wheel Drive Not For Everyone

An old mechanic friend of mine once told me, "Four-wheel drive will only get you stuck deeper, farther from home. If the weather is too bad to drive a car safely, stay home."

Four-wheel drive (4×4) directs engine power through a transfer case to all four wheels, which pull and push the vehicle forward, giving you twice as much traction. On most models, when four-wheel drive isn't engaged, the vehicle reverts to rear-drive. The large transfer-case housing makes the vehicle sit higher, giving you additional ground clearance.

Keep in mind that extended driving over dry pavement with 4×4 engaged will cause the driveline to bind and will result in serious damage. Some buyers are turning, instead, to rear-drive pickups equipped with winches and large, deep-lugged rear tires.

Many 4×4 customers have been turned off by the typically rough and noisy drive-line; a tendency for the vehicle to tip over when cornering at moderate speeds (a Ford Bronco and Isuzu Rodeo specialty); vague, trucklike handling; high repair costs; and poor fuel economy. No wonder car-based SUVs like the Toyota RAV4, Honda CR-V, and Hyundai Santa Fe are so popular: Buyers want versatility without sacrificing fuel economy, comfort, or handling.

All-wheel drive (AWD) is essentially four-wheel drive that's engaged *all* the time, a feature first popularized by Subaru. It never needs to be de-activated when running over dry pavement and doesn't require the heavy transfer case that cuts fuel economy (although some sport-utilities and pickups do use a special transfer case). AWD–equipped vehicles aren't recommended for off-roading because of their lower ground clearance and fragile driveline parts, which aren't as rugged as 4×4 components.

Rust Protection Scams

Vehicles are much less rust-prone than they were several decades ago, thanks to more durable body panels and better designs. When rusting occurs now, it's usually caused by either a poor paint job or the use of new metal panels that create galvanic corrosion or promote early paint peeling—two causes that are excluded from most rustproofing warranties. So put your $300 elsewhere and remember that the best rustproofing protection is to park the vehicle in a dry, unheated garage or under an outside carport and then wash it every few weeks. Never bring it in and out of a heated garage during the winter months, since it is most prone to rust when temperatures are just a bit above freezing; keep it especially clean and dry during that time. If you live in an area where roads are heavily salted in winter, or in a coastal region, have your vehicle's undercoating sprayed annually.

Whether you are rustproofing the entire car or just undercoating key areas, make sure to include the rocker panels (make a small mark inside the door panels on the plastic hole plugs to make sure that they were removed and that the inside was actually sprayed), the rear hatch's bottom edge, the tailgate, and the wheelwells. It's also a smart idea to stay at the garage while the work is being done to see that the overspray is cleaned up and all areas have been sufficiently covered.

Undercoating, which costs less than $100, will usually do as good a job as rustproofing. It will protect vital suspension and chassis components, make the vehicle ride more quietly, and allow you to ask a higher price at trade-in time. The only downside, which can be checked by asking for references, is that the undercoating may give off an unpleasant odour for months, and it may drip, soiling your driveway.

Surviving the Options Jungle

 The best options for your buck are a 5-speed automatic transmission, electronic stability-control (for vehicles with poor rollover scores), an anti-theft immobilizer, air conditioning, a premium sound system, and higher quality tires—features that may bring back one-third to half their value. Rustproofing makes cars easier to sell in some provinces that have salted roads in the winter, but paint protection and seat sealants are a waste of money. Most option packages can be cut by 20 percent. Extended warranties are overpriced by about 75 percent. And what will happen when the warranty runs out?

Dealers make more than three times as much profit selling options as they do selling most cars (50 percent profit versus 15 percent profit). No wonder their eyes light up when you start perusing their options list. If you must have some options, compare prices with independent retailers and buy where the price is lowest and the warranty is the most comprehensive. Buy as few options as possible from the dealer—you'll get faster service, more comprehensive guarantees, and lower prices from independent suppliers. Remember, extravagantly equipped vehicles hurt your pocketbook in three ways: They cost more to begin with and return only a fraction of what they cost when the car is resold, they drive up maintenance costs, and they often consume extra fuel.

A heavy-duty battery and suspension and, perhaps, an upgraded sound system will generally suffice for American-made vehicles. Most imports already come well equipped. An engine block heater with a timer—said by the CAA to be favoured by 39 percent of new-car shoppers—isn't a bad idea, either. It's an inexpensive investment that ensures winter starting and reduces fuel consumption by allowing you to start out with a semi-warm engine.

When ordering parts, remember that purchases from American outlets can be slapped with a small customs duty if the part isn't made in the United States; you'll pay the inevitable GST levied on the part's cost and customs duty. Finally, your freight carrier may charge a $15–$20 brokerage fee for representing you at the border.

Smart Options

The problem with options is that you often can't refuse them. Dealers sell very few bare-bones cars, SUVs, trucks, or vans, and they option-pack each vehicle with features that can't be removed. You'll be forced to dicker over the total cost of what you are offered, whether you need the extras or not. So it's not a case of "Yes or no?" but more a decision of "Is it necessary, and at what cost?"

Adjustable Pedals and Extensions

This device moves the brake and accelerator pedals forward or backward about 10 cm (4 inches) to accommodate short-statured drivers and protect them from airbag-induced injuries.

If the manufacturer of your vehicle doesn't offer optional power-adjustable pedals, there are several companies selling inexpensive pedal extensions by mail order through the Internet; for example, go to HDS Specialty Vehicles' website at *stores. yahoo.com/hdsmn/pedex.html*. If you live in Toronto or London, Ontario, check out Kino Mobility (*www.kinomobility.com*).

Adjustable Steering Wheel

This option allows easier access to the driver's seat and permits a more comfortable driving position. It's particularly useful if more than one person will drive the vehicle.

Air Conditioning

AC systems are far more reliable than they were a decade ago, and they have a lifespan of five to seven years. Sure, replacement and repair costs can hit $1,000, but that's very little when amortized over an 8- to 10-year period. AC also makes your car easier to resell.

Does AC waste or conserve fuel when a vehicle is driven at highway speeds? Interestingly, *MythBusters*, a popular *Discovery TV* program, concluded this year that, although their computer models indicated that using air conditioning with the windows up saved the most fuel, actual road tests showed that having the windows down and the AC turned off was the more fuel-efficient method of keeping the vehicle cool. However, Edmunds, a popular automotive information website, conducted their own fuel-efficiency tests and concluded that there wasn't that much difference between open or closed windows, as they point out at *www. edmunds.com/advice/fueleconomy/articles/106842/article.html*:

> While the A/C compressor does pull power from the engine wasting some gas, the effect appears to be fairly minimal in modern cars. And putting the windows down tends to increase drag on most cars, canceling out any measurable gain from turning the A/C off. But this one depends on the model you're driving. When we opened the sunroof in our SUV, the mileage did decrease even with the A/C off. Still, in our experience, it's not worth the argument because you won't save a lot of gas either way. So just do what's comfortable.

AC provides extra comfort, reduces wind noise (from not having to roll down the windows), and improves window defogging. Buy a factory-installed unit. You'll get a longer warranty and reduce the chance that other mechanical components will be damaged during installation.

Anti-Theft Systems

You'd be a fool not to buy an anti-theft system, including a lockable fuel cap, for your much-coveted-by-thieves sport-utility, van, or pickup. Auto break-ins and thefts cost Canadians more than $400 million annually; there's a one in 130 chance that your vehicle will be stolen, and only a 60 percent chance that you'll ever get it back. In fact, older pickups are particularly easy pickings for thieves. Chevrolet and GMC trucks are at the top of the list, say Calgary police, mainly because most Chrysler keys will open GM truck doors and the steering column locks are easily bypassed. Chrysler minivans are also theft-prone because of their rudimentary door lock assemblies. Car security specialist Dan Friesen told the Canadian Press in July 2001 that he's not surprised pickups are so popular: "Most of these trucks are so easy to break into, it's a joke. I tell some people they shouldn't even lock their doors because it will save them money in the end."

Since amateurs are responsible for stealing most vehicles, the best theft deterrent is a visible device that complicates the job while immobilizing the vehicle and sounding an alarm. For less than $150, you can install both a steering-wheel lock and a hidden remote-controlled ignition disabler. Satellite tracking systems like GM's OnStar feature are also very effective.

Auxiliary Lighting

Essential only for serious off-roaders, extra lighting improves safety and makes night driving less tiring. In the city, it's a pain in the butt to other drivers, who are constantly blinded by the lights' intensity and high placement.

Battery (Heavy-Duty)

The best battery for northern climates is the optional heavy-duty type offered by many manufacturers for about $80. It's a worthwhile purchase, especially for vehicles equipped with lots of electric options. Most standard batteries last only two winters; heavy-duty batteries give you an extra year or two for about 20 percent more than the price of a standard battery. A good rule of thumb is to buy the freshest and largest reserve capacity (RC) battery that will physically fit into the engine compartment. You will also want it to have a cold cranking amp (CCA) rating that meets or exceeds the car's original-equipment manufacturer's (OEM) cranking amp guidelines for your climate. Make sure you retest the battery after deep discharges or jump-starts.

Bed Protectors (Pickups)

Selling for $100–$200, these protectors range from simple mats to deluxe moulded polyethylene liners. They guard against rusting in the panel joints and bolt areas by preventing water accumulation, and they protect the cargo bed walls and tailgate from scratches and dents. These benefits help to keep resale value high.

Central Locking Control

Costing around $200, this option is most useful for families with small children, car-poolers, or drivers of pickups, minivans, and vans who can't easily slide across the seat to lock the other doors.

Child Safety Seat (Integrated)

Integrated safety seats are designed to accommodate any child more than one year old or weighing over 9 kg (20 lb.). Since the seat is permanently integrated into the seatback, it takes the fuss out of installing and removing the safety seat and then finding someplace to store it. When not in use, it quickly folds away out of sight, becoming part of the seatback. Two other safety benefits are these: You know the seat has been properly installed, and your child gets used to having his or her "special" seat in the back, where it's usually safest to sit.

Electronic Stability-Control (ESC)

The latest IIHS studies conclude that as many as 10,000 fatal crashes could be prevented if all vehicles were equipped with ESC. Its June 2006 report concluded that stability control is second only to seat belts in saving lives because it reduces the risk of fatal single-vehicle rollovers by 80 percent and the chance of having other kinds of fatal collisions by 43 percent.

A $500–$1,000 option or standard feature that's offered on half of this year's new models (a $1,500 option when bundled), ESC helps prevent the loss of control in a turn, on slippery roads, or when you must make a sudden steering correction. The system applies the brakes to individual wheels or cuts back the engine power when sensors find the vehicle is beginning to spin or skid. It's particularly useful in maintaining stability with SUVs, but is less useful with passenger coupes and sedans.

Although Honda has put ESC into all its SUVs and Chrysler plans to equip its 2007 sport-utilities with the feature, there presently isn't any federal standard governing the performance of these systems. This is worrisome, considering that not all electronic stability-control systems work as they should. In tests carried out by *Consumer Reports* on 2003 models, the stability-control system used in the Mitsubishi Montero was rated "unacceptable," BMW's X5 3.0i system provided poor emergency handling, and Acura's MDX and Subaru's Outback VDC stability systems left much to be desired.

Electric Winch

Ideal for hauling logs, boats, rocks, and stumps and getting you out of rough terrain. Serious off-roaders will find that an electric winch that can pull 675–1,350 kg (1,500–3,000 lb.) is a worthwhile $200–$350 investment.

Engines

Choose the most powerful 6- or 8-cylinder engine available if you're going to be doing a lot of highway driving, if you plan to carry a full passenger load and luggage on a regular basis, or if you intend to load up the vehicle with convenience features like air conditioning. Keep in mind that multipurpose vehicles with larger engines are easier to resell and retain their value the longest. For example, Honda's '96 Odyssey minivan was a sales dud in spite of its bulletproof reliability, mainly because buyers didn't want a minivan with an underpowered 4-cylinder powerplant. Some people buy underpowered vehicles in the mistaken belief that increased fuel economy is a good trade-off for decreased engine performance. It isn't. That's why there's so much interest in peppy 4-cylinders hooked to 5-speed transmissions, or larger engines with a "cylinder deactivation" feature.

In fact, cylinder deactivation is one feature that appears more promising than most other fuel-saving add-ons. For example, *AutoWeek* magazine found the overweight Jeep Commander equipped with a "Multiple Displacement System" still managed a respectable 13.8 L/100 km (17 mpg) on the highway in tests published in its March 2006 edition.

Honda employs a similar method, which cuts fuel consumption by 20 percent on the 2005 Odyssey. It runs on all six cylinders when accelerating and three cylinders when cruising. So far, there have been neither reliability nor performance complaints, and Honda has expanded the technology to include the 2006 Accord Hybrid.

Engine and Transmission Cooling System (Heavy-Duty)

This relatively inexpensive option can extend the life of your transmission and engine by preventing overheating when heavy towing is required.

Extended Warranties

A waste of $1,500–$2,000 for vehicles rated Recommended in *Lemon-Aid* or for vehicles sold by automakers that have written goodwill warranties covering engine and transmission failures (Ford and GM). If you can get a great price for a vehicle rated just Average or Above Average but you want protection from costly repair bills, patronize garages that offer lifetime warranties on parts listed in this guide as failure-prone, such as powertrains, exhaust systems, and brakes.

Only buy an extended warranty as a last resort, and make sure you know what it covers and for how long. Start with a $1,000 powertrain warranty if other mechanical components have a good reputation. Incidentally, auto industry insiders say the average markup on these warranties varies from 50 to 65 percent, which seems almost reasonable when you consider that appliance warranties are marked up from 40 to 80 percent.

Gas Tank (Extra Capacity)

If full-sized vans weren't such gas hogs, larger gas tanks wouldn't be necessary. Nevertheless, owners will appreciate the extra cruising range that a larger tank provides. Expect to spend about $250.

Keyless Entry (Remote)

This safety and convenience option saves you from fiddling with the key in a dark parking lot, or taking off a glove in cold weather to unlock or lock the vehicle. Try to get a keyless entry system combined with anti-theft measures such as an ignition kill switch or some other disabler. Incidentally, many automakers no longer make vehicles with an outside key lock on the passenger side.

 ## Paint Colour

Choosing a popular colour can make your vehicle easier to sell at a good price. DesRosiers automotive consultants say that blue is the preferred colour overall, but green and silver are also popular with Canadians. Manheim auctioneers say that green-coloured vehicles brought in 97.9 percent of the average auction price, while silver ones sold at a premium 105.5 percent. Remember that certain paint colours require particular care:

Black (and other dark colours): These paints are most susceptible to sun damage because of their heavy absorption of ultraviolet rays.

Pearl-toned colours: These paints are the most difficult to work with. If the paint needs to be retouched, it must be matched to look right from both the front- and side-angle views.

Red: This paint also shows sun damage, so keep your car in a garage or shady spot whenever possible.

White: Although grime looks terrible on a white car, white is the easiest colour to care for.

Power-Assisted Doors, Mirrors, Windows, and Seats

Merely a convenience feature with cars, power-assisted windows and doors are a necessity with minivans—crawling across the front seat a few times to roll up the passenger-side window or to lock the doors will quickly convince you of their value. Power mirrors are convenient on vehicles that have a number of drivers, or on minivans, vans, or trucks. Power seats with memory are particularly useful, too, if more than one person drives a vehicle. Automatic window and seat controls currently have few reliability problems, and they're fairly inexpensive to install, troubleshoot, and repair. As a safety precaution, make sure the window control has to be lifted. This will ensure no child is strangled from pressing against the switch. Power-sliding doors are even more of a danger. They are failure-prone on all makes and shouldn't be purchased by families with children.

Roll Bars

Roll bars protect sport-utility occupants from rollovers. This is an essential safety item because these vehicles have a nasty habit of overturning without warning. A good roll bar and cage kit sells for about $350.

Running Boards

Throughout this guide, I've recommended that you buy optional running boards. Far from returning you to '50s styling, running boards are practically essential for climbing into most full-sized vans, sport-utilities, and pickups. They can be purchased from independent suppliers for $65–$200, which is much less than the $250–$700 charged by the automakers.

Side Airbags

A worthwhile feature if you are the right size and properly seated, side airbags are presently overpriced and aren't very effective unless both the head and upper torso are protected. Side airbags are often featured as a $700 add-on to the sticker price, but you would be wise to bargain aggressively.

Skid Plates

A steel skid plate protects a sport-utility or pickup from rocks and other obstacles when off-roading. It should be at least a quarter-inch thick and cover the rear differential and oil pan. Some sport-utilities and pickups have a low-slung front gear housing that is easily damaged and pushes large amounts of mud and debris up into the front end, raising it to the point that front-end traction is lost.

Stow 'n' Go Seating

Pioneered by Chrysler in its minivans, Stow 'n' Go seating allows the second- and third-row seats to be folded into, not onto, the floor. Folding the seats is a one-handed operation, and the head restraints don't need to be removed. Pop the spring-loaded seats back up, and there's an in-floor storage bin under each seat. There's one caveat: These seats sacrifice comfort for versatility. But check them out anyway.

Suspension (Heavy-Duty)

Always a good idea, this inexpensive option pays for itself. It provides better handling, makes the ride more comfortable (though a bit on the firm side), and extends shock life for an extra year or two.

Tires

There are three rules to remember when purchasing tires. First, neither brand nor price is a reliable gauge of performance, quality, or durability. Second, choosing a tire recommended by the automaker may not be in your best interest, since traction and long tread life are often sacrificed for a softer ride and maximum EPA mileage ratings. And third, don't buy any new tire that's older than two years, since the rubber compound may have deteriorated because of poor handling and improper storage (if they've been stored near electrical motors). You can check the date of manufacture on the side wall of the tire.

Two types of tires are generally available: all-season and performance. "Touring" is just a fancier name for all-season tires. All-season radial tires cost from $90 to $150 per tire. They're a compromise, since according to Transport Canada, they won't get you through winter with the same margin of safety as snow tires will, and they don't provide the same durability on dry surfaces as regular summer tires. In areas with low to moderate snowfall, however, these tires are adequate as long as they're not pushed beyond their limits.

Mud or snow tires provide the best traction on snowy surfaces, but traction on wet roads is actually decreased. Treadwear is also accelerated by the use of softer rubber compounds. Beware of using wide tires for winter driving; 70-series or wider give poor traction and tend to float over snow.

Spare tires

Be wary of space-saver spare tires. They often can't match the promised mileage, and they seriously degrade steering control. Furthermore, they are usually stored in spaces inside the trunk that won't hold a normal-sized tire. The location of the stored spare can also have safety implications. Watch out for spares stowed under the chassis or mounted on the rear hatch on some sport-utilities. Frequently, the attaching cables and bolts rust out or freeze, so the spare falls off or becomes next to impossible to use when you need it.

Self-sealing and run-flat tires

Today there are two technologies available to help maintain vehicle mobility when a tire is punctured: self-sealing and self-supporting/run-flat tires.

Self-sealing: Ideal if you drive long distances. Punctures from nails, bolts, or screws up to 3/16 of an inch in diameter are fixed instantly and permanently with a sealant. A low air-pressure warning system isn't required. Expert testers say a punctured self-sealing tire can maintain air pressure for up to 200 km—even in freezing conditions. The Uniroyal Tiger Paw NailGard ($85–$140, depending on the size) is the overall winner in a side-by-side test conducted by The Tire Rack (*www.tirerack.com*).

Self-supporting/run-flat: Priced from $175 to $350 per tire, 25 to 50 percent more than the price of comparable premium tires, Goodyear's Extended Mobility Tire (EMT) run-flat tires were first offered as an option on the 1994 Chevrolet Corvette and then became standard on the 1997 model. These tires reinforce the side wall so it can carry the weight of the car for 90 km, or about an hour's driving time, even after all air pressure has been lost. You won't feel the tire go flat; you must depend upon a $250–$300 optional tire-pressure monitor to warn you before the side wall collapses and you begin riding on your rim. Also, not all vehicles can adapt to run-flat tires; you may need to upgrade your rims. Experts say run-flats will give your car a harder ride, and you'll likely notice more interior tire and road noise. The car might also track differently. The 2004 Sienna's standard Dunlop run-flat tires have a terrible reputation for premature wear. At 25,000 km, one owner complained that her Sienna needed a new set at $200 each. You can expect a backlog of over a month to get a replacement, and Toyota doesn't include any type of spare. Goodyear EMT and Pirelli PZero tires have been on the market for some time now, and they seem to perform adequately. Don't make a final choice before talking with an auto manufacturer rep about what's recommended and how your warranty will be affected.

Which tires are best?

There is no independent Canadian agency that evaluates tire performance and durability. However, the U.S.–based NHTSA rates treadwear, traction, and resistance to sustained high temperatures, etches the ratings onto the side walls of all tires sold in the States and Canada, and regularly posts its findings on the Internet (*www.nhtsa.dot.gov*). The treadwear grade is fixed at a base 100 points, and the tire's wear rate is measured after the tire is driven through a course that approximates most driving conditions. A tire rated 300 will last three times as long as one rated 100, for example.

I've come up with the following tire ratings after researching government tests and comments from consumers and industry insiders. Remember, some of the brand names may be changed from year to year for marketing reasons. Simply ask any tire specialist for the updated name of tires that are listed in this section. On the Internet, check out *www.tirerack.com/tires/surveyresults/index.jsp*.

Dunlop D65 Touring and SP20 AS: Treadwear rated 520. These tires are the bargain of the group. They provide excellent wet and dry cornering and good steering response.

Goodrich Control TA M65: Treadwear rated 360. This tire excels at snowbelt performance.

Goodyear Aquatred #3: Treadwear rated 340. This tire is a bit noisy, and its higher rolling resistance cuts fuel economy. Still, it's an exceptional performer on wet roads, and it works especially well on front-drive cars where the weight is carried over the front tires. Average performance on dry pavement.

Goodyear Regatta #2: Treadwear rated 460. This tire does everything well, including keeping tire noise to a minimum.

Michelin MX4: Treadwear rated 320. This tire gives a smoother ride and a sharper steering response than the Goodyear Aquatred. The MX1 is also an excellent winter performer.

Pirelli P300 and P400: Treadwear rated 460 and 420, respectively. These are two of the best all-around all-season tires.

Yokohama TC320: Treadwear rated 300. This is a Goodyear Aquatred knock-off that performs almost as well for half the price.

Other good tire choices are as follows: Dayton Timberline A/T, General XP, Goodrich Touring T/A HR4, Goodyear Eagle LS, Kelly Navigator Platinum TE, Pirelli P3000, and Scorpion A/T. And here are some good winter tires: Futura Euro-Metric, Goodyear Ultra Grip Ice, Michelin Arctic Alpin, and Pirelli Winter Ice Assimmetrico.

The following tires aren't recommended: Bridgestone Potenza RE 92; Continental truck tires; Cooper Lifeline Classic II; all Firestone makes; Goodrich Advantage; General Hydro 2000 and Ameri G4S; Goodyear Eagle GA, Wrangler, and WeatherHandler; Michelin XGT H4, XW4, and MXV4 Green X; Pirelli P4000 Super Touring (not to be confused with the recommended P400); and Toyo 800 Plus.

Trailer-Towing Equipment

Just because you need a vehicle with towing capability doesn't mean that you have to spend big bucks buying more power than you really need or tacking on a lot of fuel-wasting accessories. The first things you should determine before choosing a towing option are whether you need a pickup or a small van to do the job and whether your tires will handle the extra burden. For most towing needs (up to 900 kg/2,000 lb.), a passenger car, small pickup, or minivan will work just as well as a full-sized pickup or van (and will cost much less). If you're pulling a trailer that weighs more than 900 kg, most passenger cars won't handle the load unless they've been specially outfitted according to the automaker's specifications. Pulling a heavier trailer (up to 1,800 kg/4,000 lb.) will likely require a compact passenger van. You may, however, have to keep your speed at 72.4 km/h (45 mph) or less, as Toyota suggests with the 2004 Sienna.

Automakers reserve the right to change limits whenever they feel like it, so make any sales promise an integral part of your contract (see "False Advertising" in Part Three). A good rule of thumb is to reduce the promised tow rating by 20 percent. In assessing towing weight, factor in the cargo, passengers, and equipment of both the trailer and the tow vehicle. Keep in mind that five people with luggage add about 450 kg (1,000 lb.) to the load, and a full 227-litre (50-gallon) water tank adds another 225 kg (500 lb.). The manufacturer's gross vehicle weight rating (GVWR) takes into account the anticipated average cargo and supplies that your vehicle is likely to carry.

Automatic transmissions are fine for towing trailers, although there's a slight fuel penalty. Manual transmissions tend to have greater clutch wear caused by towing than do automatic transmissions. Both transmission choices are equally acceptable. Remember, the best compromise is to shift the automatic manually for maximum performance going uphill and to maintain control while not overheating the brakes when descending mountains.

Unibody vehicles (those without a separate frame) can handle most trailering jobs as long as their limits aren't exceeded. Front-drives aren't the best choice for pulling heavy loads in excess of 900 kg, since they lose some steering control and traction because of all the weight concentrated in the rear.

Whatever vehicle you choose, keep in mind that the trailer hitch is crucial. It must have a tongue capacity of at least 10 percent of the trailer's weight; otherwise, it may be unsafe to use. Hitches are chosen according to the type of tow vehicle and, to a lesser extent, the weight of the load.

Most hitches are factory-installed, even though independents can install them more cheaply. Expect to pay about $200 for a simple boat hitch and a minimum of $600 for a fifth-wheel version.

Equalizer bars and extra cooling systems for the radiator, transmission, engine oil, and steering are a prerequisite for towing anything heavier than 900 kg. Heavy-duty springs and brakes are a big help, too. Separate brakes for the trailer may be necessary to increase your vehicle's maximum towing capacity.

Transmission: Automatic, Manual, and CVT

Despite its many advantages, the manual transmission is an endangered species in North America, where manuals equip only 12 percent of all new vehicles (mostly econocars, sports cars, and budget trucks). European buyers opt for a manual transmission almost 90 percent of the time.

A transmission with four or more forward speeds is usually more fuel efficient than one with three forward speeds (hardly seen anymore), and manual transmissions are usually more efficient than automatics, although this isn't always the case.

Shoppers who want a Dodge truck with the highly recommended Cummins diesel engine but don't want to be stuck with Chrysler's infamous automatic transmission breakdowns should opt for the 6-speed transmission. Don't invest in the continuously variable transmission (CVT) used by Ford, GM, or Chrysler. GM is ditching theirs, and Ford's is just going into its third-year production. Sure, CVTs improve fuel economy by about 10 percent through the use of pulleys connected by a steel belt or chain to drive the wheels. But the system is relatively new in North America, where automakers like GM haven't quite worked the bugs out. However, CVTs have been used for decades in the rest of the world by companies like Audi, Honda, and Nissan, with few problems.

GM SPECIAL POLICY ADJUSTMENT—EXTENDED TRANSMISSION WARRANTY COVERAGE FOR VARIABLE TRANSMISSION WITH INTELLIGENCE (VTI) TRANSMISSION

BULLETIN NO.: 04020   DATE: APRIL 21, 2004

2002–04 VUE Vehicles
Equipped with VTi (M75 and M16)
2003–04 ION Quad Coupe Vehicles
Equipped with VTi (M75)

CONDITION: Saturn has determined that 2002–04 VUE and 2003–04 ION Quad Coupe vehicles equipped with the VTi transmission may experience certain transmission concerns that might affect customer satisfaction, and may require repair or replacement.

SPECIAL POLICY ADJUSTMENT: This special policy bulletin has been issued to extend the warranty on the VTi transmission assembly for a period of 5 years or 75,000 miles (120,000 km), whichever occurs first, from the date the vehicle was originally placed in service, regardless of ownership. The repairs will be made at no charge to the customer.

GM has put an optional Fiat-built CVT in its Saturn Ion and Vue since 2002 and has had to extend the warranty to deal with chronic drivetrain failures.

Unnecessary Options

Anti-Lock Brakes (ABS)

ABS is another safety feature that's fine in theory but impractical under actual driving conditions. The system maintains directional stability by preventing the wheels from locking up. This will *not* reduce the stopping distance, however. In practice, ABS makes drivers overconfident. Many still pump the brakes and render them ineffective. Total brake failure is common, and repairs are frequent, complicated, and expensive to perform.

All-Wheel Drive (AWD)

Mark Bilek, editorial director of Consumer Guide's automotive section (*auto.consumerguide.com/index.cfm*), is a critic of AWD. He says AWD systems generally encourage drivers to go faster than they should in adverse conditions, which creates trouble stopping in emergencies. Automakers like AWD as "a marketing ploy to make more money," Bilek contends.

Cruise Control

Automakers provide this $250–$300 option, which is mainly a convenience feature, for motorists who use their vehicles for long periods of high-speed driving. The constant rate of speed saves some fuel and lessens driver fatigue during long trips. Still, the system is particularly failure-prone and expensive to repair, can lead to driver inattention, and can make the vehicle hard to control on icy roadways. Malfunctioning cruise-control units are also one of the major causes of sudden acceleration incidents. At other times, cruise control can be very distracting, especially to inexperienced drivers who are unaccustomed to sudden speed fluctuations.

Adaptive cruise control is the latest evolution of this feature. It senses a vehicle ahead of you and then automatically downshifts, brakes, or cuts your vehicle's speed. This commonly occurs when passing another car or when a car passes you, and it can make for a harrowing experience. Mercedes was the first out with the feature in 2000, followed by BMW in 2002. The 2006 BMW 5 Series sells it for $2,500, Cadillac's DTS costs $1,200 more with the device, and the 2007 Toyota Avalon XLS tacks on $700 for the option.

Electronic Instrument Readout

If you've ever had trouble reading a digital watch face or resetting your VCR, you'll feel right at home with this electronic gizmo. Gauges are presented in a series of moving digital patterns that are confusing, distracting, and unreadable in direct sunlight. A trip computer and vehicle monitor that determine fuel use and how many kilometres until the tank is empty, indicate average speed, and signal component failures often accompany the electronic instrument readout system. Figures are frequently incorrect or slow to catch up.

Foglights

A pain in the eyes for other drivers, foglights aren't necessary for most drivers who have well-aimed original-equipment headlights on their vehicles.

Gas-Saving Gadgets and Fuel Additives

The accessory market has been flooded with hundreds of atomizers, magnets, and additives that purport to make vehicles less fuel-thirsty. However, tests on over 100 gadgets and fuel or crankcase additives carried out by the U.S. Environmental Protection Agency have found that only a handful produce an increase in fuel economy, and the increase is tiny. These gadgets include warning devices that tell the driver to ease up on the throttle or shift to a more fuel-frugal gear, hardware that reduces the engine power needed for belt-driven accessories, cylinder deactivation systems, and spoilers that channel airflow under the car. The use of any of these products is a quick way to lose warranty coverage and fail provincial emissions tests.

GPS Navigation Systems (Portable)

This $1,500–$2,000 navigation aid links a GPS satellite unit to the vehicle's cellular phone and electronics. For a monthly fee, the unit connects drivers to live operators who will help them with driving directions, give repair or emergency assistance, or relay messages. If the airbag deploys or the car is stolen, satellite-transmitted signals are automatically sent from the vehicle to operators who will notify the proper authorities of the vehicle's location.

Many of the systems' functions can be performed by a cellular telephone, and the navigation screens may be obtrusive, distracting, washed out in sunlight, and hard to calibrate. A portable Garmin GPS unit is more user-friendly and much cheaper.

High-Intensity Headlights

These headlights are much brighter than standard headlights, and they cast a blue hue. Granted, they provide additional illumination of the roadway, but they are also annoying to oncoming drivers, who will flash their lights at you, thinking your high beams are on. These lights are easily stolen and expensive to replace.

ID Etching

This $150–$200 option is a scam. The government doesn't require it, and thieves and joyriders aren't deterred by the etchings. If you want to etch your windows for your own peace of mind, several private companies will sell you a $15–$30 kit that does an excellent job (try *www.autoetch.net*), or you can wait for your municipality or local police agency to conduct one of their periodic free VIN ID etching sessions in your area.

Paint and Fabric Protectors

Selling for $200–$300, these "sealants" add nothing to a vehicle's resale value. Although paint lustre may be temporarily heightened, this treatment is less effective and more costly than regular waxing, and it may also invalidate the manufacturer's guarantee at a time when the automaker will look for any pretext to deny your paint claim.

Auto fabric protection products are nothing more than variations of Scotchgard, which can be bought in aerosol cans for a few dollars—a much better deal than the $50–$75 charged by dealers.

Power-Assisted Minivan Sliding Doors

Not a good idea if you have children. These doors have a high failure rate, opening or closing for no apparent reason and injuring children caught between the door and post.

Reverse-Warning System

Selling for about $500 as part of an option package, this safety feature warns the driver of any objects in the rear when backing up. Although a sound idea in theory, the device often fails to go off or sounds an alarm for no reason in practice. Drivers eventually either disconnect or ignore it.

Rollover Detection System

This feature makes use of sensors to determine if the vehicle has leaned beyond a safe angle. If so, the side airbags are automatically deployed and then remain inflated to make sure occupants aren't injured or ejected in a rollover accident. This is a totally new system that has not been proven. It could have disastrous consequences if the sensor malfunctions, as has been the case with front- and side-airbag sensors over the past decade.

Rooftop Carrier

Although this inexpensive option provides additional baggage space and may allow you to meet all your driving needs with a smaller vehicle, a loaded roof rack can increase fuel consumption by as much as 5 percent. An empty rack cuts fuel economy by about 1 percent.

Rustproofing

Rustproofing is no longer necessary since automakers have extended their own rust warranties. In fact, you have a greater chance of seeing your rustproofer go belly up than having your untreated vehicle ravaged by premature rusting. Even if the rustproofer stays in business, you're likely to get a song and dance about why the warranty won't cover so-called internal rusting, or why repairs will be delayed until the sheet metal is actually rusted through.

Be wary of electronic rustproofing. Selling for $425 to $665.99, these electrical devices claim to inhibit vehicle corrosion by sending out a pulse current to the grounded body panels, protecting areas that conventional rust-inhibiting products can't reach. There is much debate as to whether these devices are worth the cost, or if they work at all.

If you live in an area where roads are heavily salted in winter or in a coastal region, have your vehicle washed every few weeks and undercoated annually, paying particular attention to rocker panels (door bottoms) and wheelwells. Also, don't use a heated garage in winter; Canadian studies show that a heated garage will accelerate the damage caused by corrosion.

Sunroof

Unless you live in a temperate region, the advantages of a sunroof are far outweighed by the disadvantages. You're not going to get better ventilation than a good AC system would provide, and a sunroof may grace your environment with painful booming wind noises, rattles, water leaks, and road dust accumulation. A sunroof increases gas consumption, reduces night vision because overhead highway lights shine through the roof opening, and can lose you several inches of headroom.

Tinted Glass

On the one hand, tinting jeopardizes your safety by reducing your night vision. On the other hand, it does keep the interior cool in hot weather, reduce glare, and hide the car's contents from prying eyes. Factory applications are worth the extra cost, since cheaper aftermarket products (costing about $100) distort visibility and peel away after a few years. Some tinting done in the United States can run afoul of provincial highway codes that require more transparency.

Cutting the Price

Bidding by Fax or Email

Dealers are more receptive to fax and email bidding this year because showroom traffic has dwindled without "employee" discount programs. The process is quite easy: Simply fax or email an invitation for bids to area dealerships, asking them to give their bottom-line price for a specific make and model. Be clear that all final bids must be sent within a week. When all the bids are received, the lowest bid is sent to the other dealers to give them a chance to beat that price. After a week of bidding, the lowest price gets your business.

Dozens of *Lemon-Aid* readers have told me how this approach has cut thousands of dollars from the advertised price and saved them from the degrading song-and-dance routine between the buyer, sales agent, and sales manager ("he said, she said, the sales manager said").

A *Lemon-Aid* reader sent in the following suggestions for buying by fax:

> First, I'd like to thank you for writing the *Lemon-Aid* series of books, which I have used extensively in the fax-tendering purchase of my '99 Accord and '02 Elantra. I have written evidence from dealers that I saved a bare minimum of $700 on the Accord (but probably more) and a whopping $900 on the Elantra through the use of fax-tendering, over and above any deals possible through Internet-tendering and/or showroom bargaining.
>
> Based on my experience, I would suggest that in reference to the fax-tendering process, future *Lemon-Aid* editions emphasize:
>
> * Casting a wide geographical net, as long as you're willing to pick the car up there. I faxed up to 50 dealerships, which helped tremendously in increasing the number of serious bidders. One car was bought locally in Ottawa, the other in Mississauga.
> * Unless you don't care much about what car you end up with…be very specific about what you want. If you are looking at just one or two cars, which I recommend, specify trim level and all extended warranties and dealer-installed options in the fax letter. Otherwise, you'll end up with quotes comparing apples and oranges, and you won't get the best deal on options negotiated later. Also, specify that quotes should be signed—this helps out with errors in quoting.
> * Dealerships are sloppy—there is a 25–30 percent error rate in quotes. Search for errors and get corrections, and confirm any of the quotes in serious contention over the phone.
> * Phone to personally thank anyone who submits a quote for their time. Salespeople can't help themselves, they'll ask how they ranked, and often want to then beat the best quote you've got. This is much more productive than faxing back the most competitive quote (I know, I've tried that too).

Another reader, in British Columbia, was successful with this approach:

I purchased your 2005 edition *SUVs, Vans, and Trucks* earlier this year from Chapters. Thanks for all the information that helped me decide to purchase a new Honda Odyssey EX-L for a super price from a good dealer. After completing my research (and vacillating for a few weeks) I ended up issuing a faxed "request for quotation" (RFQ) from several dealerships. I can tell you that some of them were not happy and tried to tell me that Honda Canada was clamping down on this activity. In the end, one dealership did not respond and one "closer" salesperson called to attempt to get me in their dealership so he could "assess my needs." I told him that my needs were spelled out very specifically in my request but he refused to give me a price. In the end, I received five quotations by phone, fax, and email. I purchased my van in Chilliwack for about $2,200 off list. It turned out that the salesperson just started selling cars two months ago and was very appreciative of my business. The whole deal was completed in half an hour. I was in full control but treated every respondent fairly. I did not play dealers off one another and went with the lowest first offer.

Here is the fax bid request I sent to the dealers:

SAMPLE FAX BID REQUEST

WITHOUT PREJUDICE

Date: _____

Dear Sir or Madam,

I will be purchasing a new 2005 Toyota Sienna or a new 2005 Honda Odyssey and am issuing a request for quotation to several dealerships. I am willing to travel to complete a deal.

The quoted price is to *include* my requested options as well as any applicable pre-delivery inspection, administration, documentation, freight, and delivery fees. I understand that tire tax, air conditioning tax, battery tax, and provincial and federal sales tax are extra and are not required on your quotation. The dealer may sell off the lot or order the vehicle.

Please complete the attached form and either fax or email it back to me before the deadline of *5:00pm, April 14, 2005*. All respondents will be contacted after the deadline to confirm their bid. The winning bidder will then be contacted soon after to complete the transaction.

I will accept an alternate price quotation for a demonstration model with similar options, but this is not a mandatory requirement.

Please direct any questions via email to me at _____ and I will respond promptly. Alternately you may call me at my office at _____.

Sincerely,
Joe Buyer

Figuring a Fair Price

What's the Dealer's Cut?

Most new-car salespeople are reluctant to give out information on the amount of profit figured into the cost of each new car, but a few years ago, *Automotive News* gave American dealer markups based on MSRP. I've reduced the percentages a bit to reflect what Canadian dealers now receive, and I've included negotiable freight, dealer pre-delivery inspection (PDI), and administrative fees—all of which you should bargain down.

DEALER MARKUP

DEALER MARKUP (AMERICAN VEHICLES)

Base minivans: 20+ percent

High-end minivans: 22+ percent

Base pickups: 20+ percent

High-end pickups: 23+ percent

Vans and sport-utility vehicles: 22+ percent

Fully equipped, top-of-the-line vans and SUVs:
   24+ percent

DEALER MARKUP (JAPANESE VEHICLES)

Base minivans: 24+ percent

High-end minivans: 15+ percent

Base pickups: 15+ percent

High-end pickups: 17+ percent

Sport-utility vehicles: 14+ percent

Fully equipped, top-of-the-line vans and SUVs:
   17+ percent

South Korean prices are the most flexible, while Japanese and European vehicle prices are much firmer. In addition to the dealer's markup, some vehicles may also have a 3 percent carryover allowance paid out in a dealer incentive program. Finance contracts may also tack on a 3 percent dealer commission.

Can You Get a Fair Price?

Yes, but you'll have to keep your wits about you and time your purchase well into the model year—usually in late winter or spring.

New-car negotiations aren't wrestling matches where you have to pin the sales agent's shoulders to the mat to win. If you feel that the overall price is fair, don't jeopardize the deal by refusing to budge. For example, if you've brought the contract price 10 percent or more below the MSRP and the dealer sticks you with a $200 "administrative fee" at the last moment, let it pass. You've saved money and the sales agent has saved face.

Of course, someone will always be around to tell you how he or she could have bought the vehicle for much less. Let that pass, too.

To come up with a fair price, subtract one-half of the dealer markup from the MSRP and then trade the carryover and holdback allowance for a reduced delivery and transportation fee. Compute the options separately, and sell your trade-in privately. Buyers can more easily knock $2,000–$3,000 off a $20,000 base price if they wait until January or February when sales are stagnant, choose a vehicle in stock, and resist unnecessary options.

Beware of Financing and Insurance Traps

Once you and the dealer have settled on the vehicle's price, you aren't out of the woods yet. You'll be handed over to a financing and insurance (F&I) specialist, whose main goal is to convince you to buy additional financing, loan insurance, paint and seatcover protectors, rustproofing, and extended warranties. These items will be presented on a computer screen as costing only "a little bit more each month."

Compare the dealer's insurance and financing charges with those from an independent agency that may offer better rates and better service. Often the dealer gets a kickback for selling insurance and financing, and guess who pays for it? Additionally, remember that if the financing rate looks too good to be true, you're probably paying too much for the vehicle. The F&I closer's hard-sell approach will take all your willpower and patience to resist, but when he or she gives up, your trials are over.

Add-on charges are the dealer's last chance to stick it to you before the contract is signed. Dealer pre-delivery inspection (PDI) and transportation charges, "documentation" fees, and extra handling costs are ways that the dealer gets extra profits for nothing. Dealer preparation is often a once-over-lightly affair, with a car seldom getting more than a wash job and a couple of dollars' worth of gas in the tank. It's paid for by the factory in most cases, and when it's not, it should cost no more than 2 percent of the car's selling price. Reasonable transportation charges are acceptable, although dealers who claim that the manufacturer requires the payment often inflate them.

"No Haggle" Pricing Means "Price-Fixing"

All dealers bargain. They hang out the "No dickering; one price only!" sign simply as a means to discourage customers from asking for a better deal. Like parking lots and restaurants that claim they won't be responsible for lost or stolen property, they're bluffing. Still, you'd be surprised by how many people believe that if it's posted, it's non-negotiable.

No-haggle pricing is not only a deceptive practice, it's also illegal under federal price-fixing statutes. Several *Lemon-Aid* readers say some Honda dealers refuse to negotiate prices via email or fax (see page 95) because Honda Canada threatened to yank their franchise if they did so. Following *Lemon-Aid*'s formal complaint, the feds opened a formal investigation of Honda's practices.

In June 2004, Toyota Canada abandoned its Access no-haggle price strategy sales system after settling out of court a price-fixing probe undertaken by the federal Competition Bureau. Toyota is still the target of class-action lawsuits in Quebec and British Columbia, however, and the Automobile Protection Association says Toyota's actions have changed little since the settlement.

If you bought your Toyota in B.C. and feel you paid too much under Access, contact Leslie Mackoff of Mackoff & Company at *lmackoff@mackoff.ca* or call their class action hotline at 1-866-256-3853. Mackoff's class action lawsuit alleges dealers set prices unlawfully, refused to offer discounts from the Access price, and would not offer free options or extra features. Quebec buyers may file a similar claim with Daniel Belleau of the Automobile Protection Association (*www.apa.ca*), a Montreal lawyer who has also filed a class-action claim in that province.

Price Guidelines

When negotiating the price of a new vehicle, remember there are several price guidelines, and dealers use the one that will make them the most profit on each transaction. Two of the more common prices quoted are the MSRP (what the automaker advertises as a fair price) and the dealer's invoice cost (which is supposed to indicate how much the dealer paid for the vehicle). Both price indicators leave considerable room for the dealer's profit margin, along with some extra padding in the form of inflated transportation and preparation charges. If you are presented with both figures, go with the MSRP, since it can be verified by calling the manufacturer. Any dealer can print up an invoice and swear to its veracity. If you want an invoice price from an independent source, contact *CarCostCanada.com* at 1-800-805-2270.

Buyers who live in rural areas and in Western Canada are often faced with grossly inflated auto prices compared to those charged in major metropolitan areas. A good way to get a more competitive price without buying out of province is to buy a couple of out-of-town newspapers (the Saturday *Toronto Star* "Wheels" section is especially helpful) and demand that your dealer bring the selling price, preparation charges, and transportation fees into line with the prices advertised.

Another tactic is to take a copy of a local competitor's car ad to a competing dealer selling the same brand and ask for a better price. Chances are they've already lost a few sales due to the ad and will work a little harder to match the deal; if not, they're almost certain to reveal the tricks in the competitor's promotion to make the sale.

Dealer Incentives and Customer Rebates

Automobile incentives have been around ever since Henry Ford offered $40–$60 rebates on the Model T in 1914. However, rebates were first used as a sales incentive in Canada and the States during Super Bowl Sunday in 1975, just after Detroit automakers raised prices 10 percent and lost sales because of what would later be called "sticker shock." Backpedalling furiously to regain sales, automakers cut some prices immediately and added cash rebates of a few hundred dollars as an additional inducement. Sports broadcaster Joe Garagiola became the Chrysler rebate pitchman with his unforgettable tag line: "Buy a car. Get a check [$400]."

Sales incentives haven't changed much in the past 30 years. When vehicles are first introduced in the fall, they're generally overpriced; early in the new year, they'll sell for about 30 percent less. In the summer, many models will sell for almost half their original retail price through a combination of dealer sales incentives (manufacturer-to-dealer), cash rebates (manufacturer-to-customer), zero-percent interest financing (manufacturer-to-finance-company-to-customer), and discounted prices (dealer-to-customer).

The enormity of these discounts came to light last year as Detroit's Big Three engaged in cutthroat discounting early in 2005 and then followed up with even more generous "employee discounts for all" during the summer.

Smart shoppers who delay their purchases for about six months routinely shave $10,000–$13,000 off the dealer's list price.

In most cases, the manufacturer's rebate is straightforward and mailed directly to the buyer from the automaker. There are other rebate programs that require a financial investment on the dealer's part, however, and these shared programs tempt dealers to offset losses by inflating the selling price or pocketing the manufacturer's rebate. Therefore, when the dealer participates in the rebate program, demand that the rebate be deducted from the MSRP and not from some inflated invoice price concocted by the dealer.

Some rebate ads will include the phrase "from dealer inventory only." If your dealer doesn't have the vehicle in stock, you won't get the rebate.

Sometimes automakers will suddenly decide that a rebate no longer applies to a specific model, even though their ads continue to include it. When this happens, take all brochures and advertisements showing your eligibility for the rebate plan to provincial consumer protection officials. They can use false advertising statutes to force automakers to give rebates to every purchaser who was unjustly denied one.

If you are buying a heavily discounted vehicle, be wary of "option packaging" by dealers who push unwanted protection packages (rustproofing, paint sealants, and upholstery finishes) or who levy excessive charges for preparation, filing fees, loan guarantee insurance, and credit life insurance.

Rebates and Quality

Forget the old adage "you get what you pay for." Many reliable, top-performing vehicles come with rebates—they just aren't as generous as what you'll find with more mediocre choices. For example, rarely will Toyota and Honda offer more than $1,000 rebates, whereas Chrysler, Ford, and GM routinely hand out $3,000 discounts and other sales incentives. To come out ahead, you have to know how to play this rebate game by choosing quality first.

Customer and dealer incentives are frequently given out to stimulate sales of year-old models that are unpopular, scheduled to be redesigned, or headed for the axe. By choosing carefully which rebated models you buy, it's easy to realize important savings with little risk. For example, GM's $2,000 incentives are good deals when applied to its reasonably reliable compact cars, but they're not worth it when applied to the company's glitch-prone front-drive minivans. Ford's F-150 pickup and Freestar minivan rebates ($3,000 or more) also aren't sufficient to offset the greater risk of factory-related defects afflicting these failure-prone models. DaimlerChrysler rebates can be a good deal when applied to minivans but not advisable as a reason to buy the company's less reliable SUVs.

Inflated or Deflated Prices

Generally, vehicles are priced according to what the market will bear and then are discounted as the competition heats up (Chrysler and GM minivans and Ford trucks are prime examples). A vehicle's stylishness, scarcity, or general popularity can inflate its value considerably. For example, Chrysler's rear-drive Hemi engine–equipped 2006 Magnum has a prevailing market value higher than its suggested selling price, mainly because it's in a hot market niche and in short supply. Once sales slow down later in the new year, popular but overpriced vehicles usually sell at a discount (VW's New Beetle, for example). With vehicles that have an inflated value, wait two years for their popularity to subside or purchase the previous year's version. If your choice has a deflated market value (like underpowered first-year Odysseys or overly maligned South Korean models), find out why it's so unpopular and then decide if the savings are worth it. Vehicles that don't sell because of their weird styling are no problem, but poor quality control (think Chrysler Concorde and Ford Focus) can cost big bucks.

Chrysler dropped its 7-year powertrain warranty on 2006 models, and this will also be a big factor in the perceived value of its vehicles. Expect the company to be forced to add an extra $1,000 to its usual $2,000 rebates, igniting a rebate war more brutal than what was seen last year.

Leftovers

In the fall, at the beginning of each new model year, most dealers still have a few of last year's vehicles left. Some are new, and some are demonstrators with a few thousand kilometres on them. The factory gives the dealer a 3–5 percent rebate on late-season vehicles, and dealers will often pass on some of these savings to clients. But are these leftovers really bargains?

They might be, if you can amortize the first year's depreciation by keeping the vehicle for eight years. But if you're the kind of driver who trades every two or three years, you're likely to come out a loser by buying an end-of-the-season vehicle. The simple reason is that as far as trade-ins are concerned, a leftover is a used vehicle that has depreciated at least 20 percent. The savings the dealer gives you may not equal that first year's depreciation (a cost you'll incur without getting any of the first year's driving benefits). If the dealer's discounted price matches or exceeds the 20 percent depreciation, then you're getting a pretty good deal. But if the next year's model is only a bit more expensive, has been substantially improved, or is covered by a more extensive and comprehensive warranty, it could represent a better buy than a cheaper leftover.

Ask the dealer for all work orders relating to the vehicle, including the PDI checklist, and make sure that the odometer readings follow in sequential order. Remember as well that most demonstrators should have less than 5,000 km on the ticker and that the original warranty has been reduced from the day the vehicle was first put on the road. Have the dealer extend the warranty or lower the price accordingly—about $100 for each month of warranty that has expired. If the vehicle's file shows that it was registered to a leasing agency or any other third party, you're definitely buying a used vehicle disguised as a demo. You should walk away from the sale—you're dealing with a crook.

Cash Versus Financing

Let's clear up one myth right away: Dealers won't treat you better if you pay cash. They want you to buy a fully loaded vehicle and finance the whole deal. Paying cash is not advantageous to the dealer, since kickbacks on finance contracts represent an important part of the F&I division's profits. Actually, barely 8 percent of new-car buyers pay cash.

Those buyers may be making a big mistake. Financial planners say it can be smarter to borrow the money to purchase a new vehicle even if you can afford to pay cash, because if you use the vehicle for business, a portion of the interest may be tax-deductible. The cash that you free up can then be used to repay debts that aren't tax-deductible (mortgages or credit card debts, for example).

Rebates versus Low or Zero Percent Financing

If you are buying an expensive vehicle—like a luxury car or an SUV—and going for longer financing, the low-rate financing will be a better deal than the rebate. A zero percent loan will save you $80 per $1,000 financed over 24 months, or $120 per $1,000 financed over 36 months, compared with 7.5 percent financing. If you were financing a $30,000 car for two years, you'd multiply $80 × 30 and save about $2,400.

Low-financing programs have the following disadvantages:

- Buyers must have exceptionally good credit.
- Shorter financing periods mean higher payments.
- Cash rebates are excluded.
- Only fully equipped or slow-selling models are eligible.
- Buyers pay full retail price.

Remember, to get the best price, first negotiate the price of the vehicle without disclosing whether you are paying cash or financing the purchase (say you haven't yet decided). Once you have a fair price, you can then take advantage of the financing.

Getting a Loan

To borrow, you must be at least 18 years old (age of majority), have a steady income, prove that you have discretionary income sufficient to make the loan payments, and either be willing to guarantee the loan with additional collateral or have your parent or spouse as a co-signer.

Before applying for a loan, you should have established a good credit rating via a paid-off credit card and have a small savings account with your local bank, credit union, or trust company. Prepare a budget listing your assets and obligations. This will quickly show whether or not you can afford a car. Next, pre-arrange your loan with a phone call. This will protect you from much of the smoke-and-mirrors showroom shenanigans.

Incidentally, if you do get in over your head and require credit counselling, contact Credit Counselling Service (CCS), a non-profit organization located in many of Canada's major cities (*www.creditcanada.com*).

Hidden Loan Costs

Don't trust anyone. The APA's undercover shoppers have found that most deceptive deals involve major banking institutions rather than automaker-owned companies.

In your quest for an auto loan, remember that the Internet offers help for people who need an auto loan and want quick approval but don't want to face a banker. The Bank of Montreal (*www.bmo.com*) was the first Canadian bank to allow vehicle buyers to post a loan application on its website, and it promises to send a loan response within 20 seconds. Other banks, such as the Royal Bank (*www.rbc.com*), are offering a similar service. Loans are available to any web surfer, including those who aren't current BMO or RBC customers.

 Be sure to call various financial institutions to find out the following:

- The annual percentage rate on the amount you want to borrow and the rate for the duration of your repayment period
- The minimum down payment that the institution requires
- Whether taxes and licence fees are considered part of the overall cost and, thus, are covered by part of the loan
- Whether lower rates are available for different loan periods, or for a larger down payment
- Whether discounts are available to depositors and, if so, how long you must be a depositor before qualifying

When comparing loans, consider the annual rate and calculate the total cost of the loan offer: that is, how much you'll pay above and beyond the total price of the vehicle.

Dealers can finance your purchase at interest rates that are competitive with the banks' because of the rebates they get from the manufacturers and some lending institutions. Some dealers, though, mislead their customers into thinking they can borrow money at as much as five percentage points below the prime rate. Actually, they're jacking up the retail price to more than make up for the lower interest charges. Sometimes, instead of boosting the price, dealers reduce the amount they pay for the trade-in. In either case, the savings are illusory.

When dealing with banks, keep in mind that the traditional 36-month loan has now been stretched to 48 or 60 months. Longer payment terms make each month's payment more affordable, but over the long run, they increase the cost of the loan considerably. Therefore, take as short a term as possible.

Be wary of lending institutions that charge a "processing" or "document" fee ranging from $25 to $100. Sometimes consumers will be charged an extra 1–2 percent of the loan up front in order to cover servicing. This is similar to lending institutions adding "points" to mortgages, except that with auto loans, it's totally unjustified. In fact, dealers in the States are the object of several state lawsuits and class actions for inflating loan charges.

Some banks will cut the interest rate if you're a member of an automobile owners' association or if loan payments are automatically deducted from your chequing account. This latter proposal may be costly, however, if the account charges exceed the interest-rate savings.

Finance companies affiliated with GM, Ford, and Chrysler have been offering low-interest loans many points below the prime rate. In many cases, this low rate is applicable only to hard-to-sell models or vehicles equipped with expensive options. The low rate frequently doesn't cover the entire loan period. If vehicles recommended in this book are covered by low-interest loans, however, then the automaker-affiliated finance companies become a useful alternative to regular banking institutions.

Loan Protection

Credit insurance guarantees that the vehicle loan will be paid if the borrower becomes disabled or dies. There are three basic types of insurance that can be written into an installment contract: credit life, accident and health, and comprehensive. Most bank and credit union loans are already covered by some kind of loan insurance, but dealers sell the protection separately at an extra cost to the borrower. For this service, the dealer gets a hefty 20 percent commission. The additional cost to the purchaser can be significant. The federal 6 percent GST is applied to loan insurance, but PST may be exempted in some provinces.

Collecting on these types of policies isn't easy. There's no payment if your illness is caused by some condition that existed prior to your taking out the insurance. Nor will the policy cover situations like strikes, layoffs, or being fired. Generally, credit insurance is unnecessary if you're in good health, you have no dependants, and your job is secure.

Personal loans from financial institutions now offer lots of flexibility. Most offer financing (with a small down payment), fixed or variable interest rates, a choice of loan terms, and no penalties for prepayment. Precise conditions depend on your personal credit rating. Finally, credit unions can also underwrite new vehicle loans that combine a flexible payment schedule with low rates.

Leasing contracts are less flexible: There's a penalty for any prepayment, and rates aren't necessarily competitive.

Financing Scams

Financing was turned down

This scam usually begins after you have purchased the car and left your trade-in with the dealer. A few days later, you are told that your loan was rejected and that you now must put down a larger down payment and accept a higher monthly payment. Of course, your trade-in has already been sold.

Protect yourself from this rip-off by getting a signed agreement that stipulates the financing has been approved and that monthly payments can't be readjusted. Don't give up your trade-in until that agreement has been reached.

Dealer offers to pay off your existing lease or loan

The dealer will. And then the dealer will add what was paid to your new loan at a much higher interest rate. Early termination of your lease will also likely expose you to substantial penalty costs. How likely are you to be cheated when buying a new car? APA staffers posing as buyers visited 42 dealerships in four Canadian cities in early 2002. Almost half the dealers they visited (45 percent) flunked their test, and (hold onto your cowboy hats) auto buyers in Western Canada are especially vulnerable to dishonest dealers.

In Vancouver and Edmonton, dealer ads either left out important information or vehicles in the ads weren't available or were selling at higher prices. Fees for paperwork and vehicle preparation were frequently excessive, with Chrysler dealerships in Vancouver and Toronto charging the most ($299–$632). In some cases, the dealers may have double-billed the buyer. In Toronto, pre-delivery charges of $343 and $89 were levied on top of Chrysler's $955 PDI/transport fee.

Chrysler and Ford dealerships performed the worst overall, Toyota and General Motors performed best, and Mazda and Hyundai dealers were mediocre (they charged extra for items other automakers include in the base price). APA found that Toyota dealers demonstrated a superior level of product knowledge, covered all the bases more consistently, and applied the least pressure to make a sale. But Toyota dealers in the regions with Access-fixed selling prices appeared to charge substantially more.

Negotiating the Contract

The Devil's in the Details

Watch what you sign, since any document that requires your signature is a contract. Don't sign anything unless all the details are clear to you and all the blanks have been filled in. Don't accept any verbal promises that you're merely putting the vehicle on hold. And when you are presented with a contract, remember it doesn't have to include all the clauses found in the dealer's pre-printed form. You and the sales representative can agree to strike some clauses and add others.

ADDITIONAL CONTRACT CLAUSES

1. **Original contract:** This is the ONLY contract; i.e., it cannot be changed, retyped, or rewritten, without the specific agreement of both parties.

2. **Financing:** This agreement is subject to the purchaser obtaining financing at _____% or less within _____ days of the date below.

3. **"In-service" date and mileage:** To be based on the closing day, not the day the contract was executed and will be submitted to the automaker for warranty and all other purposes. The dealership will have this date corrected by the automaker if it should become necessary.

4. **Delivery:** The vehicle is to be delivered by _____, failing which the contract is cancelled and the deposit will be refunded.

5. **Cancellation:**

    (a) The purchaser retains the right to cancel this agreement without penalty at any time before delivery of the vehicle by sending a notice in writing to the vendor.

    (b) Following delivery of the vehicle, the purchaser shall have two days to return the vehicle and cancel the agreement in writing, without penalty. After two days and before thirty-one days, the purchaser shall pay the dealer $25 a day as compensation for depreciation on the returned vehicle.

    (c) Cancellation of contract can be refused where the vehicle has been subjected to abuse, negligence or unauthorized modifications after delivery.

    (d) The purchaser is responsible for accident damage and traffic violations while in possession of the said vehicle.

6. **Protected price:** The vendor agrees not to alter the price of the new vehicle, the cost of preparation or the cost of shipping.

7. **Trade-in:** The vendor agrees that the value attributed to the vehicle offered in trade shall not be reduced, unless it has been significantly modified or has suffered from unreasonable and accelerated deterioration since the signing of the agreement.

8. **Courtesy car:**

    (a) In the event the new vehicle is not delivered on the agreed-upon date, the vendor agrees to supply the purchaser with a courtesy car at no cost. If no courtesy vehicle is available, the vendor agrees to reimburse the purchaser the cost of renting a vehicle.

    (b) If the vehicle is off the road for more than five days for warranty repairs, the purchaser is entitled to a free courtesy vehicle for the duration of the repair period. If no courtesy vehicle is available, the vendor agrees to reimburse the purchaser the cost of renting a vehicle of equivalent or lesser value.

9. **Work orders:** The purchaser will receive duly completed copies of all work orders pertaining to the vehicle, including warranty repairs and the pre-delivery inspection (PDI).

10. **Dealer stickers:** The vendor will not affix any dealer advertising, in any form, on the vehicle.

11. **Fuel:** Vehicle will be delivered with a free full tank of gas.

12. **Excess mileage:** New vehicle will not be acceptable and the contract will be void if the odometer has more than 50 km at delivery/closing.

13. **Tires:** Original equipment Firestone, Bridgestone, or Goodyear tires are not acceptable.

_____   _____   _____
     Date   Vendor's Signature   Buyer's Signature

When the sales agent asks for a deposit, make sure that it's listed on the contract as a deposit and try to keep it as small as possible (a couple hundred dollars at the most). If you decide to back out of the deal on a vehicle taken from stock, let the seller have the deposit as an incentive to cancel the contract (believe me, it's cheaper than a lawyer and probably equal to the dealer's commission).

Scrutinize all references to the exact model (there is a heck of an upgrade from base to LX or Limited), prices, and delivery dates. Delivery can sometimes be delayed three to five months, and you'll have to pay all price increases announced during the interim (1–2 percent) unless you specify a delivery date in the contract that protects the price.

Make sure that the contract indicates that your new vehicle will be delivered to you with a full tank of gas. Once this was the buyer's responsibility, but now, with drivers spending over $30,000 for the average new vehicle, dealers usually throw in the tank of gas.

 ## Clauses You Should Change

You can put things on a more equal footing by negotiating the inclusion of as many clauses as possible from the sample additional contract clauses found on page 107. To do this, write in a "Remarks" section on your contract and then add "See attached clauses, which form part of this agreement." Attach a photocopy of the "Additional Contract Clauses" page and then persuade the sales agent to initial as many of the clauses as possible. Although some clauses may be rejected, the inclusion of just a couple of them can have important legal ramifications later on if you want a full or partial refund.

"We Can't Do That"

Don't take the dealer's word that "we're not allowed to do that"—heard most often in reference to your reducing the PDI or transportation fee. Some dealers have been telling *Lemon-Aid* readers that they are "obligated" by the automaker to charge a set fee and could lose their franchise if they charge less. This is pure hogwash. No dealer has ever had their franchise licence revoked for cutting prices. Furthermore, the automakers clearly state that they don't set a bottom price, since doing so would violate Canada's *Competition Act*—that's why you always see them putting disclaimers in their ads saying the dealer can charge less.

The Pre-delivery Inspection (PDI)

The best way to ensure that the PDI (written as PDE in some regions) will be done is to write in the sales contract that you'll be given a copy of the completed PDI sheet when the vehicle is delivered to you. Then, with the PDI sheet in hand, verify some of the items that were to be checked. If any items appear to have been missed, refuse delivery of the vehicle. Once you get home, check out the vehicle more thoroughly and send a registered letter to the dealer if you discover any incomplete items from the PDI.

Selling Your Trade-In

When Is the Right Time?

It doesn't take a genius to figure out that the longer one keeps a vehicle, the less it costs to own—up to a point. The Hertz Corporation has estimated that a small car equipped with standard options, driven 16,000 km (10,000 mi.), and traded each year costs approximately 6 cents/km more to run than a comparable compact traded after five years. A small car kept for 10 years and driven 16,000 km per year would cost 6.75 cents/km less than a similar vehicle kept for five years and a whopping 12.75 cents/km less than a comparable vehicle traded in each year. That would amount to savings of $20,380 over a 10-year period.

If you're happy with your vehicle's styling and convenience features and it's safe and dependable, there is no reason to get rid of it. But when the cost of repairs becomes equal to or greater than the cost of payments for a new car, then you need to consider trading it in. Shortly after your vehicle's fifth birthday (or whenever you start to think about trading it in), ask a mechanic to look at it to give you some idea of what repairs, replacement parts, and maintenance work it will need in the coming year. Find out if dealer service bulletins show that it will need extensive repairs in the near future (see Appendix I for how to order bulletins from ALLDATA). If it's going to require expensive repairs, you should trade the vehicle right away; if expensive work isn't necessary, you may want to keep it. Auto owner associations provide a good yardstick. They estimate that the annual cost of repairs and preventive maintenance for the average vehicle is from $700 to $800. If your vehicle is five years old and you haven't spent anywhere near $3,500 in maintenance, it would pay to invest in your old vehicle and continue using it for another few years.

Consider whether your vehicle can still be serviced easily. If it's no longer on the market, the parts supply is likely to dry up and independent mechanics will be reluctant to repair it.

Don't trade for fuel economy alone. Most fuel-efficient vehicles, such as front-drives, offset the savings through higher repair costs. Also, the more fuel-efficient vehicles may not be as comfortable to drive because of their excessive engine noise, lightweight construction, stiff suspension, and torque steering.

Reassess your needs. Has your family grown to the point that you need a new vehicle? Are you driving less? Are you taking fewer long trips? Let your truck or van show its age and pocket the savings if its deteriorating condition doesn't pose a safety hazard and isn't too embarrassing. If you're in sales and are constantly on the road, it makes sense to trade every few years—in that case, the vehicle's appearance and reliability become a prime consideration, particularly since the increased depreciation costs are mostly tax deductible.

Getting the Most for Your Trade-in

Customers who are on guard against paying too much for a new vehicle often sell their trade-ins for too little. Before agreeing to any trade-in amount, check out Part Four to find the selling price for your vehicle.

Now that you've nailed down your trade-in's approximate value, here are some tips on selling it with a minimum of stress:

- Never sign a new vehicle sales contract unless your trade-in has been sold—you could end up with two vehicles.
- Negotiate the price from *retail* (dealer price) down to *wholesale* (private sales).
- If you haven't sold your trade-in after two weekends, you might be trying to sell it at the wrong time of year or have it priced too high.

Private Sales

If you must sell your vehicle and want to make the most out of the deal, consider selling it yourself and putting the profits toward your next purchase. You'll likely come out hundreds of dollars ahead—buyers will pay more for your vehicle because they won't have to pay the 6 percent GST on a private sale. The most important thing to remember is that there's a large market for used vehicles in good condition in the $4,000–$5,000 range. Although most people prefer buying from individuals rather than from used car lots, they may still be afraid that the vehicle is a lemon. By using the following suggestions, you should be able to sell your vehicle quite easily:

1. Know its value. Study dealers' newspaper ads and compare them with the prices listed in this book. Undercut the dealer price by $300–$800 and be ready to bargain down another 10 percent for a serious buyer. Remember, prices can fluctuate wildly depending on which models are trendy, so watch the want ads carefully.
2. Enlist the aid of the salesperson who's selling you your new car. Offer her a few hundred dollars if she finds you a buyer. The fact that one sale hinges on the other, along with the prospect of making two commissions, may work wonders.
3. Post notices on bulletin boards at your office or local supermarkets and place a "For Sale" sign in the window of the vehicle itself. Place a newspaper ad only as a last resort.

4. Don't give your address right away to a potential buyer responding to your ad. Instead, ask for the telephone number where you may call that person back.
5. Be wary of selling to friends or family members. Anything short of perfection and you'll be eating Christmas dinner alone.
6. Don't touch the odometer. You may get a few hundred dollars more—and a criminal record.
7. Paint the vehicle. Some specialty shops charge only $300 and give a guarantee that's transferable to subsequent owners.
8. Make minor repairs. This includes a minor tune-up and patching up the exhaust. Again, if any repair warranty is transferable, use it as a selling point.
9. Clean the vehicle. Go to a reconditioning firm or spend the weekend scrubbing the interior and exterior. First impressions are important. Clean the chrome, polish the body, and peel off old bumper stickers. Remove butts from the ashtrays and clean out the glove compartment. Make sure all tools and spare parts have been taken out of the trunk. Don't remove the radio or speakers—the gaping holes will lower the vehicle's worth much more than the cost of radio or speakers. Replace missing or broken dash knobs and window cranks.
10. Change the tires. Recaps are good buys.
11. Let the buyer examine the vehicle. Insist that it be inspected at an independent garage, and then accompany the prospective buyer to the garage. This gives you protection if the buyer claims you misrepresented the vehicle.
12. Don't mislead the buyer. If the vehicle was in an accident, or some financing is still to be paid, admit it. Any misleading statements may be used later against you in court. It's also advisable to have someone witness the actual transaction in case of a future dispute.
13. Keep important documents handy. Show prospective buyers the sales contract, repair orders, owner's manual, and all other documents that show how the vehicle has been maintained. Authenticate your claims about fuel consumption.
14. Write an effective ad, if you need to use one.

Selling to Dealers

Selling to a dealer means that you're likely to get 20 percent less than if you sold your vehicle privately, unless the dealer agrees to participate in an accommodation sale. Most sellers will gladly pay some penalty to the dealer, however, for the peace of mind that comes with knowing that the eventual buyer won't lay a claim against them. This assumes that the dealer hasn't been cheated by the seller—if the vehicle is stolen, isn't paid for, has had its odometer spun back (or forward to a lower setting), or is seriously defective, the buyer or dealer can sue the original owner for fraud. Sell to a dealer who sells the same make. He or she will give you more because it's easier to sell your trade-in to customers who are interested only in that make of vehicle.

Drawing up the Contract

The province of Alberta has prepared a useful bill of sale applicable throughout Canada that can be accessed at *governmentservices.gov.ab.ca/pdf/registries/reg3126. pdf.* Your bill of sale should identify the vehicle (including the serial number) and include its price, whether a warranty applies, and the nature of the examination made by the buyer. The buyer may ask you to put in a lower price than what was actually paid in order to reduce the sales tax. If you agree to this, don't be surprised when a Revenue Canada agent comes to your door. Although the purchaser is ultimately the responsible party, you're an accomplice in defrauding the government. Furthermore, if you turn to the courts for redress, your own conduct may be put on trial.

Summary: Buy Safe and Buy Smart

Purchasing a used vehicle and keeping it for at least five years saves you the most money. It takes about eight years to realize similar depreciation savings when buying new. Giving the biggest down payment you can afford, using zero percent financing programs, and piling up as many kilometres and years as possible on your trade-in are the best ways to save money with new vehicles. Remember that safety is another consideration that depends largely on the type of vehicle you choose.

Here's a list of safety features to look for:

1. High NHTSA and IIHS crashworthiness ratings for front, offset, and side collisions as well as low rollover potential; pay particular attention to the side rating if you are a senior driver
2. Good-quality tires; be wary of "all-season" tires and Bridgestone/Firestone makes
3. Three-point belts with belt pretensioners and adjustable shoulder belt anchorages
4. Integrated child safety seats and seat anchors, safety door locks, and override window controls
5. De-powered dual airbags with a cut-off switch; side airbags with head protection; unobtrusive, effective head restraints; and pedal extenders
6. Front driver's seat with plenty of rearward travel and a height adjustment
7. Good all-around visibility; a dash that doesn't reflect onto the windshield
8. Ergonomic interior with an efficient heating and ventilation system
9. Headlights that are adequate for night driving and don't blind oncoming traffic
10. Dash gauges that don't wash out in sunlight or produce windshield glare
11. Adjustable head restraints for all seating positions
12. Delaminated side-window glass
13. Easily accessed sound system and climate controls

14. Navigation systems that don't require a degree from MIT to calibrate
15. Manual sliding doors in vans (if children are transported)

And here's a list of tips for savvy vehicle buyers:

1. Buy the vehicle you need and can afford, not the one someone else wants you to buy or one loaded with options that you'll probably never use. Take your time. Price comparisons and test-drives may take a month, but you'll get a better vehicle and price in the long run.
2. Buy in winter or later in the new year to double-dip from dealer incentives and customer rebate or low-cost financing programs.
3. Sell your trade-in privately.
4. Arrange financing before buying your vehicle.
5. Test-drive your choice by renting it overnight or for several days.
6. Buy through the Internet or by fax or use an auto broker if you're not confident in your own bargaining skills, you lack the time to haggle, or you want to avoid the "showroom shakedown."
7. Ask for at least a 5 percent discount off the MSRP and cut PDI and freight charges by at least 50 percent. Insist on a specific delivery date written in the contract, as well as a protected price in case there's a price increase between the time the contract is signed and when the vehicle is delivered. Also ask for a free tank of gas.
8. Order a minimum of options and seek a 20–30 percent discount on the entire option list. Try not to let the total option cost exceed 15 percent of the vehicle's MSRP.
9. Avoid leasing. If you must lease, choose the shortest time possible, drive down the MSRP, and refuse to pay an "acquisition" or "disposal" fee.
10. Japanese vehicles made in North America, co-ventures with American automakers, and re-badged imports often cost less than imports and are just as reliable. However, some Asian and European imports may not be as reliable as you might imagine—Kia's Sportage and Mercedes' M-Class sport-utilities, for example. Get extra warranty protection from the automaker if you're buying a model that has a poorer-than-average repair history. Use auto club references to get honest, competent repairs at a reasonable price.

Part Two

USED, NOT ABUSED

There are almost 19 million vehicles in operation in Canada and their survival rates are very high. Indeed 50 percent of the vehicles purchased 15 years ago are still on the road today. A quarter of the light trucks are still on the road after 20 years of operation.

DENNIS DESROSIERS
DESROSIERS AUTOMOTIVE CONSULTANTS
MARCH 15, 2005

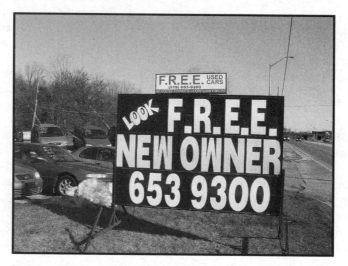

Dealers can make more money selling used than new.

DesRosiers is right, the used-car market is shifting to dealers, and owners are keeping their old vehicles longer than ever before. Although the GST favours private sales, dealers have become a major force in used-car sales in Canada: 10 years ago, dealers sold about one-third of all used cars; now they sell 44 percent. Conversely, in 1993, half of used cars were sold by their owners privately; that portion has been reduced to 38 percent today.

The used fleet mileage has almost doubled within the last 30 years. Back in the 1970s, the average car racked up 160,000 km before it was dropped off at the junk-yard. In the 1990s, the average car reached 240,000 km before being "recycled." Now, new models are expected to see 300,000 km before they're discarded.

One CAA ownership survey revealed that less than 10 percent of owners of cars five years or younger got rid of them because of reliability problems or high main-tenance costs.

Drivers gave other, far more common reasons for selling a car five years old or younger: 43 percent of owners sold because the lease had expired, 30 percent said they just wanted a change, and 21 percent said the vehicle no longer met their requirements.

Only 22 percent of owners of vehicles six to 10 years old got rid of them because of reliability problems.

For many reasons, right now is a great time to buy a used SUV, truck, or van—as long as you stay away from the many rotten products. Fortunately, you won't find as much late '70s and early '80s junk out there as there once was, and modern vehicles are safer and loaded with extra convenience and performance features. Additionally, you will find a lot of cheap product to choose from as dealers cut used prices because of pressure from zero percent interest programs and the deep discounting of new SUVs, trucks, and vans.

You don't have to feel like a cheapskate when you pass up the chance to buy a new SUV, truck, or van. An ever-increasing number of first-time car buyers are choosing used models, while only the upper third of income earners are buying new vehicles.

But dealers aren't giving anything away. Popular, car-based, 2-year-old SUVs and minivans are selling for almost two-thirds of their original price, and they aren't likely to depreciate by much more than half of their original price over five years. Shoppers are finding real bargains when they downsize their choices, or when they go to the South Korean automakers to keep costs manageable. Rather than getting a used Jeep Grand Cherokee, Ford Expedition, or GM Suburban, SUV buyers are opting for Hyundais and less expensive off-lease vehicles like the Ford Escape, Honda CR-V, Jeep Wrangler, Subaru Forester, and Toyota RAV4. Customers looking for trucks are attracted to smaller pickups like the Ford Ranger, Mazda B-series or Tribute, Nissan Frontier, or Toyota Tacoma.

Canadians aren't large-car lovers. We are small-minded when choosing what we drive. Small SUVs like the Subaru Forester, Honda CR-V, and Toyota RAV4 make up almost half of our market, but only one-quarter of the sales south of the border.

As far as minivans go, we believe that less is more and thus favour small imports over Detroit's truck-based rear-drives.

What's Wrong With Detroit?

Greed, dishonesty in giving warranty refunds, maladministration, and a penchant for selling the "deal" rather than the product, that's what.

American automakers lost the knack for making quality machines three decades ago. Suppliers of high-quality components were often rewarded with increased demands for price cuts and constantly changing parts specifications during production. Quality dropped, and owner loyalty shifted to Asian automakers. This has created a huge pool of used Chrysler, Ford, and GM products on the Canadian market that are dirt-cheap but unsafe, unreliable, and expensive to troubleshoot and repair.

Chrysler

Chrysler has been the transmission-failure king since 1991; before that, it was only a contender. The company continues to make a lot of low-quality vehicles, and their transferable 7-year/100,000 km warranty gives only buyers of 2002–04 models the protection they need when faced with Chrysler vehicles' traditional engine, transmission, and steering/suspension failures. A special extended warranty applicable to the Dakota and Durango now retroactively covers ball joint failures, which were denounced several years ago in *Lemon-Aid*. This warranty is useful when arguing for refunds on other models, as well.

Ford

Used Fords are even greater risks to your life and pocketbook than new models. Defects run the gamut, from collapsing tie-rod ends on 1997–2004 pickups to coil-spring breakage that sends 1995–98 Windstars careening out of control. And if your Explorer doesn't roll over after losing its tire tread, perhaps its windows will explode, or it may suddenly accelerate or burn up, as these reports from NHTSA's database (*www-odi.nhtsa.dot.gov/cars/problems/complain*) show:

> My 2004 Explorer was parked in a driveway with rear window towards garage door. The back window of the car along with a piece of the actual door exploded off. The piece of the door flew up into the air and came crashing back down onto the car. There was glass everywhere. Had anyone been facing the car it could have caused some serious bodily injury. Or had the car been in motion anyone inside the car could have been hurt or anyone driving behind could have been hurt.

•

While driving my 2004 Explorer, it suddenly started accelerating uncontrollably. Driver applied the brakes and the pedal went to the floor. Vehicle continued to accelerate excessively. While making a right turn driver hit the curb and flipped four times landing upside down in a ditch. Driver and passenger sustained injuries, and were transported by an ambulance to a hospital. Vehicle was towed and totaled by the insurance company.

•

While driving at approximately 20 mph [32 km/h] other vehicles were pointing at consumer's 2004 Explorer, indicating that the vehicle was on fire. Smoke was coming from the hood, the base of the chassis, the vents, and from the tire hub. The hub caps melted. The fire also disinterested the brakes. Vehicle had to be stopped by the use of the emergency brake. Dealer stated that the cause of the fire was undetermined.

The redesigned 2004 F-150 pickups were another test of Ford's commitment to quality—a test that the company failed, say 329 owners of the 2004 model who reported safety-related failures to the Washington-based NHTSA:

While driving highway speeds, the left front wheel came off the vehicle. The consumer managed to pull over and had the vehicle towed.

•

15 days after purchase of vehicle, it was in to have the rear axle assembly replaced. One year later, it had the rear diff friction plates replaced. 2 months later (right now) the rear end seals are leaking.

•

Purchased new Ford F-150 truck from dealership in April 2004. Wavy distortions in the windshield were evident. Reported defective windshield to dealership, which was then replaced in June 2004 (an approximate three-week wait was required, because dealer reported that new windshields were not available). Second windshield was also distorted, and dealer in another state said that windshield should be replaced by dealer that had installed second windshield. Third windshield replaced in January 2005, after six weeks of negotiations with Ford. This third windshield also has the wavy defect.

General Motors

GM also has its share of lemons, as Sierra and Silverado truck owners will confirm. Major engine, transmission, suspension, and brake problems have returned with a vengeance since GM redesigned its truck line in 1998 and its SUVs a bit later on. The trucks get redesigned again for 2007, and one shudders to think of what else may go wrong.

GM's reworked 1998 and later model year trucks and SUVs are worse than the Fords that were redesigned over almost the same period. GM's poor quality now rivals Ford's for diesel engine (Duramax), fuel-injector, and tranny failures. Plus, its front-drive minivans have carried "biodegradable" intake manifold gaskets since 1996.

> After the vehicle is warm, one of my 2004 Silverado injector sleeves begins to leak diesel and oil into the crankcase, causing plumes of white and black smoke to come out of the tail pipe and causes the truck to sputter. A loud sound of a valve flapping violently also is heard. The truck has been to the dealership 4 times. Each time, they say that nothing is wrong. One dealer in Monterey said that the injectors are from a 2003 model truck and are smaller than the 2004 sleeves, therefore allowing diesel and oil to leak into the crankcase. The dealership has been unwilling to correct the problem.

•

> A clunk sound emanates from the driveline of my 2004 Silverado mostly when shifting from 2nd to 3rd and from 3rd to 2nd. The clunk also occurs between no acceleration and acceleration while in 2nd gear. Occasionally the noise occurs between 1st and 2nd gear. The problem began at approximately 2000 miles [3,200 km]. It has gotten worse as I now approach 20,000 miles [32,000 km]. I am concerned about a driveline failure or damage to driveline components due to repeated torsional impacts.

But let's not just pick on Ford, GM, and Chrysler. European automakers make their share of lemons, as well. J.D. Power and Associates rank Mercedes' quality as much worse than average. If, however, you were a steady reader of *Lemon-Aid* over the past 35 years, you would have been wary of Mercedes' poor quality almost a decade ago, and you would probably have saved money buying a Toyota Highlander or Lexus 350, instead.

There's absolutely no correlation between a vehicle being safe and dependable and the amount of money that vehicle costs. In fact, almost the opposite conclusion can be reached: Cheap, simple vehicles that originally retailed for about $20,000 and have been on the market for a few years are far better buys than most vehicles costing two or three times as much. Again, J.D. Power confirms this fact.

Nevertheless, you can reduce your risk of buying a lemon by getting a used vehicle rated "Recommended" in this guide—one that has some of the original warranty still in effect. This protects you from some of the costly defects that are bound to crop up shortly after your purchase. The warranty allows you to make one final inspection before it expires, and it requires both the dealer and the automaker to compensate you for all warrantable defects found at that time, even if they are fixed after the warranty expires.

2005 and Prior GM Light Duty Truck Models
2003–2005 HUMMER H2

Some owners of light duty trucks equipped with automatic transmissions may comment that the vehicle exhibits a clunk noise when shifting between Park and Drive, Park and Reverse, or Drive and Reverse. Similarly, owners of vehicles equipped with automatic or manual transmissions may comment that the vehicle exhibits a clunk noise while driving when the accelerator is quickly depressed and then released.

Whenever there are two or more gears interacting with one another, there must be a certain amount of clearance between those gears in order for the gears to operate properly. This clearance or freeplay (also known as lash) can translate into a clunk noise whenever the gear is loaded and unloaded quickly, or whenever the direction of rotation is reversed. The more gears you have in a system, the more freeplay the total system will have.

The clunk noise that owners sometimes hear may be the result of a buildup of freeplay (lash) between the components in the driveline.

For example, the potential for a driveline clunk would be greater in a 4-wheel drive or all-wheel drive vehicle than in a 2-wheel drive vehicle. This is because in addition to the freeplay from the rear axle gears, the universal joints, and the transmission (common to both vehicles), the 4-wheel drive transfer case gears (and their associated clearances) add additional freeplay to the driveline.

In service, dealers are discouraged from attempting to repair driveline clunk conditions for the following reasons:

- Comments of driveline clunk are almost never the result of one individual component with excessive lash, but rather the result of the added freeplay (or lash) present in all of the driveline components. Because all of the components in the driveline have a certain amount of lash by design, changing driveline components may not result in satisfactory lash reduction.
- While some owners may find the clunk objectionable, this will not adversely affect durability or performance.
- For additional diagnostic information, refer to the appropriate Service Information.

Why Canadians Buy Used

We *are* different. We are frugal, unpretentious, and faithful. We don't have short love affairs—with cars or trucks, that is. We are very reluctant to trade in a vehicle or to abandon a model that suits our needs. In fact, over half of the vehicles on Canada's roads are nine years old or older, says Toronto-based industry analyst Dennis DesRosiers. We are also more conservative than Americans in our vehicle choices. We still love minivans, while Americans embrace SUVs; we buy downsized sport-utilities, while Americans go for humongous Hummers; and because of our higher fuel costs, we still support economy cars.

Cheaper Prices and No Transport or "Administration" Fees

New-vehicle prices have moderated somewhat over the past few years, but they're still quite high—Dennis DesRosiers pegs the cost of an average new vehicle at over $31,200. Insurance is another wallet buster, costing about $2,500 a year for young drivers. And once you add financing costs, maintenance, taxes, and a host of other expenses, CAA calculates the yearly outlay for a medium-sized car at over $8,252, or 36.7 cents/km; trucks or SUVs may run you about 10 cents/km more. For a comprehensive, though depressing, comparative analysis (cars versus trucks, minivans, SUVs, etc.) of all the costs involved over a 1- to 10-year period, access Alberta's consumer information website at *www.agric.gov.ab.ca/app24/costcalculators/vehicle/getvechimpls.jsp.*

Used vehicles aren't sold with $900–$1,600 transport fees or $495 "administration" charges, either. And you can legally avoid paying sales tax when you buy privately. That's right: You'll pay at least 10 percent less than the dealer's price and you may avoid the 6 percent federal Goods and Services Tax (GST) that applies in some provinces to dealer sales only.

Slower Depreciation

If someone were to ask you to invest in stocks or bonds guaranteed to be worth about one-third of their initial purchase value after four or five years, you'd probably head for the door. But you're falling into exactly this trap when you buy a new SUV, truck, or van. You will feel the depreciation bite less than passenger-car owners do, but in any new vehicle purchase, the trend is toward less value.

Now, shoppers buying a new vehicle will certainly say that the warranty and status far outweigh any inconvenience and that the initial cost will be amortized after a few years. The buyer in this example thus forks over $31,920 and then drives away in a brand new sport-utility vehicle:

COST OF A NEW VEHICLE

Purchase (2006 Ford Escape 4×4)	$28,000
Federal GST (6 percent)	$1,680
Ontario Provincial tax (8 percent)	$2,240
Total price	**$31,920**

A motorist buying that same vehicle at three years old will immediately save about $16,000. Here's how the savings would apply to Ontario residents:

COST OF A USED VEHICLE

Purchase price (2003 Ford Escape 4×4)	$15,000
No GST (if sold privately)	—
Ontario provincial tax (8 percent)	$1,200
Total price	**$16,200**

In this example, the Ford SUV buyer gets a "Recommended" set of wheels that likely has some unexpired warranty coverage left, saves $13,000 on the selling price, cuts another $2,720 in federal and provincial taxes, and avoids paying the $1,500 freight charge that would be added to the selling price of a new vehicle. Furthermore, the depreciation "hit" will be only a few thousand dollars in each of the ensuing years. And we haven't even gone into the interest savings from the $17,000.

How can you turn down a deal like this?

"Secret Warranty" Repair Refunds

Almost all automakers use secret "goodwill" warranties to cover factory-related defects long after the original warranty has expired. This creates a huge fleet of used vehicles eligible for free repairs.

We're not talking about a few months' extension. In fact, some free repairs—like those related to Mercedes engine sludge and GM diesel engines—are authorized up to 10 years or more under "goodwill" programs. Still, most secret warranty extensions hover around the 5- to 7-year mark and seldom cover vehicles whose mileage exceeds 160,000 km (100,000 mi.). This benchmark includes engine and transmission defects affecting Detroit's Big Three, Honda, Hyundai, Lexus, and Toyota. Ford's 1995–98 Windstars carry a little-known 10-year warranty extension covering front coil-spring breakage and offering free tire replacement if a tire is punctured (see NHTSA campaign on page 122).

Knowing which free repairs apply to your car will cut maintenance costs dramatically.

Incidentally, automakers and dealers claim that secret warranties don't exist, since all warranties are published in service bulletins. Although this is technically correct, have you ever tried to get a copy of a service bulletin? Or—if you did manage to get a copy—have you had the dealer or automaker say the benefits are applicable only in the States?

NHTSA CAMPAIGN ID NUMBER: 011007000

DEFECT SUMMARY: This is not a safety defect in accordance with the safety act. However, it is deemed a safety improvement campaign by the agency. Vehicle description: 1995–1998 Ford Windstar Minivans. The front coil springs could potentially fracture due to corrosion.
CONSEQUENCE SUMMARY: Some tires have deflated due to contact with a broken spring.
CORRECTIVE SUMMARY: Ford is extending the warranty for front coil spring replacement to a total of 10 years of service from the warranty start date, with unlimited mileage. This coverage is automatically transferred to subsequent owners at no charge. If either front coil spring fractures during the coverage period noted above, the dealer will replace both springs at no charge to the owner.

---

 15 secret warranties that will save you thousands

One of *Lemon-Aid's* most popular features is its annual round-up of hundreds of secret warranties authorizing free major repairs for SUVs, trucks, and vans. While most are detailed in Part Four under their respective eligible models and years, on the following pages are 15 recent programs that represent thousands of dollars in free repairs, whether you bought your vehicle new or used. Manufacturers can't weasel out of their obligations by claiming that they never wrote such a bulletin.

Service bulletins are great guides for warranty inspections, and they're useful in helping you decide when it's best to trade in your car. They're written by automakers in "mechanic-speak" because service managers relate better to them that way.

If your vehicle is out of warranty and you can't get a "goodwill" warranty extension, show these bulletins to less expensive independent garage mechanics so they can quickly find the trouble and order the most recent *upgraded* part, ensuring that you aren't just replacing one defective component with another.

Because these bulletins are sent out by U.S. automakers, Canadian service managers and automakers may deny, at first, that they even exist. (Are you listening, Chrysler and Ford?) However, when they're shown a copy, they usually find the appropriate Canadian part number or bulletin in their files. The problem and its solution don't change from one side of the border to another. Imagine American and Canadian tourists being towed across the border because each country's technical service bulletins were different! Mechanical fixes do differ in cases where a bulletin is for California only, or relates to a safety or emissions component used only in the States. But these instances are rare, indeed.

The best way to get bulletin-related repairs carried out is to visit the dealer's service bay and attach the specific ALLDATA–supplied service bulletin covering your vehicle's problems to a work order.

Free summaries of automotive recalls and technical service bulletins listed by year, make, model, and engine can be found at the ALLDATA (*www.alldatadiy.com*) and NHTSA (*safercar.gov*) websites. Like the NHTSA summaries, ALLDATA's summaries are so short and cryptic that they're of limited use. So pay the $24.95 (U.S.) subscription fee and then download the complete contents of all the bulletins applicable to your vehicle from ALLDATA.

CHRYSLER UPPER BALL JOINT EXTENDED WARRANTY

BULLETIN NO.: 02-010-04   DATE: DECEMBER 16, 2004

OVERVIEW: This bulletin involves inspecting and if necessary replacing the upper ball joints.
NOTE: The upper ball joint warranty period has been extended to 10 years or 100,000 miles [170,000 km]. Refer to Warranty Bulletin D-04-34 for complete details.
2000 – 2003 (AN) Dakota 4X2
2000 – 2003 (DN) Durango 4X2
NOTE: This bulletin applies only to the above vehicles built through December 31, 2002.

CHRYSLER UPPER BODY SEAM SEAL WATER LEAK

BULLETIN NO.: 23-002-05   DATE: JANUARY 14, 2005

OVERVIEW: This bulletin involves repairing a crack/split in the upper body seam sealer at the "B" or "C" pillar.
2003 – 2005 (RS) Town & Country/Caravan/Voyager
SYMPTOM/CONDITION: Customer may describe a visible crack/split and/or a water leak in the upper body seam sealer at the "B" or "C" pillar.
DIAGNOSIS: If the customer's description matches the Symptom/Condition, perform the Repair Procedure.

CHRYSLER SHUDDER WHILE BRAKING

BULLETIN NO.: 05-002-06   DATE: MAY 10, 2006

OVERVIEW: This bulletin involves replacing the rear brake shoes and, if necessary, the axle shafts and refacing the front brake rotors.
2005–06 (ND) Dakota
NOTE: **This bulletin applies to vehicles built on or before January 31, 2006 (MDH 0131XX).**
SYMPTOM/CONDITION: A vibration or shudder in the brake pedal when the brakes are applied at highway speeds.

FORD WELD REPAIR PROCEDURE FOR SPRING TOWER CRACKS
BULLETIN NO.: 05-1-1

FORD: 1998–2005 E-350, E-450

ISSUE: Some higher-mileage E-350 and E-450 cutaway vans may exhibit cracks in the left or right spring tower flange.

ACTION: Frame replacement is the typical recommended service procedure to address cracks in frames, and is the only repair procedure authorized under warranty. However, the frame can be repaired effectively by welding following the Service Procedure in this TSB.

FORD FRONT END SHUDDER/VIBRATION WHEN BRAKING
BULLETIN NO.: 05-5-2   DATE: NOVEMBER 18, 2004

VEHICLES BUILT BEFORE 11/18/2004

FORD: 2004–2005 F-150

ISSUE: Some 2004–2005 F-150 vehicles built before 11/18/2004 may exhibit a shudder/vibration from the front brakes when braking.

ACTION: Replace the front rotors. On vehicles built prior to 8/20/2003 also replace the rack and pinion.

GM BLAZER FUEL TANK
DATE: MARCH 14, 2005

SPECIAL POLICY ADJUSTMENT—FUEL TANK INLET CHECK VALVE FRACTURE

2002 Chevrolet TrailBlazer EXT

2002 GMC Envoy XL

CONDITION: Some customers of 2002 model year Chevrolet TrailBlazer EXT and GMC Envoy XL vehicles may comment on an SES illumination, may be accompanied by a fuel odor, and/or a few drops of fuel on the ground when refueling the vehicle. This may be caused by a fracture of a weld on the fuel tank inlet check valve (ICV). The ICV is located about the full fuel level. A fracture in this area may allow fuel vapors to pass through and allow droplets of fuel to accumulate on the side of the fuel tank as it passes over the fracture during refueling.

SPECIAL POLICY ADJUSTMENT: This special policy covers the condition described above for a period of 7 years or 70,000 miles (110,000 km), whichever occurs first, from the date the vehicle was originally placed in service, regardless of ownership. The repairs will be made at no charge to the customer.

GM NEW DESIGN WINDSHIELD/DOOR GLASS
BULLETIN NO.: 04-08-48-002B   DATE: APRIL 27, 2006

AVAILABILITY OF NEW DESIGN WINDSHIELD AND FRONT DOOR GLASS

2004–2006 Buick Rainier; 2005–2006 Chevrolet TrailBlazer, TrailBlazer EXT;

2005 GMC Envoy XUV; 2005–2006 GMC Envoy, Envoy XL; and 2005–2006 Saab 9-7X

CONDITION: Due to the difference in processing, along with the difference in the curvature of the glass, the optics of the glass may appear wavy on a cross-car view from the outside of the vehicle. This is a normal condition and the windshield glass should not be replaced for this condition. The view through the glass from the driver's position is clear and not affected.

IMPORTANT: Replace the windshield ONLY if there is a wavy condition or any type of distortion as seen from the driver's seating position that is within the wipe zone on the windshield.

GM's solution for front windshields and door windows that distort visibility is to replace them only if the driver's view is affected. Idiotic, but true.

GM PREMATURE ALUMINUM PANEL HOOD CORROSION/BLISTERING (REFINISH)

BULLETIN NO.: 01-08-51-004D   DATE: JUNE 05, 2006

2000–03 Buick LeSabre; 2002–06 Buick Rendezvous; 2000–05 Cadillac DeVille; 2003–06 Cadillac CTS; 2004–06 Cadillac SRX; 2005–06 Cadillac STS; 2006 Cadillac DTS; 1997–2002 Chevrolet Trans Sport (Export Only), Venture; 1997–2002 Oldsmobile Silhouette; 2001–03 Oldsmobile Aurora; 1997–98 Pontiac Trans Sport; 1999–2002 Pontiac Montana; 2002–03 Pontiac Bonneville

CONDITION: Some vehicles may have the appearance of blistering or bubbling paint on the top of the hood or under the hood edges and hem flanges.

GM TRANNY DEBRIS

DATE: MAY 20, 2005

INCORRECT TRANSMISSION SHIFTS, POOR ENGINE PERFORMANCE, HARSH 1–2 UPSHIFTS, SLIPS 1ST AND REVERSE, TORQUE CONVERTER CLUTCH (TCC) STUCK OFF/ON

2001–2005 GM Passenger Cars with 4T65-E Automatic Transmission
2001–2005 Buick Rendezvous
2005 Buick Terraza
2001–2004 Chevrolet Venture
2005 Chevrolet Uplander
2001–2004 Oldsmobile Silhouette
2001–2005 Pontiac Aztek, Montana
2005 Saturn Relay
with 4T65-E Transmission (RPOs M15, MN3, MN7, M76)

GM SPECIAL POLICY ADJUSTMENT—CATALYTIC CONVERTER AND FRONT EXHAUST PIPE

BULLETIN NO.: 05021   DATE: APRIL 18, 2005

1998 CHEVROLET S10
1998 GMC SONOMA
equipped with 2.2L (RPO LN2 – VIN 4) 4-cylinder engine

CONDITION: Some customers of 1998 Chevrolet S10 and GMC Sonoma model vehicles, equipped with a 2.2L (RPO LN2 – VIN 4) 4-cylinder engine, may experience illumination of the Malfunction Indicator Lamp (MIL) and/or complaints of loss of power or rattle noise. This may be due to pieces of the flex couple joint inner liner of the front exhaust pipe breaking up and tumbling into the catalytic converter, which can cause failure of the catalytic converter.

SPECIAL POLICY ADJUSTMENT: This special policy covers replacement of the front exhaust pipe and catalytic converter for the condition described above for a period of 10 years or 120,000 miles (190,000 km), whichever occurs first, from the date the vehicle was originally placed in service, regardless of ownership. The repairs will be made at no charge to the customer.

GM TRANSMISSION DELAYED ENGAGEMENT, COLD HESITATION, MALFUNCTION INDICATOR LAMP (MIL) ILLUMINATED

BULLETIN NO.: 03-07-30-011C

DATE: APRIL 4, 2005

REPLACE TORQUE CONVERTER RELIEF SPRING, TRANSMISSION FLUID ILLUMINATOR AND LUBE REGULATOR SPRING IN FRONT SUPPORT

2001–2003 Chevrolet Silverado 2500/3500 Series

2001–2003 GMC Sierra 2500/3200 Series

with Allison® 1000 Series Automatic Transmission (RPO M74)

CONDITION: Some customers may comment that the transmission has a delayed engagement, cold hesitation or may illuminate the MIL on the first start-up after sitting for a period of time.

CAUSE: Torque converter bleed down over an extended period of non-usage, usually over a week, may cause this condition.

HONDA EGR VALVE CONTAMINATION OR EGR PORT CLOGGING MAY CAUSE ENGINE HESITATION/SURGE

BULLETIN NO.: 05-026

DATE: JULY 20, 2005

1999–2002 Odyssey; 2003 Pilot

BACKGROUND: In some 1999–03 Odysseys and 2003 Pilots, the EGR system may become contaminated or clogged. If this happens, the vehicle may hesitate or surge during light acceleration, and the MIL (malfunction indicator lamp) may come on with DTC P0401 (EGR insufficient flow) or P1491 (EGR valve insufficient lift).

Because of these possible problems, affected vehicles now have a warranty extension that covers EGR port clogging and/or EGR valve sticking.

Here are the details of the extended coverage:

- On 1999–01 Odysseys thru VIN 2HKRL18..1H586575, EGR port clogging and EGR valve sticking is covered for 8 years or 80,000 miles [130,000 km], whichever occurs first.
- On 2001 Odysseys after VIN 2HKRL18..1H586575, all 2002 Odysseys, 2003 Odysseys within the affected VIN ranges, and 2003 Pilots within the affected VIN range, EGR valve sticking is covered for 8 years or 80,000 miles [130,000 km], whichever occurs first.

HONDA HARD START/POOR PERFORMANCE

BULLETIN NO.: 03-038

DATE: NOVEMBER 5, 2004

1999–01 CR-V

SYMPTOM: The engine idles roughly, is hard to start, performs poorly, or has the MIL on with DTC P0301, P0302, P0303, P0304 (cylinder misfire), or P0172 (fuel system too rich). NOTE: The exhaust valves and seats may be damaged (burnt or cracked) to further indicate that the cylinder head has a problem.

PROBABLE CAUSE: One or more exhaust valves have receded into the cylinder head.

CORRECTIVE ACTION: Inspect the valve clearance and, if necessary, replace the cylinder head.

FAILED PART: P/N 12100-P75-010, H/C 5604970

DEFECT CODE: 00503

OUT OF WARRANTY: Any repair performed after warranty expiration may be eligible for goodwill consideration by the District Parts and Service Manager or your Zone Office. You must request consideration, and get a decision, before starting work.

HONDA VEHICLE DOES NOT MOVE IN DRIVE; MIL COMES ON OR D INDICATOR BLINKS WITH A/T DTC P0730

BULLETIN NO.: 04-036   DATE: JANUARY 7, 2005

2001–04 Civic 2-door with A/T

2001–04 Civic 4-door DX, EX, LX with A/T

SYMPTOM: The vehicle does not move when you select Drive. The MIL comes on ('01–03 models) or the **D** indicator blinks ('04 models) with A/T DTC P0730 (shift control system) set.

PROBABLE CAUSE: Excessive wear in the 2nd clutch.

CORRECTIVE ACTION: Replace the A/T. Use the Honda Interface Module (HIM) to update the PCM software ('01–03 models only).

Mazda North American Operations

June 2005

2000-2003 MPV Rear Heater Pipe & Hose Assembly Warranty Extension Program SSP 65

Dear Mazda Owner:

Mazda Motor Corporation has decided to conduct a Special Service Program to extend the warranty coverage on the rear heater pipe and hose assembly on certain 2000-2003 MPV vehicles. The warranty for the rear heater pipe and hose assembly will be extended to 7 years from warranty start date, with no mileage limitation.

On certain 2000-2003 model year MPV vehicles currently or previously registered in 23 "Salt Belt" states, the accumulation of road salt may cause rust and corrosion to the rear heater pipe and hose assembly. If the rust and/or corrosion is severe, there is a possibility of an engine coolant leakage.

If your vehicle is functioning normally, there is no need to contact your dealer. We suggest keeping this letter with the vehicle's warranty information for future reference.

If your MPV is leaking engine coolant from the rear of the vehicle, please make an appointment with your Mazda dealer. If the leak is from the rear heater pipe and hose assembly, your dealer will replace the affected parts **free of charge**. The repair should take approximately one-half day to complete. However, it may take longer depending on parts availability and the service workload at your Mazda dealership.

Better and Cheaper Parts Availability

Used parts can have a surprisingly long lifespan. Generally, a new gasoline-powered car or minivan can be expected to run with few problems for at least 200,000–300,000 km (125,000–150,000 mi.) in its lifetime; a diesel-powered vehicle can easily double those figures. Some repairs will crop up at regular intervals, and, along with preventive maintenance, your yearly running costs should average about $800. Buttressing the argument that vehicles get cheaper to operate the longer you keep them, the U.S. Department of Transportation points out that the average vehicle requires one or more major repairs after every five years of use. Once these repairs are done, however, the vehicle can be run relatively trouble-free for another five years or more, as long as the environment isn't too hostile. In fact, the farther west you go in Canada, the longer owners keep their vehicles—an average of 10 years or more in some provinces.

Time is on your side in other ways, too. Three years after a model's launching, the replacement-parts market usually catches up to consumer demand. Dealers stock larger inventories, and parts wholesalers and independent parts manufacturers expand their outputs.

Used replacement parts are unquestionably easier to come by after this point. You can bargain with local garages, carefully search auto wreckers' yards, or look on the Internet. A reconditioned or used part usually costs one-third to one-half the price of a new part. There's generally no difference in the quality of reconditioned mechanical components, and they're often guaranteed for as long as, or longer than, new ones. In fact, some savvy shoppers use the information in Part Four of this guide to see which parts have a short life, and then buy those parts from retailers who give lifetime warranties on their brakes, exhaust systems, tires, batteries, etc.

Buying from discount outlets or independent garages or ordering through mail order houses can save you big bucks (30–35 percent) on the cost of new parts and another 15 percent on labour when compared with dealers' charges. Costco is another good source for savings realized through independent retailers—it sells competitively priced replacement tires and sometimes offers free rotation, balancing, and other inspections during the life of the tire.

Body parts are a different story. Although car-company repair parts cost 60 percent more than certified generic aftermarket parts, buyers would be wise to buy only original equipment manufacturer (OEM) parts supplied by automakers in order to get body panels that fit well, protect better in collisions, and have maximum rust resistance, says *Consumer Reports* in its February 1999 study. Insurance appraisers often substitute cheaper, lower-quality aftermarket body parts in collision repairs, but *Consumer Reports* found that 71 percent of policyholders who requested OEM parts got them with little or no hassle. It suggests that consumers complain to their provincial Superintendent of Insurance if OEM parts aren't provided. Ontario car owners filed a class action lawsuit against that province's major insurers, alleging that making repairs with non–OEM parts is an unsafe practice and that it violates insureds' rights.

Liberty Mutual settled the lawsuit out of court, and other insurers have become less insistent that consumers accept knock-off parts.

Does Liberty Mutual owe you a repair refund?

It sure does, if your car was repaired using used parts during the past 16 years (gulp!).

The U.S. Supreme Court has ruled that insurers must replace damaged parts with original equipment parts sold by the auto manufacturer (*Avery v. State Farm*; 1999; *www.state.il.us/court/Opinions/AppellateCourt/2001/5thDistrict/April/Html/5990830. htm*), and an Ontario class action seeking similar relief was settled on January 31, 2006 in *Albert Hague and Terrance O'Brien v. Liberty Mutual Insurance Company* (Ontario Superior Court, Case No. 01-CV-204787CP; June 14, 2004).

If you wish to participate in the settlement, you may have to complete a statutory declaration stating the following: (1) You were insured by a vehicle casualty insurance policy by Liberty Mutual (which includes Liberty Mutual Insurance Company, Liberty Insurance Company of Canada, and Liberty Mutual Fire Insurance Company) and (2) you filed a claim for the repair of your vehicle for an accident occurring between January 1, 1990, and the present in which a non–OEM crash part was specified by Liberty Mutual on the repair estimate. To obtain a copy of the settlement agreement and a form explaining how to participate, contact the Claims Administrator, Deloitte & Touche, LLP; 79 Wellington Street West, Suite 1900; P.O. Box 29; TD Centre; Toronto, Ontario; M5K 1B9.

This settlement isn't just for Liberty Mutual policyholders. *Lemon-Aid* readers throughout Canada may use the Ontario class action settlement as a bargaining chip with any insurer to get OEM parts put in their vehicles or to get a refund of the cost difference for non–OEM parts already installed, going back to 1990 (see *www.deloitte.com/dtt/cda/doc/content/Liberty%20Notice%20of%20Approval.pdf*).

European and Japanese parts

With some European models, you can count on a lot of aggravation and expense caused by the high markup and unacceptably slow distribution of parts. Because European automakers have a quasi-monopoly on replacement parts, there are few independent suppliers you can turn to for help. And junkyards, the last-chance repository for inexpensive car parts, are unlikely to carry foreign parts for vehicles that are more than three years old or are manufactured in small numbers.

Finding parts for Japanese and domestic cars and vans is no problem because of the large number of vehicles produced, the presence of hundreds of independent suppliers, the ease with which relatively simple parts can be interchanged from one model to another, and the large reservoir of used parts stocked by junkyards.

Insurance Costs Less

The price you pay for insurance can vary significantly, not only between insurance companies but also within the same company over time. But one thing does remain constant: Insurance for used vehicles is a lot cheaper than new-car coverage, and through careful comparison shopping, insurance premium payouts can be substantially reduced.

Although the cost of insurance premiums for used cars is often one-third to one-half the cost of the premiums you would pay for a new vehicle, using the Internet to find the lowest auto insurance quote and accepting a large deductible are critical to keeping premiums low.

Beware of "captive" brokers

The Consumers' Association of Canada's (CAC) latest national study on auto insurance rates released July 19, 2005, found that consumers in Ontario paid 45 percent more for their auto insurance than B.C. drivers. The average auto insurance rate in Ontario was $2,383, while it was only $1,324 in B.C.

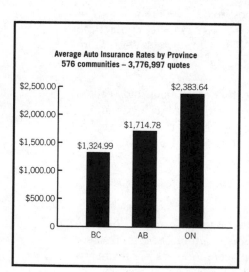

Average Auto Insurance Rates by Province
576 communities – 3,776,997 quotes

The extraordinarily high rates were charged throughout Ontario in cities such as Thunder Bay, Sault St. Marie, Sudbury, Windsor, Guelph, London, Kingston, and Ottawa. The CAC blamed the high costs on Ontario insurance brokers who, it says, may be fronts for a handful of affiliated insurers offering non-competitive rates.

Investigators say a pattern that drives up prices has emerged among so-called independent brokers. With almost 100 auto insurance companies operating in Ontario, a typical broker may sell policies from one or two insurance companies only. "Many of these brokerage firms have financial ties to insurance companies, which limits real consumer choice," said Bruce Cran, president of the Ottawa-based Association.

Use InsuranceHotline.com

One effective agency that tracks the lowest premiums is *InsuranceHotline.com*. It has created a watchdog service to alert drivers to the changes in their insurance rates and to keep their rates low. For $20 per year, the agency will automatically rerun members' profiles to ensure that they always know which insurer has the lowest rate from its database of 30 insurance companies (representing over 80 percent of the written premiums in Canada). There is no telephone access for the service; all comparisons are done online.

Surprisingly, some of the vehicles with the poorest reliability, durability, and fuel economy ratings—like General Motors' Hummer—have good insurance rates. Additionally, if you are ticketed or have one accident, your premiums can almost quadruple. When rates for a 2006 Hummer and a 2006 Honda Civic were calculated, the Civic driver only saved $49 compared to the Hummer premium. But add a police ticket and accident to the equation, and the Civic owner could pay over $2,500 more (see the chart below).

INSURANCE PREMIUMS COMPARISON

MODEL	NO CLAIMS		ONE TICKET & ONE ACCIDENT	
	LOW	HIGH	LOW	HIGH
Hummer	$1,651	$3,138	$2,812	$8,769
Honda Civic	$1,602	$3,125	$2,812	$11,271

A spreadsheet of the different insurance rates applicable to many 2006 models can be found at *www.insurancehotline.com/2006_rate_comparison.html*.

And here are some other *InsuranceHotline.com* findings:

- Family cars priced under $35,000 can cost more to insure than those that are over $35,000.
- SUVs priced under $35,000 don't always cost more to insure than a family car or a small luxury model.
- Luxury cars mean luxury premiums, costing on average about $500 more annually to insure than family cars, SUVs, muscle cars, or hybrids.
- Hybrids' fuel savings can be wiped out by higher-cost insurance premiums that rival what one would pay to insure a muscle car.

Some cars get lower collision costs than others. To know which ones, you should visit the Insurance Bureau of Canada's Vehicle Information Centre (Website: *www.ibc.ca/vehinfo.asp*; Tel: 1-800-761-6703 or 416-445-5912). You won't find a comparison of insurance premiums, but this site provides a comprehensive look at the insurance claims for the most popular private passenger vehicles. It includes collision, comprehensive, personal injury, and theft results for vehicles three or more years old. One would expect the best-rated vehicles to cost less to insure, but this isn't necessarily the case. Nevertheless, this information can help you match your insurance coverage to reflect your model's claims history.

Defects Can't Hide

You can easily avoid any nasty surprises by having your choice checked out by an independent mechanic (for $85–$100) before paying for a used vehicle. This examination before purchase protects you against any hidden defects the vehicle may have. It's also a tremendous negotiating tool, since you can use the cost of any needed repairs to bargain down the purchase price.

It's easier to get permission to have the vehicle inspected if you promise to give the seller a copy of the inspection report should you decide not to buy it. If you still can't get permission to have the vehicle inspected elsewhere, walk away from the deal, no matter how tempting the selling price. The seller is obviously trying to put something over on you. Ignore the standard excuses that the vehicle isn't insured, that the licence plates have expired, or that the vehicle has a dead battery.

You Know the Vehicle's History

Smart customers will want answers to the following questions before signing a contract: What did it first sell for, and what is its present insured value? Who serviced it? Has it had accident repairs? Are parts easily available? How much of the original warranty and/or repair warranties are left? Does the vehicle have a history of costly performance-related defects? What free repairs are available through "goodwill" warranty extensions? (See "Secret Warranties/Internal Bulletins/Service Tips" in Part Four.)

Cheap and Easy Lawsuits

In most courtrooms, lawyers win, regardless of whether you win or lose. And, after several years of being on tenterhooks, even if you do succeed, the award will likely be much less than what you lost and not worth the emotional highs and lows you endured.

But, by being just a bit creative and using the small claims courts, you'll discover there are many federal and provincial consumer protection laws that go far beyond whatever protection may be offered by the standard new-vehicle warranty. Furthermore, buyers of used vehicles don't usually have to conform to any arbitrary rules or service guidelines to get this protection.

Let's say you do get stuck with a vehicle that's unreliable, has undisclosed accident damage, or doesn't perform as promised. Most small claims courts have a jurisdiction limit of $3,000–$10,000, which should cover the cost of repairs or compensate you if the vehicle is taken back. Alberta, B.C., and Ontario now have a $25,000 ceiling—more than enough for most car purchases. That way, any dispute between buyer and seller can be settled within a few months, without lawyers or excessive court costs. Furthermore, you're not likely to face a battery of lawyers standing in for the automaker and dealer in front of a stern-faced judge. You may not even have to face a judge at all, since many cases are settled through court-imposed mediators at a pretrial meeting, usually scheduled a month or two after filing.

When and Where to Buy (Used Vehicles)

When to Buy

In the fall, dealer stocks of good-quality trade-ins and off-lease returns are at their highest level, and private sellers are moderately active. Prices are higher, but a greater choice of vehicles is available. In winter, prices decline substantially and dealers and private sellers are generally easier to bargain with because buyers are scarce and weather conditions don't help them to present their wares in the best light. In spring and summer, prices go up a bit, as private sellers become more active and increased new-car rebates bring in more trade-ins.

Private Sellers

Private sellers are your best source for cheap and reliable used vehicles because you're on an equal bargaining level with vendors who aren't trying to profit from your inexperience. A good private-sale price would be about 5 percent *more* than the rock-bottom wholesale price, or approximately 20 percent *less* than the retail price advertised by local dealers. You can find estimated wholesale and retail prices in Part Four.

Remember, no seller, be it a dealer or private party, expects to get his or her asking price. As with price reductions on home listings, a 10–20 percent reduction on the advertised price is common with private sellers. Dealers usually won't cut more than 10 percent off their advertised price.

Repossessed Vehicles

Repossessed pickups and SUVs are quite common among contractors and other small businesses that have gone bankrupt. You can usually find them at auctions, but sometimes finance companies or banks sell them, as well. Canadian courts have held that financial institutions are legally responsible for defects found in what they sell, so don't be at all surprised by the disclosure paperwork shoved under your nose. Also, as with rental-car-company transactions, these companies' deep pockets and abhorrence of bad publicity means you'll likely get your money back if you make a bad buy. The biggest problem with repossessed vans, sport-utilities, and pickups, in particular, is that they were likely abused or neglected by their financially troubled owners. Although you rarely get to test-drive or closely examine these vehicles, a local dealer may be able to produce a vehicle maintenance history by running the VIN through its manufacturer's database.

Rental and Leased Vehicles

Next to buying privately, the second-best choice for getting a good used vehicle is a rental company or leasing agency. Budget, Hertz, Avis, and National sell vehicles that have one to two years of service and approximately 80,000–100,000 km at cut-rate prices. These rental companies will gladly provide a vehicle's complete history and allow an independent inspection by a qualified mechanic of the buyer's choice, and they'll arrange for competitive financing.

Rental vehicles are generally well maintained, sell for a few thousand dollars more than privately sold vehicles, and come with strong money-back guarantees. Rental car companies also usually settle purchasers' complaints without much hassle so as not to tarnish their image with rental customers.

Rental agencies tend to keep their stock of cars on the outskirts of town near the airport, and they advertise in the local papers. Sales are held year-round as inventory is replenished. Late summer and early fall are usually the best times to get the best choice because the new rentals arrive during that time period.

Vehicles that have just come off a 3- or 5-year lease are much more competitively priced, generally have less mileage, and are usually as well maintained as rental vehicles. You're also likely to get a better price if you buy directly from the lessee rather than going through the dealership or an independent agency, but remember, you won't have the dealer's leverage to extract post-warranty "goodwill" repairs from the automaker.

New-Car Dealers

New-car dealers aren't bad places to pick up a good used SUV, truck, or van, although prices are 15–20 percent higher than those for vehicles sold privately. Dealers are insured against selling stolen vehicles or vehicles with financing or other liens owing. They also usually allow prospective buyers to have the vehicle inspected by an independent garage, offer a much wider choice of models than do private sellers, and have their own repair facilities to do warranty work. Additionally, if there's a possibility of getting post-warranty "goodwill" compensation from the manufacturer, your dealer can provide additional leverage, particularly if the dealership is a franchisee for the model you have purchased. Finally, if things do go terribly wrong, dealers have deeper pockets than most private sellers, so there's a better chance of getting a refund.

Your *Lemon-Aid* guide has levelled the playing field for the consumer when it comes to shopping for new or used vehicles. *Lemon-Aid* has also helped us consumers get the inside edge on how to protect ourselves from car manufacturers, secret warranties, goodwill service, etc.

I recently used your publication to help me in my decision to purchase a 1999 Toyota Tercel. Your *Lemon-Aid* guide also helped me avoid paying an "administration fee." I just walked out of the dealer's showroom. They must have thought I was crazy.

I didn't even have time to take my shoes off when my wife called me and said the Toyota dealership was on the telephone. She had no idea what had happened.

Suffice it to say, this wise consumer didn't pay an "administration fee" so someone could have dinner on me. If there is value in something I will pay it. If not, this customer walks. Here's to many years of carefree driving with my Toyota.

Just an off note. After 17 years of working for General Motors I thought I knew it all about vehicles, making deals, problems, defects, warranties, etc.

Was I wrong. You can never know it all. Keep publishing *Lemon-Aid* and I will keep reading it.

I'm a long-time GM employee who bought his first foreign-made vehicle with the help of Phil Edmonston. Patriotism is one thing, but blowing your hard-earned money for junk is another, just so you can wave the flag.

SINCERELY,
L.C.

"Certified" Vehicles

Almost all automakers provide "certified" used vehicles that have been refurbished by the dealer according to the manufacturer's guidelines. Sometimes, an auto association will certify a vehicle that has been inspected and has had the designated defects corrected. In Alberta, the Alberta Motor Association (AMA) will perform a vehicle inspection at a dealer's request. On each occasion, the AMA gives a written report to the dealer that identifies potential and actual problems, required repairs, and serious defects.

Automaker-certified vehicles guarantee the vehicle's mechanical fitness and provide a warranty according to the age of the vehicle. But these vehicles don't come cheap, mainly because manufacturers force their dealers to bring them up to better-than-average condition before certifying them. Choosing an older certified model can reduce the higher price, or the price can be amortized by keeping the vehicle longer.

Leasing a Used Car

With the exception of using *Leasebusters.com*, which offers extra protection, leasing a used car is a lousy idea. It's generally costlier than an outright purchase, and for most people, the pitfalls far outweigh any advantages. If you must lease, do so for the shortest time possible and make sure the lease is close-ended (meaning that you walk away from the vehicle when the lease period ends). Also, make sure there's a maximum allowance of at least 25,000 km per year and that the charge per excess kilometre is no higher than 8–10 cents.

Used-Car Dealers

Used-car dealers usually sell their vehicles for a bit less than what new-car dealers charge. However, their vehicles may be worth a lot less because they don't get the first pick of top-quality trade-ins. Many independent urban dealerships are marginal operations that can't invest much money in reconditioning their vehicles, which are often collected from auctions and new-car dealers reluctant to sell the vehicles to their own customers. And used-car dealers don't always have repair facilities to honour what warranties they do provide. Often, their credit terms are easier (but more expensive) than those offered by franchised new-car dealers.

Used-car dealers operating in small towns come from an entirely different breed. These small, often family-run businesses recondition and resell cars and trucks that usually come from within their communities. Routine servicing is often done in-house, and more complicated repairs are subcontracted out to specialized garages nearby. These small outlets survive by word-of-mouth advertising and would never last long if they didn't deal fairly with local buyers. On the other hand, their prices will likely be higher than elsewhere, due to the better quality of used vehicles they offer and the cost of reconditioning and repairing what they sell under warranty.

Auctions

First of all, make sure any auction is legitimate. Many are fronts for used-car lots where sleazy dealers put fake ads in complicit newspapers, pretending to hold auctions that are no more than weekend selling sprees.

Furthermore, you'll need lots of patience, smarts, and luck to pick up anything worthwhile. Government auctions—places where the mythical $50 Jeeps are sold—are fun to attend but highly overrated as places to find bargains. Look at the odds stacked against you: It's impossible to determine the condition of the vehicles put up for bid; prices can go way out of control; and auction employees, professional sellers, and their relatives and friends usually pick over the good stuff long before you ever see it.

To attend commercial auctions is to swim with the piranhas. These auctions are frequented by "ringers," who bid up the prices, and by professional dealers, who pick up cheap, worn-out vehicles unloaded by new-car dealers and independents. There are no guarantees, cash is required, and the vehicles' quality is apt to be as low as their prices. Remember, too, that auction purchases are subject to provincial and federal sales taxes, the auction's sales commission (3–5 percent), and, in some cases, an administrative fee of $25–$50.

If you are interested in shopping at an auto auction, remember that certain days are reserved for dealers only—so call ahead. You'll find the vehicles locked in a compound, but you should have ample opportunity to inspect them and, sometimes, to take a short drive around the property before the auction begins.

Promises and Precautions

As a buyer, you should get a printed sales agreement, even if it's just handwritten, that includes a clause stating that the vehicle has no outstanding traffic violations or liens against it. It doesn't make a great deal of difference whether the car will be purchased "as is" or as certified under provincial regulation. A vehicle sold as safety "certified" can still turn into a lemon or be dangerous to drive. The certification process can be sabotaged if a minimal number of components are checked, the mechanic is incompetent, or the instruments are poorly calibrated. "Certified" is not the same as having a warranty to protect you from engine seizure or transmission failure. It means only that the vehicle has met minimum safety standards on the day tested.

Make sure the vehicle is lien-free and has not been damaged in a flood or written off after an accident. Flood damage can be hard to see, but it impairs ABS, power steering, and airbag functioning (making deployment 10 times slower).

Canada has become a haven for rebuilt U.S. wrecks. Write-offs are also shipped from provinces where there are stringent disclosure regulations to provinces where there are lax rules, or no rules at all.

If you suspect your vehicle is a rebuilt wreck from the States, or was once a taxi, there's a useful Canadian search agency called CarProof that can quickly give you a complete history of any vehicle within a day.

 *CarProof (*www.carproof.com*)*

Operating out of London, Ontario, CarProof's services cost $29.95, $44.95, or $59.95, plus GST, per report. For your $30 plus (depending on which package you choose), you can get the following:

- **Section 1:** Vehicle information number (VIN) decode and complete vehicle description.
- **Section 2:** Report summary, which highlights the data found in the complete report.
- **Section 3:** Cross-Canada "current" vehicle registration update, which includes vehicle warning tags applied by any provincial or territorial Ministry of Transportation, such as *Normal, Salvage, Rebuilt, Non-repairable*, and *Stolen*. This section includes registration-effective dates and odometer data, if available.
- **Section 4:** Cross-Canada lien search, which reports any enforceable lien registered against the VIN in all 13 provinces and territories.
- **Section 5:** United States and Canadian vehicle history details. CarProof provides these details through a live connection to Experian Automotive. This section includes all data that would be provided in Experian's AutoCheck report, plus other insurance and registration history provided by CarProof's other data suppliers.
- **Section 6:** New import/export section. Data in this section is already accessed by CarProof and comes from Transport Canada's Registrar of Imported Vehicles (RIV) as well as from the U.S. Department of Transportation. This section reports whether a vehicle has been legally imported into either country as a used vehicle.
- **Section 7:** Odometer history. Reports any odometer records found in Canada or the United States in chronological order.
- **Section 8:** Third-party history. Includes information about aftermarket anti-theft system installations, independent inspections, and other maintenance records.
- **Section 9:** Canadian insurance history. This section provides insurance coverage information and insurance claims history from the private insurance industry all across Canada.

Information requests can be completed overnight online. Contact the company through its website, or if you prefer to talk, call 1-519-675-1415.

In most provinces, you can do a lien and registration search yourself, but it's hardly worth the effort, considering the low cost and comprehensive nature of the CarProof service.

If a lien does exist, you should contact the creditor(s) listed to find out whether any debts have been paid. If a debt is outstanding, you should arrange with the vendor to pay the creditor the outstanding balance or agree that you can put the purchase price in a trust account to pay the lender. If the debt is larger than the purchase price of the car, it's up to you to decide whether you wish to complete the deal. If the seller agrees to clear the title personally, make sure that you receive a written relinquishment of title from the creditor before transferring any money to the seller. Make sure the title doesn't show an "R" for "restored," since this indicates that the vehicle was written off as a total loss and may not have been properly repaired.

Even if all documents are in order, ask the seller to show you the vehicle's original sales contract and a few repair bills in order to ascertain how well it was maintained. The bills will show you if the odometer was turned back and will also indicate which repairs are still guaranteed. If none of these can be found, run (don't walk!) away. If the contract shows that the car was financed, verify that the loan was paid. If you're still not sure that the vehicle is free of liens, ask your bank or credit union manager to check for you. If no clear answer is forthcoming, look for something else.

Paying the Right Price

Even though prices have become considerably more moderate with large and mid-sized models, get ready for sticker shock when pricing minivans, small SUVs, and pickups. These vehicles have depreciated very little, and it's easy to get stuck with a cheap one that's been abused through hard off-roading or lack of care. Even those vehicles with mediocre reliability ratings, like the Ford F-Series pickups and Chrysler minivans, command higher-than-average resale prices for the simple reason that they're popular, though not as popular as they once were.

If you don't want to pay too much when buying used, you've got the following four alternatives:

- Buy an older vehicle. Choose one that's five years old or more and has a good reliability and durability record. Buy extra protection with an extended warranty. The money you save from the extra years' depreciation and lower insurance premiums will more than make up for the extra warranty cost.
- Look for off-lease vehicles sold privately by owners who want more than what their dealer is offering. If you can't find what you're looking for in the local classified ads, put in your own ad asking for lessees to contact you if they're not satisfied with their dealer's offer.
- Buy a vehicle that's depreciated more than average simply because of its bland styling, unpopular colour (dark blue, white, and champagne are out; silver is in), lack of high-performance features, or discontinuation.
- Buy a cheaper twin or re-badged model like a fully loaded Camry instead of a Lexus ES, a Toyota Matrix in lieu of a Pontiac Vibe, or a Plymouth Voyager instead of a Dodge Caravan.

Price Guides

The best way to determine the price range for a particular model is to read the *Lemon-Aid* values found in Part Four. From there, you may wish to get a free second opinion by accessing Vehicle Market Research International's (VMR) Canadian Used Car Prices at *www.vmrcanada.com*. It is one of the few free sources listing wholesale and retail values for used cars in Canada. The site even includes a handy calculator that adjusts a vehicle's value according to model, mileage, and options.

Black Book and *Red Book* price guides, found in most libraries, banks, and credit unions, can also be helpful. But accessing their information for free on the Internet takes a little "insider" knowledge. To access the Canadian *Black Book* values, simply copy the following URL into your web browser: *www.canadianblackbook.com/prv/ auth.cfm?token=AB04DC39ZKL01*.

If this link doesn't work, go to either *www.daimlerchrysler.ca* or *www.toyota.ca*. On Chrysler's site map, click the "Trade-in Value" link; on Toyota's site, click the "Appraise your trade-in" link in the "Vehicles" navigation menu.

Incidentally, those clever *Black Book* people don't want just anyone using their data. They sell it through an annual $146.59 subscription only, accompanied by the following warning:

> The *Canadian Black Book's Used Car Values* is published semi-monthly, for the purpose of providing confidential information to dealers, chartered banks & credit unions and insurance companies.... If you are not a licensed automotive dealer, wholesaler, financial institution or insurance company, you may be restricted in which publications and software applications you may purchase.

Now, if you want to use the *Canadian Red Book Vehicle Valuation Guide*, which seems more attuned to Quebec and Ontario sales, you can order single copies of their used car and light truck wholesale and retail price guide for $16.95 at *www. canadianredbook.com* (an annual subscription costs $95, plus PST). There are no restrictions as to who may subscribe.

You may also go to *Auto Trader* magazine's website at *www.autotrader.ca* to see at what prices other Canadians are trying to sell your vehicle.

Don't be surprised to find that many national price guides have an Eastern Ontario and Quebec price bias. They often list unrealistically low prices compared with what you'll actually see in the eastern and western provinces and in rural areas, where good used cars are often sold for outrageously high prices or simply passed down through the family for an average of eight to 10 years. Other price guides may list prices that are much higher than those found in your region. Consequently, use whichever price guide lists the highest value when selling your trade-in or negotiating a write-off value with an insurer. When buying, use the guide with the lowest values as your bargaining tool.

Financing Choices

You shouldn't spend more than 30 percent of your annual gross income on the purchase of a new or used vehicle. By keeping the initial cost low, there is less risk to you, and you may be able to pay mostly in cash. This can be an effective bargaining tool to use with private sellers, but dealers are less impressed by cash sales because they lose their kickback from the finance companies.

Credit Unions

A credit union is the best place to borrow money for a used car at competitive interest rates (8.75 percent) and with easy repayment terms. You'll have to join the credit union or have an account with it before the loan is approved. You'll also probably have to come up with a larger down payment relative to what other lending institutions require.

In addition to giving you reasonable loan rates, credit unions help car buyers in other ways. Toronto's Alterna Savings (*www.metrocu.com/Personal/Rates*), for example, has a CarFacts Centre, which provides free, objective advice on car shopping, purchasing, financing, and leasing. Their Automotive Advisors provide free consultations in person or by phone (see "Automotive Brokers and Vehicle-Buying Services" in Part One for more info).

Banks

Banks are less leery of financing used cars than they once were, and they generally charge rates that are competitive with what dealers offer. As of July 2006, the Royal Bank of Canada's interest rate on a 3-year, $15,000 used-car loan was 8.4 percent (see *www.rbcroyalbank.com/buyingacar*). The Royal Bank's rate is a reasonable benchmark for comparing rates offered by other financial institutions.

In your quest for a bank loan, keep in mind that the loan officer will be impressed by a prepared budget and sound references, particularly if you seek out a loan before choosing a vehicle. If you haven't gotten a loan, it wouldn't hurt to buy from the local dealer, since banks like to encourage businesses in their area.

The Internet also offers help for people who need an auto loan and want quick approval but don't want to face a banker. Used-car buyers can post a loan application on a bank's website, such as TD Canada Trust's Payment Advantage Auto Loan (*www.tdcanadatrust.com/lending/paal.jsp*), even if you don't have an account.

Dealers

Dealer financing isn't the rip-off it once was, but still be watchful for all the expensive little "extras" the dealer may try to pencil into the contract, because, believe it or not, dealers make far more profit on used-car sales than on new-car deals. Don't write them off for financing, though—they can finance your purchase at rates that compete with those of banks and finance companies because they agree to take back the vehicle if the creditor defaults on the loan (Mitsubishi is adrift in red ink because of its "sub-prime" bad loans to buyers). Some dealers mislead their customers into thinking they can get financing at rates far below the prime rate. Actually, the dealer jacks up the base price of the vehicle to compensate for the lower interest charges.

Dealer Scams

Most dealer sales scams are so obvious, they're laughable. But like the Nigerian supposed "lost fortune" email scam, enough stupid people get sucked in to make these dealer deceptions profitable.

One of the more common tricks is to not identify the previous owner because the vehicle either was used commercially, was problem-prone, or had been written off as a total loss after an accident. It's also not uncommon to discover that the mileage has been turned back, particularly if the vehicle was part of a company's fleet. Your best defence? Demand the name of the vehicle's previous owner and then run a VIN check through CarProof as a prerequisite to purchasing it.

It would be impossible to list all the dishonest tricks employed in used-vehicle sales. As soon as the public is alerted to one scheme, crooked sellers use other, more elaborate frauds. Nevertheless, under industry-financed provincial compensation funds, buyers can get substantial refunds if defrauded by a dealer.

Here in the following sections are some of the more common fraudulent practices you're likely to encounter.

 ### Evading Sales Tax by Shaving the Price

Here's where your own greed will do you in. In a tactic used almost exclusively by small, independent dealers and some private sellers, the buyer is told that he or she can pay less sales tax by listing a lower selling price on the contract. But what if the vehicle turns out to be a lemon, or the sales agent has falsified the model year or mileage? The hapless buyer is offered a refund on the fictitious purchase price indicated on the contract. If the buyer wanted to take the dealer to court, it's quite unlikely that he or she would get any more than the contract price. Moreover, both the buyer and dealer could be prosecuted for making a false declaration to avoid paying sales tax.

Phony Private Sales ("Curbsiders")

Individual transactions account for about three times as many used-vehicle sales as dealer sales, and crooked dealers get in on the action by posing as private sellers. Called "curbsiders," these scammers lure unsuspecting buyers through lower prices, cheat the federal government out of the GST, and routinely violate provincial registration and consumer protection regulations. Bob Beattie, executive director of the Used Car Dealers Association of Ontario, *www.ucda.org*, says his organization has found that about 20 percent of so-called private sellers in Ontario are actually curbsiders. Dealers in large cities like Toronto, Calgary, and Vancouver believe curbsiders sell half of the cars advertised in the local papers. This scam is easy to detect if the seller can't produce the original sales contract or show repair bills made out over a long period of time in his or her own name. You can usually identify a car dealer in the want ads section of the newspaper—just check to see if the same telephone number is repeated in many different ads. Sometimes you can trip up a curbsider by requesting information on the phone, without identifying the specific vehicle. If the seller asks you which car you are considering, you know you're dealing with a dealer.

Legitimate car dealers claim to deplore the dishonesty of curbsider crooks, yet they are their chief suppliers. Dealership sales managers, auto auction employees, and newspaper classified ad sellers all know the names, addresses, and phone numbers of these thieves but don't act on the information. Newspapers want the ad dollars, auctions want the action, and dealers want someplace they can unload their wrecked, rust-cankered, and odometer-tricked junkers with impunity. Talk about hypocrisy, eh?

Curbsiders are particularly active in Western Canada, importing vehicles from other provinces where they were sold by dealers, wreckers, insurance companies, and junkyards (after having been written off as total losses). They then place private classified ads in B.C. and Alberta papers, sell their stock, and then import more. Writes one Vancouver *Lemon-Aid* reader frustrated by the complicity of the provincial government and local papers in this rip-off:

> The story is the lack of sensitivity by the newspapers who turn a blind eye and let consumers get ripped off.... The newspapers are making money, ICBC [Insurance Corporation of British Columbia] is making money, the cops acknowledge wide-scale dumping on the West Coast.... Governments have no willpower to take on organized fraud.

Buyers taken in by these scam artists should sue both the seller and the newspaper that carried the original classified ad in small claims court. When just a few cases are won in court and the paper's competitors play up the story, the practice will cease.

"Free-Exchange" Privilege

Dealers get a lot of sales mileage out of this deceptive offer. The dealer offers to exchange any defective vehicle for any other vehicle in stock. What really happens, though, is that the dealer won't have anything else selling for the same price and so will demand a cash bonus for the exchange—or you may get the dubious privilege of exchanging one lemon for another.

"Money-Back" Guarantee

Once again, the purchaser feels safe in buying a used car with this kind of guarantee. After all, what could be more honest than a money-back guarantee? Dealers using this technique often charge exorbitant handling charges, rental fees, or mechanical repair costs to the customer who's bought one of these vehicles and then returned it.

"50/50" Guarantee

This can be a trap.

Essentially, the dealer will pay half of the repair costs over a limited period of time. It's a fair offer if an independent garage does the repairs. If not, the dealer can always inflate the repair costs to double their actual worth and then write up a bill for that amount (a scam sometimes used in "goodwill" settlements). The buyer winds up paying the full price of repairs that would probably have been much cheaper at an independent garage. The best kind of used-vehicle warranty is 100 percent with full coverage for a fixed term, even if that term is relatively short.

"As Is" and "No Warranty"

Neither phrase means much.

Remember, every vehicle carries a provincial legal warranty protecting you from misrepresentation and the premature failure of key mechanical or body components. Nevertheless, sellers often write "as is" or "no warranty" in the contract in the hope of dissuading buyers from pressing legitimate claims.

Generally, a vehicle with "as is" written in the contract or bill of sale usually means that you're aware of mechanical defects, you're prepared to accept the responsibility for any damage or injuries caused by the vehicle, and you're agreeing to pay all repair costs. However, the courts have held that the "as is" clause is not a blank cheque to cheat buyers and must be interpreted in light of the seller's true intent. Was there an attempt to deceive the buyer by including this clause? Did the buyer really know what the "as is" clause could do to his or her future legal rights? It's also been held that the courts may consider oral representations ("parole evidence") as an "expressed" warranty, even though they were never written into the formal contract. So, if a seller makes claims as to the fine quality of the used vehicle, these claims can be used as evidence. Courts generally ignore "as is" clauses when the vehicle has been intentionally misrepresented, when the dealer is the seller, or when the defects are so serious that the seller is presumed to have known of their existence. Private sellers are usually given more latitude than dealers or their agents.

Odometer Fraud

Who says crime doesn't pay? It most certainly does if you turn back odometers for a living in Canada.

Carfax (*www.carfax.com*) estimates that each year close to 90,000 vehicles with tampered odometers reach the Canadian marketplace—at a cost to Canadians of more than $3.56 million. This is about double the incidents one would expect based on a 2002 U.S. National Highway Traffic Safety Administration study that pegs odometer fraud at 450,000 vehicles annually. NHTSA estimates that half of the cars with reset odometers are relatively new high-mileage rental cars or fleet vehicles.

Obviously, gangs of odometer scammers ply their trade in Canada because it seems as if no one cares what they do and the average resale value of a "doctored" car can be boosted by thousands of dollars, or 10 cents profit for each mile erased from the odometer. Moreover, electronic digital odometers make tampering child's play for anyone with a laptop computer, or anyone who has sufficient skill to simply replace the dashboard's instrument panel.

Think. When was the last time you heard of a dealership being charged with odometer fraud? Probably a long time ago, if at all. And what is the punishment for those dealers convicted of defrauding buyers? Not jail time or loss of their franchises. More than likely, it'll be just a small fine.

The RCMP hate odometer-tampering complaints because rolling back a vehicle's odometer is a common crime that's hard to prove and gobbles up law enforcement man-hours. In theory, these fraud artists face $100,000 fines and two years in jail under the *Federal Weights and Measures Act*, the Canadian *Criminal Code*, and provincial consumer-protection statutes. However, in practice, few odometer tampering cases make it to court because the intent to defraud is so difficult to prove against mechanics who claim they only "fixed" the odometer, a practice allowed under Canadian federal and provincial laws.

Misrepresentation

Used vehicles can be misrepresented in a variety of ways. A used airport commuter minivan may be represented as having been used by a Sunday school class. A mechanically defective pickup that's been rebuilt after several major accidents may have plastic filler in the body panels to muffle the rattles or hide the rust damage, heavy oil in the motor to stifle the clanks, and cheap retread tires to eliminate the thumps. Your best protection against these dirty tricks is to have the vehicle's quality completely verified by an independent mechanic before completing the sale. Of course, you can still cancel the sale if you learn of the misrepresentation only after taking the vehicle home, but your chances of doing so successfully dwindle as time passes.

I'm finding it difficult finding a reasonably priced used car in the Toronto area. Many of the ads for private sales here turn out to be dealers or mechanics selling cars pretending to be private persons. Also, the prices are ridiculously inflated. Your books are a great read and have made me at least slow down and ask questions. For example, I almost got caught in a lease the other day and pulled out at the last minute. All this advertising had me believe there would be zero down, zero delivery, etc. until I found out there would be a $350 lease acquisition fee and a $250 admin. fee and all kinds of other charges, some legitimate such as licensing. However, my zero down turned into a whopping $1,200! I'm just now getting into your leasing section....

Private Scams

A lot of space in this guide has been used to describe how used-car dealers and scam artists cheat uninformed buyers. Of course, private individuals can be dishonest, too. In either case, protect yourself at the outset by keeping your deposit small and by getting as much information as possible about the vehicle you're considering. Then, after a test drive, you may sign a written agreement to purchase the vehicle and give a deposit of sufficient value to cover the seller's advertising costs, subject to cancellation if the automobile fails its inspection. After you've taken these precautions, watch out for the following private sellers' tricks.

Vehicles That Are Stolen or Have Finance Owing

Many used vehicles are sold privately without free title because the original auto loan was never repaid. You can avoid being cheated by asking for proof of purchase and payment from a private seller. Be especially wary of any individual who offers to sell a used vehicle for an incredibly low price. Check the sales contract to determine who granted the original loan, and call the lender to see if it's been repaid. Place a call to the provincial Ministry of Transportation to ascertain whether the car is registered in the seller's name. Find out if a finance company is named as beneficiary on the auto insurance policy. Finally, contact the original dealer to determine whether there are any outstanding claims.

In Ontario, all private sellers must purchase a Used Vehicle Information Package at one of 300 provincial Driver and Vehicle Licence Issuing Offices, or online at *www.mto.gov.on.ca/english/dandv/vehicle/used.htm*. This package, which costs $20, contains the vehicle's registration history in Ontario; the vehicle's lien information (i.e., if there are any liens registered on the vehicle); the fair market value on which the minimum tax payable will apply; and other information such as consumer tips, vehicle safety standards inspection guidelines, retail sales tax information, and forms for bills of sale.

In other provinces, buyers don't have easy access to this information. Generally, you have to contact the provincial office that registers property and pay a small fee for a computer printout that may or may not be accurate. You'll be asked for the current owner's name and the car's VIN, which is usually found on the driver's side of the dashboard.

There are two high-tech ways to get the goods on a dishonest seller. First, have a dealer of that particular model run a "vehicle history" check through the automaker's online network. This will tell you who the previous owners and dealers were, what warranty and recall repairs were carried out, and what other free repair programs may still apply. Second, you can use CarProof (*www.carproof.com*) to carry out a background check.

Wrong Registration

Make sure the seller's vehicle has been properly registered with provincial transport authorities; if it isn't, it may be stolen, or you could be dealing with a curbsider.

If you are selling a vehicle, protect yourself from legal liability by ensuring the registration has been transferred to the buyer. Normally, once you take the tags and give the buyer a bill of sale, you're no longer the registered owner. Nonetheless, it's a good idea to go down to the registry office to make sure the title has changed. As long as you're still listed as the owner of record, you could be sued for damages arising from an accident.

Selling Your Vehicle

Usually you will get the best price by selling to a private buyer. Expect a dealer to give you only about half as much, though you may get a bit more if the dealer sells the brand of vehicle that you're selling.

Selling privately carries its own burdens, however: several hundred dollars to make the vehicle presentable; another $100 or so for ads; prospects calling you at all times of the day and night (even after the car has been sold); and "tire kickers" who aren't serious buyers.

Worst of all, private buyers can hassle you for a complete refund of the purchase price, or for money they spent on repairs to fix defects they say you failed to disclose. Remember, they have your home address and telephone number, and nothing stops them from filing a small claims court lawsuit.

Many owners sell their old cars to dealers because they want a deal that won't come back to haunt them.

Phew, now that you are petrified by what may happen to you, keep the following in mind: Most private buyers don't mind signing a receipt that says the vehicle was sold "as is," and they accept the fact that the vehicle may have some flaws. Furthermore, Canadian courts, while tough on dealers (who are *presumed* to know which defects exist), seldom rule against private sellers, unless it's obvious there was an attempt to deceive the buyer. That's why it's a smart idea to indicate on your "as is" receipt that the buyer was offered a chance to have the vehicle inspected by a third party prior to the purchase.

Incidentally, this third-party inspection gets you a free $75–100 check-up, separates the serious buyers from the shoppers, and allows you to reduce the selling price as partial compensation for expected repairs.

USED CAR BILL OF SALE

Date: _____

Place: _____

I, _____, do hereby sell the following vehicle, _____, to _____ _____, for $_____.

This vehicle is sold AS IS. The buyer has declined to have the vehicle inspected by a third-party.

Signature: _____(seller)   Signature: _____(buyer)

Car Heaven?

Some vehicles are in such poor shape that they can't be re-sold; for them, there's always Car Heaven.

Operating as a non-profit group in Ontario, Alberta, British Columbia (Vancouver and surrounding areas only), Quebec, and the Atlantic provinces, Car Heaven is founded by the Clean Air Foundation, an organization working specifically on air quality issues in Canada. The Car Heaven Program encourages Canadians to get their old, high-polluting cars off the road sooner than they might do otherwise by giving each donor a free tow (valued at $200) and a minimum $50 or $60 charitable tax receipt. Additional incentives include bicycles, transit passes, or a $1,000 coupon toward the purchase or lease of a new GM vehicle. Incentives vary depending on the condition of your vehicle and the province in which you live. Details are available on the Car Heaven website (*www. carheaven.ca*).

Donated cars are picked up and processed by local members of the Ontario Automotive Recyclers Association (OARA) in Ontario, the Alberta Auto Recyclers and Dismantlers Association (AARDA) in Alberta, A-Part Auto Wrecking in British Columbia, Association des Recycleurs de Pièces d'Autos et de Camions (ARPAC) in Quebec, and the Automotive Recyclers Association of Atlantic Canada (ARAAC) in the Atlantic provinces. Their members are committed to the environmentally friendly processing of cars and their parts—including oil, fluids, and tires. Any reusable parts that don't produce emissions are removed and prepared for resale, but none of the vehicles donated to the program are allowed back out onto the street to continue polluting. So far, Car Heaven has raised over $1.2 million for affiliated charities.

Car Heaven covers large cities in the above-mentioned provinces, but cannot handle requests in some small communities, or may require that vehicles be dropped off.

Summary: Saving Money and Keeping Safe

You can get a reliable used SUV, truck, or van at a reasonable price—it just takes some patience and homework. Avoid potential headaches by becoming thoroughly familiar with your legal rights as outlined in Part Three and by buying a vehicle that's rated "Recommended" in Part Four. The following is a summary of the steps to take to keep your level of risk to a minimum:

1. Keep your present vehicle at least 8 to 10 years. Don't get panicked over high fuel costs—depreciation is a greater threat to your pocketbook.
2. Sell to a dealer if the reduction in GST and PST on your next purchase is greater than the potential profit of selling privately.
3. Sell privately if you can get at least 15 percent more than what the dealer offered.
4. Buy from a private party, a rental car outlet, or a dealer (in that order).
5. Use an auto broker to save time and money, but pay a set fee, not a commission.
6. Buy only a *Lemon-Aid* recommended 3- to 5-year-old vehicle with some original warranty left that can be transferred.
7. Carefully inspect front-drive vehicles that have reached their fifth year. Pay particular attention to the engine intake manifold and head gasket, CV joints, steering box, and brakes. Make sure that the spare tire and tire jack haven't been removed.
8. Buy a full-sized, rear-drive delivery van and then add the convenience features that you would like (seats, sound system, etc.) instead of opting for a more expensive, smaller, less powerful minivan.
9. Don't buy an extended warranty for a particular model year unless it's recommended in *Lemon-Aid*.
10. Have repairs done by independent garages that offer lifetime warranties.
11. Install used or reconditioned parts; demand that original parts be used for accident repairs.
12. Keep all the previous owners' repair bills to facilitate warranty claims and to let mechanics know what's already been replaced or repaired.
13. Upon delivery, adjust mirrors to reduce blind spots and adjust head restraints to prevent your head from snapping back in the event of a collision. On airbag-equipped vehicles, move the seat backward more than half of its travel distance and then sit at least 25 cm (1 foot) away from the airbag housing.
14. Ensure that the side airbags include head protection.
15. Make sure that both the dealer and automaker have your name in their computers as the new owner of record. Ask for a copy of your vehicle's history, which should be stored in the same computer. Get a $25 Internet download or data disc of all your vehicle's service bulletins from ALLDATA (see Appendix I). This will keep you current regarding the latest secret warranties, recalls, and troubleshooting tips for correcting factory screw-ups.

Part Three
FIGHTING BACK!

Would GM Lie To You?

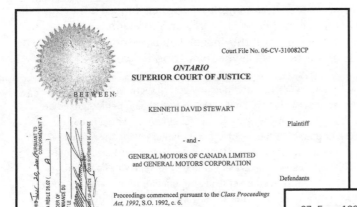

Court File No. 06-CV-310082CP

ONTARIO
SUPERIOR COURT OF JUSTICE

BETWEEN:

KENNETH DAVID STEWART

Plaintiff

- and -

GENERAL MOTORS OF CANADA LIMITED
and GENERAL MOTORS CORPORATION

Defendants

Proceedings commenced pursuant to the *Class Proceedings Act, 1992*, S.O. 1992, c. 6.

AMENDED STATEMENT OF CLAIM

This $1.2-billion class action was filed in Toronto and most other provinces early in 2006. Almost all of GM's 1995–2004 models equipped with V6 engines are implicated. Most of this GM lawsuit can be found in Appendix IV, along with new Ford engine jurisprudence.

27. From 1995 through to the present, GM concealed the nature and scope of the Intake Manifold Gasket (IMG) defect from the members of the Class and regulatory bodies in the United States and Canada. Particulars of this concealment include the fact that where any information was provided to such authorities or to the public generally, such information was incomplete or misleading in that it sought to attribute any problems to issues other than the IMG defect.

GM PAINTED ROOF ADHESIVE SEPARATION

BULLETIN NO: 05112C · DATE: JUNE 7, 2006

This program is in effect until March 31, 2007.
CONDITION: On certain 2005–06 Chevrolet Corvette vehicles, the painted roof panel may separate from its frame in some areas if it is exposed to stresses along with high temperature and humidity. The occupants of the vehicle may notice one or more of these symptoms: a snapping noise when driving over bumps, wind noise, poor roof panel fit, roof panel movement/bounce when a door or hatch is closed, or a water leak in the headliner.
CORRECTION: Dealers are to apply adhesive foam to ensure proper adhesion, or in a small number of vehicles, replace the roof panel.

GM doesn't mean *Generous* Motors. Like all automakers I've dealt with over the past 40 years, General Motors seldom admits to its mistakes, such as minivans with sliding doors that open on their own or break your arm when closing, diesel engines that self-destruct, vans with rust holes in their roofs, and cars with roofs that try to detach themselves (can you blame them?).

But Chrysler and Ford don't level with their customers, either. This is the case whether it's Chrysler's automatic transmissions that biodegrade; Dodge's trucks and SUVs that wander all over the road when their ball joints fail; or Ford's Explorers and pickups that suddenly run amok when their brakes fail or tie-rods break or that suddenly stop when their 4.6L, 5.4L, or V10 engines spit out their spark plugs. No wonder owners feel as if they need exorcists—not mechanics. The following NHTSA complaint is from the owner of a 2000 F-150:

> Two weeks ago while traveling on a two lane highway with the cruise control set at 55 mph [89 km/h], I blew the #4 plug right out of the cylinder head. Dealer quoted a price of $3668 plus tax to fix the engine. This is ludicrous! I am expected to pay this much money for a Ford design issue! I can get another engine for slightly more than that! Heck, I can get a decent commuter car for that much money! In researching this issue, I have found that this is a somewhat common problem with Ford's Triton engines. I also found an alternative method of fixing the engine, which only cost me $350, of which $300 was in the cost of the tools. I cannot believe that Ford will not admit to this engineering design problem and assist those of us who have loyally supported them for years. I guess if people are not dying, it is just seen as an easy way to overcharge people and make extra money via their service departments!

As unbelievable as it seems, these defects aren't that rare. If you've bought an unsafe or unreliable vehicle, whether new or used, and the automaker stonewalls your complaint, this part of the book is for you. My intention is to help you make a successful claim—without fear and loathing, going to court, or getting frazzled. But if going to court is your only recourse, here is 40 years' worth of information on strategies, tactics, negotiation tools, and jurisprudence to help you hang tough and either get an out-of-court settlement or win your case without spending a fortune on lawyers and research.

The Road to a Refund

Vehicles usually turn out to be bad buys for two reasons: Either they were misrepresented or they are afflicted with defects that make them unreliable or dangerous to drive. Misrepresentation is relatively easy to prove; you simply have to show that the vehicle doesn't conform to the oral or written sales representations made before or during the time of purchase. These representations include sales brochures and newspaper, radio, and television ads.

Private sales can easily be cancelled if the mileage has been turned back, if accident damage hasn't been disclosed, or if the seller is really a dealer in disguise. Even descriptive phrases like "well maintained," "driven by a woman" (is this supposed to be a positive or negative feature?), or "excellent condition" can get a seller in trouble if misrepresentation is alleged.

Defects are usually confirmed by an independent garage examination that shows the deficiencies are premature, are factory-related and not maintenance-related, or were hidden at the time of purchase. It doesn't matter if the vehicle was sold new or used. In fact, most of the small claims court victories against Ford relating to defective engines and transmissions were won by owners of used Windstars, Tauruses, and Sables who sued both the seller and the automaker.

Nipping That Lemon in the Bud

It's really not that hard to get a refund if you take it one step at a time. Vehicle defects are covered by two warranties: the *expressed* warranty, which has a fixed time limit, and the *implied*, or *legal*, warranty, which is entirely up to a judge's discretion.

Expressed warranties

The expressed warranty given by the seller is often full of empty promises, and it allows the dealer and manufacturer to act as judge and jury when deciding whether a vehicle was misrepresented or is afflicted with defects they'll pay to correct. Rarely does it provide a money-back guarantee.

Some of the more familiar lame excuses used in denying expressed warranty claims are "You abused the car," "It was poorly maintained," "It's normal wear and tear," "It's rusting from the outside, not the inside," and "It passed the safety inspection." Ironically, the expressed warranty sometimes says that there is no warranty at all, or that the vehicle is sold "as is." And, when the warranty's clauses (or lack of) don't deter claimants, some dealers simply say that a verbal warranty or representation as to the vehicle's attributes is unenforceable. Fortunately, courts routinely throw out these exclusions by upholding three legal concepts:

- Vehicles must be fit for the purpose for which they were purchased.
- Vehicles must be of merchantable quality when sold.
- Verbal promises or representations carry the strength of written warranties, and buyers and their relatives *can* testify as to what they were told.

Watch fuel economy claims

Canadian courts are cracking down on lying dealers and deceptive sales practices, and the misrepresenting of fuel economy figures is squarely in the judiciary's sights. Ontario's recently amended *Consumer Protection Act* (*www.e-laws.gov.on.ca/DBLaws/Statutes/English/o2c30_e.htm*), for example, lets vehicle buyers cancel a contract within one year of entering into an agreement if a dealer made a false, misleading, deceptive, or unconscionable representation. This includes using exaggeration, innuendo, or ambiguity as to a material fact, or failing to state a material fact if such use or failure deceives or tends to deceive consumers.

This law means that new- or used-car dealers cannot make the excuse that they were fooled about the condition or performance of a vehicle, or that they were simply providing data supplied by the manufacturer. The law clearly states that both parties are jointly liable and that dealers are *presumed* to know the history, quality, and true performance of what they are selling.

Details like fuel economy *can* lead to a contract's cancellation, if the dealer gives a higher-than-actual figure. In *Sidney v. 1011067 Ontario Inc. (c.o.b. Southside Motors)*, a precedent-setting case that was filed before Ontario's *Consumer Protection Act* was toughened, the buyer was awarded $11,424.51 plus prejudgment interest because of a false representation made by the defendant regarding fuel efficiency. The plaintiff claimed that the defendant advised him that the vehicle had a fuel efficiency of 800–900 km per tank of fuel when, in fact, the maximum efficiency was only 500 km per tank.

This consumer victory is particularly important as fuel prices soar and everyone from automakers to sellers of ineffective gas-saving gadgets make outlandishly false fuel economy claims.

Not surprisingly, sellers try to use the expressed warranty to reject claims, while smart plaintiffs ignore the expressed warranty and argue for a refund under the implied warranty, instead.

Implied warranties

The implied warranty ("of fitness") is your ace in the hole. As clearly stated in the unreported Saskatchewan decision *Maureen Frank v. General Motors of Canada Limited* (found exclusively in *Lemon-Aid* on page 190)—in which the judge declared that paint discoloration and peeling shouldn't occur within 11 years of the purchase of a vehicle—the implied warranty is an important legal principle. It's solidly supported by a large body of federal and provincial laws, regulations, and jurisprudence, and it protects you primarily from hidden dealer- or factory-related defects. But the concept also includes misrepresentation and a host of other scams.

This warranty also holds dealers to a higher standard of conduct than private sellers because, unlike private sellers, dealers are presumed to be aware of the defects present in the vehicles they sell. That way, they can't just pass the ball to the automaker or to the previous owner and then walk away from the dispute.

Dealers are also expected to disclose defects that have been repaired. For instance, in British Columbia, provincial law (the *Motor Dealer Act*) says that a dealer must disclose damages that cost more than $2,000 to fix. This is a good law to cite in other jurisdictions.

Provincial laws say a vehicle must be built to last for a reasonable period of time or else its purchase price may be refunded.

In spite of all your precautions, there's still a 10 percent chance you'll buy a lemon, says Runzheimer International. It confirms that one out of every 10 vehicles produced by the Detroit Big Three is likely to be a lemon (a figure also used by GM Vice President Bob Lutz when he was a Chrysler executive). And owners of engine- and transmission-challenged Chrysler Caravans and Ford Windstars, GM vans with peeling paint and rust holes in the roof, and failure-prone Silverados and Sierras would probably put that figure much higher.

Why the implied warranty is so effective

- It establishes the concept of reasonable durability (see "How Long Should a Part or Repair Last?" following), meaning that parts are expected to last for a reasonable period of time, as stated in jurisprudence, judged by independent mechanics, or expressed in extended warranties given by the automaker in the past (7–10 years/160,000 km for engines and transmissions).
- It covers the entire vehicle and can be applied for whatever period of time the judge decides.
- It can order that the vehicle be taken back or that a major repair cost be refunded:

> I wanted to let you and your readers know that the information you publish about Ford's paint failure problem is invaluable. Having read through your "how-to guide" on addressing this issue, I filed suit against Ford for the "latent" paint defect. The day prior to our court date, I received a settlement offer by phone for 75 percent of what I was initially asking for.

- It can help plaintiffs claim compensation for supplementary transportation, inconvenience, mental distress, missed work, screwed-up vacations, insurance paid while the vehicle was in the repair shop, repairs done by other mechanics, and exemplary, or punitive, damages in cases where the seller was a real weasel.
- It is frequently used by small claims court judges to give refunds to plaintiffs "in equity" (out of fairness) rather than through a strict interpretation of contract law.

How Long Should a Part or Repair Last?

How do you know when a part or service hasn't lasted as long as it should, or whether you should seek a full or partial refund? Sure, you have a gut feeling based on the use of the vehicle, how you maintained it, and the extent of work that was carried out. But you'll need more than emotion to win compensation from garages and automakers.

You can definitely get a refund if a repair or part lasts beyond its guarantee but not as long as is generally expected. But you'll have to show what the auto industry considers to be "reasonable durability." Automakers, mechanics, and the courts all have their own benchmarks as to what's a reasonable period of time or amount of mileage that one should expect a part or adjustment to last. Consequently, I've prepared this table to show what most automakers consider to be reasonable durability, as expressed by their original and "goodwill" warranties.

REASONABLE PART DURABILITY

ACCESSORIES		Engine (diesel)	15 years/350,000 km
Air conditioner	7 years	Engine (gas)	7 years/160,000 km
Cruise control	5 years/100,000 km	Radiator	4 years/80,000 km
Power doors, windows	5 years	Transfer case	7 years/160,000 km
Radio	5 years	Transmission (auto.)	7 years/160,000 km
		Transmission (man.)	10 years/250,000 km
BODY		Transmission oil cooler	5 years/100,000 km
Paint (peeling)	7–11 years		
Rust (perforations)	7–11 years		
Rust (surface)	5 years	**EXHAUST SYSTEM**	
Water/wind/air leaks	5 years	Catalytic converter	8–10 years/100,000 km or more
BRAKE SYSTEM		Muffler	2 years/40,000 km
Brake drum	120,000 km	Tailpipe	3 years/60,000 km
Brake drum linings	35,000 km		
Brake rotor	60,000 km	**IGNITION SYSTEM**	
Brake calipers/pads	30,000 km	Cable set	60,000 km
Master cylinder	100,000 km	Electronic module	5 years/80,000 km
Wheel cylinder	80,000 km	Retiming	20,000 km
		Spark plugs	20,000 km
ENGINE AND DRIVETRAIN		Tune-up	20,000 km
CV joint	6 years/160,000 km		
Differential	7 years/160,000 km		

SAFETY COMPONENTS			VISIBILITY	
Airbags	life of vehicle		Halogen/fog lights	3 years
ABS brakes	7 years/160,000 km		Sealed beam	2 years
ABS computer	10 years/160,000 km		Windshield wiper motor	5 years
Seatbelts	life of vehicle			

STEERING AND SUSPENSION	
Alignment	1 year/20,000 km
Ball joints	10 years/160,000 km
Coil springs	10 years/160,000 km
Power steering	5 years/80,000 km
Shock absorber	2 years/40,000 km
Struts	5 years/80,000 km
Tires (radial)	5 years/80,000 km
Wheel bearing	3 years/60,000 km

Many of these guidelines were extrapolated from Chrysler's and Ford's payouts to thousands of dissatisfied customers over the past decade, in addition to Chrysler's original 7-year powertrain warranty (applicable from 1991 to 1995 and reapplied from 2001 to 2004). Other sources of information for this chart include Ford and GM transmission warranties, outlined in their secret warranties; Ford, GM, and Toyota engine "goodwill" programs, laid out in their internal service bulletins; and court judgments where judges have given their own guidelines as to what constitutes "reasonable durability."

Download data from a "black box" data recorder to prove that your airbag, brake, or accelerator malfunctioned, regardless of whether an accident ensued. This gets around the excuse that "there was nothing wrong."

Safety features—with the exception of anti-lock brake systems (ABS)—generally have a lifetime warranty. Chrysler's 10-year "free-service" program, part of its 1993–99 ABS recall, can serve as a handy benchmark as to how long one can expect these components to last on more recent models.

Airbags are a different matter. Those that are deployed in an accident—and the personal injuries and interior damage their deployment will likely have caused—are covered by your accident insurance policy. However, if there is a sudden deployment for no apparent reason, the automaker and the dealer should be held jointly responsible for all injuries and damage caused by the airbag. You can prove their liability by downloading the data from your vehicle's data recorder. This will likely lead to a more generous settlement from the two parties and will prevent your insurance premiums from being jacked up.

Use the manufacturer's emissions warranty as your primary guideline for the expected durability of high-tech electronic and mechanical pollution-control components such as powertrain control modules (PCMs) and catalytic converters. Look first at your owner's manual for an indication of which parts on your vehicle are covered. If you come up with few specifics, ask the auto manufacturer for a list of the specific components covered by the emissions warranty. As a last resort, sue for the parts and labour costs in small claims court and then let the dealer and automaker sort it out. Usually, these claims result in a three-party split of the costs.

Getting Action

Before we go any further, let's get one thing straight: A telephone call usually won't get you much action from a corporation. Automakers and their dealers want to make money, not give it back. You must send a registered letter or an email to create a paper trail and to get attention. What's more, that correspondence must contain the threat that you will use the implied warranty against the defendant and cite powerful jurisprudence to win your small claims court action in the same region where that business operates.

On pages 180–181 are two sample complaint letters that give you much of what you'll need to invoke the implied warranty to get a refund for a bad vehicle or for ineffective repairs.

 ### Legal "Secrets" that Work for You

Send a claim letter to both the seller and the automaker and let them work out together how much they will give you back. Make sure your letter is sent to the automaker's legal affairs department (usually in Ontario) where policy is made, and not to where it's simply carried out.

Unfair sales contracts can be cancelled, but sales contracts aren't supposed to be fair. Lawyers spend countless hours making sure their corporate clients are well protected with ironclad standard-form contracts. Judges look upon these agreements, called "contracts of adhesion," with a great deal of skepticism. They know these loan documents, insurance contracts, and automobile leases grant consumers little or no bargaining power. So when a dispute arises over terms or language, provincial consumer protection statutes require that judges interpret these contracts in the way most favourable to the consumer. Simply put, ignorance can be a good defence.

Hearsay can be admitted if you introduce it in the right way. It's essential that printed evidence and/or witnesses (relatives are not excluded) be available to confirm that a false representation actually occurred, that a part is failure-prone, or that a part's replacement is covered by a secret warranty or internal service bulletin alert. If you can't find an independent expert, introduce this evidence through the automaker reps and dealership service personnel who have to be at the trial, anyway. They know all about the service bulletins and extended warranty programs cited in *Lemon-Aid*, and they'll probably contradict each other—particularly if they are excluded from the courtroom prior to testifying. Incidentally, you may wish to have the court clerk send a subpoena requiring the deposition of the documents you intend to cite, all warranty extensions relevant to your problem, and other lawsuits filed against the company for similar failures. This will make the fur fly in Oshawa, Oakville, and Windsor, and it will likely lead to an out-of-court settlement. Sometimes, the service manager or company representative will make key admissions if questioned closely by you, a court mediator, or the trial judge. For example, here are some questions to ask: Is this a common problem? Do you recognize this service bulletin? Is there a case-by-case "goodwill" plan covering this repair?

Automakers often blame owners for having pushed their vehicles beyond their limits. Therefore, when you seek to set aside the contract or to get repair work reimbursed, it's essential that you get an independent mechanic, or your co-workers, to prove the vehicle was well maintained and driven prudently.

When asking for a refund, keep in mind the "reasonable diligence" rule that requires that a suit be filed within a reasonable time after a vehicle's purchase, which usually means less than a year. Because many symptoms of factory-related deficiencies take years to appear, the courts have ruled that the reasonable diligence clock starts ticking only after the defect is confirmed to be manufacturer- or dealer-related. This allows you to make a claim up to seven years after the vehicle was originally put into service, regardless of whether it was bought new or used. If there have been negotiations with the dealer or the automaker, or if either the dealer or the automaker has been promising to correct the defects for some time or has carried out repeated unsuccessful repairs, the deadline for filing the lawsuit can be extended.

Yes, you can claim for hotel and travel costs or for compensation for general inconvenience. Fortunately, when legal action is threatened—usually through small claims court—automakers quickly up their out-of-court offer to include most of the owner's expenses because they know the courts will be far more generous. For example, a British Columbia court decision gave $2,257 for hotel and travel costs to a motorist fed up with his lemon Cadillac, and then the judge capped it off with a $5,000 award for "inconvenience and loss of enjoyment of their luxury vehicle" (*Wharton v. Tom Harris Chevrolet Oldsmobile Cadillac Ltd. and General Motors of Canada Limited*; B.C. Supreme Court, Vancouver, 1999; Docket C982104). In the *Sharman v. Ford* case (see the Windstar section in Part Four), the judge gave the plaintiff $7,500 for "mental distress" caused by the fear that his children would fall out of his 2000 Windstar equipped with a faulty sliding door.

As of March 19, 2005, the Supreme Court confirmed that car owners can ask for punitive, or exemplary, damages when a seller's or automaker's conduct has been so outrageously bad that the court wants to protect society by awarding a sum of money large enough to dissuade others from engaging in similar immoral, unethical conduct. I call this the "weasel-whacker" law. In *Prebushewski v. Dodge City Auto (1985) Ltd. and Chrysler Canada Ltd.* (2001 SKQB 537; Q.B. No. 1215), the plaintiff got $25,000 in a judgment handed down December 6, 2001, in Saskatoon. The Supreme Court upheld the judgment on March 9, 2005. The award followed testimony from Chrysler's expert witness that the company was aware of many cases where daytime running lights shorted and caused 1996 Ram pickups to catch fire. The plaintiff's truck had burned to the ground, and Chrysler had refused the owner's claim, saying it had fulfilled its expressed warranty obligations, in spite of its knowledge that fires were commonplace. The plaintiff sued on the grounds that there was an implied warranty that the vehicle would be safe. Justice Rothery gave this stinging rebuke in his judgment against Chrysler and its dealer:

> Not only did Chrysler know about the problems of the defective daytime running light modules, it did not advise the plaintiff of this. It simply chose to ignore the plaintiff's requests for compensation and told her to seek recovery from her insurance company. Chrysler had replaced thousands of these modules since 1988. But it had also made a business decision to neither advise its customers of the problem nor to recall the vehicles to replace the modules. While the cost would have been about $250 to replace each module, there were at least one million customers. Chrysler was not prepared to spend $250 million, even though it knew what the defective module might do.
>
> Counsel for the defendants argues that this matter had to be resolved by litigation because the plaintiff and the defendants simply had a difference of opinion on whether the plaintiff should be compensated by the defendants. Had the defendants some dispute as to the cause of the fire, that may have been sufficient to prove that they had not willfully violated this part of the *Act*. They did not. They knew about the defective daytime running light module. They did nothing to replace the burned truck for the plaintiff. They offered the plaintiff no compensation for her loss. Counsel's position that the definition of the return of the purchase price is an arguable point is not sufficient to negate the defendants' violation of this part of the *Act*. I find the violation of the defendants to be willful. Thus, I find that exemplary damages are appropriate on the facts of this case.

In this case, the quantum ought to be sufficiently high as to correct the defendants' behaviour. In particular, Chrysler's corporate policy to place profits ahead of the potential danger to its customers' safety and personal property must be punished. And when such corporate policy includes a refusal to comply with the provisions of the *Act* and a refusal to provide any relief to the plaintiff, I find an award of $25,000 for exemplary damages to be appropriate. I therefore order Chrysler and Dodge City to pay: Damages in the sum of $41,969.83; Exemplary damages in the sum of $25,000; Party and party costs.

Warranty Rights

The manufacturer's or dealer's warranty is a written legal promise that a vehicle will be reasonably reliable, subject to certain conditions. Regardless of the number of subsequent owners, this promise remains in force as long as the warranty's original time and kilometre limits haven't expired. Tires aren't usually covered by car manufacturers' warranties, but instead they're covered on a pro-rated basis by the tiremaker. This isn't such a good deal, because the manufacturer is making a profit by charging you the full list price. If you were to buy the same replacement tire from a discount store, you'd likely pay less without the pro-rated rebate.

But consumers have gained additional rights following Bridgestone/Firestone's massive recall of its defective ATX II and Wilderness tires in 2001. Because of the confusion and chaos surrounding Firestone's handling of the recall, Ford's 575 Canadian dealers stepped into the breach and replaced the tires with any equivalent tires that they had in stock, no questions asked. This is an important precedent that tears down the traditional wall separating tire manufacturers from automakers in product liability claims. In essence, whoever sells the product can now be held liable for damages. In the future, Canadian consumers will have an easier time holding the dealer, the automaker, and the tire manufacturer liable, not only for recalled products but also for any defect that affects the safety or reasonable durability of that product.

This is particularly true now that the Supreme Court of Canada (*Winnipeg Condominium v. Bird Construction* [1995] 1 S.C.R. 85) has ruled that defendants are liable for negligence for any designs that result in a risk to the public's safety or health. The Supreme Court reversed a long-standing policy and provided the public with a new course of action that had not existed before in Canada.

Other Warranties

In the U.S., safety restraints such as airbags and seat belts have warranty coverage extended for the lifetime of a vehicle, following an informal agreement made between automakers and NHTSA. In Canada, however, many automakers try to dodge this responsibility, alleging that they are separate entities, their vehicles are different, and no U.S. agreement or service bulletin binds them. That distinction is both disingenuous and dishonest, and wouldn't likely hold up in small claims court—probably the reason why most automakers relent when threatened with legal action.

Aftermarket products and services—such as gas-saving gadgets, rustproofing, and paint protectors—can render the manufacturer's warranty invalid, so make sure you're in the clear before purchasing any optional equipment or services from an independent supplier.

How fairly a warranty is applied is more important than how long it remains in effect. Once you know the normal wear rate for a mechanical component or body part, you can demand proportional compensation when you get less than normal durability—no matter what the original warranty says. Some dealers tell customers that they need to have original-equipment parts installed in order to maintain their warranties. A variation on this theme requires that selling dealers do routine servicing—including tune-ups and oil changes (with a certain brand of oil)—or the warranty is invalidated. Nothing could be further from the truth. Canadian law stipulates that whoever issues a warranty cannot make that warranty conditional on the use of any specific brand of motor oil, oil filter, or any other component unless that component is provided to the customer free of charge.

Sometimes dealers will do all sorts of minor repairs that don't correct a problem and then, after the warranty runs out, they'll tell you that your vehicle needs major repairs. You can avoid this nasty surprise by repeatedly bringing your vehicle to the dealership before the warranty ends. During each visit, insist that the written work order includes the specific nature of the problem, as you see it, and states that this is the second, third, or fourth time the same problem has been brought to the dealer's attention. Write all of this down yourself, if need be. This paper trail allows you to show a pattern of non-performance by the dealer during the warranty period, and it establishes that the problem is both serious and chronic. When the warranty expires, you will have the legal right to demand that it be extended on those items that consistently appear on your work orders. *Lowe v. Fairview Chrysler* (see page 206) is an excellent judgment that reinforces this important principle. In another lawsuit, *François Chong v. Marine Drive Imported Cars Ltd. and Honda Canada Inc.* (see page 206), a Honda owner forced Honda to fix his engine six times—until they got it right.

A retired GM service manager gave me another effective tactic to use when you're not sure that a dealer's warranty "repairs" will actually correct the problem for a reasonable period of time after the warranty expires. Here's what he says you should do:

> When you pick up the vehicle after the warranty repair has been done, hand the service manager a note to be put in your file that says you appreciate the warranty repair, however, you intend to return and ask for further warranty coverage if the problem reappears before a reasonable amount of time has elapsed—even if the

original warranty has expired. A copy of the same note should be sent to the auto-maker.... Keep your copy of the note in the glove compartment as cheap insurance against paying for a repair that wasn't fixed correctly the first time.

Extra-Cost Warranties

The manufacturer, the dealer, or an independent third party may sell supplementary warranties that provide extended coverage, and this coverage is automatically transferred when a vehicle is sold. They cost between $1,500 and $2,000 and should be purchased only if the vehicle you're buying is off its original warranty, if it has a reputation for being unreliable or expensive to service (see Part Four), or if you're reluctant to use the small claims courts when factory-related trouble arises. Don't let the dealer pressure you into deciding right away.

Generally, you can purchase an extended warranty at any time during the period in which the manufacturer's warranty is in effect or, in some cases, shortly after buying the vehicle from a used-car dealer. An automaker's supplementary warranty is the best choice, but it will likely cost about a third more than warranties sold by independents. In some parts of the country, notably British Columbia, dealers have a quasi-monopoly on selling warranties, with little competition from the independents.

Dealers love to sell you extended warranties, whether you need them or not, because up to 60 percent of the warranty's cost represents dealer markup. Out of the remaining 40 percent comes the sponsor's administration costs and profit margin, calculated at another 15 percent. What's left to pay for repairs is a minuscule 25 percent of the original amount. The only reason that automakers and independent warranty companies haven't been busted for

UNINSURED WARRANTIES

The UCDA continues to strongly recommend that members only offer warranties that are insured by an Ontario licensed insurer. Dealers offering insured warranty products may be liable to their customers, if the warranty company goes out of business or fails to honour its legitimate claims.

We are aware of the following companies offering warranties in Ontario. They have not provided us with any evidence that they are insured by a licensed insurer in Ontario.

A-Protect Warranty	MBI Managers
All Canadian Warranty	National Automobile Warranty
Autogard Warranty	Nationwide Warranty
AutoSure	People's Choice Warranty
Canadian Warranty Corp.	TWPro
Carrier Warranty (CWC)	Veri-Cheque Warranty
Lion's [sic] Gate Marketing	

If approached by one of these companies, or any other company not listed, we suggest that you ask them to contact the UCDA. If they won't do so, assume they are uninsured. Some companies may offer warranties that they say are underwritten, but not insured by a licensed insurer. Dealers selling these warranties may still be held responsible if legitimate claims go unpaid.

One warranty seller sued UCDA for defamation in 2002 for this cautionary advice to its dealer members. The case was thrown out of court in 2005 (*www.courts.gov.bc.ca/Jdb-txt/CA/05/02/2005BCCA0274.htm*).

operating this Ponzi scheme is that only half of the vehicle buyers who purchase extended service contracts actually use them.

It's often difficult to collect on supplementary warranties because independent companies frequently go out of business or limit the warranty's coverage through subsequent mailings. Provincial laws cover both situations. If the bankrupt warranty company's insurance policy won't cover your claim, take the dealer to small claims court and ask for the repair costs and a refund of the original warranty payment. Your argument for holding the dealer responsible is a simple one: By accepting a commission to act as an agent of the defunct company, the dealer also took on the obligations of that company. As for limiting the coverage after you have already bought the warranty policy, this is illegal and allows you to sue both the dealer and the warranty company for a refund of both the warranty and the repair costs.

Emissions-Control Warranties

These little-publicized warranties can save you big bucks if major engine or exhaust components fail prematurely. They come with all new vehicles and cover major components of the emissions-control system for up to 8 years/130,000 km, no matter how many times the vehicle is sold. Unfortunately, although owner's manuals vaguely mention the emissions warranty, most don't specify which parts are covered. The U.S. Environmental Protection Agency has intervened on several occasions, with hefty fines against Chrysler and Ford, and ruled that all major motor and fuel-system components are covered. These components include fuel metering, ignition spark advance, restart, evaporative emissions, positive crankcase ventilation (PVC), engine electronics (computer modules), and catalytic converter systems, as well as parts like hoses, clamps, brackets, pipes, gaskets, belts, seals, and connectors. Canada, however, has no governmentally defined list, so it's up to each manufacturer and the small claims courts to decide which emissions-control components are covered.

Many of the confidential technical service bulletins listed in Part Four show parts failures that are covered under the emissions warranty (stinky exhausts caused by defective catalytic converters, for example), even though motorists are routinely charged for their replacement. This Ford bulletin, applicable to the 2002–05 Taurus and Sable, shows that the automaker will pay for fuel gauge repairs under the emissions warranty. Applying the same principles to other automakers' fuel gauges, such as GM's front-drive minivans, should be a breeze.

Make sure to get your emissions system checked out thoroughly by a dealer or an independent garage before the emissions warranty expires or before having the vehicle inspected by provincial emissions inspectors. In addition to ensuring that you'll pass provincial tests, this precaution could save you up to $1,000 if your catalytic converter and other emissions components are faulty.

FORD FUEL GAUGE DOES NOT READ FULL AFTER FILLING TANK

BULLETIN NO.: 04-14-14   **DATE: MAY 2002**

Ford Taurus, Sable

ISSUE: Some 2002–05 Taurus/Sable vehicles may exhibit a fuel gauge which indicates the tank is only 7/8 full after filling the fuel tank. This may be due to the calibration of the fuel level indication unit.

ACTION: To service, remove the fuel delivery module and replace the fuel level indication unit. DO NOT REPLACE THE ENTIRE FUEL DELIVERY MODULE FOR THIS CONDITION.

WARRANTY STATUS: Eligible under provisions of new vehicle limited warranty coverage and **emissions warranty coverage**.

Operation	Description	Time
041414A	Replace Fuel Gauge tank unit (includes time to remove tank, drain and refill)	1.3hrs

 ## Psst! A Secret Warranty Update

Few vehicle owners know that secret warranties exist. Automakers issue technical service bulletins (TSBs) to dealers or the first owners of record. Consequently, motorists who find out about these policies tend to be the original owners who haven't moved or leased their vehicles. But the other group of motorists who get compensated for repairs are the ones who read *Lemon-Aid* each year, staple TSBs to their work orders, and yell the loudest.

Remember, second owners and repairs done by independent garages are included in these secret warranty programs. Large, costly repairs such as blown engines, burned transmissions, and peeling paint are often covered. Even mundane little repairs—which can still cost you a hundred bucks or more—are frequently included in these programs.

If you have a TSB but you're still refused compensation, keep in mind that secret warranties are an admission of manufacturing negligence. Try to work out a compromise by asking for a pro rata adjustment from your vehicle's manufacturer. If polite negotiations fail, challenge the refusal in court on the grounds that you shouldn't be penalized for failing to make a reimbursement claim under a secret warranty that you never knew existed!

Read on to check out a few examples of secret warranties that can save you thousands of dollars. (More extensive listings are found in Part Four's model ratings.)

Acura/Honda

1999–2003 Acura CL and TL; 1999–2003 Honda Accord, Prelude, and Odyssey

Problem: Defective automatic transmission and torque converter. **Warranty coverage:** This "goodwill" warranty extension was confirmed in the August 4, 2003, edition of *Automotive News*. Honda will fix or replace the transmission free of charge up to 7 years/160,000 km (100,000 mi.), regardless of whether you bought your vehicle new or used. The company will also reimburse owners who already paid for the repair.

2001–04 MDX

Problem: Defective front hydraulic engine mount may cause excessive vibration at idle and harsh shifting. **Warranty coverage:** This "goodwill" warranty extension will be applied up to eight years, without any mileage limitations.

Audi, Chrysler, Mercedes-Benz, Saab, Toyota, and VW

1997–2004 Audi A4; 1999–2002 Chrysler models equipped with a 2.7L V6; 1998–2002 Mercedes-Benz; 1998–2003 Saab 9-3 and 9-5; 1997–2002 Toyota and Lexus vehicles with 2.2L 4-cylinder or 3.0L V6 engines; 1997–2004 VW Passat

Problem: Engine sludge. **Warranty coverage:** Varies; usually 7–10 years/160,000 km. Automakers can't automatically deny this free repair if you don't have proof of all of your oil changes unless they can show that the sludge was caused by a missed oil change (which, according to independent mechanics, is impossible to prove). Remember, the warranty has been extended to fix a factory-related problem that occurs *despite* regular oil changes. That's why it's the automaker's responsibility.

Service bulletins, press releases, and dealer memos are all admissions of responsibility. From there, the legal doctrine of "the balance of probabilities" applies. To wit, a missed oil change *may* cause engine sludge, but a factory defect *definitely* causes engine sludge. Therefore, it's more probable that the defect caused the sludge.

Once the sludge condition is diagnosed, the dealer and automobile manufacturer are jointly liable for all corrective repairs, plus additional damages for your inconvenience, loss of use (or the cost of a loaner vehicle), and the cost to replace the oil. The automaker's owner notification letter may not have gone out to Canadian owners because it isn't required by any Canadian recall or statute. If a letter goes out, it's usually sent only to the first owners of record.

Some automakers say owners should use an expensive special oil to prevent engine sludge. This after-sale stipulation is illegal, and it can also provide owners with a reason to ask for damages, or even a refund, because it wasn't disclosed at the time of sale. All of the letter restrictions and decisions made by the dealer and the manufacturer can be easily appealed in small claims court, where the sludge letter is powerful proof of the automaker's negligence.

Chrysler

1998–2003 Dodge Durango and Dakota

Problem: Worn, rusted, and broken upper ball joints may cause steering loss, or the wheel may fall off. Over 1,000 complaints have been recorded by NHTSA. **Warranty coverage:** Chrysler has recalled the 2000–03 models and will replace defective ball joints for free up to 10 years/160,000 km (100,000 mi.). This warranty extension creates an excellent benchmark for all owners stuck with prematurely worn-out ball joints.

All Grand Cherokees

Problem: AC evaporator failure or malfunction. **Warranty coverage:** 7 years/ 115,000 km. This "goodwill" extension sets a standard for what Chrysler considers the normal durability of its ACs:

ADDENDUM TO BASIC WARRANTY

The following applies to 1993 through 1997 New Yorker, LHS, Concorde, Intrepid, Vision and Grand Cherokee vehicles equipped with factory-installed air conditioning:

> *The Basic Warranty coverage for the air conditioner evaporator has been extended to 7 years or 115,000 kilometres, whichever occurs first, from the vehicle's warranty start date.*
>
> *This extended coverage applies to all owners of the vehicle. All of the other warranty terms apply to this extension.*

Chrysler, Ford, General Motors, and Asian Automakers

All years, all models

Problem: Faulty automatic transmissions that self-destruct, shift erratically, gear down to "limp mode," are slow to shift in or out of Reverse, or are noisy. **Warranty coverage:** If you have the assistance of your dealer's service manager, expect an offer of 50–75 percent (about $2,500). File the case in small claims court, and a full refund will be offered up to 7 years/160,000 km. Acura, Honda, Hyundai, Lexus, and Toyota coverage varies between seven and eight years.

> I've just been told that I need my fourth transmission on my '96 Town & Country minivan with 132,000 miles [212,000 km] on it. I've driven many cars well past that mileage with only *one* transmission. The dealer asked Chrysler, who said they would not help me. My appeals to Chrysler's customer service department yielded me the same result.... Chrysler split some of the costs with me on the previous rebuilt replacements....

CHRYSLER TRANSMISSION DELAYED ENGAGEMENT

BULLETIN NO.: 21-004-05   DATE: JANUARY 22, 2005

OVERVIEW: This bulletin involves replacing the front pump assembly in the transmission and checking the Transmission Control Module (TCM) for the latest software revision level.

2004 (CS) Pacifica
2002 – 2004 (JR) Sebring Convertible/Sebring Sedan/Stratus Sedan
2003 (KJ) Liberty
2003 (KJ) Cherokee (International Markets)
2002 2004 (LH) 300M/Concorde/Intrepid
2002 2003 (PL) Neon
2002 2003 (PT) PT Cruiser
2002 2003 (RG) Chrysler Voyager (International Markets)
2002 2003 (RS) Town & Country/Caravan/Voyager
2003 (TJ) Wrangler

All years, all models

Problem: Premature wearout of brake pads, calipers, and rotors. Produces excessive vibration, noise, and pulling to one side when braking. **Warranty coverage:** *Calipers and pads:* Goodwill settlements confirm that brake calipers and pads that fail to last 2 years/40,000 km will be replaced for 50 percent of the repair cost; components not lasting 1 year/20,000 km will be replaced for free. *Rotors:* If they last less than 3 years/60,000 km, they'll be replaced at half the price; replacement is free up to 2 years/40,000 km.

All years, all models

Problem: A nauseating rotten-egg smell permeates the interior. **Warranty coverage:** At first, owners are told they need a tune-up. And then they're told to change the fuel and to wait a few months for the problem to correct itself. When this tactic fails, likely the catalytic converter will be replaced and the power control module recalibrated. Toyota has been particularly hard hit by this stink.

Chrysler, Ford, General Motors, Honda, Mazda, and Toyota

All years, all models

Problem: Faulty paint jobs that cause paint to turn white and peel off of horizontal panels. **Warranty coverage:** Automakers will offer a free paint job or partial compensation up to six years, with no mileage limitations. Thereafter, most manufacturers offer 50–75 percent refunds on the small claims courthouse steps.

In *Frank v. GM*, the Saskatchewan small claims court set a 15-year benchmark for paint finishes, and three other Canadian small claims judgments have extended the benchmark to seven years, second owners, and pickups.

> I wanted to let you and your readers know that the information you publish about Ford's paint failure problem is invaluable. Having read through your "how-to guide" on addressing this issue, I filed suit against Ford for the "latent" paint defect. The day prior to our court date, I received a settlement offer by phone for 75 percent of what I was initially asking for.
>
> This settlement was for a 9-year-old car. I truly believe that Ford hedges a bet that most people won't go to the extent of filing a lawsuit because they are intimidated or simply stop progress after they receive a firm no from Ford.
>
> M. D.

Chrysler, Ford, General Motors, and Hyundai

1994–2004 engine head gasket and intake manifold failures; 1998–99 Hyundai Accent

Problem: At around 60,000–100,000 km, the engine may overheat, lose power, and burn extra fuel or, possibly, self-destruct. Under the best of circumstances, the repair will take a day and cost about $800–$1,000. **Warranty coverage:** If you have the assistance of your dealer's service manager, expect a full refund up to 7 years/160,000 km, although initial offers will hover at about 50 percent of the costs. Ford Windstars and GM minivans are particularly afflicted with this defect; if you threaten small claims court action, cite the *Dufour* or *Reid* Windstar judgments (see pages 197–198).

No matter which automaker you're dealing with, filing your claim in small claims court always sweetens the company's settlement offer. Furthermore, you likely won't have to step inside a courtroom to get your refund, since most small claims court filings are settled at the pretrial mediation stage.

Engine claims are now entering a second phase where the original free repair needs to be repaired again. Car owners are told they had one kick at the can and that's it, but, once again, small claims court judges don't always see it that way.

Courts have held that the company's first repair was an admission that the product was faulty; therefore, its correction must either last a reasonable period of time or be redone.

Ford has been more upfront than GM in acknowledging its intake manifold gasket defects and much more generous in compensating owners.

GM ENGINE OIL OR COOLANT LEAK

BULLETIN NO.: 03-06-01-010A

DATE: APRIL 2003

ENGINE OIL OR COOLANT LEAK (INSTALL NEW INTAKE MANIFOLD GASKET)

2000–2003 Buick Century; 2002–03 Buick Rendezvous; 1996 Chevrolet Lumina APV; 1997–2003 Chevrolet Venture; 1999–2001 Chevrolet Lumina; 1999–2003 Chevrolet Malibu, Monte Carlo; 2000–2003 Chevrolet Impala; 1996–2003 Oldsmobile Silhouette; 1999 Oldsmobile Cutlass; 1999–2003 Oldsmobile Alero; 1996–99 Pontiac Trans Sport; 1999–2003 Pontiac Grand Am; 2000–03 Pontiac Grand Prix, Montana
2001–03 Pontiac Aztek with 3.1L or 3.4L V6 engine (VINs J, E—RPOs LGB, LA1)

CONDITION: Some owners may comment on an apparent oil or coolant leak. Additionally, the comments may range from spots on the driveway to having to add fluids.

CAUSE: Intake manifold may be leaking allowing coolant, oil or both to leak from the engine.

CORRECTION: Install a new-design intake manifold gasket. The material used in the gasket has been changed in order to improve the sealing qualities of the gasket. When replacing the gasket, the intake manifold bolts must also be replaced and torqued to a revised specification. The new bolts will come with a pre-applied threadlocker on them.

GM owners have been systematically refused engine repair refunds, despite evidence like this intake manifold internal service bulletin that shows the factory screwed up in the design and choice of materials.

Ford

1992–2004 Aerostar, Focus, Sable, Taurus, and Windstar

Problem: Defective front coil springs may suddenly break, puncturing the front tire and leading to the loss of steering control. **Warranty coverage:** Under a "Safety Improvement Campaign" negotiated with NHTSA, Ford will replace *broken* coil springs at no charge up to 10 years/unlimited mileage. The company initially said that it wouldn't replace the springs until they had broken—if you survived to submit a claim, that is—but it relented when threatened with a lawsuit. Also, 1997–98 models that are registered in either the rust-belt states or Canada have been recalled for the installation of a protective shield (called a "spring catcher bracket" in the Canadian recall) to prevent a broken spring from shredding the front tire.

1996–2004 F-Series trucks, SUVs, and Windstar vans

Problem: Sudden steering loss because of the premature wear and separation of the steering tie-rod ends. **Warranty coverage:** Presently, Ford is advising owners to have their vehicles inspected regularly. If pressed, the dealer will replace the component for free up to 5 years/100,000 km.

1999–2001 F-150 and Super Duty F-Series pickups, Econoline, Expedition, and Lincoln Navigator

Problem: Faulty engine head gaskets cause oil or coolant leakage, resulting in the loss of power, excessive fuel consumption, engine overheating, or complete engine destruction. **Warranty coverage:** Ford will repair or replace affected engines. Insiders say that the automaker is spending up to $4,500 (U.S.) to replace the engine and $800 to replace the cylinder heads and head gasket. Ford says that the faulty engines usually fail within the warranty period (according to the April 1, 2002, issue of *Automotive News*), but independent warranty data suggests they may begin to leak at any time.

1997–2001 F-150 and F-250 LD F-Series pickups, Econoline, Expedition, and Lincoln Navigator

Problem: Extensive door bottom and tailgate rusting; cracked outer door panel. **Warranty coverage:** Ford will repair or replace the door or body panels for free up to six years.

2003–05 Excursion; 2003–06 F-Super Duty; 2004–06 E-Series

Problem: 6.0L diesel engine lacks power, bucks/jerks, produces excessive smoke, and is hard to start or won't start. **Warranty coverage:** Ford will replace the diesel injectors for free up to seven years.

2004–06 F-150

Problem: Shudder and vibration when accelerating due to a misaligned rear axle pinion. **Warranty coverage:** Ford will install a shim kit for free up to six years.

General Motors

1999–2004 trucks equipped with 3.1L, 3.4L, 4.3L, 4.6L (Northstar), 4.8L, 5.3L, 5.7L (LS1), 6.0L, or 8.1L engines

Problem: Engine-damaging piston slap, engine knock, excessive oil consumption, and engine failure (see *www.pistonslap.com*):

> Excessive "piston slap" occurs because an automobile manufacturer (GM) designs and/or manufactures a defective engine in which the clearance between the piston and cylinder bore is too great. Essentially, the piston moves sideways and "slaps" or "knocks" hard against the cylinder bore and causes damage to the engine pistons and cylinders, excessive smoke emissions, excessive oil consumption, carbon buildup on piston heads, decreased mileage, and a loud and obnoxious "slapping" or "knocking" noise, all of which diminishes vehicle resale value.

Warranty coverage: GM will cover this defect for up to 5 years/100,000 km, but only on a case-by-case basis with considerable service manager jawboning. The U.S.–based *Kelley Blue Book* confirms that "a knocking engine could lower the value of a vehicle by $4,000 to $6,000 at trade-in."

1994–2000 trucks equipped with a 6.5L diesel engine

Problem: Fuel-injection pump failure. **Warranty coverage:** Up to 11 years (TSB #00064C; September 2002). This bulletin can be found on page 4.

1997–2003 Venture, TranSport/Montana, and Silhouette

Problem: Hood corrosion/blistering. **Warranty coverage:** GM will replace, repair, or repaint the roof for free up to 6 years/100,000 km.

Honda

1997–99 CR-V

Problem: Harsh-shifting automatic transmission and torque converter. **Warranty coverage:** Honda will fix or replace the transmission free of charge up to 7 years/160,000 km under a "goodwill" program, whether you bought your vehicle new or used (TSB #00-012; June 26, 2001).

1998–2003 Accord, Odyssey, and Pilot models equipped with 6-cylinder engines

Problem: Defective aluminum engine block. **Warranty coverage:** Honda will repair or replace the engine under a "goodwill" program.

1999–03 Odyssey; 2003 Pilot

Problem: Engine hesitation or surge. **Warranty coverage:** Honda will replace the EGR valve or clean the EGR port free of charge up to 8 years/128,000 km (80,000 mi.) under a "goodwill" program, whether you bought your vehicle new or used (TSB #05-026; July 20, 2005).

Jeep

1997–2005 Jeep

Problem: Water leaks from the AC onto the passenger-side carpet. **Warranty coverage:** Jeep will install an HVAC drain tube free of charge up to 7 years/160,000 km on a case-by-case basis.

Mazda

2002–03 MPV

Problem: A faulty fan control module may cause fan failure or battery drain. **Warranty coverage:** Free replacement of the fan control module.

Toyota

1997–2002 Toyota and Lexus vehicles with 2.2L 4-cylinder or 3.0L V6 engines

Problem: Sludge buildup may require a rebuilt engine. **Warranty coverage:** Toyota will repair or replace the engine at no charge up to 8 years/160,000 km (100,000 mi.), whether you bought your vehicle new or used. Toyota has said that owners will not be forced to show oil change receipts. But some dealers, apparently, haven't gotten the message:

> The service manager quietly told me that there was a "flaw" in the engine but would not elaborate. When I asked if there was a flaw why wouldn't Toyota warranty it, I was told, "Because you can't prove you did the oil change, there is no use taking it to Toyota."
>
> In May 2002 we received the letter mentioned in your article, and we took our 1998 Sienna into the dealer (after spending three weeks talking to them and producing all the oil change records except the missing one). The engine could not be rebuilt—it had to be replaced. The cost was $5,017.22, finally covered by this goodwill warranty.
>
> T. C., TORONTO

Recall Repairs

Vehicles are recalled for one of two reasons: They may be unsafe, or they don't conform to federal pollution control regulations. Whatever the reason, recalls are a great way to get free repairs—if you know which ones apply to your vehicle and you have the patience of Job.

Auto recalls are on the rise in Canada, despite automakers' claims that build quality has improved. Transport Canada says that auto recalls rose 44 percent to 3.77 million vehicles in 2004 (approximately one in six vehicles on the road). Safety experts like NHTSA's Rae Tyson ascribe this rise in recall numbers to the generic components used in many different models:

> Manufacturers are sharing drive-train components and platforms among several different models, so when you do a recall now, it will affect a lot more vehicles.

In North America, over a half-billion unsafe vehicles have been recalled by automakers for the free correction of safety-related defects since American recall legislation was passed in 1966 (a weaker Canadian law was enacted in 1971). During that time, about 28 percent of the recalled vehicles never made it back to the dealership for repairs because owners were never informed, didn't consider the defect to be that hazardous, or just gave up waiting for corrective parts.

Subsequent American legislation targets automakers who drag their feet in making recall repairs. Owners on both sides of the border may wish to cite the following NHTSA guidelines for support:

DEALER RECALL RESPONSIBILITY FOR U.S. STATES, TERRITORIES, AND POSSESSIONS

The U.S. National Traffic and Motor Vehicle Safety Act provides that each vehicle that is subject to a recall must be adequately repaired within a reasonable time after the customer has tendered it for repair. A failure to repair within 60 days after tender of a vehicle is *prima facie* evidence of failure to repair within a reasonable time. If the condition is not adequately repaired within a reasonable time, the customer may be entitled to an identical or reasonably equivalent vehicle at no charge or to a refund of the purchase price less a reasonable allowance for depreciation. To avoid having to provide these burdensome remedies, every effort must be made to promptly schedule an appointment with each customer and to repair their vehicle as soon as possible.

(GM Bulletin No.: 00064C, issued September, 2002)

 If you've moved or bought a used vehicle, it's smart to pay a visit to your local dealer. Give the dealer your address to get a "report card" on which recalls, free service campaigns, and warranties apply to your vehicle. Simply give the service advisor the vehicle identification number (VIN)—found on your insurance card or on the dash, just below the windshield on the driver's side—and have the number run through the automaker's computer system. Ask for a computer printout of the vehicle's history (or have it faxed to you, if you're so equipped) and make sure you're listed in the automaker's computer as the new owner. This process ensures that you'll receive notices of warranty extensions and emissions and safety recalls.

Regional Recalls

Don't let any dealer refuse you recall repairs because of where you live. In order to cut recall costs, many automakers try to limit a recall to vehicles in a certain designated region. This practice doesn't make sense. Cars are mobile; therefore, an unsafe, rust-cankered steering unit can be found anywhere—not just in certain rust-belt provinces or American states.

No matter where you live or drive, don't expect to be welcomed with open arms when your vehicle develops a safety- or emissions-related problem that's not yet part of a recall campaign. Automakers and dealers generally take a restrictive view of what constitutes a safety or emissions defect, and they frequently charge for repairs that should be free under federal safety or emissions legislation. To counter this tendency, look at the following list of typical defects that are clearly safety-related. If you experience similar problems, insist that the automaker fix them at no expense to yourself, including the cost of a car rental:

- Airbag malfunctions
- Corrosion affecting the safe operation of the vehicle
- Disconnected or stuck accelerators
- Electrical shorts
- Faulty windshield wipers
- Fuel leaks
- Problems with original axles, drive shafts, seats, seat recliners, or defrosters
- Seat belt problems
- Stalling or sudden acceleration
- Sudden steering or brake loss
- Suspension failures
- Trailer coupling failures

In 2001, Ford attempted to limit to five American states its recall of faulty Firestone tires. The threat of lawsuits led to an extension of the recall throughout North America. Apparently, Honda hasn't learned from Ford's experience.

In the U.S., recall campaigns compel automakers to pay the entire cost of fixing a vehicle's safety-related defect for any vehicle purchased up to eight years before the recall's announcement. Forcing automakers to extend a campaign for a reasonable period beyond eight years is usually a slam dunk in small claims court. Recalls may be voluntary or ordered by the U.S. Department of Transportation. Canadian regulations have an added twist: Transport Canada can only order automakers to notify owners that their vehicles may be unsafe; it can't force them to correct the problem. Fortunately, most U.S.–ordered recalls are carried out in Canada, and when Transport Canada makes a defect determination on its own, automakers generally comply by sending owner notification letters.

Voluntary recall campaigns, frequently called "Special Service" or "Safety Improvement Campaigns," are real problems, though: The government doesn't monitor the notification of owners; dealers and automakers routinely deny that a recall even exists, thereby dissuading most claimants; and the company's so-called fix, not authorized by any governing body, may not correct the hazard at all. Also, the voluntary recall may leave out many of the affected models, or it may unreasonably exclude certain owners.

Safety Defect Information

If you wish to report a safety defect or want to find recall info, you may access Transport Canada's website at *www.tc.gc.ca/roadsafety/recalls/search_e.asp*. You can get recall information in French or English, as well as general information on topics such as road safety or how to import a vehicle into Canada. Web surfers can now access the recall database for 1970–2005 model year vehicles, but—unlike on NHTSA's website—owner complaints aren't listed, defect investigations aren't disclosed, voluntary warranty extensions (secret warranties) aren't shown, and service bulletin summaries aren't provided. You can also contact Transport Canada directly to get additional information (Tel: 613-990-2309; TTY: 1-888-675-6863; Fax: 613-954-4731/613-998-8620; Email: *webfeedback@tc.gc.ca*).

If you're not happy with Ottawa's treatment of your recall inquiry, try NHTSA. Its website is more complete than Transport Canada's (NHTSA's database is updated daily and covers vehicles built since 1952). You can search the database for your vehicle or tires at *www.nhtsa.dot.gov/cars/problems* (Tel: 1-888-327-4236; TTY: 1-800-424-9153). You'll get immediate access to four essential database categories applicable to your vehicle and model year: the latest recalls, current and closed safety investigations, defects reported by other owners, and a brief summary of TSBs.

"Black Box" Data Recorders

Event data recorders (EDRs) the size of a VCR tape have been hidden under the seat or in the centre consoles of about 30 million airbag-equipped Ford and GM vehicles since the early '90s. Presently, about 90 percent of new cars have the devices.

To find out if your car or truck carries an EDR, go to *www.harristechnical.com/ downloads/cdrlist.pdf.*

These devices operate in a fashion similar to the flight data recorders used in airplanes. Recorded data varies, but it usually includes a vehicle's speed, the force of the impact, accelerator and braking performance, the time and speed of airbag deployment, and seat belt use prior to impact. A new NHTSA rule requires that the data be recorded from the instant a crash starts until half a second after it ends (to a maximum of 10 seconds).

Ford and GM have systematically hidden their collected data from U.S. and Canadian vehicle safety researchers who investigate thousands of complaints relating to airbags that don't deploy when they should or do deploy when they shouldn't and to anti-lock brakes that don't brake. This refusal to voluntarily share data with customers and researchers is unfortunate, because the recorders collect critical information that could lead to better-functioning safety devices.

To assist accident investigators in reconstructing crashes, the NHTSA will require that crash data compiled by EDRs must be accessible by common diagnostic tools and stored in a standard format. The rule takes effect on September 1, 2008, and will likely apply to some 2008 models and to all 2009s sold in the United States and Canada.

In the meantime, the Vetronix Corporation sells a $2,500 (U.S.) portable download device that accesses the data and stores it on any PC. Litigants can also subpoena the info through an automaker's dealer if the data is needed in court to dispute criminal charges, oppose an insurer's decision as to fault, or hold an automaker responsible for a safety device's failure.

Safety Benefits

Enthusiastically promoted by government and law enforcement agencies around the world, these data recorders have actually had a positive effect on accident prevention: A 1992 study by the European Union, cited by the Canada Safety Council, found that EDRs reduced the collision rate by 28 percent and costs by 40 percent in police fleets where drivers knew they were being monitored.

The recorders are also sending guilty people to jail, helping accident victims reap huge court awards, and prompting automaker recalls of unsafe vehicles. For example, in July 2002, New Brunswick prosecutors sent a dangerous driver to jail for two years based on his car's EDR data (see *R. v. Daley*; 2003 NBQB 20; Docket(s): S/CR/7/02; *www.canlii.org/nb/cas/nbqb/2002/2003nbqb20.html*). And GM was forced to recall more than 850,000 Cavaliers and Sunfires when its own data recorders showed that the cars' airbags often deployed inadvertently. Incidentally, California is the only jurisdiction where EDR data cannot be downloaded unless the car owner agrees or a court order is issued.

Traffic accident reconstructionists Harris Technical Services have prepared a chronological list of dozens of Canadian and American court cases related to automotive EDRs. It's available at *www.harristechnical.com/cdr5.htm*.

Three Steps to a Settlement

Step 1: Informal Negotiations

If your vehicle was misrepresented, has major defects, or wasn't properly repaired under warranty, the first thing you should do is give the seller (the dealer and automaker) a written summary (by registered mail or fax) of the outstanding problems. Stipulate a time period in which the dealer and/or automaker will need to either correct the problems or refund your money. Keep a copy for yourself, along with all your repair records. Be sure to check all of the sales and warranty documents you were given to see if they conform to provincial laws. Any errors, omissions, or violations can be used to get a settlement from the dealer in lieu of making a formal complaint.

Most vehicle owners won't take the steps outlined above, and instead, they'll try to settle things informally with a phone call. This tactic rarely works: Private sellers won't want to talk with you, and customer service agents (who recite policies but don't make them) will tell you the vehicle's warranty doesn't apply. This brush-off usually convinces 90 percent of complainers to drop their claims after some angry venting.

Nevertheless, don't take no for an answer. Contact someone higher up who has the authority to bend policies to satisfy your request. Speak in a calm, polite manner, and try to avoid polarizing the issue. Talk about co-operating to solve the problem. Let a compromise emerge—don't come in with a hardline set of demands.

An independent estimate of the vehicle's defects and the cost of repairing them is essential if you want to convince the seller that you're serious in your claim and that you stand a good chance of winning your case in court. Come prepared to use your estimate to challenge the dealer who agrees to pay half the repair costs and then tries to jack up the price 100 percent so that you wind up paying the whole shot.

Don't insist on getting the settlement offer in writing, but make sure that you're accompanied by a friend or relative who can confirm the offer in court if it isn't honoured. Be prepared to act upon the offer without delay so that if the seller or automaker withdraws it, they won't be able to blame your hesitancy.

Dealer and service manager help

Service managers have more power than you may realize. They make the first determination of what work is covered under warranty or through post-warranty "goodwill" programs, and they're directly responsible to the dealer and manufacturer for their decisions. (Dealers hate manufacturer audits that force them to pay back questionable warranty decisions.) Service managers are paid to save the dealer and automaker money while mollifying irate clients—an almost impossible balancing act. Nevertheless, when a service manager agrees to extend warranty coverage, it's because you've raised solid issues that neither the dealer nor the automaker can ignore. All the more reason to present your argument in a confident, forthright manner with your vehicle's service history and *Lemon-Aid*'s "Reasonable Part Durability" chart (see pages 156–157) on hand.

Also bring as many technical service bulletins and owner complaint printouts as you can find from websites like NHTSA's. It's not important that they apply directly to your problem; they establish parameters for giving out after-warranty assistance, or "goodwill." Don't use your salesperson as a runner because the sales staff are generally quite distant from the service staff and usually have less pull than you do.

If the service manager can't or won't set things right, your next step is to convene a mini-summit with the service manager, the dealer principal, and the automaker's rep. By getting the automaker involved, you run less risk of having the dealer fob you off on the manufacturer and you can often get an agreement where the seller and automaker pay two-thirds of the repair costs.

Step 2: Sending a Registered Letter, Fax, or Email

The pen is mightier...

If you haven't sent a written claim letter, fax, or email, you haven't really complained—or at least that's the auto industry's mindset. Send the seller and manufacturer a polite registered letter or fax that asks for compensation for repairs that have been done or need to be done, insurance costs during the vehicle's repair, towing charges, supplementary transportation costs like taxis and rented cars, and damages for your inconvenience (see the samples on pages 180–

181). If a private seller misrepresented the vehicle, there's no reason to implicate the manufacturer.

Specify five days (but allow 10 days) for either party to respond. If no satisfactory offer is made or your claim is ignored, file suit in small claims court. Make the manufacturer a party to the lawsuit, especially if an emissions warranty, a secret warranty extension, a safety recall campaign, or extensive chassis rusting is involved.

USED VEHICLE COMPLAINT LETTER/FAX/EMAIL

WITHOUT PREJUDICE

Date: _____

Name: _____

Please be advised that I am dissatisfied with my used vehicle, a (state model), for the following reasons:

1. _____
2. _____
3. _____
4. _____
5. _____

In compliance with the provincial consumer protection laws and the "implied warranty" set down by the Supreme Court of Canada in *Donoghue v. Stevenson*, *Wharton v. GM*, and *Sharman v. Ford Canada*, I hereby request that these defects be repaired without charge. This vehicle has not been reasonably durable and is, therefore, not as represented to me.

Should you fail to repair these defects in a satisfactory manner and within a reasonable period of time, I shall get an estimate of the repairs from an independent source and claim them in court, without further delay. I also reserve my right to claim up to $1 million for punitive damages, pursuant to the Supreme Court of Canada's February 22, 2002, ruling in *Whiten v. Pilot*.

I have dealt with your company because of its honesty, competence, and sincere regard for its clients. I am sure that my case is the exception and not the rule.

A positive response within the next five (5) days would be appreciated.

(signed with telephone number, fax number, or email address)

NEW VEHICLE COMPLAINT LETTER/FAX/EMAIL

WITHOUT PREJUDICE

Date: _____

Name and address of dealer: _____

Name and address of manufacturer: _____

Please be advised that I am not satisfied with my _____ (indicate year, make, model, and serial number of vehicle). The vehicle was purchased on (indicate date) and currently indicates _____ km on the odometer. The vehicle presently exhibits the following defects:

> 1. Premature rusting
> 2. Paint peeling/discoloration
> 3. Water leaks
> 4. Other defects (explain)

(List previous attempts to repair the vehicle. Attach a copy of a report from an independent garage, showing cost of estimated repairs and confirming the manufacturer's responsibility.)

I hereby request that you correct these defects free of charge under the terms of the implied warranty provisions of provincial consumer protection statutes as applied in *Kravitz v. General Motors* (1979), I.S.C.R., and *Chabot v. Ford* (1983), 39 O.R. (2d).

If you do not correct the defects noted above to my satisfaction and within a reasonable length of time, I will be obliged to ask an independent garage to _____ (choose [a] estimate or [b] carry out) the repairs and claim the amount of $_____ (state the cost, if possible) by way of the courts without further notice or delay.

I have dealt with your company because of its competence and honesty. I close in the hope of hearing from you within five (5) days of receiving this letter, failing which I will exercise the alternatives available to me. Please govern yourself accordingly.

Sincerely,

(signed with telephone or fax number)

Step 3: Mediation and Arbitration

If the formality of a courtroom puts you off or you're not sure that your claim is all that solid and don't want to pay the legal costs to find out, consider using mediation or arbitration offered by these groups: the Better Business Bureau (BBB), the Automobile Protection Association (APA), the Canadian Automobile Association (CAA), small claims court (mediation is often a prerequisite to going to trial), provincial and territorial government-run consumer mediation services, and the Canadian Motor Vehicle Arbitration Plan (CAMVAP).

> I just won my case with Chrysler Canada over my 2003 Ram SLT 4X4 quad cab truck. I've been having PCV valves freezing up (5 PCVs in 9,000 km). After one month in the shop, I went to CAMVAP to put in my claim, went to arbitration, and won. They have agreed to buy back my truck.

CAMVAP (*www.camvap.ca*) is the best known and most efficient organization offering free arbitration. Decisions are usually reached within a few months. Awards are no longer confidential (thanks to pressure exerted by the Quebec government), and the stipulation that no appeals are allowed doesn't seem enforceable, as CAMVAP says on its own website:

> If you believe that the award or result of your hearing was improper because the arbitrator erred in law or erred in his or her assessment of the facts, then you may want to consider an appeal to the courts.

The APA admits that "CAMVAP is well-run, which reduces complaints," but the group doesn't agree with CAMVAP's definition of "resolved" cases:

> The published success rate for consumers is around 61%, but 54% of consent awards and 21% of arbitrated cases were ordered back to the dealer for yet another repair. For many consumers who have gone through the arbitration process, this is not a satisfactory resolution, but in CAMVAP's statistics they appear as a successful resolution. Some consumers who went through the arbitration process contacted the APA to inform us they wanted the vehicle replaced or a monetary award and were not happy with a return trip to the dealer.

CAMVAP can be reached (toll-free) at 1-800-207-0685, and additional information can be gleaned from the following participating automobile manufacturers:

AUTOMAKER CONTACT INFORMATION

DaimlerChrysler Canada, Inc.	1-800-465-2001
	1-800-387-9983 (Quebec)
Ford Motor Company of Canada, Ltd.	1-800-565-3673
General Motors of Canada, Ltd.	1-800-263-3777 (English)
	1-800-263-7854 (French)
	1-800-263-3830 (TTY)
Honda Canada, Inc.	1-888-946-6329 (Honda)
	1-888-922-8729 (Acura)
Hyundai Auto Canada	1-800-461-8242
	1-800-461-5695 (Quebec)
Jaguar Canada, Inc.	1-800-668-6257
Kia Canada, Inc.	1-877-542-2886

Land Rover Group Canada, Inc.	1-800-346-3493
Mazda Canada, Inc.	1-800-263-4680
Mercedes-Benz Canada, Inc.	1-800-387-0100
Mitsubishi Motor Sales of Canada, Inc.	1-888-576-4878
Nissan Canada, Inc.	1-800-387-0122
Porsche Cars Canada, Ltd.	1-800-545-8039
Subaru Canada, Inc.	905-568-4959
Suzuki Canada, Inc.	905-889-2677 ext 2254
Toyota Canada, Inc.	1-888-869-6828 (Toyota)
	1-800-265-3987 (Lexus)
Volkswagen Canada, Inc.	1-800-822-8987 (Volkswagen)
	1-800-822-2834 (Audi)
Volvo Cars Canada, Ltd.	1-800-663-8255

Getting Outside Help

Don't let poor preparation scuttle your case. Ask government or independent consumer protection agencies to evaluate how well-prepared you are before going to your first hearing. Also, use the Internet and media sources to ferret out additional facts and to gather support (*www.lemonaidcars.com* is a good place to start).

Auto Industry Groups

Ontario consumers may file an online claim with the Ontario Motor Vehicle Industry Council (OMVIC) at *https://ewconsumers.omvic.on.ca/complaint/complaint. asp*. Sure, OMVIC is the dealer's self-defence lobby—made up of 9,000 registered dealers and 20,000 registered salespeople—but it has the following mandate:

> To maintain a fair, safe and informed marketplace in Ontario by protecting the rights of consumers, enhancing industry professionalism and ensuring fair, honest and open competition for registered motor vehicle dealers.

The way your complaint is handled will test the veracity of the above-stated goals.

Alberta has a similar self-regulating auto industry group, the Alberta Motor Vehicle Industry Council (AMVIC). You can visit their website at *www.amvic.org/main.htm*. During 2004, 873 consumer files were opened with AMVIC and 844 were closed. Their investigators laid 403 charges under the *Fair Trading Act* and the Canadian *Criminal Code*. Court fines of $13,400 were levied under the *Fair Trading Act*, and the courts ordered $289,281 in restitution payments. Also, AMVIC obtained $1,687,180 by mediation in restitution for victims of unfair trade practices.

Classified Ads and Television Exposés

Put an ad in the local paper describing your plight, and ask for information from people who may have experienced a problem similar to your own. This approach alerts others to the potential problem, helps build a base for a class action or a group meeting with the automaker, and puts pressure on the local dealer and manufacturer to settle with you. Sometimes the paper's news desk will assign someone to cover your story after your ad is published, or you may gain attention by setting up a website.

Television producers and their researchers need articulate consumers with issues that are easily filmed and understood. If you want media coverage, you must summarize your complaint and have visual aids that will hold the viewer's interest (viewers should be able to understand the issues with the sound turned off). Paint delamination? Show your peeling car. Bought a lemon vehicle? Show your repair bills. Holding a demonstration? Make it a "lemon" parade: Target one of the largest dealers, give your group a nifty name, and then drive past the dealership in vehicles decorated with "lemon" signs.

Federal and Provincial Consumer Affairs

The wind left the sails of the consumer movement over two decades ago, leaving consumer agencies understaffed and unsupported by the government. This has created a passive mindset among many staffers who are tired of getting their heads kicked in by businesses, deadwood bosses, and budget cutters.

Consumer affairs offices can still help with investigation, mediation, and some litigation. Strong and effective consumer protection legislation has been left standing in most of the provinces, and resourceful consumers can use these laws in conjunction with media coverage to prod provincial consumer affairs offices into action. Furthermore, provincial bureaucrats aren't as well shielded from criticism as their federal counterparts. A call to your MPP or MLA, or to their executive assistants, can often get things rolling.

Federal consumer protection is a government-created PR myth. Don't expect the staffers in the reorganized Competition Bureau (formerly the Office of Consumer Affairs) to be very helpful—they've been de-fanged and de-gummed through budget cuts and a succession of ineffective ministers. Although the beefed-up *Competition Act* has some bite in regard to misleading advertising and a number of other illegal business practices, the federal government has been more reactive than proactive in applying the law.

Nevertheless, you can lodge a formal complaint with the Competition Bureau if you encounter misleading advertising, odometer tampering, or price-fixing. Use the Online Complaint/Enquiry Form found at *www.competitionbureau.gc.ca*. An online complaint sent through this form made Toyota cease its Access price-fixing practices and pay out almost $2 million as a settlement fee.

Invest in Protest

You can have fun and put additional pressure on a seller or garage by putting a lemon sign on your car and parking it in front of the dealer or garage, by creating a lemon website, or by forming a self-help group like the Chrysler Lemon Owners Group (CLOG) or the Ford Lemon Owners Group (FLOG). After forming your group, you can have the occasional parade of creatively decorated cars visit area dealerships as the local media are convened. Just remember to keep your remarks pithy and factual, don't interfere with traffic or customers, and remain peaceful.

One other piece of advice from this consumer advocate with 40 years of experience and hundreds of pickets and mass demonstrations under his belt: Keep a sense of humour and never break off negotiations.

Finally, don't be scared off by threats that it's illegal to criticize a product or company. Unions, environmentalists, and consumer groups do it regularly (it's called "informational picketing"), and the Supreme Court of Canada in *R. v. Guinard* reaffirmed this right in February 2002. In that judgment, an insurance policy-holder posted a sign on his barn claiming the Commerce Insurance Company was unfairly refusing his claim. The municipality of St-Hyacinthe, Quebec, told him to take the sign down. He refused, maintaining that he had the right to state his opinion. The Supreme Court agreed. This judgment means that consumer protests, signs, and websites that criticize the actions of corporations cannot be banned simply because they say unpleasant things.

Typical Problems and Solutions

Sudden Acceleration, Chronic Stalling, and ABS and Airbag Failures

Incidents of sudden acceleration or chronic stalling are quite common. However, they are very difficult to diagnose, and individual cases can be treated very differently by federal safety agencies. Sudden acceleration is considered to be a safety-related problem—stalling isn't. Never mind that a vehicle's sudden loss of power on a busy highway puts everyone's lives at risk (as is the case with 2001–03 VW and Audi ignition coil failures). The same problem exists with engine and transmission powertrain failures, which are only occasionally considered to be safety-related. ABS and airbag failures are universally considered to be life-threatening defects. If your vehicle manifests any of these conditions, here's what you need to do:

1. Get independent witnesses to confirm that the problem exists. Your primary tools include an independent mechanic's verification, passenger accounts, downloaded data from your vehicle's data recorder, and lots of Internet browsing using *www.lemonaidcars.com* and Google's search engine. Notify the dealer or manufacturer by fax, email, or registered letter that you consider the problem to be a factory-induced, safety-related defect. Make sure you address your correspondence to the manufacturer's product liability or legal affairs department. At the dealership's service bay, make sure that every work order clearly states the problem as well as the number of previous attempts to fix it. (You should end up with a few complaint letters and a handful of work orders confirming that this is an ongoing deficiency.) If the dealer won't give you a copy of the work order because the work is a warranty claim, ask for a copy of the order number "in case your estate wishes to file a claim, pursuant to an accident." (This will get the service manager's attention.) Leaving a paper trail is crucial for any claim you may have later on because it shows your concern and persistence, and it clearly indicates that the dealer and manufacturer have had ample time to correct the defect.

2. Note on the work order that you expect the problem to be diagnosed and corrected under the emissions warranty or a "goodwill" program. It also wouldn't hurt to add the phrase on the work order or in your claim letters that "any deaths, injuries, or damage caused by the defect will be the dealer's and manufacturer's responsibility" since the work order (or letter, fax, or email) constitutes you putting them on "formal notice."

3. If the dealer does the necessary repairs at little or no cost to you, send a follow-up confirmation that you appreciate the "goodwill." Also, emphasize that you'll be back if the problem reappears—even if the warranty has expired—because the repair renews your warranty rights applicable to that defect. In other words, the warranty clock is set back to its original position. Understand that you won't likely get a copy of the repair bill, either, because dealers don't like to admit that there was a serious defect present and don't feel that they owe you a copy of the work order if the repair was done *gratis*. You can, however, subpoena the complete vehicle file from the dealer and manufacturer (this costs about $50) if the case goes to small claims or a higher court. This request has produced many out-of-court settlements when the internal documents show extensive work was carried out to correct the problem.

4. If the problem persists, send a letter, fax, or email to the dealer and manufacturer saying so, look for ALLDATA service bulletins to confirm that your vehicle's defects are factory-related, and report the failure by calling Transport Canada or NHTSA or by logging on to NHTSA's website. Also, call the Nader-founded Center for Auto Safety in Washington, D.C., (Tel: 202-328-7700) to get a lawyer referral and an information sheet covering the problem.

5. Now come two crucial questions: Repair the defect now or later? Use the dealer or an independent? Generally, it's smart to use an independent garage if you know the dealer isn't pushing for free corrective repairs from the manufacturer, if weeks or months have passed without any resolution of your claim, if the dealer keeps repeating that it's a maintenance item, and if you know an independent mechanic who will give you a detailed work order showing

the defect is factory-related and not caused by poor maintenance. Don't mention that a court case may ensue, since this will scare the dickens out of your only independent witness. An added bonus is that the repair charges will be about half of what a dealer would demand. Incidentally, if the automaker later denies warranty "goodwill" because you used an independent repairer, use the argument that the defect's safety implications required emergency repairs, carried out by whoever could see you first.

6. Dashboard-mounted warning lights usually come on prior to airbags suddenly deploying, ABS brakes failing, or engine glitches causing the vehicle to stall out. (Sudden acceleration usually occurs without warning.) Automakers consider these lights to be critical safety warnings and generally advise drivers to *immediately* have the vehicle serviced to correct the problem when any of the warning lights come on (advice that can be found in the owner's manual). This fact bolsters the argument that your life was threatened, emergency repairs were required, and your request for another vehicle or a complete refund isn't out of line.

7. Sudden acceleration can have multiple causes, isn't easy to duplicate, and is often blamed on the driver mistaking the accelerator for the brakes or failing to perform proper maintenance. Yet NHTSA data shows that with the 1992–2000 Explorer, for example, a faulty cruise-control or PCV valve and poorly mounted pedals are the most likely causes of the Explorer's sudden acceleration. So how do you satisfy the burden of proof showing that the problem exists and it's the automaker's responsibility? Use the legal doctrine called "the balance of probabilities" by eliminating all of the possible dodges the dealer or manufacturer may employ. Show that proper maintenance has been carried out, you're a safe driver, and the incident occurs frequently and without warning.

8. If any of the above defects causes an accident, or if the airbag fails to deploy or you're injured by its deployment, ask your insurance company to have the vehicle towed to a neutral location and clearly state that neither the dealer nor the automaker should touch the vehicle until your insurance company and Transport Canada have completed their investigation. Also, get as many witnesses as possible and immediately go to the hospital for a check-up, even if you're feeling okay. You may be injured and not know it because the adrenalin coursing through your veins is masking your injuries. A hospital exam will easily confirm that your injuries are accident-related, which is essential evidence for court or for future settlement negotiations.

9. Peruse NHTSA's online accident and service bulletin database to find reports of other accidents caused by the same failure, bulletins that indicate part upgrades, current defect investigations, and reported failures that have resulted in recalls or closed investigations.

10. Don't let your insurance company bully you. Refuse to let them settle the case if you're sure the accident was caused by a mechanical failure. Even if an engineering analysis fails to directly implicate the manufacturer or dealer, you can always plead the aforementioned balance of probabilities. If the insurance company settles, your insurance premiums will soar and the manufacturer will get away with the perfect crime.

Tires

Tire companies are far easier to deal with than automobile manufacturers because under the legal doctrine of *res ipsa loquitur* ("the thing speaks for itself," meaning, in negligence cases, that liability is shown by the failure) tires aren't supposed to fail. And when they do, smart claimants can use the *Robson v. General Motors B.C.* class action judgment to bring in the American corporation and can also refer to the Supreme Court of Canada judgment *Winnipeg Condominium No. 36 v. Bird Construction Co. Ltd.* (1995; 1 S.C.R.85), which ruled that defendants are liable in negligence for any designs that result in a public safety or health risk. This 10-year-old decision reversed a long-standing policy and provided the public with a new cause of action that had not existed before in Canada.

No wonder tire and auto companies routinely avoid liability by imputing blame to someone or something else, like punctures, impact damage, overloading, over-inflating, or under-inflating.

If you have a tire failure that conceivably puts your life in peril, consider the 10 steps outlined previously in "Sudden Acceleration, Chronic Stalling, and ABS and Airbag Failures" and add the following:

1. Access NHTSA on the Internet (see Appendix I) for current data about which tires are failure-prone and which companies are under investigation, conducting recalls, or carrying out "silent" recalls.
2. Keep the tire. If the tiremaker says an analysis must be done, permit only a portion of the tire to be taken away.
3. Plead the balance of probabilities, using friends and family to refute the tire company's contention that you caused the failure.
4. Ask for damages that are adequate to replace all the tires on your vehicle, including mounting costs.
5. Include in your damage claim any repairs needed to fix the body damage caused by the tire's failure.

Paint and Body Defects

The following settlement advice applies mainly to paint defects, but you can use these tips for any other vehicle defect that you believe is the automaker's or dealer's responsibility. If you're not sure whether the problem is a factory-related deficiency or a maintenance fault, have it checked out by an independent garage or get a technical service bulletin summary for your vehicle. The summary may include specific bulletins relating to diagnosis and correction, as well as information about ordering the upgraded parts needed to fix your problem.

Four good examples of favourable paint judgments are *Shields v. General Motors of Canada, Bentley v. Dave Wheaton Pontiac Buick GMC Ltd. and General Motors of Canada, Maureen Frank v. General Motors of Canada Limited*, and the most recent, *Dunlop v. Ford of Canada*.

In *Dunlop v. Ford of Canada* (No. 58475/04; Ontario Superior Court of Justice, Richmond Hill Small Claims Court; January 5, 2005; Deputy Judge M.J. Winer), the owner of a 1996 Lincoln Town Car, purchased used in 1999 for $27,000, was awarded $4,091.64. Judge Winer cited the *Shields* decision (below) and gave the following reasons for finding Ford of Canada liable:

> Evidence was given by the Plaintiff's witness, Terry Bonar, an experienced paint auto technician. He gave evidence that the [paint] delamination may be both a manufacturing defect and can be caused or [sped] up by atmospheric conditions. He also says that [the paint on] a car like this should last ten to 15 years, [or even for] the life of the vehicle....
>
> It is my view that the presence of ultraviolet light is an environmental condition to which the vehicle is subject. If it cannot withstand this environmental condition, it is defective....

In *Shields v. General Motors of Canada* (No. 1398/96; Ontario Court, General Division, Oshawa Small Claims Court; July 24, 1997; Robert Zochodne, Deputy Judge), the owner of a 1991 Pontiac Grand Prix had purchased the vehicle used with over 100,000 km on its odometer. Beginning in 1995, the paint began to bubble and flake, and it eventually peeled off. Deputy Judge Zochodne awarded the plaintiff $1,205.72 and struck down every one of GM's arguments that the peeling paint was caused by acid rain, UV rays, or some other environmental factor. Here are some other important aspects of this 12-page judgment that GM didn't appeal:

1. The judge admitted many of the technical service bulletins referred to in *Lemon-Aid* as proof of GM's negligence.
2. Although the vehicle had 156,000 km on its odometer when the case went to court, GM still offered to pay 50 percent of the paint repairs if the plaintiff dropped his suit.
3. The judge ruled that the failure to protect the paint from the damaging effects of UV rays is akin to engineering a car that won't start in cold weather. In essence, vehicles must be built to withstand the rigours of the environment.
4. Here's an interesting twist: The original warranty covered defects that were present at the time it was in effect. The judge, taking statements found in the GM technical service bulletins, ruled that the UV problem was factory-related, existed during the warranty period, and, therefore, represented a latent defect that appeared once the warranty expired.
5. The subsequent purchaser was not prevented from making the warranty claim, even though the warranty had long since expired, from both time and mileage standpoints, and he was the second owner.

The small claims judgment in *Bentley v. Dave Wheaton Pontiac Buick GMC Ltd. and General Motors of Canada* (Victoria Registry No. 24779; British Columbia Small

Claims Court; December 1, 1998; Judge Higinbotham) builds upon Ontario's *Shields v. General Motors of Canada* decision and cites other jurisprudence as to how long paint should last on a car. If you're wondering why Ford and Chrysler haven't been hit by similar judgments, remember that they usually settle out of court.

From *Maureen Frank v. General Motors of Canada Limited* (No. SC#12 (2001); Saskatchewan Provincial Court, Saskatoon, Saskatchewan; October 17, 2001; Provincial Court Judge H.G. Dirauf):

> On June 23, 1997, the Plaintiff bought a 1996 Chevrolet Corsica from a General Motors dealership. At the time, the odometer showed 33,172 km. The vehicle still had some factory warranty. The car had been a lease car and had no previous accidents.
>
> During June of 2000, the Plaintiff noticed that some of the paint was peeling off from the car and she took it to a General Motors dealership in Saskatoon and to the General Motors dealership in North Battleford where she purchased the car. While there were some discussions with the GM dealership about the peeling paint, nothing came of it and the Plaintiff now brings this action claiming the cost of a new paint job.
>
> During 1999, the Plaintiff was involved in a minor collision causing damage to the left rear door. This damage was repaired. During this repair some scratches to the left front door previously done by vandals were also repaired.
>
> The Plaintiff's witness, Frank Nemeth, is a qualified auto body repairman with some 26 years of experience. He testified that the peeling paint was a factory defect and that it was necessary to completely strip the car and repaint it. He diagnosed the cause of the peeling paint as a separation of the primer surface or colour coat from the electrocoat primer. In his opinion no primer surfacer was applied at all. He testified that once the peeling starts, it will continue. He has seen this problem on General Motors vehicles. The defect is called delamination.
>
> Mr. Nemeth stated that a paint job should last at least 10 years. In my opinion, most people in Saskatchewan grow up with cars and are familiar with cars. I think it is common knowledge that the original paint on cars normally lasts in excess of 15 years and that rust becomes a problem before the paint fails. In any event, paint peeling off, as it did on the Plaintiff's vehicle, is not common. I find that the paint on a new car put on by the factory should last at least 15 years.
>
> It is clear from the evidence of Frank Nemeth (independent body shop manager) that the delamination is a factory defect. His evidence was not seriously challenged. I find that the factory paint should not suffer a delamination defect for at least 15 years and that this factory defect breached the warranty that the paint was of acceptable quality and was durable for a reasonable period of time.

There will be judgment for the Plaintiff in the amount of $3,412.38 plus costs of $81.29.

Some of the important aspects of the *Frank* judgment are:

1. The judge accepted that the automaker was responsible, even though the car had been bought used. The subsequent purchaser wasn't prevented from making the warranty claim, even though the warranty had long since expired, from both time and mileage standpoints, and she was the second owner.
2. The judge stressed that the provincial warranty can kick in when the automaker's warranty has expired or isn't applied.
3. By awarding full compensation to the plaintiff, the judge didn't feel that there was a significant "betterment" or improvement added to the car that would warrant reducing the amount of the award.
4. The judge decided that the paint delamination was a factory defect.
5. The judge also concluded that without this factory defect, a paint job should last up to 15 years.
6. GM offered to pay $700 of the paint repairs if the plaintiff dropped the suit; the judge awarded five times that amount.
7. Maureen Frank won this case despite having to confront GM lawyer Ken Ready, who had considerable experience arguing other paint cases for GM and Chrysler.

Other paint and rust cases

Martin v. Honda Canada Inc. (March 17, 1986; Ontario Small Claims Court, Scarborough; Judge Sigurdson): The original owner of a 1981 Honda Civic sought compensation for the premature "bubbling, pitting, [and] cracking of the paint and rusting of the Civic after five years of ownership." Judge Sigurdson agreed with the owner and ordered Honda to pay the owner $1,163.95.

Thauberger v. Simon Fraser Sales and Mazda Motors (3 B.C.L.R., 193): This Mazda owner sued for damages caused by the premature rusting of his 1977 Mazda GLC. The court awarded him $1,000. Thauberger had also previously sued General Motors for a prematurely rusted Blazer truck and was awarded $1,000 in the same court. Both judges ruled that the defects couldn't be excluded from the automaker's expressed warranty or from the implied warranty granted by British Columbia's *Sale of Goods Act*.

Whittaker v. Ford Motor Company (1979) (24 O.R. (2d), 344): A new Ford developed serious corrosion problems despite having been rustproofed by the dealer. The court ruled that the dealer, not Ford, was liable for the damage for having sold the rustproofing product at the time of purchase. This is an important judgment to use when a rustproofer or paint protector goes out of business or refuses to pay a claim, because the decision holds the dealer jointly responsible.

See also:

- *Danson v. Chateau Ford (1976) C.P.* (Quebec Small Claims Court; No. 32-00001898-757; Judge Lande)
- *Doyle v. Vital Automotive Systems* (May 16, 1977; Ontario Small Claims Court, Toronto; Judge Turner)
- *Lacroix v. Ford* (April 1980; Ontario Small Claims Court, Toronto; Judge Tierney)
- *Marinovich v. Riverside Chrysler* (April 1, 1987; District Court of Ontario; No. 1030/85; Judge Stortini)

Using the Courts

When to Sue?

If the seller you've been negotiating with agrees to make things right, give him or her a deadline to complete the repairs and then have an independent garage check them over. If no offer is made within 10 working days, file suit in court. Make the manufacturer a party to the lawsuit only if the original, unexpired warranty is still in place; if your claim falls under the emissions warranty, a TSB, a secret warranty extension, or a safety recall campaign; or if there is extensive chassis rusting caused by poor engineering.

Which Court?

Most claims can be handled without a lawyer in small claims court, especially now that the court's jurisdiction varies between $10,000 and $25,000. Still, it's up to you to decide what remedy to pursue: that is, whether you want a partial refund or a cancellation of the sale. To determine the refund amount, add the estimated cost of repairing the existing mechanical defects to the cost of prior repairs. Don't exaggerate your losses or claim for repairs that are considered to be routine maintenance. A suit for the cancellation of a sale involves practical problems. The court requires that the vehicle be "tendered," or taken back, to the seller at the time the lawsuit is filed. This leaves you without transportation for as long as the case continues, unless you purchase another vehicle in the interim. If you lose the case, you must then take back the old vehicle and pay the accumulated storage fees. You could go from having no vehicle to having two—one of which is a clunker!

Generally, if the cost of repairs or the sales contract amount falls within the small claims court limit (discussed later), file the case there to keep your costs to a minimum and to get a speedy hearing. Small claims court judgments aren't easily appealed, lawyers aren't necessary, filing fees are minimal (about $125), and cases are usually heard within a few months. In fact, your suit is almost always best argued in the provincial small claims court to keep costs and frustrations down and to get a quick resolution within a few months.

Mr. Edmonston, I emailed you earlier in the year seeking help on my small claims case against Ford. I'm happy to report that I won my case and received a $1,900 settlement cheque from Ford in the mail yesterday! As you may recall I have a 1991 Explorer that has a significant paint peel problem.

I followed all the steps recommended by your website—ultimately I ended up in small claims court. Ford had indicated in court documents that they were going to send a representative to the hearing, but nobody showed. The judge made a quick ruling in my favour and I was out the door. I didn't even get a chance to show the load of material I had brought to make my case.

MARK G.

Here's another reason not to be greedy: If you claim more than the small claims court limit, you'll have to go to a higher court—where costs quickly add up, lawyers routinely demand 30 percent of your winnings or settlement, and delays of a few years or more are commonplace.

Small Claims Courts

Crooked automakers scurry away from small claims courts like cockroaches from bug spray, not because the courts can issue million-dollar judgments or force litigants to spend millions in legal fees (they can't), but because dealers and manufacturers don't want the bad publicity arising from the filings and eventual judgments. Other disincentives are that small claims courts can award sizeable sums to plaintiffs not represented by lawyers, and they make jurisprudence that other judges on the same bench are likely to follow.

For example, in *Dawe v. Courtesy Chrysler* (Dartmouth Nova Scotia Small Claims Court; SCCH #206825; July 30, 2004), Judge Patrick L Casey, Q.C., rendered an impressive 21-page decision citing key automobile product liability cases from the past 80 years, including *Donoghue, Kravitz*, and *Davis*. The court awarded $5,037 to the owner of a new 2001 Cummins engine–equipped Ram pickup with the following problems: It wandered all over the road; lost power, or jerked and bucked; shifted erratically; lost braking ability; bottomed out when passing over bumps; allowed water to leak into the cab; produced a burnt-wire and oil smell in the interior as the lights would dim; and produced a rear-end whine and wind noise around the doors and under the dash. Dawe had sold the vehicle and reduced his claim to meet the small claims threshold. Anyone with engine, transmission, and suspension problems or water leaking into the interior will find this judgment particularly useful.

Interestingly, "small claims" court is quickly becoming a misnomer, now that Alberta and British Columbia allow claims of up to $25,000 and most other provinces permit $10,000 filings.

There are small claims courts in most counties of every province, and you can make a claim in the county where the problem happened or where the defendant lives and conducts business. Simply go to the small claims court office and ask for a claim form (instructions on how to fill it out accompany the form). Remember, you must identify the defendant correctly, which may require some help from the court clerk (look for other recent lawsuits naming the same party). Crooks often change their company's name to escape liability; for example, it would be impossible to sue Joe's Garage (1999) if your contract is with Joe's Garage, Inc., (1984).

At this point, it wouldn't hurt to hire a lawyer or a paralegal for a brief walk-through of small claims procedures to ensure that you've prepared your case properly and that you know what objections will likely be raised by the other side. If, instead, you'd like a lawyer to do all the work for you, there are a number of law firms around the country that specialize in small claims litigation. "Small claims" doesn't mean "small legal fees," however. In Toronto, some law offices charge a flat fee of $1,000 for a basic small claims lawsuit and trial.

Remember that you're entitled to bring to court any evidence relevant to your case, including written documents such as a bill of sale or receipt, contract, or letter. If your car has developed severe rust problems, bring a photograph (signed and dated by the photographer) to court. You may also have witnesses testify in court. It's important to discuss a witness's testimony prior to the court date. If a witness can't attend the court date, he or she can write a report and sign it for representation in court. This situation usually applies to an expert witness, such as an independent mechanic who has evaluated your car's problems.

If you lose your case in spite of all your preparation and research, some small claims court statutes allow cases to be retried, at a nominal cost, in exceptional circumstances. If a new witness has come forward, additional evidence has been discovered, or key documents (that were previously not available) have become accessible, apply for a retrial. In Ontario, this little-known provision is Rule 18.4 (1).B.

Alan MacDonald, a *Lemon-Aid* reader who won his case in small claims court, gives the following tips on beating Ford over a faulty automatic transmission:

> I want to thank you for the advice you provided in my dealings with the Ford Motor Company of Canada Limited and Highbury Ford Sales Limited regarding my 1994 Ford Taurus wagon and the problems with the automatic transmission (Taurus and Windstar transmissions are identical). I also wish to apologize for not sending you a copy of this judgment earlier... (*MacDonald v. Highbury Ford Sales Limited,* Ontario Superior Court of Justice in the Small Claims Court London, June 6, 2000, Court File #0001/00, Judge J.D. Searle).

In 1999, after only 105,000 km, the automatic transmission went. I took the car to Highbury Ford to have it repaired. We paid $2,070 to have the transmission fixed, but protested and felt the transmission failed prematurely. We contacted Ford, but to no avail: Their reply was we were out of warranty, period. The transmission was so poorly repaired (and we went back to Highbury Ford several times) that we had to go to Mr. Transmission to have the transmission fixed again nine months later at a further $1,906.02.

It is at that point that I contacted you, and I was surprised, and somewhat speechless (which you noticed) when you personally called me to provide advice and encouragement. I am very grateful for your call. My observations with going through small claims court involved the following: I filed in January of 2000, the trial took place on June 1 and the judgment was issued June 6.

At pretrial, a representative of Ford (Ann Sroda) and a representative from Highbury Ford were present. I came with one binder for each of the defendants, the court and one for myself (each binder was about 3 inches thick—containing your reports on Ford Taurus automatic transmissions, ALLDATA Service Bulletins, Taurus Transmissions Victims (Bradley website), Center for Auto Safety (website), Read This Before Buying a Taurus (website), and the Ford Vent Page (website).

The representative from Ford asked a lot of questions (I think she was trying to find out if I had read the contents of the information I was relying on). The Ford representative then offered a 50 percent settlement based on the initial transmission work done at Highbury Ford. The release allowed me to still sue Highbury Ford with regards to the necessity of going to Mr. Transmission because of the faulty repair done by the dealer. Highbury Ford displayed no interest in settling the case, and so I had to go to court.

For court, I prepared by issuing a summons to the manager at Mr. Transmission, who did the second transmission repair, as an expert witness. I was advised that unless you produce an expert witness you won't win in a car repair case in small claims court. Next, I went to the law school library in London and received a great deal of assistance in researching cases pertinent to car repairs. I was told that judgments in your home province (in my case Ontario) were binding on the court; that cases outside of the home province could be considered, but not binding, on the judge.

The cases I used for trial involved *Pelleray v. Heritage Ford Sales Ltd.*, Ontario Small Claims Court (Scarborough) SC7688/91 March 22, 1993; *Phillips et al. v. Ford Motor Co. of Canada Ltd. et al*, Ontario Reports 1970, 15th January 1970; *Gregorio v. Intrans-Corp.*, Ontario Court of Appeal, May 19, 1994; *Collier v. MacMaster's Auto Sales*, New Brunswick Court of Queen's Bench, April 26, 1991; *Sigurdson v. Hillcrest Service & Acklands* (1977), Saskatchewan Queen's Bench; *White v. Sweetland*, Newfoundland District Court, Judicial Centre of Gander, November 8, 1978; *Raiches Steel Works v. J. Clark & Son*, New Brunswick Supreme Court, March 7, 1977; *Mudge v. Corner Brook Garage Ltd.*, Newfoundland Supreme Court, July 17, 1975; *Sylvain v. Carroseries d'Automobiles Guy Inc. (1981)*, C.P. 333, Judge Page;

[and] *Gagnon v. Ford Motor Company of Canada, Limited et Marineau Automobile Co. Ltée.* (1974), C.S. 422–423.

In court, I had prepared the case, as indicated above, [and] had my expert witness and two other witnesses who had driven the vehicle (my wife and my 18-year-old son). As you can see by the judgment, we won our case and I was awarded $1,756.52, including pre-judgment interest and costs.

Key Court Decisions

The following Canadian and U.S. lawsuits and judgments cover typical problems that are likely to arise. Use them as leverage when negotiating a settlement or as a reference should your claim go to trial. Legal principles applying to Canadian and American law are similar; however, Quebec court decisions may be based on legal principles that don't apply outside that province. You can find a comprehensive listing of Canadian decisions from small claims courts all the way to the Supreme Court of Canada at *www.canlii.org/index_en.html* (Canadian Legal Information Institute).

Additional court judgments can be found in the legal reference section of your city's main public library or at a nearby university law library. Ask the librarian for help in choosing the legal phrases that best describe your claim.

LexisNexis (*www.lexisnexis.com*) and FindLaw (*www.findlaw.com*) are two useful Internet sites for legal research. Their main drawback, though, is that you may need to subscribe or use a lawyer's subscription to access jurisprudence and other areas of the sites. However, there *is* a free online summary of class actions filed in Canada at *classactionsincanada.blogspot.com*. It's run by Ward Branch, one of the legal counsels in the $1.2-billion class action filed against General Motors for defective engine intake manifold gaskets.

An excellent reference book that will give you plenty of tips on filing, pleading, and collecting your judgment is Judge Marvin Zuker's *Ontario Small Claims Court Practice 2006* (Carswell, 2006). Judge Zuker's book is easily understood by non-lawyers and uses court decisions from across Canada to help you plead your case successfully in almost any Canadian court.

Product Liability

Almost three decades ago, the Supreme Court of Canada in *General Motors Products of Canada Ltd. v. Kravitz* clearly affirmed that automakers and their dealers are jointly liable for the replacement or repair of a vehicle if independent testimony shows that it is afflicted with factory-related defects that compromise its safety or performance. The existence of secret warranty extensions or technical service bulletins also helps prove that the vehicle's problems are the automaker's responsibility. For example, in *Lowe v. Fairview Chrysler* (see page 206), technical service bulletins were instrumental in showing an Ontario small claims court judge that Chrysler had a history of automatic transmission failures dating back to 1989.

In addition to replacing or repairing the vehicle, an automaker can also be held responsible for any personal damages arising from the defect. This means that lost wages, supplementary transportation costs, and damages for personal inconvenience can be awarded. However, in the States, product liability damage awards often exceed millions of dollars, while Canadian courts are far less generous.

Implied Warranty (Reasonable Durability)

The implied warranty is that powerful "other" warranty they never tell you about. It applies during and after the expiration of the manufacturer's or dealer's expressed or written warranty and requires that a part or repair will last a "reasonable" period of time. What is "reasonable" depends in large part on benchmarks used in the industry, the price of the vehicle, and how it was driven and maintained. Look at the "Reasonable Part Durability" chart on pages 156–157 for some guidelines as to what you should expect.

Judges usually apply the implied, or legal, warranty when the manufacturer's expressed warranty has expired and the vehicle's manufacturing defects remain uncorrected. For example, in *General Motors Products of Canada Ltd. v. Kravitz* (1979; 1 S.C.R. 790), the court said that the seller's warranty of quality was an accessory to the property and was transferred with it on successive sales. Accordingly, subsequent buyers could invoke the contractual warranty of quality against the manufacturer, even though they didn't contract directly with it. This precedent is now codified in articles 1434, 1442, and 1730 of Quebec's *Civil Code*.

In the following decisions, the implied warranty forced Ford to pay for its Windstars' chronic engine failures.

Dufour v. Ford Canada Ltd. (April 10, 2001; Quebec Small Claims Court, Hull; No. 550-32-008335-009; Justice P. Chevalier): Ford was forced to reimburse the cost of engine head gasket repairs carried out on a 1996 Windstar's 3.8L engine—a vehicle not covered by the automaker's Owner Notification Program, which cut off assistance after the '95 model year.

Schaffler v. Ford Motor Company Limited and Embrun Ford Sales Ltd. (Ontario Superior Court of Justice, L'Orignal Small Claims Court; Court File No. 59-2003; July 22, 2003; Justice Gerald Langlois): The plaintiff bought a used 1995 Windstar in 1998. Its engine head gasket was repaired for free three years later, under Ford's 7-year extended warranty. In 2002 at 109,600 km, the head gasket failed again, seriously damaging the engine. Ford refused a second repair. Justice Langlois ruled that Ford's warranty extension bulletin listed signs and symptoms of the covered defect that were identical to the problems written on the second work order ("persistent and/or chronic engine overheating; heavy white smoke evident from the exhaust tailpipe; flashing 'low coolant' instrument panel light, even after coolant refill; and constant loss of engine coolant"). Judge Langlois concluded that "the problem was brought to the attention of the dealer well within the warranty period; the dealer was negligent." The plaintiff was awarded $4,941 plus 5 percent interest. This figure includes $1,070 for two months' car rental fees.

John R. Reid and Laurie M. McCall v. Ford Motor Company of Canada (Superior Court of Justice, Ottawa Small Claims Court; Claim No. #02-SC-077344; July 11, 2003; Justice Tiernay): A 1996 Windstar, bought used in 1997, experienced an engine head gasket failure in October 2001 at 159,000 km. Judge Tiernay awarded the plaintiffs $4,145 for the following reasons:

> A Technical Service Bulletin dated June 28, 1999, was circulated to Ford dealers. It dealt specifically with "undetermined loss of coolant" and "engine oil contaminated with coolant" in the 1996–98 Windstar and five other models of Ford vehicles. I conclude that Ford owed a duty of care to the Plaintiff to equip this vehicle with a cylinder head gasket of sufficient sturdiness and durability that would function trouble-free for at least seven years, given normal driving and proper maintenance conditions. I find that Ford is answerable in damages for the consequences of its negligence.

New-Vehicle Defects

Bagnell's Cleaners v. Eastern Automobile Ltd. (1991; 111 N.S.R. (2nd), No. 51, 303 A.P.R., No. 51 (T.D.)): This Nova Scotia company found that the new van it purchased had serious engine, transmission, and radiator defects. The court held that there was a fundamental breach of the implied warranty and that an exclusionary clause could not protect the seller.

Burridge v. City Motor (10 Nfld. & P.E.I.R.; No. 451): This Newfoundland resident complained repeatedly of his new car's defects during the warranty period and stated that he hadn't used his car for 204 days after spending almost $1,500 for repairs. The judge awarded all repair costs and cancelled the sale.

Davis v. Chrysler Canada Ltd. (1977; 26 N.S.R. (2nd), No. 410 (T.D.)): The owner of a new $28,000 diesel truck found that a faulty steering assembly prevented him from carrying on his business. The court ordered that the sale be cancelled and that $10,000 in monthly payments be reimbursed.

Fox v. Wilson Motors and GM (February 9, 1989; Court of Queen's Bench, New Brunswick; No. F/C/308/87): A trucker's new tractor-trailer had repeated engine malfunctions. He was awarded damages for loss of income, excessive fuel consumption, and telephone charges under the provincial *Sale of Goods Act*.

Gibbons v. Trapp Motors Ltd. (1970; 9 D.L.R. (3rd), No. 742 (B.C.S.C.)): The court ordered the dealer to take back a new car that had numerous defects and required 32 hours' worth of repairs.

Johnson v. Northway Chevrolet Oldsmobile (1993; 108 Sask. R., No. 138 (Q.B.)): The court ordered the dealer to take back a new car that had been brought in for repairs on 14 different occasions. Two years after purchasing the vehicle, the buyer initiated a lawsuit for the purchase price of the car and for general damages. General damages were awarded.

Julien v. GM of Canada (1991; 116 N.B.R. (2nd), No. 80): The plaintiff's new diesel truck produced excessive engine noise. The plaintiff was awarded the $5,000 cost of repairing the engine through an independent dealer.

Magna Management Ltd. v. Volkswagen Canada Inc. (May 27, 1988; Vancouver (B.C.C.A.); No. CA006037): This precedent-setting judgment allowed the plaintiff to keep his new $48,325 VW while awarding him $37,101—three years after the car was purchased. The problems had to do with poor engine performance.

Maughan v. Silver's Garage Ltd. (Nova Scotia Supreme Court; 6 B.L.R., No. 303, N.S.C. (2nd), No. 278): The plaintiff leased a defective backhoe. The manufacturer had to reimburse the plaintiff's losses because the warranty wasn't honoured. The court rejected the manufacturer's contention that the contract's exclusion clause protected the company from lawsuits for damages resulting from a latent defect.

Murphy v. Penney Motors Ltd. (1979; 23 Nfld. & P.E.I.R.; No. 152, 61 A.P.R., No. 152 (Nfld. T.D.)): This Newfoundland trucker found that his vehicle's engine problems took his new trailer off the road for 129 days during a 7-month period. The judge awarded all repair costs, as well as compensation for business losses, and cancelled the sale.

Murray v. Sperry Rand Corp. (Ontario Supreme Court; 5 B.L.R., No. 284): The seller, dealer, and manufacturer were all held liable for breach of warranty when a forage harvester didn't perform as advertised in the sales brochure or as promised by the sales agent. The plaintiff was given his money back and reimbursed for his economic loss, based on the amount his harvesting usually earned. The court held that the advertising claims acted as a warranty.

Oliver v. Courtesy Chrysler (1983) Ltd. (1992; 11 B.C.A.C., No. 169): Over a 3-year period, a new car showed symptoms of numerous defects, which the dealer attempted to fix, to no avail. The plaintiff put the car in storage and sued the dealer for the purchase price. The court ruled that the car wasn't roadworthy and that the plaintiff couldn't be blamed for putting it in storage rather than selling it and purchasing another vehicle. The purchase price was refunded, minus $1,500 for each year the plaintiff used the car.

Olshaski Farms Ltd. v. Skene Farm Equipment Ltd. (January 9, 1987; Alberta Court of Queen's Bench; 49 Alta. L.R. (2nd), No. 249): The plaintiff's Massey-Ferguson combine caught fire after the manufacturer had sent two notices to dealers informing them of a defect that could cause a fire. The judge ruled under the *Sale of Goods Act* that the balance of probabilities indicated that the manufacturing defect caused the fire, even though there was no direct evidence proving that the defect existed.

Western Pacific Tank Lines Ltd. v. Brentwood Dodge (June 2, 1975; B.C.S.C., No. 30945-74; Judge Meredith): The court awarded the plaintiff $8,600 and cancelled the sale of a new Chrysler New Yorker with badly adjusted doors, water leaks into the interior, and electrical short circuits.

Used-Vehicle Defects

Fissel v. Ideal Auto Sales Ltd. (1991; 91 Sask. R. 266): Shortly after the vehicle was purchased, its motor seized. The dealer refused to replace it, even though the car was returned on several occasions. The court ruled that the dealer had breached the statutory warranties in sections 11 (4) and 11 (7) of the *Consumer Products Warranties Act*. The purchasers were entitled to cancel the sale and recover the full purchase price.

Friskin v. Chevrolet Oldsmobile (72 D.L.R. (3d), 289): A Manitoba used-car buyer asked that his contract be cancelled because of a chronic stalling problem. The garage owner did his best to correct the problem, but despite his good intentions, the Manitoba *Consumer Protection Act* allowed for the cancellation of the sale.

Graves v. C&R Motors Ltd. (April 8, 1980; British Columbia County Court; Judge Skipp): The plaintiff bought a used car on the condition that certain deficiencies be remedied, but they never were. The buyer was promised a refund, but it never arrived. He brought suit, claiming that the dealer's deceptive activities violated the provincial *Trade Practices Act*. The court agreed, concluding that a deceptive act that occurs before, during, or after the transaction can lead to the cancellation of the contract.

Hachey v. Galbraith Equipment Company (1991; 33 M.V.R. (2d) 242): The plaintiff bought a used truck from a dealer for hauling gravel. Shortly thereafter, the truck's steering failed. The plaintiff's suit was successful because expert testimony showed that the truck wasn't roadworthy. The dealer was found liable for damages for being in breach of the implied condition of fitness for the purpose for which the truck was purchased, as set out in section 15 (a) of the New Brunswick *Sale of Goods Act*.

Henzel v. Brussels Motors (1973; 1 O.R., 339 (C.C.)): The dealer sold this used car while brandishing a copy of the mechanical fitness certificate as proof that the car was in good shape. The plaintiff was awarded his money back because the court held the certificate to be a warranty that was breached by the car's subsequent problems, caused by defects.

Johnston v. Bodasing Corporation Limited (February 23, 1983; Ontario County Court (Bruce); No. 15/11/83; Judge McKay): The plaintiff bought a used 1979 Buick Riviera for $8,500 that was represented as being "reliable." Two weeks after the car's purchase, its motor self-destructed. Judge McKay awarded the plaintiff $2,318 as compensation to fix the Riviera's defects.

One interesting aspect of this particular decision is that the trial judge found the *Sale of Goods Act* applied in this case, notwithstanding the fact that the vendor used a standard contract that said there were no warranties or representations. The judge also accepted the decision in *Kendal v. Lillico* (1969; 2 Appeal Cases, 31), which indicates that the *Sale of Goods Act* covers not only defects that the seller ought to have detected, but also latent defects that even his utmost skill and judgment couldn't have spotted. This places a very heavy onus on the vendor, and it should prove useful in similar actions in other common-law provinces with laws similar to Ontario's *Sale of Goods Act*.

Kelly v. Mack Canada (53 D.L.R. (4th), 476): The plaintiff bought two trucks from Mack Sales. The first, a used White Freightliner tractor and trailer, was purchased for $29,742. It cost him over $12,000 in repairs during the first five months, and another $9,000 was estimated for future engine repairs. Mack Sales convinced Kelly to trade in the old truck for a new Mack truck. Kelly did this, but, shortly thereafter, the new truck had similar problems. He sued for the return of all his money, arguing that the two transactions were really one.

The Ontario Court of Appeal agreed and awarded Kelly a complete refund. It stated, "There was such a congeries of defects that there had been a breach of the implied conditions set out in the *Sale of Goods Act*."

Although Mack Sales argued that the contract contained a clause excluding any implied warranties, the court determined that the breach was of such a magnitude that the dealer couldn't rely on that clause. The dealer then argued that because the client used the trucks, the depreciation of both should be taken into account in reducing the award. This contention was refused on the grounds that the plaintiff never had the product he bargained for and that in no way did he profit from the transaction. The court also awarded Kelly compensation for loss of income while the trucks were being repaired as well as the interest on all of the money tied up in both transactions from the time of purchase until the final judgment.

Morrison v. Hillside Motors (1973) Ltd. (1981; 35 Nfld. & P.E.I.R. 361): A used car advertised to be in "A-1" condition and carrying a 50/50 warranty developed a number of problems. The court decided that the purchaser should be partially compensated because of the ad's claim. In deciding how much compensation to award, the presiding judge considered the warranty's wording, the amount paid for the vehicle, the model year of the vehicle, its average life, the type of defect that occurred, and how long the purchaser had use of the vehicle before its defects became evident. Although this judgment was rendered in Newfoundland, judges throughout Canada have since used a similar approach for more than a decade.

Neilson v. Maclin Motors (71 D.L.R. (3d), 744): The plaintiff bought a used truck on the strength of the seller's assurances that the motor had been rebuilt and that it had 210 hp. The engine failed. The judge awarded damages and cancelled the contract because the motor hadn't been rebuilt, it didn't have 210 hp, and its transmission was defective.

Parent v. Le Grand Trianon and Ford Credit (1982; C.P., 194; Judge Bertrand Gagnon): After paying $3,300 for a used 1974 LTD, the plaintiff sued the Ford dealer 19 months later for his money back because the car was prematurely rusted out. The dealer replied that rust was normal, there was no warranty, and the claim was too late. The court held that the garage was still responsible. The plaintiff was awarded $1,500 for the cost of rust repairs.

"As is" clauses

Since 1907, Canadian courts have ruled that a seller can't exclude the implied warranty as to fitness by including such phrases as "there are no other warranties or guarantees, promises, or agreements than those contained herein." See *Sawyer-Massey Co. v. Thibault* (1907; 5 W.L.R. 241).

Adams v. J&D's Used Cars Ltd. (1983; 26 Sask. R. 40 (Q.B.)): Shortly after the vehicle's purchase, its engine and transmission failed. The court ruled that the inclusion of "as is" in the sales contract had no legal effect and, therefore, the dealer had breached the implied warranty set out in Saskatchewan's *Consumer Products Warranties Act*. The sale was cancelled, and all monies were refunded.

Leasing

Ford Motor Credit v. Bothwell (December 3, 1979; Ontario County Court (Middlesex); No. 9226-T; Judge Macnab): The defendant leased a 1977 Ford truck that had frequent engine problems, characterized by stalling and hard starting. After complaining for one year and driving 35,000 km (22,000 mi.), the defendant cancelled the lease. Ford Credit sued for the money owing on the lease. Judge Macnab upheld the cancellation of the lease and ordered Ford Credit to repay 70 percent of the amount the plaintiff had paid during the leasing period. Ford Credit was also ordered to refund the repair costs, even though the corporation claimed that it should not be held responsible for Ford's failure to honour its warranty.

Schryvers v. Richport Ford Sales (May 18, 1993; B.C.S.C., No. C917060; Justice Tysoe): The court awarded $17,578.47, plus costs, to a couple who paid thousands of dollars more in unfair and hidden leasing charges than if they had simply purchased their Ford Explorer and Escort. The court found that this price difference constituted a deceptive, unconscionable act or practice, in contravention of the *Trade Practices Act*, R.S.B.C. 1979, c. 406.

Judge Tysoe concluded that the total of the general damages awarded to the Schryvers for both vehicles would be $11,578.47. He then proceeded to give the following reasons for awarding an additional $6,000 in punitive damages:

> Little wonder Richport Ford had a contest for the salesperson who could persuade the most customers to acquire their vehicles by way of a lease transaction. I consider the actions of Richport Ford to be sufficiently flagrant and high handed to warrant an award of punitive damages.
>
> There must be a disincentive to suppliers in respect of intentionally deceptive trade practices. If no punitive damages are awarded for intentional violations of the legislation, suppliers will continue to conduct their businesses in a manner that involves deceptive trade practices because they will have nothing to lose. In this case I believe that the appropriate amount of punitive damages is the extra profit Richport Ford endeavoured to make as a result of its deceptive acts. I therefore award punitive damages against Richport Ford in the amount of $6,000.

Salvador v. Setay Motors/Queenstown Chev-Olds (Hamilton Small Claims Court; Case No.1621/95): The plaintiff was awarded $2,000 plus costs from Queenstown Leasing. The court found that the company should have tried harder to sell the leased vehicle, and at a higher price, when the "open lease" expired.

See also:
- *Barber v. Inland Truck Sales* (11 D.L.R. (3rd), No. 469)
- *Canadian-Dominion Leasing v. Suburban Super Drug Ltd.* (1966; 56 D.L.R. (2nd), No. 43)
- *Neilson v. Atlantic Rentals Ltd.* (1974; 8 N.B.R. (2d), No. 594)
- *Volvo Canada v. Fox* (December 13, 1979; New Brunswick Court of Queen's Bench; No. 1698/77/C; Judge Stevenson)
- *Western Tractor v. Dyck* (7 D.L.R. (3rd), No. 535)

Return of security deposit

Dealers routinely keep much of a lease customer's security deposit when the lease expires. However, this action can always be challenged. In the following claim, settled out of court, Ontario lawyer Harvey Goldstein (*www.loop.on.ca/goldstein*) forced GMAC Financial Services and a GM dealer to refund his $525 security deposit:

1. The Plaintiff Claims:
    (A) Return of his security deposit of $525.00; and a finding that no amount is owing to the Defendants;
    (B) Alternatively, damages in the above amount;
    (C) Prejudgment interest on $525.00 at the rate of 2% per month (24% per annum) from June 22, 2005, to the date of this Claim, and thereafter on the date of payment or Judgment at the rate of 4% per annum, pursuant to Section 128 of the Courts of Justice Act, R.S.O. (1990) as amended;
    (D) Post-judgment interest at the post-judgment rate of interest, pursuant to Section 129 of the Courts of Justice Act, R. S. O. (1990) as amended;
    (E) His costs of this action;
    (F) Punitive damages in an amount to be determined; and
    (G) Such further and other relief as this Honorable Court deems just and proper...

    ...

4. On or about June 10, 2005 the Plaintiff advised the Defendant North York Chevrolet Oldsmobile Ltd that he wanted it to inspect the said vehicle for chargeable damage prior to its return or that he be present when it was inspected after its return to the said Defendant.
5. The said Defendant advised that it had no control over the inspection process and that the Defendant GMAC Leaseco Limited would inspect the vehicle only after the lease expired, the vehicle was returned to the dealer and the Plaintiff was not present.
6. The Plaintiff sent an email on June 10, 2005 to the Defendant GMAC Leaseco Limited asking it for an inspection prior to the vehicle being returned.
7. The said Defendant did not respond to the request.
8. The Plaintiff called and spoke with a representative of the said Defendant on June 17, and wrote her a letter sent by fax the same day, again asking that an inspection be scheduled in his presence. The said Defendant did not respond to the letter.
9. On June 23, 2005, the Plaintiff again called the said Defendant. He was told that it had no record of the vehicle being returned to the dealership.
10. Shortly thereafter, the Plaintiff called the Defendant North York Chevrolet Oldsmobile Ltd to enquire as to the status of his security deposit. The said Defendant advised that it had no record of the vehicle being returned to it.
11. Not having heard from either Defendant, the Plaintiff called the Defendant GMAC Leaseco Limited on July 15, 2005. He was advised that he owed the said Defendant $550.00, less the amount of the security deposit held by it. He was further advised that details of its claim to that amount could be found on the said

Defendant's website. He was told that it did not inspect the said vehicle until July 7, 2005, 15 days after it was left in the dealership's service bay. He was told that the vehicle was at an auction and that he could not inspect the alleged damages for which the Defendants claimed compensation. He was advised that no adjustment would be made to their claim even though the vehicle was returned with 20,000.00 kilometers less than allowed by the lease agreement. Further, he was told that the alleged damages to the vehicle were not repaired prior to sending it to auction.

12. The Plaintiff denies that the vehicle required repairs claimed by the Defendants and puts them to the strict proof thereof.

13. The Plaintiff further claims that the process by which the Defendants seek to claim compensation from him is unfair open to abuse and contrary to the principles of natural justice. The Defendants pay the fee of the alleged independent inspectors and deny the Plaintiff the opportunity to dispute the charges in any meaningful fashion. Further, its delay in inspecting the vehicle for 15 days, leaves open the question of when, if ever, the damages occurred.

Repairs

Faulty diagnosis

Davies v. Alberta Motor Association (August 13, 1991; Alberta Provincial Court, Civil Division; No. P9090106097; Judge Moore): The plaintiff had a used 1985 Nissan Pulsar NX checked out by the AMA's Vehicle Inspection Service prior to buying it. The car passed with flying colours. A month later, the clutch was replaced, and numerous electrical problems ensued. At that time, another garage discovered that the car had been involved in a major accident, had a bent frame and a leaking radiator, and was unsafe to drive. The court awarded the plaintiff $1,578.40 plus three years of interest. The judge held that the AMA set itself out as an expert and should have spotted the car's defects. The AMA's defence—that it wasn't responsible for errors—was thrown out. The court held that a disclaimer clause couldn't protect the association from a fundamental breach of contract.

Insurance repairs

Don't let a repairer put used or off-brand parts in your car. In *Avery v. State Farm*, the U.S. Supreme Court ruled that insurers must replace damaged parts with original equipment manufacturer (OEM) parts (1999; *www.state.il.us/court/Opinions/AppellateCourt/2001/5thDistrict/April/Html/5990830.htm*). An Ontario class action lawsuit seeking similar relief was settled on January 31, 2006, in *Albert Hague and Terrance O'Brien v. Liberty Mutual Insurance Company* (Ontario Superior Court; Case No. 01-CV-204787CP; June 14, 2004). For information about participating in the settlement, see page 129.

Secret Warranties

It's common practice for manufacturers to secretly extend their warranties to cover components with a high failure rate. Customers who complain vigorously get extended warranty compensation in the form of "goodwill" adjustments.

In *François Chong v. Marine Drive Imported Cars Ltd. and Honda Canada Inc.* (May 17, 1994; British Columbia Provincial Small Claims Court; No. 92-06760; Judge C.L. Bagnall), Mr. Chong was the first owner of a 1983 Honda Accord with 134,000 km on the odometer. He had six engine camshafts replaced—four under Honda "goodwill" programs, one where he paid part of the repairs, and one via this small claims court judgment.

In his ruling, Judge Bagnall agreed with Chong and ordered Honda and the dealer to each pay half of the $835.81 repair bill for the following reasons:

> The defendants assert that the warranty, which was part of the contract for purchase of the car, encompassed the entirety of their obligation to the claimant, and that it expired in February 1985. The replacements of the camshaft after that date were paid for wholly or in part by Honda as a "goodwill gesture." The time has come for these gestures to cease, according to the witness for Honda. As well, he pointed out to me that the most recent replacement of the camshaft was paid for by Honda and that, therefore, the work would not be covered by Honda's usual warranty of 12 months from date of repair. Mr. Wall, who testified for Honda, told me there was no question that this situation with Mr. Chong's engine was an unusual state of affairs. He said that a camshaft properly maintained can last anywhere from 24,000 to 500,000 km. He could not offer any suggestion as to why the car keeps having this problem.

> The claimant has convinced me that the problems he is having with rapid breakdown of camshafts in his car is due to a defect, which was present in the engine at the time that he purchased the car. The problem first arose during the warranty period and in my view has never been properly identified nor repaired.

Automatic transmission failures (Chrysler)

Lowe v. Fairview Chrysler-Dodge Limited and Chrysler Canada Limited (May 14, 1996; Ontario Court, General Division, Burlington Small Claims Court; No. 1224/95): The judgment, in the plaintiff's favour, raised important legal principles relative to Chrysler:

- Technical dealer service bulletins are admissible in court to prove that a problem exists and that certain parts should be checked out.
- If a problem is reported prior to a warranty's expiration, warranty coverage for the problematic component(s) is automatically carried over after the warranty ends.
- It's not up to the car owner to tell the dealer or automaker what the specific problem is.

- Repairs carried out by an independent garage can be refunded if the dealer or automaker unfairly refuses to apply the warranty.
- The dealer or automaker cannot dispute the cost of the independent repair if they fail to cross-examine the independent repairer.
- Auto owners can ask for and win compensation for their inconvenience, which amounted to $150 in this judgment.

Court awards quickly add up. Although the plaintiff was given $1,985.94, with the addition of court costs and prejudgment interest, plus costs of inconvenience fixed at $150, the final award amounted to $2,266.04.

False Advertising

Truck misrepresentation

Goldie v. Golden Ears Motors (1980) Ltd. (Port Coquitlam; June 27, 2000; British Columbia Small Claims Court; Case No. CO8287; Justice Warren): In a well-written eight-page judgment, the court awarded the plaintiff $5,000 for engine repairs on a 1990 Ford F-150 pickup in addition to $236 in court costs. The dealer was found to have misrepresented the mileage and sold a used vehicle that didn't meet Section 8.01 of the provincial motor vehicle regulations (it had unsafe tires plus a defective exhaust and headlights).

In rejecting the seller's defence that he disclosed all information "to the best of his knowledge and belief," as stipulated in the sales contract, Justice Warren stated:

> The words "to the best of your knowledge and belief" do not allow someone to be willfully blind to defects or to provide incorrect information. I find as a fact that the business made no effort to fulfill its duty to comply with the requirements of this form.... The defendant has been reckless in its actions. More likely, it has actively deceived the claimant into entering into this contract. I find the conduct of the defendant has been reprehensible throughout the dealings with the claimant.

This judgment closes a loophole that sellers have used to justify their misrepresentation, and it allows for the cancellation of the sale and the awarding of damages if the vehicle doesn't meet highway safety regulations.

MacDonald v. Equilease Co. Ltd. (January 18, 1979; Ontario Supreme Court; Judge O'Driscoll): The plaintiff leased a truck that was represented as having an axle stronger than it really was. The court awarded the plaintiff damages for repairs and set aside the lease.

Seich v. Festival Ford Sales Ltd. (1978; 6 Alta. L.R. (2nd), No. 262): The plaintiff bought a used truck from the defendant after being assured that it had a new motor and transmission. It didn't, so the court awarded the plaintiff $6,400.

Used car sold as new (demonstrator)

Bilodeau v. Sud Auto (Quebec Court of Appeal; No. 09-000751-73; Judge Tremblay): This appeals court cancelled the contract and held that a car can't be sold as new or as a demonstrator if it has ever been rented, leased, sold, or titled to anyone other than the dealer.

Rourke v. Gilmore (January 16, 1928; published in *Ontario Weekly Notes*, Vol. XXXIII, p. 292): Before discovering that his "new" car was really used, the plaintiff drove it for over a year. For this reason, the contract couldn't be cancelled. However, the appeals court instead awarded damages for $500, which was quite a sum in 1928!

Vehicle not as ordered

Whether you're buying new or used, the seller can't misrepresent the vehicle. Anything that varies from what one would commonly expect, or from the seller's representation, must be disclosed prior to signing the contract. Typical scenarios are odometer turnbacks, accident damage, used or leased cars sold as new, new vehicles that are the wrong colour or the wrong model year, or vehicles that lack promised options or standard features.

Chenel v. Bel Automobile (1981) Inc. (August 27, 1976; Quebec Superior Court; Judge Desmeules): The plaintiff didn't receive his new Ford truck equipped with Jacob brakes, essential for transporting sand in hilly regions. The court awarded the plaintiff $27,000, representing the purchase price of the vehicle less the money he earned while using the truck.

Lasky v. Royal City Chrysler Plymouth (February 18, 1987; Ontario High Court of Justice; 59 O.R. (2nd), No. 323): The plaintiff bought a 4-cylinder 1983 Dodge 600 that was represented by the salesman as being a 6-cylinder model. After putting 40,000 km on the vehicle over a 22-month period, the buyer was given her money back, without interest, under the provincial *Business Practices Act*.

False fuel economy claims

Sidney v. 1011067 Ontario Inc. (c.o.b. Southside Motors): This is a precedent-setting case that awarded a used-car buyer $11,424.51 plus prejudgment interest because of a false representation made by the defendant regarding fuel efficiency. This judgment puts new-car dealers and automakers on notice that the courts will strictly interpret their gas mileage claims. And, because hardly anyone comes within 10 percent of the fuel efficiency that they claim, we'll likely see more lawsuits of this nature in the future.

Damages (Punitive)

Punitive damages (also known as exemplary damages) allow the plaintiff to get compensation that exceeds his or her losses as a deterrent to those who carry out dishonest or negligent practices. These kinds of judgments, common in the U.S., sometimes reach hundreds of millions of dollars. Canadian courts, however, seldom award substantial punitive damages.

Nevertheless, there have been a few relatively recent cases where the Supreme Court has shocked the business establishment by levying huge exemplary damage awards. One such case was the *Whiten v. Pilot Insurance Co.* decision rendered in 2002. In this case, the plaintiff's home caught fire and burned to the ground, destroying all of the home's contents and killing three pet cats. Pilot Insurance made a single $5,000 payment for living expenses and covered the family's rent for a couple of months, and then they cut off the rent payments without forewarning the family. The insurance claim went to trial, based on the respondent's allegation that the family had torched their own home, even though the local fire chief, the respondent's own expert investigator, and its initial expert all said there was no evidence whatsoever of arson. The original trial jury awarded the plaintiff compensatory damages and $1 million in punitive damages. Pilot Insurance fought this decision at the Court of Appeal, where the punitive damages award was reduced to $100,000. The case was then taken all the way to the Supreme Court, where the trial jury's unprecedented award of $1 million was restored:

> The jury's award of punitive damages, though high, was within rational limits. The respondent insurer's conduct towards the appellant was exceptionally reprehensible. It forced her to put at risk her only remaining asset (the $345,000 insurance claim) plus $320,000 in costs that she did not have. The denial of the claim was designed to force her to make an unfair settlement for less than she was entitled to. The conduct was planned and deliberate and continued for over two years, while the financial situation of the appellant grew increasingly desperate. The jury evidently believed that the respondent knew from the outset that its arson defence was contrived and unsustainable. Insurance contracts are sold by the insurance industry and purchased by members of the public for peace of mind. The more devastating the loss, the more the insured may be at the financial mercy of the insurer, and the more difficult it may be to challenge a wrongful refusal to pay the claim.

Punitive damages are rarely awarded in Canadian courts against automakers. When they are given out, it's usually for sums less than $100,000. In *Prebushewski v. Dodge City Auto (1985) Ltd. and Chrysler Canada Ltd.*, the plaintiff got $25,000 in a judgment handed down in 2001 and confirmed by the Supreme Court in 2005 (see "Getting Action," earlier in Part Three). The court basically said aggrieved car owners may sue for much more than the depreciated value of what they bought under provincial consumer protection statutes. The Supreme Court reaffirmed the power of the lower courts to assess an additional financial penalty to punish automakers who treat their customers unfairly and to ensure they don't repeat the offense.

Vlchek v. Koshel (1988; 44 C.C.L.T. 314, B.C.S.C., No. B842974): The plaintiff was seriously injured when she was thrown from a Honda all-terrain cycle on which she had been riding as a passenger. The court allowed for punitive damages because the manufacturer was well aware of the injuries likely to be caused by the cycle. Specifically, the court ruled that there is no firm and inflexible principle of law stipulating that punitive or exemplary damages must be denied unless the defendant's acts are specifically directed against the plaintiff. The Court may apply punitive damages "where the defendant's conduct has been indiscriminate of focus, but reckless or malicious in its character. Intent to injure the plaintiff need not be present, so long as intent to do the injurious act can be shown."

See also:
- *Granek v. Reiter* (Ontario Court, General Division; No. 35/741)
- *Morrison v. Sharp* (Ontario Court, General Division; No. 43/548)
- *Schryvers v. Richport Ford Sales* (May 18, 1993; B.C.S.C., No. C917060; Judge Tysoe)
- *Varleg v. Angeloni* (B.C.S.C., No. 41/301)

Provincial business practices acts cover false, misleading, or deceptive representations and allow for punitive damages should the unfair practice toward the consumer amount to an unconscionable representation (see *Canadian Encyclopedic Digest (C.E.D.)*, 3rd Edition, s. 76, pp. 140–45). And here are some specific cases to keep in mind:

- Exemplary damages are justified where compensatory damages are insufficient to deter and punish. See *Walker et al. v. CFTO Ltd. et al.* (1978; 59 O.R. (2nd), No. 104; Ontario C.A.).
- Exemplary damages can be awarded in cases where the defendant's conduct was "cavalier." See *Ronald Elwyn Lister Ltd. et al. v. Dayton Tire Canada Ltd.* (1985; 52 O.R. (2nd), No. 89; Ontario C.A.).
- The primary purpose of exemplary damages is to prevent the defendant and all others from doing similar wrongs. See *Fleming v. Spracklin* (1921).
- Disregard of the public's interest, lack of preventive measures, and a callous attitude all merit exemplary damages. See *Coughlin v. Kuntz* (1989; 2 C.C.L.T. (2nd); B.C.C.A.).
- Punitive damages can be awarded for mental distress. See *Ribeiro v. Canadian Imperial Bank of Commerce* (1992; Ontario Reports 13 (3rd)) and *Brown v. Waterloo Regional Board of Comissioners of Police* (1992; 37 O.R. (2nd)).

In the States, punitive damage awards have been particularly generous. Do you remember the Alabama fellow who won a multi-million dollar award because his new BMW had been repainted before he bought it and the seller didn't tell him so? The case was *BMW of North America, Inc. v. Gore* (517 U.S. 559, 116 S. Ct. 1589; 1996). In this case, the U.S. Supreme Court cut the damages award and established standards for jury awards of punitive damages. Nevertheless, million-dollar awards are still quite common.

For example, an Oregon dealer learned that a $1-million punitive damages award wasn't excessive under *Gore* and under Oregon law. The Oregon Supreme Court determined that the standard it set forth in *Oberg v. Honda Motor Company* (888 P.2d 8; 1996), on remand from the Supreme Court, survived the Supreme Court's subsequent ruling in *Gore*. The court held that the jury's $1-million punitive damages award, 87 times larger than the plaintiff's compensatory damages in *Parrott v. Carr Chevrolet, Inc.* (2001 Ore. LEXIS 1; January 11, 2001), wasn't excessive. In that case, Mark Parrott sued Carr Chevrolet, Inc., over a used 1983 Chevrolet Suburban under Oregon's *Unlawful Trade Practices Act*. The jury awarded Parrott $11,496 in compensatory damages and $1 million in punitive damages because the dealer failed to disclose collision damage to a new-car buyer.

Class Action Settlements

TFI Module Class Action Settlement: *Howard v. Ford Motor Company* (U.S.); *Barbara Reid v. Ford Motor Company* (B.C.); and *Royal Fine Cars, Reuben Covello, and Justin Lauria v. Ford Motor Company* (Ontario).

In October 2006, B.C.'s Supreme Court approved a $1.5 million class action settlement from Ford of Canada for a defect in its thick film ignition (TFI) engine computer module. The settlement is related to these class actions and involves more than a dozen different models built from 1983 to 1995. It principally covers B.C. and Ontario residents; however, claims from other provinces and territories will be accepted by Ford on a case-by-case basis.

According to the plaintiffs, the TFI module is an integral part of the solid state ignition system used by Ford in most of its vehicles. It regulates the current that creates the ignition spark and was mounted on the distributor above the engine block, where it could be damaged by overheating.

Ford has agreed to pay up to $325 each to those who replaced the module or need the part replaced. See *www.tfisettlement.com* for information about the U.S. settlement. Information about the Ontario and B.C. settlement can be found at *www.classproceedings.ca/present%20cases%20ford.htm* or by contacting *craber@stevensonlaw.net* or 416-599-7900.

Part Four

VEHICLE RATINGS: THE GOOD, THE BAD, AND THE UGLY

Wipe Away the Swan Fat

Over the years I've been wined and dined by car firms at the Burj Al Arab in Dubai, the Carlton in Cannes, the Regent in Hong Kong, the Fairmont in San Francisco, the George V in Paris, the Arts in Barcelona, the Hyatt in Beaver Creek, the Phoenician in Phoenix, the Byblos in St Tropez…there's no point going on because the list is endless. Once, Alfa Romeo took me to the Cipriani in Venice. It actually had a press launch for a car in a city with no roads. It was great but I spent so much time flying round the world, wiping swan fat from round my chops with the silken underpants of Vietnamese virgins, that in my first year of motoring journalism I earned $5000.

JEREMY CLARKSON
BBC TV *TOP GEAR*

A Necessary Evil?

Look, let's face it—I don't like cars, SUVs, trucks, or vans. They're considered to be a necessary evil, but they're also one of the main reasons why the poor stay poor, why corporate ethics have moved from the absolute to the relative, and why air pollution is worse than ever.

Okay, do you understand where I'm coming from? Automobiles are appliances. Although some do their job efficiently over the years, the social and economic costs inherent to auto ownership are becoming more than we can afford. And, like appliances, the more time vehicles save us, the more time we waste in their care and feeding. We get more done, but then we find that we have more to do.

No, it's not only about fuel costs, highway safety, and pollution. There's also an awesome psychological burden associated with auto ownership that few people consider when buying their first car.

First, you become anti-social. You see other drivers as morons with driving skills far inferior to your own, or as predators who seek to cut you off or steal your parking spot at the first opportunity. The surrounding environment becomes abstract as the landscape whizzes by you. Your concentration is focused on the radio, now called the "sound system," and the cell phone, where there's always one more call to be made. Then there's all the paperwork to do, bills to pay, and maintenance to schedule and argue about. And don't forget the hours lost each day commuting to work, school, and social events.

Perhaps it does seem odd that I discuss the dark side of vehicle ownership in an auto guide. But what better place? Furthermore, by following the many smart buying tips outlined in the first three parts of this book, your costs and frustrations can be contained. In fact, my enthusiasm for used vehicles is driven by the realization that the simplest way to stay above the fray is to recycle the vehicles that have already been built.

The March of the Penguins

There's an interesting and entertaining natural phenomenon that occurs every time I attend the annual auto shows in Montreal, Toronto, and Vancouver. As I walk by each automaker's kiosk, fronting dozens of beautifully spiffed new cars and trucks, the manufacturers' reps follow me cautiously, almost in lock-step fashion. Decked out in similarly styled suits and waddling along in unison, they play out a scene reminiscent of the movie *March of the Penguins*, except no one lays an egg (at least, not literally).

All car journalists (an oxymoron?) know it's tough rating new and used vehicles without selling out to the car industry. This fact has been repeatedly confirmed by some of the best writers and broadcasters who are critical of automobile manufacturers. Yet, the road to auto harlotry is so subtle that few people can resist compromising their integrity: The smooth-talking car pimps are always there to say how much their company admires your work, but then they tell you how much better your articles would be with more balance.

Then these car pimps invite you on their trips to Japan and Europe, where they give you hats, jackets, specially prepared vehicles, and interviews with the top brass. They even sponsor annual journalism awards to make sure their coterie of friendly scribes spouts the party line.

You feel like nobility; they see you as a whore.

Good rating systems will downgrade models when customer complaints and service bulletins confirm performance and reliability failings, as seen with the Nissan Titan pickup (brake, rear end, and powertrain failures) and the Suzuki Vitara/XL7 (overall poor performance).

Keeping Ratings Honest and Fair

Lemon-Aid has managed to be both honest and fairly accurate (okay, I did mistakenly recommend the Dodge Aspen and Ford Windstar, years ago) for more than 35 years by following these simple rules:

- Ratings should be used primarily as a comparative database, where the low-ranked or recommended models reappear in different driving tests and owner surveys. The best rating approach is to combine a driving test with an owner survey rating past models (only *Consumer Reports* does this).
- The responses must come from a large owner pool (such as the more than one million responses from *Consumer Reports* subscribers). Anecdotal responses should then be cross-referenced, updated, and given depth and specificity through NHTSA's safety complaint prism. Responses must again be cross-referenced with automaker internal service bulletins to determine the extent of a particular defect over a specific model and model-year range and to alert owners to the types of problems that are likely to occur.
- Rankings should be predicated upon important characteristics measured over a significant period of time, unlike "Car of the Year" beauty contests, owner-

perceived values, or J.D. Power surveys that consider only problems that are experienced after three months of ownership (the three-year survey results are more relevant).

- Ratings must come from unimpeachable sources. There shouldn't be any conflicts of interest such as advertising or consultant ties, or self-serving tests done under ideal conditions.
- Beware of self-generated fuel economy ratings used by automakers in complicity with the federal government. *Automotive News* recently found that Honda and Toyota hybrids get 20 percent less "real world" gas mileage (44 mpg, or 5 L/100 km) than advertised because hybrids require a particular style of driving to be fuel efficient, short trips penalize the efficiency of hybrids more than regular cars, air conditioning penalizes hybrids more, and colder climates increase fuel consumption. *Consumer Reports* found a 40 percent shortfall.
- Tested cars must be bought rather than borrowed and serviced rather than pampered as part of a journalists' fleet lent out for ranking purposes. Automakers must not be members of the ranking body. Also, all automakers need to be judged equally. For example, at one time Toyota didn't accept weekend car journalist "roundup" tests as valid; the company refused to lend its vehicles to the events, so it was penalized. Toyota now participates enthusiastically…sigh.

Key Factors

A good sport-utility, van, or pickup must be reasonably priced, crashworthy, easy to handle, and durable (lasting 10–15 years). And don't believe for one moment that the more you spend, the better the vehicle. For example, the Honda Pilot and Toyota Highlander are two great performers that rival luxury SUVs costing over $10,000 more, like the Acura MDX, BMW X5, Infiniti FX35, and Lexus RX330. The extra money only buys you more features of dubious value and newer, unproven technology like rear-mounted video cameras.

A good vehicle choice should cost no more than about $800 per year to maintain, and it should provide you with a 40–50 percent resale value after five years of use. Parts and servicing costs shouldn't be excessive, as CBC TV's *Marketplace* found to be the case with some Mazda dealers, and dealer servicing must be easily accessible, unlike Land Rover's, Mercedes', and Kia's service.

Fuel economy isn't all that important when you're buying used, because all of your other savings should easily compensate for the extra fuel costs. We don't recommend electric and gasoline engine hybrids, which are found in some SUVs and trucks, because their fuel economy can be 40 percent worse than what the automakers report, their long-term reliability is unknown, their batteries can cost $8,000 (U.S.) to replace, their retail prices are incredibly high, and their potential resale values are no better than those of similar vehicles equipped with conventional engines. For example, a 2001 Prius that originally sold for $29,990 is now valued at a disappointing $14,000 (and we're only three years away from the expiration of that $8,000-battery warranty).

Depreciation *is* an important consideration. Vehicles that hold their value well after four years won't be bargains now, but they will still have considerable equity in them should you have to sell because of a cash flow emergency. And, yes, models that depreciate slowly are usually seen as dependable vehicles that hold up better than others over the long run.

Four years ago, Toronto auto consultant Dennis DesRosiers put out the following list of which automaker's vehicles he believed held their value best. I have inserted an asterisk (*) next to the choices I disagree with, and then I added a few companies (**). However, most of his ratings make sense.

DESROSIERS' DEPRECIATION RATINGS

47.9 percent depreciation after four years is average

ABOVE AVERAGE		BELOW AVERAGE	
Acura**	Lexus	Dodge	Isuzu
BMW**	Mazda	Chrysler	Mitsubishi**
GM*	Mercedes*	Ford	Nissan*
Honda	Subaru*	GMC**	Suzuki*
Jeep	Toyota		
Infiniti*			

Here's where I disagreed while updating this chart: Real-world resale values appear to me to be much lower than average for Mercedes, General Motors, Infiniti, and Subaru. The first two companies have been shunned by buyers who have gotten word of their products' declining quality, and resale values have further eroded because of massive new-car rebates and dealer sales incentives. Infiniti resale values have declined primarily because the company has propped up a waning leasing market through unrealistically high buy-back offers. And buyers see Infinitis as overpriced to begin with. Used Subarus lose their value quickly because all-wheel drive is no longer that unusual, and new models are deeply discounted due to poor sales figures over the past three years.

Nissan and Suzuki resale values have improved because new models are attractively styled (Nissan), fuel-efficient, and inexpensive (Suzuki).

Lemon-Aid Ratings

Lemon-Aid uses mostly owner feedback and confidential service bulletins to rate vehicles. We don't try to curry any automaker's favour. Our guides are ad-free, and we don't depend on free "loaner" vehicles. We don't play favourites, even with car companies who traditionally turn out some of the better-made vehicles, like Honda, Mazda, Nissan, and Toyota. For almost a decade, we have chastised and down-rated these companies for their sliding-door, automatic transmission, and engine glitches—problems now covered by generous extended warranties. Additionally, *Lemon-Aid*'s 2002 price-fixing complaint against Toyota led to the company's $2-million settlement with Ottawa a year later. In 2006, we filed a similar complaint against Honda and are awaiting the outcome.

Customer comments alone do not make a scientific sampling, and that's why we use them in conjunction with other sources of information. Owner complaints, combined with inside information found in service bulletins, are a good starting point to cut through the automakers' hyperbole and to get a glimpse of reality.

This guide emphasizes those important new features that add to a vehicle's safety, reliability, road performance, and comfort, and it points out those changes that are merely gadgets and styling revisions. Also noted are important changes to be made in the future, including the ending of model lines. In addition to the "Recommended" or "Not Recommended" rating (the current year's rating is reflected in the number of stars beside the vehicle's name), *Lemon-Aid* summarizes each vehicle's strong and weak points.

What the Ratings Mean

Recommended

This rating indicates a "Best Buy," and it's almost exclusively the domain of Asian automakers. Interestingly, some vehicles that are identical but marketed and serviced by different automakers, like the Ford Ranger and Mazda B-series pickups, may have different ratings. This variation occurs because servicing and after-warranty assistance may be better within one dealer network than another.

Recommended vehicles usually combine a high level of crashworthiness with good road performance, few safety-related complaints, decent reliability, and a better-than-average resale value. Servicing is readily available, and parts are inexpensive and easy to find.

Above Average

Vehicles in this class are pretty good choices. They aren't perfect, but they're often more reasonably priced than their competition. Most vehicles in this category have quality construction, good durability, and plenty of safety features as standard equipment. On the downside, they may have expensive parts and servicing, too many safety-related complaints, or only satisfactory warranty performance—one or all of which may have disqualified them from the Recommended category.

Average

Vehicles in this group have some deficiencies or flaws that make them a second choice. In many cases, certain components are prone to premature wear or breakdown, or some other aspect of long-term ownership is problematic. An Average rating can also be attributed to such factors as substandard assembly quality, the lack of a solid long-term reliability record, a number of safety-related complaints, or some flaw in the parts and service network.

Below Average

This rating category denotes an unreliable vehicle that may have also had a poor safety record. Improvements may have been made to enhance durability or safety. An extended warranty is advised.

 ### Not Recommended

Chances of having major breakdowns or safety-related failures are omnipresent. Inadequate road performance and poor dealer service, among other factors, can make owning one of these vehicles a traumatic and expensive experience.

Vehicles that have not been on the road long enough to assess, or that are sold in such small numbers that owner feedback is insufficient, are either Not Recommended or left unrated.

Model Features and Model History

These sections outline the vehicle's specifications and the differences between model years. The "Model History" section provides information on the evolution of the vehicle, including redesigns and modifications.

Technical data

Note that towing capacities differ depending on the kind of powertrain/suspension package or towing package you buy. Remember that there's a difference between how a vehicle is rated for cargo capacity or payload and how heavy a boat or trailer it can pull.

In the ratings, cargo capacity is measured with the vehicle's rear seat up and expressed in cubic feet. With the rear seat folded or removed, the cargo capacity becomes much larger. The gross vehicle weight rating (GVWR) is the vehicle's own weight plus the weight of the maximum load it's rated to carry. Subtracting the curb weight from the GVWR gives you the vehicle's maximum payload capacity.

Cost analysis

Each vehicle's manufacturer's suggested retail price (MSRP) is given, and *Lemon-Aid* also tells you what percentage of a vehicle's cost is the dealer's markup. Bargain the markup down by half the amount or more. Other charges, such as pre-delivery inspection (PDI) and transportation, can also be reduced by at least 50 percent. The ongoing discount war means the markup will be even lower this year. Alternately, if you can get a copy of the Canadian invoice price (look at *www.carhelpcanada.com* or *www.carcostcanada.com*), offer a price that is comparable to what the U.S. employee discount percentage would be (check U.S. automakers' websites).

GM fired the opening salvo in June 2005 when it extended huge employee discounts to all buyers in the States ("Employee Discount for Everyone"). The price-cutting was substantial and successful—it pushed GM's U.S. market share from May 2005's 26 percent to 30.3 percent in June, a figure that hadn't been seen since September 2004.

Through August of 2006, auto sales in Canada were booming due to our sizzling resource economy and solid housing market. On the other hand, U.S. sales continued their decline: Total American sales were down by 5 percent, while the Canadian year-to-date total gained 0.4 percent. The U.S. sales decline was led by a 12 percent decline for Ford U.S.A.—contrasting with a 28.6 percent rise for Ford in Canada. Consequently, Chrysler, Ford, and GM will continue discounting to keep their share of the market in both countries; however, Canadian rebates and discounts won't be quite as generous as those given out in the States.

Toyota had record sales on both sides of the border in 2006, with huge discounts tied to its aggressive end-of-model-year sales, the popularity of its more fuel-efficient hybrids, and the launching of a number of improved models. European automakers are setting up their own incentive programs in the fall, led by Volkswagen. These sales incentives are expected to rely heavily on discounts, low leasing charges, and end-of-the-year sales.

Canadian dealers of all makes are clamouring for deep discounts because they fear the sales surge may be soon followed by weaker sales in the late fall. Additionally, buyers see the American discount percentages and want to apply them to Canadian prices, so dealers who don't offer similar price cuts fear they will lose sales.

The price cuts on 2006 and 2007 models can be found on most automakers' websites. And a full analysis of discounts offered in Canada versus the listed manufacturer's suggested retail price (MSRP) can be downloaded in PDF form from *OnTheHoist.com*.

Says Kurt Binnie at *OnTheHoist.com*:

> By releasing the employee pricing to the general public, GM is providing a benchmark against which all of their car sales can be held until they change their pricing model. This could have ramifications that last far beyond the obvious "I bought it this month instead of in the next few months" impact this promotion will have on sales. Now

the general public knows that a large SUV can be a $10,000 USD money-maker and what all of the new models are worth with some hard bargaining...

 ## Quality and Reliability

Lemon-Aid bases its quality and reliability evaluations on owner comments, confidential technical service bulletins (TSBs), and government reports from NHTSA safety complaint files, among other sources. We also draw on the knowledge and expertise of professionals working in the automotive marketplace, including mechanics and fleet owners.

As you read through the quality and reliability ratings (safety is more of a mixed bag), you'll quickly discover that most Asian automakers are far ahead of DaimlerChrysler, Ford, GM, and European manufacturers in maintaining a high level of quality control in their vehicles. Although GM's SUV and minivan quality control has improved a bit as of late, you wouldn't believe it after looking over Silverado/Sierra truck complaints recorded by NHTSA at *www.nhtsa.dot.gov/cars/ problems/complain*. The redesigned 2007 trucks will likely be just as failure-prone, with new problems joining the old ones.

The following legend is used to show a vehicle's relative degree of overall reliability. The numbers lighten as the rating becomes more positive:

❶	❷	❸	❹	❺
Unacceptable	Below Average	Average	Above Average	Excellent

Warranty performance

I'm more impressed by performance than promise. A manufacturer's warranty is a legal commitment that the product it sells will perform in the normal and customary manner for which it's designed. It's an important factor in this edition's ratings, and a warranty is judged by how fairly it's applied—not by what it promises.

For example, Ford and General Motors are stricter in their warranty and extended warranty payouts than Chrysler or the Asian automakers. Europeans are the worst—they often demonstrate a scornful arrogance when customers question the quality or reliability of their products. The fact that Volkswagen Canada operates mostly out of the States adds another layer of indifference to the equation in Canada—as seen in its recent warranty-extension debacle over ignition coil failures and its reluctant admission that VW engines were afflicted with oil sludge.

Chrysler's pullback from its 7-year/115,000 km powertrain warranty to 5 years/100,000 km starting with its 2005 models is worrisome. In the past, the company's automatic transmission and engine failures have clustered around the 5-year mark, often forcing owners with shorter warranties to pay up to $3,000 to fix what are essentially factory defects.

Smart shoppers have noted this shift to less warranty coverage and are paying a premium for 2003 and 2004 models carrying unexpired powertrain warranties. Similar powertrain warranties sold by independent agencies often cost between $1,500 and $2,000. Vehicles with less warranty coverage are worth less, says Charlie Vogelheim, executive editor of the *Kelley Blue Book*:

> I will say that a vehicle under warranty is worth more than a vehicle that's not. That's a known fact. And we always see a marked drop in vehicle value once it falls out of warranty, either by calendar or by miles.

Besides protecting owners from costly powertrain repairs, manufacturers' warranties are particularly important in covering expensive computer hardware and software defects. Considering that the typical passenger car uses 70 or more tiny, powerful on-board computers that control key components—such as safety devices and the engine, transmission, emissions-control, and fuel-delivery systems—failures will likely occur more frequently as these electronic systems become more sophisticated.

European automakers like Mercedes, BMW, and VW admit that they've been hit hard by electronic glitches related to computer malfunctions, and IBM estimates that automakers generally spend $2–$3 billion a year fixing software problems.

 ## Road (and Off-Road) Performance

Off-roading requires sufficient low-range power (torque) and lots of ground clearance, which can make a vehicle more likely to tip. The suspension has to be adequate to take the punishment of off-roading challenges. ABS can be hazardous when used off-road, because you can't lock the brakes to build up a vehicle-decelerating wedge of earth in front of the wheels. Consequently, when the ABS sensors kick in to prevent wheel lock-up, it seems as if you have no brakes at all. This is especially evident when descending a hill, where the driver is forced to shift into low gear and reduce speed to a crawl. Stability-control is another feature that may promise much more than it delivers on some models (early BMWs, for example).

 ## Safety Summary

Some of the main features weighed in the safety ratings are a model's crashworthiness and insurance claims experience (as assessed by NHTSA and various insurers' groups, including the Highway Loss Data Institute and the IIHS), the availability of standard safety features, and front and rearward visibility. Also listed here are summaries of safety-related complaints that will astound and worry you. Many of the quotes in this section are taken from NHTSA's complaints database.

Front and side crash protection figures are taken from NHTSA's New Car Assessment Program. Vehicles are crashed into a fixed barrier, head-on, at 56 km/h (35 mph). NHTSA uses star rankings to express the likelihood of the belted occupants being seriously injured. The higher the number of stars, the greater the crash protection. NHTSA's side crash test represents an intersection-type collision with a 1,368 kg (3,015 lb.) barrier moving at 62 km/h (38.5 mph) into a standing vehicle. To replicate the front of a car, the moving barrier is covered with material that has "give."

NHTSA COLLISION RATINGS: CHANCE OF SERIOUS INJURY		
	FRONT	SIDE
5	10% or less	5% or less
4	11% to 20%	6% to 10%
3	21% to 35%	11% to 20%
2	36% to 45%	21% to 25%
1	46% or greater	26% or greater

NHTSA ROLLOVER RATINGS: CHANCE OF TIPPING OVER	
	ROLLOVER RISK
5	Less than 10%
4	Between 10% and 20%
3	Between 20% and 30%
2	Between 30% and 40%
1	Greater than 40%

IIHS rates head-restraint, frontal offset, and side crash protection as "good," "acceptable," "marginal," or "poor." In the Institute's 64 km/h (40 mph) offset test, 40 percent of the total width of each vehicle strikes a barrier on the driver's side. The barrier's deformable face is made of an aluminum honeycomb, which makes the forces in the test similar to those involved in a frontal offset crash between two vehicles of the same weight, each going just less than 64 km/h.

The 50 km/h (31 mph) side-impact test performed by IIHS is carried out at a slower speed than the NHTSA test, but it uses a barrier with a front end shaped to simulate the typical front end of a pickup or SUV. The Institute also includes the degree of head injury in its ratings.

Secret Warranties/Internal Bulletins/Service Tips

A *Lemon-Aid* exclusive, confidential technical service bulletins (TSBs) are listed for each rated model to give readers the ammunition to get free repairs.

Some vehicles have more TSBs than others, but this doesn't necessarily mean they're lemons. It may be that the listed problems affect only a small number of vehicles, or that problems are minor and easily corrected. TSBs should also be used to verify that a problem was correctly diagnosed, the correct upgraded replacement part was used, and the billed labour time was fair.

Costs

Here we list the manufacturer's suggested retail price (MSRP) for standard models at press time, the price's negotiability, and the range of the dealer's markup, including freight and other added fees.

If the dealer's price is more than 3 percent higher than the price indicated in *Lemon-Aid*, ask for a copy of the manufacturer's notice to the dealer of the MSRP increase. You can confirm the MSRP figure by accessing each manufacturer's website, or by visiting *www.carcostcanada.com*. Once you discover the latest MSRP, negotiate a reduction, keeping in mind whether the price is "firm" or "negotiable."

SPORT-UTILITY VEHICLES

Mercedes Hits a Pothole

Spend $25,000 on a car that doesn't run the way you expect it to, and you get pretty angry. Spend $50,000 or $100,000, and you get really angry. Just listen to the anguished howls of Mercedes-Benz owners on websites like *troublebenz.com*, *lemonmb.com*, and *www.mercedesproblems.com* as they vent about the latest mishap to afflict their Benzes. Depending on the model, the complaints range from faulty key fobs and leaky sunroofs to balky electronics that leave drivers and their passengers stranded. Regardless of the severity, a single sentiment runs through the gripes: This shouldn't be happening to a Mercedes.

ALEX TAYLOR III
FORTUNE
OCTOBER 13, 2003

Large SUVs—Low Prices

Although insurance premiums have moderated, high fuel costs and interest rates continue to savage full- and mid-sized SUV sales, forcing Detroit's Big Three to drop negotiated prices by up to tens of thousands of dollars and causing the market to shift to downsized and "crossover" models. Automakers say reduced prices are only temporary, but independent industry sources believe lower "real" prices will continue well into the new year due to deep discounting led by DaimlerChrysler, an over-supply of unpopular models, and shoppers' demands for sweeter rebates and other sales incentives.

Large SUVs, like the Ford Expedition and Excursion, the Jeep Grand Cherokee, and the GM Suburban, Yukon, and Tahoe, are selling for a song—three-year-old vehicles are worth less than 50 percent of their original MSRP. Beside depreciation and steep gas prices, SUV shoppers are put off by high insurance costs and the increasingly complex mechanical and electronic systems associated with these Goliaths that compromise both their safety and reliability.

Dealers are responding with $5,000–$10,000 discounts on leftover 2006 and 2007 models, while used prices spiral downward to match the incentives. But some behemoths like the Ford Excursion, GM Suburban, and Hummer H1 can't even be given away and, therefore, have been discontinued. Furthermore, the Ford Expedition, Lincoln Navigator and Aviator, and Mercedes M series are at the top of the hit list—even though Mercedes-Benz is in denial that its sport-utility models are in peril. In fact, no SUV larger than Honda's CR-V or Toyota's RAV4 has a secure future.

Small sport wagons—like the Ford Escape, Honda CR-V, Hyundai Tucson, Mazda Tribute, and Toyota RAV4—are doing well this year because they offer more reasonable prices, better fuel economy, and easier handling than do the larger SUVs. Shoppers have simply downsized their choices rather than switching to another kind of vehicle. Instead of scintillating 0–100 km/h performance, buyers are looking for fuel economy bragging rights and innovative convenience and safety features.

Ford's small Escape SUV (above) and the identical Mazda Tribute are two successful Detroit models that perform well, are fairly reliable, and aren't overpriced.

And don't forget the fastest growing segment of SUVs: "crossover" car-based sport-utilities and tall wagons that take on SUV attributes and blend cargo-carrying versatility with carlike comfort and handling. Prime examples of these fusions are the Chrysler Pacifica, Honda Pilot, Mitsubishi Outlander, Nissan Xterra, Pontiac Vibe, Subaru Forester, and Toyota Matrix.

Car- or Truck-Based?

SUV buyers must decide whether they would rather have the ruggedness and increased towing capability of a truck-based SUV or the ride comfort, more predictable handling, and increased crashworthiness of a car-based version or a crossover. For example, the car-based Chrysler Pacifica is much closer to being a station wagon than what many of us think of as an SUV. It has one of the best highway rides of any SUV, plus exceptional handling and one of the lowest rollover risks among SUVs tested. Furthermore, its fuel economy is almost equal to that of a minivan or large sedan. Is it any wonder that sales of truck-based SUVs have been flat for five years, while sales of car-based and crossover vehicles have grown steadily?

Don't assume that all truck-based models have similar towing capabilities. The Chevy Tahoe/GMC Yukon and Ford Expedition can tow more than 4 tons. Chevrolet's TrailBlazer has more than double the torque of the Buick Rendezvous, whose towing capacity maxes out at 1,600 kg (3,500 lb.) with the optional towing package; the standard towing limit is just 1 ton.

The United States military made its contribution to the SUV craze with its Jeep lineup (now a division of DaimlerChrysler) and the Hummer (now marketed by General Motors). Imagine, what was designed for use as a military vehicle during World War II has now become the toy of baby-boomer G.I. Joes who miss the irony of a German company (Daimler-Benz), once part of Hitler's war machine, selling Jeeps to Americans:

> Daimler-Benz avidly supported Nazism and in return received arms contracts and tax breaks that enabled it to become one of the world's leading industrial concerns. (Between 1932 and 1940 production grew by 830 percent.) During the war the company used thousands of slaves and forced laborers including Jews, foreigners, and POWs.
>
> *THE STRAIGHT DOPE*
> *www.straightdope.com/classics/a5_078.html*

Now, a final word for that 5 percent of us who do enjoy off-roading. Listing "adventure" as the top reason for choosing SUVs, buyers stress that they expect outstanding off-road performance combined with good handling, a comfortable ride, good traction, and high ground clearance.

Don't be a sucker. You want lots of off-road comfort? Stick to Montreal's Beaver Lake or Vancouver's Stanley Park.

A soft suspension and precision handling are inversely proportional to true off-road capability, though some automakers are providing vehicles that offer a good compromise. Bear in mind that real off-roading takes place at about 15 km/h and can be a kidney-pounding, white-knuckle experience (kind of like driving early MGs, Triumphs, and Ladas).

Hatchback and Wagon Alternatives

Hatchbacks and wagons can be good alternatives to SUVs if you don't need to accommodate more than five passengers or carry very much cargo. Some pros and cons you may wish to consider are outlined in the chart "Wagons versus SUVs."

WAGONS VERSUS SUVS

WAGON ADVANTAGES

- Reasonable pricing
- Low rollover risk
- Good handling, braking
- Many advanced safety features
- Good fuel economy
- Low step-in height

SUV ADVANTAGES

- Competitive prices and slow depreciation on smaller models
- Good front visibility and predictable driving in winter and on rough terrain
- Seat five to nine passengers with lots of seating flexibility
- Lots of cargo room and easy loading and unloading
- 907–2,270 kg towing capability
- Truck frame good for heavy-duty off-roading
- Car-based models are relatively fuel-efficient and easy to handle when compared to minivans and trucks
- Versatile performance
- Post-1997 models have safety features similar to those found in cars
- Impressive crashworthiness scores for car-based models

WAGON DISADVANTAGES

- Lower view of the road in front
- Less passenger, cargo room
- Difficult to access small third-row seats; limited seating flexibility
- Low towing capability
- Limited off-roading, even with AWD

SUV DISADVANTAGES

- Overpriced, fuel-thirsty, with high insurance premiums
- Accessories, such as running boards, roll bars, and sophisticated anti-theft systems, are expensive but essential
- Inferior handling, rough riding, moderate to very high rollover risk
- Increased risk of injury to children
- Inferior braking
- Truck frames may be deadly to small cars in multi-vehicle crashes, and in crashes with other trucks
- Awkward to enter and exit, difficult to access third row seats, smaller rear doors, and high step-in height
- Lower crashworthiness scores for truck-based models
- Good off-road performers are poorly suited for highway or city use, and vice versa

Part- or Full-Time 4×4?

There are two types of 4×4 vehicles: part-time and full-time. Part-time 4×4 should be engaged when roads are wet, muddy, or snow covered. The four wheels are locked together to turn at the same speed. On dry pavement, driving in 4×4 mode may strain the drivetrain and damage the driveline components (check the owner's manual).

Full-time 4×4 (also called "all-wheel drive," or AWD) is a more sophisticated system that permits driving on any surface, all the time. A centre differential lets all four wheels turn at different speeds. If front or rear wheels lose traction, sensors send more power to those wheels. Most buyers prefer the convenience of all-wheel drive, and most automakers are moving in that direction.

Keep in mind that while a 4×4 drivetrain will help you keep traction on muddy, snowy roads, it does little to aid cornering ability and is practically useless in improving braking.

 ## Safety

One of the main reasons buyers choose sport-utility vehicles is for the safety advantages they offer. The large windshield and high seating give you a commanding view of the road ahead, though your rear vision may be obstructed by side pillars, rear head restraints, or the spare tire hanging off the back end. As we react more slowly with age, this increased forward visibility comes in handy (a few extra seconds of warning can make a big difference). Improvements have also been made with three-point seat belts in the front and rear, seat belt pretensioners, optional adjustable brake and accelerator pedals, four-wheel anti-lock brakes, electronic stability control, a high centre brake light, adjustable head restraints on all seatbacks, side head-protecting airbags, side-door beams, and reinforced roofs to protect occupants in rollovers.

Most large SUVs will protect you fairly well in a frontal collision—while creaming whoever hits you. But rollovers are an ever-present safety risk, particularly with early production models that were made through the mid-1990s (we're talking Suzuki, Isuzu, and Ford Bronco) and that poster child for rollovers, Ford's 1992–2004 Explorer. SUVs with electronic stability-control reduce this hazard.

 ## Reliability and Quality

In the last decade, many domestic and imported SUVs were rushed to market with serious quality and performance deficiencies. Mercedes' 1997–2005 M-Class luxury sport-utilities, for example, are nowhere near as reliable as Jeep's entry-level Liberty and the SUVs produced by Asian automakers.

DaimlerChrysler, Jeep, and Ford have a long way to go to close the quality gap. Dodge's Durango has a barely acceptable reliability score. Jeep's Cherokee and Grand Cherokee have been afflicted with serious powertrain, AC, brake, and body defects, and the new Jeep Commander is unproven. And don't forget the Ford Explorer, the most popular SUV ever produced. It has a terrible reputation for poor quality control and reliability, plus it shows signs of a plethora of safety-related factory mistakes, highlighted by sudden, unintended acceleration, rollovers (a problem first raised with the previous Bronco series), and under-hood fires.

GM's post-2000 SUVs are the best of Detroit's worst. Their relatively recent redesigns have improved overall safety and performance, but reliability is still the pits, with serious engine, transmission, and fit-and-finish defects. After three to five years of use (about when the warranty ends), buyers would be wise to get an extended warranty or dump these vehicles.

SPORT-UTILITY RATINGS

RECOMMENDED

Chrysler TJ, YJ Wrangler (2003–07)
Ford Escape/Mazda Tribute (2005–07)
Honda CR-V (2002–07)
Honda Pilot (2003–07)

Hyundai Santa Fe (2007)
Hyundai Tucson (2007)
Toyota RAV4 (2006–07)
Toyota Sequoia (2005–07)

ABOVE AVERAGE

Acura MDX (2006–07)
Acura RDX (2007)
Chrysler Liberty (2005–07)
Ford Escape/Mazda Tribute (2004)
Ford Escape Hybrid (2005–07)
Honda CR-V (1997–2001)
Honda Element (2003–07)
Hyundai Santa Fe (2001–06)
Infiniti FX35, FX45 (2003–07)
Infiniti QX4 (1997–2003)
Kia Sportage (2005–07)
Lexus GX 470, LX 470 (1998–2007)

Lexus RX 300, RX 330 (1999–2003)
Mitsubishi Outlander (2007)
Nissan Pathfinder (2006–07)
Nissan Murano (2005–07)
Nissan Xterra (2005–07)
Nissan X-Trail (2005–07)
Subaru Forester (2006–07)
Toyota Highlander (2001–07)
Toyota Highlander Hybrid (2006–07)
Toyota RAV4 (1997–2005)
Toyota 4Runner (1996–2007)
Toyota Sequoia (2001–04)

AVERAGE

Acura MDX (2001–05)
BMW X3 (2004–07)
BMW X5 (2007)
Chrysler Cherokee, Grand Cherokee (2002–07)
Chrysler Liberty (2002–04)
Chrysler Pacifica (2004–07)
Chrysler TJ, YJ Wrangler (1987–2002)
Ford Escape/Mazda Tribute (2002–03)
General Motors Escalade, EXT,
    Denali (1995–2007)
General Motors Suburban, Yukon, Tahoe
    (2002–07)
General Motors/Suzuki Tracker/Sidekick, Vitara,
    Grand Vitara, XL-7 (1994–2007)

Hyundai Tucson (2006)
Kia Sorrento (2005–07)
Lexus LX 450 (1997)
Lexus RX 300, RX 330, RX 350 (2004–07)
Mitsubishi Endeavour (2004–07)
Mitsubishi Montero (2004–06)
Mitsubishi Outlander (2004–06)
Nissan Armada (2007)
Nissan Pathfinder (1990–2006)
Nissan Xterra (2003–04)
Subaru Forester (1994–2005)
Subaru Impreza (1997–2007)
Toyota 4Runner (1986–95)

BELOW AVERAGE

BMW X5 (2000–06)
Ford Aviator, Explorer, Mountaineer, Sport,
    Sport Trac (2003–07)
Ford Escape/Mazda Tribute (2001)
Ford Excursion (2000–05)
Ford Expedition (1997–2007)
General Motors Aztek, Rendezvous (2001–07)

Infiniti QX56 (2004–07)
Kia Sorento (2003–04)
Kia Sportage (2000–02)
Mitsubishi Montero (2003)
Mitsubishi Outlander (2003)
Nissan Armada (2005–06)
Nissan Murano (2003–04)

General Moters Envoy, TrailBlazer,
    Rainier (2002–07)
General Motors Suburban,
    Yukon, Tahoe (1995–2001)
Hyundai Tucson (2005)

Nissan Pathfinder (1987–89)
Nissan Xterra (2000–02)
Subaru Tribeca (2006–07)
Subaru WRX (2002–07)

NOT RECOMMENDED

Chrysler Cherokee, Grand Cherokee
    (1985–2001)
Chrysler Commander (2006–07)
Chrysler Compass, Patriot (2007)
Chrysler Durango (1998–2007)
Ford Aviator, Explorer, Mountaineer,
    Sport, Sport Trac (1991–2002)
Ford Navigator (1997–2007)
General Motors Blazer, Envoy, Jimmy
    (1995–2005)

General Motors Equinox (2005–07)
General Motors Suburban, Yukon,
    Tahoe (1985–94)
Hyundai Veracruz (2007)
Lexus RX 400h (2006–07)
Nissan Armada (2004)
Saab 9-7X (2005–07)
Saturn Vue (2002–07)

Note: Additional models may be found in Appendix II.

Acura

| **MDX** | ★★★★ |

RATING: Above Average (2006–07); Average (2001–05). Why spend $52,500 for a warmed-over Odyssey when you can do better with the cheaper and larger Honda Pilot? Sure, it has a few less horses, but odds are you won't feel it. **Strong points:** Drives and rides like a car; good acceleration with plenty of low-end grunt; well-appointed, roomy interior with a standard third-row seat. Scheduled to get a fuel-frugal engine cylinder deactivation. **Weak points:** No low-speed transfer case; transmission failures on early models; stability-control on 2001–03 models doesn't deliver promised performance; rivals have better designs. Lots of road, drivetrain, and exhaust system noise; on early models, imprecise steering has insufficient feedback; third-row seat is adequate for small adults or children only; earlier models have a tacky-looking interior with lots of plastic garnishing;

2007 TECHNICAL DATA

POWERTRAIN (REAR-DRIVE)
Engine: 3.7L V6 (300 hp); Transmission: 5-speed auto.

DIMENSION/CAPACITY
Passengers: 2/3/2; Wheelbase: 108.3 in.; H: 68.2/L: 190.7/W: 78.5 in.; Headroom F/R: 4.0/4.0 in.; Legroom F/R: 41/30 in.; Cargo volume: 42 cu. ft.; Fuel tank: 72.7L/premium; Tow limit: 5,000 lb.; Load capacity: 1,160 lb.; GVWR: 5,732 lb.; Turning circle: 40 ft.; Ground clearance: 5 in.; Weight: 4,541 lb.

problematic fit and finish; climate controls are difficult to access and indicator lights wash out in sunlight; navigation system isn't user-friendly; lots of wind noise (many owners complain of poor body construction); high MSRP, freight/PDI charges are way out of line, and no haggle policy borders on price-fixing; mediocre real-world fuel economy, and requires premium fuel; limited seatback adjustment and thigh support; steering wheel can't be adjusted for reach, forcing small drivers to sit perilously close to the airbag housing; and mediocre braking performance. **New for 2007:** A redesigned 2007 MDX with a lower and wider stance, a more powerful engine, and possibly a fuel-saving cylinder deactivation.

MODEL HISTORY: Introduced as a 2001 model, the MDX initially carried a 212-hp 6-cylinder engine. It seats seven and is longer than the rival five-seat BMW X5 and Lexus RX 300. Its second- and third-row bench seats conveniently fold flat with the load floor (the last row is suitable for small children only). **2002**—Some noise-reduction measures. **2003**—More power, a new transmission, and a standard anti-skid system; a Honda clone called the Pilot is introduced. **2004**—Updated styling, a tire-pressure monitor, and head-protecting side curtain airbags. **2005**—A larger fuel tank, an improved hands-free cell phone link, and a standard CD changer. **2006**—No significant changes.

COST ANALYSIS: Priced at $52,500, the 2007 is practically identical to the 2006 ($51,600). The 2007's extra horsepower is a dealmaker. **Best alternatives:** You want comparable performance for about $12,000 less? Try a Honda Pilot (the MDX's cheaper cousin) for its additional passenger/cargo hauling capability, or a Nissan Xterra or Toyota Highlander. The Volvo XC90 and ML320/350/500 have very good cargo room with all the rows down, but they have neither comparable cargo room behind the second row nor a comparable level of quality control. **Rebates:** Look for $7,000+ rebates on the 2006 this year and $5,000 on the 2007 models early next year as the competition heats up. **Delivery/PDI:** $1,430. **Warranty:** Bumper-to-bumper 3 years/60,000 km; powertrain 5 years/100,000 km; rust perforation 5 years/unlimited km. **Supplementary warranty:** Not needed. **Options:** Vehicle comes fully loaded, except for the non-essential navigation system, rear backup camera, and DVD player. Replace the stock Goodyear tires with Michelins or their equivalent (see *tirerack.com* owner reports) for a better, quieter ride. Change only the radio speakers for improved audio quality. The roof crossrails aren't adjustable and are a bit wider than those on other SUVs, making it difficult to get roof cargo carriers that will fit. **Depreciation:** Lower than average. **Insurance cost:** Much higher than average. **Parts supply/cost:** Parts are reasonably priced and easily found in the Odyssey/Honda generic parts bin. **Annual maintenance cost:** Less than average. **Highway/city fuel economy:** 10.4/13.9 L/100 km, but many owners say their fuel consumption is much higher. Cylinder deactivation is a definite plus.

 QUALITY/RELIABILITY: Reliability shouldn't be a problem, unless you actually believe this vehicle can go off-road. If so, make sure you get an extended warranty and find a friendly garage. **Owner complaints:** Automatic transmission and front spring failures; repair of the recalled transmission not effective; alloy wheel cracks; a rotten-egg exhaust smell; engine hesitation around 60 km/h; moonroof leaks water; an exhaust droning noise when underway; a metallic clanging and rumbling heard at 2000 rpm; squeaks and rattles (dash, door lock, and tailpipe); brake-caliper clicking and clunking; gas tank sloshing; wind noise; and a high-speed harmonic drone. The auto AC mode is slow to cool the car in stop-and-go driving; AM reception is poor; Bose radio may have too much bass; driver's seat-back doesn't go vertical enough for some; seats have insufficient thigh and back support; and seat memory settings are gradually lost. **Warranty performance:** Average.

 ROAD PERFORMANCE: Acceleration/torque: Smooth, quiet, and sustained acceleration; one of the best among V6 competitors (0–100 km/h: 8.7 seconds). The 2003 model has 20 extra horses. **Transmission:** Flawless shifting with the only trans-axle available, the 5-speed automatic. **Steering:** Vague, with insufficient feedback. **Routine handling:** A bit cumbersome, particularly when cornering, as body lean becomes more evident. This unsteady behaviour becomes worse as the speed increases or if the steering correction is more severe. Say Consumers Union testers: "The MDX does not inspire confidence in emergency handling, even with its new stability-control." Firm suspension also jostles occupants when passing over uneven pavement (the Lexus RX 300/330 and Toyota Sequoia handle this better). The lack of a low-speed transfer case limits this SUV's off-roading prowess. **Braking:** Unimpressive; they're difficult to modulate until you adapt to their sensitivity with a lighter foot.

 SAFETY SUMMARY: Airbags: Front and side. **ABS:** Standard; disc/disc. **Head restraints F/R:** 2001–02: ★★★; 2003–04: ★★★★. **Visibility F/R:** ★★★★.

SAFETY COMPLAINTS: 2001—Chronic stalling on the highway. • Many automatic transmission breakdowns: Automatic transmission suddenly downshifted, causing loss of control; front wheels suddenly locked up because of transmission failure. • Seat belts won't hold a child booster seat securely. • Airbag failed to deploy. **2002**—Sudden acceleration. • Transmission can be shifted from Park to Reverse without key in ignition. • Cell phones or laptops in the cabin can disable the airbag feature:

> Consumer stated whenever an electric device like a cell phone or laptop computer was used, the airbags deactivated until the device was turned off. Consumer felt as though he didn't have any control over the airbag system. The dealer stated a cell phone or laptop could not be on or near the seats.

• Seat belts tighten progressively once buckled. **2002–03**—Transmission failures. **2003**—Airbag failed to deploy. • Front spring breakage. • Sudden acceleration. • Navigation system gives incorrect information. • Seat belt crosses at driver's neck.

• Front seat belt locks up. **2004**—Tire slipped off the rim and vehicle went out of control, despite stability-control feature. • Vehicle continued in Reverse after it was shifted into Drive. • Passenger injured by deployment of side airbag:

> During a collision the passenger fell to the side window and airbags deployed, resulting in head injuries. Passenger was transported by ambulance to the hospital.

2005—Chronic stalling and hard starts. • Airbag malfunction warning light constantly illuminated.

Secret Warranties/Internal Bulletins/Service Tips

2001—Throttle bracket buzzes or rattles. • Clunking when braking or accelerating, thought to be caused by front lower control arm. • Noisy power-steering pump. • Supplementary restraint system (SRS) unit internal failure. • Product update/secret warranty relative to the seat belt harness. • Second-row seat may not fold down or recline. • Water dripping from the outside mirror. • Loose rear wiper arm. • Loose or detached seatback panel covered by a TSB. **2001–02**—V6 engine oil leaks. • Missing speed-sensor plug. • Brief hesitation when accelerating. • Cranks, but won't start. • Loose driver's seat. • Thumping from sloshing fuel. • Under-hood buzzing or rattling. • Booming noise from rear of vehicle at 90–100 km/h. • Squeaking noise from the middle roof area and the moonroof. • Broken seat belt tongue-stopper button. **2001–03**—Faulty remote audio controls. • Dash or front strut creaking or ticking. **2001–04**—Noise and judder from the rear when turning. • Clunking brakes (see bulletin). • Buzzing from the front blower motor. • Glove box light stays on. **2002–03**—Remedy for front damper noise. **2003**—Sunroof water leaks will be fixed for free under TSB #03-018, issued June 2003. **2004**—Correction for an exhaust system drone. • Subwoofer rattling noise. **2004–05**—Free tire valve cap replacement.

REAR BRAKE CLUNK NOISE	
BULLETIN NO.: 04-009	DATE: MARCH 23, 2004

2001–04 MDX

SYMPTOM: The rear brake calipers clunk when you first apply the brakes after changing the direction of the vehicle.

PROBABLE CAUSE: The outer shims on the rear brake pads do not allow the pads to slide easily when you press the brake pedal. This causes the outer pad to hit hard during a change of direction, resulting in a clunk.

MDX PROFILE

	2001	2002	2003	2004	2005	2006
Cost Price ($) (firm)						
MDX (25%)	47,000	48,000	49,000	50,300	50,800	51,600

Used Values ($)

MDX ▲	21,000	26,000	30,000	37,000	41,000	—
MDX ▼	19,000	24,000	28,000	35,000	39,000	—

Reliability	④	⑤	⑤	⑤	⑤	—
Crash Safety (F)	—	⑤	④	⑤	⑤	⑤
Side	—	⑤	⑤	⑤	⑤	⑤
Offset	⑤	⑤	⑤	⑤	⑤	⑤
Rollover	—	④	④	—	④	④

BMW

X3	★ ★ ★

RATING: Average (2004–07). BMW downsizes and disappoints, although the 6-cylinder engine enhances overall performance. **Strong points:** High seating gives a good view of the road; a new X3 costs $14,000 less than an X5; the 3.0L engine, optional until this year, provides an impressive power range and towing capability for a compact SUV; a full complement of high-tech safety features. **Weak points:** The 2.5L engine is underpowered; overall highway performance isn't up to the 3 Series standard. Ride is hard and choppy. Bland styling, and lacks many standard features found on other $50,000 compact SUVs. Long shifter throws; slower and less precise steering than the competition; heavier and about 15 percent less fuel efficient than a Lexus RX; cargo-carrying capacity can't touch the Honda CR-V or Ford Escape; doesn't project the same quality cachet as other BMWs; service bulletins show serious engine and automatic transmission failures on early models; and an excessively high freight and preparation charge. Incredibly, there have been no crashworthiness tests carried out yet. **New for 2007:** A major facelift—including front and rear styling; a cabin upgrade; and a standard twin-cam 3.0L inline 6-cylinder engine that produces 260 hp at 6600 rpm and 225 lb-ft of torque at 2500 rpm, an increase of 35 hp and 11 lb-ft of torque over the previous 3.0L. A 6-speed manual will be a standard feature, and a new 6-speed Steptronic automatic transmission will be offered as a no-cost option.

2007 TECHNICAL DATA

POWERTRAIN
Engine: 3.0L 6-cyl. (260 hp);
Transmissions: 6-speed man. • 6-speed Steptronic auto.

DIMENSION/CAPACITY
Passengers: 2/3; Wheelbase: 110 in.;
H: 65.9/L: 180/W: 73 in.; Headroom F/R: 4.0/3.0 in.; Legroom F/R: 42/27.5 in.; Cargo volume: 33 cu. ft.; Fuel tank: 67L/premium; Tow limit: 3,500 lb.; Load capacity: 1,005 lb.; GVWR: 4,993 lb.; Turning circle: 39 ft.; Ground clearance: 7.5 in.; Weight: 4,065 lb.

All ratings on a numbered scale where ⑤ is good and ❶ is bad. See page 220 for a more detailed description.

COST ANALYSIS: Be wary of the first-series 2004 X3; choose instead a $45,000 2007 model for a better-performing BMW. Also, stay away from the 2.5L powerplant, and hold out for the 3.0L, instead. **Best alternatives:** The Honda CR-V or Pilot, Infiniti FX35, Lexus RX series, and Nissan Murano. **Rebates:** Look for $3,000 rebates on leftover 2006s by year's end. **Delivery/PDI:** $1,595. **Warranty:** Bumper-to-bumper 4 years/80,000 km; rust perforation 12 years/unlimited km. **Supplementary warranty:** A good idea with the 2004 model. **Options:** The X3 gets an updated 3.0L inline 6-cylinder engine, which it shares with the 3 Series. It uses the latest technology, like variable valve timing, to deliver 260 hp—35 hp stronger than the engine in last year's model. A new 6-speed automatic transmission replaces the previous 5-speed as a no-cost option. A 6-speed manual transmission remains standard. High-intensity headlights may be too bright. **Depreciation:** Slower than average. **Insurance cost:** Higher than average. **Parts supply/cost:** Average. **Annual maintenance cost:** Higher-than-average repair costs with the first-year 2004s; average for later years. Cheaper independent garages won't touch these vehicles, adding to their servicing costs. **Highway/city fuel economy:** *2.5L 6-cyl.: 8.9/13.6 L/100 km; 3.0L 6-cyl.: 8.8/13.8 L/100 km.*

QUALITY/RELIABILITY: 2004 models appear to have serious quality and reliability problems, judging by BMW's internal service bulletins. **Warranty performance:** Better than average, probably because BMW is seeking increased market share for the X3.

ROAD PERFORMANCE: Acceleration/torque: BMW's smallest SUV offers a wimpy, torque-challenged 184-hp 2.5L and a better-performing 3.0L inline-six. **Transmission:** Power is handled smoothly in 3 Series fashion via a 6-speed manual and permanent all-wheel-drive system. **Steering:** Very responsive and precise. **Routine handling:** Very good, but the ride is a bit bumpy, making for constant steering corrections. Emergency handling is compromised by the X3's stiff suspension. **Braking:** Excellent.

SAFETY SUMMARY: Airbags: Standard. **ABS:** Standard; disc/disc. **Safety belt pretensioners:** Front. **Traction control:** Yes. **Head restraints F/R:** ★★★. **Visibility F/R:** ★★★★/★★★.

SAFETY COMPLAINTS: 2004—Vehicle suddenly accelerated and crashed through garage wall. • A faulty Steptronic system caused the vehicle to suddenly surge forward. • Automatic transmission wouldn't go into Drive after vehicle was parked overnight; can be shifted without first stepping on the brakes. • Multiple electronic problems (dash gauges, AC, and ignition system). • High-intensity headlights are too bright. • Vehicle doesn't come with a Door Ajar warning light or buzzer. • Original-equipment tires leak air. **2005**—Sudden acceleration. • The passenger-side airbag is often disabled because of a sensor failure.

Secret Warranties/Internal Bulletins/Service Tips

2004—Radio reception problems. • Delayed cold engagement of automatic transmission. • Engine head bolt threads pull out of block. • Engine cylinder head leaks (see bulletin). 2004–05—Noise emanating from the door frame area. 2005—Engine runs poorly due to faulty ignition coil. • Trunk lid won't latch. • Engine drivebelt tensioner noise. • Windshield whistling. • Panoramic-roof gurgling. • The AC produces a strong musty smell.

OIL LEAKAGE FROM CYLINDER HEAD

BULLETIN NO.: B11 201 04   DATE: FEBRUARY 4, 2004

LOW MILEAGE OIL LEAKAGE FROM CYLINDER HEAD
All with M54 Engine

CAUSE: Porosity in the cylinder head casting between the oil pressure supply passage and the spark plug tubes. Replace the cylinder head.

X3 PROFILE

	2004	2005	2006
Cost Price ($) (soft)			
X3 2.5i (23%)	44,600	44,800	44,800
X3 3.0i (25%)	49,800	49,900	50,100
Used Values ($)			
X3 2.5i ▲	33,000	41,000	
X3 2.5i ▼	31,000	39,000	—
X3 3.0i ▲	38,000	44,000	—
X3 3.0i ▼	36,000	42,000	—
Reliability	③	④	—

X5   ★★★

RATING: Average (2007). Below Average (2000–06). Way overrated by car journalists who enjoy the BMW cachet on BMW's dime. Sure, the X5 has lots of power and convenience features, but its high-speed performance isn't all that impressive. Quality control is still way below average, particularly when it comes to electronic hardware and program software (Mercedes and VW are also feeling the byte bite). **Strong points:** Rapid acceleration with plenty of torque in all gear ranges; nimble low-speed handling; good braking; first-class interior; a wide array of standard safety, performance, and convenience features; and a "good" crashworthiness rating from IIHS. **Weak points:** No low-range gearing for off-roading; high-speed handling seriously compromised by this wagon's choppy, unstable ride and excessive weight; lots of engine noise; complicated navigation system controls; tall step-up and narrow doorways; loading is made difficult by the high liftover; unusually small interior makes for limited rear-seat and cargo space (the small X3 and most competitors are roomier); atrocious premium fuel economy; and an unusually large number of safety-related recalls and owner complaints (confidential BMW service bulletins show manufacturing mistakes are the source of most problems). **New for 2007:** The car is slightly restyled. Next year it's likely to be longer, wider, and taller than the current model, and unlike the 2006 Mercedes M-Class, this X5 will offer the option of a third-row seat.

2007 TECHNICAL DATA

POWERTRAIN
Engines: 3.0L 6-cyl. (225 hp) • 4.4L V8 (315 hp) • 4.8L V8 (355 hp); Transmissions: 5-speed man. • 6-speed auto. • 6-speed manumatic

DIMENSION/CAPACITY
Passengers: 2/3; Wheelbase: 111 in.; H: 67/L: 184/W: 73.7 in.; Headroom F/R: 4.0/4.5 in.; Legroom F/R: 42/28.5 in.; Cargo volume: 35.5 cu. ft.; Fuel tank: 93L/premium; Tow limit: 5,000 lb.; Load capacity: 1,260 lb.; GVWR: 5,860 lb.; Turning circle: 40 ft.; Ground clearance: 7.5 in.; Weight: 4,652 lb.

MODEL HISTORY: 2001—A V8-powered X5 4.4i and 6-cylinder 3.0i edition debuted in Canada after a year in the States. **2002**—A high-performance 4.6is model gave BMW a high-performance counterpunch against Mercedes-Benz's ML 500/ML55 AMG. **2004**—New front-end styling, AWD system, and V8 engine; a high-performance model was added mid-year; and a standard 6-speed transmission was added.

COST ANALYSIS: This $59,400-to-start sport wagon isn't worth its high price, although some of the excess cost will be recovered through a higher-than-average resale value. Unless you want the fuel-thirsty 4.8L V8 ($98,100), stick with the 3.0L 6-cylinder. Be wary of the smaller V6 engine coupled with a manual transmission—clutch action is rough and hard to modulate. **Best alternatives:** When it comes to off-roading, the X5 is blown away by the prowess of the Toyota Land Cruiser or Lexus RX 300/330 and other less-expensive SUVs. Even Land Rover's Range Rover outperforms the X5 in off-road driving. Think seriously of getting a BMW 5 Series wagon for storage capability and performance. Forget Nissan's FX35 if you want a comfortable ride and lots of storage capacity. **Rebates:** Look for $5,000 rebates on leftover 2006s by year's end. **Delivery/PDI:** $1,795. **Warranty:** Bumper-to-bumper 4 years/80,000 km; rust perforation 12 years/unlimited km. **Supplementary warranty:** A good idea. **Options:** Rear-obstacle warning system and 5-speed automatic transmission with manual shift capability are worthwhile investments. Sport package low-profile tires will bounce you around on rough pavement. **Depreciation:** A bit slower than average. **Insurance cost:** Much higher than average. **Parts supply/cost:** Average. **Annual maintenance cost:** Predict higher-than-average repair costs, if owner complaints already recorded and dealership servicing costs for passenger cars are any indication. Cheaper independent garages won't touch these vehicles, adding to their servicing costs. **Highway/city fuel economy:** *6-cyl.:* 10.6/15.6 L/100 km; *V8:* 11.9/16.4 L/100 km.

QUALITY/RELIABILITY: Overall reliability has been quite poor, judging by owner complaints on the Internet (*www.roadfly.com*, among others) and by BMW's internal service bulletins. Aside from the X5's many recall campaigns, owners report a number of safety-related defects that are indicative of poor quality control. Many of the owner complaints go to the heart of the X5's reliability, as well as its overall safety. **Warranty performance:** Average. It would be comforting to see the company expend as much energy eliminating defects at the factory level.

ROAD PERFORMANCE: Acceleration/torque: Both the 6-cylinder and V8 provide acceptable acceleration. **Transmission:** Smooth and quiet shifting. **Steering:** Impressive steering is very responsive and accurate, though a bit heavy when parking. Power-adjustable steering wheel keeps small-statured drivers away from the airbag housing. **Routine handling:** Acceptable. Emergency handling, however, is quite poor. The ride is choppy, requiring constant steering corrections. The car doesn't inspire handling confidence when pushed; it seems ready to tip over, despite its stability-control feature. **Braking:** Excellent, with no fading after successive stops.

SAFETY SUMMARY: 2001–03 models have received a "Best Pick" offset crash rating from IIHS. Before you purchase this vehicle, make sure the headlight illumination is adequate. On some model years, the gas and brake pedals are poorly designed; anyone with a size 12 or larger shoe can inadvertently hit the wrong pedal. **Airbags:** Standard. There have been reports that airbags on the 2000 models didn't deploy during head-on collisions. **ABS:** Standard; disc/disc. **Safety belt pretensioners:** Front. **Traction control:** Yes. **Head restraints F/R: ★★★. Visibility F/R: ★★★★/★.**

SAFETY COMPLAINTS: 2000—Vehicle suddenly leaps forward or stalls. • Airbags fail to deploy. • Engine runs rough and warning light is constantly lit. • Door latch will not release; driver had to crawl out through the window. • Rear doors open while vehicle is underway. • Hooking mechanism fails to hold up shade and flies across vehicle. • Poorly designed brake pedals won't accept a large foot. **2000–03**—Headlight illumination is blinding. • Windshield shatters for no reason. **2001**—ABS light remains lit. • Fuel leakage into the passenger's compartment from the fuel-pump seal. • Inadvertent deployment of front airbags. • Chronic stalling problem with 3.0L engines. • Parked vehicle rolled away because of emergency brake failure. • Transmission loses First, Second, and Fifth gears because of faulty electronic chip. • Transmission often shifts into Neutral. • Bent suspension control arm caused prematurely worn-out tires. • Front door design can injure one's head. • Front door locks occupants inside vehicle. • Seat heater burns leather and occupant's skin. • Recall should be expanded to include other fire-prone fans. **2001–02**—Sudden brake failure. • Faulty electronic side-view mirrors. **2002**—

Rear blind spot contributed to fatal accident. • While driving, driver-side door suddenly opened. • Floor mat may cause throttle to stick. • Airbag light stays lit. • Power windows won't stay up. • Wipers come on for no reason. • Fragile bumpers. **2002–03**—Frequent major electrical system failures. **2003**—Headlights may suddenly cut out while driving. **2004**—Engine suddenly surges, causing unintended acceleration. • Despite recall fix for stalling, vehicle continues to stall. • Chronic electrical system shutdowns. • Transmission shuts down while engine is running.

Secret Warranties/Internal Bulletins/Service Tips

All years: Troubleshooting tips for a Check Engine light that's constantly lit. • Intermittent electrical faults related to circuits in the upper rear hatch. • Rough running, black smoke, and starter may stay engaged. • Service action covers deburring the exhaust tailpipes. • Troubleshooting AC musty odours. • Squealing, groaning, or grinding noise when turning the steering wheel. • Steering-wheel vibration at idle. • Brake pedal rattling. • Popping, clicking clutch pedal. • Front-door window or door seal noise. • Outer door releases fail to operate in freezing weather. • Service action to replace the passenger-side mirror. **2000**—Window regulators produce squeaking, clicking, and creaking noises on vehicles built before May 2000. • Some vehicles may lack the electrically adjustable steering column that is a standard feature on U.S. models. • Fuel-tank vent-line fitting weld may be faulty, allowing gas fumes to enter the passenger compartment; dealer will re-weld it under a "product update campaign" (read, secret warranty) as per TSB #16-5200. • Incorrect fuel gauge readings. • Faulty windshield wiper blades. • Generator whine on AM band. **2000–01**—Poor starting, no-starts, and erratic shifting. **2001**—Battery drain from Alpine radio hookup. • Faulty interior light in luggage compartment. **2002**—Campaign to troubleshoot faulty Check Engine light. • Loose air intake boot. • Defective rear hatch switch. • Inoperative AC blower. • Brake pedal rattling. • Correcting steering squealing, grinding, or groaning. **2002–03**—Hard shift or no-shift condition (automatic transmission). **2004**—Engine head bolt threads pull out of block. • Defective engine cylinder head (see X3). • Hydraulic belt tensioner installation. • Campaign to troubleshoot Low Oil Level warning. • Cold weather may damage the engine valve cover. • Harsh downshifts. • Delayed cold engagement of automatic transmission. • Difficulty coding navigation system; erratic performance. • Replace alternator belt tensioner to silence annoying noise. • Poor radio reception. • Defective keyless entry. • Telematic inspection/replacement campaign. • Rear hatch latch electrical failure campaign. • Headlight condensation. • Transmission suddenly self-destructed. **2004–05**—Compass loses calibration.

	2000	2001	2002	2003	2004	2005	2006
Cost Price ($) (soft)							
X5 (23%)	—	56,960	56,900	57,800	58,500	58,800	59,400
X5 4.4i (25%)	—	—	68,900	69,800	71,400	69,800	72,100
X5 4.6is	—	—	93,900	94,500	—	—	—
X5 4.8is (30%)	—	—	—	—	96,500	96,500	98,100
Used Values ($)							
X5 ▲	—	26,000	30,000	37,000	46,000	52,000	—
X5 ▼	—	23,000	28,000	34,000	40,000	49,000	—
X5 4.4i ▲	—	—	38,000	45,000	53,000	58,000	—
X5 4.4i ▼	—	—	36,000	43,000	51,000	54,000	—
X5 4.6is ▲	—	—	50,000	62,000	—	—	—
X5 4.6is ▼	—	—	48,000	59,000	—	—	—
X5 4.8is ▲	—	—	—	—	70,000	81,000	—
X5 4.8is ▼	—	—	—	—	68,000	78,000	—
Reliability	④	④	④	④	❸	❸	—
Crash Safety (F)	—	—	—	⑤	⑤	⑤	⑤
Side	—	—	—	④	④	④	④
Offset	—	⑤	⑤	⑤	⑤	⑤	⑤
Rollover	—	—	—	❸	—	❸	—

DaimlerChrysler

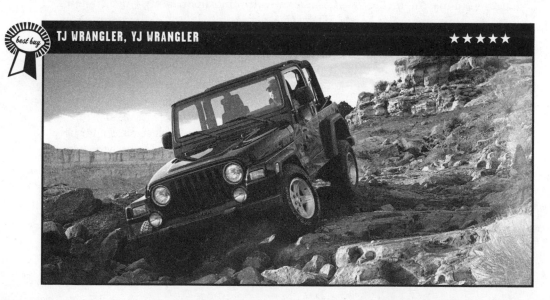

TJ WRANGLER, YJ WRANGLER ★★★★★

best buy

2007 TECHNICAL DATA

POWERTRAIN (4X4)

Engine: 3.8L 6-cyl. (205 hp); Transmissions: 6-speed man. • 4-speed auto.

DIMENSION/CAPACITY

Passengers: 2/2; Wheelbase: 95.4 in.; H: 69.4/L: 160/W: 71.7 in.; Headroom F/R: N/A; Legroom F/R: 41.1/34.9 in.; Cargo volume: 11.9 cu. ft.; Fuel tank: 72L/regular; Tow limit: 1,000–3,500 lb.; Load capacity: 400 lb.; GVWR: 3,094–3,333 lb.; Turning circle: 36 ft.; Weight: 3,510 lb.

RATING: Recommended (2003–07); Average (1987–2002). A direct descendant of the original Jeep—the 1941 Willys MB—this should be the first choice for all off-roaders. It's primitive, capable, and fun to drive. Plus, the Wrangler's not a bad looker for Saturday night cruising along Yonge or Burrard streets, and short commutes with the 4-speed automatic are a breeze (2003 and later models). Here are your best choices: Get either an improved, second-series 2007 model for both on- and off-roading capabilities, or get a 2003–06 version equipped with the 4-speed automatic tranny, for better highway performance while burning less fuel. **Strong points:** The 2007 model offers more standard features and handles much better than earlier versions. Entry-level models are reasonably priced, depreciate slowly, are attractively styled, and have comfortable front seating. Also, controls and displays are nicely laid out, though controls on older models aren't as user-friendly. Low-speed handling is fairly competent, making the Wrangler a versatile off-roader. For concerned parents out there: The Wrangler also has good frontal, offset, and rollover crashworthiness ratings. **Weak points:** Pre-2007 base models are bereft of many standard features; rough and noisy ride; vague, imprecise steering; mediocre braking; cramped rear seating; little storage space; the canvas top is a chore to open; plastic windows don't stay clean for long; high step-in; chronic powertrain and body shortcomings; poor fuel economy; and many reports of engine- and steering-column-related fires. **New for 2007:** Completely redesigned and given more power, more interior room, better off-road capability, and more on-road refinement. A four-door Unlimited debuts.

MODEL HISTORY: Early CJs and YJs were equipped with a wimpy, fuel-thirsty 4.2L straight-six motor mated to either a 4- or 5-speed manual or a 3-speed automatic transmission. **1991**—A powerful, better-running 180-hp 4.0L engine replaced the 4.2L 6-cylinder. For off-roading use, skip the 6-cylinder; you are much better off with a 4-cylinder engine, particularly on later models. Unfortunately, the 3-speed automatic shifts harshly and saps power from the engine. This isn't the best vehicle for everyday use: Pre-1997 versions have good low-speed manoeuvrability that is compromised by dismal crashworthiness scores; mediocre high-speed handling; a rough, noisy ride; and worse-than-average braking. **1997**—YJ replaced by the TJ and is much improved from safety, quality, comfort, and performance perspectives. The chassis, steering, and suspension refinements make the Wrangler more carlike in its handling and much more stable on the road. **1999**—Upgraded rotary climate controls and a larger standard fuel tank. **2000**—Sport and Sahara got a more refined, quieter 6-cylinder powerplant along with an upgraded 5-speed manual shifter. **2003**—An optional 4-speed automatic is introduced. SE models use the Liberty's 147-hp 2.4L 4-cylinder engine, and the X, Sport, Sahara, and Rubicon versions now carry a 190-hp 4.0L inline-six powerplant. **2004**—Unlimited gets a wheelbase that's 25 cm (10 in.) longer than other Wranglers and 38 cm (15 in.) longer overall, adding 5 cm (2 in.) of rear legroom and more cargo volume. A tilt steering wheel is standard. **2005**—A 6-speed manual transmission replaced the 5-speed. **2007**—A new 205-hp 3.8L V6 with 15 more horses than the 4.0L V6; electronic stability-control (ESP); electronic roll mitigation; dual-stage airbags, seat-mounted side airbags, and an occupant classification system (OCS); increased ground clearance; larger wheels and tires; enhanced Dana solid front and rear axles; Command-Trac and Rock-Trac transfer cases; new electric axle lockers; and a revamped front sway bar. Additionally, you get a stiffer frame, a 5 cm (2 in.) longer wheelbase, a 9 cm (3.5 in.) wider track, lower spring rates, better brakes, and a retuned suspension. The larger interior gives 12 cm (4.6 in.) more hip room and 13 cm (5.1 in.) inches more shoulder room, combined with an additional 5 cm (2 in.) in the front and 2.5 cm (1 in.) more in rear-seat legroom. The three-piece modular hardtop is also new this year.

COST ANALYSIS: Priced at $23,600–$33,160 (SE/Rubicon) before generous rebates and discounts are applied, this is the smallest and least expensive (we're talking bare-bones here) Jeep you can find. Fortunately, a base model without too many options should suit most driving needs. The Unlimited's extended wheelbase adds to rear-seat comfort, and the 2005's 6-speed manual improves fuel economy and performance. The 2003–04 versions, with their longer powertrain warranty and base engine and automatic transmission improvements, should be better buys than earlier versions. **Best alternatives:** Other comparable sport-utilities worth a look are the GM Tracker (V6), Suzuki Sidekick, Honda CR-V or Element, Hyundai Tucson, Subaru Forester, and Toyota RAV4. But remember, none of these other models can follow the Wrangler off-road. **Rebates:** $2,500–$4,500 on the 2006; nothing for the 2007s, which are destined to sell for their full list price and come fully loaded. **Delivery/PDI:** $1,050. **Warranty:** Bumper-to-bumper 3 years/60,000 km; powertrain 5 years/100,000 km; rust perforation 5 years/160,000 km. **Supplementary warranty:** Strongly recommended now that Chrysler's 7-year warranty has been axed. **Options:** For serious off-roading, opt for the 6-cylinder powerplant and 5-speed manual transmission. Keep an eye out for the optional suspension system, which includes larger shock absorbers and heavy-duty springs. An aftermarket anti-theft system is also a plus. **Depreciation:** Much slower than average. **Insurance cost:** Above average. **Parts supply/cost:** Above-average supply. Servicing from dealers can get expensive, so you'll want to frequent independent service agencies after the warranty expires. **Annual maintenance cost:** Higher than average without the 7-year warranty. A spotty service record at Jeep dealerships inflates maintenance costs. **Highway/city fuel economy:** The 6-speed manual and 6-cylinder engine give you the best fuel economy. *2.4L 4-cyl. and auto.:*

12.1/15.7 L/100 km; *4.0L 6-cyl. and man.:* 11.6/15.4 L/100 km; *6-cyl. and auto.:* 11.7/16.8 L/100 km.

QUALITY/RELIABILITY: Average. Factory-related defects have always plagued these vehicles, but not as much now as before. Premature front brake wear is a frequent complaint. Owners say that the 5-speed and 6-speed manual transmissions don't shift smoothly. The 6-speed grinds when going into Reverse, or it pops out of Reverse. The 5-speed constantly grinds when shifting or when in Neutral when the clutch is depressed; the shifter won't come out of or go into gear; it may suddenly pop out of gear; it sticks in Second gear when hot, or when accelerating in First or Second; and the Fifth gear suddenly disengages. One dissatisfied owner said, "There have now been four transmissions in my Jeep, and all have had problems with noise, shifting into and out of gear, and getting stuck in gear." Another owner had to replace the transmission at 600 km. Watch out for transfer-case malfunctions, piston knocking on 1991–96 models, engine overheating, engine and transfer-case oil leaks, worn-out suspension (ball joints, especially) and steering components, and ignition-component malfunctions. Body welds and seams are susceptible to premature rusting, and there have been frequent complaints about peeling paint and water leaks. The worst leaks occur at the bottom of the windshield frame. An easy way to check for this is to examine the underside of the frame to see if there's excessive rust. This has consistently been a problem area for Jeeps; hence all of the ads for aftermarket windshield frames. The good news is that you can replace the windshield frame and all of the seals relatively cheaply. **Warranty performance:** Average.

ROAD PERFORMANCE (2006 MODELS): Acceleration/torque: Off-road capability is impressive with the 4-cylinder engine, thanks to gobs of low-end torque when it's shifted into low range (torque lb.-ft.: 140 at 3500 rpm). Smooth, above-average acceleration and torque with the 6-cylinder engine (0–100 km/h: 10.5 sec.). The 2.4L 4-cylinder engine is noisy and lacks the power for serious hauling; it's especially sluggish when hooked to the automatic transmission. Says one owner, "This Jeep loses power at 100 km/h and, even when the accelerator pedal is floored, won't increase speed." **Transmission:** The 3-speed automatic shifts harshly and saps power from the engine. **Steering:** Clumsy; vehicle tends to wander on the highway. **Routine handling:** The ride is harsh and bouncy on all but the smoothest roads, and there's considerable body roll when cornering. Handling is mediocre on the highway but outstanding off-road. P225/75R tires cause the vehicle to wander. Doesn't take curves very well, owing to the short wheelbase and high centre of gravity. Good ground clearance and stiff suspension for off-roading. **Braking:** Unacceptably long braking distance (100–0 km/h: 47 m), with or without ABS.

SAFETY SUMMARY: Insurance industry figures show a much higher-than-average number of accident injury claims, aggravated by a high incidence of sudden rollovers when drivers exceed the Jeep's very low tolerance for sporty driving. In fact, Jeeps, along with the Ford Bronco and Suzuki Samurai, have always been among the SUVs most frequently cited in rollover deaths. There are lots of recall campaigns to check out. There have also been reports of front seat belts that fail to retract and interfere with the door latch as well as seat belts that failed to restrain occupants in a collision. **Airbags:** Front airbags are standard; side airbags are available on later models. Many complaints that the airbags fail to deploy or are late deploying, or that the Airbag light stays on. **ABS:** Optional, but not offered on all models; disc/drum. Upgraded a few years ago, brakes continue to be problematic. **Head restraints F/R: ★★. Visibility F/R: ★★★★★/★.**

SAFETY COMPLAINTS: Owners report chronic engine stalling when accelerating or decelerating, clutch master and slave cylinder leaks, premature brake wear, and brake failure. There have been several incidents of sudden brake loss where the pedal went all the way to the floor with no braking effect (corrected by replacing the master cylinder). Other brake complaints include a seal leak in the power-brake booster that might cause a brake failure; the brake drum not keeping its shape; the vehicle pulling to left when braking; the rear brakes suddenly locking up while driving in the rain and approaching a stop sign; and the vehicle going into open throttle position when the brakes are applied. There have also been many instances where drivers mistook the accelerator for the brake because the pedals are so close together. There have been many complaints of airbag failures, fuel-tank leaks, fuel-pump failures, and malfunctioning fuel gauges. **1995–2003**—Manual and automatic transmission failures. • Gas and brake pedals are too close together. **1999**—Exhaust manifold leaks. • Vehicle rolls back when in gear. **2000**—Under-hood fire. • Right rear wheel separated from vehicle. • Vehicle went into Reverse after being shifted into Drive. **2001**—Many engine-related steering-column fires. • Sudden, unintended acceleration in Reverse gear. • Rear brakes often fail to engage. • Sudden steering lock-up. • Camshaft sensor binding and breaking, causing vehicle to stall. • Broken rear axle seal. • Manual tranny pops out of Third gear and grinds as the clutch is let out. • Premature wearout of the rear brake pads. • Faulty catalytic converter. **2002**—Manual transmission shifts poorly between Fourth and Fifth gear. • Defective dash cluster. • Intermittent stalling and rough running. • Vehicle accelerates when foot is taken off the gas pedal. **2003**—Airbags failed to deploy. • Manual and automatic transmission malfunctions and failures. • Driveshaft fell out while driving. • Vehicle slips into Neutral from Drive. • Sudden axle and steering failure. • Seat belts unlatch too easily. • Seat is angled to the left. • Driver's foot ends up half on accelerator pedal and half on brake pedal. **2004**—Driver mistook accelerator pedal for brakes. • Sudden stalling caused by defective crankshaft position sensor. • Airbags didn't deploy. • Engine and transmission oil leak. • Defective manual transmission. • Front left axle seal leak. • Gas-line leaks cause fumes to enter the cabin. • Chronic stalling. • Seized front brakes. • Front brakes vibrate violently when applied. • Cracked driver-seat frame. • Seat belt doesn't retract. • Cloth top came off while vehicle was underway (driver had to hold it down with his hand). • Window pops open. **2005**—Automatic transmission failure. • Sudden acceleration:

I was sitting at a stop sign with my foot resting on the brake. I was not pressing the pedal actively, but the brakes were applied. The jeep surged forward. My foot was nowhere near the gas pedal, yet the jeep revved and moved about a foot. I pressed hard on the brake and it stopped, but took a second to rev back down.

www.rubiconownersforum.com

• Defective steering stabilizer responsible for steering shudder. • Partial loss of control when passing over bumps or railroad tracks. • Carpet caused accelerator pedal to stick. • Carbon monoxide leakage into cabin. • Seat belt gets caught in door.

Secret Warranties/Internal Bulletins/Service Tips

1996–99—A noisy cold transmission may signal the need to replace the transmission regulator valve. **1997–99**—Measures to reduce disc brake rotor pulsation, transfer-case shifter and universal-joint noise, and tailgate rattles or knocks; diagnostic tips for plugging water leaks. • AC evaporator freeze-up tips. **1997–2002**—Water leaks under the passenger-side carpet. **1997–2005**—Tips on repairing a leak in the engine rear main oil seal. **1997–2006**—Tips on plugging door leaks. **1999–2000**—Interior roof sagging and water accumulation can be corrected through the installation of foam blocks under an extended warranty. **1999–2001**—Tips for correcting windshield/cowl water leaks. **1999–2004**—A rough idle may require the installation of a fuel-injector insulator sleeve. **2001–05**—If the vehicle tends to drift, install upgraded ball joints and get Jeep to pay half the cost up to five years of use:

LEAD OR DRIFT TO EITHER SIDE OF ROAD

BULLETIN NO: 02-006-04   DATE: AUGUST 20, 2004

SPECIAL OFFSET BALL JOINT ALLOWS ADJUSTMENT TO CASTER AND CAMBER ANGLES

This bulletin involves the replacement of one or both front upper ball joints when front end alignment specifications can not be obtained using normal alignment practices.

2001–05 Wrangler

2001–04 Grand Cherokee

2001 Cherokee

SYMPTOM/CONDITION: The customer may experience a slight lead or drift to either side of the road. This condition may occur when there is no driver input to the steering system, or when the driver must maintain a constant input to the steering system in order to maintain a straight ahead direction of the vehicle.

2003—Delayed or temporary loss of transmission engagement and harsh 4–3 downshift (NHTSA TSB #2100503, June 20, 2003). • Manual transmission may have defective Third gear weld. • 4.0L engine crankshaft burr. • Faulty fuel-injector wiring connections. **2003–04**—Automatic transmission leaks:

AUTOMATIC TRANSMISSION FLUID LEAK

BULLETIN NO.: 21-003-04   DATE: MARCH 9, 2004

FLUID SEEPAGE FROM AREA OF REAR OUTPUT SHAFT RETAINER

OVERVIEW: This bulletin involves the replacement of the NV-241 transfer case rear output shaft retainer/extension housing and related seals.

2003–04 (TJ) Wrangler

2003–06—Drivebelt noise countermeasures:

ENGINE—DRIVE BELT CHIRPING

BULLETIN NO.: 07-001-06   DATE: FEBRUARY 15, 2006

2.4 ENGINE—CHIRP-LIKE SOUND FROM ACCESSORY DRIVE BELT

OVERVIEW: This bulletin involves the installation of a new serpentine accessory drive belt and on some vehicles a revised drive belt routing.

MODELS: 2003–2006 Wrangler; 2003–2005 Liberty, Cherokee

2005—Manual 6-speed won't stay in gear.

TJ WRANGLER, YJ WRANGLER PROFILE

	1998	1999	2000	2001	2002	2003	2004	2005	2006
Cost Price ($) (firm)									
TJ, YJ (20%)	118,575	19,205	19,445	20,355	21,000	21,340	21,995	22,910	23,600
Used Values ($)									
TJ, YJ ▲	5,000	6,500	8,000	9,500	11,500	13,000	15,500	17,500	—
TJ, YJ ▼	4,500	5,500	7,000	8,500	10,500	12,000	14,000	16,000	—
Reliability	❸	❸	❸	❸	❹	❹	❹	❹	—
Crash Safety (F)	—	❹	❹	❹	❹	❹	❹	❹	❹
IIHS Side	❷	❷	❷	❷	❷	❷	❷	❷	❷
Offset	❸	❸	❸	❸	❸	❸	❸	❸	❸
Rollover	—	—	—	❸	❸	❸	—	❹	❹

CHEROKEE, GRAND CHEROKEE   ★★★

RATING: Average (2002–07); Not Recommended (1985–2001). Oh, how the mighty have fallen. Jeep's Cherokee and Grand Cherokee were perennial bestsellers a decade ago when the Japanese and South Korean competition was practically non-existent. Now, they are also-ran SUVs that have no future due to their mediocre performance and poor quality control. As with the Wrangler, the Cherokee's forte

All ratings on a numbered scale where ⑤ is good and ❶ is bad. See page 220 for a more detailed description.

is its superior off-roading capability (it was replaced in 2002 by the Liberty). For highway cruising, off-roading, or city use, the Grand Cherokee is the better choice of the two. **Strong points:** Powerful V8 and plenty of cargo space (Grand Cherokee); easy handling; a comfortable ride; and a smooth-shifting transmission, when it's not in the shop for repairs. Good fuel economy and smooth, integrated drivetrain performance with the 6-cylinder. A comprehensive 7-year powertrain warranty on 2002–2004 versions. **Weak points:** Abrupt throttle tip-in; restricted rear visibility; high fuel consumption with the Grand Cherokee; an unreliable powertrain and fuel system; cheap, rattle-prone interior trim; low door openings make for difficult entry and exit; uncomfortable rear seating; an unusually high number of safety-related complaints; and severe rusting around fenders, wheel-wells, doors, and door handles. *Cherokee:* The high step-up and narrow rear doors make entry and exit difficult. Back-seat access is also problematic. **New for 2007:** Standard curtain airbags and stability-control. A 3.0L turbo common-rail diesel (CRD) engine will arrive at Jeep dealerships in the first quarter of 2007. Built by Mercedes-Benz, the new diesel produces 215 hp and gets an estimated highway/city fuel economy of 10.2/12.38 L/100 km (23/19 mpg).

2001 CHEROKEE TECHNICAL DATA

POWERTRAIN
Engine: 4.0L 6-cyl. (190 hp); Transmissions: 5-speed man. • 3-speed auto. • 4-speed auto.
DIMENSION/CAPACITY (4-DOOR)
Passengers: 2/3; Wheelbase: 101.4 in.; H: 63.9/L: 167.5/W: 69.4 in.; Headroom F/R: N/A.; Legroom F/R: 41.4/35 in.; Cargo volume: 36.5 cu. ft.; Fuel tank: 76L/regular; Tow limit: 5,000 lb.; Load capacity: N/A; GVWR: 4,550–4,900 lb.; Turning circle: 38 ft.; Ground clearance: N/A; Weight: 3,150 lb.

2007 GRAND CHEROKEE TECHNICAL DATA

POWERTRAIN (REAR-DRIVE OR 4X4)
Engines: 3.7L 6-cyl. (210 hp) • 3.0L 6-cyl. diesel (215 hp) • 4.7L V8 (235 hp) • 5.7L V8 (330 hp) • STR8 6.1L V8 (420 hp); Transmission: 5-speed auto./man.
DIMENSION/CAPACITY
Passengers: 2/3; Wheelbase: 109.5. in.; H: 67.7/L: 186.6/W: 73.3 in.; Headroom F/R: N/A; Legroom F/R: 41.7/35.5 in.; Cargo volume: 34.5 cu. ft.; Fuel tank: 78L/regular; Tow limit: 3,500–6,500 lb.; Load capacity: 1,050–1,100 lb.; GVWR: 4,889–6,200 lb.; Turning circle: 37.4 ft.; Ground clearance: 7.0 in.; Weight: 4,441 lb.

MODEL HISTORY: Cherokee and its early partner, the Wagoneer, were the first four-door Jeeps designed under the tutelage of American Motors (boy, do I miss the straight-talking Bill Pickett, AMC Canada's former prez). Intended to be downsized and upgraded replacements for the old full-sized wagons, they were an instant success. They kept AMC afloat until the Chrysler buyout.

Transmission choices include 4- or 5-speed manuals and 3- or 4-speed automatics. The 3-speed automatic is the most reliable; the manuals have heavy clutches and notchy shifting. The smaller engines are jokes in such large vehicles, most of which are available with optional, larger engines. These Jeeps wander at highway speeds (now a Dodge truck/SUV problem; see *Dawe v. Courtesy Chrysler* in Part Three), and the numb power steering doesn't help. They aren't a pleasure to manoeuvre or park around town. Interiors are spacious—although the spare tire reduces interior space—and will easily and comfortably accommodate five people on long rides.

Early Cherokees and Wagoneers have very poor repair histories. Buyers should be especially wary of the 4-cylinder engine; premature brake wear; the electrical system; the fuel system; and the failure-prone, expensive-to-repair 4×4 system.

The 1995–2001 Cherokees provide smoother, more integrated drivetrain performance (later models offered full-time AWD) and give better fuel economy. However, interior room is still limited, standard features are few, rear visibility is restricted, and brakes remain troublesome. These later models are apparently less failure-prone, although long-term reliability remains questionable.

Grand Cherokee

Early Grand Cherokees are just as failure-prone as other early Jeeps. The 1995–98 Grand Cherokees are easier to handle, give a more comfortable ride, and are equipped with an optional 5.9L V8. On the minus side, you'll still find limited rear seating, a difficult entry and exit, high fuel consumption, and uncertain powertrain reliability. Since the Grand Cherokee is afflicted with the same failure-prone parts as the Cherokee, we see chronic engine and transmission failures, poor-quality hardware, sloppy assembly, oil leaks, electrical system glitches, and brakes that often fail and are in need of frequent servicing. The Selec-Trac 4×4 system continues to be expensive to maintain and glitch-prone (this has dramatically worsened over the past few years). **1999**—Grand Cherokee is longer, wider, roomier, and generally more refined. A new optional 235-hp 4.7L V8 replaced the base 4.0L 6-cylinder, used since the early '60s in American Motors' Ramblers. A Dana-built Quadra-Trac transmission was added, and a restyled exterior gave this upscale Cherokee a more modern look. Brakes and steering components were upgraded as well. **2003–04**—Improved steering and brake feel; additional storage space. These models still suffer from poor quality control, which afflicts the engine, transmission, brakes, AC, and body fit and finish. **2005**—A major redesign softened the Grand Cherokee's road manners in favour of on-road comfort without sacrificing its off-road prowess. A re-engineered suspension improved the ride via three 4×4 systems and a longer and wider platform. The new models offer three engines, including a new 325-hp 5.7L Hemi V8 with cylinder deactivation. **2006**—Introduction of the Grand Cherokee SRT8, Jeep's first high-performance SUV. Powered by a 6.1L 420-hp Hemi, early reports are that it posts 0–100 km/h in under 5 seconds, beating the Porsche Cayenne Turbo and BMW X5. Other nice features: a lighter-weight four-wheel drive system, a modified suspension, upgraded brakes and exhaust, and a fresh-air induction system that allows for a fording depth of up to 48 cm (19 in).

COST ANALYSIS: Selling for $39,470/$52,900 (Laredo/Overland 5.7L), a used second-series (made after March) 2005 is your best bet, once all of the rebates are deducted from what is an unrealistically high retail price. Stay away from the new diesel powerplant. It has been totally redesigned, and its Mercedes roots guarantee a fair amount of start-up glitches. Plus, it will have to handle reformulated fuel in 2007. Wait on the upgraded diesels coming out with the 2008 models. **Best alternatives:** *Cherokee:* When compared with the 2002 Liberty, a used 2001 Cherokee (its last model year) offers more base power, sells for thousands less, and is much more reliable (31 NHTSA–logged safety complaints versus 177). *Grand Cherokee:* The 2003 and 2004 Grand Cherokee returned heavily discounted with some important upgrades, like a longer warranty, that make it a better choice than earlier models. Other 4×4s worth a look are the Honda CR-V, Hyundai Tucson or Santa Fe, Nissan Xterra or X-Trail, and Toyota's RAV4 or 4Runner. **Rebates:** Prices will be cut by several thousand dollars to keep up with GM's deep discounting. Also, look for $2,000–$3,500 rebates on last year's leftovers. **Delivery/PDI:** $1,050. **Warranty:** Bumper-to-bumper 3 years/60,000 km; powertrain 5 years/100,000 km; rust perforation 5 years/160,000 km. **Supplementary warranty:** A good idea for the powertrain of any model not covered for 7 years. **Options:** Get an anti-theft system, or kiss your vehicle goodbye. Choose your tires carefully. Off-road rubber with an aggressive tread isn't conducive to comfortable highway driving. *Grand Cherokee:* Get the 4.7L V8 for the best overall performance; the Hemi 5.7L doesn't give the fuel economy promised. **Depreciation:** A bit slower than average. **Insurance cost:** Average, but higher than average for the Grand Cherokee. **Parts supply/cost:** Moderately priced parts that are usually easily found. Owners report waits of several months for recall campaign parts. **Annual maintenance cost:** Higher than average without the 7-year warranty. Spotty service record at Jeep dealerships. The drivetrain is particularly expensive to repair. **Highway/city fuel economy:** *Cherokee: 2.5L 4-cyl. and auto.: 10.0/13.4 L/100 km; 4.0L 6-cyl. and auto.: 10.2/15.0 L/100 km; 4.0L 6-cyl. and 4×4: 10.4/14.9 L/100 km. Grand Cherokee: 3.7L V6 and auto.: 10.3/14.2 L/100 km; 4.0L 6-cyl.: 10.4/14.7 L/100 km; 4.0L 6-cyl. and 4×4: 10.4/14.9 L/100 km; 4.7L V8 and 4×4: 11.1/16.3 L/100 km; 5.7L Hemi V8: 11.2/16.5 L/100 km.*

QUALITY/RELIABILITY: Although not as badly built as the Ford Explorer, quality control is quite poor. Transmission, brake, and fuel-system problems continue to dog Chrysler—and its customers. An inadequate base warranty and a spotty service record at Jeep dealerships compound a poor overall reliability record for the Cherokee. Long-term reliability doesn't look good for the Grand Cherokee, either, despite its recent makeover. AWD components are expensive to maintain after the fourth year of use.

The transfer cases and axles are unreliable, noisy, and prone to early wearout. A misalignment of the gears produces a loud humming noise emanating from the ring gear and pinion gear. Although dealers have attempted to fix the problem by realigning the gears, the noise continues to this day.

Another quality problem is the binding of the wheels in the Quadra-Trac system when the outer wheel can't rotate faster than the inner wheel during a turn, causing excessive noise and premature wear. Electrical system and body deficiencies continue to plague these redesigned models, and everything points toward these vehicles being hazardous, underperforming, and costly to maintain as they age. **Owner-reported problems:** *Cherokee:* Knocking connecting rods on 6-cylinder engines. Selec-Trac 4×4 often requires expensive servicing after a few years of use or high mileage. Transmission bangs or clunks when shifting. Steering failures. Engine and ABS warning lights stay on. Frequent and expensive brake repairs because of warped rotors and cracked shoes. Excessive vibration and pulling when brakes are applied. Electrical system shorts, power windows fail, and rear wipers won't work. Premature shock absorber and tie-rod wearout, resulting in uneven tire wear. Alloy wheels can fuse to the drums. AC leaks and failures, and engine and transfer-case oil leaks. *Grand Cherokee:* Engine difficult to start when hot and acts as if it's starved for fuel. Chronic automatic transmission failures. Rear-end whine on acceleration. Excessive steering wander and noisy operation (honking). Premature wearout of original-equipment tires and ball joints; electrical and fuel-system glitches; poorly performing and expensive-to-maintain brakes; and subpar body hardware and paint. It's hard to secure loads to the roof rack. Premature rusting of the undercarriage, steering spindle, brake lines, and exhaust. **Warranty performance:** Very tight-fisted in handling warranty claims.

 ROAD PERFORMANCE: Acceleration/torque: *Cherokee:* The 6-cylinder engine provides a smooth and powerful performance with brisk acceleration (0–100 km/h: 9 sec.). The 2.5L 4-cylinder engine is noisy and lacks the power for serious hauling, and it is especially sluggish when hooked to the automatic transmission. *Grand Cherokee:* Plenty of power with the inline 6-cylinder and V8 engines. The V8s accelerate to 100 km/h about as fast as the Ford Explorer. Excellent engines for off-roading, and the Hemi 5.7L provides impressive all-around performance, when it's not stalling out. **Transmission:** *Cherokee:* Smooth-shifting automatic, but it's the 5-speed manual gearbox that gives the best performance. *Grand Cherokee:* Usually shifts smoothly in all gear ranges (if working properly). Occasional abrupt throttle response can cause jerky shifting. **Steering:** *Cherokee:* Precise, with good road feedback. Many reports that the steering will suddenly veer to the right at highway speeds. *Grand Cherokee:* Fairly good, as a result of the 2000's enhancements. Suspension geometry requires constant steering corrections to keep vehicle on the highway. **Routine handling:** *Cherokee:* Average at moderate speeds. The ride is harsh and bouncy when the going gets rough. Doesn't take curves graciously, and likes to wander on the highway. *Grand Cherokee:* Ride comfort is augmented by a three-link rear axle. Handling is precise, with improved high-speed cornering stability. The Quadra-Trac system has a "Vari-Lok" feature that provides a mechanical lock in the low-range position for extra traction. Many complaints that the vehicle tends to wander all over the road. **Emergency handling:** *Cherokee:* Average. Good ground clearance and stiff suspension for off-roading. *Grand Cherokee:* Good. Cornering is well controlled, and handling is predictable and precise. Little body roll. **Braking:** *Cherokee:* Average (100–0 km/h: 41 m). *Grand Cherokee:* Very good (100–0 km/h: 40 m with the V8). Some plowing in hard stops. Braking upgrades have followed years of criticism related to sudden brake failure, poor braking performance, and the premature wearout of expensive major brake components.

 SAFETY SUMMARY: Location of fuel tank makes it vulnerable, leading to fires in rear-end collisions. In *Rolf v. Winger* (Jackson County, Missouri; October 2001), lawyers obtained a $5.7-million verdict in a wrongful death case where the driver was killed when his Jeep Cherokee was rear-ended by a drunk driver. The collision caused the gas tank on the Cherokee to explode on impact. Confidential settlements were reached before trial with DaimlerChrysler and the pub where the drunk driver became intoxicated. (The case was tried against the remaining defendants, including the drunk driver's employer.) There are also many complaints that the low-beam headlights give insufficient illumination. Be wary of tow figures given out by salespeople. They are often wrong; in particular, salespeople often don't divulge the lower rating for manual transmissions. **Airbags:** *Grand Cherokee:* Side airbags are standard. There have been many reports of airbags not deploying when they should and deploying when they shouldn't. **ABS:** 4W optional on Cherokee; standard on Grand Cherokee. ABS failures characterized by pedal going to the floor with no braking action and extended stopping distances. **Traction control:** Optional on Grand Cherokee. **Head restraints F/R:** *Cherokee: 1997:* ★; *1998–99:* ★★/★; *2001:* ★. *Grand Cherokee: 1996–97:* ★; *1999:* ★; *2001:* ★; *2002–04:* ★★/★. **Visibility F/R:** *Cherokee:* ★★★★★/★; *Grand Cherokee:* ★★★★★/★★.

SAFETY COMPLAINTS: All years: Under-hood fires. • Ignition switch and steering column overheated. • Fuel leakage from the gas tank. • Transfer-case leakage causes fire to ignite in exhaust system area. • Engine-mount bolts shear off, causing the engine to fall down. • Easy to mistake accelerator for brake pedal. • Brake rotors corrode, crack, and warp. • Brake rotor failure causes extended stopping distance and vibration when braking. • Frequent replacement of the master cylinder and proportioning valve. • Sudden, unintended acceleration, especially with vehicles equipped with a 4.7L engine:

> Local carwash employee entered into my 2005 Jeep Grand Cherokee. When ignition was turned on, the vehicle redlined and accelerated off of conveyor. Employee hit the brakes with no response. It collided with another vehicle and went through a towel cabinet and a brick wall. Four employees and myself were nearly killed. I took the driver out of the vehicle and while no one was in it, it was still trying to drive through the wall on its own (nothing was touching the accelerator).

• Frequent automatic transmission and differential failures. • Transfer-case grinding, fluid leakage, and failure. • Automatic transmission jumped from Park to Reverse. • Transmission allows vehicle to roll away even though it's in Park. • Power-steering bracket shears off, causing steering loss. • Complete electrical failure and sudden stalling. • Airbag, ABS, and Check Engine lights come on for no reason. • Erratically functioning interior and exterior lights. • Headlights dim when the AC engages. • Frequent AC malfunctions. • Water leakage through improperly welded seam near dash causes chronic electrical shorts. • Water leaks from dash and doors. • Doors fall off because of defective hinges. **1998**—Dash panel fire. • Driver-side mat jams the accelerator. • Tire-jack platform is too small. • Right rear wheel fell off. • Stabilizer bar broke. • Left rear axle shaft failed. • Warped door. • Fuel gauge reads one-quarter tank when it's empty. **1999**—Rear seat belt won't secure a child safety seat. **2000**—Right rear door latch caught on fire while driving. • One fire in the under-hood area believed to be caused by the headlight switch shorting out. • Leaking gas comes out of hoses (which appear to be dry-rotted) between gas tank filler and fuel tank. • Fuel leakage from tailpipe; fumes entered passenger compartment; dealer replaced fuel injectors and PCM. • Check Engine light comes on all the time (often it's a loose gas cap, defective #5 spark plug, or ignition coil). • Sudden stalling with loss of brakes and steering. • Premature transmission failure. • Rear axle misalignment causes vehicle to sway to the side of the road. • Excessive steering-wheel vibrations. • Steering lock-up while driving in a parking lot. • Plastic fuel tank is located too close to the rear bumper. • Headlights work intermittently. • Rear tailgate glass shattered for unknown reason. **2001**—Suspension, steering, and driveline fell off vehicle. • Cam sensor failures cause vehicle to lose all power. • Brake failures. • Airbag didn't deploy during collision. • Headlights suddenly went out. • Seat belt abraded from catching on door latch. • Horn is hard to access. • Incorrect speedometer readings. • Brake and gas pedal too close together. **2002**—Waits of several months for recalled parts. • Airbags fail to deploy. • Check Engine light comes on, and vehicle suddenly stalls in traffic • Brake goes to the floor without any braking effect. **2003**—Rear axle mounting bolt snapped. • Rear end sways left and right while driving. • Dashboard reflects onto windshield at night. • Driver-seat instability. **2004**—Faulty electronic control module (ECM) causes chronic stalling. • Complete brake failure. • Imprecise steering. • Sunroof exploded while driving. • Power outlet wiring can easily overheat under a 20-amp load. **2005**—Driver's knee can hit the ignition switch, shutting off vehicle. • Hemi engine loss of power; sudden acceleration. • Chronic stalling. • Shift lever stuck in Park. • Automatic transmission self-destructed just after transmission seal recall fix. • Owners state the powertrain recall doesn't fix the problem. • Differential seal leaks fluid, grinds. • Windows won't open in cold weather if water seeps through the housing. • Seat belts are too short. • Sudden loss of power-steering fluid resulted in loss of steering ability. • Head restraint tilts driver's head too far forward. • Heated seats may burn occupant:

> I am a paraplegic and was a passenger in a 2005 Grand Cherokee with heated seats. It was a cool day and I turned on the seats. The heated seats burned both cheeks of my butt. I am confined to a bed until the burns heal.

• Tire jack won't lift vehicle high enough to change a tire.

Secret Warranties/Internal Bulletins/Service Tips

1993–2003—Paint delamination, peeling, or fading. **1999–2000**—Harsh upshifts or downshifts may require the reprogramming of the transmission control module (TCM) or powertrain control module (PCM) under the emissions warranty, says TSB #21-09-00, published September 15, 2000. • Front axle whines or moans, rear-end whines at speeds greater than 65 km/h, long cranking times to start, steering-gear honks on turns, slow-to-retract seat belts, an intermittent bump felt when stopping, front-seat binding or sticking, brake roughness or pedal pulsation when brakes are applied, and cold air leaking into the passenger footwell are all addressed in Jeep's bulletins for these two model years. • A worn-out O-ring (quad ring) in the fuel-module assembly may be the cause of long cranking before starts. **1999–2001**—A front axle whine may require extensive repairs to correct, says TSB #03-001-01 Rev A. **1999–2003**—Many anecdotal reports of Chrysler paying for brake caliper and rotor replacement after the warranty has expired. **1999–2004**—Rough-running engine (see bulletin).

HOT START MISFIRE, ROUGH IDLE

BULLETIN NO.: 18-031-03   DATE: SEP. 5, 2003

4.0L ROUGH ENGINE IDLE AFTER RESTART FOLLOWING A HOT SOAK

This bulletin involves the installation of a fuel injector insulator sleeve.

2000–04 (TJ) Wrangler
1999–2004 (WJ) Grand Cherokee
2000–01 (XJ) Jeep Cherokee

• Front-door wind noise. • Suspension noise. **2001**—Harsh upshifts; a clunk or shudder noticed when accelerating. • Exhaust boom when idling. • Honking noise when turning. • Front axle whine. • Troubleshooting geartrain sound that enters into the passenger compartment. • Remedy for climate-control setting that may be too warm or too cool. **2001–02**—Vehicle runs rough or exhibits a bucking or hesitation. • Excessive vibration and brake-pedal pulsation. **2001–03**—Steering-wheel pop or tick noise. • **2002**—4.7L engine crankshaft problems. • Brake roughness; front-brake pulsation.

• Premature fuel-nozzle shutoff when fuelling. • Faulty seat cushion heater. • Inadvertent activation of panic alarm. **2002–03**—Front-door wind noise. • Shift/speed control improvements. • Transmission may only operate in Second gear. **2002–04**—Engine idle gets progressively rougher as the engine warms up. **2003**—Crankshaft burr. • Erratically shifting automatic transmission may require a re-calibrated PCM or TCM. • Automatic transmission may overheat. • A "customer satisfaction program" will fix the automatic transmission's torque converter for free. • Power-steering moan or whine. **2003–04**—Liftgate glass lifts up in wet conditions. **2004**—Rough cold engine operation. **2005**—Faulty connection may cause automatic tranny to "limp" home. • Remedy for diesel hard starts. • Water leaks at front pillar. • AC compressor growl. • Power-steering whine. • Roof rack wind turbulence. • Tailgate secondary seal may be loose, misaligned, or wrinkled. • Improved AC settings. **2005–06**—Improved temperature-control settings. • Troubleshooting tips to correct a rear suspension squeak. • Tips on removing windshield ring marks. **2006**—Loose, binding front-door window.

CHEROKEE, GRAND CHEROKEE PROFILE

	1998	1999	2000	2001	2002	2003	2004	2005	2006
Cost Price ($) (soft)									
Base 4X2	21,425	22,460	22,460	—	—	—	—	—	—
Cherokee 4X4	23,645	24,680	24,680	28,550	—	—	—	—	—
Gr. Cherokee (25%)	34,980	36,295	38,860	—	—	—	—	—	—
Gr. Cherokee 4X4 (25%)	34,980	36,295	38,860	39,790	39,005	39,225	39,775	38,990	39,955
Used Values ($)									
Base 4X2 ▲	3,000	4,500	6,000	—	—	—	—	—	—
Base 4X2 ▼	2,500	3,500	5,000	—	—	—	—	—	—
Cherokee 4X4 ▲	5,000	5,500	7,500	9,500	—	—	—	—	—
Cherokee 4X4 ▼	4,500	5,000	6,000	8,000	—	—	—	—	—
Gr. Cherokee ▲	6,000	7,500	9,000	—	—	—	—	—	—
Gr. Cherokee ▼	5,000	6,500	7,500	—	—	—	—	—	—
Gr. Cherokee 4X4 ▲	7,500	8,500	10,500	13,500	16,000	18,500	23,500	27,500	—
Gr. Cherokee 4X4 ▼	6,500	7,500	9,000	12,000	14,500	17,000	22,000	26,000	—
Reliability	③	③	③	③	③	④	④	④	—
Crash Safety (F)	—	③	③	③	—	—	—	—	—
Grand Cherokee	③	③	③	③	③	③	③	⑤	⑤
Side	—	③	③	③	—	—	—	—	—
Grand Cherokee	—	④	④	④	④	④	④	⑤	⑤
Offset	②	②	②	②	—	—	—	—	—
Grand Cherokee	—	②	②	②	②	②	②	—	—
Rollover	—	—	—	②	②	②	—	④	③

 COMMANDER ★

RATING: Not Recommended (2006–07). This huge SUV makes no sense whatsoever, and it's living on borrowed time. It's essentially a $40,865–$51,055, seven-passenger, supersized Grand Cherokee with undersized tires that's been stretched by 5 cm (2 in.). You get the same Grand Cherokee platform and off-road capability with similar overall highway performance and reliability. However, first-year glitches and the dropping of Jeep's 7-year powertrain warranty will likely mean long-term maintenance costs will be higher. Buyers have the choice of a

2007 TECHNICAL DATA

POWERTRAIN (REAR-DRIVE OR 4X4)
Engines: 3.7L V6 (210 hp) • 4.7L
V8 (235 hp) • 5.7L V8 (330 hp);
Transmission: 5-speed auto./man.

DIMENSION/CAPACITY
Passengers: 2/3; Wheelbase: 109.5.
in.; H: 71.9/L: 188.5/W: 74.8 in.;
Headroom F/R: 42.1/35.7 in.;
Legroom F/R: 41.7/35.5 in.; Cargo
volume: 34.5 cu. ft.; Fuel tank:
77.6L/regular; Tow limit: 3,500–7,200
lb.; Load capacity: 1,230–1,620 lb.;
GVWR: 4,889–6,200 lb.; Turning
circle: 37 ft.; Ground clearance: 9.9
in.; Weight: 4,441 lb.

Commander combines Willys Wagon, Wagoneer, and Cherokee styling.

rather lacklustre 3.7L V6, a more suitable 4.7L V8, or a 5.7L Hemi V8 and of three full-time 4×4 systems. The V6 comes with a 5-speed automatic transmission, while a multi-speed automatic is used with both V8s. Two models are available with two- or four-wheel drive and a towing capacity of 1,590 kg (3,500 lb.).

Styling is rather bland, squarish, and utilitarian. The three passenger-seat rows provide raised "theatre" seating, and the second and third rows fold flat. Some major design miscues include a minuscule third seat that's too small for most adults, fake-looking riveted fender flares, three sunroofs, four driver-side air vents, and a huge rear overhang. Two important safety features found on the Commander are electronic stability-control and electronic roll mitigation, a system that selectively deploys side curtain airbags as directed by sensors whenever a rollover appears imminent. Incidentally, although the Commander's front and side crashworthiness ratings have been excellent, NHTSA tests have concluded it has an average tendency to roll over—in spite of the standard stability-control.

Jeep is selling this gas-guzzler while most shoppers are downsizing their SUV choices in reaction to higher fuel prices and insurance premiums. This means smart buyers will wait at least until the spring of 2007 to get a cheaper, better quality Commander. Expect the Commander to carry a profit margin of at least 25 percent of its MSRP, which will help pay for the estimated $8,000 in rebates and discounts that should be available in the new year. **New for 2007:** Nothing significant.

 SAFETY COMPLAINTS: 2006—Sudden, unintended acceleration or total loss of power:

I have purchased a 2006 Jeep Commander. It has 6,000 miles [9,660 km] on it. At 4,200 miles [6,760 km] it started stalling for no apparent reason. It has done it in stop and go traffic and has done it when I was traveling at 35 mph [56 km/h]. Other Jeep Commander owners are experiencing the same problem. See Jeep Commander thread at *Edmunds.com*.

• Engine self-destructed. • Headrests can't be removed, making it impossible to secure a child booster seat:

The Commander headrests seem to be fixed in place. They just seem to move forward when you flip the seat down to access the third row. To make matters worse, they are fixed in a slightly forward position, which forces the booster seat to pitch forward. I can correct that slightly by reclining the seat back, but, in the Commander, the second row seat only slightly reclines. In any case, the booster can't be installed properly or safely, according to the manual.

• Tire jack bent under weight of the vehicle. • Windshield is easily cracked by small pebbles.

Secret Warranties/Internal Bulletins/Service Tips

2006—Improved temperature-control settings. • Troubleshooting tips to correct a rear suspension squeak. • Loose, binding front-door window. • Interior water leaks and excessive wind noise.

The Compass is priced right, but for most off-roaders, it doesn't look right.

RATING: Not Recommended during their first year on the market. Although this rating may seem harsh, it follows Jeep's history of putting out glitch-ridden first-year vehicles that are a nightmare to own. Both the Cherokee and Liberty, for example, needed almost three years to work out many of their factory-related defects and to convince dealers to stock up on parts. The Patriot is essentially a Compass with a different suspension and styled more along the lines of the Liberty.

Compass—a carlike Jeep

As much as the Commander is the wrong SUV launched at the wrong time, the Compass and Patriot may be two crossover SUVs that are right on target, at least on paper. Jeep's first front-drive-based SUVs, these two vehicles are designed to capitalize on the public's shift to compact sport-utilities. The first fruit of a trium-virate venture with Mitsubishi and Hyundai, they combine the packaging and functionality of an SUV with the performance, handling, fuel economy, and price of a compact car or small pickup, thus rivaling established models like the Toyota RAV4, Honda CR-V, and Ford Escape. Other competitors are the Honda Element, Hyundai Tucson, Kia Sportage, Mazda Tribute, Mitsubishi Outlander, Nissan Xterra or X-Trail, Pontiac Torrent, and Toyota FJ Cruiser.

Both vehicles use the Dodge Caliber platform and are about 13 cm (5 in.) longer and 360 kg (800 lb.) heavier than the Liberty. A fuel-efficient and quiet-running 172-hp 2.4L 4-cylinder engine may be hooked to a 5-speed manual transaxle or an optional continuously variable transaxle (CVT) that is said to improve fuel economy by 5 percent. The CVT itself has an AutoStick option that allows for the manual control of a simulated 6-speed. Although CVT transaxles have been used in Japanese vehicles for many years without any reliability problems, American models, notably Saturn's Vue, have had serious problems with their CVTs—another reason why buyers should delay the purchase of a first-year Compass or Patriot.

An optional full-time 4×4 system enhances overall driving performance and includes a number of standard features like Brake Traction Control, Electronic Stability Program (ESP), Brake Assist, Electronic Roll Mitigation (ERM), and anti-lock brakes. Off-roaders will also appreciate the 20 cm (8 in.) of ground clearance. Additional standard features include side curtain airbags, a fold-flat vinyl load floor, an AM/FM CD radio with an auxiliary audio input jack, cloth seats, tilt steering wheel, dome and cargo lights, floor mats, and a centre console sliding armrest.

The manufacturer's suggested retail price (MSRP) for the 2007 entry-level Compass is $17,995 (not including a $1,050 freight and PDI fee). The MSRP for 4×4 models is $19,995.

Patriot—a "Jeeplike" Compass

The Patriot takes the Compass up a couple of notches in styling and performance capability. It has more of the Jeep's traditional rugged look and, unlike the Compass, can be made into a Trail Rated off-roader with the Freedom Drive II off-road package that offers full skid plates and automatic four-wheel drive with a locking low-range gear for no-worry off-roading. The package also includes 17-inch all-terrain outline white letter (OWL) tires and aluminum wheels, a full-sized spare tire, an air-filtration system, tow hooks, fog lamps, and a seat-height adjuster—all for an estimated price that varies from $22,985 to $28,485, plus the same freight and PDI fee as the Compass.

The Patriot has the rugged Jeep styling the Compass lacks, but extra-cost off-road capability may be a tough sell.

Family ties

When you buy the car, you marry the family, and the three members of this auto alliance have their share of dysfunctional elements. For example, in the '80s when Chrysler teamed up with Mitsubishi to produce several generations of Colts, they made small cars with a good reputation for quality control, and the small auto-maker began riding the crest of a surge in small-car sales.

Then all hell broke loose.

From the late 1990s through 2004, seven top Mitsubishi executives were arrested and charged in Japan with covering up safety recalls and falsifying defect reports, including a failure that killed a driver. Then the press found evidence that the company regularly made payoffs to Yakuza crime bosses for protection from union leaders and disgruntled stockholders. Reacting to the scandals and mounting losses, the parent company in 2005 forced the resignation of Mitsubishi's president, chairman, and vice chairman. DaimlerChrysler's Mercedes masters in Germany were horrified, and they soon began cutting their ties with Mitsubishi.

Not soon enough, though. Shortly thereafter, the company was hit by lawsuits alleging a pattern of systematic sexual harassment of women at Mitsubishi's Illinois assembly plant. Although these suits were settled, Chrysler ran for cover and sold off its 37 percent interest in the company. Interestingly, now it has come to light that Mercedes-Benz, Hitler's favourite employer of slave labour, has its own hands full fending off allegations of sexual harassment, illegal payoffs, maladministration, and poor quality control.

Now, with both Mitsubishi and Hyundai in the picture, both the Dodge Caliber and its Compass/Patriot spin-off may turn out to be bestsellers. Healthy early Caliber sales certainly point in this direction. On the other hand, all three automakers have a lot of catching up to do. In the 2006 edition of J.D. Power and Associates Initial Quality Study, Mitsubishi placed 23rd out of 37 brands ranked, and the Eclipse is the company's only bestseller; Hyundai has a full plate pulling its Kia subsidiary sales out of the mud and launching delayed new products; and Chrysler is stuck with a huge inventory of large trucks and SUVs that nobody wants (don't even mention Dodge's B-Van replacement, the $39,135 Mercedes Sprinter).

LIBERTY, NITRO ★★★★

RATING: Above Average (2005–07); Average (2002–04). This heavier, more versatile successor to the Cherokee has many reliability and quality problems, most of which are clustered around its first three model years. More recent models have had fewer deficiencies reported, but they haven't been on the road that long, nor do they have a 7-year powertrain warranty to cover the Jeep's automatic transmission failures. **Strong points:** A 7-year powertrain warranty on the 2002–04 models; good towing capability for a V6; very comfortable ride; generous interior volume; practical, versatile interior; well-appointed and offers a nice array of standard and optional safety features. A tight turning circle, low-range gearing, load-levelling shocks, and a front skid plate enhance off-road performance (while mediocre quality control compromises safety and performance). **Weak points:** The 2001 Jeep Cherokee came

2007 LIBERTY TECHNICAL DATA

POWERTRAIN
Engine: 3.7L V6 (210 hp); Transmissions: 6-speed man. • 4-speed auto. • 5-speed auto.

DIMENSION/CAPACITY
Passengers: 2/3; Wheelbase: 104.3 in.; H: 70.2/L: 174.4/W: 71.6 in.; Headroom F/R: 6.0/7.0 in.; Legroom F/R: 40/28.5 in.; Cargo volume: 35 cu. ft.; Fuel tank: 78L/regular; Tow limit (V6): 5,000 lb.; Load capacity: 1,150 lb.; GVWR: 5,350 lb. (av.); Turning circle: 37 ft.; Ground clearance: 6.5 in.; Weight: 4,125 lb.

with a peppy 190-hp inline 6-cylinder engine; Liberty's pre-2006 base engine is a 150-hp, underpowered, Cirrus-sourced 4-cylinder. There's little reserve power for passing and merging. The 160-hp 2.8L turbodiesel is a joke. It gets only three extra miles per gallon over the V6, provides lethargic acceleration, and sounds like a farm tractor. Selec-Trac 4×4 is not as user-friendly as rivals' AWD; there's excessive swaying, rocking, and jiggling on uneven roads; the steering is less responsive than that of the RAV4; and independent front suspension can limit off-roading prowess. The 2001 Cherokee also offered an extra 2.5 cm (1 in.) of ground clearance and a heavy-duty suspension for serious off-roading. The Liberty has compromised rear-seat comfort; rear visibility that's blocked by a spare tire; a driver's seat that is positioned closer to the door than usual and could use additional lumbar and lateral support; a high step-in and narrow door openings; a bulging heater box that protrudes into the cabin area; no folding centre rear armrest; 4×4 gear whine (a Jeep trademark for years) and excessive engine clatter, turbo whistle, and tire and wind noise; cheap-looking plastic interior trim; and surprisingly poor fuel economy for a compact SUV. **New for 2007:** Liberty's small 2.8L 4-cylinder diesel engine has been dropped because it doesn't meet the tougher federal emissions standards that will be taking effect next year. The Nitro, a Liberty-derived Dodge sport-utility, enters the marketplace in late 2006 as a 2007 model. A restyled exterior uses flat surfaces, crisp lines, and a downsized version of the macho crosshair grille to set this spin-off apart from its Liberty brother. Nitro's interior space feels a bit larger than the Liberty's, and its "Load and Slide" textured vinyl cargo floor slides for easy loading and unloading.

In the U.S., Nitros will come with standard rear-wheel drive; in Canada it is expected that only four-wheel drive models will be available.

Marketed as a mid-sized alternative to the Durango SUV, the Nitro has a 3.7L 210-hp SOHC V6 coupled to a full-time 4×4 and a 4-speed automatic. A high-performance SRT version will be offered for 2008.

MODEL HISTORY: Introduced as a 2002 model, the Liberty is a four-door that's longer, wider, taller, and generally roomier than the Cherokee it replaced; it has less cargo space and ground clearance, however. It also weighs a lot more than its predecessor, which eats into its fuel economy figures. **2002**—Given larger, stronger brake rotors and drums than the Cherokee (brake problems remain a constant complaint) and a new ABS system with electronic brake force distribution. **2003**—Standard four-wheel disc brakes. **2006**—A 160-hp 2.8L 4-cylinder diesel engine debuted on the 2006 models and then was dropped for the 2007 model year.

COST ANALYSIS: *Liberty:* Priced at $29,815/$33,560 (Sport/Limited), the 2007 Liberty is overpriced; try a 2006 version for about $7,000 less. Stay away from the little 4-banger. It's the same failure-prone beastie used on the Cirrus (complete with biodegradable head gaskets). It's completely overwhelmed by the Liberty's extra weight, although it does manage to eke out a 900 kg (2,000 lb.) tow rating. If you choose the torquier turbodiesel, fuel economy will benefit, but acceleration is still sluggish and long-term reliability is unknown. The V6 is the best choice. It's fairly powerful, with plenty of low-end grunt, and can tow up to 2,265 kg (5,000 lb.) when equipped with the optional towing package. *Nitro:* This year's Nitro base price varies between $27,000–$42,000, depending on the model or equipment chosen. **Best alternatives:** A new Honda CR-V, Nissan Xterra, or Toyota RAV4. The 2001 Jeep Cherokee isn't a bad choice, either. **Rebates:** Look for $3,000 rebates or low-financing deals on both vehicles. **Delivery/PDI:** $1,050. **Warranty:** Bumper-to-bumper 3 years/60,000 km; powertrain 5 years/100,000 km; rust perforation 5 years/160,000 km. **Supplementary warranty:** A comprehensive extended warranty is a wise buy because this vehicle is so poorly made. **Options:** Get the V6 engine, 4-speed automatic transmission, and Selec-Trac full-time 4×4. Larger 16-inch tires are a performance plus. Here are two worthwhile, though overpriced, option packages worth considering: a trailer towing package ($480), which includes an engine oil cooler, Class 3 trailer hitch, and 7-pin wiring harness; and a convenience package ($2,485), which includes air conditioning, CD changer, roof rack, deluxe steel wheels, full-sized spare tire, power front windows with one-touch-down feature, and a tilt steering wheel. **Depreciation:** Slower than average. **Insurance cost:** Average. **Parts supply/cost:** Expect high parts costs and month-long waits until the parts supply line gets filled. **Annual maintenance cost:** Average, thanks to the 7-year extended powertrain warranty. **Highway/city fuel economy:** *4-cyl.:* 9.4/11.8 L/100 km; *2.8L turbodiesel:* 8.0/10.5 L/100 km; *V6:* 10.7/12.4 L/100 km.

QUALITY/RELIABILITY: Average. **Owner complaints:** Ongoing reliability problems compromise the Liberty's safety and performance. **Warranty performance:** DaimlerChrysler's warranty performance is about average.

ROAD PERFORMANCE: Acceleration/torque: Plenty of power with the V6, although it could use more high-end grunt for highway cruising. Diesel engine acceleration is woefully slow and keeps the engine high-revving with lots of clatter and turbo whine. **Transmission:** Quite versatile over a variety of roads. For ordinary day-to-day driving on dry roads, 4×2 is fine; on wet or snow-covered roads, full-time 4×4 enhances stability and traction; for gravel and dirt roads, part-time 4×4 provides more traction; and for steep, slippery inclines, 4×4 Low gives you lots of engine braking and pulling power. **Steering:** Fairly accurate and predictable, though less so with the diesel-equipped version. **Routine handling:** A firm, jittery ride. The Liberty's drivetrain and body are more vibration-prone and noisy than the Cherokee's. Unibody construction and independent front suspension provide more carlike handling than a body-on-frame design. The low ground clearance limits the Liberty's off-road capability. **Braking:** Works quite well. Off-roaders will appreciate that the ABS system is defeated when the transfer case is placed in Low and that it has been redesigned to limit false activation on bumpy surfaces.

 SAFETY SUMMARY: Airbags: Front. **ABS:** Optional; disc/drum. **Safety belt pretensioners:** Front. **Traction control:** No. **Head restraints F/R:** ★★★★★/★★★. **Visibility F/R:** ★★★★★/★★★.

SAFETY COMPLAINTS: You would think this Mercedes-backed SUV would avoid most of the factory-related mistakes that have plagued so many Chrysler/Jeep vehicles. Think again. Government probes have logged over 100 safety complaints on the 2002–05 models. This is an astounding figure, given that the Liberty was Mercedes' first chance to show it could produce a top-quality vehicle in cooperation with Chrysler. This raises the question: How could Mercedes bosses allow such poorly designed junk to be rushed into production?

It's because they're turning out junk themselves. In fact, Mercedes' own product quality has been judged to be unacceptable by J.D. Power and the U.S. National Automobile Dealers Association (NADA).

All years: Many complaints of electrical fires, faulty airbags, no brakes, sudden acceleration, chronic stalling, transmission failures, excessive on-road vibration, and recall snafus, with owners not being notified, parts not being available, and the correction not fixing the problem. **2002**—Fire ignited at right side of vehicle. • Vehicle tips over quite easily. • Transmission went from Park to Reverse and rolled over when started. • Vehicle easily rolled over from a side impact. • Vehicle rolled over when wheel/axle suddenly collapsed. • Side airbags deployed while driving. • Low suspension allows underside to be easily damaged; makes off-roading unsafe. • Part of steering wheel fell off while driving. • Front seats propelled forward when braking. **2003**—Vehicle suddenly shuts down because of chronic fuel-pump failures. • Front ball joint/strut mount failures. **2004**—Airbag-induced injuries:

> While driving at 25 mph [40 km/h], the driver-side airbag deployed for no logical reason. The consumer lost control of the vehicle and collided with an embankment. The vehicle never ran over anything or hit anything before the mishap. The consumer

suffered a sprained wrist, a concussion and trauma to his back. The consumer also reported that before the airbag deployed, electrical currents from the steering wheel were shocking whoever drove the vehicle.

• Fuel smell in cabin, and then a fire ignited. • Hood latch failure. • Goodyear Wrangler tire tread separation. **2005**—Sudden acceleration caused by a defective accelerator pedal pressure sensor. • Chronic stalling. • Airbags failed to deploy during a severe collision. • Excessive steering-wheel play; vehicle tends to wander all over the highway, forcing driver to constantly make steering corrections. • Plastic fuel tank and its mounting increase the possibility of fuel leakage from minor impacts. • Premature wearout of the lower front ball joints:

> The bolt holding the lower A-arm came off, and the whole assembly was sitting on the ground and had made a huge hole in the tire. Lucky this did not happen going up the steep and windy roads over the mountain, otherwise she would have definitely got into an accident. We called the Chrysler roadside assistance and had the Jeep towed to the dealer. The next day we called the dealer, [and] they gave us a loaner car. About a week later we picked up the Jeep, [and] they had replaced both front ball joints and replaced the tire with a brand new one. We only had our '05 Renegade for just over a year and about 31,000 miles [50,000 km] on it.

• Airbag Off light comes on when an adult sits in the passenger seat:

> Airbag Off light comes on with adult in passenger seat. Seems to go off only over 110 lb. Many adult passengers around 100 lb, and thus do not have safety of system on. Been to dealer three times. They say nothing can be done.

• Tire jack bent under the weight of the vehicle. • Gas sloshes out of a full tank.

Secret Warranties/Internal Bulletins/Service Tips

2002—Remedy for skunk-like odour. • Front engine-compartment harness may have an intermittent loose ground. • Loss of crankshaft position sensor signal. • Troubleshooting 45RFE transmission solenoids. • Radiator oil cooler contamination. • Longer-than-normal crank time prior to start. • Reduced power-steering assist when steering wheel is turned quickly. • Excessive wind buffeting. • Software improvement for unlatching flip-up glass. • Flickering panel lights or display. • Difficulty refuelling. • Exhaust rattle caused by flange bolt springs. • Front-end creaking noise. • Wind whistle from Mopar brush guard or front air deflector. • AC drain water leaks under passenger-side carpet are caused by a factory

---

BRAKE MOANING
BULLETIN NO.: 05-001-04   DATE: JANUARY 13, 2004

REAR DISC BRAKE MOAN
This bulletin involves the replacement of the rear disc brake pads and rotors. 2003–04 Liberty (Domestic Market) The customer may experience a rear brake moan-like sound during light or no brake application pressure. This condition is more likely to occur when the brakes are cool (first use) and ambient temperatures are below 50°F [10°C]. The moan-like sound may be intermittent.

mistake, says TSB #24-012-01. **2003**—An erratically shifting automatic transmission may require a re-calibrated PCM or TCM. • Harsh-shifting countermeasures. • Scored 3.7L engine crankshaft. • Insufficient body sealer in cowl area. **2003–04**—Liftgate glass lifts up. • AC won't cool or heat properly. • Harsh downshifts. • Excessive brake noise (see bulletin). • **2004**—Slow gear engagement after a cold start requires reprogramming of the PCM. **2005**—Faulty connection may cause automatic tranny to "limp" home. • Remedy for diesel hard starts. **2005–06**—Improved hill-climbing capability in Reverse. • Ring marks on glass. • Manual 6-speed won't stay in gear.

LIBERTY PROFILE

	2002	2003	2004	2005	2006
Cost Price ($) (soft)					
Liberty Sport (22%)	22,800	24,490	25,695	27,360	29,815
Liberty Limited (23%)	28,680	29,790	30,675	33,420	33,555
Used Values ($)					
Liberty Sport ▲	11,500	14,500	17,000	20,000	—
Liberty Sport ▼	10,000	13,000	15,500	18,000	—
Liberty Limited ▲	13,000	17,500	21,000	24,000	—
Liberty Limited ▼	11,500	16,000	19,500	22,000	—
Reliability	③	④	④	④	—
Crash Safety (F)	⑤	⑤	⑤	⑤	⑤
Side	⑤	⑤	⑤	⑤	⑤
Offset	②	②	②	②	②
Rollover	②	③	③	③	③

bad buy **DURANGO, ASPEN** ★

RATING: Not Recommended (1998–2007). **Strong points:** Powerful V8 engines provide brisk acceleration with plenty of low-end torque for trailering heavy loads; lots of passenger and cargo room; a 7-year powertrain warranty on the 2002–04 models; and a comfortable ride. **Weak points:** 2005–07 models don't get the extended powertrain warranty; poor acceleration with the V6; excessive fuel consumption because of the Durango's heft, especially with the more powerful engines; chronic Hemi engine stalling; unacceptable emergency handling; unsteady road manners; sudden jerks when passing over bumps; harsh and abrupt downshifts; obstructed rear visibility; difficult rear entry and exit; and insufficient rear-seat padding. The climate-control system won't blow air on the floor and your face at the same time (on the earlier models); the drivetrain's durability is problematic; ball joints are biodegradable (also a Dakota failing); the vehicle is fuel-thirsty; and a painfully loud pounding noise is heard while cruising with the rear windows down. **New for 2007:** The 4.7L V8 engine features standard E85

All ratings on a numbered scale where ⑤ is good and ❶ is bad. See page 220 for a more detailed description.

2007 TECHNICAL DATA

POWERTRAIN (FRONT-DRIVE OR 4X4)
Engines: 3.7L V6 (210 hp) • 4.7L V8
(235 hp) • 5.7L Hemi V8 (335 hp);
Transmissions: 4-speed auto. • 5-speed
auto.

DIMENSION/CAPACITY
Passengers: 3/3/2; Wheelbase: 119.2 in.;
H: 74.3/L: 201/W: 76 in.; Headroom F/
R1/R2: 3.5/3.5/3.5 in.; Legroom F/R1/R2:
41/27.5/28 in.; Cargo volume: 44.5 cu. ft.;
Fuel tank: 102L/regular; Tow limit: 8,700
lb.; Load capacity: 1,260 lb.; GVWR:
6,600 lb.; Turning circle: 43 ft.; Ground
clearance: 6.0 in.; Weight: 5,335 lb.

compatibility that allows drivers the choice of using ethanol, gasoline, or any mixture of the two. The exterior has been restyled and second-row bucket seats have been added. The new Aspen is described by Chrysler as an "elegant" Durango.

MODEL HISTORY: Essentially a re-badged Dakota pickup, the $42,750/$49,145 (SLT/Limited) Durango is larger than the Jeep Grand Cherokee but shorter than the Ford Expedition. It underwent a redesign in 2004, where it got heavier and more complex. Interestingly, the Durango's 5.7L Hemi V8 has a 3,950 kg (8,700 lb.) towing capacity, giving this mid-sized truck as much hauling power as some costlier full-sized sport-utilities. A few 1998–2005 models carry the then-standard V6, but most Durangos have been ordered with the more robust 4.7L, 5.2L, 5.7L Hemi, and 5.9L optional V8 engines. **1999**—Added rear-wheel drive, a rear power outlet, steering-wheel-mounted radio controls, and heated mirrors. **2000**—The standard V6 was replaced by the 4.7L V8, suspension was upgraded, and a sporty R/T package was introduced. **2001**—A standard electronic transfer case, interior upgrades, 15-inch wheels, and a tilt steering column. The 5.2L V8 was dropped. **2003**—An upgraded 5-speed automatic transmission; standard four-wheel disc brakes. **2004**—A reworked, larger chassis, more power, an improved ride and handling, additional interior luxury features, and a slightly restyled front end. This SUV also gains almost 180 kg (400 lb.). The Durango is now offered with rear-wheel drive and two all-wheel-drive systems, one with low-range gearing. **2005**—Addition of a new optional navigation system. Three engines are available: a new 3.7L V6, a 4.7L V8, and a newly optional 5.7L Hemi V8 with almost 100 more horses than the largest previous engine. **2006**—The Hemi V8 comes with a fuel-saving cylinder deactivation feature called MDS (Multi-Displacement System), borrowed from Chrysler's Hemi-powered car lines.

COST ANALYSIS: Buy a second-series 2004 or later model. The 2006's cylinder deactivation feature has so far not generated any reports of malfunctions, so it's not as risky a buy as first thought. This year's exterior restyling doesn't justify the Durango's higher cost. **Best alternatives:** Check out the Honda Pilot, Nissan Xterra, and Toyota Highlander. **Options:** Get the 4.7L V8 or 5.2L V8 engine. Although the Hemi option pays for itself at resale time, the engine is still relatively unproven and has elicited serious reliability and performance complaints over the past several years. An anti-theft system is a must-have. **Rebates:** $5,000+ rebates likely by year's end. **Delivery/PDI:** $1,175. **Depreciation:** Fairly rapid; slower if equipped with the Hemi engine. **Insurance cost:** Above average. **Parts supply/ cost:** Parts have been moderately priced and plentiful because of the availability of competitively priced parts from the Dakota parts bin. Expensive brake and drive-train servicing. **Annual maintenance cost:** Average. **Warranty:** Bumper-to-bumper 3 years/60,000 km; powertrain 5 years/100,000 km; rust perforation 5 years/160,000 km. **Supplementary warranty:** An extended warranty is a must. **Highway/city fuel economy:** *3.7L V6:* 11.0/15.9 L/100 km; *4.7L V8:* 12.0/17.4 L/100 km; *5.7L Hemi V8:* 12.1/18 L/100 km; *5.9L V8:* 13.2/18.9 L/100 km.

QUALITY/RELIABILITY: Quality control has declined markedly. Body components and trim items still seem to be blue-light specials. For additional owner comments, go to *www-odi.nhtsa.dot.gov/cars/problems/complain.* **Owner-reported problems:** Chronic stalling (Hemi engine); engine crankshaft, drive shaft, differential, motor mount, ball joint (covered by a 10-year extended warranty), and wheel bearing failures; chronic drivetrain whines and howls; electrical system and brake defects (spongy brakes, warped rotors); chronic AC failures, dash rattles, and premature differential bearing failures. **Warranty performance:** Average. **Likely failures:** Automatic transmission, steering, ball joints, and control arms:

> 2003 Dodge Durango upper ball joint failed on interstate at 65 mph [105 km/h]. Right front wheel and assembly separated from vehicle, causing single-car accident. Skidded into guard rail. Damage estimated at $10,000 plus.

Other problem spots are brake rotors and pads; centre wheel caps, which may fly off; AC compressor and evaporator; and water leaks.

ROAD PERFORMANCE: Acceleration/torque: Although the V6 may look like a bargain, it's not powerful enough for a vehicle this large. The 4.7L V8 is the best compromise for most driving chores. If you intend to tow a trailer or carry a full load of passengers, move up to the huskier 5.7L. **Transmission:** Automatic transmission downshifts can be abrupt at times. The floor-mounted transfer-case lever can be a stretch for some drivers. **Routine handling:** 2004 models provide easier handling and a more pleasant ride. Some body lean and front-end plowing in fast turns. **Emergency handling:** Acceptable. Not as ponderous as most vehicles this size. Cornering is well controlled and handling is more crisp and predictable on the 2004 version. **Steering:** Good, most of the time. Very responsive, with lots of road feedback. **Braking:** Mediocre (100–0 km/h: 43 m with the 4.7L V8).

SAFETY SUMMARY: Side-view mirror is too large to see around and blocks view when making turns. Owners report long waits for recall repairs that in some cases don't improve performance, notably the recent recall to fix the ABS brake system. **Airbags:** Reports of airbags failing to deploy. **ABS:** Standard; on rear wheels only. **Head restraints F/R:** *2004:* ★★★★; *1999–2003:* ★. **Visibility F/R:** ★:

I have a 2005 Dodge Durango. The way the vehicle is engineered there are serious blind spots. This is observed when the driver looks to his [or her] right. The passenger side "B" pillar is in their direct view. The way the front cockpit is designed you can't see overhead street lights while stopped or approaching a stop bar. There are also blind spots to the passenger side and rear and driver's side rear of the driver.

SAFETY COMPLAINTS: All years: Sudden acceleration and frequent stalling. • Vehicle wanders all over the road. • Transmission/differential breakdowns. • Collapsing ball joints (warranty extended). • Loss of brakes. • Electrical fires. • Violent shaking. **1998–99**—Child accidentally moved shift lever out of Park, causing vehicle to roll into lake. • Horn failure. • Power windows go down by themselves and won't go back up. • Brakes slow, but won't completely stop vehicle when in Reverse on an incline. • Rear-liftgate support rod broke. **2000**—Accelerator tends to stick. • Loss of all electrical power. • Vehicle can be put into gear without pressing the brake pedal; child placed transmission into Drive, and vehicle took off. • Goodyear tire blowouts and tread separation. • Defective brake retainer spring caused loss of braking ability and cracked the rim. • Steering-wheel lock-up while driving, which had to be jerked free; dealer suggested that the clock spring broke. • Steering wheel fell off. • Seat belt fails to release when release button is fully depressed. **2001**—Left front wheel flew off vehicle. • Suspension causes vehicle to go out of control over uneven roads. • Steering will suddenly pull to the left or right. • Surging when cruise control is engaged. • Child pulled vehicle out of gear without touching brakes. • Middle fold-down rear seat doesn't lock properly; when brakes applied, it hit driver in head, causing a concussion. • Second-row seat leaves a sharp edge exposed when it's tumbled forward for rear access. • Cracked fuel tank. **2002**—Vehicle slips into gear without keys in the ignition. • Passenger-side window suddenly shattered. • Exhaust fumes come in through back door. **2003**—Early engine failure caused by oil system defect. • Faulty ABS braking pump results in extended stopping distance. • Erratically performing cruise control. • Door locks and unlocks for no reason. **2004**—Instrument-cluster fire. • Misfiring caused by water getting into the spark plug area. • Complete loss of steering. • Polymer bumper cracks in cold weather. • Rear wiper fell out. • Unsafe speed control on Hemi-equipped models causes engine to race when going downhill. • Rear-view mirror creates a serious blind spot. **2005**—154 safety complaints already logged by NHTSA. • Vehicle shakes violently when driven with rear windows down. • Accident caused by snapped tie rod:

When I got out and walked around to the driver's side, I saw my left front tire laying flat parallel with the ground, pinned partially under the vehicle. All of the components of the tire (the brakes, suspension, brake line, etc.) were still attached to the tire. Where the upper ball joint should have been, there was a large crack in the metal, and the tie rod was snapped. There was damage to the front left side of the vehicle due to the impact with the pillar.

• Fuel spurts out when refuelling (covered by a recall). • Sudden acceleration caused by the accelerator sticking. • Chronic stalling when going uphill, decelerating, or shifting into Reverse from a cold start:

> I have a 2005 Hemi Durango Limited with 3,300 miles [5,300 km] on it. Since new, the vehicle has occasionally died when making low speed turns. The dealer has informed me that the PCM flash provided by Dodge has not corrected the problem and they are still working on a fix. Overall the vehicle has stalled five times. I have also filed a similar complaint for my '05 Ram 2500 with the Hemi engine.

• Sudden steering loss:

> My firm represents several passengers and the personal representatives of the estates of two decedent[s] who were killed when a 2005 Dodge Durango lost steering control on the Florida Turnpike. The vehicle is a rental vehicle from Dollar [Rent A] Car. It may be a case where the bolts in the steering were missing.

Secret Warranties/Internal Bulletins/Service Tips

All years: Internal service bulletins cover the following problems: Engine knocking, stalling, poor performance, vehicle bucking during wide-open throttle operation, and transmission and suspension defects. **1998–2003**—Upper and lower ball joints, control arm, and bushing failures. Chrysler has extended the warranty to 10 years/160,000 km (100,000 mi.) on the 2000–2003 Durangos and Dakotas. On other model years, Chrysler sometimes offers a 50 percent replacement refund, which doesn't help much when applied to the full retail charge. Stand your ground and ask that the 10-year extension be applied (see CanadianDriver, "Chrysler recalls 600,000 Dodge Durangos, Dakotas," *www.canadiandriver.com/news/041213-2.htm*). **1999**—Engine overheating. • Hard starts and stalling. • Poor AC performance. • Faulty rear AC. • Front-end squeaking or creaking. • Brake grinding or growling. **2000**—The central timer module can be short-circuited by electromagnetic interference from airports, military installations, power fields, etc. When this happens, many of the vehicle's electrical systems will go haywire. Ask Chrysler to install a free revised module. • Harsh upshifts or downshifts can be smoothed out by reprogramming the PCM or TCM under the emissions warranty. • A front axle noise on acceleration may be fixed by replacing the right-side front axle bearing. • Driveline noise, vibration. **2000–01**—If the malfunction indicator light (MIL) comes on, indicating a TCC/OD solenoid performance problem, consider replacing the transmission pressure-boost valve cover plate. **2001**—Spark knock when accelerating. • Prohibition against oil additives. • Drivetrain noise and vibration. • Constant velocity joint-boot integrity (the joint boot wears out quickly). • Troubleshooting transmission warning lights. • Silencing a noisy suspension. • Steering column pop or snap. **2000–04**—AC water leak into passenger area. **2002–2003**—An erratically shifting automatic transmission may require a re-calibrated PCM or TCM. •

All ratings on a numbered scale where ⑤ is good and ❶ is bad. See page 220 for a more detailed description.

Automatic transmission may overheat. • A "customer satisfaction program" will fix the automatic transmission's torque converter for free. • Brake pads will be replaced for free to cure excessive vibration (Bulletin No.: 05-007-03). • Water leak at the B-post seam and roof. 2004—AC/heater fluttering. • Suspension squawk or screech. • Campaign to correct left-front door flange rusting. • Exhaust system drone. 2004–05—Tips for eliminating a steering snapping or ticking sound. • Troubleshooting a malfunctioning AC. • Installation of improved brakes to reduce vibration and shudder. 2005—Idle vibration and body resonance. • Wind noise at top of rear door. • AC hissing. 2005–06—Ring marks on glass.

DURANGO PROFILE

	1998	1999	2000	2001	2002	2003	2004	2005	2006
Cost Price ($) (negotiable)									
4X2	—	36,705	37,750	—	—	—	—	—	—
4X4 (26%)	36,560	38,070	39,115	38,410	38,060	38,765	41,975	42,750	43,820
Used Values ($)									
4X2 ▲	—	8,500	10,000	—	—	—	—	—	—
4X2 ▼	—	7,500	8,500	—	—	—	—	—	—
4X4 ▲	8,500	10,000	11,500	13,500	16,000	19,000	24,000	28,000	—
4X4 ▼	7,500	9,000	10,000	12,000	14,500	17,000	22,000	26,000	—
Reliability	3	3	3	3	3	3	3	3	—
Crash Safety (F)	2	2	2	4	4	4	5	5	5
Side	—	—	—	—	—	—	—	5	—
Offset	3	3	3	3	3	3	—	—	—
Rollover	—	—	—	3	3	3	3	3	3

PACIFICA ★★★

RATING: Average (2004–06). Forget the hype: This is neither a performance nor an off-road vehicle; it's more like your dad's luxury station wagon—or a mini-minivan with four swing-out doors. **Strong points:** A comfortable ride and quiet interior; lots of front- and middle-row seating space and storage areas; easily accessible seat controls; a cargo floor that's low enough for easy loading and unloading; excellent front and side crashworthiness scores, and three-point seat belts for all six seats; impressive ventilation system; and a 7-year powertrain warranty on 2004 models. **Weak points:** Seriously overpriced new models; abrupt transmission shifts remain a problem through the 2006 model year; second-row seats accommodate only two occupants, making it necessary for whoever picks the shortest straw to sit in the cramped third-row seat bereft of a seatback head restraint; restricted rear visibility; unproven body and mechanicals; and excessive fuel consumption. **New for 2007:** A 4.0L single overhead cam (SOHC) aluminum V6 engine mated to an all-new 6-speed transmission. Safety features include all-row side curtain airbags, Electronic Stability Program (ESP), Electronic Throttle Control (ETC), traction control, and an available ParkView rear backup camera.

MODEL HISTORY: The $37,050 ($42,915 for AWD models) Pacifica is an SUV, minivan, and station wagon all rolled into one. It's a big, tall vehicle that appears much lower and longer than it really is. Second- and third-row seats fold flat, and those in the third row split 50/50. Built in Windsor, Ontario, on the same production line as Chrysler's minivans, Chrysler calls it a "sports tourer" and cringes every time it's referred to as a "mini-minivan." It's actually wider, heavier, and almost as long as the Chrysler Town & Country minivan.

> **2007 TECHNICAL DATA**
>
> **POWERTRAIN (FRONT-DRIVE OR AWD)**
> Engines: 3.8L V6 (210 hp) • 4.0L V6 (255 hp) • Transmissions: 4-speed auto. • 6-speed auto.
> **DIMENSION/CAPACITY**
> Passengers: 2/2/2; Wheelbase: 116.3 in.; H: 66.5/L: 198.9/W: 79.3 in.; Headroom F/R1/R2: 5.5/5.0/N/A in.; Legroom F/R1/R2: 41/29/25.5 in.; Cargo volume: 36 cu. ft.; Fuel tank: 87L/regular; Tow limit: 3,500 lb.; Load capacity: 1,165 lb.; GVWR: 6,600 lb.; Turning circle: 42 ft. Ground clearance: 5.0 in.; Weight: 4,635 lb.

Pacifica's V6 uses both a front-drive and all-wheel-drive powertrain (an on-demand 4×4 system, transferring power to the rear wheels when the front wheels lose traction). The 4-speed automatic transmission includes an AutoStick manual-shift feature. DaimlerChrysler Canada expects 70 percent of Pacificas to be all-wheel-drive models. Handling and ride are enhanced through a strut-type suspension in the front and a multi-link independent suspension in the rear, featuring automatic load levelling.

Safety features include standard four-wheel disc brakes with ABS, a tire-pressure monitoring system, three-row head curtain airbags, adjustable pedals, and driver-side inflatable knee bolsters.

COST ANALYSIS: Buy a 2007 model made after March 2006 to distance yourself from the powertrain's first-year production glitches and from overpriced intro models. With just a few options, the Pacifica's price tag can hit $50,000—the price for an AWD Town & Country, or his-and-hers entry-level Caravans. **Best alternatives:** Try the Honda Pilot, Lexus RX series, Nissan Murano, or Toyota Highlander. **Options:** The most expensive and non-essential include a $1,200 video system and a navigation system with a small screen located in the instrument cluster (bright sunlight washes out the navigation map). Traction control is not available for all-wheel-drive Pacificas, but it comes standard on front-drive models. **Rebates:** Expect huge rebates of $5,000+ early in the new year, when Chrysler's dealer/customer sales incentives start to kick in. **Delivery/PDI:** $1,200. **Depreciation:** Faster than average. **Insurance cost:** Fairly costly. **Parts supply/cost:** Parts aren't easily found and are relatively expensive. **Annual maintenance cost:** Predicted to be costlier than average. **Warranty:** Bumper-to-bumper 3 years/60,000 km; powertrain 5 years/100,000 km; rust perforation 5 years/160,000 km. **Supplementary warranty:** An extended warranty would be a wise buy until long-term reliability has been established. **Highway/city fuel economy:** 8.7/13.4 L/100 km. Owners say fuel consumption is much more than advertised because of the vehicle's heft and rather high drag coefficient.

QUALITY/RELIABILITY: Quality control has been fair. Clanging noise when shifting from Park to Reverse. Some recurring deficiencies that aren't safety related are a constant popping and clicking caused by a defective power transfer unit, frequent stalling when turning, an inoperative climate control screen, and driver-side water leaks. **Warranty performance:** Predicted to be average.

ROAD PERFORMANCE: Acceleration/torque: The new V6 performs reasonably well but may not be powerful enough for a 2,100 kg (4,635 lb.) vehicle when pushed. Earlier engines are annoyingly loud when climbing long grades or passing at high speeds. **Transmission:** Some gear-hunting and occasional abrupt shifts. The 4-speed automatic also kicks down for long periods when the vehicle is fully loaded or going uphill. This year's tranny behaves less erratically, so far (let's keep our fingers crossed). **Routine handling:** Fairly nimble. **Emergency handling:** Feels top-heavy; some body lean in hard cornering. Fairly wide turning circle. **Steering:** Not much steering feel; road feedback is limited. **Braking:** Large four-wheel disc brakes perform quite well, with little fade, even under heavy use.

SAFETY SUMMARY: NHTSA–rated five-star occupant protection in front and side collisions. Rear visibility is seriously compromised by the car's high beltline and the thick rear side pillars. Backing up and lane changing can be scary. **Airbags:** Front and side curtain. **ABS:** Standard; on all four wheels. **Visibility F/R: ★:**

> The first incident occurred backing up in my bank parking lot…bam! Where did that pole come from? Cost: $850. My deductible: $500. The second occurrence happened in my driveway. Again, backing up. This time, the coast was clear before I got into the car. Next thing I heard as I was looking back was a crunch. Between $5K and $8K damage to the other vehicle. Oh, I wasn't going any more than 5 mph [8 km/h]! Thing is, even after the accident, I still didn't see the car when I looked back to see what the ?#$@ happened!

SAFETY COMPLAINTS: Many reports that the glass roof exploded. **2004**—About 80 safety-related complaints registered by NHTSA up to July 2006. • Chronic stalling continues despite recall fix. • Drivers often inadvertently hit the ignition key with their knee, thereby shutting off the vehicle while underway. • Transmission shifts abruptly, slips, or flares, especially when the AC is enabled. • Transmission stuck in Drive. • Rear control arm fractured, and inner tie-rods had to be replaced:

It was found via NY state inspection at about 27,000 miles [43,450 km] that the right front tie rod end was worn to the point of near failure, which would have the potential to cause the front right wheel to fall off.

• Many reports of ignition switch failures. • Incorrect fuel gauge readings ($750 U.S. fuel-tank replacement). • Lower front bumper falls off (also reported on the 2005 model) • Gas tank is easily punctured. • Sharp door edge cuts the leg of exiting occupants. • Headlights won't work (not part of recall). **2005**—Over 148 safety incidents registered, many of them recounting hair-raising "adventures" caused by the Pacifica suddenly stalling in traffic or on the highway (also confirmed by *www.edmunds.com*):

I have owned a 2005 Chrysler Pacifica for seven months. Over that period, I have documented a total 6 stalling events. The common trigger seems to be deceleration while turning or slightly turning either left or right. The speeds during the stalling events have twice occurred at highway speeds and four times while decelerating from speeds of 30–45 [48–72 km/h] to near 0. On one occasion, while at 45–50 mph [72–80 km/h] and changing lanes to the right, the vehicle stalled, affecting the steerability, and the car ran off the road, striking a hard object that caused the front tire to blow out and [the] destruction of the front rim and bending [of] the rear rim...the dealer failed to notify us of the 2004 recall for the same type of stalling event.

• Sudden acceleration. • Side airbags failed to deploy on impact. • Automatic transmission failure. • Excessive shimmying and steering-wheel vibrations, despite having replaced both lower control arms. • Extreme shaking when braking. • Faulty ABS wheel brake sensors cause ABS warning light to stay lit. • Headlights go on and off on their own.

Secret Warranties/Internal Bulletins/Service Tips

2004—An erratically shifting automatic transmission may require a re-calibrated PCM or TCM. • Rattling front splash shield. • Interior materials may give off an offensive odour. **2004–05**—Remedy for a rough-running engine or idle fluctuation. • Inoperative power seats or adjustable pedals. • Inoperative steering-wheel tilt mechanism. • Correction for a popping, clicking sound. • Front strut squeaking, squawking. • Tips on silencing a front/rear rattle. • Replacing the front suspension lower control arms may eliminate a suspension clunk or rattle. • Dip, sag in centre of instrument panel. • Troubleshooting water leaks into the passenger compartment or leaks found on the front floor. • Seat belts may stink:

BULLETIN NO.: 23-026-04 REV. A   DATE: JULY 30, 2004

OVERVIEW: This bulletin involves replacing the seat belt assembly and removing the foam material behind the seat belt retractor.

MODELS: 2004–2005 Pacifica

SYMPTOM/CONDITION: The vehicle operator may describe a foul odor from the front seat belt(s). The odor does not originate from the seat belt but from the foam to plastic cup material interaction. Under warm ambient temperatures, the foam gives off an odor which permeates the plastic cup behind the seat belt retractor, into the seat belt itself. Replacing only the seat belt assembly will not correct the condition.

Imagine a $36,000 car with stinky seat belts. Labour cost is one hour, but the entire job should be *gratis*.

2005—Front-door glass sticks or binds. **2005–06**—Headliner gap at front door weather stripping. • Circular marks on the glass.

PACIFICA PROFILE

	2004	2005	2006
Cost Price ($) (soft)			
Base (23%)	39,995	36,065	37,495
Used Values ($)			
Base ▲	22,000	24,000	—
Base ▼	20,500	22,500	—
Reliability	④	④	—
Crash Safety (F)	⑤	⑤	⑤
Side	⑤	⑤	⑤
Offset	⑤	⑤	⑤
Rollover	④	④	④

Ford

2006 EXPLORER TECHNICAL DATA

POWERTRAIN (4X2 OR 4X4)

Engines: 4.0L V6 (210 hp) • 4.6L V8 (239 hp); Transmissions: 5-speed auto. • 6-speed auto.

DIMENSION/CAPACITY

Passengers: 2/3/2; Wheelbase: 114 in.; H: 67.7/L: 190/W: 72 in.; Headroom F/R1/R2: 3.0/4.5/5.5 in.; Legroom F/R1/R2: 41.5/29/27.5 in.; Cargo volume: 45.5 cu. ft.; Fuel tank: 79L/regular; Tow limit: 3,500 lb.; Load capacity: 1,325 lb.; GVWR: 5,421 lb.; Turning circle: 39 ft.; Ground clearance: 7.5 in.; Weight: 4,515 lb.

RATING: Below Average (2003–2007); Not Recommended (1991–2002). Although the 2005–06 models seem much improved from a reliability standpoint, be wary. We have been misled in the past with Explorers that literally fell apart after accumulating some mileage. They are particularly prone to rolling over through the 2001 model year (and up until the 2004 Sport Trac). The Lincoln Aviator is essentially a baby Navigator spun off from the Explorer 4×4. Mountaineers are 1997 Mercury spin-offs with chrome and standard luxury features. Not quite a pickup truck, not quite an SUV, the Sport Trac takes elements from both to create a vehicle able to transport five passengers and carry tall objects in the small rear bed. Remember the Ford Ranchero? **Strong points:** The redesigned 2002–04 Explorers are a big improvement from a performance point of view, though quality is still abysmally low. Well appointed, with many standard safety features; a good 4.6L V8 power-train matchup that gives you much-needed power without too severe a fuel penalty (when compared with the thirsty V6); stable and forgiving handling when performing routine and emergency manoeuvres; steering is accurate and smooth; comfortable ride; permanent, full-time 4×4; versatile seven-passenger seating; attractively styled. The redesigned model has larger doors for easier entry and exit and a lower step-up. Lots of cargo space—more than the Chevrolet Blazer or Jeep Cherokee. Impressive crashworthiness scores and insurance injury claim data, except for head restraint performance. All trucks, SUVs, and crossovers are now covered by a longer base warranty. **Weak points:** The 5- and 6-year base warranties are still inadequate to deal with chronic factory defects. There's a clustering of safety-related defects around 2002 because of the Explorer's redesign that model year. Unacceptable off-road performance: slow, noisy acceleration with the base powerplant, hard riding over rocky terrain at slow speeds, and slow steering response. Excessive road noise and fuel consumption with the V6 engine (11.5–16.8 L/100 km, or 17–25 mpg). Power driver-seat and seat-heater controls are hard to access; short drivers may have trouble reaching the pedals because of the driver-seat cushion; interior takes a while to warm up on very cold days; inconveniently located passenger-side fuel-filler door; step bars (remember when they were called running boards?) are too narrow to be useful; and the 2007 Sport Trac's door handles aren't very user-friendly, making it difficult to close the doors. **New for 2007:** Ford has boosted its warranty coverage to 5 years/100,000 km on trucks, SUVs, and crossovers and to 6 years/110,000 km on Lincoln products. *Aviator:* Now more a sport wagon than a traditional SUV, Lincoln's 2007 Aviator will have a smaller, sleeker profile and two rows of adjustable seating surrounded by a restyled interior. It will use the same platform as the Ford Fusion, Mercury Milan, and Lincoln Zephyr and target primarily the Lexus RX 330's consumer base. Power will be provided by a 3.5L 245-hp V6 coupled to a 6-speed automatic transmission, harnessed to either a front-drive or all-wheel-drive configuration. *Explorer:* More accessible inside door handles and a longer warranty. *Sport Trac:* After a year's hiatus, this redesigned half-SUV, half-truck Explorer spin-off is longer, wider, and taller than its previous iteration. Other improvements include more safety features, like Roll Stability Control; an independent rear suspension; and a choice of either a 4.0L V6 or 4.6L V8 engine. Incidentally, previous Sport Tracs were exclusively V6-powered. Available in rear- or four-wheel drive, 6-cylinder versions use a 5-speed automatic transmission, while the V8 is mated to a 6-speed automatic.

MODEL HISTORY: The Explorer was introduced in 1991 as a compact sport-utility that combined the solidity of a truck with carlike handling. Despite its Firestone and quality woes, it remains the top-selling sport-utility in North America. It's available with two or four doors and in 4×2 or 4×4 modes. The V6 engine can be hooked to a 5-speed manual with Overdrive or a 5-speed automatic with Overdrive. The Control-Trac 4×4 system is controlled by a dial on the instrument panel and has three modes. Unlike a traditional 4×4 system, Control-Trac can be left in 4×4 all the time. 4×4 High is a constant 50/50 front/rear split, and it should be used only on loose or slippery road surfaces. 4×4 Low is a low-range gear for climbing steep hills or for travelling on very poor roads. The vehicle must be stopped and the transmission put into Neutral to engage or disengage the low range.

Explorers have generous cargo space, large doors, and lots of rear headroom and legroom. The 4.0L V6 engine does a respectable job of pulling the Explorer's hefty weight, but passing power is underwhelming. **1993**—Upgraded ABS brakes work in both 4×2 and 4×4 modes. **1995**—Dual airbags, four-wheel ABS, and Control-Trac 4×4 that can be left on all the time. **1996**—Four-door versions were given a V8 engine, and a new SOHC V6 mated to a redesigned 5-speed automatic was added. **1996**—Arrival of the 205-hp 4.0L V6, addition of a new electronic transfer case, and the debut of the Mercury Mountaineer, just as Ford Canada was sacking its Mercury dealers. **1999**—An improved braking system, a 5-hp boost for the 4.0L V6 (210 hp), optional side airbags, a sonar sensing system that warns drivers of objects behind the vehicle when backing up, a slight revamping of the exterior, and the addition of a new four-door XLS series. **2000**—Debut of the Explorer

Sport Trac as a 2001 model. **2001**—Explorer Sport arrives. Automatic transmission became standard, and a 210-hp V6 replaced the standard 160-hp V6. **2003**—Sport Trac gets four-wheel disc brakes and an optional side curtain airbag system. Side airbags have been dropped on the Sport model. **2004**—The two-door Explorer Sport was dropped, leaving only the pickup/SUV combo. **2006**—A more powerful V8 engine, a quieter V6, upgraded frame, and updated front, rear, and interior styling.

Overall, 1995–2001 models are good performers, although they still have some traditional quirks. For example, the 160-hp 4.0L V6 is slow to accelerate and even slower when hauling a full passenger load. It's noisy and not as refined as the new V6—or the old V8, for that matter. The 210-hp 4.0L V6, on the other hand, is a smoother-running engine that gives better fuel economy, but much less than one would expect. Expect impressive acceleration with the V8 engine. Though smoother than the Jeep Grand Cherokee's 5.2L, it's not quicker and, again, you will pay a huge fuel penalty.

Year 2002–05 models have a split personality: The Sport and Sport Trac were carried over unchanged, which means they remain tippy and unreliable, while the four-door 4×4 was substantially reworked for 2002, taking on additional safety features and becoming more powerful, roomy, and carlike in its comfort and handling. Its "smart" airbags deploy at different speeds, depending on the severity of the crash and whether or not occupants are wearing seat belts. Buyers also get a more powerful standard 4.0L V6 engine and, for the first time, an optional 4.6L V8. Although it's 3.0 cm (1.2 in.) shorter than the 2001, width and wheelbase were increased by 4.8 and 5.3 cm (1.9 and 2.1 in.), respectively. The cargo area behind the second row seat is 7 percent bigger, and the new optional third-row seating makes the Explorer a seven-seater. Suspension, steering, and drivetrain improvements also reduce the chances of rollovers, but the risk is still serious.

WHY THE EXPLORER IS A BAD SUV

COST ANALYSIS: The 2006–07 models are much improved, but way overpriced: Explorer costs $39,999–$51,299, Sport Trac is $38,299, and Aviator is $62,000. Still, the standard stability control and the extra features are important additions that are worth a few extra loonies. This extra cost can be shaved, however, by waiting for prices to fall drastically once competition heats up in the first quarter of 2007 as Ford attempts to crawl out from under a huge inventory of unsold Explorers (sales are down about 40 percent). It's also interesting to note that a new Sport Trac 4×2 is about $8,000 cheaper than the Explorer 4×4, but after a few years, it's actually worth about $1,000 more than the Explorer. Aviators cost about $20,000 more than an Explorer 4×4, but this difference is narrowed by $12,000 after a year's depreciation. **Best alternatives:** Some competitors worth checking out are the Nissan Pathfinder Xterra or X-Trail, Hyundai Santa Fe or second-series Veracruz, and Toyota 4Runner, Sequoia, or Highlander. Forget about the luxury European SUVs: BMWs and Mercedes' M-Class have a worse quality control record and a much heftier sticker price, plus both are returning this year with major redesigns, which means there's a greater chance of things going wrong (mostly fuel-delivery and electrical systems and electronics) and mechanics will be on the downside of the learning curve. **Rebates:** Look for zero percent financing and $5,000+ rebates on the 2006–07 models. The 2007 base price will likely fall to about $30,000 in the new year if fuel prices continue to rise. **Delivery/PDI:** $1,200. **Warranty:** Bumper-to-bumper 5–6 years/60,000–110,000 km; rust perforation 5 years/unlimited km. **Supplementary warranty:** A toss-up on the 2007s; essential on earlier models. **Options:** Order the 239-hp 4.6L V8; the base 210-hp V6 engine's lacklustre performance isn't worth the fuel economy trade-off. Shorter drivers will want the power-adjustable brakes and accelerator pedals. Stay away from Bridgestone, Goodyear Wrangler, and Continental tires. Michelin Cross Terrain tires are an excellent alternative. The $700 side curtain airbags add head protection for those in the first two rows, but their safety is questionable. The Reverse-Sensing system, which sounds an audible warning when backing up too close to another vehicle or obstacle, has been glitch-prone—learn to turn your head. **Depreciation:** Higher than average. **Insurance cost:** Unusually high. **Annual maintenance cost:** Average during the warranty period. Driveline, fuel system, brake, suspension/steering, and electrical defects cause maintenance costs to rise after the third year of ownership. **Parts supply/cost:** Parts are expensive but easily found. **Highway/city fuel economy:** *4.0L V6 and auto.:* 11.5/16.8 L/100 km; *4.6L V8 with 4×4:* 12.5/17.8 L/100 km.

QUALITY/RELIABILITY: Reliability record is dismal, particularly with the V6 and V8 engines. St. Louis Ford employees say that the optional 4.6L V8 engine "has been blowing head gaskets and overheating big time." Furthermore, according to these sources, cars and trucks equipped with 4.6L and 5.4L V8 engines are burning oil because of engine blocks that were improperly cast, causing the #2 cylinder bore to fail. The powertrain control modules (PCM) on early 2002 Explorers were allegedly programmed with corrupted software. Some Explorers have been repaired up to five times to correct driveline defects.

Ford just replaced the differential on my 2002 4×2 Explorer. I took it in with gear howling and clunking. When I tried to get more specifics about what happened and why, I was stonewalled by "It was worn out." The SUV is one year old, [with] 16,000 miles [25,600 km], [and] used like a family car. As I was leaving, the service writer quietly confided she didn't know what happened but I was the fourth such replacement this week. This is not a large dealership so the repair ratio sounds really bad.

Owner-reported problems: A perusal of owner comments indicates that these SUVs will likely continue to have serious factory-related defects that will probably include automatic transmission failures, fuel-system glitches, air conditioning system malfunctions, premature brake wear and noise, and brake failures. **Warranty performance:** Much worse than average. The company's staff is overwhelmed by complaints from owners who are poorly served by an inadequate base warranty.

1998–2006 defects

Components with a high failure history include the engine, cooling, fuel, and electrical systems; automatic transmission; brakes; AC; suspension; and body hardware. Here are some specific problem areas: AC remains on a high setting; Airbag service light stays on for no reason; transmission lacks power on acceleration; faulty speed sensor; excessive drivetrain vibration throughout vehicle; automatic transmission fluid leakage at the radiator; premature fuel-pump failure; steering binding; and engine knocking. One owner replaced the engine at 15,000 km, but the new engine made the same knocking noise, which the dealer now describes as being normal. **Other problem areas:** Defective 4×4 electronic module; roof shakes and an ear-piercing sound occurs when rear windows are lowered while cruising; overwhelming rotten-egg, sulphur, fuel, and oil-burning smells; and a rusted-out fuel-filler pipe that leaks fuel and allows dirt to contaminate fuel in the gas tank:

> I thought your readers should be made aware of a problem we experienced on a 1999 Ford Explorer Sport.
>
> The fuel-filler pipe rusted out at the top of the inlet pipe right behind the inlet area. The area is subjected to road splash and the rust out point is not visible from beneath the car. The local mechanics could not find the cause of the problem and the vehicle was eventually towed to a dealer where the problem was finally figured out. The total bill was $2,500 because the cause was so obscure. Ford would not pay for the rust out, [which] caused damages, water and dirt in fuel lines, new fuel pump, etc.

•

> I had a serious problem with my 2001 Explorer as described and found on the bottom of page 232 and top of page 233 of your book [*Lemon-Aid SUVs, Vans, and Trucks 2006*]. My costs to date exceed $6,000. Two dealerships failed to diagnose the problem. *www.cartalk.com* led me to solving the problem myself, after dealerships

and Ford tried to explain my vehicle is out of warranty. I had a lawyer write Ford, giving them 21 days before I proceed to Division Court. Your book helped me in establishing [that] a secret warranty [exists] between Ford and Utilimaster Corporation. In Sept. 2002, Utilimaster issued a confidential bulletin #03101937: "Fuel Pump and Fuel Neck Retrofit Replacement" for Ford and Utilimaster employees. It says: "In USPS Flex fuel vehicles built in the years 1999–2001, the fuel pump may corrode from the use of ethanol fuel"! I have checked Ford bulletins, recalls, Transport Canada, ALLDATA, etc. Service managers are not aware of the problem and seem surprised when I show them the actual parts with Ford part numbers stamped on them. A Ford representative called to tell me they won't do anything, and that their quality control department has not reported a problem.

The premature rusting of the fuel filler neck could have caused a fire. I have had 4 fuel pumps burn out prematurely due to lack of pressure in the system. Interesting is that muffler exhaust and tail pipe original equipment are still intact. Even if the secret warranty is not effective, there is an implied warranty. The dealer says he won't or can't do anything, so I am suing the dealer and Ford for $10,000.00 (the maximum in Ontario's Division Court).

Owners also complain about the flimsy front bumper; cracked moulding under the rear light; sticking rear door handle; door handles that are easily broken; ice and slush entering the door panels, causing the doors to freeze shut; water leaks into the interior; running-board cracks and paint peeling; and a broken power driver's seat:

I bought a 2002 Ford Explorer last April (2004) with an extended mechanical warranty for 5 years. The original full warranty [had] run out. Last week, the driver's electric seat got stuck in my driving position and we were not able to move the seat forward or backwards. We took the car into our local Ford Dealership where they told us that a metal cable had snapped. Unfortunately, they stated they are not able to simply replace the cable but instead have to replace the Power Tracking System. This system costs $662 plus labor and tax. I think this is absolutely outrageous but I have been unable to find a wreckers' yard with the equivalent part, and have been told we are not able to swap the passenger (manual) seat with the electric driver seat. To top this off, the new power-tracking system has a warranty which only lasts 1 year, so we are very concerned that this may happen every year and we have to pay $1,000/year for a seat. The dealership stated that our warranty will not cover this and so we have had to order this part from the dealer as we need the car to commute.

ROAD PERFORMANCE: Acceleration/torque: The overhead cam 210-hp V6 is an adequate all-around performer that puts the rougher 2001 base V6 to shame. The V8 engine, however, provides a more versatile power supply. The engine is smoother—though not quicker—than the Jeep Grand Cherokee's 4.7L V8, but you'll pay a fuel penalty. With the standard Class 2 towing package on models equipped with the V6 or V8 engines, towing capacity is 1,600 kg (3,500 lb.). Add a Class 3 or 4 towing package, and V6-equipped models will tow 2,500 kg (5,500 lb.); V8-equipped Explorers max out at 3,200 kg (7,000 lb.). **Transmission:** Mostly smooth-shifting, until about the third year or 100,000 km. **Routine handling:** Handles like a large sedan and rides better as the load is increased. The V8 handles better because the engine is positioned lower and farther back in the frame, improving steering responsiveness, reducing wallowing, and making the Explorer less nose-heavy. **Emergency handling:** Good on dry highways. The tendency to fishtail when cornering under speed or on hard acceleration has been reduced with the new independent rear suspension. Ford engineers have raised the ground clearance without raising the ride height. **Steering:** Precise and predictable. Some steering-column noise. **Braking:** Very good (100–0 km/h: 41 m). The suspension could be stiffer to reduce body roll in turns. With a light load, the ride gets choppy on bumpy roads; off-road, the suspension frequently bottoms out. Owners report vehicle has a propensity for hydroplaning on wet roads. Automatic transmission low-speed driveline vibration and occasional jerky shift when changing from Second to Third under light acceleration. Inadequate ground clearance and excessive front and rear overhangs preclude serious off-roading. On-road handling is not as responsive as the Jeep Grand Cherokee. The redesigned Explorer needs to go on a diet to lose about 180 kg (400 lb.).

 SAFETY SUMMARY: Now, a question everyone's asking: Is the Explorer more dangerous than other vehicles if it has a blowout? Absolutely. Just look at NHTSA's 2004 rollover ratings: Sport Trac (virtually unchanged post-Firestone) got an "Unacceptable" two-star ranking, while the re-engineered Explorer (with steering and suspension upgrades) scored three stars. In August 2004, a Fort Meyers, Florida, jury rendered a $2-million negligence judgment against Ford after seeing internal documents that showed that the company was aware of a stability problem with Explorers manufactured through the 2001 model year.

Ford's PR mantra is that Explorer owners are being killed and injured *only* because of faulty Firestone tires, while Firestone maintains that the Explorer's faulty design *sends* the vehicle out of control. Firestone's finger pointing has been buttressed by the *Washington Post*'s October 9, 2000, analysis of 27,000 fatal and non-fatal sport-utility accidents from 1997 to 1999. The study's conclusions:

> The Explorer has a higher rate of tire-related accidents than other sport-utility vehicles—even when equipped with Goodyear tires; the Explorer was 53 percent more likely than other compact SUVs to roll over when an equipment failure such as faulty brakes, bald tires, or blowouts caused an accident; in 187 fatal blown-tire

accidents, the Explorer rolled over 95 percent of the time, compared with 83 percent for other SUVs.

Before we close the file on Ford's Firestone fiasco, keep in mind that safety investigators have recently seen a surge in Firestone blowout rollovers due to Firestone spare tires. Apparently, the spares were never replaced during the last recall. Watch out!

Many owners report excessive engine knocking and premature engine replacement in vehicles that have yet to reach 10,000 km. When the Explorer stalls, brakes and steering are lost, the Check Engine light comes on, and the driver has to wait a few minutes before the vehicle can be restarted. Automatic transmission malfunctions and failures are still quite common with low-mileage Explorers. Poor braking or no brakes are a frequent complaint. Other safety-related complaints include fires erupting in the rear of the vehicle and within the rear-view mirror wiring harness; no seat belt for the rear middle seat; seat belts failing to retract or detaching from the wall anchor; the power steering locking up or leaking fluid; the wheel separating when backing up; front-brake rotor warping; the emergency brake not stopping the vehicle; and tail lights filling with water when it rains. **Airbags:** Side airbags are optional. Many reports of airbags failing to deploy or deploying for no reason. **ABS:** 4W is standard; disc/disc. **Safety belt pretensioners:** Standard. **Traction control:** Standard. **Head restraints F/R:** *1997–2001:* ★; *2002:* ★★/★; *2003–04:* ★★★/★★. **Visibility F/R:** ★★★★★.

SAFETY COMPLAINTS: All years: Ford has confirmed, albeit reluctantly, that brake fluid could leak through the cruise control's deactivation switch into the system's electrical components, leading to corrosion, a buildup of electrical current, overheating, and fire. Apparently, fires caused by the cruise-control deactivation switch go back as far as 1994, with Ford's recent recall of the 1998 model Explorer. In September 2005, Ford recalled 3.8 million pickups and SUVs from the 1994–2002 model years, including the top-selling F-150 pickup, because of the concerns over engine fires. Then, after announcing another massive recall in August 2006, NHTSA closed a nearly 2-year investigation into the switch fires. The agency had received 1,472 complaints connected to the problem, including 65 reports of fires. • Vehicle lacks stability on the highway; it tends to bounce around and veer off to one side or the other, and it's excessively prone to hydroplaning on wet roadways. • Because it has no rear leaf springs, the Explorer becomes even more unsteady when engaged for towing. • Sudden acceleration or stalling, often related to erratic cruise-control operation. • Sticking accelerator pedal and throttle linkage. • Engine overheating. • After driving the vehicle through water, engine died when water was sucked into engine because the air intake is located on bottom of vehicle. • Fuel, water pump, and ignition module failures. • Transmission slips in forward gears, Overdrive light comes on, and vehicle loses power. • Overdrive failures. • Repeated transmission failures caused by defective planetary gear. • Repeated transfer-case failures. • Excessive drive-shaft vibration. • Brake master cylinder and fluid-line failures. • Emergency parking brake won't stay engaged. • Brake pedal sticks. • Repeated brake failures. • Brake lock-up. • Power-steering pump fluid leakage. • Steering lock-up. • Front-end suspension failure. • Faulty rear liftgate support assembly allows hatch to fall. • Horn pad failure. • Driver's seat belt fails to retract. • Rear seat belts are hard to unbuckle. • Driver-seat frame breaks. • Inside rear door handles break. • Power-door lock and antenna failures. • Electric door locks will disengage while driving. • Steering wheel came off steering column because of missing bolt. • Power-steering failure. • Steering-column failure. • Gas gauge failure. • Under-dash wiring short caused a fire to ignite. • Fire erupted in the centre console. • Overheated ignition electronic control unit caught fire. • Engine fire. • Engine failure. • Power-seat switch failure. • Aluminum wheels cause tires to go flat. • Spare tire is too small. • Speed control failure. • Rear-view mirror sits too low; obstructs forward vision. • Fuel spews out of fuel-filler tube, no matter how slowly it is filled. • Anti-sway bar pulled loose from suspension when vehicle was pulling into a parking lot. • Axle bearing assembly failure. **2000**—Firestone tire failures are paramount, with new allegations that the wheel rims aren't symmetrically round, making for difficult tire mounting. A number of tires have failed that weren't in the Firestone recall. **2001**—Sudden, unintended acceleration. • Cruise-control deactivation switch failure caused an under-hood fire. • Rear-view mirror sparked a fire in the dash wiring.

> While attempting to back up a 2001 Explorer, [the vehicle] caught fire without warning. The driver was pronounced dead at the scene.

> •

> Vehicle was parked in the garage for an hour when all of a sudden it caught on fire along with consumer's home. Results showed that there was a short with the cruise control switch under the hood.

• Exhaust fumes invade the passenger compartment. • While driving, gas line exploded. • Driver-side window shattered while cruising at 100 km/h. • Reports of windshield suddenly shattering. • Vehicle rolled over when turning to avoid another vehicle. • Hitting a water puddle causes vehicle to flip and roll onto its side. • When driving 110 km/h, 4×4 suddenly kicked in, causing transmission to downshift, and vehicle suddenly accelerated. • Transmission Overdrive suddenly disengages. • Gearshift sticks in Park; vehicle can roll backward even though transmission is engaged in Drive or Park. • Wheel fell off when backing out of the driveway. • Lug nuts loosen while driving. • Sudden steering loss. • Front-suspension lower ball joint failure at 50,000 km. • Rear suspension unsafe for towing a boat. • Sudden brake lock-up while driving 35–40 km/h. • When brakes were applied during a panic stop, pedal went to the floor without braking. • Premature brake rotor replacement. • Excessive rear-end sag, and rear axle jumps when load is placed in the cargo area. • Bolt that attaches the seat belt for the integrated child safety seat comes apart. • During rear impact, driver-seat frame broke, causing seat to collapse backward. • Broken seat-track weld. • Front and rear shoulder belts ride up on occupants' necks and slip off small-statured people. • Seat belts fail to retract. • Sudden loss of all electrical power. • Windshield wiper failure; wipers are activated when you hit a bump or use the turn signal, or may stop suddenly in rainy weather. • Inadequate defrosting. • Brake lights don't work during gentle braking. • Overheated CD player melts CD. • Sudden loss of power to lights, odometer, speedometer, wipers, and power windows. • Incorrect fuel gauge reading. • Key is hard to turn in the ignition. • Goodrich tire-tread separation. **2002**—Over 300 safety-related complaints, similar to other model years. • Tail light fire. • No airbag deployment. • Hydraulic liftgate cylinder arm often comes off. • Window explodes and blows out the rear door:

> Four hours after new 2002 Explorer was picked up from the dealer, glass tailgate exploded on being closed gently. Rear window shattered with such force that metal components of the door were badly bent and scratched. Glass was scattered over a radius of 20 feet [6 metres], including into the back seats and onto the roof. My right leg was cut in three places…. The entire door was replaced by the dealer. Unless recalled, this apparently common defect will result in serious injury.

Ford has a "Safety Improvement Program," NHTSA #01I010000, which will fix the defect for free. It is not a recall. • Vehicle rolls away while in Park. • Three out of five wheel lug nuts were sheared off. • Intermittent steering lock-up while driving. • Head restraints sit too low; could snap one's neck in a rear-end collision. • Door handles are easily broken. • Smoky rear-view mirror. • Message Center dash light is too dim. • Headlights suddenly fail. • Rear-view mirror obscures forward vision. **2003**—Same old complaint patterns relating mainly to the engine, transmission, brakes, and electrical system. • Sudden unintended acceleration in Drive as well as in Reverse gear. • Driver's airbag deployed when key was put into the ignition. • Airbags failed to deploy. • Fire ignited in the engine compartment's front right side. • ABS brakes perform poorly. • Many complaints that the rear lift glass shatters for no reason, despite recall fix; right-side window has a history of shattering, as well. • Liftgate window frequently pops open. • Defective engine, transmission, drive shaft, and steering clock spring. • Faulty sensor module causes the ignition, seats, and other electrical features to fail. **2004**—Under-hood fire. • Sudden acceleration when parking. • No-start, stalling. • Running board broke when stepped upon. • Excessive vibration. • Steering wheel sticks when turning; power steering suddenly disengages. • Misleading fuel gauge. **2005**—Both front airbags deployed for no reason. • Constant stalling • Automatic transmission malfunctions; long shift delay. • Leaking axle seals. • It's easy to confuse the accelerator and brake pedals. • Frequent loss of power steering and braking. • Tailgate latch won't hold. • Multiple electrical shorts cause Explorers to play out a scene from *Close Encounters of the Third Kind*:

> While driving at no specific speed all the windows went up and down, the driver seat moved forward and backward, the radio came on and went off, and the air conditioner

came on and went off. Also, while attempting to apply brake pressure the brakes vibrated and a clunking noise was heard from the rear of the vehicle. The dealership inspected the vehicle and unknown repairs were made; however the repairs did not remedy the problem.

Secret Warranties/Internal Bulletins/Service Tips

All years: Press Ford for "goodwill" warranty coverage if your AC fails within 5 years/80,000 km. **1991–97**—Transmission slippage may be caused by a damaged fluid-pump support seal. **1993–2004**—Paint delamination, peeling, or fading. • A buzzing or rattling noise coming from underneath the vehicle indicates the need to secure the heat shield. **1994–98**—TSB #98-18-5 has lots of tips on eliminating side-door wind noise. **1995–99**—Service the air blend door if AC doesn't cool the interior. **1995–2002**—Automatic transmission defects (see bulletin). • **1996–2000**—A rubbing sound heard from the rear during right-hand turns may be caused by insufficient clearance between the muffler hanger rod and the rear drive shaft. **1997–98**—Troubleshooting tips for tracking down and eliminating side-door wind noise. • Sticking throttle, surging, and hesitation can be corrected by installing a new throttle body assembly, says TSB #98-21-22. • To eliminate a front-end suspension clunk, replace the stabilizer bar and insulators. • How to restore loss of electrical and 4×4 capability. **1997–99**—Excessive vibration or boom at idle, or hearing a grunt, groan, or moan noise at idle may require the installation of an exhaust system Y-brace. • Cold condensate dripping from the AC system onto the heated exhaust-gas oxygen sensor could be the cause of backfiring, stalling, or a rough idle. **1997–2000**—Transmission fluid may leak between the radiator transmission oil cooler and the transmission oil cooler fitting because of insufficient thread sealer on the transmission oil cooler fitting; install O-ring #W705181-S onto the oil cooler fitting. **1997–2001**—Hesitation on acceleration or when turning may be caused by cavitation in fuel pump; install a revised fuel pump and sender assembly, says TSB #00-20-1. **1997–2002**—Troubleshooting a constantly lit MIL light. **1998–2000**—A buzzing or grinding noise heard during a shift from Second to Third gear with a manual transmission usually signals the need to replace the 3–4 synchronizer assembly. **1998–2001**—4×4 front axle squealing or whistling countermeasures. **1999**—Automatic transmission slipping, delayed shifting, or no engagement may be solved by a new EPC solenoid and bracket. **1999–2001**—Vibration, shake, or a resonance noise at speeds in

---

NO 2ND, 3RD GEAR/ NO ENGINE BRAKING

BULLETIN NO.: 03-22-10   **DATE: NOV. 10, 2003**

1995–2001 EXPLORER
1995–2002 RANGER
1996–97 AEROSTAR
2000–02 EXPLORER SPORT
2001–02 EXPLORER SPORT TRAC
1997–2001 MOUNTAINEER

ISSUE: Some vehicles may exhibit the following shift and engagement conditions:
• No 2nd Gear
• No 3rd Gear
• No Engine Braking In Manual 1st.
ACTION: The main control valve body separator plate may need to be updated to the latest level.

excess of 72 km/h may be caused by an imbalance in one or more of the driveline components. **1999–2002**—Engine timing chain rattling:

2000–05—Ford has a special kit to correct seat belts that are slow to retract. • Paint blistering caused by contaminated coating is a "smoking gun" bulletin for owners wanting their vehicle repainted at Ford's expense:

2001—AC stays on high setting. • Manual transmission buzzing or grinding. • Automatic transmission fluid leakage at the radiator. • Rear rubbing noise when making right-hand turns. **2002**—Engine coolant seepage. • Harsh shifting and shuddering may simply require re-calibration of the PCM. • Automatic transmission ticking, whine, or howl. **2002–04**—4.6L engine ticking; replace the cylinder head and cam assembly with part #4L3Z-6049-AA (RH) or #4L3Z-6049-BA (LH). • Inoperative rear power windows. **2002–2005**—Rear AC moan, buzz, groan. • Driveline vibration, boom. • Rear axle noise, binding, or vibration:

REAR AXLE SHUDDER/CHATTER/BIND/VIBRATION	
BULLETIN NO.: 04-24-20	DATE: DECEMBER 13, 2004

LIMITED SLIP AXLE CHATTER, SHUDDER, BINDING SENSATION, OR VIBRATION DURING LOW-SPEED TURNING MANOEUVERS

2002–2005 Crown Victoria, Mustang, Explorer; 2003–2005 Expedition; 2004–2005 F-150; 2002–2005 Town Car; 2003–2005 Navigator; 2002–2005 Grand Marquis, and Mountaineer.

ISSUE: Vehicles equipped with 8.8" limited slip rear axle may exhibit a chatter, shudder, a binding sensation, or a vibration during low-speed turns. On 4x4 vehicles, the sensation may appear to be originating from the front axle or the steering gear.

ACTION: First verify the condition. On 4x4 trucks, ensure that the vehicle is in 2WD to isolate the rear axle. On all vehicles, turn the wheel fully right (or fully left) and then accelerate the vehicle. If the condition is verified to be in the rear axle, replace the limited slip clutch pack.

• Noisy axle hub bearings. • Rear half-shaft axle leaks. • Ford will fix vehicles that are hard to shift from Drive to Park. • AC hooting upon light acceleration. • Back glass hard to close. • Damaged liftgate glass applique. **2002–2006**—Fuel gauge drops to Empty or is slow to reset after a refuel. **2003**—Incorrectly installed gear-driven camshaft-position sensor synchronizer assemblies can cause engine surge, loss of power, and a lit MIL light. • Front axle leaks fluid from the vent tube. • Rear driveline click, creak, or pop. • Squeaking accelerator pedal. **2003–05**—Inoperative AC; compressor leakage. **2004–05**—Hard starts are likely caused by a miscalibrated powertrain control module. • Delayed, harsh shifts or delayed acceleration. • Cracked leather seat cushions. **2004–06**—Excessive runout vibration.

AVIATOR, EXPLORER, SPORT TRAC PROFILE

	1998	1999	2000	2001	2002	2003	2004	2005	2006
Cost Price ($) (very soft)									
Explorer 4X2	28,995	28,995	—	—	—	—	—	—	—
4X4 (26%)	30,095	30,095	29,995	35,400	37,700	37,795	39,140	39,140	39,999
Sport Trac (25%)	—	—	—	27,050	28,440	30,840	31,155	31,295	—
Aviator (30%)	—	—	—	—	—	58,950	59,240	59,895	—
Used Values ($)									
Explorer 4X2 ▲	5,000	6,000	—	—	—	—	—	—	—
Explorer 4X2 ▼	4,500	5,000	—	—	—	—	—	—	—
4X4 ▲	6,500	7,500	9,000	10,000	11,500	14,500	21,000	25,000	—
4X4 ▼	5,500	6,500	8,000	8,500	10,000	13,000	19,500	23,500	—
Sport Trac ▲	—	—	—	10,500	13,500	16,000	19,000	22,000	—
Sport Trac ▼	—	—	—	9,000	12,000	15,000	18,000	20,500	—
Aviator ▲	—	—	—	—	—	27,000	33,000	37,000	—
Aviator ▼	—	—	—	—	—	25,000	31,000	35,000	—

All ratings on a numbered scale where ⑤ is good and ❶ is bad. See page 220 for a more detailed description.

Reliability	②	②	②	②	❶	❶	❶	③	—
Crash Safety (F)	④	④	④	④	④	④	④	④	⑤
Side	—	⑤	⑤	⑤	⑤	⑤	⑤	⑤	⑤
Offset	③	③	③	③	⑤	⑤	⑤	⑤	⑤
Rollover	—	—	—	②	③	③	③	③	③
Sport Trac	—	—	—	—	②	②	②	—	—

Note: Mountaineers aren't sold in Canada.

EXPEDITION, NAVIGATOR ★★/★

2007 TECHNICAL DATA

POWERTRAIN (4X4)

Engine: 5.4L V8 (300 hp); Transmission: 6-speed auto.

DIMENSION/CAPACITY

Passengers: 2/3/3; Wheelbase: 119 in.; H: 76.7/L: 206.5/W: 91.8 in.; Headroom F/R1/R2: 2.5/4.0/3.5 in.; Legroom F/R1/R2: 40.5/29.5/28 in.; Cargo volume: 86 cu. ft.; Fuel tank: 106L/regular; Tow limit: 9,200 lb.; Load capacity: 1,400 lb.; GVWR: 8,000 lb.; Turning circle: 42 ft.; Ground clearance: 7.0 in.; Weight: 5,578 lb.

RATING: *Expedition:* Below Average (1997–2007); *Navigator:* Not recommended (1997–2007). The Lincoln Navigator is a re-badged Expedition, selling for a $25,000 premium and saddled with tons of chrome and plastic cladding along with a sad history of powertrain and fit and finish glitches identical to the Expedition's. **Strong points:** Powerful engines suitable for heavy hauling; excellent ride and visibility; lots of passenger room; and a luxury, carlike interior. **Weak points:** Hard to park or drive in the city; rough 5.4L V8 performance; lethargic steering; ride is a bit busy at low speeds; limited rear-seat access and cargo space; slow to heat or cool; entry is hampered by a high step-in and lack of a grab handle on the driver's side; poor fuel economy; poor quality control; and an unusually large number of performance- and safety-related complaints, particularly since the 2003 model redesign. **New for 2007:** Expedition's new independent rear suspension provides a much better ride than previous versions. There's also a stiffer chassis and a new interior with third-row seats that fold flat. The new Expedition EL is 37.6 cm (14.8 in.) longer and has an additional 0.7 cubic metres (24 cubic feet) of cargo space behind the third-row seat. More safety features include standard safety content like seat-mounted side airbags, three-row curtain airbags, and electronic stability-control with rollover protection.

MODEL HISTORY: Based on the F-150 pickup and offered only as a four-door, the Expedition and Navigator handle serious trailer-towing with more comfort than a pickup or a van. They have a nine-passenger potential if you use the optional third-row bench seat. The full-time 4×4 is taken from the Explorer, along with four-wheel ABS disc brakes. On one hand, both the 4.6L and 5.4L V8s are peppy, even though they can't match the torque and fuel economy of the Tahoe's diesel engines. On the other hand, both V8 engines experience a similar delay when accelerating, as do the Tahoe and Yukon. Keep in mind that these vehicles have many serious safety-related problems, reported repeatedly to NHTSA. Ditch the Firestone tires; many tires that weren't on the recall list have been defective.

1999—A small power boost, an upgraded Command-Trac 4×4 system that provides 4×4 when needed, and optional power-adjustable gas and brake pedals. **2000**—Standard power-adjusted foot pedals, a rear sonar backing-up alert system, a revised centre console, and optional side airbags. **2003**—An independent rear suspension, stiffer chassis, increased towing capability of 4,035 kg (8,900 lb.), improved braking and stability, and a third-row, foldable seat. Third-row passengers gained lots of legroom but lost some shoulder room. The 4.6L V8 gets a bit more horsepower. Navigators were given exceptionally large seats and tweaks to reduce vibrations and noise. Optional power-deployed running boards that pop out when the door is opened and a remote-controlled aluminum liftgate were also added. **2004**—Wider availability of 2003's new features.

COST ANALYSIS: Go for the 2006 with stability-control or a 2007 version, which offers a quieter, smoother ride and more creature comforts; the $45,199/$55,099 (XLT/Limited) prices are unrealistic and can be easily cut by $7,000–$12,000, so haggle aggressively with the knowledge that sales are plummeting. **Best alternatives:** GM's large SUVs, like the Tahoe and Yukon (with an extended warranty), are far more nimble, reliable, and fuel-efficient.

The Expedition EL is designed to compete against the Chevrolet Suburban. Toyota's Highlander and 4Runner are also worth a look. If they won't do, consider a Nissan Pathfinder or the Lexus LX 450 or 470. **Rebates:** Look for $8,000+ rebates on the 2006 models and $5,000 on this year's version early in the new year. New Lincolns aren't worth the extra $25,000 you pay; a 1998 version sells for only $1,500 more than the Expedition as of August 2006. **Delivery/PDI:** $1,200. **Warranty:** Bumper-to-bumper 5–6 years/60,000–110,000 km; rust perforation

FORD EXPEDITION OR GM TAHOE/YUKON?

	2007 FORD EXPEDITION	2007 CHEVROLET TAHOE
Height	76.7 in.	76.9 in.
Length	206.5 in.	202.0 in.
Width	91.8 in.	79.0 in.
Wheelbase	119.0 in.	116.0 in.
Curb weight	5,578 lb.	5,233 lb.
Standard engine	5.4L V8	4.8L V8
Transmission	6-speed auto.	4-speed auto.

5 years/unlimited km. **Supplementary warranty:** An extended warranty is a good idea. **Options:** Stay away from any Firestone or Continental tires: Both the 16- and 17-inch Firestone tires have a history of sudden tread separation, while Continental tires simply lose chunks of tread. Bridgestone tires should be boycotted as well. Be wary of the moonroof option—many complaints of water leaks and wind noise have been reported. Consider the 5.4L powerplant with its sturdier transmission (the E40D instead of the 4R70W), 20 additional horses, and extra torque. Other recommended options are adjustable accelerator and brake pedals, and running boards. **Depreciation:** Much faster than average (sales are down almost 40 percent). **Insurance cost:** Higher than average. **Parts supply/cost:** Body parts are often back-ordered, but moderately priced mechanical parts are easily found either in the Explorer or F-Series bins. **Annual maintenance cost:** Costlier than average. **Highway/city fuel economy:** *4.6L V8:* 12.2/17.6 L/100 km; *4.6L V8 and 4×4:* 13.4/19.1 L/100 km; *5.4L V8:* 12.1/16.6 L/100 km.

 QUALITY/RELIABILITY: Overall quality control and reliability are way below average and got worse with the 2003 revamped model. There's also a disturbingly high rate of safety-related complaints that suggest a "What, me worry?" attitude among Ford engineers. After all, how much engineering prowess does it take to prevent wheels from falling off or the rear hatch from falling on someone's head? Or to reduce the enormous amounts of brake-dust buildup on the front and back wheels after driving only a few kilometres? Continental General and Firestone tires have a history of tread retention problems (this is my polite way of saying that they could be crap). **Owner-reported problems:** Inadequate troubleshooting of sudden acceleration or stalling; 4.6L engine piston-slap noise with cold starts; rough idling caused by a faulty throttle cable; excessive steering play requiring constant correction; chronic electrical shorts for all model years, affecting everything from gauges and lights to engine and transmission performance; transmission failures; excessive rear differential noise; engine oil leaks lead to engine replacement within first year of ownership; defective fuel-pump sensors; poor braking, high brake maintenance costs (chronic rotor warpage and brake dust everywhere), and excessive brake noise; automatic-adjusting side mirrors constantly readjust themselves to the wrong setting; and assorted clunks, rattles, and wind noise. The 2005 models are just as unreliable, as this owner reports:

> If you remove your foot from the brake the vehicle will roll out of control. The transmission will shift at odd times as you are driving. Rear passenger dome light flickers when you turn it on with the switch in the back. Driver door does not latch unless it is shut hard. In addition to the above the following new defects have been found: turn signals will sometimes not work at all. When making a sharp turn the rear end will slip. You can feel it not holding the road. Outside fumes are sucked into the vehicle. Any smell or exhaust from this or other vehicles is pulled inside. The leather on the front seats has turned black.

Warranty performance: Mediocre.

ROAD PERFORMANCE: Acceleration/torque: 0–100 km/h: 9.9 seconds (about a second slower than the Tahoe) with the 2000's base engine; expect much better acceleration with the 2001 model's additional horses. **Transmission:** Well-spaced gearing shifts imperceptibly, without any gear hunting when traversing hilly terrain. **Steering:** Overly sensitive at lower speeds. **Routine handling:** Smooth, comfortable ride that's above average for a sport-utility. The variable-assist steering is fairly precise at lower speeds and gives adequate feedback from the road. Leaving the Expedition in AWD improves handling considerably. Parking is more like docking. **Emergency handling:** Above average. The Expedition's tight chassis and supple suspension keep the vehicle on track, without the wallowing and nose-diving evident in many other sport-utilities in its class. **Braking:** Adequate, but not impressive (100–0 km/h: 45 m).

 SAFETY SUMMARY: An Ontario law firm (*www.willbarristers.com*) has filed a class action petition against Ford for defective door latches on 1997–2000 model year Expeditions, Navigators, and F-Series trucks. It will cost about $994 per four-door vehicle to replace the door latches, which have opened in side-impact crashes and rollover accidents. Many class actions have been filed in the States over this defect, and Ford has settled one lawsuit out of court (*www.defectivedoor.com/news/texas_settlement.html*). There have also been many cases where the wheel lug nuts sheared and the wheel flew off (it was later recalled). But the kicker is that even the spare tire is dangerous: Several reports state the spare-tire cable broke while turning a corner, causing the spare tire to fly away. Also, an inaccurate fuel gauge indicates one-quarter tank full when you are actually out of gas. Many incidents have been reported of unintended, sudden acceleration, which has been blamed on a variety of causes. Horn design makes it difficult to activate in an emergency. Some complaints of insufficient low-beam illumination and an annoying dashboard reflection onto the front windshield. **Airbags:** Side airbags are optional. There have been reports of airbags failing to deploy and the Airbag light staying on for no reason. **ABS:** 4W is standard; disc/disc. ABS failure or lock-up often caused by faulty sensor or ABS module. **Traction control:** Optional. **Head restraints F/R:** ★★/★; *2003–04:* ★★★★★/★★★. **Visibility F/R:** ★★★★★.

SAFETY COMPLAINTS: All years: Fire ignites while vehicle is parked. • Cruise control fails to disengage when brakes are applied. • Chronic engine head gasket failures and oil leaks; Check Engine light comes on as coolant leaks onto plugs and #3 and #4 coil packs. • Too much steering play. • Excessive front-end wandering. • Tie-rod end and torsion bar failures. • Excessive suspension vibration. • Transmission failures. • Slips while in gear. • Rear axle failure. • Seat belt failures. • Plastic running board is slippery. • Rear hatch latch cylinders fail, allowing hatch to fall on owner's head. • Inoperative power windows. • Windows shatter for no reason. • Defective gas cap causes Check Engine light to come on and makes for poor driveability. • Gas and brake pedal are too close. **1999**—Vehicle exploded while getting gas. • Pitman arm suddenly detached from the steering gear. • Rear door hinge cut off child's finger as door was opened. • Vehicle started twice on its own without the key in the ignition. • Rear brake caliper seizure scored rotor: $1,000 repair. • Rear-view mirror backing peels off. • Cracked hood welds. **2000**—Sudden loss of engine power when accelerating, especially when fuel tank is less than one-quarter full. • Suspension and steering combination makes the vehicle wander all over the road. • Over-sensitive steering also makes vehicle hard to control; one report that it almost tipped over. • Three bolts that hold the steering gearbox came apart. • In some cases, the steering assist may cut on and off. • Plastic fuel tank is quite vulnerable to leakage from road debris punctures. • Jack failures. • Driver-side seat belt clip won't go into buckle—apparently a common problem. **2001**—Sudden, unintended acceleration when brakes were applied. • Stalling; unable to restart. • Child shifted vehicle into Neutral without touching brake pedal. • Vehicle surges forward, despite brakes being applied. • Brake pedal fell to the floor when brakes were applied. • Adjustable gas pedal will sometimes get stuck under floor mat. • Vibration, moan at highway speeds. • Door lock is easily thwarted. • Driver-side seat belt unlatches. • Wheel lug nuts won't stay tight; wheel flew off vehicle. • Passengers sickened by white powder coming out of air vents. • Vehicle stalls and won't start when on an incline with one-quarter tank of fuel left. **2002**—Airbags failed to deploy. • Vehicle fishtailed out of control. • Sudden acceleration when braking. • Steering-wheel lock-up. **2003**—Fires ignited from the seat-heating system because of a loose gas line and an overheated fuse. • Early failure of power-train components.

> The driver-side tie-rod has broken twice. Both times [were] without warning. The dealer has fixed it once and now it is back to the dealer for the second time for same problem. The manufacturer took information from the consumer, but she has not heard back from them. Passenger-side rear window does not go down [when master switch is activated]. Door Ajar light does not go off. Left front ball joint separated, then vehicle hit sign. Lower control arm broken, upper ball joint bad, spindle broken, sway bar link broken, CV boot torn, and axle pulled out of front differential. Tie-rod end on left side broken and vacuum hub cracked on spindle and tire and rim damaged. Also fender liner ripped out. Spindle, upper control arm, lower control arm, CV boot replaced. Clip for axle vacuum hub and wheel and tire, removed front differential to reinstall, axle and clip replaced wheel and tire and performed alignment. Damage to hood when knuckle split.

• Drive shaft and tie-rod broke while vehicle was underway. • Sudden acceleration. • Vehicle jumped from Park to Reverse. • Gas leaks from the filler cap area. • Continental tire blowouts. • Brake failures and premature rotor, caliper wearout. **2004**—Sudden, unintended acceleration:

> The vehicle transmission was in the Park position while waiting on a slow train. When engaging the transmission into the Drive position, after the train had passed, the vehicle uncontrollably fully accelerated on its own. To avoid a serious collision with oncoming traffic, the driver turned the vehicle onto the railroad tracks where it

came to a stop after damaging two wheels and high centering on the tracks. This is a very dangerous vehicle.

• Steering wheel sticks when turning. • Still excessive brake wear and brake dust everywhere (a TSB confirms this problem). • Faulty tire-pressure monitor. • Throttle sticks, especially when the cruise control is engaged. • Total brake loss. • Serious Continental tire defects continue. **2005**—Sudden, unintended acceleration is still a problem:

> Vehicle was being driven in a parking lot. We stopped to allow a car to pull out of the parking space. The brake was released to allow the car to slowly roll into the parking space when it suddenly accelerated. My wife plowed [on] the brakes as the vehicle came close to running over pedestrians walking by. Dealer checked and found nothing wrong. This is one of two incidents in a 3 month period. This vehicle is a major catastrophe waiting to happen, please beware of the danger.

• Airbag failed to deploy. • Automatic transmission slipped from Park into Reverse while idling. • Transmission wouldn't shift.

Secret Warranties/Internal Bulletins/Service Tips

All years: Free fuel gauge/sender replacement under ONP #97B17, Supplement 1 (a secret warranty). • Front engine-cover oil leaks. • No-starts in cold weather. **1997–98**—Fuel may leak from the spring lock couplings at the fuel rail. **1997–99**—Vibration or shimmy above 70 km/h may require an upgraded drive shaft. • Diagnostic tips for correcting a front differential moaning, whining, or buzzing in the speakers and a whistling noise when driving with the AC off. • An exhaust system crack or break between the muffler and tailpipe may require a new drive shaft, muffler, and tailpipe assembly. **1997–2000**—A hesitation upon acceleration or while turning may be caused by fuel-pump cavitation because of fuel sloshing away from the filter sock in the fuel-tank reservoir. Ford TSB #00-20-1 says a new fuel pump should be installed if other possible causes have been eliminated. **1997–2001**—Under a little-known extended warranty, Ford will repair or replace 5.4L engines with faulty head gaskets on the 1999–2001 F-150 and Super Duty F-Series pickups, Econoline, Expedition, and Lincoln Navigator. **1997–2002**—Throttle sticks in very cold weather. **1998**—Erratic speedometer readings require the installation of an upgraded unit. • A free service kit is available to add an extra 25 mm to the narrow running boards. • TSB #98-17-21 gives a comprehensive listing of the probable causes of rattles and squeaks. • Electrical accessories that short out may be contaminated by water leaks, says TSB #98-9-13. **1999–2000**—Install a clutch pack kit under warranty to silence rear axle chattering (on vehicles with a limited slip rear axle) when turning or cornering, says TSB #00-8-4. **2000**—A new side intake manifold gasket will correct a coolant leak from the passenger-side intake manifold. **2000–05**—Correction for seat belts that are slow to retract. **2001**—No-starts, stalling with the 7.3L engine. • Engine stalls when vehicle is shifted into

Reverse. • A buck or jerk may be felt with cruise control engaged. • Turbo hooting. • Ford admits investigating cam sensor failures (which lead to loss of power, engine shutdown, and no-starts). • Sudden loss of Second gear; vehicle won't move. • Delayed shifts. • Sway bar clunk and popping. • Front shaft seal leakage. • Water-pump shaft seal leakage. • Higher-than-normal steering effort required. • Incorrect oil pressure readings. 2002—Engine cylinder head leaks. • 5.4L engine power loss. • Engine vibration at idle, and droning noise when accelerating. • Lack of fuel pressure. • Driveline vibration at 100 km/h. • Loose axle bearing; axle-tube seal leakage. • Excessive braking required when decelerating. • Front suspension noise. • Heater core leaks. • Faulty ignition-switch lock cylinder. • Air leak in air suspension. • Excessive wind noise. 2003—Frequent no-starts. • Front axle groan, hum, or vibration. • Powertrain fluid leaks from the rear half-shaft seal. • Transmission fluid leaks at the transmission oil cooler. • Rear axle whine. • Electrical shorts may cause gauge, alarm, radio/DVD, and door lock failures. • Power-steering leaks, noise, vibration. 2003–04—Intermittent loss of cooling. • Excessive brake dust on wheels. 2003–05—Rear axle seal leak (see bulletin). 2003–06—Preventing electrical battery drain. 2004–06—Tips for correcting front brake vibration or shudder. 2005—Remedy for engine knocking or ticking when warmed up. • Inoperative seat heaters. 2005–06—Rough idle (4×2 only). • Hesitation or lack of power when shifting.

REAR AXLE SEAL LEAKS	
BULLETIN NO.: 04-10-5	DATE: MAY 25, 2004

AXLE SEAL LEAKS
2003–04 EXPEDITION, NAVIGATOR
ISSUE: Some vehicles may exhibit fluid leaks from the rear halfshaft axle seal. This may occur when the halfshaft spline comes in contact with the inner diameter of the axle seal. The leak may be more pronounced in cold weather.
ACTION: To service order and install Axle Seal Kit 3L1Z-4A109-BA. Review the revised instruction sheet and obtain the required tools before beginning any repairs. Also refer to the following installation service tips.

EXPEDITION, NAVIGATOR PROFILE

	1998	1999	2000	2001	2002	2003	2004	2005	2006
Cost Price ($) (very negotiable)									
Expedition 4X2	36,495	37,495	—	—	—	—	—	—	—
Expedition 4X4 (30%)	39,595	40,595	41,195	40,855	41,255	43,270	46,800	48,245	45,199
Navigator (30%)	52,548	63,765	68,690	66,425	66,425	69,995	72,625	73,195	75,899

Used Values ($)									
Expedition 4X2 ▲	8,500	11,000	—	—	—	—	—	—	—
Expedition 4X2 ▼	7,500	9,500	—	—	—	—	—	—	—
Expedition 4X4 ▲	9,000	11,500	13,500	16,000	18,000	21,000	25,000	30,000	—
Expedition 4X4 ▼	8,500	10,000	12,000	14,500	16,500	19,000	23,000	27,500	—
Navigator ▲	10,500	12,500	14,500	19,000	23,000	32,000	40,000	47,000	—
Navigator ▼	9,500	11,000	13,000	17,500	21,000	30,000	38,000	44,000	—
Reliability	❷	❷	❷	❷	❷	❶	❷	❸	—
Crash Safety (F)	④	④	④	⑤	⑤	⑤	⑤	⑤	⑤
Rollover	—	—	—	❷	❷	—	—	—	❸

Note: A used 4×2 Navigator is worth about $2,000 less than a 4×4.

PART FOUR • SPORT-UTILITY VEHICLES

EXCURSION ★★

2005 TECHNICAL DATA

POWERTRAIN

Engines: 5.4L V8 (255 hp) • 6.0L TD V8 (325 hp) • 6.8L V10 (310 hp); Transmissions: 4-speed auto. • 5-speed auto.

DIMENSION/CAPACITY

Passengers: 3/3/2; Wheelbase: 137 in.; H: 80/L: 226/W: 80 in.; Headroom F/R1/R2: 6.5/6.0/4.0 in.; Legroom F/R1/R2: 41.5/31/28.5 in.; Cargo volume: 48 cu. ft.; Fuel tank: 167L/regular; Tow limit: 7,600–11,000 lb.; Load capacity: 1,630 lb.; GVWR: 8,600–9,200 lb.; Turning circle: 50.4 ft.; Ground clearance: 8.5 in.; Weight: 6,680–7,770 lb.

RATING: Below Average (2000–05). Recipe for building an Excursion: Take an F-350, replace the bed with three rows of seats, and ditch the tailgate. This unreliable, gas-guzzling Godzilla SUV was doomed from the start. **Strong points:** Well appointed, powerful 6.8L V10 gas engine, standard stability-control, good optional powertrain match for highway cruising or city commuting, automatic 4×4, versatile interior, good passenger room, comfortable seating, and a low floor for easy access and loading. **Weak points:** Slow acceleration with the base 5.4L and 6.0L diesel powerplants, unacceptable off-road performance, excessive engine noise, mediocre handling, obstructed rear visibility, poor head restraint protection, no crashworthiness data, and non-existent fuel economy. Government safety investigators have recorded an unusually high number of safety-related complaints. Owners also report that the suspension cannot handle the towing weight recommended by Ford.

MODEL HISTORY: Gone but not forgotten, the Excursion is a restyled version of Ford's three-quarter-ton Super Duty pickup, equipped with a standard 255-hp 5.4L V8 engine on its 4×2s and a choice of a 310-hp 6.8L V10 or a 325-hp 6.0L turbodiesel

All ratings on a numbered scale where ⑤ is good and ❶ is bad. See page 220 for a more detailed description.

V8 powerplant on the 4×4 versions. A dash-mounted switch permits shifting on the fly; however, unlike the GM competition, Ford's 4×4 system can't be used on dry pavement.

First launched in 1999 to compete against GM's full-sized Chevrolet Suburban SUV, the 2001 Excursion got a beefed-up 250-hp 7.3L diesel powerplant and additional entertainment and convenience features. Since then, it has returned each model year relatively unchanged. Its last model year was 2005.

COST ANALYSIS: Only used models are available, and they are no "bargain," despite their bargain prices. **Best alternatives:** The redesigned Suburban looks to be a better choice because of its better quality, its handling, and performance refinements. **Warranty:** Bumper-to-bumper 3 years/60,000 km; rust perforation 5 years/unlimited km. **Supplementary warranty:** An extended warranty is essential. **Options:** Nothing worth the extra money, unless you absolutely need running boards. Stay away from Firestone and Bridgestone tires. **Depreciation:** Much faster than average—a 2000 Excursion 4×4 that sold for $47,000 new is now worth about…$12,000! **Insurance cost:** Goes in the other direction; sky-high premiums. **Annual maintenance cost:** Average during the warranty period; fairly costly once the warranty expires. **Parts supply/cost:** Parts are moderately priced and easily found, since they all come from Ford's truck parts bin. **Highway/city fuel economy:** *5.4L V8:* 12.1/16.7 L/100 km; *6.8L V10:* 13.0/20.0 L/100 km.

QUALITY/RELIABILITY: Amazingly bad for a vehicle this expensive. Next time someone suggests that "you get what you pay for" in vehicle quality, show the service bulletin references for luxury SUVs like the Excursion, Expedition/Navigator, BMW X5, and Mercedes M series. **Owner-reported problems:** Steering instability and poor handling; drive shaft, differential, motor mount, and wheel bearing failures; chronic drivetrain whine and howl; electrical system problems; poor braking, high brake maintenance costs (chronic rotor warpage), and excessive brake noise; and assorted clunks, rattles, and wind noise. Excessive vibration at cruising speed (not tire related); vehicle bounces all over the road and nosedives as front shocks bottom out; hard to control the vehicle when towing a trailer. **Warranty performance:** Average but expected to get worse now that the Excursion is no longer sold and Ford is concentrating on the sale and servicing of smaller SUVs and trucks.

SAFETY SUMMARY: No head restraints or shoulder belts on centre rear seats. Vehicle has yet to be crash-tested by NHTSA. **Airbags:** Side airbags are optional. Front and side airbags have failed to deploy in collisions. **ABS:** Standard; disc/disc. **Head restraints F/R:** ★. **Visibility F/R:** ★★★★★/★★.

SAFETY COMPLAINTS: 2000—A plethora of Firestone tire failures (check that spare!). • Cracked fuel tank leaked gasoline. • Passenger-side Airbag light stays lit because of a short circuit in the system. • Transmission fluid leaked onto drive shaft, causing a fire. • Transmission popped out of gear while vehicle was parked (a common Ford failure seen over the past three decades). • Sudden breakage of the right front tie-rod end. • Turbocharger malfunctions cause oil leaks and stalling. • Drive shaft fell out because of loose bolts. • Complete brake failure when approaching intersection. • Brakes pulsate violently. • Poor steering and handling compromise safety. • Poorly designed suspension causes vehicle to move laterally on dry pavement. • Severe shaking and vibrating while driving over 90 km/h. • Excessively sharp seat tracks injured two people. • Jack won't align with suspension pins and may suddenly fail. • If you close the rear tri-doors in the wrong order, the rear window glass may explode. 2001—Tie-rod end fell off; complete steering loss. • Spark plug popped out of the engine head (a similar incident was reported on the 2002 model):

> The 3rd spark plug on the [right-hand] side of the engine blew out and took the cylinder head threads with it. $3,000 to repair. The Ford inspector refused to admit fault on Ford's part, yet the service manager at the dealership told me that the plug blowout was no fault of mine.

> I have found hundreds of identical incidents. It's about time Ford is forced to be responsible.

• Frequent failure of the transmission gasket seal and main central valve. • Failed wheel bearings can't be serviced. • Grease leaks onto brake rotors. • Rear-end instability when passing over uneven terrain. • Cruise control surges when set at 110 km/h. • Chronic brake rotor warpage. • Driver-side seat belts unlatch. 2002—Under-hood fire. • No airbag deployment. • Sudden acceleration. • Chronic stalling. • Spark plug popped out of the engine head. • Rough roads cause sudden loss of steering control. • Steering binds. • Vehicle shakes excessively when rear windows are open while underway. • Loose seat belt bolt pulled out. 2003—Vehicle (gas and diesel) suddenly shuts down. • Diesel fuel leaks from the fuel filter onto the engine:

> Faulty fuel injectors in the 6.0L diesel engine resulting in excessive amounts of diesel fuel to enter the oil crankcase. Oil level in crankcase is diluted with fuel to the extent of being measured on the dipstick by several inches and flash point of oil reduced to half of the flash point of the oil.

• Total automatic transmission failure. • Early ball joint replacement. • Hatchback window shattered for no reason. • High-intensity headlights blind other drivers. • Seat belts failed to lock. • Overheated power-window switch. 2004—Under-hood fire. • Engine surges and stalls while cruising. • Cruise control goes on and off when descending a hill. • Early transmission replacement. • Vehicle frequently goes out of alignment. • ABS brake failure. • Premature brake rotor wearout. • Firestone side wall blowout saga continues. • Limited spring travel causes suspension to "bottom out" easily. • Passenger window suddenly exploded. • Exhaust fumes enter the cabin. **2005**—Automatic transmission slips and jerks into gear. • Faulty electrical unit. • Windows won't roll down. • Locks don't work. • Radio malfunctions. • Suspension won't support the extra weight of a trailer that's much lighter than the recommended maximum towing weight. • Frame is easily bent. • Brake lines leak fluid.

Secret Warranties/Internal Bulletins/Service Tips

All years: Front brake caliper rattling. **2000**—Engine knocking. • Because of low fuel pressure, diesel engine may produce a loud knocking or cackle noise. • The Reverse Park Aid may sound a false alarm if contaminated by debris in the system. **2000–03**—Rough idle or hesitation when accelerating is covered in TSB #03-9-11. **2000–04**—Front hubs won't lock or disengage. • Repair tips for diesel engine vacuum pumps that won't run, or that run continuously. • 4×4 system may be compromised, and climate control may default to defrost. **2000–05**—Seat belts are slow to retract. **2001**—No-starts, stalling with the 7.3L engine. • Engine stalls when vehicle is shifted into Reverse. • Ford admits investigating cam sensor failures (which lead to loss of power, engine shutdown, and no-starts). • Sudden loss of Second gear; vehicle won't move. • Delayed shifts. • Turbo hooting. • Sway bar clunks and pops. • Front shaft seal leaks. • Water-pump shaft seal leaks. • A buck or jerk may be felt with cruise control engaged. • Higher-than-normal steering effort required at low speeds. • Incorrect oil pressure readings. **2002**—Heater core leaks. • Ignition switch lock cylinder is faulty. • Engine cylinder heads leak oil or coolant. • Oil contamination in the cooling system. • Vehicle pulls to one side when braking. • Popping noise from the floorboard area. • Increased low-speed steering effort required. • Hard starts; battery won't charge. **2003**—Special Customer Satisfaction Program to enhance cold-weather engine performance (reduces rough idle). • Special Customer Satisfaction Program #03B05 to replace ICP sensor. • Exhaust noise and loss of power. • Remedy for faulty adjustable pedals. • Correction for starter failures. **2003–04**—Steering grunt, moan on left-hand turns. **2003–05**—Inoperative AC; compressor leakage. *Diesel engines:* **2003–04**—Diesel fuel in the oil may cause the engine to run rough or lose power. • Troubleshooting tips for water in diesel fuel and a warning light that won't shut off. • Diesel engine misfiring or no-starts may be caused by a defective fuel-injection control module (TSB #04-18-06). TSB # 04-17-13 says diesel hard starts or no-starts can also be traced to a faulty glow-plug control module. • Diesel engine excessive accessory drivebelt squeal or squawk; turbo-induced moan, groan. • Overall poor diesel engine performance requires a revised computer module calibration (TSB # 03-20-12) and the following countermeasures (see bulletins) • **2003–**

> ### DIESEL ENGINE—DRIVEABILITY/ OIL FUEL DILUTION
>
> BULLETIN NO.: 04-9-3   DATE: MAY 11, 2004
>
> **DRIVEABILITY—RUNS ROUGH, LOW POWER**
>
> 2003–04 EXCURSION, F SUPER DUTY 2004 ECONOLINE
>
> **ISSUE:** Some vehicles equipped with the 6.0L diesel engine may exhibit engine oil diluted with fuel (OIL LEVEL MAY APPEAR OVER FULL), runs rough and/or a low power condition.

05—Additional diagnostic and repair tips for 6.0L diesel-equipped models that misfire, lose power, buck and jerk, produce excessive smoke, are hard to start, or won't start (injector failure is the prime suspect, but the TSB delves into other causes as well). **2004**—6.0L diesel low-power and oil leak diagnostic tips. • Diesel engine may buck, jerk, or stumble after deceleration down long grade with the cruise control engaged. • Turbo-induced diesel engine exhaust moan, drone.

EXCURSION PROFILE

	2000	2001	2002	2003	2004	2005
Cost Price ($) (very negotiable)						
4X2 XLT	46,219	42,481	45,925	46,940	48,945	51,510
4X4 XLT	47,695	47,245	56,460	56,880	52,905	54,370
Used Values ($)						
4X2 XLT ▲	12,000	14,000	18,000	23,000	28,000	33,000
4X2 XLT ▼	10,500	13,000	17,000	21,000	26,000	31,000
4X4 XLT ▲	13,500	16,000	20,000	25,000	32,000	36,000
4X4 XLT ▼	12,500	15,000	19,000	23,000	30,000	34,000
Reliability	②	②	②	②	②	③

Ford/Mazda

best buy | **ESCAPE/TRIBUTE, ESCAPE HYBRID** | ★★★★★

All ratings on a numbered scale where ⑤ is good and ❶ is bad. See page 220 for a more detailed description.

2007 TECHNICAL DATA

POWERTRAIN

Engines: 2.3L 4-cyl. (153 hp) • Hybrid (155 hp) • 3.0L V6 (200 hp); Transmissions: 5-speed man. • 4-speed auto. • CVT Hybrid

DIMENSION/CAPACITY

Passengers: 2/3; Wheelbase: 103 in.; H: 69.7/L: 175/W: 70 in.; Headroom F/R: 4.5/5.0 in.; Legroom F/R: 40.5/28 in.; Cargo volume: 29.3 cu. ft.; Fuel tank: 62L/regular; Tow limit: 3,500 lb.; Load capacity: 900 lb.; GVWR: 4,120–4,520 lb.; Turning circle: 40 ft.; Ground clearance: 8.0 in.; Weight: 3,580 lb.

RATING: *Escape/Tribute:* Recommended (2005–07); Above Average (2004); Average (2002–03); Below Average (2001). One of the most improved vehicles in Ford's lineup. *Escape Hybrid:* Above Average (2005–07). Improvements on 2005 model year vehicles correct the quality, power, and performance deficiencies of previous models. Up to the 2003 model year, the Escape/Tribute promised a lot but delivered a low-quality SUV that would frequently stall or suddenly accelerate at any time. Interestingly, Mazda dealers generate fewer servicing complaints. **Strong points:** *2005 and later models:* A smoother driveline; a more powerful base engine; an automatic tranny is now available with the base engine; a quieter cabin; less V6 engine noise and vibration; more standard equipment and a longer powertrain warranty on the 2007s. *Pre-2005 models:* Quick 6-cylinder acceleration; good manoeuvrability; plenty of passenger space and cargo room, almost equal to the Explorer; well laid-out and easy-to-read instruments and controls; good visibility; easy-to-fold rear seatbacks; and rear liftgate's flip-up glass gives quick access to cargo. **Weak points:** Although NHTSA gives the Escape an "Average" rollover rating, independent tests carried out by *Consumer Reports* conclude the vehicle is "tippy." *2005 and later models:* Only rated "Acceptable" for offset crashworthiness by the IIHS. *Pre-2005 models:* Poorly equipped and underpowered, with unimpressive snow traction; historically poor-quality Ford-designed engines and transmissions. There's a sluggish 4-cylinder and a V6 that needs more high-end grunt for long upgrades; you won't find a base 4-cylinder, front-drive model with an automatic transmission; no low-speed transfer case; bumps can be jolting; entry and exit are compromised by a high step-in; side mirrors are on the small side; excessive engine and road noise; and a significant number of safety- and performance-related complaints clustered around the 2001 first-year lineup. **New for 2007:** The powertrain warranty has been extended to 5 years/100,000 km.

MODEL HISTORY: Launched as 2001 models, both the Escape and Tribute combine a carlike ride and handling—thanks to an independent rear suspension and front MacPherson struts—with the ability to drive in the snow and carry up to five passengers and their luggage. Neither vehicle is an upsized car or a downsized truck—they're four-doors that sip fuel, look like sport-utilities, and drive like sedans. **2005**—Foremost, you get a quieter engine and 26 more horses with the new 2.3L Duratec 4-banger, which raises towing capability from 454 kg (1,000 lb.) to 680 kg (1,500 lb.). The V6 engine has one less horse (200 hp), but uses upgraded engine mounts and computers to smooth out the idle and improve throttle response. Safety is also enhanced with "smart" seat sensors that can prevent airbag deployment if a child or small adult is seated, dual-stage airbags, head restraints and three-point safety belts for all seats, side curtain airbags, and larger diameter four-wheel disc and anti-lock brakes. The Escape and Tribute's front structure has been reinforced to better protect occupants in offset frontal crashes. Other enhancements include an improved 4×4 system that is fully automatic (it no longer needs to be switched on); front shocks that are larger in diameter; a new stabilizer system; a floor-mounted shifter; new headlights, foglights, grille, and front and rear ends; different gauges; upgraded seat cushions; more storage space; additional sound-absorbing materials (though it still lets in excessive wind noise); and alloy wheels. *Escape Hybrid:* This gasoline-electric hybrid is equipped with a 2.3L 4-cylinder engine, a 65-kilowatt electric motor, and a 28-kilowatt generator. It has off-road and towing capability, plus acceleration comparable to the 200-hp Escape V6 engine. The 2005 Mariner, a Mercury version of the Escape (sold only in the States), debuted in the fall of 2004.

COST ANALYSIS: Get a second-series 2005 model 4×2 version for the upgraded quality control, additional equipment, and about $8,000 off the original $23,000 sales price. The MSRP for a 2006 front-drive GX is $24,595 ($2,000 more for the V6), $27,395 for the AWD version (a V6 will cost about $2,500 more), and $36,499 for the fully loaded Limited V6 4×4. A new Hybrid will cost $33,599 for the base model and an additional $2,000 for the 4×4 variant. All of the above new prices will likely be increased by $500 to $1,000 in the late fall of 2006, with the largest increase reserved for the red-hot hybrids. There is almost a 20 percent dealer profit cushion figured into the base prices; most models are selling close to list. **Best alternatives:** Roughly the size of a Ford Focus sedan, the base Escape XLS 4×2 targets the low-priced, compact sport-utility market presently dominated by the Honda CR-V, Jeep Cherokee, Nissan Xterra, Pontiac Vibe, and Toyota RAV4 and Matrix. It costs considerably less than a V6-equipped Ford Explorer 4×4, yet the Escape is nearly the same width and height as the Explorer. **Rebates:** These compact SUVs are hot, so expect only modest discounting and low financing rates. **Delivery/PDI:** *Escape:* $1,200; *Tribute:* $1,390 (the extra $190 for the Mazda version is unacceptable). **Warranty:** Bumper-to-bumper 3 years/60,000 km; powertrain 5 years/100,000 km; rust perforation 5 years/unlimited km. *Hybrid:* Essentially the same, except for an 8 year/160,000 km electrical components warranty. **Supplementary warranty:** Yes, at least for the powertrain. **Options:** AWD, if you really need it; 1,588 kg (3,500 lb.) towing package; sunroof reduces headroom considerably. Convenient snap-in pet barrier and mountain-bike hauler from Ford Outfitters. **Depreciation:** Quite slow. **Insurance cost:** Average for a small SUV. **Parts supply/cost:** Few complaints so far. Generic powertrain parts aren't hard to find, though electronics can be expensive and hard to troubleshoot. Long delays for parts needed for recall campaigns. **Annual maintenance cost:** Expected to be higher than average once first-year models lose base warranty protection. **Highway/city fuel economy:** *4-cyl. 2.3L:* 7.3/9.7 L/100 km; *Hybrid 2.3L:* 7.0/6.6

L/100 km (remember, hybrids are more economical in the city); *V6 3.0L:* 9.9/13.3 L/100 km. Notwithstanding the above fuel economy estimates, owners often report their vehicles burn much more fuel than estimated.

 QUALITY/RELIABILITY: Both companies have a poor record for quality control during the first few years their vehicles are on the market. Numerous secret warranty programs (Ford now calls these "Special Service Instructions," or SSIs) are used to correct problems like chronic stalling, a sticking cruise control, the steering wheel and rear wheels falling off, and leaking fuel lines. Off-roading capability is compromised by the profusion of dust and dirt that works its way into the cabin. **Owner complaints:** Vehicle was out of service 36 days while dealer looked for cause of raw-fuel smell entering cabin; chronic stalling and hard starts; engine oil leaks (engine crankshaft out of spec); transmission refuses to go into gear; automatic transmission won't upshift at 85 km/h; lost Reverse gear; automatic transmission gearshift handle gets stuck halfway down when changing gears because of a design flaw; transmission fluid leaks; excessive front brake dust turns wheels black; frequent short circuits; rear defogger won't shut off; alternator light comes on intermittently; cruise control turns itself off; faulty side windows; ice forming on front wheels causes excessive vibrations; lots of squeaks, rattles, and wind noise; poor fit and finish; the internal support beam on the rear passenger door contracts and pulls the door panel inward, causing a dimpling effect in six separate areas; tires make a humming noise; engine hesitates when AC is engaged; AC makes a loud, cyclic sound; mildew odour from AC and vents; can't remove key from ignition. **Warranty performance:** Average. Ford's SSI secret warranty programs are a giant step backward from its ONPs, which notified all owners.

 ROAD PERFORMANCE: Acceleration/torque: Good performance with the 2005–07 models, but earlier 4-cylinder engines were overwhelmed by the wagon's heft. The V6 performs well, though it's a bit rough and could use some more power for passing and merging. **Transmission:** Smooth and quiet shifting, though the automatic transmission's long-term reliability is still worrisome. The automatic transmission lever blocks access to controls for the rear defogger, parking lights, and radio; transmission levers are often knocked inadvertently into Neutral when adjusting the radio. Dial-up 4×4 engagement is a pain on 2004 and earlier versions. **Steering:** Above average. **Routine handling:** Surprisingly good for a wagon. Easy to manoeuvre in tight places. Corners very well at high speeds, with only a bit of body lean. Taut four-wheel independent suspension may be too firm for some, but it enhances handling considerably. **Braking:** Brakes perform very well, with little fading after successive stops; there's some nosedive, however.

 SAFETY SUMMARY: Ontario lawyer Harvin Pitch has filed a class action petition on behalf of a Toronto couple injured when their 2003 Tribute rolled over in New Mexico. The ensuing rollover caused brain damage to the seat-belted passenger. Two issues are raised: That SUVs are unsafe because they have a propensity to roll over, and that the Tribute's passenger roof is not strong enough to absorb the rollover crush. (Harvin Pitch may be reached at *hpitch@teplitskycolson.com*.) Five three-point seat belts and five height-adjustable head restraints. **Airbags:** Front and side. Owners have reported that airbags may go off without warning, may fail to deploy in a collision, or are disabled when an adult sits in the front passenger seat. **ABS:** Optional; disc/drum; standard on the Hybrid. **Safety belt pretensioners:** Front. **Head restraints F/R:** *2001:* ★; *2002–04:* ★★★★★/★★★. **Visibility F/R:** ★★★★★.

SAFETY COMPLAINTS: Chronic stalling, sudden unintended acceleration (gas pedal sticking), airbag and brake malfunctions, and frequent transmission replacements are major problems through the 2003 model year. **2001–04**—Rear wiper arm failure. • Headliner sagging. *Escape:* **2001**—Fuel vapours enter passenger compartment via ventilation ducts (to fix, tighten bolts on the left-side intake manifold). • Fuel leakage around fuel injectors. • Fuel line clip failed, causing loss of power, and fuel was sprayed onto hot engine. • Vehicle rolled over unexpectedly while driving 25–40 km/h. • CV joints and front axle fell off vehicle. • Transmission failures. • Clutch cable often comes off when driving. • Automatic transmission pops out of Drive into Neutral while underway. • Sudden, unintended acceleration when shifting into Reverse or First gear, or when taking foot off the accelerator. • When going downhill, vehicle often suddenly loses all electrical power and shuts down on the highway with loss of steering and brake assist (faulty EGR valve suspected as the cause of the problem). • Chronic electrical problems. • Left rear wheels suddenly locked up, pulling vehicle into traffic. • Vehicle pulls randomly to the right or left when steering wheel is let go. • Steering is too tight. • Sometimes steering tugs a bit to one side and then freezes, brakes won't work, and Check Engine light comes on (engine still running). • Part of power-steering system fell out of car when it was put into Park. • Rear seats don't lock properly. • Car seatback collapsed in collision. • Left rear seat belt frequently jams. • Windshield wiper failures; 6-week delay for recall fix. *Tribute:* **2001**—Fuel smell still enters cabin (after recall). • Wiring harness fire. • Erratic shifting. • Transmission will slip if vehicle has been sitting for an extended period of time. • Faulty rear-differential seal caused differential to self-destruct. • Sudden loss of steering and brakes. • Power steering cuts out when making a left turn; steering often locks up. • Loss of steering caused by a broken tensioner belt. • Steering linkage fell off vehicle while underway. • Frequent brake failures; brake master cylinder replaced. • Windshield wiper failures (after recall). • Headlights collect moisture. • Power windows and sunroof stopped working. • Side mirror vibrates excessively. **2002**—Over 400 complaints reported to federal investigators (50–100 would be normal). • Sudden acceleration. • Brake and steering failures. • Reports of water entering the passenger compartment. • Transmission fluid and engine oil leaks. • Wipers that skip over the windshield. **2003**—Prone to roll over; roof cannot support crush forces (see lawsuit information in "Safety Summary"). • Jammed throttle control cable. • Automatic transmission locked up and was replaced. • Brake and accelerator pedals placed too close together. • Brake pads separated; loss of braking ability. • Stalls at intersections. • Suspension failure while driving. • Driver-side door hinge failed, allowing door to fall off. • Tire side wall blowouts; tread separation (Continental ContiTrac). **2004**—Sudden, unintended acceleration; chronic stalling. • Automatic transmission failure:

> The "needle bearings" in the "planetary bearing" had failed. They disintegrated. Small metal fragments worked throughout the transmission, resulting in excessive internal damage.

• Door locks self-activate. • Window short-circuits. • Vehicle may pull sharply to one side or gain speed when descending a hill with the cruise control engaged. • Rolls backwards when stopped on an incline. • Fuel spillage because filler pipe doesn't trip gas pump automatic shutoff. **2005**—Chronic stalling remains a problem. • Sudden acceleration. • Airbags failed to deploy. • Transmission failure. • Broken door latch:

> Right rear passenger door latch broke and door came open while driving. We had to secure door with a nylon strap to get to our destination. It is a good thing we are firm believers in seat belt use or this might have ended in a tragedy as the seat next to [the] door was occupied.

Hybrid: **2005**—Only three complaints registered by NHTSA. • Stalling (believed to be caused by a faulty water pump and fuse).

Secret Warranties/Internal Bulletins/Service Tips

All years: Engine hydromount insulator and rear drive shaft replacement. • No forward transmission engagement (yes, the forward clutch piston, the cause of so many Windstar and Taurus/Sable failures, once again rears its ugly head). • Rear axle pinion seal leak. • Driveline grinding and clicking. • Possible leak in the transmission converter housing near the cooler line. • Intermittent loss of First and Second gears. • Manual transmission gear shifter buzz or rattle in Third or Fourth gear is being investigated by Ford technicians. • Possible causes for a lit MIL warning light. • EGR failures. • Fuel-pump whine heard through speakers (a Ford problem since 1990). • Vehicles with 3.0L engines may show a false "low coolant" condition. • ABS light may stay lit. • AC temperature-control knob may be hard to turn or adjust. **2001–02**—Harsh, delayed upshifts • Defective door latches. • Power-steering leaks. **2001–03**—Steering squeaking noise. • 3.0L engine stalling remedy (see bulletin) • **2001–04**—Engine misfire troubleshooting tips. • Correction for a sagging rear headliner. **2001–05**—Diagnostic and repair tips for steering pull and drifting. • Poor shifting in cold weather; install a Cooler Bypass Kit. • Slow-to-retract seat belts. • Instrument panel vents hard to adjust. **2001–06**—3.0L engine ticking noise. • Driveline whine. **2002**—Coolant, oil leakage from engine cylinder head area. • Defective Duratec engines. • Heater core leaks. • Brake squealing. • Wheels make a clicking sound. **2003**—Automatic transmission shudder and whine. • Powertrain throttle body service replacement. • Front

ENGINE CONTROLS/EMISSIONS—IDLE DIP/INTERMITTENT STALL

BULLETIN NO.: 02-23-1   DATE: NOVEMBER 25, 2002

2001–03 ESCAPE

ISSUE: Some vehicles equipped with the 3.0L Duratec engine may exhibit an intermittent engine quit and restart condition. This is usually a one-time event during closed throttle deceleration with no Diagnostic Trouble Codes (DTCs) and no Malfunction Indicator Lamp (MIL). Due to the intermittent nature of the condition and the multiple potential causes of the condition, the complete bulletin checklist, and all appropriate part replacements should be performed regardless of whether the condition can be duplicated by the technician. Otherwise, customers may experience the intermittent condition and be forced to return to the dealership. If the vehicle is no longer eligible for warranty coverage, discuss this service with the customer before performing.

wheel bearing noise. • Rear shock leak and noise. **2003–04**—False activation of Parking Assist ("Stop! Stop! There's something behind you! Just kidding."). You know what's most worrisome? Ford says this device may be operating as it should. **2003–06**—Inoperative AC; compressor leakage:

A/C—COMPRESSOR LEAKING/INOPERATIVE

BULLETIN NO.: 06-4-9   DATE: MARCH 6, 2006

A/C COMPRESSOR NOT OPERATIONAL / LOW FREON-SHAFT SEAL LEAKS (REPLACE THE AC SHAFT SEAL)

FORD: 2003 Escort; 2003–2006 Focus, Mustang, Taurus; 2003 Explorer Sport, Windstar; 2003–2005 Excursion, Explorer Sport Trac; 2003–2006 Escape, F-150, F-Super Duty, Ranger; 2004–2006 Freestar; and 2006 Low Cab Forward.

LINCOLN: 2002 Blackwood and 2006 Mark LT.

MERCURY: 2003–2005 Sable; 2004–2006 Monterey; and 2005–2006 Mariner.

2005—Engine overheating. • An engine oil leak from the oil dipstick or front/rear crankshaft seals can be fixed by installing a Heated PCV Kit. • Rear brake noise. **2005–06**—Hard starts may require a recalibrated powertrain control module (PCM); the half-hour labour charge is covered by the emissions warranty, says TSB #05-26-1. • Excessive steering vibration likely caused by faulty Continental tires, which will be replaced under an extended warranty. *Hybrid:* **2005**—Rear brake noise. **2005–06**—Driveline whine. • Fuel tank slow to fill; frequent pump shut-offs.

ESCAPE/TRIBUTE, ESCAPE HYBRID PROFILE

	2001	2002	2003	2004	2005	2006
Cost Price ($) (negotiable)						
XLS 4X2 (18%)	21,310	21,510	21,595	21,895	22,995	22,999
XLS 4X4 (18%)	23,960	24,190	27,495	27,825	28,125	28,399
Tribute 4X2 (17%)	22,150	22,415	22,790	22,790	24,495	24,595
Tribute 4X4 (17%)	24,800	25,065	25,575	25,445	27,295	27,395
Hybrid 4X2 (20%)	—	—	—	—	33,195	33,599
Hybrid 4X4 (20%)	—	—	—	—	35,925	36,399
Used Values ($)						
XLS 4X2 ▲	8,500	10,500	11,500	12,500	15,500	—
XLS 4X2 ▼	7,500	9,000	10,000	11,500	14,000	—
XLS 4X4 ▲	10,000	11,500	15,000	16,000	17,500	—
XLS 4X4 ▼	9,000	9,500	14,000	15,000	16,000	—
Tribute 4X2 ▲	9,000	10,500	11,500	14,000	16,500	—
Tribute 4X2 ▼	8,000	9,500	10,000	12,000	15,000	—
Tribute 4X4 ▲	10,000	12,000	13,000	15,000	17,500	—
Tribute 4X4 ▼	9,000	10,500	11,500	13,500	16,000	—
Hybrid 4X2 ▲	—	—	—	—	24,000	—
Hybrid 4X2 ▼	—	—	—	—	22,000	—
Hybrid 4X4 ▲	—	—	—	—	25,500	—
Hybrid 4X4 ▼	—	—	—	—	23,500	—
Reliability	②	②	②	③	③	—
Crash Safety (F)	⑤	⑤	⑤	⑤	④	④
Side	⑤	⑤	⑤	⑤	⑤	⑤
Offset	②	②	②	②	③	③
Rollover	③	③	③	—	③	③

General Motors

AZTEK, RENDEZVOUS ★★

RATING: Below Average (2001–07). More luxury minivans than sporty SUVs; neither vehicle is any match for the Asian competition. The Rendezvous is scheduled to be dropped by December 2006, and it will be replaced by the 2008 Buick Enclave later the following year. **Strong points:** Quiet, comfortable ride; one of the more affordable seven-passenger SUVs; tight steering; lots of passenger and storage room; low step-in and large doors; uses regular fuel. **Weak points:** The 3.4L V6 lacks the kick of GM's new inline-six; interior materials don't say "Buick luxury"; one-piece tailgate. Very expensive for what little you get. If you want four-

2006 RENDEZVOUS TECHNICAL DATA

POWERTRAIN

Engines: 3.5L V6 (201 hp) • 3.6L V6 (245 hp); Transmission: 4-speed auto.

DIMENSION/CAPACITY

Passengers: 2/3/2; Wheelbase: 112 in.; H: 69/L: 187/W: 74 in.; Headroom F/R1/R2: 4.5/6.0/1.0 in.; Legroom F/R1/R2: 40/29.5/24 in.; Cargo volume: 45 cu. ft.; Fuel tank: 70L/regular; Tow limit: 3,500 lb.; Load capacity: 1,215 lb.; GVWR: 4,986–5,218 lb.; Turning circle: 40 ft.; Ground clearance: 6.0 in.; Weight: 3,900 lb.

wheel discs, for example, you have to get the higher-end AWD version, or if you want the better-suited 3.6L V6, you have to opt for the more expensive Ultra. Rear hatch is often coated with road grime that can't be removed because there's no rear wiper. Over-the-shoulder visibility is hampered by the thick side roof pillars, and front body corners are hard to see. Large doors could be a problem when parking in tight spaces. Poor acceleration; mediocre handling and road holding; no low-range gearing and low ground clearance make off-roading a no-no. The Rendezvous has a more jiggly ride, and its additional seating isn't that comfortable; plus, to access the more-than-ample storage areas, you have to remove the seats. Imprecise steering has insufficient feedback; marginal head restraint and offset crash scores; excessive road, tire, and engine noise; mediocre fuel economy; and spotty quality control highlighted by hard starts, chronic stalling, and engine intake manifold failures afflicting all model years. **New for 2007:** No more optional V6. A dead "minivan" walking, GM will likely dump the Rendezvous at the end of the 2007 model year.

MODEL HISTORY: Essentially minivan/SUV crossovers, the Aztek and Rendezvous are practically identical, except the Rendezvous' wheelbase is an extra 10 cm (4 in.) longer and accommodates third-row seating. Both have been sales flops, despite the Rendezvous' designation by *Consumer Reports* as a "Recommended" buy—an opinion *Lemon-Aid* doesn't share.

The Aztek is built on a shorter Montana minivan platform, while the Rendezvous' larger wheelbase allows for more, but not as comfortable, seating. The Aztek is especially roomy, with more cargo room than a Ford Explorer, and is capable of carrying a bicycle upright. The Rendezvous excels in storage capacity too, once you remove the seats. These vehicles are also full of innovative features, like a centre console that doubles as a portable cooler and three special packages for biking, camping, and hiking. The Aztek's stiff suspension makes for an uncomfortable ride, though, and is likely to cause more severe rattling as the vehicle ages. The Rendezvous provides a more forgiving, gentler ride. Driving performance is minivan-boring, though, with considerable under-steer, sluggish steering, and mediocre handling; it takes almost 11 seconds to reach 100 km/h.

The Rendezvous comes with standard ABS and four-wheel disc brakes, found on the Aztek on AWD models only. Second-row seating is provided by a three-person split bench or by twin-bucket seats. The optional two-passenger third-row seat folds flush with the floor. **2002**—A revised front end and a spoiler added to the Aztek. **2003**—A rear-seat DVD player, upgraded wheels, and a tire-inflation monitoring system. **2004**—An all-new, plush AWD Rendezvous Ultra equipped with a 242-hp 3.6L V6. **2005**—The Aztek's last model year. **2006**—3.6L V6 dropped for the 2007 model year.

COST ANALYSIS: Best alternatives: Prices will change little, with the 2007 Rendezvous costing about $29,000/$42,000 for the CX and CXL Plus, respectively. The 2006 entry-level Rendezvous CX (both front-drive and AWD) is listed at about $4,000 less than the 2005s. This price cut means the 2006s will sell used for about what a 2005 will bring, making a used 2006 the better deal, if you can wait a year or so. If you can downsize a bit to save fuel and insurance costs, consider the Honda CR-V, Hyundai Santa Fe or a second-series Veracruz, and Toyota's RAV4. **Rebates:** These mid-sized SUVs attract hefty $8,000+ rebates and zero percent financing as GM seeks to unload its bloated large and mid-sized SUV inventory. **Delivery/PDI:** $1,170. **Warranty:** Bumper-to-bumper 3 years/60,000 km; powertrain 3 years/60,000 km; rust perforation 5 years/unlimited km. **Supplementary warranty:** Yes, bumper-to-bumper coverage is a must-have. **Options:** AWD, if you really need it. Stay away from the distracting and not-always-accurate rear obstacle detection feature as well as the head-up instrument display. **Depreciation:** Faster than average. **Insurance cost:** Higher than average. **Parts supply/cost:** Few complaints so far. These SUVs use generic Montana parts that are found everywhere and are usually reasonably priced. **Annual maintenance cost:** Expected to be just a bit higher than average once the warranty expires. **Highway/city fuel economy:** 8.3/12.6 L/100 km.

QUALITY/RELIABILITY: Owner complaints: Engine, front wheel bearing, and AC failures are commonplace. **Warranty performance:** Fair.

SAFETY SUMMARY: Airbags: Front and side. **ABS:** Standard; disc/drum. **Safety belt pretensioners:** Yes. **Traction control:** Optional. **Head restraints F/R:** *Aztek:* ★★; *2003 Aztek:* ★★★/★★; *Rendezvous:* ★★★/★★. **Visibility F/R:** *Aztek:* ★★★/★; *Rendezvous:* ★★★. Exterior rear-view mirrors cause a huge blind spot.

SAFETY COMPLAINTS: All years: Fill hose enters gas tank at a very vulnerable location. • Airbags failed to deploy in a collision. • Rear spoiler obstructs vision. • Water leaks or heavy condensation in the tail lights. • Horn is hard to blow. • **2001**—Numerous reports of rollover accidents where occupants were ejected. • Vehicle fire caused by shorted wiring harness. • Steering tie-rod/drive bar failed, sending vehicle out of control. • Delayed automatic transmission shifts, slippage, extended shifts, or flaring during cold operation. • Transmission grinding. • Growling noise when sitting in Park on a hill or slope with the engine running and the parking brake not applied. • Rear brake failure. • Excessive vibration while driving. • Instrument panel may be warped rearward of the defroster outlet. •

Water may enter the passenger compartment near the H-back module. • GM says windshield distortion could be caused by car washes. • Rear liftgate will not release the secondary latch position when opened automatically. • Wiper blades hit each other. • Airbag light comes on intermittently. • Shock absorber rattling. *Aztek:* **2001**—Rear brake failures. • Stalling. • Excessive vibration above 100 km/h, said to be caused by a faulty drive shaft. • Dealer says front wheels cannot be realigned without bending the frame. • Rear wipers are hard to find. • Faulty rear door security-lock lever. **2002**—Engine surges when braking. • Brakes work intermittently. **2003**—ABS control unit failure. • Vehicle's rear end skips about when passing over highway bumps. *Rendezvous:* **2002**—Chronic differential leak. • Vehicle won't stay in gear while stopped on an incline. • Car stalls when changing gears. • Sudden loss of all electrical power. • Loss of steering when right axle spindle gear broke. • Parts for airbag recall aren't available. • Faulty sending unit causes inaccurate fuel gauge readings. • Water enters and soaks the front carpet. • Wind blows door back, breaking hinge. **2003**—Engine, transmission, and brake failures. • Electrical shorts; blown fuses. **2004**—Gas tank neck snapped off. • Chronic stalling. • Transmission failure. • Radio and horn would self-activate. • Unable to open windows and rear doors. • Middle seat belt securing baby seat suddenly unlatched. **2005**—Sudden, unintended acceleration. • Chronic stalling, possibly related to the ignition relay recall on the 2004 model. • Instrument panel cannot be read under certain daylight conditions. • Incorrect fuel gauge readings. • ABS and AWD warning lights are often lit.

Secret Warranties/Internal Bulletins/Service Tips

All years: Harsh transmission shifts while Check Engine light is on. • Poor engine and transmission performance. • Rear axle seal leaks. • Hard start, no-start, stalling, and fuel gauge fluctuation. • Muffler heat shield rattle. **2001**—No forward, delayed forward, or the automatic transmission may lock in Reverse. **2001–02**—Customer Satisfaction Program (secret warranty) regarding the brake booster power piston, valve springs replacement, and dead battery replacements. • Grinding noise, or failure of 4-speed automatic transmission to engage when shifting into Drive or Reverse. **2001–03**—Faulty intake manifold may cause coolant/oil loss (TSB #03-06-01-O10A). • Defective AC, compressor. • Exhaust rattle, buzz. • Radio speaker static. **2001–05**—No Reverse, Second, or Fourth gears (Bulletin #00-07-30-022B says to replace the reaction sun shell with a more durable, heat-treated part). **2001–06**—Hard start, stalling, inoperative gauges, and lit warning lights can all be traced to water leaking onto the C305 connector, says TSB #01-08-45-005D. **2002**—Hard shifting, shuddering with automatic transmission (TSB #02-07-30-039B). **2002–03**—Engine exhaust manifold defect correction:

ENGINE OIL OR COOLANT LEAK (INSTALL NEW INTAKE MANIFOLD GASKET)

2000–03 Buick Century	1996–2003 Oldsmobile Silhouette
2002–03 Buick Rendezvous	1999 Oldsmobile Cutlass
1996 Chevrolet Lumina APV	1999–2003 Oldsmobile Alero
1997–2003 Chevrolet Venture	1996–99 Pontiac Trans Sport
1999–2001 Chevrolet Lumina	1999–2003 Pontiac Grand Am, Montana
1999–2003 Chevrolet Malibu, Monte Carlo	2000–03 Pontiac Grand Prix
2000–03 Chevrolet Impala	2001–03 Pontiac Aztek with 3.1L or 3.4L V-6 Engine.

CONDITION: Some owners may comment on an apparent oil or coolant leak. Additionally, the comments may range from spots on the driveway to having to add fluids.

CORRECTION: Install a new design intake manifold gasket. The material used in the gasket has been changed in order to improve the sealing qualities of the gasket. When replacing the gasket, the intake manifold bolts must also be replaced and torqued to a revised specification. The new bolts will come with a pre-applied threadlocker on them.

2002–04—Tips on silencing an engine boom or drone noise (install a revised torque tube mount). 2003—Long, hard starts, rough idle, and clogged fuel injectors. *Rendezvous:* 2002—Wet carpet in the passenger footwell produces a foul odour. • Water enters passenger compartment at the area of the H-back module. 2002–06—Noisy steering can be silenced by replacing the inner tie-rod boot, says TSB #06-02-32-005.

AZTEK, RENDEZVOUS PROFILE

	2001	2002	2003	2004	2005	2006
Cost Price ($) (very negotiable)						
Aztek	29,255	29,255	29,500	28,180	28,655	—
GT 4X4	36,185	36,185	36,985	34,060	35,895	—
Rendezvous (23%)	—	30,995	31,545	32,440	32,750	28,610
Rendezvous 4X4 (25%)	—	34,995	35,595	36,415	36,940	32,020
Used Values ($)						
Aztek ▲	8,500	10,500	12,500	14,500	18,000	—
Aztek ▼	7,000	9,500	11,000	13,000	16,000	—
GT 4X4 ▲	9,000	11,500	14,500	17,000	18,500	—
GT 4X4 ▼	8,000	10,500	13,000	15,500	17,000	—
Rendezvous ▲	—	13,500	15,500	17,500	20,000	—
Rendezvous ▼	—	12,000	14,000	16,000	18,500	—
Rendezvous 4X4 ▲	—	14,500	16,500	19,500	22,500	—
Rendezvous 4X4 ▼	—	13,500	15,500	18,000	21,000	—

Reliability	②	③	③	③	③	—
Crash Safety (F) (4X4)	③	③	③	③	③	③
Side (Aztek)	⑤	⑤	⑤	⑤	—	—
Rendezvous	—	③	③	—	⑤	⑤
Offset (Aztek)	②	②	②	②	②	—
Rendezvous	—	③	③	③	③	③
Rollover	③	③	③	—	—	—

---

bad buy | **BLAZER, ENVOY, JIMMY**

2005 TECHNICAL DATA

POWERTRAIN

Engine: 4.3L V6 (190 hp); Transmissions: 4-speed auto. OD • 5-speed man. OD

DIMENSION/CAPACITY (2D)

Passengers: 2/3; Wheelbase: 100.5 in.; H: 64/L: 176.8/W: 68 in.; Headroom F/R: N/A; Legroom F/R: 42.4/35.6 in.; Cargo volume: 29.8 cu. ft.; Fuel tank: 71L/regular; Tow limit: 5,600 lb.; Load capacity: 838–2,000 lb.; GVWR: 5,000–5,300 lb.; Turning circle: 34.8 ft.; Ground clearance: 8 in.; Weight: 3,866 lb.

RATING: Not Recommended (1995–2005). These are three of the worst SUVs you could possibly buy. Blazer and Jimmy are identical, and both were dropped after the 2005 model year. **Strong points:** Reasonably well appointed; full-time AutoTrac 4×4 shifts on the fly and can be used on dry pavement; comfortable ride; nice handling; comfortable seating and sufficient headroom and legroom for all but the last row of passengers; plenty of cargo space, and expanding the cargo room by folding the rear seat is a snap; low noise levels. **Weak points:** Blazer embodies a decade's worth of safety-related problems, poor quality, and mediocre performance. Drivers have had to contend with a gas-guzzling engine that quickly runs out of steam; poor emergency handling; a hard, jiggly ride; and GM's subpar fit and finish. The thick centre and rear roof pillars and the tinted rear windows compromise rear visibility; rear interior access is restricted; and the short, hard rear seats can make for a harsh ride.

MODEL HISTORY: These are identical two-door and four-door mid-sized sport-utility vehicles, incorporating 4×2 and 4×4 drive and based on the GM S-series pickup platform. Part-time 4×4 (InstaTrac) is standard with all models, while the optional AutoTrac system delivers full rear-drive power until road conditions require it to automatically readjust the power ratio to other wheels. The only available engine is a 4.3L V6, rated at 190 hp and hooked to a 4-speed automatic transmission with Overdrive. Only two-door models come with a 5-speed manual gearbox.

The compact Blazer and Jimmy were first launched in 1983 as spin-offs of the full-sized GM Blazer and Jimmy—1970 SUV offshoots of GM's full-sized trucks. Although the Blazer and Jimmy are identical, separate GM divisions market them.

All ratings on a numbered scale where ⑤ is good and ❶ is bad. See page 220 for a more detailed description.

The Envoy, a Jimmy clone with some styling twists and more standard features, was launched in 1998, dropped for the 2001 model year, and then revived as a totally different 2002 model. However, the Jimmy and Blazer continued to soldier on as cheaper alternatives to Chevrolet's larger, more powerful TrailBlazer and the resurrected GMC Envoy.

The redesigned 1995–98 models aren't really all that different—GM didn't want to cannibalize sales of its full-sized Blazer, Yukon, and Tahoe. Nevertheless, interior noise was muffled, and cargo room was increased by mounting the spare tire beneath the rear end. **1996**—A Vortec V6 with five fewer horses became the standard powerplant. **1999**—An upgraded 4L60-E automatic transmission and optional AutoTrac transfer case that automatically engages 4×4 when needed. **2000**—Some engine, exhaust system, manual transmission, and ABS enhancements, but horsepower remained the same. Vehicles equipped with the ZR2 package were given an upgraded axle ratio to improve shifting and acceleration. Watch the payload rating though; some vehicles were sold with incorrect payload ratings. **2003**—A new fuel injection system, and some trim changes. A mid-year cost-cutting change replaced the front-drive's disc brakes with drums. **2005**—Four-door models are relegated to fleets.

COST ANALYSIS: Best alternatives: These are cheap SUVs to buy used from phased-out fleet sales, but what savings you get up front will be quickly eaten up in accelerated depreciation and high maintenance payouts. Check out the Hyundai Tucson, Nissan Xterra or X-Trail, and Toyota Highlander, Sequoia, or 4Runner. **Warranty:** Bumper-to-bumper 3 years/60,000 km; rust perforation 6 years/160,000 km. **Supplementary warranty:** An extended warranty is a good idea. **Options:** Rear window defroster, remote keyless entry, power door locks, engine block heater, and an upgraded sound system are worth considering. Have a transmission oil cooler installed. Get a sophisticated anti-theft system, or you'll keep your Blazer for only a few days. **Depreciation:** Quite rapid. **Insurance cost:** Average. **Annual maintenance cost:** Higher than average. **Parts supply/cost:** Parts are inexpensive from independent suppliers and widely available. **Highway/city fuel economy:** High fuel consumption in city driving. V6 4×2: 10.4/14.4 L/100 km; V6 4×4: 12.2/17.8 L/100 km.

QUALITY/RELIABILITY: Below Average. **Owner-reported problems:** Fuel injection glitches; noisy and roughly shifting transmissions; electrical system shorts, causing blown fuses and brake light, hazard light, and turn signal failures; excessive steering-wheel play makes the vehicle wander all over the road and difficult to control at times; excessive engine knocking; front suspension noise; body assembly and paint application have been below standard. **Warranty performance:** Below average. Don't get your hopes up if you're beyond the warranty period. GM is tight-fisted in allocating after-warranty compensation, especially on vehicles that are no longer sold.

SAFETY SUMMARY: These vehicles have registered an extraordinarily large number of accident injury claims. The IIHS collected data on traffic accidents involving passenger vehicles and small-sized trucks from 2000–03 on U.S. highways and calculated the death rates of drivers for each vehicle. In March 2005, it released its report, concluding that Blazer drivers are at the highest risk of death. About 308 Blazer drivers per 1 million would die if their cars were involved in accidents; the average death rate for all vehicles was 87 per 1 million.

Airbags: Standard side. Reports of airbags failing to deploy. **ABS:** Standard 4W; disc/disc. **Head restraints F/R:** *1996:* ★★★/★★/★; *1997:* ★; *1999:* ★★★/★★/★; *2001–02:* ★★★/★. **Visibility F/R:** ★★★★/★.

SAFETY COMPLAINTS: 1999–2000—Wiring-harness and other, non-specific, underhood fires. • Plastic fuel tank is easily punctured. • Accelerator pedal sticks. • Cruise control still engaged when brakes are applied. • Chronic stalling when decelerating (likely fuel-pump failure). • Premature automatic transmission failure; leaks, delayed and harsh shifting are the first signs of eventual breakdown. • Transfer case gets stuck in 4×4 High and Low. • Jumps out of First gear when accelerating. • Right wheel came off because of a missing cotter pin that locked the spindle in place. • Spare-tire cable broke, allowing tire to fly off. • Defective locking nut on the steering shaft allows the steering wheel to come off in the driver's hands. • Inner tie-rod and ball joint failure. • ABS light remains lit for no apparent reason. • Complete loss of braking. • Brake pedal went to floor with little braking effect. • On bumpy and rough surfaces, brake pedal goes soft and then stiffens. • When applying brakes while going downhill, vehicle fishtails out of control. • A weak spring causes the driver and passenger seats to slide back and forth. • Bad switch causes sudden headlight failure. • Windshield wipers work poorly. • Exhaust fumes invade cabin. • Seat belt retractor failed to restrain driver in a collision. • Horn goes off by itself. • In cold weather, driver-side window shattered as passenger door was closed. • Liftgate may suddenly fall because of collapsing support struts. • Interior and exterior light failures. **2001**—Airbags failed to deploy. • Power-steering hose fell off. • Malfunctioning brake lights said to be covered by a "silent" recall. • Theft-deterrent alarm goes off for no reason. • Brake pedal hits floor without activating brakes. • Faulty rear hatch actuator. • Vehicle accelerates when foot is taken off the accelerator. **2002**—Sudden acceleration. • Extreme buffeting when driving with rear window open. • 4×4 suddenly engages, locking up wheels. • 4×4 fails to engage. • Sudden tie-rod failure. • Faulty electronic mirror memory. • Seat belt continually retracts while worn. • Faulty camshaft position sensor. • Fuel tank leak, fuel line fell off, and incorrect fuel gauge readings. **2003**—Airbags didn't deploy. • Manual and automatic transmission fall into Neutral when driving. • Incorrect fuel gauge readings. • Fuel splashes outside of tank when refuelling. • Unacceptably long braking distance. **2004**—Sudden, unintended acceleration. • Loss of steering control when passing over bumpy roads. • Excessive rusting of the brake rotors and ABS module failure. • Water leaks into the B-pillar, soaking the seat belt webbing. • Spare tire is mounted in the rear, where it blocks almost all rear visibility.

Secret Warranties/Internal Bulletins/Service Tips

All years: No Reverse, Second, or Fourth gear (replace the reaction sun shell with more robust, heat-treated parts, says TSB #00-07-30-022B; November 18, 2004). • Hood hinge rattling. **1993–2002**—Paint delamination, peeling, or fading. **1997–98**—A variety of service bulletins outline steps to correct the following: engine high idle/flare when shifting gears; excessive ticking noise in ambient temperature; a blower fan that runs continuously with the ignition off; rough idling after vehicle has sat overnight; and instrument panel rattles. **1999**—If the front wheels slip while in 4×4, consider replacing the transfer-case clutch plates and front-drive axle lubricant. **1999–2000**—Before spending big bucks for engine head gasket repairs or the replacement of costly emissions components to fix a hot-running engine or stop coolant loss, first replace the radiator cap and polish the radiator filler neck. • GM's infamous "driveline clunk" has been carried over in another "don't worry about it" bulletin sent to dealers. **1999–2001**—TSB #01-07-30-038B indicates transmission malfunctions likely caused by debris plugging the bleed orifice of the 2–3 shift solenoid. • A faulty ignition switch may cause the transmission to stick in Third gear. **1999–2004**—Transmission debris may cause poor performance:

A/T—4L60-E/4L65-E MIL ON/DTC P0757/SLIPPING

BULLETIN NO.: 01-07-30-038B   **DATE: JANUARY 26, 2004**

DTC P0757 SET, SES LAMP ILLUMINATED, POOR PERFORMANCE OF TRANSMISSION, TRANSMISSION SLIPPING (CLEAN TRANSMISSION VALVE BODY AND CASE OIL PASSAGES OF DEBRIS)

1999–2004 Passenger Cars and Light Duty Trucks
2003–04 HUMMER H2 with 4L60-E/4L65-E Automatic Transmission

CONDITION: Some customers may comment on any of the following conditions:

• The SES lamp is illuminated.

• No 3rd and 4th gear.

• The transmission does not shift correctly.

• The transmission feels like it shifts to Neutral or a loss of drive occurs.

The vehicle freewheels above 48 km/h (30 mph). High RPM needed to overcome the freewheeling.

The most likely cause is chips or debris plugging the bleed orifice of the 23 shift solenoid (367). This will cause the transmission to stay in 2nd gear when 3rd gear is commanded and return to 1st gear when 4th gear is commanded.

• Inaccurate fuel gauge readings. **2000–03**—Hard-to-close doors. **2001**—Harsh shift remedies. • Premature wearout of automatic transmission and clutch components. • Automatic transmission 2–4 band or 3–4 clutch damage. • Transmission sticks in Third gear, MIL light stays on, and instrument cluster is inoperative. •

Transmission slips when placed in 4×4. • No-starts, hard starts, and stalling while Security light flashes. • Rear suspension popping noise. • Rear roof corrosion or perforation. • Corroded trailer pre-wire harness. • Muffler rattling. • Light flickering. **2001–02**—Poor engine performance and erratic shifting. • Service Engine light comes on, and transmission feels like it has slipped into Neutral. **2001–05**—Tips on correcting a harsh 1–2 upshift. **2002**—Diagnostic tips for loss of Third or Fourth gear. • Wet carpet and mildew odour in the front passenger-seat area. **2003–05**—Lack of power in high ambient temperatures. **2004**—Transmission fluid leak, inoperative gears, no movement, case cracked or broken at 2–4 servo (repair transmission and install new retaining ring).

BLAZER, ENVOY, JIMMY PROFILE

	1997	1998	1999	2000	2001	2002	2003	2004	2005
Cost Price ($) (negotiable)									
Blazer/Jimmy 4X2	27,160	28,800	26,899	28,305	—	—	—	—	—
Blazer/Jimmy 4X4 (25%)	29,015	30,655	28,750	31,005	32,085	28,770	29,270	29,350	26,045
Envoy	—	43,805	45,185	45,185					
Used Values ($)									
Blazer/Jimmy 4X2 ▲	3,000	3,500	4,500	5,500	—	—	—	—	—
Blazer/Jimmy 4X2 ▼	2,500	3,000	4,000	4,500	—	—	—	—	—
Blazer/Jimmy 4X4 ▲	3,500	4,500	5,500	6,500	8,000	11,000	12,500	13,500	15,500
Blazer/Jimmy 4X4 ▼	3,000	4,000	5,000	6,000	6,500	9,500	11,000	12,000	14,000
Envoy ▲	—	8,000	9,000	11,000	—	—	—	—	—
Envoy ▼	—	6,500	7,500	9,500	—	—	—	—	—
Reliability	❶	❷	❷	❷	❷	❷	❷	❸	❸
Crash Safety (F)									
Blazer 4d	❸	❹	❸	❸	❸	❸	❸	❸	❸
Side	—	—	❺	❺	❺	❺	❺	❺	❺
Offset	❶	❶	❶	❶	❶	❶	❶	❶	—
Rollover	—	—	—	—	❶	❶	❶	—	—

ENVOY, TRAILBLAZER, RAINIER, (SAAB) 9-7X ★★/★

RATING: Below Average (2002–07); 9-7X: Not Recommended (2005–07). Offering five- and seven-passenger seating, these mid-sized sport-utilities are bigger, wider, and roomier than the Blazer/Jimmy they replace. The TrailBlazer is the least luxurious; Buick's Rainier, the newest and cushiest; and the 9-7X, a Saab facsimile that offers little that is new or innovative and is the least popular of the group. **Strong points:** Good acceleration in all gear ranges; high tow rating; AutoTrac 4×4 can be left engaged on dry pavement and has low-range gearing for off-road use; comfortable ride; easy city manoeuvring, thanks to the relatively tight turning radius; less

All ratings on a numbered scale where ⑤ is good and ❶ is bad. See page 220 for a more detailed description.

tippy than competitors, with a higher centre of gravity; plenty of headroom and legroom, plus ample cargo space; rear seating for three adults; and supportive seats. **Weak points:** Overpriced; truck-like handling (vague steering and excessive body lean in turns) without the standard stability-control feature found on post-2005 models; excessive vibration and droning with the 6-cylinder engine; white-knuckle braking because of numb and spongy brakes; sudden stops lead to severe nosedive and steering instability; ground clearance that's 3.0 to 3.3 cm (1.2 or 1.3 in.) lower than the competition compromises off-road prowess; front seats lack lateral support; climate controls are hard to adjust by feel; rear visibility is blocked by head restraints and rear pillars; tacky-looking interior; excessive wind noise; awkward loading because of the rear hatch's high sill; and awful real-world fuel economy. **New for 2007:** TrailBlazer ditches its extended-length seven-passenger models. This is the Rainier's last model year.

MODEL HISTORY: With the debut of these four-door, five-passenger wagons, GM repositioned the Blazer as an entry-level, smaller SUV. Each of these models is larger than the model it replaces, although they all share the same styling details, rear-drive and 4×4 platforms, and mechanical components. **2003**—Seven-passenger stretched version (the Yukon's only size advantage is its 10 cm (4 in.) of extra width and its optional 5.3L 285-hp V8). **2004**—TrailBlazer returned unchanged. Arrival of the Envoy XUV, an SUV with a number of pickup features. It's basically an XL Envoy with a sliding rear roof and a small pickup bed. **2005**—The Buick Rainier gets more power and an upgraded interior and tires. **2006**—A standard vehicle stability and anti-skid system, an Active Fuel Management feature that selectively deactivates four of the V8's cylinders for fuel-saving cruising, and a freshened exterior. Envoy Denali models get 18-inch wheels and an SS model equipped with a 6.0L V8. Optional side airbags have been upgraded to deploy during rollovers.

Rainier

Selling for $49,350, Buick's mid-sized, five-passenger Rainier goes into its third year just as buyers begin downsizing their SUV choices to compact SUVs in the $30,000 range. Look for heavy discounting, rapid depreciation, and the dropping of the model midway through 2007.

Saab 9-7X

This is a GM truck-wagon with European styling that includes a Saab-style dashboard and the ubiquitous centre-console-mounted ignition switch. Handling is more driver-oriented through steering, suspension, and brake system enhancements. Due to abysmally poor sales, it's doubtful this Saab spin-off will last through the 2007 model year. And, when it *is* taken off the market, its resale value will plummet and servicing will become even more problematic.

COST ANALYSIS: All of these vehicles are way overpriced and are selling only with huge discounts. For example, the 2007 TrailBlazer's $31,820–$42,960 (LS/LT 4×4) base price is quite soft this year and can easily be bargained down by about $8,000. The 2006 models are practically identical and cheaper, still. Be wary of the even cheaper 2005s—they lack the all-important standard stability-control package, an essential safety feature for this class of vehicle. **Best alternatives:** The Lexus RX 300/330 and Toyota Highlander or 4Runner. **Rebates:** Look for $8,000+ rebates and low-financing rates. **Delivery/PDI:** $1,150. **Warranty:** Bumper-to-bumper 3 years/60,000 km; powertrain 3 years/60,000 km; rust perforation 6 years/160,000 km. **Supplementary warranty:** A wise buy. **Options:** Air suspension makes for a less jolting ride, but it degrades handling. Dual exhausts will give you 30 extra horses, and skid plates are essential to counteract undercarriage damage from excessive suspension dive. **Depreciation:** Likely to be much faster than average. **Insurance cost:** Higher than average. **Parts supply/cost:** Most parts seem to be reasonably priced and easy to find. **Annual maintenance cost:** Expected to be higher than average once these models go off warranty. **Highway/city fuel economy:** 11.2/16.0 L/100 km.

QUALITY/RELIABILITY: Likely failures: Automatic transmission; transfer case; brake rotors (excessive rusting and scoring), linings, and ABS module; electrical (shorts); and fuel systems (leaks). Fit and finish deficiencies include water leakage at the driver-side B-pillar (seat belt will be wet), excessive wind noise, and constant clicks and rattles. Usually, GM will fix the problem or pay compensation after a small claims lawsuit is filed, as was the case with this Albertan Rainier owner:

> Phil, SUCCESS! I sued GM in small claims as per your recommendation. They waited 2-and-a-half months (until 1 week before the court appearance) and asked if they could have a field engineer look at the Rainier. The field engineer (truly a good guy) took the vehicle for 3 days, ultimately duplicated the concern, identified it as a problem with the transfer case, changed the case oil and solved the problem—21 hours before the court date. Interestingly—I had surmised to both dealerships and to GM's regional service manager that exact theory.
>
> As this was just a pre-trial conference, the judge advised me my case was at best shaky (I had sued for cost of inconvenience—which is not covered in the warranty—and for the cost to buy out the remainder of my lease). As the problem was resolved, the judge told me I would have at best a big uphill fight. As I only got a resolution because

of the filing of the suit, I asked GM to at least cover the costs of the court filing and to make an offer if they were interested in keeping me as a customer. I was offered $1,000—which I accepted.

So—to recap—cost to solve actual problem—under $100. GM's legal fees—several thousand for sure plus all the "darts" they threw at the problem (A/C upgrades, sway bars, trailing arms, bushings, slip-yolk services, and six rental vehicles).

Ultimately, my goal was to have the problem fixed, which they did, and I came out $800 bucks ahead after the cost of the court fee. Thanks for your assistance.

TIM

 SAFETY SUMMARY: Airbags: Front. **ABS:** Standard; disc/disc. **Traction control:** Optional; stability-control is a standard feature on 2006 and later models. **Head restraints F/R:** *2002:* ★★; *2003–04:* ★★★. **Visibility F/R:** ★★★★★/★★.

SAFETY COMPLAINTS: 2002—Detached fuel lines. • Airbag failed to deploy. • Transfer-case and 4×4 failures. • Stalling caused by oil seeping onto the camshaft position sensor wiring harness. • Loss of steering, loose steering. • Sudden tie-rod failure. • Horn doesn't blow. • Faulty brake light switch. • Wind blows lightweight hood away. • Front passenger window suddenly shattered. • Side-view mirrors change position at random. • Dash lights and gauges go blank. • Seat belt locks up too easily; has no slack. **2003**—Transfer-case failure. • Brake failure. • Wiper motor works erratically. • Rear window shattered for no reason. • Seat belts pin occupants against the seat. • Jack handle is too short to safely change the tire. **2004**—Engine surging. • Temporary loss of steering control when passing over bumpy terrain. • Tie-rod steering-arm adjusting sleeve may rust out prematurely. • Loose plastic running board cut driver's leg. • Security and dome lights remain lit. **2005**—Seat belt doesn't restrain driver sufficiently in a collision. • Voltage fluctuates, causing lights to go dim (a common problem mentioned in GM bulletins). • Windshields can distort view (see "Secret Warranties/Internal Bulletins/Service Tips."):

> The windshield in my 2005 Chevrolet TrailBlazer was defective from the factory. It had such bad ripples in the glass that it made me feel as if I were looking through a pair of bifocals. After a couple of trips back to the dealer I finally convinced them to replace it! The new one is better but still has flaws in it. I've been looking at other TrailBlazers now and see the same defect in many other vehicles.

Secret Warranties/Internal Bulletins/Service Tips

1999–2004—TSB #01-07-30-038B indicates transmission malfunctions likely caused by debris plugging the bleed orifice of the 2–3 shift solenoid. **2002**—4.2L engine cylinder bore liner cracking will be repaired under a Special Policy

AWD/4WD SYSTEM INOPERATIVE

BULLETIN NO.: 02-04-21-006D   **DATE: MARCH 24, 2004**

INOPERATIVE 4WD/AWD LAMPS, INOPERATIVE 4WD/AWD SYSTEM (REPROGRAM TRANSFER CASE CONTROL MODULE)

2004 Buick Rainier

2002–04 Chevrolet TrailBlazer, TrailBlazer EXT

2003–04 Chevrolet Avalanche, Silverado, Suburban, Tahoe

2002–04 GMC Envoy, Envoy XL

2003–04 GMC Sierra, Yukon, Yukon XL

2004 GMC Envoy XUV

2002–04 Oldsmobile Bravada

(Bulletin # 03019; June 2003) up to 7 years/160,000 km (100,000 miles). • Service Engine light comes on, and transmission feels like it has slipped into Neutral. • Delayed transmission shift, harsh shift, and shudder. • Transfer case may be poorly calibrated, causing erratic operation. • Poor engine performance and transmission slips. • Diagnostic tips for loss of Third or Fourth gear. • Surging in First gear. • Campaign (secret warranty) to replace the left and right front lower control arm brackets. • Excessive noise from the fan and side mirror. • Service Engine or Service 4×4 light stays on. • Loss of electrical power to dash. • Front axle seal high-pitched noise emanating from the front of vehicle. • Roof rack howling. • Heater may not warm driver's feet. 2002–03—Rear axle whine. • Drivetrain shudder or binding. • Faulty ignition switch may cause transmission to stick in Third gear. • Front drive axle noise. • AC blows warm air. • Inoperative AC. • Steering-column noise remedies. • Adjust striker on hard-to-close doors. • Front carpet gets wet because of poor weather stripping. 2002–04—Liftgate unlatches on bumpy roads. • Scratched side window glass. • Front hood rattles. • Jammed seat belt retractor. • Inoperative 4×4/AWD (see bulletin). • 2003—Transmission slippage. 2003–04—GM will replace the fuel-tank fill-up pipe and lower hose under "goodwill" to prevent "spit back" when refuelling. 2003–05—An inoperative AC blower may need a new blower motor control module. • Steering moan, groan, shudder, or vibration when turning may be caused by a defective steering gear (see bulletin). 2004—Harsh transmission shifts. 2004–05—Front-end oil leaks. 2004–06—GM's solution for front windshields and door windows that distort visibility is to replace them only if the driver's view is affected. Idiotic, but true (see bulletin on page 124).

STEERING NOISE WHEN TURNING

BULLETIN NO.: 04-02-32-007A   **DATE: DECEMBER 1, 2004**

STEERING SYSTEM MOAN, GROAN, SHUDDER AND/OR VIBRATION-TYPE NOISE DURING LOW-SPEED TURNING MANOEUVERS (REPLACE STEERING GEAR)

2004–2005 Buick Rainier; 2003–2005 Chevrolet TrailBlazer, TrailBlazer EXT;

2003–2005 GMC Envoy, Envoy XL; 2004–2005 GMC Envoy XUV; 2003–2004 Oldsmobile Bravada.

	2002	2003	2004	2005	2006
Cost Price ($) (negotiable)					
Envoy 4X2 (25%)	37,995	37,195	41,475	39,390	32,320
Envoy AWD (25%)	37,995	37,195	41,820	42,715	41,505
Envoy XUV (26%)	—	—	41,895	42,830	33,615
Envoy XUV AWD (28%)	—	—	31,025	46,150	42,800
Rainier AWD (30%)	—	—	49,245	49,645	49,350
Trailblazer 4X2 (25%)	34,600	37,500	39,705	38,670	31,820
Trailblazer AWD (29%)	37,455	—	40,120	41,945	40,955
Used Values ($)					
Envoy 4X2 ▲	16,000	17,500	22,000	23,000	—
Envoy 4X2 ▼	14,500	16,000	20,000	21,000	—
Envoy AWD ▲	17,500	19,000	23,000	26,000	—
Envoy AWD ▼	16,500	17,500	21,000	24,000	—
Envoy XUV ▲	—	—	22,000	26,000	—
Envoy XUV ▼	—	—	21,000	24,000	—
Envoy XUV AWD ▲	—	—	25,000	29,000	—
Envoy XUV AWD ▼	—	—	23,000	27,000	—
Rainier AWD ▲	—	—	28,000	34,000	—
Rainier AWD ▼	—	—	26,000	31,000	—
Trailblazer 4X2 ▲	14,000	17,000	21,000	23,000	—
Trailblazer 4X2 ▼	12,500	16,000	19,000	21,000	—
Trailblazer AWD ▲	17,500	—	22,000	26,000	—
Trailblazer AWD ▼	16,000	—	20,000	24,000	—
Reliability	③	③	③	③	—
Crash Safety (F)	③	③	③	③	③
Side	⑤	⑤	⑤	⑤	⑤
Offset	②	②	②	②	—
Envoy	②	②	②	②	—
Rollover	③	③	③	③	③

ESCALADE, ESCALADE ESV, EXT, SUBURBAN, TAHOE, YUKON, YUKON XL, DENALI ★★★

RATING: *Escalade, EXT, and Denali:* Average (2001–07); Average with an extended warranty (1995–2000); *Suburban, Yukon, Tahoe:* Average (2002–07); Below Average (1995–2001); Not Recommended (1985–94). Brawny, large SUVs for buyers who lack imagination, the GMC Yukon and Denali and the Cadillac Escalade share the basic Tahoe/Suburban design but differ in styling, options, and price. Although these models are some of GM's best-performing large SUVs, they can't match the Japanese competition in overall reliability and quality control. Plus, over $43,000 for the cheapest model in this series is way too much. Used

2007 TECHNICAL DATA

POWERTRAIN (4X2/4X4)

Engines: 4.8L V8 (295 hp) • 5.3L V8 (320 hp) • 6.0L V8 (355 hp) • 6.2L V8 (380 hp) • 8.1L V8 (325 hp); Transmissions: 4-speed auto. • 6-speed auto. (Denali)

DIMENSION/CAPACITY (TAHOE/SUBURBAN)

Passengers: 3/3/3; Wheelbase: 116–130 in.; H: 77/L: 202–222/W: 79 in.; Headroom F/R1/R2: 5.0/4.5/1.0 in.; Legroom F/R1/R2: 40.5/29.5/28.5 in.; Cargo volume: 65–75 cu. ft.; Fuel tank: 98L/regular; Tow limit: 8,200 lb.; Load capacity: 1,395 lb.; GVWR: 6,500–7,000 lb.; Turning circle: 42 ft.; Ground clearance: 8.5 in.; Weight: 5,233 lb.

models, at about half that price, perhaps. New? You've gotta be kidding—or a former CEO of Nortel. **Strong points:** A good variety of competent engines that are great for trailering; standard stability-control; a fuel-saving cylinder-deactivation feature; lavishly appointed; a good array of instruments and controls; a large and comfortable cabin that adds passenger and cargo space with the redesigned 2007s; high ground clearance; a rattle-resistant body; and slow depreciation. The Suburban and Yukon XL are the largest heavy-hitters of this group, and they actually acquit themselves quite well, with reasonably predictable handling and more than enough power for most driving needs. **Weak points:** Incredibly expensive. The 4-speed automatic transmission wastes fuel and hinders powertrain performance. *2006 and earlier models:* A high step-up takes some acrobatics, the wide turning circle complicates parking, and braking is barely acceptable; bizarre electrical short-circuits; biodegradable fuel pumps; premature brake wear; excessive suspension and steering vibrations; vague steering; a suspension that provides a too-compliant, wandering ride; and excessive road and engine noise. A constant stream of reports that the airbags failed to deploy in a collision; Escalade models have been particularly failure-prone. **New for 2007:** More power (the standard 5.3L V8 comes with 320 hp versus 295), new styling, a larger interior, and additional features like second-row seats that automatically fold to provide third-row access, a revised navigation system, a power liftgate, and a rear obstacle detection feature. These improvements make for more agile handling, much better steering and braking responses, and a more comfortable and controlled ride.

MODEL HISTORY: These full-sized, four-door rear-drives and 4×4s haven't lost much of their popularity over the last few years in spite of their large size, excessive fuel consumption, so-so reliability, and atrocious fit and finish. Except for a wimpy base 275-hp V8 powerplant (not available on newer models), the full array of engines are capable of hauling almost any load, towing a trailer, or carrying up to nine passengers.

The GMC Yukon 4×4 (and its twin, the Tahoe) came on the scene in 1992 when GMC gave the Jimmy name to its smaller sport-utility wagon line and re-badged the big one as the Tahoe/Yukon.

During the 1995 model year, Blazers became Tahoes and a four-door version with standard driver-side airbags was added. The base V8 engine lost 10 horses (210 hp), but the following year, the 5.7L V8s got 50 more horses (250 hp) and a 4-speed automatic transmission became standard (no more manual). **1997**—A standard passenger-side airbag. **1998**—An optional full-time 4×4 system called AutoTrac that can be used on any surface. **1999**—Luxury trappings were added to the Yukon, which was then designated the Denali. **2000**—Wider and taller vehicles, the Tahoe and Yukon adopted a new V8 engine, front side airbags, and a seating capacity that grew from six to nine passengers. The familiar two-door version was dropped. **2001**—New engine cylinder heads. The 6.0L V8 gained 20 hp. An 8.1L 340-hp V8 for the Suburban 2500. **2002**—More standard features, such as AC, power windows, power front seats, heated power mirrors, and rear climate controls. **2003**—New entertainment options, an anti-skid system, four-wheel steering, and adjustable pedals. **2006**—No more Quadrastar; Yukons get a 5.3L V8 that uses gasoline and ethanol. Standard stability-control.

Pre-2000 models are set on GM's C/K truck platform and have been available with a variety of V8s over the years. The best choice, though, is the 5.7L gas engine mated to an electronic 4-speed automatic. This matchup provides gobs of torque at low rpm, making these part-time 4×4s great for towing, stump pulling, or mountain climbing.

Transmission alternatives are limited to your choice of 4-speeds: the manual or the automatic. Standard-equipment hubs must be locked manually before shifting into 4×4 on early models. The diesel provides a good compromise between power and economy, although it has been plagued by malfunctions for decades and has never been the equal of the Cummins. Overall reliability is only average, and declining.

Suburban, Yukon XL

Although it's classed as a full-sized SUV, the Suburban is really a combination of a station wagon, a van, and a pickup. It can carry nine passengers, tow just about anything, and go anywhere with optional 4×4.

These vehicles didn't change much until the launch of the 2000 models. **1995**—A four-door version and standard driver-side airbag. **1996**—5.7L V8s got 50 more horses (250 hp), and the 7.4L gained 60 horses (290 hp) and push-button 4×4. **1997**—Standard passenger-side airbag and upgraded, middle-seat height-adjustable shoulder belt anchors.

2000—Chevrolet restyled the Suburban by setting it on the Silverado/Tahoe/Yukon platform and using generic parts from the same parts bin. With the change-over, GMC's Suburban name was swapped for the Yukon XL, while the Chevrolet division soldiered on, keeping the Suburban name alive.

Both the Suburban and Yukon XL are GM's largest sport-utilities: 37.3 cm (14.7 in.) longer than the Ford Expedition but 18.8 cm (7.4 in.) shorter than the Excursion. Handling was improved considerably, but fuel economy remained atrocious. Improvements include a wider and taller body; new 5.3L and 6.0L V8 engines that replace the 5.7L and 7.4L engines, and a turbocharged diesel V8; an automatic transmission with tow/haul mode for smoother shifting; standard front side airbags; and four-wheel disc brakes. Rear leaf springs have been replaced by rear coil springs.

2001—Suburban got an upgraded 6.0L V8 in addition to a totally new 340-hp 8.1L V8. The upscale Yukon Denali (the Cadillac Escalade's big brother) moved to GM's new full-sized platform. Until the changeover, when it became the Yukon XL, the Suburban was a Hummer in civilian garb, and like the Hummer, it's far less sturdy than it looks. 2005—The StabiliTrak anti-skid system became standard for all Tahoe and 1500 models, and swing-out rear cargo doors are gone. 2006—An Active Fuel Management cylinder shut-off system saves gas while cruising.

Cadillac Escalade

This is GM's pop culture party wagon, favoured by rich pop stars and "make the people pay" politicos. Cadillac's first truck, the 1999 Escalade 4×4, was nothing more than a warmed-over GMC Yukon Denali covered with ugly, poorly designed side cladding in an effort to disguise its parentage. The redesigned 2002 Escalade got many improvements, including an EXT version (a Suburban/Avalanche clone with additional luxury features), a 6.0L V8, and a more refined AWD system. 2003—A longer ESV and Escalade EXT, an all-dressed version of the Chevrolet Avalanche SUV/pickup truck. Other changes include standard power-adjustable gas and brake pedals and second-row bucket seats for the wagons. 2004—A tire-pressure monitor, trailering package, and satellite radio were added. A new Platinum Edition offered a standard navigation system and 20-inch wheels. 2005—An improved cooling system and upgraded interior trim and gauges. 2006—Standard electronic stability-control.

COST ANALYSIS: The 2006 and 2007 model year costs vary considerably, depending on the model and powertrain configuration. For example, your cheapest 2007 model Tahoe 4×2 will likely cost about $43,995, and a fully equipped Escalade 4×4 ESV Platinum sells for close to $100,000. The 2007 Yukons and Suburbans are no bargains, either, selling for $44,615 and $48,000, respectively. Even a base Escalade will set you back $78,030. For this kind of money, Lexus and Toyota are mighty attractive. **Best alternatives:** Choose a 2007 model for the interior and performance upgrades. If you're looking for a used vehicle, try to find a Suburban with the 7.4L V8 engine—the 5.7L is barely adequate for this behemoth. Don't become mesmerized by a luxury nameplate on a practically identical model. For example, a new 2000 Cadillac Escalade originally retailed for about $30,000 more than a Suburban, but there's only a few thousand dollars separating the two vehicles' resale values today. When looking for other choices, remember that few other similar-class vehicles equal the Suburban for sheer size. Alternatively, a full-sized van or extended minivan might be a better choice if off-road capability isn't a priority. If size isn't your primary concern, look to other, more reliable SUVs that are less costly to operate. **Rebates:** $10,000 rebates and zero percent financing should continue well into 2007. **Delivery/PDI:** $1,350. **Warranty:** Bumper-to-bumper 3 years/60,000 km; rust perforation 6 years/160,000 km. **Supplementary warranty:** An extended warranty is a good idea but not critical. **Options:** You won't find many bare-bones models because dealers want the extra profit gained from selling these SUVs fully loaded. The transmission oil cooler, rear window defogger, engine block heater, and upgraded sound system are all worthy add-ons. Consider buying running boards ($300) if you plan to carry people who will have difficulty stepping up into the vehicle. Don't accept less-reliable Firestone or Bridgestone tires. **Depreciation:** Mind-spinning as fuel costs rise. Beware of paying a premium for the nameplate. **Insurance cost:** Insurance industry statistics indicate that these full-sized vehicles have a substantially lower-than-average number of accident injury claims, but the cost of insurance is way above average. Surprised? **Annual maintenance cost:** Higher than average. The early Suburban's many mechanical and body deficiencies boost its upkeep costs. One saving grace, however, is that it can be serviced practically anywhere. Escalade's redesign will probably result in higher maintenance costs once the warranty expires. **Parts supply/cost:** Good supply and inexpensive. There have been long waits for transfer-case replacements. Competition from independent suppliers keeps prices down. **Highway/city fuel economy:** *Tahoe and Yukon 4.8L, with or without 4×4:* 12.7/16.9 L/100 km; *Tahoe, Suburban, Yukon, Yukon Denali, and Yukon XL 5.3L 4×4:* 12.6/17.1 L/100 km; *6.0L:* 12.5/17.3 L/100 km.

 QUALITY/RELIABILITY: The best of the Detroit Big Three...ho-hum. Overall reliability has improved during the past three years, and resale value is still fairly high. **Owner-reported problems:** Lots of driveability complaints relating to excessive wander and vibrations. Other complaints pertain to the brakes, electrical, fuel, and exhaust systems (popping and pinging). A loose oxygen-sensor connection is the reason why the Check Engine light is often activated. Body assembly and paint application is below standard. **Warranty performance:** Average.

 SAFETY SUMMARY: The vehicle will wander, requiring constant steering correction, particularly when buffeted by crosswinds. Airbags frequently fail to deploy, causing severe trauma. The early Suburbans are too large for safe off-road use—no surprise for most people. Braking is terrible—one of the worst in the sport-utility class (100–0 km/h: 50 m). Although standard four-wheel ABS first appeared on 1992 models, it has been failure-prone and not very effective. NHTSA reports 1,755 complaints, 604 accidents, and 142 injuries related to ABS failures on 1992–98 versions. In spite of the above findings, injury claim rates reported by insurance companies have been judged to be much better than average—perhaps the drivers are more reliable than the brakes. **Airbags:** Standard side airbags (Escalade). **ABS:**

Standard four-wheel; disc/disc. **Traction control:** Optional. **Head restraints F/R:** ★. **Visibility F/R:** ★★★★★.

SAFETY COMPLAINTS: All years: Sudden, unintended acceleration. • Engine head gasket and exhaust manifold, transmission, steering, ABS brake and brake drum, tire, door lock, and airbag failures. • Vehicle wanders, vibrates excessively, and jerks to one side when braking. • Seat belt tightens progressively. • Gas tank leaks fuel. • Fuel pumps often need replacing. • Gas fumes permeate the interior. • Rear liftgate window exploded. • Chronic electrical failures. *Tahoe, Yukon:* **1997**—Long stopping distance after pedal goes all the way to the floor. • Vehicle fails to slow down sufficiently when driver takes foot from accelerator pedal. • Engine misses when AC is engaged. • Lack of rear stabilizer bar results in poor high-speed stability. • Faulty differential pinion gear seal. • Rear axle failure. • Chassis fluid leaks onto brake rotors. **1998**—Steering bolt failed, leading to steering loss. • Excessive vibrations when braking, usually caused by premature rotor and pad wearout. • Brakes suddenly grab in rainy weather. • Poor fuel-tank design allows fuel to leak out the filler spout whenever vehicle is parked on an incline. • Electrical problems cause AC surging, flickering lights and switches, and an instrument panel that's hot to the touch. • Rear middle seat belt failure. **2000**—Steering broke loose and caused complete loss of steering control. • Tie-rod fell off, causing serious steering difficulties. • Child had to be cut free from locked up seat belt. • Windshield wipers don't stay in contact with the windshield. • Factory roof rack came off vehicle while hauling a lightweight kayak. • Passenger windows don't operate properly. • Fuel smell invades the interior. • Driver's seat rocks back and forth while accelerating and decelerating. • Mirror is mounted in such a way that it blocks visibility. **2000–04**—Steering-wheel clunk. **2001**—Erratic shifting, slipping, jerking, and clunking. • Sudden stalling. • Catalytic converter glowing red. • Stones lodge between the brake calipers and wheel rims. • Finger cut from lowering head restraint. **2002**—Loose steering feels unstable, causes vehicle to wander. • Faulty transmission; delayed shifts. **2003**—Faulty steering linkage. • Vehicle can be shifted out of Park without pressing the brake pedal. • Rear passenger doors don't lock properly. • Leaking gas tank. • High beam light is too bright. **2005**—Airbags failed to deploy during a head-on collision. • Overheated fuel-pump wiring. • Wheels intermittently lock up while driving. • Transmission slips from Drive to Neutral. • Goodyear P265/70R25 M&S on-/off-road tires are easily punctured by stones getting into the tread. *Suburban, Yukon XL:* **1997**—Steering is too sensitive and doesn't tighten up as speed increases. • Side door doesn't lock/close. **1998**—Sudden steering loss. • Engine oil leak caused by oil plug failure. • AC compressor failure. • Electrical components stay on when ignition is turned off. • Power-window regulator failure causing window to stick and rattle. • **1999–2000**—Emergency brake failed, allowing vehicle to roll downhill. • Battery acid ran down the negative cable and caused the brake line to rupture. • Loss of rear braking caused by leakage of brake cylinder fluid. • Fuel leakage from fuel injector and regulator. • All lights (including headlights) go off intermittently. • Driver-side door handle broke. • Rear power windows often fail in the up or down position. • Window may shatter for no reason. • Rear left shoulder belts don't stay connected. • Unable to secure child safety seat into the middle position because of seat belt's location. • Driver's seat caught fire. • Driver's seat rocks back and forth upon acceleration and deceleration. • Several cases where rear wheel flew off after lug nuts failed. • Cracked trailer hitch. • Spare-tire jack won't hold vehicle. **2001**— Total electrical shutdown. • Simultaneous failure of steering and brakes. **2002**—Headlights are aimed too high. • Dash lights reflect into mirror. • Dashboard lights are too bright. • Gas tank hard to refuel, causes premature shutoff. • Liftgate window exploded. **2003**—Vehicle rolled over and airbags failed to deploy. • Vehicle lunged forward, once stopped. • Sudden brake loss. • Premature tie-rod wearout. • Steering shaft failure and differential leaking. • Steering clanking silenced by packing grease around the steering shaft. • Frequent fuel-pump replacements. • Exhaust produces explosive noises. • Vehicle registers no gas when the tank is full. • Excessive shoulder belt tension. • Cab reverberation causes ear pain (not a problem with later models). • Many complaints of exploding back liftgate windows. **2004**—All airbags failed to deploy, despite being in a high-speed collision that totally destroyed a new Escalade. The same thing happened with a Tahoe after a side-impact rollover. Also, OnStar failed to activate. • Vehicle fails to accelerate when merging into traffic. • Sharp pull to the right when accelerating, and then vehicle snaps to the left when foot is taken off the accelerator. • Excessive on-road vibration at 110 km/h; vehicle becomes very unstable. • When key is in the ignition Accessory position, one can shift out of Park without first applying the brake:

> When key is in the ACCESSORY position, vehicle can be put into gear without the brake being applied. A 3-year-old child died after shifting into gear a parked 1997 Chevy Tahoe.

• Defroster doesn't clear entire windshield and stops working intermittently. • When using the turn signal, the flashers are activated. • All memory presets for seats, mirrors, pedals, etc. are lost when vehicle is restarted or once it is underway; driver's seat moves forward unexpectedly. • Child safety seat latch is not secure. • When accelerating from a stop, transmission jumps into gear after a long delay. • Complete transmission replacement followed by chronic electrical system failures:

> The entire electric system failed in April, when radio, and other electric functions failed. Also, the Low PSI light did not illuminate when the tire went flat. This happened after the repair of electric system. Transmission failed, and had to be replaced. There were several bulletins regarding the stability control and electric systems, but dealer denied any problem with the stability control.

• While driving, tailgate window fell inward. • Inoperative emergency brake. • Static electricity shock when exiting vehicle. *Yukon:* Rear window suddenly exploded. • Instrument panel gives bizarre readings or simply goes out when vehicle is started. • Chronic stalling. • Denali steering pump failed a few days after purchase. • Headlight fuse burns out constantly. • Excessive exhaust popping, cracking, gurgling noise. • Spare-tire security device doesn't work as described in manual. *Suburban:* **2005**—Vehicle was parked on a hill and rolled backward. • Sudden brake loss. • OnStar frequently fails to work. • Firestone Wilderness tires lose air. *Yukon XL:* Frequent no-starts. • Transmission shifts harshly when put into Reverse, or is slow to engage Drive. • Stability Trac fails to activate. • Driver's seat moves on its own; inoperative seat memory. • Satellite radio loses frequency. • Rear heater inoperative. • Extremely loud, popping exhaust. • Excessive steering vibrations. *Escalade:* **2004**—A high-speed frontal collision and no airbag deployment:

> Involved in a horrific auto accident with another vehicle. Hit in front passenger and front part of vehicle (by radiator area) at high speed. (45–55 mph [72–88 km/h] with no skid marks). Unbelievably, none of our four airbags deployed. We and hundreds of our friends are in total disbelief when [we] see the condition [our] vehicle was left in. We were injured, but by [the] grace of God, injuries were not life threatening.

• Vehicle flipped over and not one of the four airbags deployed. **2005**—Another incident where the airbag failed to deploy in a head-on collision. • On EXT models, the horn often fails to sound if used infrequently.

Secret Warranties/Internal Bulletins/Service Tips

Tahoe, Yukon: **1992–99**—Upgraded rear brake shoes will eliminate brake lead and pull and reduce front brake wear. **1993–2002**—Paint delamination, peeling, or fading. **1993–2005**—No Reverse, Second, or Fourth gear may be caused by a defective reaction sun gear. **1994–99**—Hard starts on vehicles equipped with a 6.5L diesel engine may signal the need to replace the shut-off solenoid. **1995–2000**—No-starts or hard starts can be eliminated by replacing the crankshaft position sensor. **1996–97**—Excessive engine noise can be corrected by installing upgraded valve-stem oil seals. **1996–98**—Diagnosing causes of fluid leak near front wheels or front engine area. • Vehicles equipped with a 6.5L diesel engine that experience hard upshifts may need to reprogram the PCM/VCM. **1996–99**—Engine bearing knocking on vehicles equipped with a 5.7L V8 may be silenced by using a special GM countermeasure kit. **1996–2000**—Hard starts, backfires, or an unusual grinding sound when starting can all be addressed by replacing the crankshaft position sensor. **1998**—Engine stalling or surging and a slipping transmission may signal the need to repair the auxiliary oil cooler or replace the transmission torque converter. • Tips for fixing water leak at the driver-side windshield or just below the instrument panel. **1998–2000**—GM, at no charge, will repaint the outside rear-view mirror housing if it turns a chalky, dull colour. • Stalling or surging following a stop may be corrected by re-calibrating the PCM settings. • A transfer-case bump or clunk on acceleration is usually caused by a slip-stick condition between the rear propeller-shaft slip yoke and the transfer-case output shaft. It can be eliminated by using a new transfer-case fluid that contains a better friction modifier, says TSB #99-04-21-004. **1999**—If the front wheels slip while in 4×4, consider replacing the transfer-case clutch plates and front-drive axle lubricant. • A steering-column squeak noise may be silenced by replacing the steering-wheel SIR module coil assembly. *Tahoe, Yukon, Escalade:* **1999–2000**—Engine may misfire, water may mix with fuel, or the Service Engine light may come on if water has entered through the EVAP canister. Correct the problem by installing a new EVAP canister vent solenoid. **1999–2004**—Transmission failure caused by debris in the 2–3 shift solenoid bleed orifice. **2000**—If the steering column makes a clunking noise, it may signal the need to change the upper intermediate steering-shaft assembly. **2000–03**—Excessive engine noise:

ENGINE—KNOCKING OR LIFTER NOISE

BULLETIN NO.: 02-06-01-038   DATE: DECEMBER 2002

ENGINE KNOCK OR LIFTER NOISE (REPLACE O-RING)

2001–02 Chevrolet Camaro	2002–03 Chevrolet Avalanche
2001–03 Chevrolet Corvette	2000–03 GMC Yukon, Yukon XL
2001–02 Pontiac Firebird	2001–03 GMC Sierra
2002–03 Cadillac Escalade, Escalade EXT	with 4.8L, 5.3L, 5.7L or 6.0L V8 Engine (VINs V, T, Z, G, S, N,
2000–03 Chevrolet Suburban, Tahoe	U – RPOs LR4, LM7, L59, LS1,
2001–03 Chevrolet Silverado	LS6, LQ9, LQ4)

CONDITION: Some customers may comment on an engine tick noise. The distinguishing characteristic of this condition is that it likely will have been present since new, and is typically noticed within the first 161–322 km (100–200 mi.). The noise may often be diagnosed as a collapsed lifter. Additionally, the noise may be present at cold start and appear to diminish and then return as the engine warms to operating temperature. This noise is different from other noises that may begin to occur at 3,219–4,828 km (2,000–3,000 mi.).

2000–04—Remedies for a steering-wheel clunk and inoperative power windows. **2001**—Fuel-tank leakage. • Harsh shifts. • 2–4 band or 3–4 clutch damage. • Rear heater puts out insufficient heat. • Carpet may be wet or have a musty odour. **2003–04**—Inoperative AWD. • Noisy, inoperative power window. • Faulty heated seats. **2004–06**—Instrument panel ticking and poor AC performance. • Automatic transmission shudder due to water intrusion (see bulletin). *Suburban, Yukon XL:* **1992–99**—Upgraded rear brake shoes will eliminate brake lead and pull and will reduce front-brake wear. **1996–99**—Engine bearing knocking on vehicles equipped with a 5.0L or 5.7L V8 may be silenced by using a special GM countermeasure kit to service the crankshaft and select-fit undersized connecting rod bearings. **1998**—Tips for fixing a water leak at the driver-side windshield or just below the instrument panel. • Engine stalling or surging and a slipping transmission may signal the need to repair the auxiliary oil cooler or replace the

SHUDDER/WATER IN TRANSMISSION

BULLETIN NO.: 05-07-30-017B

DATE: FEBRUARY 17, 2006

AUTOMATIC TRANSMISSION/TORQUE CONVERTER CLUTCH (TCC) SHUDDER, WATER IN TRANSMISSION (REPAIR TRANSMISSION AND SEAL COWL AREA)

2004–2006 Cadillac Escalade; 2004–2006 Chevrolet Avalanche, Silverado, Suburban, Tahoe; 2004–2006 GMC Sierra, and Yukon models with 4L60-E (RPO M30), 4L65-E (RPO M32) or 4L70-E (RPO M70) automatic transmissions.

CONDITION: Some customers may comment on a shudder condition at approximately 64–80 km/h (40–50 mph) when the TCC engages.

CAUSE: This condition may be caused by water in the automatic transmission fluid (ATF). Water may enter the transmission by dripping from the cowl area onto the handle of the transmission fluid level indicator.

transmission torque converter. **1998–99**—If you can't engage the 4×4 mode, it may be necessary to replace the transfer-case actuator/shift detent plunger. **1999**—If the front wheels slip while in 4×4, consider replacing the transfer-case clutch plates and front-drive axle lubricant. • AC blows hot air because of faulty inlet actuator. **1998–2000**—If only all of the Suburban's problems were this easy to solve: A transfer-case bump or clunk on acceleration is usually caused by a slip-stick condition between the rear propeller shaft-slip yoke and the transfer-case output shaft. It can be eliminated by using a new transfer-case fluid that contains a better friction modifier, says TSB #99-04-21-004. • Increased accelerator pedal effort can be fixed by replacing the throttle body. • Silence front-door rattling by replacing the door window regulator bolts. **2000–04**—Remedies for a steering-wheel clunk and inoperative power windows. **2000–05**—Tips on silencing a differential whine are found in TSB #03-04-17-001E. **2001**—Fuel-tank leakage. • Harsh shifts. • 2–4 band or 3–4 clutch damage. • Rear heater puts out insufficient heat. • Carpet may be wet or have a musty odour. **2002–03**—Second-row footwell carpet may be wet with dirty water. GM will seal the rear wheelhouse under warranty (Bulletin #03-08-57-001; May 2003). **2002–04**—Suspension clunk, slap. GM will replace the spring insert and insulator for free (see Silverado "Secret Warranties/Internal Bulletins/Service Tips"). **2002–05**—Outside rear-view mirrors may fold in at highway speeds. **2003**—Harsh automatic transmission 1–2 shifting, slipping caused by a faulty pressure control solenoid (Bulletin #03-07-30-020; May 2003). **2003–04**—Inoperative front power window. **2003–05**—Inoperative AC blower motor should be replaced (hmmm...sounds like a defect to me). • Tires go flat slowly because of defective grommet. • Faulty AC and audio (replace RSA module). • Front suspension rattle, squeak. **2004–06**—See "Shudder/Water in Transmission" bulletin. **2005–06**—Troubleshooting a steering-column shaft clunk. *Escalade:* Many of the aforementioned TSBs also apply to the Escalade. **2002–06**—Discoloured cargo covers or body cladding (seen as a chalky colour) will be corrected under a secret warranty.

All ratings on a numbered scale where ⑤ is good and ❶ is bad. See page 220 for a more detailed description.

ESCALADE, SUBURBAN, TAHOE, YUKON PROFILE

	1998	1999	2000	2001	2002	2003	2004	2005	2006
Cost Price ($) (negotiable)									
Escalade (30%)	—	63,055	63,805	63,805	72,700	74,970	70,675	71,405	78,030
Suburban (29%)	33,965	34,620	34,620	37,905	45,875	46,670	46,680	49,820	47,000
Tahoe, Yukon (30%)	31,155	31,555	33,305	31,715	42,680	42,530	44,105	45,615	43,455
4X4 (30%)	34,155	34,555	36,715	35,010	46,895	50,385	42.530	48,870	47,785
Yukon XL (30%)	—	—	34,620	35,760	46,895	47,290	44,720	50,415	47,665
Used Values ($)									
Escalade ▲	—	13,000	16,000	23,000	28,000	36,000	42,000	47,000	—
Escalade ▼	—	11,500	15,000	21,000	26,000	34,000	39,000	44,000	—
Suburban ▲	8,500	10,500	13,000	15,000	18,000	23,000	27,000	33,000	—
Suburban ▼	8,000	9,000	11,500	14,000	16,000	21,000	25,000	30,000	—
Tahoe, Yukon ▲	9,000	10,000	12,000	15,000	16,500	21,000	26,000	31,000	—
Tahoe, Yukon ▼	8,000	9,000	11,000	14,000	15,500	20,000	24,000	29,000	—
4X4 ▲	10,000	11,000	13,000	16,000	18,500	23,000	27,000	33,000	—
4X4 ▼	9,000	10,500	12,500	15,000	17,500	21,000	25,000	31,000	—
Yukon XL ▲	—	—	13,500	17,000	19,000	23,000	28,000	32,000	—
Yukon XL ▼	—	—	12,500	16,000	18,000	22,000	26,000	30,000	—
Reliability									
Tahoe, Yukon	③	③	③	③	③	③	③	③	—
Suburban, Yukon XL	②	③	③	③	③	③	③	③	—
Crash Safety (F)									
Suburban, Yukon XL	—	④	—	④	④	④	④	④	④
4X4	④	④	—	—	④	④	—	—	—
Denali 4d	—	④	④	④	—	④	④	—	—
Tahoe/Yukon	—	④	④	③	③	④	③	③	④
4X4	—	④	③	③	③	④	—	—	—
Escalade	—	④	④	—	③	④	④	④	④
4X4	—	④	④	—	③	④	④	④	—
Rollover (Escalade)	—	—	—	—	③	③	—	③	③

General Motors/Suzuki

2004 VITARA TECHNICAL DATA

POWERTRAIN (REAR-DRIVE/ PART-TIME 4X4)

Engines: 2.0L 4-cyl. (127 hp) • 2.5L V6 (165 hp) • 2.7L V6 (183 hp); Transmissions: 5-speed man. • 3-speed auto. • 4-speed auto.

DIMENSION/CAPACITY (VITARA)

Passengers: 2/3/2; Wheelbase: 97.6 in.; H: 67.3/L: 152/W: 64.8 in.; Headroom F/R: 39.9/39.6 in.; Legroom F/R: 41.4/35.9 in.; Cargo volume: 30 cu. ft.; Fuel tank: 66L/regular; Tow limit: 1,000 lb.; GVWR: 3,373–3,593 lb.; Load capacity: 870–895 lb.; Ground clearance: 7.2 in.; Turning circle: 37 ft.; Weight: 2,450 lb.

RATING: Average (1994–2007). Although *Consumer Reports* designates the XL-7 a "Recommended" buy, *Lemon-Aid* believes this rating is way too high considering the vehicle's failings, particularly the absence of side-impact protection on pre-2006 models. Yes, Suzuki has a reputation for building affordable, durable, quality small cars, but many of its SUVs lack real 4×4 performance, important safety features, and an acceptable level of quality control. The players in this market segment are the Honda Pilot; Hyundai Tucson, Veracruz, and Santa Fe; Jeep Liberty; Kia Sorento; Lexus Highlander; Nissan Murano, Xterra, and X-Trail; and Toyota 4Runner. **Strong points:** *Vitara and Grand Vitara 2006 and later models:* A much different vehicle that's less truck-like on the road, thanks to the fully independent suspension and new unibody construction, which also gives rear-seat passengers more room. A competent 2.7L V6 and permanent four-wheel drive offer low-range gearing and a locking differential. Standard side-/head-protection airbags and stability-control. On earlier model years, the Grand Vitara is the better performer, with its minimal body lean when cornering and good emergency handling and braking. Lots of front and rear passenger space, but having three passengers in the rear remains a tight squeeze. **Weak points:** *2005 and earlier Vitara and Grand Vitara models:* The 4-cylinder engine is weak and rough-running; part-time 4×4 isn't suitable for dry pavement; stiff riding; sluggish automatic transmission; frequent downshifting with the base Vitara; skimpy interior appointments; the heater is slow to warm the interior on sub-freezing days and employs a noisy fan; the AC struggles to keep the Vitara cool; the accelerator is placed too far left; seats feel cheap, are inadequately padded, and lack thigh support; seatbacks lack shoulder and lower back support; driver's seat doesn't adjust for height, making it hard for short drivers to get a clear view; spare tire further restricts rear visibility; and lots of axle whine and road, wind, and engine noise invade the cabin. *XL-7:* The 2007 versions have been redesigned in a similar fashion to the 2006 Grand Vitara. Notwithstanding this improvement, earlier models fall short in many areas: four-wheel drive is usable only on dry pavement; so-so fuel economy;

a stiff and jerky ride; excessive body lean when cornering; little steering feedback; mushy braking doesn't inspire confidence; lots of engine, road, and tire noise; cheap-looking interior materials; the narrow cabin provides only average legroom; seat cushions don't provide enough leg support; third-row headrests obstruct rearward visibility; high fuel consumption; rapid depreciation; and inadequate occupant crash protection and poor quality as highlighted in *Consumer Reports'* owner surveys and crash test results as well as bulletins gathered by *Lemon-Aid*. **New for 2007:** *XL-7:* Redesigned and set on the Chevrolet Equinox/Pontiac Torrent Theta platform used last year for the Grand Vitara, the truck-like XL-7 has been transformed into a unibody crossover that's slightly wider and taller but nearly 25 cm (10 in.) shorter than last year's version. The wimpy 185-hp V6 has been replaced with a 250-hp variant.

MODEL HISTORY: Introduced as a GM/Suzuki co-venture in 1989, these vehicles have been quite successful as entry-level 4×4s for city dwellers who want off-roading allure. They will provide some off-road thrills (if they're not pushed too hard), but they're more show than go.

The Tracker and Sidekick, available as a two-door convertible and a four-door wagon, come with a standard 1.6L 4-cylinder powerplant. The 1997 Sport version, sold only by Suzuki, carries a 1.8L 4-cylinder with dual overhead camshafts, rated at 120 hp. The GM Tracker and Vitara are built in Ontario and use similar designs and components.

All of these cars have been quite primitive in construction and performance; however, their overall reliability is more than reasonable, considering their low retail prices.

Vitara

The Vitara is longer, wider, taller, and handles much better than the Sidekick it replaced. It's essentially an entry-level version of the Grand Vitara and carries a smaller 2.0L 127-hp 4-cylinder engine and less standard equipment. Nevertheless, it projects a more solid appearance, has a more refined interior, and exhibits less noise and vibration than its primitive predecessor. It was dropped for the 2005 model year.

Grand Vitara

The 2006 and 2007 models have undergone a major redesign that enhances safety, performance, and interior comfort. However, reliability and quality control on the newest models is still to be determined. The top-of-the-line 2005 and earlier Grand Vitara is wider, longer, and taller than its predecessor, the Sidekick Sport, plus it gives a more supple ride. It comes with an adequate, though not very powerful, 24-valve 2.5L 165-hp V6 powerplant, shared with GM's Tracker. Other standard features include a full-sized spare tire and four-wheel ABS on any "+" model. Peppy in the lower gears (good for off-roading), the engine quickly loses steam in the higher gear ranges (a drawback to highway cruising). It has competent road holding and handling, though the handling isn't as carlike as the Honda CR-V's or Toyota RAV4's.

Inside, there's plenty of headroom, armroom, and legroom, but the interior is somewhat narrow. The rear seats and seatbacks fold flat, adding to cargo capacity, and there are plenty of small trays, bins, and compartments to store things.

Tracker/Vitara/Grand Vitara: **1999–2000**—The four-door carried a standard 2.0L 16-valve 120-hp 4-cylinder engine, shift-on-the-fly 4×4, rack-and-pinion steering, and revised interior and exterior styling. **2002**—Standard air conditioning, AM/FM cassette stereo, and child-seat tethers. The base 1.6L engine was dropped in favour of the more powerful 127-hp 2.0L version. The Tracker also got the Suzuki V6 it had been lusting for, since many buyers found the 4-banger inadequate. **2003**—An upgraded dash and centre console. **2004**—Tracker's last model year. *Grand Vitara:* **2000**—First year on the market. **2002**—V6 engine gets 10 more horses. **2003**— Given a new dash, aluminum wheels, smaller rear head restraints, and interior upgrades. **2006**—Totally redesigned with help from GM's Torrent/Equinox platform and parts bin.

XL-7

Through the 2006 model year, this mid-sized SUV is basically a larger Grand Vitara wagon, built on a truck-type platform, with a side-hinged rear cargo door and seating for five with a split folding second-row seat or seven with an available split folding third-row seat. A 185-hp V6 with a 5-speed automatic transmission is the only powertrain. XL-7 offers rear-wheel drive or four-wheel drive that shouldn't be left engaged on dry pavement but has low-range gearing. ABS is standard. Side airbags may be available with the 2007 models.

Towing capacity is 1,360 kb (3,000 lb.). City driving is no problem, but the car lacks adequate power for worry-free highway passing and merging, especially when carrying more than two adults. You often have to run the car full out and endure considerable engine noise and tire drone.

The harsh, bouncy suspension is annoying, and cornering under speed results in excessive noseplow, tire scrub, and body lean. The car doesn't track well when encountering crosswinds, which easily blow it off course. Steering feedback is minimal, and braking is only adequate despite the ABS.

The narrow cabin gives barely adequate leg, hip, and shoulder room. Narrow rear seats are somewhat hard. Head restraints have been given a five-star top rating for occupant protection, although rear head restraints have cut visibility considerably. Figuring out how to fold the second-row seat takes an engineering degree.

XL-7: **2002**—The V6 engine gained 13 horses, and a user-friendly rear child-seat anchor system was installed. The Standard model adopted five-passenger seating, losing its third-row seat. Other versions kept the seven-passenger seating. Standard and Plus 4WD models came with ABS, and 4WD versions used heated door mirrors. **2003**—Five-passenger seating was standard, with a third-row seat optional, including rear air conditioning. **2004**—A mild facelift, new model names, and a new 5-speed automatic transmission. **2005**—A tire-pressure monitor was added to the 2005 model. **2006**—Fewer models and added standard features. The more fuel-efficient 5-speed manual has been dropped. Neither front side airbags nor curtain side airbags are offered.

COST ANALYSIS: Get the much-improved 2006 Grand Vitara ($24,495), or wait for the redesigned 2007 XL-7 ($31,000) scheduled to hit showrooms in late 2006. An $11,000 2003 Tracker 4×4 convertible is one of the best micro-convertible buys around. **Best alternatives:** For serious off-roading, look to a 2004 or later Jeep Wrangler or Liberty. For pretend off-roading, consider the Honda CR-V, Hyundai Santa Fe, Subaru Forester, and Toyota RAV4, or, if you really want to splurge, look at a Toyota Highlander. **Rebates:** $3,500–$4,000 on the 2006s; low-interest financing plans worth about $3,000. 2006 XL-7s will carry huge discounts in the $5,000 range, and 2007 versions will offer $3,000 rebates and low-interest loans during the beginning of the year. **Delivery/PDI:** $995. **Warranty:** *Suzuki:* Bumper-to-bumper 3 years/80,000 km; rust perforation 5 years/unlimited km. *GM:* Bumper-to-bumper 3 years/60,000 km; rust perforation 6 years/160,000 km. **Supplementary warranty:** An extended warranty is a good idea for the redesigned 2006 and 2007 models; previous versions can do without. **Options:** Stick with the manual tranny; an automatic will sap too much power and eat into fuel economy. **Depreciation:** Average; faster than average with 2005 and earlier models. **Insurance cost:** Average. **Annual maintenance cost:** Average repair costs; easily repaired at independent garages and Chevrolet or Suzuki dealerships. **Parts supply/cost:** Good supply. Parts are usually reasonably priced. **Highway/city fuel economy:** *2.0L:* 8.4/10.3 L/100 km; *V6:* 10.2/12.6 L/100 km. Fuel consumption (regular fuel) has been about 25 percent more than what government-inspired figures show.

QUALITY/RELIABILITY: Suzuki's models haven't been plagued by the large number of owner complaints and service bulletin admissions of poor quality that we've seen with some Nissans and Toyotas and with most of Detroit's offerings. Still, prudent buyers will opt for a second-series 2006 Grand Vitara or 2007 XL-7 to dodge any first-year quality glitches that may be present. Although this hasn't been a problem with Suzuki's previous revamped models, the Equinox platform and other components have had a large number of quality problems during the past two years, and these problems are likely to carry over to the Grand Vitara and XL-7. Conversely, quality control on 2005 and earlier models is above average. Defects haven't led to a lot of shop downtime or rendered these cars unreliable, and repairs are usually quite simple and relatively easy to perform. **Owner-reported problems:** Most owners' complaints target poor handling caused by underperforming brakes, steering, and suspension components. There are also a number of gripes relative to excessive vibrations and road and engine noise. Other failure-prone components are the serpentine belt, electrical system, catalytic converter, and muffler/exhaust system. Some owners report early transmission failures. Poor body fit and finish allows water and wind to enter the cabin. **Warranty performance:** Average. Although warranty performance and dealer servicing are unimpressive, these vehicles aren't very dealer-dependent, so it doesn't matter a great deal.

SAFETY SUMMARY: These lightweights are very vulnerable to side-wind buffeting. **ABS:** Optional 4W. Later models have standard rear ABS; disc/drum. **Head restraints F/R:** *Tracker 2d 1997:* ★; *1999:* ★★★; *2001:* ★★★★★/★★★; *2002–03:* ★★★; *Tracker 4d 2001:* ★★★★★/★★★; *2002–03:* ★★★★★; *Grand Vitara 1999–02:* ★★★; *2003–05:* ★; *2006:* ★★; *Grand Vitara XL-7 2003–04:* ★★★★★; *2005–06:* ★. **Visibility F/R:** ★★★/★★.

SAFETY COMPLAINTS: All years: Sudden, unintended acceleration. • Airbags failed to deploy. • Brake failures. • Lots of road wander. • Premature tire wearout and poor tire and wheel design compromise handling. *Sidekick/Tracker:* **1996–99**—Airbag light lit for no reason. • Engine EGR valve failures. • Frequent automatic transmission breakdowns, electrical shorts, chronic stalling, sudden brake loss, and emergency brake and AC failures. • Water leaking through the AC assembly causes chronic window fogging and blows the turn signal indicator fuse. **2000**—Rear side-window air vents allow exhaust fumes to enter cabin. • Steering linkage suddenly fails when turning. • Complete brake failure. • Continuously low brake-fluid level causes failure of front and rear calipers. • Brake and accelerator pedals are too close together. • Loose plastic inner fender damaged by tire. • Inadequate peripheral visibility. • GM's wiper blade material takes the shape of the windshield in its rest position and doesn't clean the windshield when needed. • Weather stripping doesn't clear rain from windows when they're rolled up or down. • Headlights don't adequately light up the road. • Hard to stay in lane when driving with the top off. • Automatic light sensor is designed to turn on the lights when it gets dark; however, it seldom works properly. **2001**—Drive shaft failure. • Driver tapped brakes to disengage cruise control, brakes locked up, and vehicle went out of control. • Extended braking stopping distance. *Vitara, Grand Vitara:* **1999**—Excessive vibration at 100 km/h. • Electrical shorts (a common Suzuki failing). • Excessive brake fade. • Stalling and surging (stuck accelerator). • Defective motor mounts. **2000**—Vehicle pulls right when accelerating and vibrates excessively. **2001**—Blown oil line dripped oil on hot exhaust and caused a fire. • Vehicle is tippy when cornering. **2002**—Brakes grind when stopping. **2003**—Vehicle flipped over, and airbags didn't deploy. **2004**—Accelerator stuck after recall fix for sudden acceleration. • Vehicle suddenly lost power and hit a tree; airbags didn't deploy. *Grand Vitara:* **2002**—Brake and gas pedal are set too close together. • Fuel-filler door fell off. • Passenger seat belt frequently locks up and doesn't retract fully. **2003**—No airbag deployment. • Rear seat belt shredded in half. **2004**—Airbags failed to deploy. **2005**—Don't leave vehicle while engine is idling; doors often self-lock. *XL-7:* **2002**—Door armrest caught on fire due to a defective fuse nearby. • Shredded rear seat belt. • Many complaints of bad Bridgestone original-equipment tires. **2003**—Accelerator pedal stuck. • Automatic transmission slippage. **2004**—Airbags failed to deploy. • Premature failure of the passenger-side seat airbag sensor. **2005**—Windshield rake makes it almost impossible to see behind the vehicle.

Secret Warranties/Internal Bulletins/Service Tips

All years: 4×4 may not fully engage, or it may pop out of gear. • Get rid of an annoying engine ticking noise by purging the air from the valve lifters. • *Tracker:* **1989–2003**—Troubleshooting automatic transmission slipping. **1999–2003**—Engine ticking. • Serpentine belt frayed or squealing. • Brake pulsation, vibration. *Vitara:* **1999**—Vitaras equipped with 2.0L engines may not start in cold temperatures because of a faulty ECM/PCM program (TSB #TS06-01-03099). *Tracker and Vitara:* **1999–2000**—On vehicles equipped with a manual transmission, the engine may idle poorly until it warms up; reprogram the PCM under the emissions warranty. • Manual transmission gears that clash when shifting may require a new synchronizer spring kit. • If the transmission won't upshift after downshifting with cruise control engaged, chances are the cruise-control module is at fault. • An inoperative or malfunctioning (blows warm air) AC may simply require a new O-ring. **1999–2002**—Windows bind and tip forward. **1999–2003**—Oil level reads low. **2001**—Excessive driveline vibration. • Frayed serpentine belt. • Instrument panel squeaks and rattles. • Heating, ventilation system may not work properly. • Ignition key sticks in the ignition. **2002**—Air leaks out of dash vents; AC air leaks. • Windows bind. **2003**—Oil seepage from left front of engine. *Grand Vitara and XL-7:* **1999–2002**—Engine rattling can be silenced by adjusting the timing-chain tensioner, says TSB #TS07 04213R. **1999–2003**—Engine oil leaks (see bulletin).

OIL LEAKS FROM LEFT FRONT OF ENGINE
BULLETIN NO.: TS 06 02244R2 WS

GRAND VITARA/XL-7
1999–2003 models

CONDITION: Engine oil leaking down left front of engine.

CORRECTION: If the condition appears to be only light (weepage/seepage) it may be due to dirt accumulating on engine protective coating applied during manufacturing. This condition can be corrected by cleaning the affected area.

If the condition is oil leaking down left front of engine, remove the timing cover and thoroughly clean the sealing surfaces of the cover block and cylinder head of any oil, old sealer, and dirt. Replace the front crankshaft seal and reseal; paying particular attention to the areas noted in this bulletin.

TRACKER/SIDEKICK, VITARA, GRAND VITARA, XL-7 PROFILE

	1998	1999	2000	2001	2002	2003	2004	2005	2006
Cost Price ($) (negotiable)									
Tracker 4X4	18,630	19,400	19,710	21,395	21,395	21,500	25,605	—	—
Sidekick S/T	16,495	—	—	—	—	—	—	—	—
Sidekick H/T	18,295	—	—	—	—	—	—	—	—
Vitara	19,995	20,795	18,695	18,695	18,695	20,295	21,995	—	—
Grand Vitara (19%)	23,495	23,495	23,995	24,495	23,995	23,995	24,995	25,595	24,495
Vitara XL-7 (17%)	—	—	—	28,995	26,495	26,995	27,495	29,495	29,495
Used Values ($)									
Tracker 4X4 ▲	4,000	5,500	7,000	8,000	9,500	11,000	14,500	—	—
Tracker 4X4 ▼	3,000	4,500	6,000	7,000	8,500	10,000	13,500	—	—
Sidekick S/T ▲	4,500	—	—	—	—	—	—	—	—
Sidekick S/T ▼	3,500	—	—	—	—	—	—	—	—
Sidekick H/T ▲	5,000	—	—	—	—	—	—	—	—
Sidekick H/T ▼	4,000	—	—	—	—	—	—	—	—
Vitara ▲	—	5,000	6,000	7,500	9,000	11,000	12,500	—	—
Vitara ▼	—	4,000	5,000	6,500	8,000	10,000	11,000	—	—
Grand Vitara ▲	5,000	6,500	7,500	9,000	11,000	13,000	15,500	17,500	—
Grand Vitara ▼	4,000	6,000	6,500	8,000	10,000	12,000	14,000	16,500	—
Vitara XL-7 ▲	—	—	—	10,000	12,000	14,500	18,000	20,000	—
Vitara XL-7 ▼	—	—	—	8,500	10,500	13,000	16,500	18,500	—
Reliability									
Sidekick, Tracker	3	4	4	4	4	4	5	—	—
Vitara, Grand Vitara	—	4	4	4	4	4	5	5	—
Vitara XL-7	—	—	—	4	4	4	5	5	—
Crash Safety (F)									
Sidekick, Tracker 2d	—	—	—	4	4	4	4	—	—
Vitara	—	—	—	4	4	4	4	—	—
Grand Vitara	—	—	—	4	4	4	4	4	4
Side (Vitara)	—	—	—	4	4	4	4	—	—
Grand Vitara	—	—	—	—	5	5	5	5	5
Tracker	—	—	—	4	4	4	4	—	—
Offset (all)	—	3	3	3	3	3	3	3	3
Vitara XL-7	—	—	—	5	5	5	5	5	—
Rollover (Tracker)	—	—	—	3	3	3	—	—	—
Vitara	—	—	—	3	3	3	—	—	—
Grand Vitara	—	—	—	3	3	3	—	—	4

All ratings on a numbered scale where 5 is good and 1 is bad. See page 220 for a more detailed description.

2005 TECHNICAL DATA

POWERTRAIN (4X2/4X4)

Engine: 3.4L V6 (185 hp); Transmission: 5-speed auto. OD

DIMENSION/CAPACITY (4D)

Passengers: 2/3; Wheelbase: 112.5 in.; H: 69.3/L: 188.8/W: 71.4 in.; Headroom F/R: 6.0/5.0 in.; Legroom F/R: 42.5/33 in.; Cargo volume: 33 cu. ft.; Fuel tank: 75L/regular; Tow limit: 3,500 lb.; Load capacity: 1,294 lb.; GVWR: 5,070 lb.; Turning circle: 44 ft.; Ground clearance: 6.5 in.; Weight: 3,845 lb.

RATING: Not Recommended (2005–07). The Equinox is an international parts bin: It's designed in the United States, engineered and built in Canada, powered by a Chinese engine, and loaded with parts from Japan, Mexico, and the Philippines. Usually, vehicles with so many outsourced parts are found on the bottom rung of the quality/reliability ladder, and Equinox seems to prove the rule. **Strong points:** Well-equipped and reasonably priced, this is one of the largest, most powerful compact SUVs available. Other pluses are its versatile drivetrain, carlike unibody frame, and fully independent suspension that smoothes out the ride. A unique sliding rear seat slides fore and aft to accommodate long-legged passengers, and an adjustable shelf behind the rear seats can be used as a picnic table. Received a five-star rating for front and side occupant crash protection and a four-star rating for rollover prevention. **Weak points:** Uses an unproven Chinese-bred V6 instead of the more reliable and peppy Honda 3.5L V6 used in the 2004 Saturn Vue. Mediocre handling; suspension bottoms out noisily when passing over bumps; no low-range gearing for off-roading; rear drum brakes instead of better-performing discs; wide turning circle makes for tough handling in tight areas; power-window controls are found on the centre console instead of on the doors; seats could use more side support and may be too firm for some; no third-row seat available; rear hatch doesn't have separately opening glass; rear suspension housings intrude into rear cargo space; and the Equinox uses many of the Saturn Vue's quality-challenged mechanical components. Owners also report that the interior literally stinks—giving off an odour that's part dead animal and part propane. **New for 2007:** Revised suspension and steering systems, restyled interior, and additional standard safety features like ABS and traction control. Optional curtain side airbags now include sensors for rollover deployment. Equinox's instrument panel, radio, and climate controls have also been redesigned. No word about the interior's gassy animal smell.

★★★★★

HIGHEST GOVERNMENT SAFETY RATING.

The Chevrolet Equinox received a 5-Star Rating for the driver and front passenger in the frontal crash test and for front and rear seat occupants in the side-impact crash test.

Sure, the Equinox has a good crash-safety rating, but who wants to drive a car that smells like a dead animal?

MODEL HISTORY: A replacement for GM's Suzuki-*cum*-Chevrolet Tracker, the five-passenger Equinox distinguishes itself from the rest of the SUV pack by offering standard V6 power, a 5-speed automatic transmission, and a comfortable ride. Although it uses many of the Vue's underpinnings (without the plastic body panels), it has a longer wheelbase and a wider body.

COST ANALYSIS: The 2007 Equinox LS FWD costs $25,375; the LT FWD, $27,540; the LS AWD, $27,985; and the LT AWD, $30,250. The same 2005 models, used, would cost you $17,500–$18,000, $18,500–$19,000, $19,000–$20,000, and $19,500–$21,000, respectively. Buyers would be wise to get a 2007 model for the improvements and to distance themselves as far as possible from the multitude of first-year defects that afflict the 2005s. **Best alternatives:** Honda CR-V, Hyundai Santa Fe, Mazda Tribute, Nissan X-Trail, Subaru Forester, and Toyota RAV4. **Rebates:** $3,000–$5,000 on the 2006s, and about half as much on the 2007s in early 2007. Low-financing programs will be applicable to both model years. **Delivery/PDI:** $1,100. **Warranty:** Bumper-to-bumper 3 years/60,000 km; powertrain 5 years/100,000 km; rust perforation 5 years/unlimited km. **Supplementary warranty:** A bumper-to-bumper warranty is essential. **Options:** Nothing worth buying. **Depreciation:** Faster than average. **Insurance cost:** Average. **Parts supply/cost:** Body parts are often back ordered; mechanical and electronic components are easily found. All parts will be a bit pricey until independent suppliers are out in force. **Annual maintenance cost:** Predicted to be higher than average, inasmuch as these vehicles are somewhat dealer-dependent. **Highway/city fuel economy:** 8.6/12.7 L/100 km.

QUALITY/RELIABILITY: Likely failures: Engines and engine head gaskets; DEX-COOL apparently corroding the engine and cooling system—one owner says the engine coolant smells like rotten meat:

> Bad odor coming from vents. DEX-COOL is corroding cooling system and engine. 17,000 miles [27,360 km] have had it in 3 times for entire coolant system flush...still is unbearable. Be aware, this is not an isolated case. After extended drive (greater than 30 minutes) results [are] light-headedness, headache, or watery burning eyes. It leaves a film of antifreeze vapor on the windshield, on the inside. GM does not consider this vehicle inoperable. Go figure. GM has done little to satisfy our needs, they pay for new hoses and flush—which obviously doesn't work. 900 dollars a pop, for the same result.

Other problem areas are as follows: automatic transmission; AC condenser; rear-drive clutch unit; electrical system; front struts; fit and finish (water leaks, squeaks and rattles, and loose moulding); early wearout of the front brake calipers and rotors; and fuel economy is far worse than what is advertised.

SAFETY COMPLAINTS: 2005—Airbags failed to deploy in a collision. • Sudden stalling when accelerating. • Car shuts down when going down a steep incline. •

Accelerator pedal sticks. • When turning into a parking space, vehicle suddenly accelerated. • Sudden acceleration when backing up:

> While backing out from the car port, vehicle accelerated in reverse. Vehicle went down an incline and was totalled. Consumer stated the dealer told him that transmission had an adaptive learning transmission.

• Engine fumes enter the cabin causing headaches and dizziness:

> I had about 300 miles [480 km] on the car and it started smelling of a propane odor/dead animals. Took it to dealer and they flushed the coolant system but the odor returned. Then the car overheated due to the coolant system. They put a new thermostat and flushed once again. Still a bad odor, the car leaks water and it runs hot. I have had the car in the shop three times and they still cannot fix the odor.

• Transmission fails to shift into Fourth gear. • Brake failure. • Defective suspension struts. • The design of the coil-spring mount leaves a razor-sharp edge on the strut. • Erratic steering produces too-sharp steering corrections. • Repeated windshield cracks. • When driving with the rear windows down, car produces a flat-tire sound. • Faulty window regulators. • No assist handles. • Driver's head restraint tilted too far forward. • Cupholder blocks the emergency brake. • Standing water in the tire well. • Dome light filled with water after vehicle passed through a car wash. • Tailgate collapsed when the left strut gave out.

Secret Warranties/Internal Bulletins/Service Tips

2005—Automatic transmission hesitation, flare; harsh cold shifts. • No Reverse, Second, or Fourth gears. • Harsh 1–2 upshift. • Transmission growl, moan, and shudder at low speeds. • Steering groan, hiss, or grinding when turning. • Inadequate AC cooling. • Liftgate strut bracket deformation. • Parasitic battery drain. • Vehicle glass distortion. • Chrome wheel pitting and dust accumulation. • Popping noise on bumps. • Front- and rear-end rattle. • Troubleshooting wind noise. • Loose, missing plastic wheel-nut covers. • Spoiler not properly fastened on rear hatch. • Door handle sticks out, won't latch. • Tips on eliminating interior odours.

Honda

best buy CR-V/RDX ★★★★★/★★★★★

RATING: Recommended (2002–07); Above Average (1997–2001). *RDX:* Above Average (2007). The CR-V is a compact SUV that's both fun and functional. For the 2007 model year, it's joined by an upscale spin-off—the Acura RDX. Both vehicles are practically identical, except for some minor design differences (like the RDX's horizontally mounted tail lights) and the Acura's additional standard features. **Strong points:** The small power boost and improved chassis added in 2002 give additional interior room (interior volume has grown by 8 percent) and provide improved functionality. Lots of interior room and standard features; impressive steering and handling, particularly around town; easy front entry and exit; top-quality fit and finish; comfortable seating with lots of passenger room; innovative use of storage space; flip-folding seats are easily stored; plastic cargo floor panel *cum* picnic table; outstanding NHTSA front crashworthiness scores; good fuel economy; and superior reliability. **Weak points:** Acceleration is somewhat compromised on vehicles equipped with an automatic transmission, though the 2005 4-beater rivals many V6 competitors; no low-range gearing for off-roading; a long history of severe steering pull to the right when accelerating ("torque steer"); jittery ride on less-than-perfect roadways; excessive engine and road noise; 2005 redesign reduced front legroom slightly; rear cargo door opens to

2007 TECHNICAL DATA

POWERTRAIN (FRONT-DRIVE/4X4)
Engine: 2.4L 4-cyl. (166 hp);
Transmission: 5-speed auto.
DIMENSION/CAPACITY
Passengers: 2/3; Wheelbase: 103.1 in.;
H: 66.1/L: 177.9/W: 71.6 in.; Headroom
F/R: 4.5/4.0 in.; Legroom F/R: 40.0/30.0
in.; Cargo volume: 32 cu. ft.; Fuel tank:
58L/regular; Tow limit: 1,500 lb.; Load
capacity: 850 lb.; GVWR: 4,165 lb.;
Turning circle: 37 ft.; Ground clearance:
6.5 in.; Weight: 3,560 lb.

the street, rather than the curb; not suitable for true off-roading; and may be tippy in a side impact (1999–2001 models), according to NHTSA crash results. "Marginal" IIHS offset crash rating on earlier models, and head restraints scored poorly, as well. Unlike the Toyota RAV4, there's no third-row seat. **New for 2007:** A new platform borrowed from the Civic, and a restyled interior and exterior that includes a new swing-up tailgate and a hiding spot underneath the cargo floor for the spare tire. These changes make the car wider and shorter than last year's model and enhance ride and handling, especially in turns. Cargo is also easier to load and unload; however, the spare tire is more difficult to access with a full load.

MODEL HISTORY: The 2002–05 models don't look that different from their predecessors, though they are a bit longer, wider, and higher. The interior, however, underwent a major change, with more space for both passengers and cargo, and more user-friendly features and controls.

The CR-V's Civic-based platform incorporates a four-wheel independent suspension that shortens the nose and frees up more rear cargo room. Steering components have also been modified. The base 160-hp 2.4L I-VTEC 4-cylinder engine is offered with either a 5-speed manual or a 4-speed automatic transmission (through the 2004 models).

The CR-V is offered in three trim levels, all offering full-time 4×4. Combining sport-utility styling with minivan versatility, this SUV is essentially a restyled Civic with 4×4 capability added. Since its '97 launch, the car changed little until the revamped 2002 came out. **1998**—Front-drive comes equipped with either a standard 5-speed manual transmission or optional automatic. **1999**—Picked up 20 more horses and an Overdrive On-Off switch. **2001**—Standard-issue ABS and user-friendly child-seat tether anchors added to the EX and SE. **2002**—Restyled and given more power, interior room, and features, like a side-hinged tailgate and new interior panels. **2004**—A front-passenger power door lock switch. **2005**—Standard curtain side airbags, skid control, and ABS; an upgraded 5-speed automatic transmission; and minor styling changes.

COST ANALYSIS: Selling for $29,300/$30,800/$34,200 (LX/EX/EX-L), Honda's 2006 models are outclassed by the more refined 2007 models, which should cost between $700 and $1,000 more. Don't expect much discounting or price-haggling—Honda's 2006 inventory is almost all gone, and there's a waiting list for the 2007s. Blame buyers downsizing in the wake of higher fuel prices. **Best alternatives:** In theory, a used, upgraded second-series 2002 would be the best buy from quality and price perspectives, but there aren't many available. The 2001 or earlier CR-Vs are acceptable, but they are poor second choices because they're underpowered and overpriced for what they offer. Take solace in knowing that, even if you pay too much for a Recommended model, you can drive this bantam 4×4 until you outgrow it and then trade it in for almost as much as you paid originally. Good second choices are the Hyundai Tucson or Santa Fe, Subaru Forester, and Toyota RAV4. **Rebates:** Mostly low-financing programs. **Delivery/PDI:** $1,455. **Warranty:** Bumper-to-bumper 3 years/60,000 km; powertrain 5 years/100,000 km; rust perforation 5 years/unlimited km. **Supplementary warranty:** Honda's impressive quality control makes an extended warranty unnecessary. **Options:** Make sure a moonroof doesn't reduce your headroom to an uncomfortable degree. Be wary of the cruise control—it's quirky, and when it's engaged, you may find that the car won't hold its speed over hilly terrain. One other bit of advice: Because of their design, CR-Vs tend to sandblast the paint off the side-door bottoms. Invest in a pair of $25 mudflaps. Also, steer clear of the original-equipment Bridgestone and Firestone tires. Owners report poor performance on wet roads and premature failures. Try Michelin, Yokohama, or Pirelli, instead. **Depreciation:** Much slower than average. **Insurance cost:** Average. **Parts supply/cost:** Parts are easily found and reasonably priced (they come mostly from the Civic parts bin). **Annual maintenance cost:** Well below average; easily repaired at independent garages. **Highway/city fuel economy:** Estimated to be 8.9/10.9 L/100 km.

QUALITY/RELIABILITY: Traditionally beyond reproach, but quality has slipped a bit lately. **Owner-reported problems:** Harsh shifting on the 1997–99 models, and high-rev shifting, slipping, pulsing, and surging on the 2000 version. The 1999–2001 CR-Vs also have a history of engine failures caused by defective cylinder heads (see "Secret Warranties/Internal Bulletins/Service Tips," below). Other reported problems include minor body trim defects, premature front brake wear and vibrations, drive shaft popping noises, accessories that malfunction (particularly the sound system and AC), and electrical glitches. **Warranty performance:** Like most other automakers, Honda frequently extends its warranty through "goodwill" policies that cover generic factory-related defects. The company denies this is the case, but, interestingly enough, almost all of its service bulletins include a paragraph stating that post-warranty goodwill compensation will be considered if requested by the dealer. Be wary, though. Sometimes owners are asked to show maintenance receipts as a prerequisite for "goodwill" repairs. Stand your ground, as did this American *Lemon-Aid* reader:

> My 2001 Honda CR-V started to run rough and stall. The engine light came on 79,000 miles [127,000 km]. The codes retrieved were P0300, P0302, P0302, P0304. These are misfire codes. A repairman stated that Honda has a well known defect in their 1999–2001 Honda CR-V which valves cause internal damage to their engine, and it should be under "GOODWILL" warranty. The dealer said it would not fix it unless I have proof of "Honda Dealer" Maintenance, which I don't have....
>
> I refused and dealer later offered to do the repair for $500.

ROAD PERFORMANCE: Acceleration/torque: The 2005's more powerful, upgraded engine is faster accelerating from a standing start and is less prone to hunting for the right gear when pressed. Manual transmissions need to downshift less frequently, as well. Generally, though, the CR-V is slow to accelerate when loaded—add passengers and an automatic transmission, and you're likely to get passed by bicycling seniors. Nevertheless, the engine's increased low-end torque adds 227 kg (500 lb.) to the towing rating (680 kg/1,500 lb.). **Transmission:** The 5-speed manual is precise, with short throws and easy shifting, while the automatic is quick and smooth. The full-time 4×4 disengages under braking, allowing the ABS system to engage. **Steering:** Many reports of severe "torque steer," where vehicle pulls hard to the right when accelerating. Variable-assisted steering, however, is nimble and accurate, and it provides just the right boost for highway and city driving. On the downside, the 2002 modifications have reduced road feel. **Routine handling:** The CR-V isn't tippy and handles remarkably well. Excellent ride over smooth surfaces. The car's small size doesn't handle road imperfections well, making for a bumpy, jittery ride. Forget about off-roading: There's no locking feature for the centre differential and no low-range 4×4 capability. **Emergency handling:** Very good, partly because of the four-wheel independent suspension and precise steering. Little body lean when cornering under power. **Braking:** Better than average, with good directional control and little fading after repeated applications.

 SAFETY SUMMARY: When compared with Toyota, Honda has had fewer safety-related defects reported to NHTSA. One recurring complaint, though, is that large occupants can't use the original-equipment seat belts. Note also that the CR-V flipped over in 1999 side-impact tests carried out by NHTSA. **Airbags:** There's a concern that the steering-wheel design is on an angle, which could result in an injury if the airbag deploys at an angle. There have been reports of airbags failing to deploy or deploying inadvertently. In one incident, the vehicle was going about 25 km/h when the driver's airbag suddenly exploded. The vehicle went off the road, flipped over, and injured the driver. **ABS:** Standard; disc/disc. **Seat belt pretensioners:** Standard. **Head restraints F/R:** *1997:* ★★★; *1998:* ★★; *2001:* ★★★/★★; *2002–03:* ★★★★★; *2005–06:* ★. **Visibility F/R:** ★★★★★.

SAFETY COMPLAINTS: All years: Sudden acceleration. • Chronic stalling. • ABS lockup. • Bridgestone tire blowouts. **1997**—Seatback collapsed. • ABS lock-up. • Cruise control doesn't maintain speed going up or down a hill. • Cruise control activates without warning at highway speeds. **1998**—Low-speed rear-ender pushed tailpipe into the fuel tank. • Accelerator sticks. • Knuckle arm broke, causing left front tire to come off. • Loss of steering while driving. • Steering locked up while making a right turn. • Cruise control often malfunctions. • Vehicle pulls to the right at any speed. • Front brake rotors need replacing after only 5,000 km. • Seat belt unlatched when brakes were applied. **1999**—Engine cylinder failure causes excessive vibration and stalling. • Automatic transmission slams into First gear. • Hatch window blew out while driving. **2000**—Bumper assembly caught fire. • Vehicle rolled over; A-pillar collapsed and killed driver. • Automatic transmission takes an inordinate amount of time to go into First gear and doesn't hold car when stopped in traffic on an incline. • Unacceptable slippage, poor traction of Bridgestone tires on wet pavement. • Excessive shimmying and front suspension vibration when accelerating. • Chronic steering-wheel vibrations. **2001**—Chronic stalling. • Short drivers find airbags point toward their faces. • Rear wheel lock-up while turning caused head-on collision (clutch failure suspected). • Driver's seatback collapsed in rear-ender. • Seat belt tightens uncomfortably. **2002**—Hood suddenly flew open while cruising. • Loud popping noise when braking and changing direction (replacing the brake pads doesn't fix the problem). • Vehicle hesitates when accelerating, or surges and then stalls. • Dim driver-side headlight. **2003**—Hood flew up. • Airbags failed to deploy. • Driver-side and rear centre seat belts unbuckled when car was rear-ended. • Steering wheel doesn't return to normal position after making a turn. **2004**—Many reports of engine fires after oil has been changed. • Gas pedal stuck. • Wheel froze while making a turn. • Stress fractures in windshield. • Airbag failed to deploy. • Wheel lug bolt broke off. • Constant stalling. • Removable picnic table caused serious head injuries in a rollover accident. • Gas spews out of filler tube when refuelling. • Water can enter the fuel tank from gas-cap vent. • Door lock doesn't function with key as indicated in the owner's manual. • No seat belt extender available. **2005**—Engine caught fire after oil change. • Sudden, unintended acceleration. • Airbags fail to deploy, or deploy for no reason:

> Airbags deployed (both front and side) while driving through a mall parking lot. The obstruction of view caused the vehicle to run into a light pole. The driver sustained a broken arm, fractured cheek, dislocated nose and jaw, and 8 stitches in her lip.

• Dozens of complaints that the vehicle pulls sharply to the right when accelerating:

> Purchased 2005 Honda CR-V for teenaged daughter in December 2004. Her mother drove the car for the first time on March 5, 2005, and was unfamiliar with the severe torque steer present in the vehicle. After making a right turn onto a major highway under hard acceleration, the steering wheel slipped from my wife's hands and the car struck the curb on the right side of the road. This blew both tires on the right side. At my own expense, I had all four tires replaced and a four-wheel alignment done at an independent dealer. Torque steer is still very prevalent.

• Failure of the CV joint protective boot. • Windshield is easily chipped. • Defective Bridgestone tires.

Secret Warranties/Internal Bulletins/Service Tips

All years: Keep in mind that Honda service bulletins almost always mention that "goodwill" extended warranties may be applied to any malfunction. **1997–98**—If the ABS light remains lit, check first for a faulty wheel-speed sensor, says TSB #98-041. • Tips on correcting a noisy driver's seat. • Replace the AC expansion valve under a "goodwill" warranty as a possible cure for dashboard noise (hissing, moaning, or whistling) when the AC is engaged. • Wind whistling from the top of the windshield may be corrected by applying additional sealant to the windshield moulding—another "goodwill" claim. **1997–99**—Harsh shifting caused by faulty solenoid; subject to free "goodwill" repair. • Front suspension clunking can be corrected by replacing the upper-arm flange bolts. • Cargo-cover end-caps come off. **1997–2001**—Differential noise. **1998**—Correcting wind noise coming from the door mirror area and a clunking noise from the power-window motor. **1997–2001**—Engine cylinder head failures causing poor engine performance covered by a secret warranty (see bulletin). **2000**—Information regarding shudder or vibration upon hard acceleration. • The remedy for differential moan during turns. • Malfunctioning Low Fuel light. **2001**—Rear differential noise. • Water leaks into the interior. **2002**—Rattling from the passenger grab handle area and above the doors. **2002–03**—A front brake clicking noise is caused by faulty lower retaining clips on the front brake pad that may be replaced for free under a "goodwill" program. • Engine stumbles or stalls after a stop. • Vehicle pulls to the right:

VEHICLE DRIFTS TO THE RIGHT

BULLETIN NO.: 03-004   DATE: JANUARY 21, 2003

2002–03 CR-V 4WD WITH A/T

SYMPTOM: The vehicle drifts or pulls to the right while driving at highway speeds.

CORRECTIVE ACTION: Realign the damper spring on the upper spring seat.

OUT OF WARRANTY: Any repair performed after warranty expiration may be eligible for goodwill consideration by the District Parts and Service Manager or your Zone Office. You must request consideration, and get a decision, before starting work.

• Misaligned door glass. **2003**—Coolant in the oil pan. **2002–04**—Troubleshooting a rear brake grinding noise. • Correcting harsh or noisy automatic transmission downshifts when slowing down. **2002–05**—Remedy for a rattle, grind, or growl coming from the A-pillar of the right-front side of the vehicle when turning left. • Troubleshooting rear seat belt retractor rattles/squeaks.

HARD START/POOR PERFORMANCE/MIL ON/MISFIRE DTC

BULLETIN NO.: 03-038   **DATE: NOVEMBER 5, 2004**

1999–2001 CR-V – ALL

SYMPTOM: The engine idles roughly, is hard to start, performs poorly, or has the MIL on with DTC P0301, P0302, P0303, P0304 (cylinder misfire), or P0172 (fuel system too rich).

PROBABLE CAUSE: One or more exhaust valves have receded into the cylinder head.

CORRECTIVE ACTION: Inspect the valve clearance and, if necessary, replace the cylinder head.

OP#	DESCRIPTION	FRT
110345	Check/adjust valve clearance only	0.8
110163	Check valve clearance, and replace cylinder head with new assembly	6.9

WARRANTY CLAIM INFORMATION: In warranty: The normal warranty applies.

Failed Part: P/N 12100-P75-010

        H/C 5604970

Defect Code: 00503

Symptom Code: 03203

Out of warranty: Any repair performed after warranty expiration may be eligible for goodwill consideration by the District Parts and Service Manager or your Zone Office. You must request consideration, and get a decision, before starting work.

INSPECTION PROCEDURE

1. Remove the cylinder head cover, and check the valve clearance on all exhaust valves.
   - If any of the valve clearances are below 0.09 mm, go to step 2.
   - If any of the valve clearances are between 0.09 and 0.16 mm, adjust the valves to specification (0.16 to 0.20 mm) Return the vehicle to the customer.
   - If the clearances are within specification, disregard this bulletin and look for other possible causes (ignition, fuel injection, etc.).
2. Ask the customer if the valves were adjusted shortly before the problem occurred.
   - If the valves were recently adjusted, readjust the valves to specification.
   - If the valves were not adjusted, proceed to REPAIR PROCEDURE.

REPAIR PROCEDURE: Replace the cylinder head: The exhaust valves and seats may be damaged (burnt or cracked) to further indicate that the cylinder head has a problem.

CR-V PROFILE

	1998	1999	2000	2001	2002	2003	2004	2005	2006
Cost Price ($) (firm)									
LX (20%)	25,800	26,000	26,000	26,300	26,900	27,300	27,200	28,200	29,300
Used Values ($)									
LX ▲	7,000	8,500	10,500	12,500	15,500	18,000	20,500	22,500	—
LX ▼	6,000	7,500	9,000	11,000	14,500	16,500	18,500	21,000	—

All ratings on a numbered scale where ⑤ is good and ❶ is bad. See page 220 for a more detailed description.

Reliability	④	④	⑤	⑤	⑤	⑤	⑤	⑤	—
Crash Safety (F)	④	④	④	④	⑤	⑤	⑤	⑤	⑤
Side	—	⑤	⑤	⑤	⑤	⑤	⑤	⑤	⑤
IIHS Side	—	—	—	—	❷	❷	❷	⑤	⑤
Offset	❷	❷	❷	❷	⑤	⑤	⑤	⑤	⑤
Rollover	—	—	—	❸	❸	❸	—	④	④

ELEMENT ★★★★

2007 TECHNICAL DATA

POWERTRAIN (FRONT-DRIVE/4X4)

Engine: 2.4L 4-cyl. (166 hp);
Transmissions: 5-speed man. • 5-speed auto.

DIMENSION/CAPACITY

Passengers: 2/2; Wheelbase: 101.4 in.; H: 70.4/L: 169.2/W: 71.5 in.; Headroom F/R: 4.5/4.0 in.; Legroom F/R: 40.0/30.0 in.; Cargo volume: 25.1 cu. ft.; Fuel tank: 60L/regular; Tow limit: 1,500 lb.; Load capacity: 675 lb.; Turning circle: 34.9 ft.; Ground clearance: 6.9 in.; Weight: 3,380 lb.

RATING: Above Average (2003–07). Honda launched this oddly styled SUV as a youth magnet, but has only succeeded in giving soccer moms and baby boomers a minivan alternative. **Strong points:** It's almost the same size as a CR-V, with a better package, and it costs thousands of dollars less. Other notable features include a limited, though adequate, powertrain; a roomy, versatile interior; an unusually large cargo door opening; a low liftover; a sliding roof partition that allows it to carry bulky items like kayaks, fishing poles, and surfboards; interior tie-down hooks; and a dash that allows for Internet access. Predicted slow depreciation; first-year Honda defects usually aren't that serious. **Weak points:** No 6-cylinder option; engine is noisy when pushed; mediocre passing performance; doesn't corner very well; unusual driving position; gauges are sometimes difficult to see; the front windshield is more vertical than most and seems far away from the driver; lack of a third seat in rear; side windows don't roll down; poor stereo sound; some high-speed wind noise; side crashworthiness rated "Poor" by the IIHS; 20 cm (8 in.) shorter than the Civic coupe; looks a bit like the 2003 Hummer H2. **New for 2007:** A slight restyling (new headlights and grille); seat-integrated front safety belts allow for much easier rear passenger access; 10 more horses; a 5-speed automatic transmission; and standard side curtain airbags and Vehicle Stability Assist. An all-new sporty variation, the Element SC, will also debut with a sport-tuned suspension and "Street Custom" styling.

MODEL HISTORY: A CR-V clone based on the Civic platform, the tall, square-looking Element is a crossover sport wagon SUV launched in early 2003 and priced in the $24,000–$29,000 range. Aimed at the youth market with its rugged exterior styling, buyers get the versatility of an SUV, the cargo-hauling capability of a pickup, and the interior access of a minivan.

Campers are well served by front- and second-row seats that fold flat for sleeping. The second-row seats can be folded away to the side, or removed to make more room for sports equipment and other toys.

Powered by a 166-hp 2.4L 4-cylinder engine coupled with a 5-speed automatic transmission or a 5-speed manual, the Element's powertrain and light weight make it a good all-around performer. Nonetheless, the lack of a V6 engine compromises its sporty pretensions.

COST ANALYSIS: Smart buyers will opt for the more refined 2007 version over the 2006. The 2007 vehicle's additional features are well worth the slightly higher cost: 2006 models sell for $24,200/$27,200/$29,500 (Base/Y/Y4WD), with minimal discounting; 2007s are expected to cost about $1,000 more. **Best alternatives:** The Honda CR-V, Hyundai Santa Fe GLS, Nissan X-Trail or Xterra, Subaru Forester, and Toyota Highlander AWD. **Rebates:** Few rebates because of the limited production. **Delivery/PDI:** $1,455. **Warranty:** Bumper-to-bumper 3 years/60,000 km; powertrain 5 years/100,000 km; rust perforation 5 years/unlimited km. **Supplementary warranty:** A waste of money. **Options:** Nothing that's necessary. **Depreciation:** Much slower than average. **Insurance cost:** Average. **Parts supply/cost:** Average. **Annual maintenance cost:** Less than average. **Highway/city fuel economy:** 8.5/11.1 L/100 km.

QUALITY/RELIABILITY: Likely failures: Windshield cracks plus minor fit and finish, electrical system, AC, and sound system glitches.

SAFETY SUMMARY: The driver's and front passenger's shoulder belts are attached to the rear doors. This means front occupants must unbuckle their seat belts before the rear passengers can open the rear doors (assuming the front doors are open). This problem has been corrected on the 2007 model. Windshield pillars are quite thick, and they occasionally obscure vision when turning. **Airbags:** Front and side. **ABS:** Optional; disc/disc. **Safety belt pretensioners:** Front. **Head restraints F/R:** *2003–06:* ★. **Visibility F/R:** ★★★/★.

SAFETY COMPLAINTS: 2003–05—Many complaints related to windshield cracking (covered by a "goodwill" policy on a case-by-case basis). **2003**—Extensive low-speed collision damage. • Loose rear torsion bar nut. **2004**—Fire occurred in driver-side door. • Airbag deployed for no reason. • Loose driver's seat rocks back and forth. **2005**—You cannot open the back door unless the front door is opened first. • Airbags deploy for no reason, or fail to deploy.

Secret Warranties/Internal Bulletins/Service Tips

2003—Windshield cracks in the lower corners because of an uneven flange surface (TSB #03-028; issued May 6, 2003). • Driver's seat rocks back and forth. • Troubleshooting ABS problems. **2003–04**—Correcting harsh or noisy automatic transmission downshifts when slowing down. • What to do when the tailgate rattles, Hatch Open indicator is on, and interior light is lit. **2003–05**—Noisy front seatback. **2005**—Axle seal leaks.

ELEMENT PROFILE

	2003	2004	2005	2006
Cost Price ($) (firm)				
Base (20%)	23,900	23,900	24,000	24,200
Used Values ($)				
Base ▲	14,500	17,000	19,000	—
Base ▼	13,000	16,000	17,500	—
Reliability	⑤	⑤	⑤	—
Crash Safety (F)	⑤	⑤	⑤	⑤
Side	⑤	⑤	⑤	⑤
IIHS Side	❶	❶	❶	❶
Offset	⑤	⑤	⑤	⑤
Rollover	❸	—	—	—

best buy

PILOT ★★★★★

RATING: Recommended (2003–07). Think of the Pilot as a large, upscale minivan with all-wheel drive—a cheaper alternative to the Acura MDX. **Strong points:** Roomier and more powerful than most of the mid-sized competition; good acceleration with the AWD V6 powertrain; can tow a small trailer or boat (1,588–2,040 kg/3,500–4,500 lb.); drives and rides like a nicely balanced luxury car where comfort, performance, and handling are optimized; has seating for eight with three-point seat belts for all; has a reasonably equipped, versatile, and roomy interior with lots of cargo space; and the second- and third-row seats fold flat. **Weak points:** No side curtain airbags; front headrests are mounted too far back, causing neck pain and strain; lacks low-range gearing for off-road use; transmission shifts a bit slowly when accelerating at 100 km/h; steering is a bit heavy during parking manoeuvres; high-speed corrections are somewhat slow because of the tires' high side walls; a fair amount of body lean is present when cornering, and front-end noseplow occurs in high-speed turns and sudden stops; the steering wheel can be a long reach for some drivers; high fuel consumption; rear hatch door doesn't have a convenient, separate rear liftglass; entry and exit are made difficult by the Pilot's trucklike height; rear legroom is at a premium; the third-row seat is best suited for small kids because access is hampered by a narrow passageway and the limited forward travel of the second-row seats; visibility is hindered by thick front roof pillars. **New for 2007:** A slight restyling (mostly to the hood, grille, and headlights).

2007 TECHNICAL DATA

POWERTRAIN
Engine: 3.5L V6 (255 hp); Transmission: 5-speed auto.

DIMENSION/CAPACITY
Passengers: 2/3/3; Wheelbase: 107 in.; H: 70.6/L: 188/W: 78 in.; Headroom F/R1/R2: 7.5/6.0/2.5 in.; Legroom F/R1/R2: 41/29/24.5 in.; Cargo volume: 42.5 cu. ft.; Fuel tank: 77L/regular; Tow limit: 4,500 lb.; Load capacity: 1,320 lb.; Ground clearance: 5.0 in.; Turning circle: 40 ft.; Weight: 4,435 lb.

MODEL HISTORY: Introduced as a 2003 model, the Pilot borrows the basic design of its chassis and powertrain from the MDX. The Pilot differs from its more expensive brother with more conservative styling, a softer suspension, larger wheels, and a shorter body that's slightly wider and taller than the Acura and seats eight passengers versus the MDX's seven. The Odyssey-sourced V6 240-hp engine coupled to a full-time all-wheel-drive unit enhances overall performance. Four-wheel independent suspension ensures fairly good handling and a comfortable ride. The Pilot is built in Alliston, Ontario, along with the Honda Odyssey, Honda Civic, Acura 1.7EL, and Acura MDX. **2005**—15 more horses, a standard anti-skid system with the EX-L, a tire-pressure monitor, a larger fuel tank, and a slight restyling.

COST ANALYSIS: With 2006 models selling for $39,400/$41,901/$44,500 (LX/EX/EX-L), go for the 2006 model if you can get at least a 10 percent discount. **Best alternatives:** Infiniti QX4, Lexus RX 300/330, and Toyota Highlander AWD or Sequoia. **Rebates:** Look for $3,000 rebates in the late fall. **Delivery/PDI:** $1,455. **Warranty:** Bumper-to-bumper 3 years/60,000 km; powertrain 5 years/100,000 km; rust perforation 5 years/unlimited km. **Supplementary warranty:** Not needed. **Options:** Nothing that's necessary. **Depreciation:** Slower than average, but soaring fuel prices and Detroit discounting will likely speed up depreciation a bit by year's end. **Insurance cost:** Has been higher than average. **Parts supply/cost:** Parts have been moderately priced and easily found in the MDX/Odyssey generic parts bin. **Annual maintenance cost:** Much less than average. **Highway/city fuel economy:** 9.7/14.1 L/100 km.

QUALITY/RELIABILITY: Likely failures: Quite a few first-year glitches were reported to government safety agencies, but things seem to have settled down with the latest models. Still, watch out for engine oil leaks, excessive steering vibration, electrical problems (low or no alternator output), body glitches (body and bumper paint defects), an inoperable horn, intolerable cabin wind noise, and an annoying thunking noise from the gas tank.

 SAFETY SUMMARY: Airbags: Front and side. **ABS:** Standard; disc/disc. **Safety belt pretensioners:** Front. **Head restraints F/R:** 2003–05: ★ (cloth seats); 2003–05: ★★ (leather seats); 2006: ★★★★★ (LX seats). **Visibility F/R:** ★★★★/★★★★★.

SAFETY COMPLAINTS: 2003—Vehicle rolled over after driver made a small steering correction. • Small road imperfections make the Pilot suddenly veer left or right. • Airbags failed to deploy. • Engine oil leakage caused by damaged timing belt and valves. • Intermittent hard starts. • ABS brake lock-up. • Power-steering pulley breakage. • Head restraints are too low for tall occupants. • Shoulder straps cut across neck. • Intolerable noise and turbulence is produced when cruising with the windows open. • Weak headlights. **2004**—Automatic transmission suddenly downshifted on its own. • Transmission recall parts aren't available. • Hard starting because of poor electrical connection. • Alarm goes off whenever car is started. • Airbag constantly disables itself. • Weak low beam headlights. • Plastic fuel tank is easily punctured. • Interior cabin light flickers on and off, door locks cease to function, and window won't go down. • Passenger window shattered after a drop in temperature. • Severe wind buffeting when driving with the rear windows down. • Excessive vibration when driving over 100 km/h. • Sunroofs are failure-prone and they leak and create wind and vibration noise. **2005**—Airbag deployment caused severe burns to the driver's hands. • Loss of braking ability caused by brake master cylinder failure. • Sudden loss of steering. • Vehicle would start on its own; not equipped with a remote starter. • Non-adjustable, doughnut-style head restraints are literally a pain in the neck (see *www.edmunds.com*). • Middle second-row seat belt is mounted too far forward on the ceiling so that it passes the shoulder and sits near the neck and cheek. • Instrument panel data is hard to see in daylight. • Frequent complaints of excessive steering vibration (check *www.hondapilot.org/forums*) that is *not* corrected by re-balancing or changing the tires. Don't waste your money.

Secret Warranties/Internal Bulletin/Service Tips

2003—V6 engine oil leaks. • Noisy power-steering pump, front strut and damper, hood air deflector, dash, and fuel tank (fuel sloshes when accelerating or stopping). • Security system won't arm. • Steering vibration. • Power-window failure. • HomeLink remote system can't be programmed. • Third-row seat won't fold, tilt, slide, or recline. • Right rear suspension clicking. **2003–04**—Noise and shudder when turning. • Rear brake clunk. **2003–05**—Accessory-hood air deflector cracks. **2005**—Tire valve stem cap replacement campaign.

	2003	2004	2005	2006
Cost Price ($) (firm)				
Base (23%)	41,000	38,800	39,000	39,400
Used Values ($)				
Base ▲	25,000	28,000	31,000	—
Base ▼	23,500	26,500	29,000	—
Reliability	④	⑤	⑤	—
Crash Safety (F)	⑤	⑤	⑤	⑤
Side	⑤	⑤	⑤	⑤
Offset	⑤	⑤	⑤	⑤
Rollover	④	④	④	④

Hyundai

SANTA FE ★★★★★

best buy

RATING: Recommended (2007); Above Average (2001–06). This year, Santa Fe will go upscale in price, size, and equipment, while Tucson anchors the entry-level spot. **Strong points:** Smooth-shifting automatic transmission; small turning circle; very comfortable ride; generous occupant space; practical, versatile interior; well appointed; competitively priced; and good build and finish quality. **Weak points:** *2006 and earlier models:* Underpowered with the 4-cylinder; little V6 reserve power; engine struggles with too-tall second gearing; no low-range gearing; mediocre braking (with rear drum brakes); head restraint protection is rated "Poor"; excessive engine noise; and thirsty around town. **New for 2007:** More power and features. It's 18 cm (7 in.) longer, 2.5 cm (1 in.) wider, almost

All ratings on a numbered scale where ⑤ is good and ❶ is bad. See page 220 for a more detailed description.

5 cm (2 in.) taller, and set on a new wheelbase with a 7.4 cm (2.9 in.) increase in track width. All this was done to distance the car from its cheaper Tucson brother by increasing interior room and adding an optional third-row seat for seven-passenger seating. The base 2.7L engine has been given a 15-hp boost, while the new 3.3L V6 provides 30 more horses than the previous 3.5L engine. ABS, traction/anti-skid control, and front side and side curtain airbags are now standard safety features.

MODEL HISTORY: Hyundai's first sport-utility was seen as essentially a Sonata with SUV amenities. It's about the same size as the Honda CR-V or the Ford Escape, but it's a bit wider and its interior room is slightly larger than either of the aforementioned vehicles. Attractively styled, with a user-friendly cockpit, comfortable seating, and lots of storage area, the Santa Fe has appealed mostly to budget-minded buyers looking for SUV versatility.

Less appealing is the Santa Fe's highway performance. The car's heavy weight combined with the puny 4-cylinder engine hampers performance considerably. And the 185-hp V6 powerplant's additional 35 horses still don't give this SUV wannabe sufficient power to overcome its heft. All the more reason to save your loonies for the 2007, equipped with a new 242-hp V6. On all models, handling is good, with responsive steering and a comfortable ride. The 4×4 system works efficiently, too, without any harshness or undue noise. There isn't any low-range gear; instead, a limited-slip rear differential does the job.

This mid-sized SUV, nevertheless, has lots of potential because of its many standard features, reasonable price, and comprehensive warranty. Furthermore, the powertrain shortcomings may not be very important if your driving requirements don't include a lot of high-speed commuting or trailering. **2003**—Front side airbags, an upgraded optional CD changer, and a garage door opener. **2005**—No more 4-cylinder engine.

COST ANALYSIS: Buy a 2007 base FWD GL model with the 185-hp 2.7L V6 and a 5-speed manual transmission for about $25,995. The AWD GL Premium with the 242-hp 3.3L V6 and a standard 5-speed automatic starts at $30,095. Fully loaded with AWD, leather, power driver's seat and electric sunroof, the GLS tops out at $35,995—about $5,000 less than many competitors. A side-airbag-equipped 2003 Santa Fe V6 is also a good buy if it has some of the original factory warranty left. **Best alternatives:** Check out the Ford Escape, Honda CR-V or Element, Hyundai

2007 TECHNICAL DATA

POWERTRAIN
Engines: 2.7L V6 (185 hp) • 3.3L V6 (242 hp); Transmissions: 5-speed man. • 4-speed auto. • 5-speed auto.

DIMENSION/CAPACITY
Passengers: 2/3; 2/3/2 Wheelbase: 106.3 in.; H: 67.9/L: 184.1/W: 74.4 in.; Headroom F/R: 4.0/4.0 in.; Legroom F/R: 40/29 in.; Cargo volume: 33.5 cu. ft.; Fuel tank: 72L/regular; Tow limit: 2,800–3,500 lb.; Load capacity: 880 lb.; GVWR: 5,240 lb.; Turning circle: 35.8 ft.; Ground clearance: 8.1 in.; Weight: 3,793 lb.

Tucson (2006–07), Jeep Liberty, Mazda Tribute, Nissan Xterra, Subaru Forester, and Toyota RAV4. **Rebates:** Look for $3,000 rebates early in the new year on the 2006 models. The 2007s will likely not be discounted by much or have any sizeable rebates. **Delivery/PDI:** $1,545. **Warranty:** Bumper-to-bumper 5 years/100,000 km; powertrain 5 years/100,000 km; rust perforation 5 years/unlimited km. **Supplementary warranty:** Not necessary. **Options:** The GL option is a must for the V6 engine. **Depreciation:** Slower than average. **Insurance cost:** Average. **Parts supply/cost:** Santa Fe shares the compact Sonata platform, so parts should be easily found and reasonably priced. **Annual maintenance cost:** Lower than average. **Highway/city fuel economy:** The 2007 2.7L is rated at 8.4/11.3 L/100 km, while the more powerful 3.3L can be expected to deliver 8.8/12.2 L/100 km.

QUALITY/RELIABILITY: Hyundai's quality control is a heck of a lot better than Detroit's Big Three and practically as good as Honda or Toyota. **Owner-reported problems:** Remarkably few complaints reported so far, although there's been a smattering of engine and transmission problems mentioned. **Warranty performance:** Much better than average, but as sales increase, the company has become more insensitive to customer claims. We have now come full-circle since Hyundai angered Pony, Stellar, and Excel owners by denying warranty claims in the '70s, '80s, and '90s. **Likely failures:** The automatic transmission, electrical system, cruise control, catalytic converter, speedometer, alternator, and fit and finish (water leaks, door misalignment, and paint peeling under the hood). In rainy weather, air intake sucks water into the engine and shorts out the mass air sensor (MAS).

SAFETY SUMMARY: For some drivers, the rear-view mirror obstructs the right-side view. **Airbags:** Front, side, and side curtain. **ABS:** Standard or optional; disc/drum; disc/disc on some recent models. **Safety belt pretensioners:** Front. **Traction control:** Optional and standard. **Head restraints F/R:** *2001–06:* ★. **Visibility F/R:** Vision is clear in the front and rear.

SAFETY COMPLAINTS: All years: Engine hesitates and then surges, causing unintended acceleration. • Windshield cracking. • Alternator failures drain battery and cause instruments and gauges to malfunction. • Check Engine light is constantly lit. **2001**—Fire ignited in the starter. • Airbags failed to deploy. • Steering wheel locks up while driving. • Sudden, unintended acceleration. • Chronic stalling and hesitation when accelerating. • Accelerator and pedal set too close together. • Power-steering belt shredded repeatedly. • Refuelling is difficult because gas pump shuts off prematurely. • Defective speedometers and alternators replaced under a secret "goodwill" warranty. **2002**—Coolant leak onto engine caused fire. • Premature failure of the transmission and engine. • Passenger window suddenly shattered. • Loose wheel lug bolts. **2003**—Engine camshaft and axle failures. • Steering wheel wouldn't lock. **2004**—Vehicle will suddenly pull to the left while underway. • Complete brake failure; vehicle out of service for a month. • Sudden, unintended acceleration. • Airbag deployed for no reason. • Jerky automatic transmission engagement. **2005**—Sudden, unintended acceleration when the vehicle is put into Reverse. • Computer-assisted gas pedal on vehicles equipped with a 3.5L V6 causes a dangerous delay in acceleration, followed by a sudden surging:

> The optional 3.5 engine is equipped with a computer operated acceleration throttle engine. This new set up is very poorly designed, has a few second delay and then the car darts off fast, sometimes spinning all drive wheels on dry pavement. I bought a 4 wheel drive unit for our rain, snow covered roads in Oregon, however it's much [worse in these types] of conditions. I've almost rear ended the car ahead of me several times and also have to have one foot on brake pedal in heavy traffic or where I have to stop for people crossing the street.

• Traction control allows wheels to slip in the snow. • Vehicle "bucks" whenever cruise control is deactivated. • Side front airbag is often disabled when an adult passenger occupies the seat. • Airbags failed to deploy.

Secret Warranties/Internal Bulletins/Service Tips

All models/years: No movement in Drive or Reverse. **2001**—A faulty automatic transaxle oil temperature sensor or solenoid may be the cause of poor shifting or no-shifts. • Troubleshooting a harsh gear engagement. • Fluid may leak from the area around the automatic transmission torque converter. • Harsh or delayed Park–Reverse or Park–Drive engagement. • Engine runs and idles roughly. • Inoperative or intermittent operation of the sport mode switch. • Noise from rear wheels. • Front-door wind noise. • Poor AM reception. **2001–02**—Delayed, erratic, and harsh shifts. • Front suspension knocking. **2001–03**—Cruise control disengages on its own. • Automatic transmission erratic performance or whining. • Headlight dimming. **2003**—Cruise control doesn't downshift. • 2.7L V6 engine oxygen sensor upgrade.

SANTA FE PROFILE

	2001	2002	2003	2004	2005
2006					
Cost Price ($) (negotiable)					
GL (20%)	25,250	21,050	21,050	22,595	20,995	20,995
GLS (23%)	29,250	29,500	29,950	30,195	30,395	30,585
Used Values ($)					
GL ▲	10,500	11,500	13,000	14,500	16,500	—
GL ▼	9,500	11,000	12,000	13,000	15,000	—
GLS ▲	12,000	13,500	16,500	20,000	22,000	—
GLS ▼	10,500	12,500	15,000	18,500	20,500	—

Reliability	④	④	④	⑤	⑤	—
Crash Safety (F)	—	⑤	⑤	⑤	④	④
Side	—	⑤	⑤	⑤	⑤	⑤
IIHS side	—	③	③	③	③	③
Offset	⑤	⑤	⑤	⑤	⑤	⑤
Rollover	—	③	③	—	③	③

Note: 2002 base model price was cut because Hyundai GL reverted to front-drive from AWD.

TUCSON ★★★★

2007 TECHNICAL DATA

POWERTRAIN
Engines: 2.0L 4-cyl. (140 hp) • 2.7L V6 (173 hp); Transmissions: 5-speed man. • 4-speed manumatic

DIMENSION/CAPACITY
Passengers: 2/3; Wheelbase: 103.5 in.; H: 66.1/L: 170.3/W: 70.7 in.; Headroom F/R: 5.0/4.0 in.; Legroom F/R: 41/29 in.; Cargo volume: 22.7 cu. ft.; Fuel tank: 58L/regular; Tow limit: 2,000 lb.; Load capacity: 860 lb.; GVWR: 4,431 lb.; Ground clearance: 7 in.; Turning circle: 39 ft.; Weight: 3,240 lb.

RATING: Above Average (2007); Average (2006); Below Average (2005). With this Kia Sportage twin, you get a lot of features for your money, but a competent 4-cylinder engine isn't one of them. **Strong points:** Fairly cheap; well-equipped with standard side airbags and stability control; NHTSA five-star front and side crashworthiness ratings; excellent braking; very comfortable ride; roomy interior; and good fit and finish. **Weak points:** Underpowered and "undergeared"; bland interior; mediocre handling; sluggish steering; limited rear visibility; numerous first-year factory-related deficiencies; noisy suspension; IIHS gives it an "Average" for offset and side crash protection, and head restraints are rated "Poor" for occupant protection; and poor fuel economy. **New for 2007:** Nothing significant.

MODEL HISTORY: Hyundai's second and smallest sport-utility is built on a strengthened and stretched Elantra platform powered by the Elantra's engine and offering the addition of four-wheel drive. The interior looks fairly low-tech and uses cheap-looking plastics everywhere. The optional 2.7L V6 is harnessed to a "manumatic" 4-speed automatic transmission, a setup that leads to excessive gear-hunting, imprecise automatic-to-manual shifting, and compromised fuel economy. What's really needed is a conventional 5-speed, or for the Santa Fe's 3.3L 242-hp V6 to handle the Tucson's heft.

While we're on the subject of weight, the Tucson is heavier than either the Honda CR-V or Toyota RAV4, so true handling enthusiasts will want to throw their lot in with the RAV4 or Ford Escape/Tribute to get their performance thrills.

All ratings on a numbered scale where ⑤ is good and ❶ is bad. See page 220 for a more detailed description.

COST ANALYSIS: The 2006 models are reasonably priced at $20,596/$24,095/ $25,695/$27,995 (GL/GL AWD/GL V6/GL AWD V6), and the 2007 version price hikes will average from $700 to $1,000. Since there are no real improvements this year, buy a 2006 Tucson. Don't invest in a 2005 unless it has been thoroughly checked over, is incredibly cheap, and has much of the original warranty left. Also, try to find an improved second-series version that was built after March 2005. Prices for used 2005s are fairly firm and are as follows: *FWD GL: $14,000–$16,000; FWD GL V6: $16,500–$18,000; 4WD GL V6: $18,500–$20,500; 4WD GLS V6: $24,000–$25,500.* **Best alternatives:** Ford Escape, Honda CR-V, Jeep Liberty, and Toyota RAV4. **Rebates:** Look for $2,500 rebates early in the new year. **Delivery/PDI:** $1,545. **Warranty:** Bumper-to-bumper 5 years/100,000 km; powertrain 5 years/100,000 km; rust perforation 5 years/unlimited km. **Supplementary warranty:** Not necessary. **Options:** The V6 engine is a must-have to compensate for the 4-banger's lack of passing power. **Depreciation:** Average. **Insurance cost:** Average. **Parts supply/cost:** Tucson's Elantra-sourced parts are easily found and reasonably priced. **Annual maintenance cost:** Rather high for the first-year 2005s; predicted to be lower than average for the 2006 and 2007 models. **Highway/city fuel economy:** *2.0L 4-cyl.:* 7.9/10.6 L/100 km; *V6:* 8.4/11.9 L/100 km.

QUALITY/RELIABILITY: Although the 2005 first-series models were somewhat glitch-ridden, overall quality control is quite good. **Owner-reported problems:** Owner gripes concern failures related to the cruise control, automatic transmission, manual transmission shift-lever cable assembly, and stability-control module. Poor fit and finish; water pours in from behind the glove box:

> Upon removing the glove box and pulling out the cabin filter, I noticed the water coming down through the AC system...similar complaint filed on service bulletins. Car was parked on a 10 degree angle nose end down. Water leak through and near electrical components and near passenger side airbag. Loss of airbag integrity with unknown damage if any. Mold and mildew damage is a potential health issue as well.

Warranty performance: Better than average, but service is a big disappointment. **Likely failures:** The automatic transmission, electronics, cruise control, stability-control system, and ABS brakes.

SAFETY SUMMARY: Airbags: Standard front, side, and side curtain. **ABS:** Standard; disc/disc. **Safety belt pretensioners:** Front. **Traction control:** Standard. **Head restraints F/R:** *2006:* ★. **Visibility F/R:** Good overall.

SAFETY COMPLAINTS: 2005—Side and side curtain airbags failed to deploy. • A faulty ESP (stability-control) module can cause the vehicle to stall and the ABS to suddenly engage, and can result in the vehicle going out of control. This has happened to vehicles that have been recalled and "fixed" for the problem and to cars that aren't included in the recall:

> There is a recall on this vehicle by Hyundai however due to the VIN number this car is not included. The problem is there is an ESP (stability control) which activates one of the wheels and causes the vehicle to swerve in the direction of the braking. In this case, the vehicle locked up and the consumer nearly lost control while driving about 40 mph [64 km/h] and the right front wheel and brake locked up.

• Manual and automatic transmissions suddenly fail to go into gear. • Power steering fails while passing through small pools of water on the road. • Passenger-side airbag is disabled even though an adult is sitting in the seat.

⌕ecret Warranties/Internal Bulletins/Service Tips

2005—No movement in Drive or Reverse. • Fluid may leak from the area around the automatic transmission torque converter or between the transaxle and the transfer case. • Correcting harsh gear engagement. • Tips on silencing a rattling sunroof.

VERACRUZ

RATING: Not Recommended during its first year on the market. Prices will be quite firm during the first few months following the launch, and then high fuel prices and a cooling of the market next fall should make for much better deals. **New for 2007:** Everything.

MODEL HISTORY: Not much history, yet. Named after the Mexican state, this mid-sized SUV will be unveiled at the North American International Auto Show in January and will go on sale during the second quarter of 2007. It will compete with the upcoming Saturn Outlook and GMC Acadia and with the Honda Pilot, Nissan Murano, Subaru B9 Tribeca, and Lexus RX 350. Power will be provided by a 265-hp 3.8L V6 coupled to a 6-speed automatic transmission. Its unibody architecture promises carlike driving dynamics. Front-drive will be standard, with all-wheel drive optional. As with all Hyundai SUVs, side and side curtain airbags as well as electronic stability-control/anti-skid capability are standard features. A fold-into-the-floor third-row seat that can seat two passengers will increase the maximum passenger load to seven. It will be larger than the Honda Pilot and have more cargo volume than the full-sized Mercedes-Benz GL (plus, it'll cost a lot less). Speaking of cost: The Veracruz is slotted a bit above the Santa Fe in size and price and is expected to sell for $30,000+.

Infiniti

FX35, FX45   ★★★★

RATING: Above Average (2003–07). A luxury SUV for buyers secretly wanting a sports sedan. **Strong points:** The FX35 rivals BMW's X5 in its carlike handling. Excellent acceleration, steering response, and braking; good fuel economy; and predicted to be more reliable than the competition. Few safety-related complaints. **Weak points:** The AWD lacks low-range gearing and is not intended for off-roading. An uncomfortable, stiff, jerky ride when going over road imperfections. A wide turning circle complicates parking and in-town manoeuvring. Annoying tire noise and excessive exhaust roar. The sports sedan driving position isn't for everyone; its low driver's position, sloping roof, and high doorsills create a claustrophobic feeling. The sporty interior limits cargo space, and the narrow rear windshield impairs visibility. The power front seat and dash- and steering-mounted controls are confusing and not user-friendly. Child safety seat installation is even less user-friendly. Head-restraint occupant protection rated "Marginal" by IIHS. Premium fuel is required. **New for 2007:** A minor restyling; the next redesign is scheduled for the 2009 models.

MODEL HISTORY: Launched in 2003, this crossover model is a high-performance, five-passenger, four-door wagon spin-off of Infiniti's G35 sedan. The FX35 comes with a 3.5L V6 and rear-drive or all-wheel drive, while the FX45 has a 4.5L V8 and comes only with AWD. Every FX has ABS, anti-skid/traction control, front side torso airbags, head-protecting side curtain airbags, and xenon headlights. The FX45 uses an innovative Lane Departure Warning system that alerts the driver when the vehicle has wandered outside of the designated traffic lane. The FX35 rides on 18-inch wheels; the FX45 offers a standard sport suspension with 20-inch wheels. The 2006 models got exterior styling tweaks and a redesigned centre console.

COST ANALYSIS: Go for a discounted 2006 ($54,500 and $62,400), since the 2007s are practically the same. This year's models will cost a few thousand dollars more, but this difference can be wiped out by patiently shopping the 2007 discounts and rebates. Remember, Infiniti dealers are crying for new products and

2007 TECHNICAL DATA

POWERTRAIN (4X4)
Engines: 3.5L V6 (280 hp) • 4.5L V8 (315 hp); Transmission: 5-speed manumatic
DIMENSION/CAPACITY
Passengers: 2/3; Wheelbase: 112 in.; H: 65/L: 189.1/W: 77 in.; Headroom F/R: N/A; Legroom F/R: 4.5/4.0 in.; Cargo volume: 29 cu. ft.; Fuel tank: 90L/premium; Tow limit: 3,500 lb.; Load capacity: 950 lb.; GVWR: 5,164–5,462 lb.; Ground clearance: 7.0 in.; Turning circle: 42 ft.; Weight: 4,295 lb.

slashing prices on carried-over inventory. If buying used, all the previous models are good buys except for the more glitch-ridden, first-year 2003s. **Best alternatives:** The FX beats BMW's X5 in almost every category. The Lexus RX 300/330 or a second-series 2007 ES 350 and the Toyota Highlander are good alternatives from a reliability and performance perspective. **Rebates:** $3,000–$5,000 price cuts are quite likely in the late fall as Detroit's SUV discounting picks up speed. **Delivery/PDI:** $1,577 (a 10 percent increase). **Warranty:** Bumper-to-bumper 4 years/100,000 km; powertrain 6 years/100,000 km; rust perforation 7 years/unlimited km. **Supplementary warranty:** Not necessary. **Options:** The Touring and Sport packages don't give you much for your money. **Depreciation:** Although average, depreciation is much faster than one would think; 2003s often go for almost half their original cost. **Insurance cost:** Higher than average. **Parts supply/cost:** Average parts supply, but relatively costly electronic and body parts. **Annual maintenance cost:** Lower than average, so far, but most vehicles are still on warranty. **Highway/city fuel economy:** *V6:* 9.9/14.4 L/100 km; *V8:* 11.2/15.6 L/100 km. Owners report real-world fuel consumption is much higher than these figures.

 QUALITY/RELIABILTY: Better than average. **Owner-reported problems:** Transfer-case failures, premature front and rear brake-caliper and rotor wear and noise, and body trim defects. **Warranty performance:** Average; owners mention that problems are seldom fixed on the first servicing visit.

 SAFETY SUMMARY: Child safety seats are hard to install because the lower anchor points aren't very accessible. **Airbags:** Side airbags are standard. Reports of airbags failing to deploy. **ABS:** Standard 4W; disc/disc. **Safety belt pretensioners:** Standard. **Head restraints F/R:** 2003–06: ★★. **Traction control:** Standard. **Visibility F/R:** ★★★/★.

SAFETY COMPLAINTS: *FX35:* **2003**—Many complaints that the driver's seat rocks back and forth, thereby possibly increasing crash forces during a collision. • Front axle and differential separation. • Sudden loss of steering control. • Passenger-side front seat belt would not release and had to be cut away. • When activating the turn blinker switch, the headlights are inadvertently turned off due to the close proximity of the headlight switch. **2004**—Child safety seats are difficult to install or remove. • Erratic cruise-control operation; not maintaining set speed. • Fuel gauge continues to give inaccurate readings, even with a new fuel sender. • Mud flaps on all four wheels cause ice buildup, hampering steering. • When door locks are forced open, windows roll down automatically. **2005**—Sudden, unintended acceleration. *FX45:* **2003**—Sudden, unintended acceleration when stopping at a stoplight. • Drive shaft fell out from under the vehicle while underway on the highway. • Vehicle suddenly downshifted while underway on the highway. • A child moved the gearshift lever from Park without the key in the ignition or the brakes depressed. • Similar front-seat rocking complaints to the FX35's. • Many complaints of front windshields cracking (see *www.freshalloy.com*). **2004**—Bright brake and turning lights blind others driving behind the vehicle.

Secret Warranties/Internal Bulletins/Service Tips

2003–05—Tips on adjusting a too-high-idle rpm. • Correcting excessive steering-column play. • Ways to fix driver-seat rocking are outlined in TSB #ITB05-018A. • Inoperative door mirror kit available. • A fuel tank that's difficult to refuel requires a new shutter valve. 2003–06—Troubleshooting cold hard starts. 2005—Remedy for front brake noise.

FX35/FX45 PROFILE

	2003	2004	2005	2006
Cost Price ($) (soft)				
FX35 (30%)	52,700	52,700	52,900	54,500
FX45 (30%)	60,200	60,200	60,500	62,400
Used Values ($)				
FX35 ▲	32,000	37,000	43,000	—
FX35 ▼	30,000	35,000	41,000	—
FX45 ▲	36,000	43,000	47,000	—
FX45 ▼	34,000	41,000	44,000	—
Reliability	④	④	⑤	—
Crash Safety (F)	—	⑤	⑤	⑤
Side	—	⑤	⑤	⑤
Offset	⑤	⑤	⑤	⑤

QX4, QX56   ★ ★

2007 TECHNICAL DATA

POWERTRAIN (4X4)

Engine: 5.6L V8 (315 hp); Transmission: 5-speed auto.

DIMENSION/CAPACITY

Passengers: 2/3/3; Wheelbase: 123.2 in.; H: 78.7/L: 206.9/W: 78.8 in.; Headroom F/R1/R2: N/A; Legroom F/R1/R2: 41.8/41.9/32.2 in.; Cargo volume: 20 cu. ft.; Fuel tank: 105L/premium; Tow limit: 8,900–9,000 lb.; Load capacity: Varies; GVWR: 6,622 lb.; Ground clearance: 10.6 in.; Turning circle: 41 ft.; Weight: 5,631 lb.

RATING: Below Average (2004–07); Above Average (1997–2003). With its more powerful engine and better-than-average quality control, the QX4 is the better choice—too bad 2003 was its last model year. The QX56 is an Infiniti clone of the Pathfinder Armada SUV (with 10 extra horses), a spin-off of the Nissan Titan. Its 2004 model redesign hurt overall reliability and performance. **Strong points:** QX4: Reasonably priced, with a long list of standard features, and it depreciates slowly. Impressive acceleration on 2001 and later models; attractively styled, mostly posh interior; front seats are especially supportive; automatic 4×4; cargo bay has a low, wide opening; excellent front and side crashworthiness scores, and few safety- and quality-related complaints. *QX56:* A powerful base engine; towing capacity is almost double that of its competitors. Can carry up to eight passengers more comfortably than most luxury models. Impressively responsive handling, thanks to the independent, load-levelling suspension. NHTSA gave the 2006 and 2007 models a four-star frontal crashworthiness rating and a three-star rollover rating. **Weak points:** *QX4:* Feeble acceleration with earlier models; rear-wheel-only ABS; rear drum brakes; limited rear legroom and cargo space; no third-row seat; fake wood interior trim; interior door handles are too small; rear windows don't roll all the way down; small, narrow rear door openings; useless running boards; and it's a gas-guzzler. Average reliability. Low ground clearance and large bumpers limit off-road capabilities. Below-average offset crashworthiness and head restraint scores. *QX56:* Major braking defects and other serious quality deficiencies. It's way overpriced for what you get, it depreciates rather dramatically, and it's also a gas-guzzler. The QX56's cargo area is long and rather shallow, providing less maximum cargo capacity than an Escalade or Navigator. A stiff ride is accompanied by excessive engine noise. Too much interior plastic trim (doors and dash top). **New for 2007:** Nothing important.

MODEL HISTORY: In 1997, Nissan waved its magic wand and created another Infiniti out of what was once a Nissan—in this case, a Nissan Pathfinder. Don't be surprised—it had been done before with the Altima/G20 and Maxima/I30. What is surprising, though, is that people buy these high-priced clones simply because they carry the Infiniti moniker. **2001**—A larger 240-hp 3.5L V6 engine on the QX4; reworked instrument panel; improved power-window controls; xenon headlights (you'll love 'em; your neighbours won't); minor exterior restyling; a new roof rack; and a redesigned grille. The previous model had only a 3.3L 170-hp V6 with lower torque. It barely provided adequate performance for the 1,810+ kg (4,000+ lb.) truck.

COST ANALYSIS: A 2007 QX56 goes for about $80,000, but getting a 2006 shaves off several thousand dollars—all before substantial rebates and discounting. Cheaper, used 2004–05 models are money traps: You'll pay big bucks to correct quality deficiencies, and lose money and time. **Best alternatives:** Pre-2001 QX4 models changed little over the years, so look for the cheapest model available. If you want convenience upgrades and 40 extra horses with the V6, a 2001 model with a March 2001 or later build plate is the best choice (the build plate is usually found on the inside edge of the driver's door or door pillar). Credible alternatives would be the Cadillac Escalade, GMC Yukon or Denali, and Toyota Land Cruiser, in addition to the Lexus RX 300/330, Nissan Xterra, and Toyota Highlander. **Rebates:** Look for $5,000–$7,000 discounts or zero percent financing programs. **Delivery/PDI:** $1,653. **Warranty:** Bumper-to-bumper 4 years/100,000 km; powertrain 6 years/110,000 km; rust perforation 7 years/unlimited km. **Supplementary warranty:** Not needed. **Options:** A second-row bench seat to accommodate an eighth passenger. **Depreciation:** Faster than average. **Insurance cost:** Higher than average. **Parts supply/cost:** Good parts supply, but relatively costly. Body parts may be back-ordered. **Annual maintenance cost:** Lower than average, since most of these cars are still under warranty. **Highway/city fuel economy:** *QX4:* 11.8/15.8 L/100 km; *QX56:* 12.1/18.1 L/100 km.

QUALITY/RELIABILTY: Infiniti quality control is no better than average. **Owner-reported problems:** Automatic transmission slippage; many complaints of premature front brake wear, vibration, and noise; minor electrical glitches; driver window won't roll up; body trim defects, door clicking or creaking, paint peeling, and windshield wiper fluid that discolours paint; liftgate and backup sensors beep for no reason; and headliner squeaks and rattles. **Warranty performance:** Average.

SAFETY SUMMARY: Airbags: Side airbags are standard. Reports of airbags failing to deploy. **ABS:** Standard 4W; disc/drum; disc/disc. **Safety belt pretensioners:** Standard. **Traction control:** Optional; standard. **Head restraints F/R:** *1997:* ★; *1999:* ★★; *2001–03:* ★★★★. **Visibility F/R:** ★★★★★. **Maximum load capacity:** *QX4:* 860 lb.

SAFETY COMPLAINTS: All years: Hesitation, followed by sudden acceleration. • Airbags failed to deploy. **1999**—Sudden loss of steering control; steering lock-up; excessive vibration. • Excessive drive shaft vibration. • Distorted front windshield. **2000**—Under-hood fire. **2001**—Airbags failed to deploy. • Stalling when going uphill. • Early automatic transmission replacement. • Complete brake failure. **2002**—Rear suspension bottoms out with four passengers in the car. • Inaudible turn signal indicator. **2003**—Severe rear brake pulsation. **2004**—Passenger's airbag turns off intermittently because of passenger's "light" weight (120 lb.). • Airbags failed to deploy. • Brakes continue to wear out early, and suspension system degrades steering control:

> Infiniti QX56 has brake system design flaw. Front brakes need replacement on average every 4,000–6,000 miles [6,400–9,700 km]. Brake rotors are too small, which causes rotor warpage. As a result, the steering wheel shutters back and forth when brakes are applied. There is no fix for this from Nissan. This brake design flaw also affects similar platforms, such as the Armada and the Titan. There also is a design flaw in the front end, which causes the steering wheel to shake violently when going over bumps at speeds in excess of 45 mph [70 km/h]. Hitting certain bumps in the road can cause the front end to go into resonance, thus shaking the steering wheel enough to lose control of vehicle.

• Sudden loss of cruise control cuts engine power. • Parked vehicle rolled downhill. • False backup alerts. **2005**—Brakes overheat and wear out prematurely, causing severe shaking when braking. **2006**—Four left rear axle bolts sheared off.

Secret Warranties/Internal Bulletins/Service Tips

All years: Brake vibration, excessive vehicle shake, noise, and premature wear are covered in service bulletin Reference ITB00-024b, published August 30, 2004. **1997–2000**—Remedy for steering-wheel vibration and brake pedal pulsation. • Service tips to silence a rear hatch that squeaks or rattles. **1998–2000**—Tips on troubleshooting hard starts at high elevations or low temperatures after vehicle has been parked for a few hours. **2001**—Automatic transmission flares on the 1–2 shift when accelerating from a hard stop and then backing off on the throttle. • Engine won't start, or intermittently fails to start. • Incorrect engine idle speed. • Steering fluid leak near the pump-hose fitting. **2001–02**—Transfer-case oil leak, clunk, or stuck in Low gear. • Steering-column noise. • Speaker static. • Navigation system freezes. **2002–03**—Roof rack whistle. **2002–05**—Adjusting a too-high idle speed. **2003–04**—Vibration/shudder may be related to low engine oil. **2004**—No-starts and transmission malfunctions. • No-start in extreme cold. • Engine knocking. • Inoperative cruise control. • Rear axle clicking. • Front brake shudder. • Inoperative second-row seat actuator. • AC humming. • Inoperative navigation system. • Cabin buffeting noise. **2004–05**—Vehicle won't start. • Poor cooling at idle. • TSB #BR04-004e gives many troubleshooting tips to correct brake shudder, pedal vibration, and vehicle shake. • Mushy brakes; long brake pedal travel. • Fluid leaks from automatic transmission air-cooler line. • Free body control module sub-harness to improve electrical connection for trailering. • Fuel gauge always reads full. • AC condenser fan rattles. • Door clicks and creaks. **2005**—Free replacement of the third-row seat belt buckle. **2004–06**—AC wets front-passenger carpet

QX4, QX56 PROFILE

	1998	1999	2000	2001	2002	2003	2004	2005	2006
Cost Price ($) (negotiable)									
QX4	45,000	45,700	45,500	48,000	48,000	48,800	—	—	—
QX56 (30%)	—	—	—	—	—	—	69,550	75,900	78,200
Used Values ($)									
QX4 ▲	9,000	10,500	14,000	16,000	19,000	24,000	—	—	—
QX4 ▼	8,000	9,500	12,500	15,000	17,000	22,000	—	—	—
QX56 ▲	—	—	—	—	—	—	45,000	52,000	—
QX56 ▼	—	—	—	—	—	—	42,000	49,000	—
Reliability	④	⑤	⑤	⑤	⑤	⑤	❸	❸	—
Crash Safety (F)	—	④	④	④	④	—	—	—	④
Side	—	⑤	⑤	⑤	⑤	⑤	—	—	—
Offset	❷	❷	❷	❷	❷	❷	—	—	—
Rollover	—	—	—	❸	❸	❸	—	—	❸

All ratings on a numbered scale where ⑤ is good and ❶ is bad. See page 220 for a more detailed description.

Kia

2002 TECHNICAL DATA

POWERTRAIN (4X4)
Engine: 2.0L 4-cyl. (130 hp);
Transmission: 4-speed auto.

DIMENSION/CAPACITY
Passengers: 2/3; Wheelbase: 92.9 in.;
H: 65/L: 56.4/W: 68.1 in.; Headroom F/R:
N/A; Legroom F/R: 44.5/31.1 in.; Cargo
volume: 30 cu. ft.; Fuel tank: 60L/regular;
Tow limit: 2,000 lb.; Load capacity: 900
lb.; GVWR: 4,156 lb.; Turning circle: 37
ft.; Ground clearance: 7.9 in.; Weight:
3,365 lb.

2007 TECHNICAL DATA

POWERTRAIN (4X4)
Engines: 2.0L 4-cyl. (140 hp) • 2.7L V6
(170 hp); Transmissions: 5-speed man. •
4-speed auto.

DIMENSION/CAPACITY
Passengers: 2/3; Wheelbase: 103.5 in.;
H: 66.7/L: 171.3/W: 70.9 in., Headroom
F/R: 5.0/4.0 in.; Legroom F/R: 41/29 in.;
Cargo volume: 23.6 cu. ft.; Fuel tank:
58L/regular; Tow limit: 2,000 lb.; Load
capacity: 860 lb.; GVWR: 4,519 lb.;
Turning circle: 35.4 ft.; Ground clearance:
7.7 in.; Weight: 3,344 lb.

RATING: Above Average (2005–07); Below Average (2000–02). On the one hand, the 2005–07 Sportage is a Hyundai Tucson twin that's a better-than-average choice and fairly dependable, thanks to the Hyundai DNA transplant. On the other hand, the 2000–02 model is an entirely different SUV that lacks refinement, is a poor highway performer, and has one of the worst quality-control records in its class. There were no 2003 or 2004 models. **Strong points:** The 2005 and later models are reasonably priced and subject to deep discounting. They also scored a three-star crashworthiness rating in IIHS's offset crash tests. Pre-2005s are dirt cheap, reflecting their poor reputation. **Weak points:** The 2005–06 models scored a one-star rating for head-restraint protection. Pre-2005 models are slow, hard riding, clumsy, and unstable. They have posted unimpressive crashworthiness scores and face an uncertain future with a limited dealership network. As if that's not enough, there are other deficiencies, including brake failures and the premature wearout of the brake rotors and calipers, a constantly shifting automatic transmission, a part-time 4×4 that's not suited for dry pavement use, uneven interior ventilation, a noisy engine and fan, obstructed rear visibility with the raised convertible top, and tight rear seating. **New for 2007:** Nothing important; the 2005 model incorporated the last redesign.

MODEL HISTORY: *Pre-2005:* The early Sportage is a rudimentary compact sport-utility that's an unimpressive performer and full of expensive-to-repair powertrain and body poor-quality "surprises." It's offered as a five-passenger, four-door wagon or a four-passenger, two-door convertible. The only engine available is an anemic 130-hp 2.0L 4-cylinder attached to either a rear-drive or 4×4 system.

The 2005 Sportage is a different car entirely, and it's the only one worth consideration. It uses the Hyundai Tucson's carlike platform, along with Hyundai's 4- or 6-cylinder engines and front-drive or all-wheel drive. Entry-level LXs come with a 140-hp 4-cylinder and a 5-speed manual or 4-speed automatic transmission. LX V6s and EXs offer a gutsier 173-hp V6 that's hobbled a bit by the automatic tranny (the only choice available). Optional AWD lacks low-range gearing and uses a dashboard switch that locks in a 50/50 front/rear torque split. Standard safety features include anti-lock four-wheel disc brakes, traction control, an anti-skid system, front side airbags, and head-protecting side curtain airbags.

COST ANALYSIS: Selling for about $20,000, the 2005 Sportage LX is identical to the 2006 and 2007 models and, thus, represents the better buy. **Best alternatives:** Consider Honda's CR-V, Hyundai's Tucson or Santa Fe, and Toyota's RAV4. Nissan's Xterra and Toyota's Highlander are good second choices. **Rebates:** $2,000 discounts will come out in the late fall. **Supplementary warranty:** Not needed for 2005–07 models, but essential for earlier versions. **Depreciation:** A bit slower than average on recent models; quite fast with early versions. **Insurance cost:** Higher than average. **Annual maintenance cost:** High for early models; predicted to be below average for the 2005 and later versions. **Parts supply/cost:** Parts aren't easily found, but they are reasonably priced. **Highway/city fuel economy:** *Pre-2005:* 10.3/11.9 L/100 km with an automatic transmission; *2005–06 4-cyl:* 7.9/10.6 L/100 km; *2005–06 V6:* 8.4/11.9 L/100 km.

QUALITY/RELIABILITY: Best with current models. The J.D. Power and Associates Initial Quality Study placed Kia either at or near dead last in its annual surveys from 1993–2003, forcing the company's American CEO to admit that "up until 1999, the company wasn't focused on quality." Subsequent Power dependability surveys carried out on the 2006 models still show Kia near the bottom of the ladder; however, Kia and MINI were designated the two "most improved" nameplates, and the 2006 Sportage was given a "Better than Average" quality rating. **Owner-reported problems:** *2000–03:* Fuel and electrical system malfunctions; transmission glitches; AC water leaks; premature catalytic converter, brake pad, and rotor replacement; and poor body fit and finish (rattles, paint peeling, doors often ajar, and wind noise from all doors). *2005–06:* Rear-end squeaking related to the axle spindle. Fuel tank can be "over-filled"—it must then be removed and repaired for about $300. Fragile front and rear windshield wipers and wiper arms:

> The rear wiper arm of the Kia Sportage is made of weak plastic and cannot withstand going through a car wash. The first car wash it went through ripped off the wiper blade and cover over the installation nut. The second car wash then broke the arm.

Warranty performance: Average.

SAFETY SUMMARY: Airbags: Kia includes a unique knee-level airbag to protect the lower extremities. **ABS:** Optional 4W; disc/drum. **Head restraints F/R:** *1997:* ★★★; *1999:* ★★★; *2001–02:* ★★; *2005–06:* ★. **Visibility F/R:** ★★★★★/★. **Maximum load capacity:** *1999 EX:* 860 lb.

SAFETY COMPLAINTS: All years: Fumes enter passenger compartment when driving. • Defective front hub assembly won't let driver shift into 4×4 on the fly. • During highway driving, vehicle vibrates excessively. • Vehicle veers from right to left because of faulty suspension. • When driving, 4×4 comes on and off on its own, leading to vehicle almost going off the road. • Brake lights won't turn off • Sudden failure of the turn signals and flashers. • Seat belts tighten uncomfortably on their own. • Gears grind as they shift into Third or Fourth. • Excessive shaking when braking. • Airbag and ABS lights stay on. • Driver-side shoulder belt doesn't work. • Water leaks through the door frame. **2001**—Chronic stalling. • Complete brake failure. • Low-speed rear-ender caused seatback to collapse. • Vehicle pulls to one side upon acceleration, or it rocks side to side when turning. • Dash indicators fail from blown fuse. • Fuel tank hard to refuel. **2001–02**—Airbags failed to deploy. • Very loose steering. • Check Engine light is constantly lit. • Doors won't latch unless pulled up when closing. **2002**—Fire ignited from oil dripping onto the exhaust manifold. • Gasoline leaks from the vehicle. • Airbags failed to deploy. • Airbag light is constantly lit. • Panel lights go out intermittently. • Steering locks up or has excessive play. • Prematurely worn brake rotors and calipers. • Rear seats move backward or forward when accelerating or braking. • Filler spout spits out fuel. • Driver's door suddenly swings open or freezes shut. • Windows lock up. • Plastic fan blades broke off and struck the radiator. • Water seeping into the hub assembly wears out wheel hubs. **2005**—Airbags failed to deploy in several collisions. • Fuel filler leaks gas. • Electronic stability system causes braking at the wrong time and pulls car in the direction of the braking wheel (see bulletin reference in "Secret Warranties/Internal Bulletins/Service Tips," below). • Recall repairs took five weeks to perform.

Secret Warranties/Internal Bulletins/Service Tips

2001–02—Free catalytic converter replacement under emissions campaign #022. • Front windows won't close at freeway speeds. • Airbag warning light stays lit. • Cooling-fan blade cracking. **2005–06**—Reprogramming campaign to improve the functioning of the electronic stability system (ESP) detailed in TSB #056, published November 2005.

SPORTAGE PROFILE

	2000	2001	2002	2005	2006
Cost Price ($) (negotiable)					
Sportage (19%)	20,995	20,995	22,095	19,995	21,095

Used Values ($)					
Sportage ▲	5,000	7,000	9,000	15,000	—
Sportage ▼	4,000	6,000	8,000	13,500	—
Reliability	❶	❶	❶	④	
Crash Safety (Offset)	❷	❷	❷	❸	❸
IIHS Side	—	—	—	❸	❸

Note: Although there are no recent NHTSA frontal crash tests, the 1997 model (not sold in Canada) garnered three stars. Also, the 2005 jump in the reliability rating is due primarily to the use of more Hyundai-sourced parts.

SORENTO ★★★

2007 TECHNICAL DATA

POWERTRAIN (4X4)

Engine: 3.5L V6 (192 hp); Transmissions: 5-speed man. • 5-speed auto.

DIMENSION/CAPACITY

Passengers: 2/3; Wheelbase: 107 in.; H: 69.3/L: 179.8/W: 74.6 in.; Headroom F/R: 3.0/3.5 in.; Legroom F/R: 40/27.5 in.; Cargo volume: 30.5 cu. ft.; Fuel tank: 80L/regular; Tow limit: 3,500 lb.; Load capacity: 1,145 lb.; GVWR: 5,467 lb.; Turning circle: 39 ft.; Ground clearance: 7.0 in.; Weight: 4,500 lb.

RATING: Average (2005–07); Below Average (2003–04). Kia has a history of having poor quality control with models in their early years and then bailing out when the model doesn't sell. The Sorento has, apparently, escaped that fate. **Strong points:** Competitively priced with lots of standard features, a competent engine, a roomy interior, and a comprehensive warranty. Both low-range gearing and good ground clearance enhance the Sorento's off-road capabilities. **Weak points:** So-so acceleration, mediocre handling and braking, a jolting ride, poor fuel economy, cheap-looking seat upholstery, and a tacky plastic dash. **New for 2007:** The Sorento returns relatively unchanged; the next redesign is scheduled for 2009.

MODEL HISTORY: This SUV crossover *cum* Honda Pilot copycat carries passenger-car genes in a compact SUV body. Although the "torque on demand" 4×4 system is better suited to navigating slippery surfaces than cavorting off-road, the Sorento's full- and part-time low range gearing gives it a decided off-road advantage over Honda's models. Other off-road assets are a wide track, fully independent suspension, high ground clearance, and short front and rear overhangs.

The Sorento's wheelbase is almost as large as the Pilot's, and it has a similar 3.5L V6 powerplant. You won't find the Pilot's third-row seating, though, or the high quality control and resale value found with most Hondas. **2004**—A 5-speed manual transmission. **2005**—Addition of an upgraded 5-speed automatic transmission.

COST ANALYSIS: Choose a 2005 version with its upgraded automatic tranny because it is practically identical to more recent models. The 2006s are priced at $27,895/$34,625/$38,695 (LX/EX/EX Luxury) and should be discounted by about 15 percent. If not, pay about $700 more for a 2007. **Best alternatives:** The Honda CR-V or Pilot, Hyundai Tucson or Santa Fe, Nissan Murano, and Toyota Highlander are all good choices. **Rebates:** Look for $3,000 rebates or zero percent financing programs early in the new year. **Delivery/PDI:** $1,395 (for a Kia?). **Warranty:** Bumper-to-bumper 5 years/100,000 km; powertrain 5 years/100,000 km; rust perforation 5 years/100,000 km. **Supplementary warranty:** Always a smart idea with Kia, though judging by the Sportage evolution, the 2005 and later products are apparently better made. **Options:** Side running boards. **Depreciation:** Average. **Insurance cost:** Higher than average. **Parts supply/cost:** Average; reasonably priced. **Annual maintenance cost:** Average. **Highway/city fuel economy:** 10.9/14.9 L/100 km.

QUALITY/RELIABILITY: Average, and getting better; poor dealer servicing is now the source of most complaints. **Owner-reported problems:** Many owners of 2003–06 Sorentos report crankshaft/accessory pulley and vibration damper bolt failures, causing the loss of power steering capability:

> This problem affects 2003 to 2006 Kia Sorento V6 engines. Many owners have had multi failures of this bolt, the updated bolts fail too. Kia is trying to hide this serious problem and has no intention of a real fix. My 2005 and others are afraid to drive our Kia Sorentos.

Automatic transmission slips out of gear; prematurely worn-out brake rotors and calipers; excessive drive shaft and brake pedal vibration; and fuel and electrical system malfunctions (chronic starting problems, clock not working, lights and gauges inoperative). **Warranty performance:** Average. **Likely failures:** Automatic transmission, fuel and electrical systems, accessories, and brakes.

SAFETY SUMMARY: Thick roof pillars cut visibility, but the large side mirrors compensate somewhat. The 2006–07 models earned a five-star crashworthiness rating for side passenger protection; 2006s also scored well for frontal crash protection (four stars) and were given three stars for rollover prevention. **Airbags:** Standard front, side, and side curtain airbags. **ABS:** Optional 4W; disc/disc. **Head restraints F/R:** 2003–06: ★. **Visibility F/R:** ★★★.

SAFETY COMPLAINTS: 2003—Sudden acceleration; airbags failed to deploy. • Many complaints of hard starts and no-starts, thought to be related to the fuel pump. • Power-steering failures. • Defective front axle (gear oil leakage). • Drive shaft installed upside down. • Automatic transmission self-destructed. • Excessive on-road vibration. • Harmonic balancer's main bolt sheared off, causing severe vibration. • Front axle causes tire to wear faster on the inside. **2004**—Hard starting continues despite multiple fuel-pump replacements. • Hesitation upon acceleration. • Steering assembly failed, spewing fluid onto the engine. • Delayed gear shifts. • When in 4×4, it feels as if the emergency brake is on. • Rear differential bearing failure. • Automatic transmission grinds and then breaks down. • Brakes engaged for no reason. • Excessive on-road vibration despite having drive shaft replaced. • Speedometer reads fast. 2005—Sudden acceleration blamed on faulty engine intake manifold. • Sudden loss of power. • Many reports of quirky airbag sensors that deactivate airbag as if underweight occupant was seated; occupants are advised not to lean on the door or to sit too far forward, or they may disable the system. • Airbags failed to deploy. • Power steering goes out. • Electrical shorts cause light failures and hard starts. • Low-beam headlights overheat and burn out prematurely:

> I have had the headlights replaced twice. They both went out within a day of each other. The first time, I had to pay $129.00 U.S. and the car was less than a year old. The second time, they replaced it under warranty. This is serious. A lot of Kia owners are complaining, but Kia says nothing is wrong.

• Key cannot be removed from the ignition. • Gas spurts out when refuelling.

Secret Warranties/Internal Bulletins/Service Tips

2003—Enhanced power-steering feel. • Hood anti-corrosion treatment. • Rattling heard from the jack compartment. • Service campaign to inspect and re-position the driver's seat belt–buckle wire harness. 2004—Engine misfiring or white smoke signal an engine cylinder head leak. • Hesitation on cold starts. 2005—Free correction of malfunctioning front airbag sensors. • Free wheel guard installation to prevent snow and ice clogging the evaporative air filter.

SORENTO PROFILE

	2003	2004	2005	2006
Cost Price ($) (negotiable)				
Sorento (22%)	29,795	29,845	29,995	27,895
Used Values ($)				
Sorento ▲	16,000	19,500	22,000	—
Sorento ▼	15,000	18,000	20,000	—
Reliability	②	③	④	—
Crash Safety (F)	④	④	④	④
Side	⑤	⑤	⑤	⑤
Offset	③	③	③	③
Rollover	③	—	—	③

All ratings on a numbered scale where ⑤ is good and ❶ is bad. See page 220 for a more detailed description.

Land Rover

Because of their limited production, Land Rover SUVs are included in Appendix II.

Lexus

2007 RX 350 AND 2007 RX 400H TECHNICAL DATA

POWERTRAIN (AWD)

Engines: 3.5L V6 (230 hp) • 3.5L V6 (270 hp) • 3.3L V6 (208 hp) + Electric (68 hp); Transmissions: 5-speed auto. • 6-speed auto. • CVT

DIMENSION/CAPACITY (RX 350)

Passengers: 2/3; Wheelbase: 107 in.; H: 66.1/L: 186.2/W: 72.6 in.; Headroom F/R: 3.0/4.0 in.; Legroom F/R: 41/29.5 in.; Cargo volume: 34.5 cu. ft.; Fuel tank: 73L/regular; Tow limit: 3,500 lb.; Load capacity: 1,385 lb.; GVWR: 5,245–5,520 lb.; Turning circle: 40 ft.; Ground clearance: 7.1 in.; Weight: 4,065 lb.

DIMENSION/CAPACITY (RX 400H)

Passengers: 2/3; Wheelbase: 107 in.; H: 66.4/L: 187.2/W: 72.6 in.; Headroom F/R: 3.0/4.0 in.; Legroom F/R: 41/29.5 in.; Cargo volume: 34.5 cu. ft.; Fuel tank: 65 L/regular; Tow limit: 3,500 lb.; GVWR: 5,245–5,520 lb.; Turning circle: 37.4 ft.; Ground clearance: 7.1 in.; Weight: 4,365 lb.

RATING: *RX 300, RX 330, RX 350:* Average (2004–07); Above Average (1999–2003). The rating has been lowered post-2003 because of Toyota's engine sludge problems, dangerous automatic transmission delayed shifts, complete loss of braking ability, sudden acceleration, and inadequate, theft-prone headlights. These vehicles are not suitable for serious off-roading. *RX 400h:* Not Recommended (2006–07). Ridiculously expensive and unproven, it's essentially a more fuel-frugal RX 330 with plenty of horsepower and full-time AWD. If you must go "green," get a cheaper used Toyota Highlander and keep one more new vehicle off the roads. **Strong points:** *RX 300:* Strong powertrain performance; handles well; fully equipped; top-quality mechanical components and fit and finish; pleasant riding (better than the Acura MDX and Mercedes' M series); plenty of passenger room; very comfortable seating; lots of small storage areas; easy entry and exit; and slow depreciation. Reliability has been its strong suit over many years. *RX 330:* Quieter, longer, wider, slightly taller, a bit more powerful, and with a longer wheelbase than its predecessor. Comfortable rear seats are adjustable and are easily folded out of the way. Better interior ergonomics, and ride comfort doesn't deteriorate with a full load. Much better emergency handling than with the RX 300. Improved fuel economy; can take regular unleaded fuel. Predicted to be quite reliable. **Weak**

points: *RX 300:* Pricey, and it's too big and heavy for sporty handling. No low-range gearing for off-roading, and traction control is optional. Thick roof pillars obstruct outward visibility. Head restraint crashworthiness for 2004–06 models rated "Poor" by IIHS. Instrument displays wash out in direct sunlight. Tilt steering wheel may not tilt sufficiently for some drivers. Expect some wind noise, squeaks, and rattles in addition to wind roar from the moonroof. Limited rear storage area, with a high liftover and excessive wind noise. Takes premium fuel. *RX 330:* Additional power is undermined by the added kilos. Dangerous shift delay when downshifting with the automatic transmission. There's considerable body lean when cornering, the suspension bottoms out easily and there's excessive bouncing and body roll with original-equipment shocks, and steering could be more sensitive. Front and rear seat cushions lack thigh support. Thick rear roof panels obstruct visibility. No third-row seating, and the sloping rear end cuts into cargo space. The power rear door is slow to open, and the moonroof takes up too much headroom. Reduced ground clearance. The optional navigation system screen washes out in sunlight. High freight charges would make Tony Soprano proud. Overpriced when compared to the Toyota Sienna or Highlander. *RX 400h:* Way overpriced, simply to avoid a few extra trips to the gas station. The long delivery wait means that you may be charged more a few months later, unless your contract price is "protected." Makes you a captive customer of Toyota/Lexus and limits where you can go for servicing. The $8,000 (U.S.) battery replacement cost may require a bank loan to pay off. Crashworthiness hasn't been tested yet. Unusually long time for the vehicle to start; slow and vague steering; and the instrument panel power gauge is too small. The 18-inch wheels and beefy P235/55R18 tires don't enhance fuel efficiency. **New for 2007:** *RX 330:* Morphs into the RX 350 and now carries a 3.5L V6 that boosts horsepower from 223 to 270. A 6-speed automatic transmission is also new this year. The next redesign is scheduled for the spring of 2008. *RX 400h:* Returns relatively unchanged.

MODEL HISTORY: The RX is a compact luxury sport-utility based partly on Toyota's passenger-car platform. It's a bit longer and wider than a Jeep Grand Cherokee, and it's sold as either a front-drive or permanent all-wheel drive. Available only with a 4-speed automatic transmission and a Camry/Lexus ES 300–derived, upgraded 220-hp V6, the RX 300 handles competently on the highway but isn't suitable for off-roading because of its lack of low-range gearing and its tall, four-door wagon body.

First launched in Canada as a 1999 model, the RX 300 was a pioneer "crossover" SUV that combined minivan versatility with the practicality of a 4×4 drivetrain, suitable for light tasks. And as practically the only game in town for its first several years on the market, many critics ignored this Lexus' many shortcomings and aging design. Now all that's changed, with Acura, Ford, Nissan, Hyundai, and Toyota raising the bar with their cutting-edge SUVs and, in Toyota's case, with a revamped Sienna minivan that offers the same features and performs just as well—for a lot less money.

RX 330 and 350

Introduced as a 2004 replacement for the RX 300, Lexus calls the RX 330 a "luxury utility vehicle." And yes, it does eclipse the old model with its many luxury features and extra-cost gadgets, extra interior room, and an upgraded powertrain. But, in many ways, competing minivans have more utility, more room inside, more seats, and even, as in the Toyota Sienna, four-wheel drive. All they lack is the RX 330's luxury cachet.

The RX 330 and 350 offer a good ride, a plush and innovative interior, great all-around visibility, plenty of power, all-wheel drive, and better-than-average quality and reliability. Not bad for a bestselling SUV cobbled together from ES 330, Camry, and Sienna parts. **2005**—Roll-sensing side curtain airbags, rain-sensing wipers, and an eight-way power passenger seat.

RX 400h

The RX 400h Lexus hybrid debuted last year as a 2006 model, joining other hybrid models like Toyota's Prius and Highlander, Honda's Insight and Civic, and Ford's Escape. Toyota hopes that by putting the hybrid system in a luxury Lexus, it will get back the high costs of hybrid technology—an impossible feat with a $30,000 Toyota Prius. In fact, industry insiders say Toyota loses thousands of dollars with each Prius sale.

In addition to the hybrid fuel system, your 12,000 extra loonies buy you a vehicle stability-control system, leather upholstery, power tilt/telescoping steering wheel, power moonroof, DVD navigation system with rear backup camera, six-disc CD changer, HID headlights with adaptive lighting, and 18-inch wheels.

The 3.3L 230-hp engine is detuned to just 208 horses; however, when coupled to the 68-hp electric motor, there's a net gain in horsepower. Like the Prius, it operates mainly by allowing the gasoline and electric motors to kick in when the engine load varies. For example, the electric motor is used when accelerating from a stop or in city traffic, while the gasoline engine is useful for highway cruising. If you floor the accelerator, both motors work in unison to give you the extra horsepower needed (posting 0–100 km/h acceleration scores of about 7 seconds). Nevertheless, Lexus hybrid technology isn't as refined as that of the Honda Accord hybrid, which shuts down half the engine's cylinders when carrying a light load to save even more gas.

Fortunately, there's no need to recharge the battery pack. That's done by the gasoline-engine generator. Toyota guarantees the battery for eight years. A new pack will cost about $8,000 U.S., or a few thousand dollars more than what the vehicle will be worth.

Other reasons to be wary of a hybrid-equipped vehicle: Fuel economy is hyped by 15–40 percent; cold weather performance isn't as fuel-efficient; repairs and servicing are dealer-dependent; highway rescuers are wary of cutting through the high-voltage electrical system to save occupants; there's no long-term reliability data; the vehicles have a faster-than-average rate of depreciation; and you have to drive several hundred thousand kilometres to amortize the hybrid's start-up costs.

COST ANALYSIS: The 2006 RX 400h sells for about $62,000, or $12,000 more than the $50,500 AWD RX 330. The 2007 versions of both vehicles will likely cost a couple thousand dollars more. **Best alternatives:** *RX 330 and 350:* Consider buying a Toyota Highlander as a cheaper, more reliable, and more refined alternative. Any used RX 300 is also a good buy. Other vehicles worth considering are the Nissan Murano and the Toyota 4Runner. **Rebates:** Not likely. **Delivery/PDI:** $1,775. **Warranty:** Bumper-to-bumper 4 years/80,000 km; powertrain 6 years/110,000 km; rust perforation 6 years/unlimited km. *RX 400h:* 96 months/160,000 km (applies to the battery control module, hybrid vehicle control module, hybrid vehicle battery, and the inverter/converter). **Supplementary warranty:** Not necessary for the RX 330; a prudent idea with the RX 400h. **Options:** The $7,000+ Premium and Ultra Premium Package bundled options are a waste of money. The moonroof has generated many complaints about excessive wind noise entering the cabin. **Depreciation:** Slower than normal, but not slow enough to pay for a new battery pack. **Insurance cost:** Above average. **Parts supply/cost:** Parts are taken from the Camry bin and are reasonably priced. **Annual maintenance cost:** Average. **Highway/city fuel economy:** *RX 300:* 9.7/13.0 L/100 km; *RX 330:* 9.0/12.8 L/100 km; *RX 400h:* 8.1/7.5 L/100 km. (Remember that hybrids save the most fuel in city use, where the electric motor proves its worth.)

QUALITY/RELIABILITY: Good quality control for most years except 2004, where brake, transmission, and headlight failures reign. Hybrid quality and durability is still unproven. **Owner-reported problems:** The automatic transmission lurches between gears and lags in shifting at low speeds, making the car vulnerable to rear-enders. The fuel gauge gives inaccurate readings, and there have been some minor electrical shorts, prematurely worn brake calipers and warped rotors, excessive brake noise, and a variety of interior squeaks and rattles. Also, there are some body trim defects, and the instrument panel display may be too dim. *RX 400h:* The continuously variable transmission has had a checkered past, with early failures reported by other automakers (like Saturn); independent repairers are unable to service it. Sudden, unintended acceleration and engine surging make for risky winter driving. **Warranty performance:** Lousy on the 2004. Shame on Toyota/Lexus for telling its RX 330 customers that it's "normal" to drive with a dangerously defective transmission:

> The automobile has a latent defect and is inherently dangerous. In November 2003, I attempted to back up in a crowded parking lot, and while in reverse, I pressed the accelerator—there was a lag and the vehicle then accelerated backward very rapidly,

striking another vehicle. I assumed the fault was my own (since in moving my foot from the accelerator to the brake, my foot was caught under the brake because the pedals are close together, but that is another item) and after the vehicle was repaired (approximately $7,000 worth of damage) I resumed driving the vehicle. On June 29, 2004, again I was attempting to back up and again the vehicle was in reverse and again when I pressed on the accelerator, there was a lag and then again the vehicle accelerated rapidly backwards, striking a building. It is estimated that the damage to the vehicle is over $10,000, and I do not know what the cost of the damage to the building is. Interestingly, as well, in neither case did the airbags deploy. The second incident received some local press coverage, and on July 8, 2004, I received a call from a visitor to Massachusetts from Florida who had heard about the second incident.... [O]n July 1, 2004, that driver, while in a parking lot, had also had sudden rapid acceleration and had struck a building.... [She] also stated that she had heard of a third incident in Massachusetts of a Lexus RX 330 striking a building following sudden acceleration. The faulty transmission, coupled with the power and torque of the vehicle and the resulting sudden acceleration, is a serious defect; I will not drive the vehicle again. The response of the Lexus dealer when the incidents were reported to it was silence.

SAFETY SUMMARY: Airbags: Standard front and head-protection side airbags; a driver's knee airbag. There have been reports of airbags failing to deploy. **ABS:** Standard; disc/disc. **Safety belt pretensioners:** Standard. **Traction control:** Standard. **Head restraints F/R:** *1999:* ★★★; *2001–03:* ★★★★★; *2004–06:* ★ **Visibility F/R:** ★★★★★/★★. **Maximum load capacity:** *1999:* 880 lb.; *2001:* 840 lb.

SAFETY COMPLAINTS: All years: Sudden, unintended acceleration. • Airbags failed to deploy. **1999**—Engine overheating and under-hood fires. • Car suddenly accelerated when shifted from Reverse to Drive. • Right rear axle sheared in two, causing the wheel to fall off and vehicle to roll over. **2000**—During hard acceleration from a standing start on dry pavement, the left front tire loses traction and spins free, causing vehicle to veer to the left. • A power distribution problem in the transfer case causes the wheels to lock up at 100 km/h. • Displays on the instrument panel are too dim. • If the wireless remote entry is used to lock the vehicle with an occupant inside, that person may be trapped inside if he or she doesn't exit the vehicle within 30 seconds. • When vehicle is travelling at 70–100 km/h, air entering through the open sunroof makes the whole vehicle shake and produces a horrendous noise. • Original-equipment tires aren't acceptable for off-roading. **2001**—Engine compartment burst into flames after slowly accelerating from a stop. • Transmission jumped from Park to Reverse. • Defective jack. **2002**—Vehicle rolls backward when stopped on a hill. • Sunroof doesn't offer pinch protection. • Cupholders are too shallow. **2003**—Airbags failed to deploy. • Major rear blind spot. **2004**—139 safety-related incidents reported; a few dozen would be normal. Most of the complaints concern transmission lag and lurch, accompanied by sudden acceleration. • Cruise control would not release. • Many complaints that brakes failed because of a faulty brake booster. • Side airbags failed to deploy. •

Suspension defect causes car to pull into oncoming traffic. • Poor headlight illumination:

> The headlights on a 2004 RX 330 have cost me a lawsuit against dealer. Drove car second night, 3 miles [5 km], on country roads. I had motion sickness after that experience. Every time I hit a bump, the car lights would bounce, as if on a spring. The line from lights goes across center of windshield at eye level. The driver can't see beyond 20 ft [6 m]. When looking beyond 20 ft, you see total darkness. When passing a person on the side of the road you can only see them from the knees down. Very scary driving the RX 330 at night.

• Dash reflects onto the windshield. • Wipers don't clean effectively. • Suspension bottoms out with a 320 kg (700 lb.) load. • Hatch closed on driver's neck. • Rear window shattered for no reason. **2005**—Automatic transmission delay when downshifting or when accelerating. • Xenon headlights are often stolen. • Headlight low beam falls short. • White taillight lens reflects sunlight and can blind drivers following the vehicle. • Exhaust fumes are sucked into the cabin if the rear hatch is left ajar. *RX 400h:* **2006**—Erratic cruise-control operation. • Vehicle constantly pulls to the left. • Sudden, unintended acceleration and engine surging make for risky winter driving:

> The vehicle does not gear down while going down an icy road. There are no 1st, 2nd or 3rd gears. There is no way to stop the vehicle from hydroplaning. The dealership determined that this is the way the vehicle is designed to operate. Consumer no longer owns the vehicle and feels this is a safety hazard.

Secret Warranties/Internal Bulletins/Service Tips

All years: Free engine sludge repairs. • Lexus blames rotten-egg exhaust smells on fuel, not on its vehicles. **1999**—If the MIL alert comes on, you may have to install an improved air/fuel ratio sensor under the emissions warranty. • A 2–3 shift shudder can be corrected by installing an upgraded transaxle valve body. • Tips on improving the driver-side door master switch. • To reduce noise and vibration at idle speeds, a dynamic damper has been added to the centre exhaust pipe. • There are dozens of bulletins that address the correction of various squeaks and rattles found throughout the vehicle. • Countermeasures are outlined to reduce wind-rushing noise from the moonroof wind deflector panel. **1999–2000**—Glove box rattling and front suspension noise. **1999–2001**—Measures to silence front brake squeal (see bulletin). **2000**—Correction for noisy front wheel bearing. • Low-speed drivetrain noise and vibration will be corrected for free up to

---

BRAKES—FRONT SQUEAL NOISE

BULLETIN NO.: BR001-02   DATE: MARCH 22, 2002

1999–2001 RX 300

To reduce brake squeal noise, which may occur during brake application while backing up and/or while turning, the front brake disc rotor, the anti-squeal shim, the pad support plate, ** and the brake pad ** have been modified. This warranty is in effect for 48 months or 50,000 miles [80,000 km], whichever occurs first, from the vehicle's in-service date.

6 years/116,000 km (72,000 mi.), says TSB #SU007-02, dated November 22, 2002. • More glove box rattles. • Outside mirror stress cracks. **2001–03**—Front seatback popping or clicking. • Inoperative mirror compass. **2002**—Drivetrain vibration. **2002–03**—Troubleshooting front brake vibration. **2002–06**—Diagnosis and repair of vehicles that pull excessively to one side. **2003**—Remedy for ABS brake noise. **2004**—Free replacement of the exhaust manifold converter assemblies under "Special Service Campaign" #3LE to curb excessive exhaust noise. Lexus has a deal with Enterprise Rent-A-Car to pay $47 per day for a rental if the dealer has no loaner vehicles available. Additionally, owners will get a free full tank of gas, a free car wash up to $20, and a refund for repairs done at a "remote facility" (this probably means an independent garage). One replacement per car is authorized, and there are no ownership, time, or mileage restrictions. • A brake booster upgrade. • Front brake vibration remedy. • Coolant may leak from a crack in the base of the radiator. "Limited Service Campaign" #4LF says Lexus will replace radiators for free through October 31, 2007, and allow for a $45 daily rental rebate. • Drone, vibration upon acceleration. • AC groaning, moaning; diminished blower speed. • Inoperative power back door. • Deceleration hump/thump. • Front suspension creaking and knocking. • Hatch area creak or tick. • Glove box and instrument panel rattles. • Rear wiper upgrade. **2004–05**—No-start in cold weather. • Toyota/Lexus suggests a remedy for "poor shift quality" in an August 11, 2003, bulletin (#TC005-03). Owners say this didn't fix the lagging and lurching shifts. In May 2005, Toyota proposed another remedy and revised the earlier service bulletin, which kept its original bulletin number • Front-door window noise. • Troubleshooting dash rattles. • Free headlight theft-prevention kit. **2004–06**—Rear door-stay improvement. **2005**—Upgraded front brake rotors should silence a high-pitched front brake squeal. **2005–06**—Unacceptable power backdoor operation.

RX 300/RX 330 PROFILE

	1999	2000	2001	2002	2003	2004	2005	2006
Cost Price ($) (negotiable)								
RX (28%)	46,000	46,640	53,000	51,250	51,600	49,900	50,200	50,500
Used Values ($)								
RX ▲	16,000	20,000	23,000	27,000	32,000	39,000	43,000	—
RX ▼	15,000	18,000	21,000	25,000	30,000	37,000	41,000	—
Reliability	⑤	⑤	⑤	⑤	⑤	❷	❸	—
Crash Safety (F)	—	—	④	④	④	⑤	⑤	—
Side	—	—	⑤	⑤	⑤	⑤	⑤	—
Offset	⑤	⑤	⑤	⑤	⑤	⑤	⑤	⑤
Rollover	—	—	❸	❸	❸	—	—	—

Note: Unlike other hybrids, the RX 400h hardly depreciated at all during its first model year; a used 2006 (its first year) is worth close to 95 percent of its original selling price.

2007 GX 470 TECHNICAL DATA

POWERTRAIN (4X4)

Engine: 4.7L V8 (263 hp); Transmission: 5-speed auto.

DIMENSION/CAPACITY

Passengers: 2/3/3; Wheelbase: 109.8 in.; H: 74.6/L: 188.2/W: 74 in.; Headroom F/R1/R2: 4.0/6.0 in./N/A; Legroom F/R1/R2: 41.5/29/24 in.; Cargo volume: 43.7 cu. ft.; Fuel tank: 87L/premium; Tow limit: 6,500 lb.; Load capacity: 1,329 lb.; GVWR: 6,200 lb.; Turning circle: 41 ft.; Ground clearance: 7.5 in.; Weight: 4,825 lb.

RATING: Above Average (1998–2007); Average (1997). **Strong points:** Strong, smooth V8 engine performance; car-like handling; an adjustable suspension; hill-descent control; user-friendly instrumentation and controls; lots of passenger and cargo room; comfortable seating; pleasant ride; excellent fit and finish; and exceptional reliability. "Good" head-restraint crashworthiness score (LX 470). **Weak points:** Acceleration is only fair, the brakes are overly sensitive, and the ride can be busy. Difficult middle-row entry and exit; antiquated rear-seat folding system (Honda's Pilot gets it right); cramped third-row seats; side-opening tailgate can be inconvenient; lots of tire and wind noise; and poor fuel economy. Owners report automatic transmission "thumping." Head restraints and roof pillars may obstruct rear vision. "Poor" head-restraint crashworthiness score (LX 450 and 2003–06 GX 470). No front or side crashworthiness data. **New for 2007:** Nothing important.

GX 470

MODEL HISTORY: Having made its debut in early 2003, the GX 470 is a mid-sized, four-door luxury SUV that bridges the price and performance gap between the RX 300 series and the LX 470. With promised seating for eight adults (don't be too hopeful), this newer entry has a minivan's passenger-carrying capability without the minivan "mommy-mobile" cachet.

Set on a modified truck platform and lacking an independent rear suspension, the GX 470 doesn't have as comfortable a ride and isn't as manoeuvrable as its car-based brethren. Downhill Assist Control helps drivers maintain control on very steep descents (I still think independent rear suspension would be more useful). **2005**—35 extra horses, a roll-detection sensor, a rear-view camera, and a tire-pressure monitor.

LX 450

MODEL HISTORY: Even though it was only around for the 1997 model year, the LX 450 offered a full array of safety, comfort, and convenience features that included full-time 4×4 and a nicely appointed interior. Additionally, owners were attracted to the SUV's benchmark quality, first-class assembly, and slow rate of depreciation. Many buyers, however, have been a bit reluctant to buy what is essentially a Land Cruiser with extra side cladding and prominent wheel arches. Other minuses: The LX 450 has ponderous handling and is a gas-guzzler equipped with a small fuel tank. The 450's 212-hp 4.5L inline 6-cylinder is hooked to an electronically controlled 4-speed automatic transmission.

LX 470

MODEL HISTORY: Launched in early 1998, the 230-hp 4.7L V8-equipped LX 470 still has all of its Land Cruiser trappings and a few additional features that are all its own, including a 2,903 kg towing capacity, adaptive variable suspension, stability-control, automatic height control, rear air conditioning, side running boards, and an in-dash CD changer. The 470 comes with only an automatic transmission, however.

The V8 engine, based on that of the Lexus LS 400, provides lots of low- and mid-range torque, essential to propel the 470's extra heft to 100 km/h in less than 10 seconds. Off-roading is no problem, either, thanks to the transfer case's low-range gearing and a centre differential that locks in low range for better traction. These SUVs can seat up to eight passengers, though the third-row seat isn't suitable for anyone larger than a pre-teen. Other sport-utilities have more room but not as much off-road capability.

2000—Standard vehicle stability-control, power sunroof, and illuminated running boards. **2002**—Navigation system becomes a standard feature. **2003**—Additional airbags, a small horsepower boost, a new gated shifter for the 5-speed automatic, improved steering and brakes, a voice-controlled navigation system, 18-inch wheels, rain-sensing windshield wipers, radio controls on the steering wheel, and a new grille, bumper, headlights, and lower rear hatch. **2004**—A rear-view camera was added.

COST ANALYSIS: The 2007 GX 470 and LX 470 will cost about $68,000 and $101,000, and they aren't much different from the 2006s. Earlier versions have about 35–40 fewer horses. **Best alternatives:** Some credible Toyota alternatives are the 4Runner or Sequoia. **Rebates:** Expect $5,000 discounts and attractive leasing programs to kick in by early 2007. **Delivery/PDI:** $1,775. **Warranty:** Bumper-to-bumper 4 years/80,000 km; powertrain 6 years/110,000 km; rust perforation 6 years/unlimited km. **Supplementary warranty:** Not necessary. **Options:** None. **Depreciation:** Much slower than average. **Insurance cost:** Above average. **Annual maintenance cost:** Average. **Parts supply/cost:** Parts are often back-ordered and can be costly. **Highway/city fuel economy:** *GX:* 11.4/15.7 L/100 km; *LX:* 12.9/17.9 L/100 km.

SAFETY SUMMARY: Amazingly, these luxury toys have never been crash-tested by NHTSA. **Airbags:** Standard front, side, and side curtain airbags. Reports of airbags failing to deploy. **ABS:** Standard 4W; disc/disc. **Safety belt pretensioners:** Standard. **Traction control:** Standard. **Head restraints F/R:** *1997 LX 450:* ★; *1999:* ★★★; *2001–03 LX 470:* ★★★★; *2003–06 GX 470:* ★. **Visibility F/R:** ★★★★/★★.

SAFETY COMPLAINTS: *GX 470:* **2004**—Airbags failed to deploy. • Excessive drive shaft vibration. • Loose steering; vehicle wanders all over the road, requiring constant steering corrections. • Premature wearout of brake rotors and calipers. • Child safety seat cannot be installed to perform safely. • Footrest jams under the brake pedal. *LX 470:* **1999**—Airbag failed to deploy. **2000**—Sudden, unintended acceleration. **2003**—Airbags failed to deploy. **2004**—Engine surges when the AC compressor is activated. • Gas tank will only fill up two-thirds of the way.

Secret Warranties/Internal Bulletins/Service Tips

GX 470: **2002–06**—A correction for steering that pulls vehicle to one side. **2003–04**—Rear drive shaft clunk, thump. • Driveline vibration, groan. • AC cools the vehicle poorly. • A rotten-egg exhaust odour signals the need to install an upgraded catalytic converter. • Field fix for a difficult-to-open rear door. **2003–05**—No-start in cold weather. • Highway-speed steering flutter. **2005**—Inaccurate fuel gauge. *LX 470:* **1998–99**—AC noise can be silenced by replacing the expansion valve. • Roof rack wind noises may be caused by improperly installed crossbars. **1998–2000**—If the AC fan continues to run after the ignition has been turned off, it's likely caused by a corroded relay. Lexus has a repair kit that will correct the problem. • To eliminate a transfer-case buzzing at moderate speeds, TSB #NV008-00 suggests installing an upgraded high-speed output gear and shift lever assembly. • The in-dash CD player and changer may work erratically. Lexus will replace it under warranty. **1998–2003**—Steering-column noise/roughness. **1998–2006**—Correction for a booming exhaust at idle. **2001–02**—Front brake vibration. • Continuous alarm chime noise. • Upgrade to reduce telescopic steering-wheel noise and enhance smoothness. **2002**—Brake vibration. • Noisy, rough telescopic steering. • Upgraded rear-view mirror. **2001–06**—Ways to silence A-pillar wind noise. **2002–06**—A correction for steering that pulls vehicle to one side. **2004–06**—Inconsistent ride height.

GX470, LX 470 PROFILE

	1998	1999	2000	2001	2002	2003	2004	2005	2006
Cost Price ($) (negotiable)									
GX 470 (30%)	—	—	—	—	—	—	66,800	67,700	68,400
LX 450 (30%)	82,000	83,265	83,265	90,100	90,600	98,200	99,950	100,400	101,400

Used Values ($)								
GX 470 ▲	—	—	—	—	—	—	51,000	56,000	—
GX 470 ▼	—	—	—	—	—	—	49,000	54,000	—
LX 470 ▲	18,000	22,000	28,000	34,000	43,000	51,000	65,000	75,000	—
LX 470 ▼	16,000	20,000	26,000	32,000	40,000	48,000	62,000	72,000	—
Reliability	⑤	⑤	⑤	⑤	⑤	⑤	⑤	⑤	—
Crash Safety (Offset/GX)	—	—	—	—	—	⑤	⑤	⑤	⑤

Mercedes-Benz

Because of their limited production, Mercedes SUVs are covered in Appendix II.

Mitsubishi

ENDEAVOR ★★★

2007 TECHNICAL DATA

POWERTRAIN (PERMANENT AWD)
Engine: 3.8L V6 (225 hp); Transmission: 4-speed manumatic
DIMENSION/CAPACITY
Passengers: 2/3; Wheelbase: 108.3 in.; H: 67.3/L: 190.2/W: 73.6 in.; Cargo volume: 40.7 cu. ft.; Fuel tank: 81L/ premium; Tow limit: 3,500 lb.; GVWR: 5,250 lb.; Turning circle: 38.4 ft.; Ground clearance: 8.3 in.; Weight: 3,847 lb.

RATING: Average (2004–07). A decent-performing mid-sized SUV that was spun off the 2004 Galant sedan platform, giving it carlike handling and a comfortable ride. **Strong points:** A strong 225-hp 3.8L V6; a liftgate with separate opening glass; "Good" IIHS offset crashworthiness scores; and an NHTSA five-star rating for front- and side-impact crashworthiness. **Weak points:** Off-roading is compromised by the lack of low-range gearing; cornering produces excessive body lean; fuel-thirsty; head-restraint protection rated "Poor" by IIHS; and side curtain airbags are unavailable. Depreciation is more rapid than usual. **Best alternatives:** Honda Pilot, Nissan Pathfinder, and Toyota Highlander or 4Runner. **New for 2007:** Nothing significant; Mitsubishi is putting its development and marketing money into the redesigned Outlander.

MODEL HISTORY: This mid-sized SUV carries five passengers and offers front-drive or all-wheel drive. Safety features include four-wheel disc brakes, a tire-pressure monitor, 17-inch alloy wheels, standard front and side airbags (XLS and Limited), traction control (2WD XLS and 2WD Limited), and ABS (optional on the 2WD LS). The Endeavor has been priced around $35,000 for the past three model years; however, dealer discounts of up to 20 percent are quite common. There is also the car's rapid depreciation to consider: A used 2004 that sold originally for $34,000 is now worth only $19,000, and a 2005 goes for between $21,000 and $23,000. This is good news if you buy used, but it's a bit distressing if you have to sell within the first five years.

QUALITY/RELIABILITY: Average. **Likely failures:** Automatic transmission (whine and flaring); brake pads and rotors; power windows, door locks, and plastic outside door handles; windshield wiper motor; heater core; AC (debris collects in the housing and blower motor); and radiator (it's easily punctured due to the large grille opening and the absence of a shield or deflector, and it costs about $700 to replace). Water leaks into the driver's footwell area due to a plugged AC hose. Front windshield may shatter, and liftgate glass may also shatter as the liftgate is closed.

Secret Warranties/Internal Bulletins/Service Tips

2004—Power seats operate poorly. • Troubleshooting tips for eliminating a body whistle produced when the vehicle is underway. **2004–05**—A spark knock, engine ping, and delayed shift may be caused by a miscalibrated powertrain control module (PCM). • Troubleshooting tips to reduce gear whine. • Shift delay and/or no Overdrive. • Shift flare when going from Second to Third gear. • Steering column noisy when turning. • Poor AC performance. • AC water leaks. • Plugged HVAC drain. • Torn seat side seam (cloth seats). • Body noise diagnosis and repair. • Water leaks into the rear of the vehicle. • Fuel tank is hard to fill.

ENDEAVOR PROFILE

	2003	2004	2005	2006
Cost Price ($) (negotiable)				
Base (22%)	32,497	33,998	34,298	34,998
Used Values ($)				
Base ▲	17,000	19,500	22,000	—
Base ▼	15,000	18,000	20,000	—
Reliability	❷	❸	❸	—
Crash Safety (F)	④	④	④	⑤
Side	⑤	⑤	⑤	⑤
Offset	❸	❸	❸	⑤
Rollover	❸	—	—	—

All ratings on a numbered scale where ⑤ is good and ❶ is bad. See page 220 for a more detailed description.

2006 TECHNICAL DATA

POWERTRAIN (PERMANENT AWD)
Engine: 3.8L V6 (215 hp); Transmission:
5-speed manumatic

DIMENSION/CAPACITY
Passengers: 2/3/2 Wheelbase: 109.7
in.; H: 71.5/L: 190.2/W: 74.8 in.; Cargo
volume: 39.8 cu. ft.; Fuel tank: 90L/
premium; Tow limit: 3,500 lb.; GVWR:
5,997 lb.; Turning circle: 37.4 ft.; Ground
clearance: 8.6 in.; Weight: 4,718 lb.

RATING: Average (2004–06); Below Average (2003). There's nothing fundamentally wrong with Mitsubishi's cars (like the low-cost Colt compacts, the 1991–99 3000GT, and the Stealth sporty coupe), but the SUVs look much better than they drive. And charging $50,000 for a Montero is close to committing a felony. The problem is the company itself: It's always one step away from bankruptcy, its officials are doing jail time for concealing defects and paying Yakuza mobsters to hush irate stockholders, and DaimlerChrysler has slashed its investment in Mitsubishi while treating its former partner with benign neglect. Chrysler's action will, undoubtedly, negatively impact warranty claims and servicing. Plus the dropping of the Montero this year will drive down resale values and complicate servicing even more. **Strong points:** Seats seven, and features lots of passenger and cargo room. The classy interior has well-designed seats; an attractive, user-friendly dash and cabin controls; and good fit and finish. There's also low-range gearing for off-roading; anti-skid and traction control, beginning with the 2003s; and ABS on four-wheel disc brakes. A good reliability record is another plus. *Montero Sport:* Overall performance is quite similar to the Montero, although the Sport's crashworthiness ratings are better. NHTSA gives frontal crashworthiness for the 2001–04 models four stars and side protection for the 2002–04 models five stars. IIHS also rates the Sport "Good" in providing offset crash protection. **Weak points:** The V6 is adequate for highway use, but it requires a full throttle for passing and merging, hurting fuel economy. A tightly sprung chassis degrades handling and ride comfort. Lots of body lean in turns, and steering isn't as precise as the Japanese competition's. Problematic rear-seat access. IIHS says 2001–06 Monteros give only "Average" offset crash protection and have head restraints that are "Average," as well. The Montero also has a high propensity to roll over: *Consumer Reports* magazine found the 2001–03 models tend to roll over under hard cornering, a conclusion also reached by NHTSA in its two-star rollover rating given to the 2001–04 models. Rear head restraints block rearward vision and have been judged by the IIHS as giving "Poor" collision protection. Rapid depreciation—the top-of-the-line 2005 Limited sold for almost $50,000 new and is now worth less than $30,000. *Montero Sport:* Overpriced and quick to lose resale value. For example, the entry-level 2003 Sport sold for $32,497; its resale price now varies between $14,000 and $16,000. It's more trucklike than the Montero, resulting in poor handling, an uncomfortable ride, considerable wind and engine noise, and excessive fuel consumption. Entry and exit are made difficult by the low roofline and high floor. The narrow rear bench seat is uncomfortable. Head restraints have been ranked "Below Average," and the 2004 and later models don't come with standard side airbags, though 2003 and earlier models did. **New for 2007:** Montero will be dropped from production during the 2006 model year.

MODEL HISTORY: Going into its 12th year in the States, Mitsubishi's sales have been a roller coaster ride that now looks like it has evened out. Sales and profits are picking up, and the company is putting out acceptable and competitively priced products. Development and marketing money is tight, though, so don't look for many loonies to be spent on improving the 2007 lineup, except for the Outlander's redesign. Montero owners, on the other hand, are the not-so-proud owners of an auto "orphan" that has been axed to pay for Mitsubishi's new model realignment.

The base Montero uses a 215-hp 3.8L V6 coupled to a 5-speed manumatic transmission. The Sport employs a 197-hp variant and seats five passengers, rather than seven. Montero also offers a third-row bench seat that folds flush with the cargo floor. Standard features include front side airbags; ActiveTrac 4×4, suitable for prolonged use on dry pavement; low-range gearing; ABS; anti-skid/traction control; rear air conditioning; and a power sunroof. Side curtain airbags aren't available. **2004**—Standard front side airbags become optional. **2005**—17-inch wheels.

QUALITY/RELIABILITY: Likely failures: Owner complaints have targeted airbag (failure to deploy), tie-rod, brake (rotors and pads), Bridgestone tire, and electrical system failures. Chronic stalling is also a common complaint. The 1999–2003 Sport models are noted for costly speedometer failures, covered in TSB #03-23-002.

Secret Warranties/Internal Bulletins/Service Tips

All models/years: Engine pinging diagnosis. **1997–2005**—Diagnosis and correction of body squeaks when turning. **2001–04**—Rear seat won't unlatch. **2004**—Shift delay and/or no Overdrive. **2005**—Engine valve lifter noise diagnosis.

MONTERO PROFILE

	2003	2004	2005	2006
Cost Price ($) (very soft)				
Montero Sport	32,497	—	—	—
Montero	48,507	48,550	48,748	48,598
Used Values ($)				
Montero Sport ▲	16,000	—	—	—
Montero Sport ▼	14,500	—	—	—
Montero ▲	21,000	26,000	32,000	—
Montero ▼	19,000	24,000	30,000	—

All ratings on a numbered scale where ⑤ is good and ❶ is bad. See page 220 for a more detailed description.

Reliability	❷	❷	❸	—
Crash Safety (F/Sport)	❹	—	—	—
Side (Sport)	❺	—	—	—
Offset (Sport)	❸	—	—	—
Rollover (Sport)	❷	—	—	—

Note: There are no recent NHTSA crashworthiness ratings for the Montero. The last frontal crash test gave the 1997 model a three-star designation.

OUTLANDER ★★★★

2007 TECHNICAL DATA

POWERTRAIN (PERMANENT AWD)
Engine: 3.0L V6 (220 hp); Transmission: 6-speed auto.

DIMENSION/CAPACITY
Passengers: 2/3; 2/3/2 Wheelbase: 105 in.; H: 66.1/L: 182.7/W: 70.9 in.; Cargo volume: 39.3 cu. ft.; Fuel tank: 59L/regular; Tow limit: 3,500 lb.; Load capacity: 970 lb.; GVWR: 4,431 lb.; Turning circle: 39 ft.; Ground clearance: 8.5 in.; Weight: 3,527 lb.

RATING: Above Average (2007); Average (2004–06); Below Average (2003). Mitsubishi is finally giving the 2007 Outlander the much-needed powertrain and handling enhancements that this little SUV has lacked since its debut. **Strong points:** *2006 and earlier models:* The redesign producing 20 more horses and a quieter cabin for 2004 was a good start, but more power is needed and steering/suspension geometry isn't sufficiently refined. Stable handling. Longer than most SUVs in the compact class, so there's plenty of cargo room. Prices are heavily discounted, and depreciation is fairly dramatic. The front-drive 2006 sells for $23,998 before $2,000–$3,000 rebates and discounting; add another $1,000 for the upgraded 2007. **Weak points:** *2006 and earlier models:* Weak, noisy engine; fuel-thirsty; automatic transmission constantly downshifts; not suitable for off-roading; steering is way too light; and there's too much body lean. Other minuses are the narrow body, excessive road noise, weak dealer network, and "Poor" IIHS–rated side crashworthiness. **Best alternatives:** Honda CR-V, Hyundai Tucson, and Toyota RAV4. **New for 2007:** A new platform that accommodates seven seats, versus last year's five, and a 220-hp 3.0L V6 hooked to a 6-speed automatic transmission. This setup provides 60 more horses than last year's puny 4-beater. Also new are standard stability and traction control, a lower centre of gravity, side and side curtain airbags, a lowered cargo floor, and a tailgate extension flap/seat capable of supporting up to 180 kg (400 lb.)

MODEL HISTORY: This compact SUV was originally a spin-off of Mitsubishi's Lancer, which explains its carlike handling and ride. Unfortunately, the Lancer's 140-hp 2.4L 4-banger is no match for the larger and heavier Outlander, even with its transmission set in manual mode. On top of that, the lack of low-range gearing compromises its off-road capability. Smart buyers will opt for a used 2004 version with its 20 extra horses and other improvements. The Outlander seats five comfortably, though tall occupants may wish for a bit more legroom. It also offers good all-around visibility and is easy to enter and exit. **2005**—A manual transmission, upgraded airbags, four-wheel disc brakes, updated styling, and new Limited features.

QUALITY/RELIABILITY: Likely failures: Brake pads and rotors, and interior and exterior trim.

SAFETY COMPLAINTS: 2003–05—Shift flare when going from Second to Third gear.

OUTLANDER PROFILE

	2003	2004	2005	2006
Cost Price ($) (firm)				
Outlander	26,757	24,458	23,348	23,998
Used Values ($)				
Outlander ▲	12,500	14,000	16,500	—
Outlander ▼	11,500	13,500	15,000	—
Reliability	❸	❸	❸	—
Crash Safety (F)	❹	❹	—	—
Side	❺	❺	—	—
IIHS Side	❶	❶	❶	—
Offset	❺	❺	❺	❺
Rollover	❸	—	—	—

Nissan

MURANO ★★★★

RATING: Above Average (2005–07); Below Average (2003–04). The Murano is essentially a tall Altima AWD with serious steering, alternator, and transmission problems afflicting its first two model years. **Strong points:** Powerful, responsive engine, carlike handling, an easily accessed interior, and plenty of passenger and cargo room. **Weak points:** Some serious reliability and safety deficiencies up to the 2005 model year (like leaking fuel tanks). A stiff ride; poor rear visibility; and limited off-road use. Fit and finish may disappoint. **New for 2007:** Nothing significant; a redesign is planned for the 2008 model year.

MODEL HISTORY: This is a stylish five-passenger, mid-sized SUV crossover wagon that's essentially a tall wagon with 4×4 capability. Built on the Altima sedan's

All ratings on a numbered scale where ❺ is good and ❶ is bad. See page 220 for a more detailed description.

platform, the $38,798 Murano uses a permanently engaged all-wheel-drive system as well as front-drive. Wearing huge 18-inch wheels and equipped with a continuously variable transmission (CVT) hooked to a 245-hp 3.5L V6, the Murano combines performance with comfort. It features standard four-wheel disc brakes with Brake Assist (BA) and Electronic Brakeforce Distribution (EBD).

With its 245 horses and CVT transmission, the Murano accelerates effortlessly, posting some of the fastest times in its class. The car rides comfortably with little jostling of passengers when passing over uneven terrain. The SE's sport-tuned suspension adds very little to ride quality.

2007 TECHNICAL DATA

POWERTRAIN (PERMANENT AWD)
Engine: 3.5L V6 (245 hp); Transmission: CVT

DIMENSION/CAPACITY
Passengers: 2/3; Wheelbase: 111.2 in.; H: 66.5/L: 187.6/W: 74 in.; Headroom F/R: 3.5/5.0 in.; Legroom F/R: 40/29 in.; Cargo volume: 32.6 cu. ft.; Fuel tank: 82L/premium; Tow limit: 3,500 lb.; Load capacity: 1,055 lb.; GVWR: 4,918–5,051 lb.; Turning circle: 40 ft.; Ground clearance: 5.5 in.; Weight: 3,847 lb.

On the downside, the CVT has been troublesome and takes some getting used to (it slips rather than shifts), and third-row seating isn't available. The body feels cheap. There's lots of wind buffeting with the windows or sunroof open, first-year models were plagued by a variety of squeaks and rattles, and the doors don't sound solid when closed. The optional navigation system is complicated to operate. Furthermore, despite the Murano's rugged looks, it can't handle serious off-roading, and its towing ability is quite limited at 1,587 kg (3,500 lb.) when equipped with a $750 tow package.

COST ANALYSIS: Best alternatives: The Honda Pilot and Toyota Highlander. **Rebates:** $5,000 by year's end. **Delivery/PDI:** $1,314. **Warranty:** Bumper-to-bumper 3 years/60,000 km; powertrain 5 years/100,000 km; rust perforation 5 years/unlimited km. **Supplementary warranty:** Not needed. **Options:** Navigation system and "Cold Package" (heated seats and mirrors) add $3,000 to the price with little benefit. **Depreciation:** Slower than average. **Insurance cost:** Much higher than average. **Annual maintenance cost:** Average. **Parts supply/cost:** Parts aren't easily found and can be expensive. **Highway/city fuel economy:** 6.8/11.7 L/100 km.

QUALITY/RELIABILITY: Better-than-average quality, which is all the more surprising considering that the 2004 redesigned Altima, Armada, Maxima, Quest, and Titan versions have been plagued by unreliable components and poor fit and finish. **Owner-reported problems:** Poor fuel economy; sudden loss of power; faulty engine computer module (ECM), throttle body, engine oil seals, and AC amplifier; no current through PIN connectors; CVT transmission won't hold vehicle stopped on an incline; transmission and alternator failures; chronic ABS brake failures (actuator and sensor); premature brake wear; a variety of interior squeaks and rattles; and shock absorber thunking. **Warranty performance:** Fallen to below average.

 SAFETY SUMMARY: Adjustable pedals. **Airbags:** Front, rear, and side. **ABS:** Standard 4W; disc. **Head restraints F/R:** 2003–05: ★; 2006: ★★. **Visibility F/R:** ★★★★★/★.

SAFETY COMPLAINTS: All years: Airbags fail to deploy. • Brake calipers and rotors wear out prematurely. **2003**—Sudden, unintended acceleration. • Early transmission failure. • Vehicle vibrates violently when driven with the rear windows down. • Front seat rocks, causing driver's seat belt to tighten progressively. • Suspension is hard and stiff; with a full load, the Murano tends to bounce around. • Doors randomly lock themselves. • Rear roof pillars block view rearward. • Wipers clog easily; can't be raised to wipe off accumulated snow and ice without opening the hood. • Ineffective defroster system. • False Open Door alert. **2003–04**—Complete loss of power steering; sometimes occurs when turning steering wheel rapidly. • Alternator failure causes stalling, loss of power, and no-starts; preceded by the illumination of the Brake and Battery warning lights (see *www.nissanmurano.org*):

> 2004 Nissan Murano SE AWD with only 1,901 miles [3,000 km] had the alternator fail today. The car completely lost power, leaving me unable to accelerate or use power steering or braking functions. Occurred on local city streets—had this occurred on the highway, travelling at highway speeds, it could have easily led to an accident.

• Early replacement of the CVT transmission and transfer case. **2004**—Shifts out of Park without the keys in the ignition. • Gas tank is vulnerable to puncture from road debris. • Loose, leaking power-steering line. • Low brake pedal causes foot to hit the accelerator pedal. • Wipers get bent out of shape. • Headlight switch moves too easily; it inadvertently turns off the lights. • Xenon headlights are easily stolen. **2005**—Gas tank leaks fuel and is vulnerable to damage from road debris:

> Noticed gas leaking on the parking lot. I proceeded to Jamestown, NY (50 miles [80.5 km]), to take the car to the closest Nissan dealer. Signature Nissan 716-664-0175 discovered that something had gone through the gas tank and I would need to replace it. He showed me how the gas tank drops down and has a smooth unprotected surface facing forward where [road debris] (whatever it was that hit the tank) went through the plastic surface.

• Cruise control cuts out, and vehicle suddenly slows down when ascending or descending hills. • Transmission often slips into "limp" mode. • Chronic throttle body failures cause stalling or loss of power. • Vehicle suddenly jumps to the right when passing over bumps. • Alternator failures continue despite a recall to correct the problem. • Child safety seats difficult to install. • Distorted windshields. • Windshield washer spray nozzle doesn't adequately clean passenger-side windshield.

All ratings on a numbered scale where ⑤ is good and ❶ is bad. See page 220 for a more detailed description.

2002–03—Engine fails to start. • Automatic transmission clicking noise. • ABS or Airbag light may remain lit. • Doors lock and unlock intermittently, front window rolls down, and alarm sounds. • Centre console lid is hard to close. • Inoperative interior courtesy lamps. 2003–04—Front brake vibration. • Defective sunroof. • Door glass ticking. 2003–06—Hard starts, no-starts in cold weather may call for the replacement of the power distribution module (PDM).

MURANO PROFILE

	2003	2004	2005	2006
Cost Price ($) (negotiable)				
Murano (17%)	39,500	37,700	37,900	38,998
Used Values ($)				
Murano ▲	24,000	26,000	29,500	—
Murano ▼	22,500	24,000	27,500	—
Reliability	❸	❸	❹	—
Crash Safety (F)	❹	—	❹	❺
Side	❺	❺	❺	❺
Offset	—	❺	❺	❺
Rollover	❹	❹	❹	❹

PATHFINDER, ARMADA   ★★★★/★★★

RATING: *Pathfinder:* Above Average (2006–07); Average (1990–2005); Below Average (1987–89). *Armada:* Average (2007); Below Average (2005–06); Not Recommended (2004). Performance wasn't the early Pathfinder's strong suit, and you still have to pay big bucks for the LE's more refined drivetrain and performance enhancements. **Strong points:** The powerful and smooth 4.0L V6 matches some V8s for impressive acceleration and reserve power while delivering good fuel economy and a 2,720 kg (6,000 lb.) towing capability. Standard stability-control provides acceptable handling and a stiff ride. Little road or wind noise, and plenty of cargo room. The quiet interior is nicely finished with plenty of standard convenience and comfort features plus third-row seating. An attractive and user-friendly dashboard is at the head of the class in terms of clear instrumentation and easily accessed controls. SE and LE transmissions have low-range gearing on recent models. Very slow depreciation. **Weak points:** Handling can get scary at times, as the vehicle tends to wander over the highway and twists violently when passing over bumps. Weak suspension. Second- and third-row seats are cramped. Side and head-protection airbags are optional. Limited visibility to the rear. Gas hogs. *Pathfinder: 2004 and earlier models:* Lethargic engine. Part-time 4×4 isn't to be used on dry pavement, subpar emergency handling, and unimpressive braking. Vehicle can be hard to control when going over a bump. Difficult entry and exit

2007 PATHFINDER TECHNICAL DATA

POWERTRAIN (REAR-DRIVE/AWD)

Engine: 4.0L V6 (270 hp); Transmission: 5-speed auto. OD

DIMENSION/CAPACITY

Passengers: 2/3/2; Wheelbase: 112.2 in.; H: 73.3/L: 187.6/W: 72.8 in.; Headroom F/R: 2.5/3.5 in.; Legroom F/R: 42.4/34.2 in.; Cargo volume: 17.4 cu. ft.; Fuel tank: 80L/premium; Tow limit: 1,186–1,424 lb.; Load capacity: 1,415 lb.; GVWR: 5,050–5,300 lb.; Turning circle: 40 ft.; Ground clearance: 8.3 in.; Weight: 4,682 lb.

2007 ARMADA TECHNICAL DATA

POWERTRAIN (PERMANENT AWD)

Engine: 5.6L V8 (305 hp); Transmission: 5-speed auto.

DIMENSION/CAPACITY

Passengers: 2/3/3; Wheelbase: 123 in.; H: 69/L: 207/W: 79 in.; Headroom F/R1/R2: 6.0/5.0/0.5 in.; Legroom F/R1/R2: 41.5/33.5/27 in.; Cargo volume: 58.5 cu. ft.; Fuel tank: 106L/regular; Tow limit: 9,100 lb.; Load capacity: 1,375 lb.; GVWR: 6,800 lb.; Turning circle: 44 ft.; Ground clearance: 9.0 in.; Weight: 5,715 lb.

because of a high step-up and doors that aren't wide enough to permit easy access. Rear has barely adequate leg space and restricted visibility. Rear seats lack sufficient back support and aren't easily folded out of the way. Standard running boards on the LE are more decorative than practical. No third-row seating. A history of sudden, unintended acceleration. Poor fuel economy. *Armada:* Terrible safety and reliability history. **New for 2007:** *Pathfinder:* Nothing significant. *Armada:* A minor restyling.

MODEL HISTORY: Introduced in 1987, the Pathfinder has developed slowly over the years. Originally based on the Nissan pickup, it was seriously underpowered until 1990, when multipoint fuel injection was added to the 3.0L V6, which boosted horsepower from 153 to 180. **1991**—A four-door body came on the scene. **1993**—Better side-impact protection. **1994**—The LE 4×4 luxury model debuts, and a new instrument panel is introduced. **1995**—Debut of a 4×2 version of the LE. **1996**—Redesigned model is more powerful, longer, taller, wider, and 91 kg (200 lb.) lighter. The new engine is a 3.3L 168-hp V6 hooked to a part-time 4×4 powertrain (not for dry pavement) with shift-on-the-fly. Also, a unibody platform, dual airbags, and standard four-wheel ABS. **1997**—Door map pockets, and an Infiniti QX4 clone. **1999**—A mid-year facelift. **2001**—Given a 3.5L V6 (240–250 hp). The QX4's on-demand All-Mode drivetrain given to the LE, making it okay for dry pavement, though the SE's system can't be used on dry pavement. Other new features are standard cruise control and a restyled interior. **2002**—A slight restyling, and larger wheels. **2003**—Traction control, front side/curtain airbags, and user-friendly child-seat anchors were offered for the first time. **2005**—Redesigned as a larger, more luxurious version of the Xterra, the 2005 Pathfinder was given a 270-hp 4.0L V6, independent double-wishbone front and rear suspensions, and a standard third-row seat for seven-passenger seating. A 5-speed automatic is the only transmission available.

The four-door Pathfinder, introduced in 1990, gives a bit better access to the rear seat. But entry and exit are still problematic, with a high step-up and doors that are still not wide enough, though they are larger than in previous years. Recent models have the spare tire mounted under the vehicle, where it's more vulnerable to premature corrosion and highway contaminants.

The base engine until 1996 is a wimpy 3.0L V6, developed for passenger cars; it does a respectable job in pulling the Pathfinder's substantial weight, but it lacks the low-end torque of an Explorer or Cherokee.

Handling isn't the Pathfinder's strong suit, either. There's lots of body roll in turns, and braking distance is unacceptably long. Some people will find the ride harsh, owing to the stiffer suspension and Nissan's adoption of a unibody frame instead of the separate body-on-frame construction used in most large sport-utilities.

The 3.3L V6 delivers so-so acceleration, and it's noisy when pushed; a more refined and efficient 3.5L V6 replaced it in March 2000. It was then replaced by the much better performing 4.0L V6 in 2005.

Armada

A new Pathfinder Armada arrived in 2004 and then ditched the Pathfinder name for 2005. Built on the Nissan Titan pickup platform, it's a larger, meaner-looking SUV with more angular lines, a 305-hp 5.6L DOHC V8, and a 5-speed automatic that it shares with the Titan. Armada's long wheelbase gives it a longer interior with plenty of cargo room. The short front and rear overhangs add to the Armada's manoeuvrability. Interior amenities provide exceptional versatility, roominess, and flexibility—including standard fold-flat second- and third-row seats; the most second-row legroom in the full-sized, light-duty SUV class; and a full-length overhead console.

COST ANALYSIS: Used second-series 2005s look like the best deal for price and quality. The 2006–07 versions (S/SE/Off-Road/LE) are mostly carryovers and don't merit their higher prices ($37,498/$41,198/$42,198/$47,298). **Best alternatives:** The Honda Pilot; Lexus RX 300/330; Nissan Murano, X-Trail, or Xterra; and Toyota Highlander. **Rebates:** $5,000 rebates and zero percent financing. **Delivery/PDI:** $1,307. **Depreciation:** Slower than average for the Pathfinder; Armada is faster than average. **Warranty:** Bumper-to-bumper 3 years/60,000 km; powertrain 5 years/100,000 km; rust perforation 5 years/unlimited km. **Supplementary warranty:** Not needed. **Options:** Worthwhile options include electronic stability- control (ESC), remote keyless entry, theft-deterrent system, rear window defroster and wiper, and air conditioning. Not recommended are fender flares (standard on the LE) and large tires that will make turning in tight corners more difficult. Don't take original-equipment Firestone or Bridgestone tires. **Insurance cost:** Higher than average. **Annual maintenance cost:** Average; easily repaired by independent garages. **Parts supply/cost:** Parts are widely available and of average cost. **Highway/city fuel economy:** *3.5L V6:* 11.1/14.2 L/100 km; *4.0L V6:* 10.4/15.5 L/100 km.

QUALITY/RELIABILITY: Powertrain components, electronics, and brakes are often troublesome. Paint and trim are acceptable, but body hardware quality has been below average for some time. The Pathfinder's overall reliability is average; Armada's is way below average, with even more complaints relating to poor-quality brakes. **Owner-reported problems:** The engine intake manifold, automatic transmission, electrical and cooling systems, brakes, and exhaust components are problematic. Owners also report underbody squeaks and vibration:

> My 2005 Nissan Pathfinder LE has a loud squeak/vibration coming from the under-body. Dealer (Ramsey Nissan—Ramsey, NJ) has confirmed that the source of the loud squeak/vibration is due to the change in design for the "fuel pump spring assembly." Apparently, the 2004 Pathfinder had a 2 spring design which was changed to a 1 spring design in 2005. Once the fuel tank becomes pressurized (car running for approximately 10 minutes), a loud, constant, and obtrusive squeak/vibration comes from underneath the car. To date, Nissan does not have a fix for this which is unacceptable since the vibration is coming from a critically sensitive area such as the fuel tank. This is an expensive vehicle that should not sound and feel like it is 10 years old.

Brakes can be extremely noisy, particularly when applied while the vehicle is in Reverse. Armada owners report excessive wind noise; roof, door, and dash rattles; a harmonic hum that occurs when the defroster is activated; and leaking sunroofs. **Warranty performance:** Warranty service and customer relations are below average, particularly since Nissan sales have taken a nosedive during the past year.

ROAD PERFORMANCE: Acceleration/torque: The 4.0L V6 transforms the Pathfinder into an impressively powerful SUV. Power is delivered smoothly with little engine noise. **Transmission:** Usually functions smoothly, but there are some reports of delayed downshifts when passing. Long-term durability may be a problem. LE's 4×4 is more useful and refined than the SE's system. **Steering:** A bit vague and over-assisted at times. Turning radius is larger than the competition's. **Routine handling:** Barely acceptable. The vehicle tends to wander and shake when passing over bumps—poor brakes, shocks, and steering are the chief culprits. Ride is a bit jarring. **Emergency handling:** Not good. Moderate body lean in turns. Armada handling is particularly poor. **Braking:** Average in controlled tests; bad in real-world practice.

SAFETY SUMMARY: The 2006 and 2007 Pathfinders and Armadas earned four stars for frontal crash protection and a three-star rollover rating. **Airbags:** Optional side and head-protection side airbags. **ABS:** Standard 4W. **Safety belt pretensioners:**

Standard. **Traction control:** Optional; standard. **Head restraints F/R:** *1997:* ★; *1999:* ★★★/★★; *2001–03:* ★★/★; *2005–06:* ★★. **Visibility F/R:** ★★★★★/★ **Maximum load capacity:** *1996:* 1,060 lb.; *2001:* 1,030 lb.

SAFETY COMPLAINTS: All years: Many reports of sudden, unintended acceleration after coming to a stop. • Airbag failures. • Sudden loss of steering control, lock-up. • ABS brake lock-up and failure. • Transmission failure. • Gas and brake pedals are set too close. **1999**—Electrical arcing beneath hood at right front fender, along wiring harness from ABS actuator to fuse block; caused wiring insulation to ignite while vehicle was parked. • Steering-wheel lock-up caused driver to lose control. • Complete engine and brake failure on a hill with no guardrail. • When in 4×4 High, 4×2 High won't engage. • Excessive vibration felt throughout vehicle while driving 70 km/h, and then a severe front-end shimmy kicks in around 100 km/h. • Sudden steering lock-up. • Premature tread wear, blowouts with Bridgestone tires. • Front driver-side strut, housing, and bearings self-destructed. **2000**—Excessive steering-wheel vibration (steering rack replaced). • ABS doesn't work properly on wet pavement. **2001**—Brake pedal takes too much effort to stop vehicle; extended stopping distances are the result. • All gauges and instruments fail intermittently. • Steering pull and excessive body vibration at 100 km/h. • Passenger-side window suddenly exploded. • Strut-tower bolt broke. • Although rated to pull 2,250 kg (5,000 lb.), vehicle flipped while pulling a 1,400 kg (3,100 lb.) trailer. **2002**—Stuck throttle. • Rear window fell out. **2003**—Excessive shaking when brakes are applied. **2004**—Pathfinder has 13 complaints logged in NHTSA's database; Armada has 124. **2005**—Rear hatch flies open while underway. • Entire electrical system shuts down during highway travel. *Pathfinder:* **2004**—Automatic "roll-up" windows can be dangerous to children. • Brake failure caused a collision. • Multiple brake problems include early wearout of rotors and pads, grinding, and vibration. • Brake wiring harness interferes with foot travel from accelerator to brake pedal. **2005**—Rear suspension can barely support four passengers. • Excessive highway wander and violent shaking occurs when passing over a bump:

> 2005 Nissan Pathfinder becomes very unstable at highway speeds when hitting a bump. The vehicle rocks violently diagonally and sways out of the lane. It also bottoms out constantly [ever] since it was new with no load in it. Dealer has attempted a fix by reprogramming the vehicle dynamic control, this has not fixed the problem. This vehicle is extremely unsafe to drive at any speed above 40 mph [64 km/h]. Driver feels as if he has lost total control when hitting a bump. I followed my wife when she was driving the vehicle and it appears that the rear shocks are trying to over-compensate for every little bump as they are jumping up and down like crazy as the vehicle drives over bumps.

Armada: **2004**—Surging, stalling engine. • Early brake pad wearout, rotor warpage, and master cylinder failures:

Fourth time since April 2004: The 2004 Pathfinder [Armada]'s brakes deteriorate to the point of imminent failure. The steering wheel vibrates and shakes, the brake pedal travel increases, and brakes become unresponsive. Rotors have been cut, pads replaced, rotors replaced, caliper "kits" installed, pins replaced, grease applied, etc. The problem keeps returning. Many other annoyance type problems as well...rattles, navigation system failure, radio replaced, overhead console cracked, replaced window motors and switches, poor wheel alignment from factory.

The Nissan Armada has been designed with a much inferior brake system [with regard to its size and weight]. They have cut costs by installing a Nissan Frontier brake system, which weighs about half the weight of a Nissan Armada. This has caused the brakes to give out every 5,000 miles [8,000 km] and also creates an unsafe braking system. It also allows the vehicle to dive when braking, not giving a safe braking reaction time. The dealerships have constantly replaced my brakes (three times within 15,000 miles [24,000 km]) and did admit that Nissan has admitted to [using] an inferior braking system.

• Middle seat shoulder strap won't unbuckle; failed in a collision, tossing child and safety seat forward. • Third-row centre seat belt failed. • Airbag sensor shuts off airbags even if a 110-pound occupant is seated. • Low tire-pressure warning light comes on in cold temperatures. • Stuck fuel gauge. • Window regulators break easily. **2005**—Brake failures continue unabated, apparently due to brakes that are undersized for this size of this vehicle. • When passing over bumps, steering wheel jerks sharply to one side; it feels loose and sloppy. • Windshield glass distorts visibility.

Secret Warranties/Internal Bulletins/ Service Tips

All years: Brake noise, vibration, and pulling to one side are diagnosed in a comprehensive bulletin #NTB00-033B, issued August 30, 2004. • Brake pedal slowly drops to the floor. • Vehicle wanders. **1996–99**—If the MIL light comes on, it may be because of poor grounding between the intake manifold and the engine cylinder head. • TSB #96-032 addresses hard starting and no-starts. **1996–2002**—Transfer-case noise or hard shifting. **1999–04**—Engine overheating or coolant problems traced to a faulty radiator cap. **2000–02**—Rear suspension bottoms out. **2001**—Computer module may have incorrect idle setting. • Power-steering fluid leak near the pump hose

---

FRONT BRAKE VIBRATION/ PULSATION/JUDDER

BULLETIN NO.: NTB03-091   DATE: OCTOBER 8, 2003

BRAKE JUDDER FROM FRONT BRAKES
2001–03 Pathfinder (R50)
While braking, a steering wheel shake, body vibration, or brake pedal pulsation (also known as "brake judder"), especially during high speed braking.

ACTIONS:

- Check front wheel bearing axial end play.
- "Turn" the front brake rotors using an On-Car Brake Lathe.
- Install the new front brake pads and hardware kit (see Parts Information).
- Burnish the brake pads.

All ratings on a numbered scale where ⑤ is good and ❶ is bad. See page 220 for a more detailed description.

fitting. **2001–02**—Transfer case stuck in 4×4 Low. • Troubleshooting navigation system malfunctions. • Steering-column noise when turning. • Front brake problems (see bulletin). **2001–04**—Headlight fogging. **2002**—Roof rack noise or poor appearance. **2002–05**—Idle speed too high. **2003**—ABS light stays lit. • Roof rack whistles. • Tire pressure monitor stays lit. **2003–04**—Oil leak in transfer case. **2004**—Special campaign to tighten the differential's left front flange-fixing bolt to prevent oil leakage or excessive noise. **2005**—Defective power seat (driver-side). • Free body control module sub-harness. • AC clunk, thump noise. • Popping noise from rear of headliner. • Poor AM radio reception. • Engine and sunroof rattles. **2005–06**—Right front seatback rattles and moves sideways. • Tailgate rust near licence plate. *Armada:* **2004**—No-starts in cold temperatures likely caused by a defective powertrain control module. • Remedies for brake vibration, etc., are found in bulletin #NTB04-066b, issued August 31, 2004. • Tips on silencing AC humming. • Rear axle clicks. • Countermeasures for a brake pedal that feels mushy or has too much travel. • Wind noise from rear side-door window. • Sunroof water leaks. • Cracked overhead DVD console. • Faulty cruise control. • Inoperative navigation system. • Booming noise when passing over rough roads. • Slow tire leak. **2004–05**—Free body control module sub-harness.

PATHFINDER, ARMADA PROFILE

	1998	1999	2000	2001	2002	2003	2004	2005	2006
Cost Price ($) (soft)									
Pathfinder 4X4 (27%)	30,898	33,800	34,700	34,700	34,700	34,200	34,200	36,500	37,698
Armada (30%)	—	—	—	—	—	—	53,500	53,500	54,498
Used Values ($)									
Pathfinder ▲	8,000	10,000	12,000	14,000	16,000	19,000	23,000	26,000	—
Pathfinder ▼	7,500	9,000	10,500	13,000	14,500	17,500	22,000	24,000	—
Armada ▲	—	—	—	—	—	—	35,000	41,000	—
Armada ▼	—	—	—	—	—	—	33,000	39,000	—
Reliability	❸	❸	❹	❹	❹	❹	❹	❹	—
Armada	—	—	—	—	—	—	❶	❸	—
Crash Safety (F)		❹	❹	❹	❹	—	—	❹	❹
Side	—	❺	❺	❺	❺	❺	❺	❺	❺
Offset	❷	❷	❷	❷	❷	❷	❷	—	—
Rollover (2X4)	—	—	❷	❷	❷	❷	—	—	❸
4X4	—	—	—	❸	❸	❸	—	❸	❸

2007 TECHNICAL DATA

POWERTRAIN (REAR-DRIVE/4X4)
Engine: 4.0L V6 (265 hp); Transmissions:
6-speed man. • 5-speed auto.
DIMENSION/CAPACITY
Passengers: 2/3; Wheelbase: 106.3
in.; H: 74.9/L: 178.7/W: 72.8 in.;
Cargo volume: 13.7 cu. ft.; Fuel tank:
80L/regular; Tow limit: 5,000 lb.; Load
capacity: 1,138 lb.; GVWR: 5,200 lb.;
Turning circle: 37.7 ft.; Ground clearance:
9.5 in.; Weight: 4,275 lb.

RATING: Above Average (2005–07); Average (2003–04); Below Average (2000–02). **Strong points:** Reasonably priced, a competent off-roader and highway cruiser (with the 4.0L V6), smooth-shifting automatic transmission, good braking, interior space for five adults, well laid-out instruments and controls, elevated rear seats, and good handling and ride. Engine and transmission skid plates and a short front overhang enhance its off-road prowess. Depreciation is quite slow, and first-year quality-control problems were minimal. **Weak points:** The underpowered 4-cylinder and early V6 engines are most suitable for off-road use where torque is more important than speed, but they could still use a few more horses. The supercharged V6 doesn't impress and requires premium fuel. All three older engines are noisy and fuel thirsty. The part-time 4×4's low-range gearing could be lower, steering is a bit over-assisted for highway driving, and the pre-2002 knee-banging handbrake is an irritant. Early-model dash gauges are hard to read, and small rear-door openings complicate entry and exit. To get more cargo space with 2004 and earlier versions, you must first remove the flimsy blocks of foam that were passed off as the rear-seat cushions. Seats are hard and lack thigh support. There's insufficient rearward seat travel for tall drivers. Some engine, wind, and road noise. **New for 2007:** Nothing important.

MODEL HISTORY: Essentially a $34,000 Frontier and Pathfinder spin-off, the Xterra is a four-door, five-passenger sport-utility vehicle that's longer and wider than the Jeep Cherokee. Its fully loaded top price is a few loonies less than what one would pay for an unadorned Pathfinder. The 2004 and earlier models came with a base 2.4L 4-cylinder (XE version) or an optional 3.3L V6 or supercharged variant. Top-line models offer rear-drive or 4×4; however, the 4×4 isn't to be used on dry pavement. **2001**—Minor revisions. **2002**—An optional supercharged V6 and limited slip differential. **2003**—An additional 10 horses, optional head-protecting side curtain airbags, an anti-skid system, 16-inch alloy wheels, optional tire pressure monitoring, side step rails, 90 more watts for the entertainment system, a new driver-seat height and lumbar support adjuster, and dual 12-volt power outlets. **2005**—Redesigned as a smaller version of Nissan's Titan and Frontier pickups, the 2005 Xterra now uses the Pathfinder's platform, but with a solid rear axle instead of the independent one used by Pathfinders. The 4-banger is replaced by a more powerful V6 coupled to new transmissions that equip the 350Z. In addition to being wider and taller, the wheelbase has been stretched a couple of inches, enhancing ride comfort and interior room, most of which is given to rear-seat passengers. Seats are more practical and comfortable; there's a newly available fold-down front passenger seat (great for skis); the instrument panel has been revised; and the radio and climate controls in the centre console have been made more user-friendly. The roof rack has a latching lid, ground clearance is higher, and the Off-Road model now uses high-performance gas shocks.

COST ANALYSIS: Best alternatives: Get a larger, more powerful, second-series used 2005 for $23,000—it's practically identical to the new 2006 or 2007 versions that will cost a whopping $33,748 and $34,500, respectively. Other vehicles worth considering are the Honda CR-V, Hyundai Tucson or Santa Fe, and Toyota RAV4 or Highlander. **Rebates:** $3,500 rebates, and zero percent financing. **Delivery/PDI:** $1,276. **Warranty:** Bumper-to-bumper 3 years/60,000 km; powertrain 5 years/100,000 km; rust perforation 5 years/unlimited km. **Supplementary warranty:** Not necessary. **Options:** Stability-control is a worthwhile option for the 2005 and later models. Stay away from the dealer-ordered Firestone/Bridgestone tires. **Depreciation:** Very slow. **Insurance cost:** Above average. **Annual maintenance cost:** Less than average. **Parts supply/cost:** Good supply of relatively inexpensive parts. **Highway/city fuel economy:** 2.4L: 9.2/12.6 L/100 km with a manual transmission; 3.3L: 11.4/14.2 L/100 km with a manual transmission, 11.1/14.8 L/100 km with an automatic; 3.3L and 4×4: 11.9/14.5 L/100 km with a manual tranny, 11.7/15.6 L/100 km with an automatic; 4.0L: 10.4/14.0 L/100 km with a manual, 10.4/15.0 L/100 km with an automatic. Be careful with this last estimate: "Real-world" owner reports say fuel consumption on vehicles equipped with an automatic gearbox is actually 15–20 percent higher than the government/industry figures.

QUALITY/RELIABILITY: Owner-reported problems: Complaints of transmission failures; oil, transmission fluid, and coolant leaks; cooling system problems; assorted squeaks and rattles; steering clunk or rattle; front bumper rattling; AC idler pulley whine and compressor continuing to run when defogger is switched off; electrical short circuits. Engine drivebelt fails frequently; Check Engine light comes on because of a faulty fuel tank, canister, or valve assembly; Airbag warning light stays lit; erratic speedometer performance; excessive fuel consumption; paint chipping and blisters; grille stains from the windshield wiper fluid; and the premature rusting of the front-wheel spindles. **Warranty performance:** Below average.

ROAD PERFORMANCE: Acceleration/torque: Sluggish 4-cylinder performance, though the non-supercharged V6 is an adequate performer. Supercharged version is peppier, but no more so than larger V6 engines offered by the competition or found with the 2005–07 Xterra. **Transmission:** Smooth and quiet shifting with the automatic gearbox. **Steering:** Competent steering that's a bit vague on-centre. **Routine handling:** Corners well, with minimal body lean; however, the Xterra's truck platform doesn't react well to sudden steering corrections. **Emergency handling:** Acceptable, though the steering feels too loose at higher speeds. **Braking:** Quite good; some fading after successive stops.

SAFETY SUMMARY: Airbags: Optional side airbags. Reports of airbags failing to deploy. **ABS:** Standard 4W; disc/drum. **Safety belt pretensioners:** Standard. **Traction control:** Standard. **Head restraints F/R:** *2000:* ★★★/★★; *2001:* ★★★★; *2002–03:* ★★★/★★; *2005–06:* ★. **Visibility F/R:** ★★★★★. **Maximum load capacity:** *Pre-2005:* 885 lb.

SAFETY COMPLAINTS: All years: Sudden acceleration. • Airbag malfunctions. • Vehicle pulls sharply when braking. **2000**—Vehicle was parked with engine running and then suddenly took off. • On one wheel, three of the six studs failed, and on the other wheel, five of the six studs failed. • Rear end suddenly goes out of control. • Stalling at full throttle. • Driver's seat belt doesn't buckle. • ABS light comes on for no reason. **2001**—Fuel splashes out of filler tube when refuelling (Nissan will replace the tank for free, if pushed). • Right rear wheel and axle flew off vehicle. • Centre seat belt won't adequately accommodate a child safety seat. • Windshield wipers stop intermittently. • Dash lights are way too dim. **2002**— Sudden loss of power and stalling. • Vehicle wanders all over the road. • When keyless remote entry was activated, airbag deployed. • Axle bearing inner seal failure. **2003**—Vehicle suddenly went out of control when brakes were lightly applied. • General Grabber tire blowout. • Complete brake loss. • Driver-side upper ball joint collapsed, leading to loss of steering. • Brake and gas pedals are mounted too close together. **2004**—Engine fire caused by a faulty fuel-line clamp. • Side mirrors show distorted images. • Fuses ignited. • Cruise control causes engine to surge. • Wobbly gear; takes forever to get out of 4×4. • Dash lights and gauges operate erratically. **2005**—Recall corrective parts are slow to arrive (trailer hitch).

Secret Warranties/Internal Bulletins/Service Tips

All years: Cracked right-hand exhaust manifold. **1999–2004**—Coolant problems may be caused by a defective radiator cap. **2000**—If the MIL light comes on, it may be because of poor grounding between the intake manifold and the engine cylinder head. • Idle fluctuation can be eliminated by updating the ECM program. • Tips on troubleshooting Xterra squeaks and rattles. **2000–02**—Troubleshooting a noisy transfer case and hard shifting. • Bearing noise. • Coolant leak from intake manifold water outlet. **2001**—Idle fluctuation when coasting to a stop with the clutch depressed. • Roof paint damage at lower edge of roof rack air dam. • Paint chipping at the rear of the hood or top of the fender area. • Water may have entered the distributor assembly. • V6 engines may experience a rough idle or engine vibration at idle. **2001–02**—Goodwill warranty will replace faulty window regulators free of charge (see bulletin). **2001–04**—Headlight fogging. **2002**— Engine knocking noise. • Coolant leak from intake manifold water outlet. •

Steering pull during braking. • Airbag warning light continually flashes. • Malfunctioning engine MIL warning light. • Bearing noise from transfer case area. • Oil leak from the front transfer-case oil seal. **2002–04**—Cold engine rattle or clatter. **2003**—ABS light stays lit. • All lights shut down. • AC won't turn off. **2004**—Tips on silencing engine clatter when starting up in cold weather. • Remedies for brake shudder. • Special campaign to tighten the differential's left front flange-fixing bolt to prevent oil leakage or excessive noise. **2005**—Free body control module sub-harness to improve electrical connection for trailering. **2005–06**—Rear leaf spring squeaks. • Right front seatback rattles and moves sideways.

WINDOW REGULATOR REPLACEMENT

BULLETIN NO.: NTB03-118   DATE: DECEMBER 10, 2003

VOLUNTARY SERVICE CAMPAIGN CAMPAIGN I.D. #: PU306 & PU307

2001 Altima

2001–02 Frontier

2001–02 Xterra

Nissan has identified that certain models may experience unexpected or difficult operation of the windows. The primary cause is extended high temperature conditions affecting the window regulator system. Nissan has initiated a Voluntary Service Campaign to replace the affected window regulators with the improved design. In other areas where this incident is not expected to occur, Nissan is extending the warranty on the vehicles should a future repair be needed.

XTERRA PROFILE

	2000	2001	2002	2003	2004	2005	2006
Cost Price ($) (negotiable)							
Xterra (12%)	29,998	28,498	29,498	29,798	29,798	32,700	33,748
Used Prices ($)							
Xterra ▲	10,500	12,500	15,000	17,500	21,000	24,000	—
Xterra ▼	9,000	11,000	14,000	16,000	19,500	22,500	—
Reliability	④	⑤	⑤	⑤	⑤	⑤	—
Crash Safety (F)	④	④	④	④	④	④	④
Side	④	④	④	④	⑤	⑤	⑤
Offset	③	③	③	③	③	—	—
Rollover	—	②	②	②	—	—	③

X-TRAIL ★★★★

RATING: Above Average (2005–07). Nissan's X-Trail isn't very high-tech, and it's not as refined as the Honda and Toyota competition. The small, five-passenger SUV

2007 TECHNICAL DATA

POWERTRAIN (REAR-DRIVE/4X4)

Engine: 2.5L 4-cyl. (165 hp);
Transmissions: 5-speed manual. •
4-speed auto.

DIMENSION/CAPACITY

Passengers: 2/3; Wheelbase: 103.3
in.; H: 65.9/L: 175.4/W: 69.5 in.; Cargo
volume: 29.2 cu. ft.; Fuel tank: 60L/
regular; Tow limit: 2,000 lb.; Ground
clearance: 7.8 in.; Weight: 3,121 lb.

has been on sale in the rest of the world (excluding the United States) since the end of 2000, which means that Nissan's engineers have had ample time to work out the early-production bugs (a problem still afflicting recent Altimas, Maximas, Quests, and Titans). **Strong points:** Few first-year reliability problems, and competitively priced. The 4-cylinder engine is quiet and smooth. A huge, easy-to-operate sunroof makes the cabin seem more spacious than it is, and there's very little wind buffeting with the sunroof open. Good outward visibility due mainly to the high seating. Centre-mounted dash gauges are a bit disconcerting, though, but they are easier to see than looking through the steering wheel. You will find the ride a bit stiff but comfortable. The 8.1/10.8 L/100km (highway/city) fuel consumption rating is fairly realistic. There isn't any IIHS or NHTSA crashworthiness data available because the X-Trail isn't sold in the States; however, European, Japanese, and Australian crash testers have given the 2001 and later X-Trail a four-star rating for occupant protection in offset collisions (see *users.tpg.com.au/mpaine/ncaplist.html*). **Weak points:** A little sluggish at 80–110 km/h (expect a 0–100 km/h time of just over 10 seconds), and the automatic tranny is hesitant to downshift. Vague steering. Some jarring when going over bumps, potholes, and cracks. Problematic rear-seat access. Some tire noise as well as squeaks and rattles from the hatch, dash, and pedals. Head restraints are positioned too far back and seem to be bargain-basement prototypes—you can feel the seatback flex when you put your head on it. The power-window switch isn't very accessible on the 2006 models. **New for 2007:** No significant changes.

MODEL HISTORY: The X-Trail was launched in Canada as a 2005 model and is based on the Nissan C (compact) car platform used by the Sentra. Equipped with a fully independent suspension and all-wheel drive, 2007 versions sell for $26,098 for a front-drive XE, $27,498 for the AWD version, and $33,798 for the LE AWD. Resale values are also fairly high. A second-series 2005 base front-drive that sold originally for $26,000 now fetches $18,500–$20,000. Similarly, a 2005 AWD variant that once sold for $27,200 is now worth $21,000–$22,000. A 5-speed manual is available, but only on the all-wheel-drive versions. X-Trail competes in the small SUV niche that includes the Honda CR-V, Ford Escape, Mazda Tribute, Jeep Liberty, Subaru Forester, Toyota RAV4, Hyundai Santa Fe, Mitsubishi Outlander, Saturn VUE, Suzuki Vitara/Grand Vitara, and Chevrolet Tracker and Equinox.

The X-Trail is powered by a peppy 2.5L 165-hp 4-cylinder Sentra/Altima engine that'll give the small Honda and Toyota SUVs a run for their money. Both the

5-speed manual and 4-speed automatic transmissions work effortlessly, making this a fun car to drive if you have a bias toward cruising rather than off-roading. A fully independent suspension, responsive steering, and exceptionally well-performing four-wheel vented disc brakes with ABS enhance handling. A Snow-Mode switch, standard on all front-drive models, is particularly useful in that it retards engine power to provide extra traction in slippery conditions.

The X-Trail's unusually tall and boxy styling takes a little bit of getting used to, but it does provide a surprisingly large amount of interior room, many cleverly located storage compartments, plenty of legroom and headroom, a low step-in height, and a nice view of the road (though the extra-wide rear D-pillars obstruct the view somewhat).

Saab

 9-7X ★

RATING: Not Recommended (2005–07). This is a GM "Saabrolet," so refer to the TrailBlazer's rating. GM has ruined the Saab cachet by making its latest models a parts bin for a hodge-podge of components used in GM's quality-challenged cars and trucks, and by assembling these "creations" in the States. Saab, for its part, continues to drain GM's resources with vehicles nobody wants, a marketing strategy that's bizarre at best ("Born from jets"?), and a dealership body that fled for the hills years ago. Take Saab's 9-7X crossover SRV, for instance: It's a warmed-over GM TrailBlazer/Rainier built in Ohio. This is the second Saab neither assembled in Sweden nor sold in Europe (the 9-2X AWD sports compact was the first). It's also the only Saab that doesn't offer a manual transmission. GM figured that a European SUV that's serviced by an atrophied dealer body and not even built or sold in Europe was just the ticket to goose American sales, proving that corporate leaders can exhibit just as much arrogance and stupidity as politicians. Really, who wants to buy a discontinued TrailBlazer from Saab? In fact, a TrailBlazer SS is thousands of dollars cheaper and offers 100 more horses. On top of that, the 9-7X's name is a major turn-off for buyers who are used to names that depict something, and aren't just a jumble of letters and numbers for the "wink, wink, nudge, nudge" car *cognoscenti*. Reminds one of the departed and unlamented Ford/Merkur XR4Ti of a few decades ago. Apparently, to those whom the gods wish to destroy, they first give unintelligible nameplates.

Strong points: The ride is smoother, lower, and more refined than that of an Envoy, Blazer, Rainier, or TrailBlazer. The 2005–07 models earned an "Average" three-star frontal crash-protection rating from NHTSA. The V8 engine is responsive and powerful. No reliability complaints have yet been registered against the

2005–07 models. **Weak points:** Poor gas mileage, despite GM's active fuel management (a cylinder-deactivation feature). Mediocre braking. A limited and demoralized dealership network. Priced higher than GM's own alternatives. Rapid depreciation. Likely to be axed after the 2007 model year, a move that will further drive down resale values and add to servicing woes. **New for 2007:** No significant changes. GM recently killed a planned Subaru-based 9-6X, but next year, the automaker still intends to bring out a large, American-made crossover wagon similar to the 2007 Saturn Outlook. It will likely replace the 9-7X in the 2008 model year.

MODEL HISTORY: With a $50,900 base price, the 9-7X is Saab's first-ever SUV. Fortunately, hefty discounts and rebates can easily cut the high retail price by $7,000 to $10,000. Although this is a TrailBlazer clone, there are a few Saab features that have been retained, like the centre console ignition key and the distinctive air vents and cockpit. It has a wheelbase of 2.87 metres (113 inches), is 4.91 metres (193 inches) long, and can carry up to 1.16 cubic metres (41 cubic feet) of luggage in the trunk with the seats up. There's a standard 60/40 split rear seat and a trailer hitch receiver and cover. The V8 model is estimated to have a maximum towing capacity of 2,950 kg (6,500 lb.).

For a dash of European performance, the 9-7X uses a double A-arm front suspension with coil springs; a multi-link, electronically controlled rear air suspension; a low ride height; a thick front stabilizer; and stiff rear upper control arm bushings. The front end has been stiffened, and steering response and precision have also been enhanced.

Two engines are available: a 275-hp 4.2L in-line 6-cylinder and a 300-hp 5.3L V8. Both engines are teamed with a 4-speed automatic transmission, standard all-wheel drive, and a limited slip differential. **Best alternatives:** The Acura TSX, Audi A4, and Volvo S40 or V50.

Saturn

 VUE ★

RATING: Not Recommended (2002–07). You couldn't buy a worse SUV, and that includes the Ford Explorer and defunct Lada Niva. Honda gave a new heart to this dying patient with its V6, while GM cut it off at the knees with its failure-prone CVT transmission. **Strong points:** Honda's 3.5L V6 and 5-speed automatic transmission work well in the Odyssey and Pilot, and they do just as well with the lighter Vue. Some other pluses are dent-resistant plastic side body panels; head-protecting side curtain airbags; average handling and a comfortable ride; easily

2007 TECHNICAL DATA

POWERTRAIN (FRONT, 4X4)

Engines: 2.2L 4-cyl. (143 hp) • 3.5L
V6 (250 hp). • 2.4L 4-cyl. (170 hp);
Transmissions: 5-speed man. • CVT •
4-speed auto. • 5-speed auto.

DIMENSION/CAPACITY

Passengers: 2/3; Wheelbase: 106.6 in.;
H: 66.5/L: 181.3/W: 71.5 in.; Headroom
F/R: 6.0/6.0 in.; Legroom F/R: 43.1/32.4
in.; Cargo volume: 36.5 cu. ft.; Fuel tank:
63L/regular; Tow limit: 1,500 lb. (3,500
lb. with the V6); Load capacity: 1,175 lb.;
GVWR: 4,598–4,839 lb.; Turning circle:
42 ft.; Ground clearance: 6.5 in.; Weight:
3,740 lb.

accessible and clearly marked instruments and controls; a low step-in height and trunk liftover; and an adequate, versatile interior that includes a split-folding seat to accommodate long objects. **Weak points:** Mediocre acceleration with the base 2.2L engine; the GM–bred 3.0L V6 had a history of factory-induced glitches that compromised performance and overall powertrain reliability; CVT automatic transmission isn't very durable, and it's hard to service; AWD is slow to engage; it's not a serious off-roader (no low-range gearing, for example); there's excessive torque steer (twisting) when accelerating and excessive body roll and rocking in turns; there's lots of noseplow when stopping; the vague steering is too light at low speeds; there's excessive engine noise when accelerating and lots of road noise; the driver's visor is too low; the seats aren't as comfortable as those offered by competitors; the liftgate doesn't have separate opening glass; there are no ceiling-mounted grab handles for easier entry and exit; the second-row seats are firmer and not as comfortable as the front seats; the rear seats are too low; cheap-looking interior and plastic trim; the vehicle is rated "Poor" in IIHS side-impact crash tests, and it almost rolled over in NHTSA tests; and quality control is below average. **New for 2007:** A 170-hp gas-electric hybrid model. The 2008 model will be re-engineered and restyled by GM's Daewoo subsidiary.

MODEL FEATURES: The part-time 4×4 Vue is a conventionally styled, late-arriving (midway through the 2002 model year) compact SUV that targets cars in the Ford Escape and Honda CR-V class. The Vue runs in the rear of the SUV pack and uses as its chief selling point the mantra that Saturn is a "different" car company that cares about its customers. Don't you believe it. When the warranty expires, it's "Goodbye, Charlie."

2003—Expanded powertrain combination. **2004**—Honda's 250-hp V6 engine replaces the unreliable GM–bred powerplant. It delivers lots of power on regular fuel and offers a high degree of reliability and durability. A new Red Line "high-performance" version sits 2.5 cm (1 in.) lower, uses a tighter suspension, offers better-performing 18-inch wheels, and sports a racier appearance. Horsepower remains the same, no matter what the salesman says. **2005**—Red Line enhanced high-performance handling and cosmetic improvements. A slight body makeover with changes to the hood, grille, and headlights as well as an updated interior, radio, centre stack, and door trim.

COST ANALYSIS: Unless you want to take a chance on GM's first-year 2007 hybrid for almost $30,000 (I suggest a Ford Escape hybrid, instead), consider buying a used 2004 with a Honda engine for about $15,000. **Best alternatives:** Ford Escape, Honda CR-V or Element, Hyundai Tucson or Santa Fe, Jeep TJ or Liberty, Mazda Tribute, Nissan Xterra or X-Trail, Subaru Forester, and Toyota Highlander or RAV4. **Rebates:** $4,000 rebates to clear out the 2006s. **Delivery/PDI:** $1,150. **Warranty:** Bumper-to-bumper 3 years/60,000 km; powertrain 5 years/100,000 km; rust perforation 5 years/unlimited km. **Supplementary warranty:** Absolutely. **Options:** I recommend the Honda-sourced V6 engine and traction control along with side curtain airbags. The hybrid option is to be avoided during its first year on the market. Replace historically poor-performing Firestone and Bridgestone original-equipment tires with Michelins. **Depreciation:** Faster than average. **Insurance cost:** Average. **Parts supply/cost:** Parts can be costly; hybrid parts and servicing costs are expected to be particularly high. **Annual maintenance cost:** Higher than average. **Highway/ city fuel economy:** *2.2L:* 7.4/10.4 L/100 km; *2.2L:* 7.8/11.9 L/100 km; *Hybrid:* Not yet available, but other hybrids typically post "real" figures up to 40 percent more than the predicted fuel consumption.

QUALITY/RELIABILITY: Below average—with unreliable powertrain, brake, and body components—plus there's a mountain of service bulletins that cast doubt on the Vue's long-term dependability. Honda engines in later models are fairly dependable. Hybrid engines are major unknowns. **Owner-reported problems:** Engine knocking; automatic transmission and suspension failures; hard downshifts; horn is hard to operate; steering-column thumping; there's a plethora of electrical malfunctions; anti-lock brakes hammer excessively; frequent brake caliper and rotor replacement; the cupholder's so low as to be useless; water collects in the roof rack pin wells; and there are excessive wind, rattling, and brake noises. **Warranty performance:** When you first buy the car new, dealers will welcome you with open arms. But after the warranty expires, you'll get arm gestures of a different sort! Let's just say after-warranty assistance is parsimonious, at best.

SAFETY SUMMARY: Vehicle has a reputation for being tippy at highway speeds:

> 2005 Saturn Vue feels like it is going to tip over when taking sharp turns. This is particularly noticeable when driving at high rates of speed but within the posted speed limits such as leaving the interstate freeways onto adjoining on ramps/off ramps which tend to have various curves in the road. The car feels scary when this happens and requires a complete reduction of speed by the driver with all other nearby cars and SUVs passing by with no visible similar handling problem.

Airbags: Optional side airbags. Numerous reports of airbags failing to deploy. **ABS:** Optional; standard. Front disc/rear drum. There have been many complaints of ABS failures and the premature wearout of brake components. **Head restraints F/R:** *2002–06:* ★★. **Visibility F/R:** ★★★★. **Maximum load capacity:** *2002:* 825 lb.

SAFETY COMPLAINTS: All years: Loss of steering, transmission failure, airbag malfunction, chronic stalling and surging, and horn is hard to activate. **2002**—Transmission fluid lines are vulnerable to road debris. **2002–03**—Airbags failed to deploy. • Reduced Power light comes on, and vehicle shuts down. • Torque steer jerks car to the right when accelerating. **2003**—Transmission breakdown (variable drive unit). • Vehicle slides backward when stopped on a hill. • Inside door latches couldn't open the door. • Incorrect speedometer readings. • Electrical short circuit in the signal/headlight control stalk. • Headlight and daylight driving lights burn out, and vehicle stalls when it rains. **2004**—Side airbags failed to deploy. • Rear suspension collapsed when changing lanes. • Cruise control would not disengage. • Recall repairs related to the Rear Drive Module cause excessive front-wheel spin and torque steer when accelerating. • Manual transmission failure. • When the brakes were applied, the automatic transmission shifted to Neutral. • Vehicle continues to roll even though brakes are applied. • Chronic electrical shorts. • Corrosion from bolt holes in roof-rail mounting. • Rear window shattered when side door was closed. **2005**—Airbags failed to deploy, or deployed without inflating. • Vehicle rolls backward when in Drive. • CVT transmission slippage:

> If the car is cold, the computer will prevent the transmission from being engaged, to avoid transmission damage. They also said that the slipping in the transmission was "normal operation" for the CVT transmission. Well, I did not have this issue happen when I test drove the car, and for approximately 5 months after. I do not have the problem for a week or so after an oil change. I feel that there is a blatant performance problem with the CVT (continuous variable transmission). Continuous implies that the transmission varies "continuously." I can assure you, if my car had done this while I was test driving it, I never would have bought the car. It is a safety hazard, and makes me extremely anxious when I am driving, as there is no way to anticipate when it will happen. Saturn has repeatedly stated that this "slipping" is normal. I have found several web sites on the web with people complaining of this exact problem.

Also, see GM's "What, me worry?" service bulletin at the end of "Secret Warranties/Internal Bulletins/Service Tips."

Secret Warranties/Internal Bulletins/Service Tips

2001–06—Diagnosis for trannies stuck in Second or Third gear, harsh upshifts, and an upshift/downshift clunk. **2001–07**—No-starts can be traced to either stripped battery threads or a faulty battery bolt. **2002**—Engine flare during 2–3 upshifts. • Timing-belt coolant contamination. • Rattle or tapping noise from steering-column shroud area. • Creaking noise may come from left or right rear of vehicle while driving. • Front-seat squeaking. • Troubleshooting a defective MIL light. • Rear-seat cushion cover is baggy or loose along the bottom edge. • Horn design makes it difficult to activate at night. • AC and lower condenser are exposed to road debris. **2002–03**—No-starts, stalling, a rough-running engine, and a poor idle may all be caused by a stuck engine intake manifold pressure-relief valve. • A

BLUE SMOKE AT START-UP
BULLETIN NO.: 04-06-01-010   DATE: APRIL 2004

(Inspect Valve Stem Seal Color and Perform Service
Procedure)
2000–04 Saturn L-Series
2002–03 Saturn VUE with 3.0L V6
This condition may be caused by leaking valve seals
(on engines with brown seal color) or excessive
clearance between valve stem and valve guide.

OIL LEAKS IN SUB-FREEZING TEMPS.
BULLETIN NO.: 04-06-01-001   DATE: JANUARY 2004

**OIL LEAKS FROM ENGINE AFTER SUB-FREEZING
TEMPERATURES**
(Remove Ice/Water from Positive Crankcase
Ventilation (PCV) Hose and Re-route Hose)
2002–03 Saturn VUE Vehicles
with 3.0L V6 Engine

NO SHIFT/NO GEAR ENGAGEMENT
BULLETIN NO.: 03-07-30-023   DATE: NOVEMBER 2003

**VEHICLE DOES NOT SHIFT OR MOVE AFTER RUNNING FOR A PERIOD OF TIME AND/OR CHECK ENGINE
LIGHT IS ON AND DTC P0741 IS SET**
(Replace Torque Converter, Valve Body, Clean Out Transaxle and Install New Flex Plate Bolts and Washers)
2002–03 Saturn VUE

history of faulty valve seals and poor cold-weather engine performance (see bulletins). • Powertrain vibration when AC is activated. • A moan/growl noise and vibration from rear of vehicle can be corrected by replacing the rear-drive module's limited slip clutch drum. • Torque converter shudder, vibration. • Shudder, vibration in Reverse. • Transaxle whine. • Starter stays engaged after start-up. • Electrical accessories fail intermittently. • Fluid leak caused by loose VTI transaxle-converter housing bolts. • Transmission won't go into gear (see bulletin). • Noisy upper steering column. • Incorrect speedometer and fuel gauge readings. • Insufficient AC cooling and heating. • Instrument panel condensation. • Fluid drips onto driver's floormat. • Engine compartment whistling and chirping. • Front-end squeaking. • Buzzing, grinding, and growling from rear of vehicle when fuel pump is activated. • Clunk, pop, or click when accelerating or decelerating. • Upgraded liftgate latching system. **2002–04**—Free replacement of the rear lateral link assembly, a suspension component that may fail during hard cornering. A one-day rental ($35 U.S.) is authorized. **2002–05**—Free tranny case cover assembly and filter if transmission won't shift into Drive or Reverse. **2002–06**—Front-end rattle. • Front-seat squeaking. • Excessive windshield wind noise. • Free replacement of the instrument panel cluster if the lenses are broken, cracked, scratched, or cloudy. **2003–05**—Automatic transmission grind or rattle when starting up requires the replacement of the case cover assembly, torque converter, and filter. **2003–06**—Excessive A-pillar wind noise. **2004**—Special warranty policy adjustment for the CVT transmission. • Hard starts. • Moan, growl, and vibration when turning. • Steering rattle. • Suspension pop, clunk noise. • AC hissing. • Exhaust system rattle or buzz. • Drone noise between 80 and 120 km/h. • Outside rearview mirror cracking. **2004–05**—Remedy for an inoperative cruise control. **2004–06**—Incredibly, GM says delayed CVT transmission shifts are "normal":

All ratings on a numbered scale where ⑤ is good and ❶ is bad. See page 220 for a more detailed description.

TRANSAXLE SHIFT LAG AND/OR HESITATION DURING WARM-UP FOLLOWING INITIAL START-UP— NORMAL CHARACTERISTIC, NO SERVICE NECESSARY

2004–2006 Saturn VUE with 5AT 5-Speed Automatic Transaxle

The 5AT transaxle (RPO MJ7/MJ8) is a 5-speed, electronically controlled, automatic transaxle featuring transaxle shift calibration that adjusts and assures consistent shift feel. However, transaxle shift feel adaptation on the 5AT automatic transaxle does not initiate until after the first series of shifts are completed, after a cold soak (i.e. when the vehicle parked for extended periods of time). The Saturn VUE SAT automatic transaxle shift calibration is designed to provide optimum shift feel during normal driving, and more specifically, during normal operating temperatures (transaxle fluid temperatures of 65–110°C [150–230°F]).

This method of providing consistent shift feel is to ensure the best possible shift feel during the ideal operating temperatures. Because of this programming, some customers may experience shift performance that is described as firm or a sensation of a slight up shift lag when comparing the shift feel after warm up to pre-warm up operating modes.

During initial pre-warm up periods, customers may experience a lag/delay during 1–2, 2–3 upshift after accelerating from a stop, or during acceleration during a rolling stop. The delayed 1–2/2–3 upshift can occur between the speeds of 32–48 km/h (20–30 mph), during the initial warm up period. As the transaxle fluid warms, the transaxle control module (TCM) calibration is optimized to refine shift feel for smoothness and responsiveness during the normal range of temperatures experienced.

The shift feel characteristics experienced by customers is considered a normal characteristic. There is no need to attempt a repair for cold shift performance.

VUE PROFILE

	2002	2003	2004	2005	2006
Cost Price ($) (negotiable)					
Base Vue (21%)	21,565	21,980	22,745	23,095	22,995
4X4 (22%)	26,055	27,595	26,390	26,595	29,795
Used Values ($)					
Base Vue ▲	10,500	12,500	14,000	15,000	—
Base Vue ▼	9,000	11,000	13,000	14,000	—
4X4 ▲	12,000	14,500	16,500	18,500	—
4X4 ▼	10,500	13,000	15,000	17,000	—
Reliability	❷	❷	❸	❸	—
Crash Safety (F)	⑤	⑤	⑤	⑤	⑤
Side	⑤	⑤	⑤	⑤	⑤
IIHS Side	❶	❶	❶	❶	❶
Offset	⑤	⑤	⑤	⑤	⑤
Rollover	❸	❸	❸	❸	❸

Subaru

FORESTER, IMPREZA, TRIBECA, WRX ★★★★/★★★/★★/★★

2007 FORESTER TECHNICAL DATA

POWERTRAIN (AWD)

Engines: 2.5L 4-cyl. (173 hp) • 2.5L turbo (230 hp); Transmissions: 5-speed man. • 4-speed auto.

DIMENSION/CAPACITY

Passengers: 2/3; Wheelbase: 99.4 in.; H: 62.5/L: 176.6/W: 68.1 in.; Headroom F/R: N/A; Legroom F/R: 43.6/33.7 in.; Cargo volume: 31.9 cu. ft.; Fuel tank: 60L/regular, premium; Tow limit: 2,400 lb.; Load capacity: 900 lb.; GVWR: 4,120 lb.; Turning circle: 38 ft.; Ground clearance: 8.1 in.; Weight: 3,165 lb.

2007 IMPREZA TECHNICAL DATA

POWERTRAIN (AWD)

Engines: 2.5L 4-cyl. (173 hp) • 2.0L turbo (227 hp) • 2.5L turbo (230 hp) • 2.5L turbo (300 hp); Transmissions: 5-speed man. • 6-speed man. • 4-speed auto.

DIMENSION/CAPACITY

Passengers: 2/3; Wheelbase: 100 in.; H: 60/L: 174/ W: 69 in.; Headroom F/R: 5.0/1.5 in.; Legroom F/R: 43.1/32.4 in.; Cargo volume: 19.5 cu. ft.; Fuel tank: 60L/regular, premium; Tow limit: 2,000 lb.; Load capacity: 830 lb.; GVWR: 4,120 lb.; Turning circle: 40 ft.; Ground clearance: 5.0 in.; Weight: 3,290 lb.

RATING: *Forester:* Above Average (2006–07); Average (1994–2005). *Impreza:* Average (1997–2007). *WRX:* Below Average (2002–07). The WRX has been downgraded mainly because of its tricky handling and its reliability issues (powertrain, brake, and steering). *Tribeca:* Below Average (2006–07). Living on borrowed time, the Tribeca is overweight and overpriced, and it's outclassed by the competition. Except for the Forester, Subaru's model lineup is mostly the bland leading the bland. There's nothing remarkable about Subaru except for its early use of AWD for its entire lineup as a desperate move to stave off bankruptcy in the mid-1990s. Incidentally, the company isn't in great financial shape right now. Quality control has declined markedly over the past four years, and customer service has suffered equally. Smart shoppers will choose a cheaper Asian SUV until Subaru lowers its prices and raises performance and quality-control levels. The 2006 Forester improvements are a good start. **Strong points:** Some long-awaited performance and size improvements. A refined AWD drivetrain; a powerful WRX engine, and good acceleration with the base 2.5L; competent handling, without any torque steer; impressive crashworthiness; well-appointed base models; and a nice control layout. **Weak points:** Generally stiff-riding, and the Outback Sport doesn't ride as comfortably or handle as well as other Imprezas. Problematic entry and exit; the coupe's narrow rear window and large rear pillars hinder rear visibility; wagon has limited cargo volume; heater is insufficient, and air distribution is inadequate;

comfort is compromised by the WRX's short wheelbase, suspension, and 16-inch tires; front- and rear-seat legroom may be insufficient for tall drivers; small doors and entryways restrict rear access; the WRX requires premium fuel; and there's a surprisingly large number of safety-related complaints that include complete brake loss, chronic surging, and stalling. **New for 2007:** No significant changes until the 2008 Impreza redesign and the Forester's revamped 2009 model. *Impreza:* The 2007 Spec B gets standard stability-control, a Torsen rear differential, and the WRX STI's 6-speed manual transmission. *Outback/Legacy/B9 Tribeca:* All will be slightly changed for the 2008 model year.

MODEL HISTORY: The full-time 4×4 Impreza is essentially a shorter Legacy with additional convenience features. It comes as a four-door sedan, a wagon, and an Outback Sport Wagon, all powered by a 165-hp 2.5L flat-four engine. The rally-inspired WRX models have a more powerful 227-hp 2.0L turbocharged engine, lots of standard performance features, a sport suspension, an aluminum hood with a functional scoop, and higher-quality instruments, controls, trim, and seats. The 2003 Impreza and WRX were carried over unchanged.

Another Subaru spin-off, the Forester, is a cross between a tall wagon and a sport-utility. Based on the shorter Impreza, the Forester adds eight horses to the Legacy Outback's 2.5L 165-hp engine and couples it to a 5-speed manual transmission or an optional 4-speed automatic. Its road manners are more subdued and its engine provides more power and torque for off-roading than most vehicles its size.

1993—Impreza's first year on the market. **1995**—Entry-level Imprezas got coupe and Outback models as well as optional AWD. **1996**—A mix of front-drives and all-wheel drives along with a new sport model, a new Outback Wagon (for light off-roading), and larger engines. **1997**—Additional power and torque, a restyled front end, and a new Outback Sport Wagon. **1998**—The Impreza got a revised dash and door panels. The Brighton was dropped, and the high-end 2.5 RS was added. **1999**—Stronger engines, more torque, and upgraded transmissions. **2002**—The 2.2L 4-cylinder was dropped, along with Subaru's pretensions for making affordable entry-level cars. Totally redesigned models include the 2.5 TS Sport Wagon, 2.5 RS sedan, Outback Sport Wagon, WRX sporty sedan, and Sport Wagon. There is no longer a two-door version available. *Impreza:* **2004**—New front end with larger headlights and a restyled interior and exterior. **2006**—Expected to get a small horsepower increase, an enhanced front end, additional airbags, and a freshened interior. *Forester:* **1999**—A quieter, torquier engine; a smoother-shifting transmission; and a more solid body. **2000**—Standard cruise control (L) and limited slip differential (S). **2003**—Improved interior materials, an upgraded suspension, and enhanced handling and ride quality. You'll also find larger tires and fenders as well as revised head restraints and side-impact airbags. **2004**—A turbocharged 210-hp 2.5L 4-banger, and a racier appearance. **2006**—More power, and a slightly restyled interior and exterior. The 2006 turbocharged XT adds 20 hp via a redesigned engine intake manifold (this could be troublesome in the future); other models get eight more horses, for a total of 173. A retuned suspension enhances ride smoothness and handling response, and there's improved braking feel on all models. Ground clearance has been slightly increased, an alarm system is now standard, and the 5-speed manual transmission isn't available with L.L. Bean models. *WRX:* **2003**—An AWD car for the high-performance crowd, the WRX is a goofy-looking, squat little wagon/SUV with a large rear end and a 227-hp 2.0L 4-cylinder engine mated to a high-boost turbocharger. **2004**—A 300-hp engine. **2006**—The 2.5L gets 20 extra horses (230).

Tribeca (B9)

Named after either a small neighbourhood in New York City or a vitamin pill, the $42,000, five-passenger base 2006 Tribeca is Subaru's latest crossover SUV. It's sized between the Forester and Legacy Outback. Its on- and off-road performance is that of a slightly bigger Legacy—impressive body control, a comfortable and supple ride (even with standard 18-inch wheels), and an adequate steering response that's muted by the car's heft.

And heft is the Tribeca's most serious drawback. Although its swoopy styling gives it an aerodynamic appearance, the car's estimated 15.0 L/100 km (18.0 mpg) fuel consumption rating combined with its small gas tank mean you'll quickly get to know your gas station operators on a first-name basis.

Furthermore, the car lags in many other areas. For example, take its power-to-weight ratio: Tribeca has to haul 8.8 kg (19.4 lb.) per pound-foot of torque, while most of the competitors only need to pull around 7–8 kg (16–17 lb.). Even Nissan's fuel-thirsty Murano betters the Tribeca in the power-to-weight category. Also, the B9 has the smallest amount of rear legroom, at 87 cm (34.3 in.), and the shortest combined front/rear legroom, at 194 cm (76.6 in.), in a

2007 TRIBECA TECHNICAL DATA

POWERTRAIN (AWD)
Engines: 3.0L 6-cyl. (250 hp);
Transmissions: 5-speed manumatic
DIMENSION/CAPACITY
Passengers: 2/3, 2/3/2; Wheelbase: 108.2/189.8 in.; H: 66.4/W: 189.8/ L:73.9 in.; Headroom F/R: N/A; Legroom F/R: 42.3/34.3 in.; Cargo volume: 37.5 cu. ft.; Fuel tank: 64L/ premium; Tow limit: 3,500 lb.; Load capacity: 1,560 lb.; GVWR: 4,120 lb.; Turning circle: 37.4 ft.; Ground clearance: 8.4 in.; Weight: 4,155 lb.

field where most automakers offer 198–200 cm (78–79 in.). It also has one of the smallest cargo capacities and the smallest third-row cargo capacity.

Other minuses include spongy braking and excessive tire noise when cruising; the steering wheel blocks the view of the fuel and temperature gauges; the view rearward is obscured by thick rear pillars; and the small, hard-to-access third-row seats are for kids only, offering no legroom if the second-row seats are pushed rearward.

With the Tribeca, Subaru undoubtedly did a pretty nice job of moving up in scale and class, but it has seriously misjudged the car's limited market potential. It screams "big SUV" at a time when buyers are downsizing their choices because of high fuel costs and inflated price tags for large Asian SUVs. Moreover, it will be an uphill battle to move the traditionally conservative, "function-over-form" Subaru commuter upscale. Despite its non-conformist looks and smooth boxer-six engine, I'm betting Subaru owners will walk away feeling betrayed.

COST ANALYSIS: Stay away from the Tribeca, at least until 2007 when first-series glitches will likely be remedied and the $42,000 price will be discounted by about 20 percent. The 2007 base Impreza RS starts at $23,495 and is identical to the 2006. Both models are a better choice than the less-refined 2005. Just remember to budget an extra $1,500 for an extended powertrain warranty to protect you from premature and repeated clutch failures. Cheaper 2002 redesigned Imprezas or an upgraded 2003 Forester are also good second choices. WRX versions are expensive Imprezas that equal the sporty performance of the Audi A4 and BMW 3 Series—cars costing $10,000 more. But can you handle the brake failures and quirky handling? **Best alternatives:** Excellent alternatives are the Toyota Matrix/Pontiac Vibe front-drive or AWD models. If you really don't need a 4×4, here are some front-drives worth considering: Honda Civic, Hyundai Elantra, Mazda3, and Toyota Corolla. Other alternatives are the Honda Pilot EX AWD and the Lexus RX 330 four-door AWD. **Rebates:** Subaru is cash hungry, so look for $4,000 rebates on all models. **Delivery/PDI:** $1,495. **Warranty:** Bumper-to-bumper 3 years/60,000 km; powertrain 5 years/100,000 km; rust perforation 5 years/unlimited km. **Supplementary warranty:** Not needed. **Options:** Larger tires smooth out the ride. **Depreciation:** Slower than average. Foresters hold their value best of all. WRX versions depreciate rapidly. **Insurance cost:** Higher than average. **Parts supply/cost:** Parts aren't easy to find and can be costly; delayed recall repairs. **Annual maintenance cost:** Higher than average. Mediocre, expensive servicing is hard to overcome because independent garages can't service key AWD components. **Highway/city fuel economy:** *2.5L:* 7.2/10.3 L/100 km; *WRX 2.0L Turbo:* 8.0/11.8 L/100 km; *2.5L Turbo:* 9.1/13.4 L/100 km.

QUALITY/RELIABILITY: Poor sales are negatively affecting the quality of servicing and warranty work. Mediocre quality control, and Subaru reps sometimes cop too much of an attitude when faced with serious safety-related complaints:

While attempting to slow my 2003 WRX for a corner on a well groomed, dry gravel road, the ABS system of the car initiated a mode that would not allow the car's brakes to function at all. During the episode (which has been and can be recreated) pedal pressure and pedal height was maintained as during normal braking operations. The brakes would not work despite the fact that I was standing with both feet on the brake pedal. I am in the process of disconnecting my ABS. Subaru North America claims that I'm nuts.

There's a history of premature powertrain, fuel system, and brake failures and some body panel and trim fit and finish deficiencies. Servicing quality is spotty. **Owner-reported problems:** Poor engine idling, cooling; frequent cold-weather stalling; manual transmission malfunctions (mostly clutch chatter and shudder); rear wheel bearing failures; alloy wheels cause excessive vibration; suspension clunks; premature exhaust system rust-out and early brake wear; minor electrical short circuits; catalytic converter failures; doors don't latch properly; water leaks and condensation problems from the top of the windshield or sunroof; windshield scratches too easily; and paint peeling. **Warranty performance:** Has declined markedly during the past couple of years (especially in relation to brake and clutch complaints).

SAFETY SUMMARY: Huge fold-away side mirrors. Front shoulder belts can be uncomfortable, and rear seat belts may be hard to buckle up. The 2006 and 2007 model Tribecas earned a five-star rating for frontal and side crashworthiness; rollover protection was given four stars. IIHS rated the 2006 Impreza's side and offset crashworthiness as "Good." **Airbags:** Numerous reports of airbags failing to deploy; also reports of airbags injuring passengers or deploying but not inflating. **ABS:** Standard. There have been many complaints of ABS failures and the premature wearout of brake components. **Head restraints F/R:** *Forester 1999:* ★★/★; *2001–02:* ★★★/★★; *2003:* ★★★★★; *2006:* ★★★★★. *Impreza 1995:* ★★; *1997:* ★★/★; *2001:* ★★; *2002–03:* ★★★; *2005–06:* ★★★★★; *Impreza WRX: 2004–06:* ★★. **Visibility F/R:** *Coupe:* ★★★★★/★★. **Maximum load capacity:** *Forester 1998–2003:* 900 lb.

 SAFETY COMPLAINTS: *Impreza:* **All years:** Sudden acceleration, stalling, transmission failures, steering loss, airbag malfunctions, brake and engine lights continually on, and front seats move fore and aft. **1999**—Engine failure caused by a cracked #2 piston. • When accelerating or decelerating, vehicle will jerk because of excessive play in the front axle. • Front bumper skirt catches on parking blocks; the bumper twists and rips off. • Total loss of braking capability. • The centre rear seat belt's poor design prohibits the installation of many child safety seats. **2000**—A mountain of complaints relative to the loss of braking and premature wearout of key brake components. **2001**—ABS overreacts when braking over an irregular surface. • Rear wheel bearings fail repeatedly. • Factory-installed anti-theft device disables the starter. **2002**—Chronic brake failures. • Brake rotors are frequently scored after only a few kilometres. • Many reports of blown transmissions. • First gear is hard to engage. **2003**—Sudden, unintended acceleration; brake pedal wouldn't respond. • Very poor braking when passing over rough surfaces:

> On my 2003 Subaru Impreza Outback Sport, the anti-lock brakes are dangerous. If you hit a bump while braking, it will trigger the ABS—and result in an almost complete loss of braking ability. I notice a bulletin is listed for the WRX only, but this is a major problem in my car as well.

• Seat belt ratchets tighten and refuse to unlock. • Windshield chips easily. **2004**—Airbags failed to deploy. • Vehicle won't go into gear. • Complete loss of brakes. • Raw fuel smell in the cabin. • Car wanders all over the road because of defective suspension struts. **2004–05**—Windshield is easily cracked. **2005**—Chronic rear strut failure. • Fuel odour inside the cabin. • Side window shatters spontaneously. *Forester:* **2000**—Driver burned from airbag deployment. • Sudden loss of transmission fluid. • Driver's seatback may suddenly recline because seat belt gets tangled up in the recliner lever. • Frequent wheel bearing failures. • Fuel-filler cap design is too complicated for gas station attendants to put on properly, which causes the Check Engine light to come on. Driver, therefore, has to pay dealer to reset the Check Engine light. **2001**—Rear wheel bearings broke. • Brake and accelerator pedals are too close together. • In a collision, airbags failed to deploy and seat belt didn't restrain occupant. • In a similar incident, shoulder belt allowed driver's head to hit the windshield. • Headlights don't illuminate the edge of the road and are either too bright on High or too dim on Low. • Alarm system self-activated, trapping a baby inside the car until fire rescue arrived. **2002**—Dangerous delay and then surging when accelerating forward or in Reverse. • Surging at highway speeds and stalling at lower rpm. • Transmission failure; gears lock in Park intermittently. • Intermittent backfire when shifting the manual transmission. • Open wheel design allows snow and debris to pack in the area and throw wheel out of balance, creating dangerous vibrations. • High hood allows water onto the engine. (Note: The preceding comments apply to the Forester but can be relevant to Impreza owners, too.) **2003**—When backing vehicle into a parking space, the hill-holder feature activates, forcing the driver to use excessive throttle in Reverse. • Brake pedal went to floor without braking. • Heater, defroster failure. • Five doors but only one keyhole makes for difficult access when the keyless entry fails. *WRX:* **2001**—Brake rotors are easily grooved, degrading braking ability. **2002**—First gear is hard to engage. **2002–03**—Windshield cracking. • Chronic ABS brake failures. • Fuel smell in the cabin caused by fuel pooling in the engine manifold recess. **2003**—Increased braking distance when brakes are applied on an uneven surface. **2004**—Defective Bridgestone tires. • Failure-prone, clunking struts will not rebound, causing the rear end to sag and degrading handling. **2005**—Tricky handling is still a problem.

Secret Warranties/Internal Bulletins/Service Tips

All years: Bulletins relate to the automatic transmission popping out of gear. • At least three bulletins deal with manual transmission malfunctions. • Diagnostic and repair tips are offered on transfer clutch binding and/or bucking on turns. • Troubleshooting tips on a sticking anti-lock brake relay are offered. This problem is characterized by a lit ABS warning light or the ABS motor continuing to run and buzz when the ignition is turned off. • A rotten-egg smell could be caused by a defective catalytic converter. It will be replaced, after a bit of arguing, free of charge up to five years under the emissions warranty. **1999**—A broken air intake chamber box will cause stalling during start-up and the Check Engine light to remain lit. **1999–2002**—Sliding seat belt latch. **2000**—Growling noises from the engine area. • Automatic Transmission light flashing. • Low brake pedal adjustment procedure. **2000–01**—Front oxygen air/fuel sensor cracking. **2001–03**—Premature brake pad wear. **2002–03**—Insufficient AC cooling. **2003**—Defective 4EAT transmission parking pawl rod. • Clutch pedal sticking. *WRX:* **2004–05**—Tips on silencing a noisy rear differential.

SPORT-UTILITY VEHICLES • PART FOUR

FORESTER, IMPREZA, WRX PROFILE

	1998	1999	2000	2001	2002	2003	2004	2005	2006
Cost Price ($) (negotiable)									
Forester (24%)	26,695	26,695	26,895	28,395	28,395	27,995	27,995	27,995	27,995
Impreza sedan (22%)	21,695	21,995	21,995	22,196	21,995	22,995	22,995	22,995	23,495
WRX (26%)	—	—	—	—	34,995	34,995	35,495	35,495	35,495
Used Values ($)									
Forester ▲	6,000	7,500	10,500	13,000	15,000	17,000	19,500	22,000	—
Forester ▼	5,000	6,500	9,000	12,000	13,500	16,000	18,000	20, 000	—
Impreza sedan ▲	5,000	6,000	7,000	9,500	11,500	13,500	15,500	18,000	—
Impreza sedan ▼	4,000	5,000	6,000	8,000	10,000	12,000	14,000	16,500	—
WRX ▲	—	—	—	—	16,500	19,000	23,000	27,000	—
WRX ▼	—	—	—	—	15,000	17,000	21,000	25,000	—
Reliability	❸	❸	❸	❸	❹	❹	❹	❹	—
Crash Safety (F)									
Forester	—	❹	❹	❹	❹	❺	❺	❺	❺
Impreza	—	—	—	—	❹	❹	—	—	❹
Side (Forester)	—	—	—	❺	❺	❺	❺	❺	❺
Impreza	—	—	—	—	❹	❹	—	—	❹
IIHS Side	—	—	—	—	❺	❺	❺	❺	❺
Offset (Forester)	—	❺	❺	❺	❺	❺	❺	❺	❺
Impreza	—	—	—	—	—	❺	❺	❺	❺
Rollover (Forester)	—	—	—	❸	❸	❸	❹	❹	❹
Impreza	—	—	—	—	❹	❹	—	—	❹

All ratings on a numbered scale where ❺ is good and ❶ is bad. See page 220 for a more detailed description.

Toyota

RATING: Recommended (2006–07); Above Average (1997–2005). An impressive all-around performer, suitable for limited off-road tasks with an exciting array of long-awaited 2004 and 2006 enhancements. **Strong points:** *All years:* Full-time 4×4; adequate 4-cylinder acceleration (but it may still be too tame for some), good handling, and smooth riding (the four-door model has a handling advantage over the two-door version); all passengers have more than enough headroom and legroom; the four-door has more cargo space than most passenger cars, but the two-door version reduces that cargo capacity by half; the split rear bench seat folds for extra cargo space; easy access and a low liftover; the four-door is nicely equipped, while the two-door is spartan, though adequate; incredibly high resale value; and legendary reliability. *2006–07 models:* A V6 and a small horsepower boost for the 4-cylinder engine; additional cabin space allows for more cargo room and optional seven-passenger seating. The 2007s carry standard side curtain airbags (formerly a $750 option). **Weak points:** *2006–07 models:* V6 throttle is super-sensitive and tough to modulate, leading to jerky acceleration and rough low-speed shifts; no manual transmission available; drivers may want more legroom; cheap-looking glove box lid and headliner; wide rear roof pillars obstruct rearward view; second-row seats give insufficient legroom; third-row seats hard to access; cargo door is hinged on the passenger side, exposing people loading the vehicle to traffic; no separately opening hatch glass. *2005 and earlier models:*

Automatic gearbox and 4×4 reduces engine performance (front-drive is faster); excessive road and engine noise; rearward visibility is seriously compromised by the RAV4's convertible top, high headrests, and spare-tire placement. **New for 2007:** Standard front seat-mounted side airbags and roll-sensing front and rear head/side curtain airbags.

MODEL HISTORY: Selling for almost $30,000, the RAV4 is a cross between a small car and an off-road wagon with a tall roof, and it marks Toyota's entry into the mini-sport-utility market. "RAV4" stands for "Recreational Active Vehicle with four-wheel drive." It has attractive lines, a high profile, and two drivetrains: permanent 4×4 or front-drive, which doesn't include low-range gearing but has a locking centre differential.

2007 TECHNICAL DATA

POWERTRAIN (FRONT-DRIVE/4X4)
Engine: 2.4L 4-cyl. (166 hp) • 3.5L V6 (269 hp); Transmissions: 4-speed auto. • 5-speed auto.

DIMENSION/CAPACITY
Passengers: 2/3; 2/3/2; Wheelbase: 104.7 in.; H: 66.3/L: 181.1/W: 68 in.; Headroom F/R: 6.5/4.0 in.; Legroom F/R: 41.5/29.0 in.; Cargo volume: 38.5 cu. ft.; Fuel tank: 60L/regular; Tow limit: 1,500–3,500.; Load capacity: 825 lb. (1,144 lb. on manual-shift front-drive models); GVWR: 4,535–4,865 lb.; Turning circle: 37 ft.; Ground clearance: 7.0 in.; Weight: 3,444 lb.

The RAV4 is based on the Camry platform and features a four-wheel independent suspension and unibody construction; the 2005 and earlier models ride and handle like a stiffly sprung, small-wheelbase car. Like Honda's CR-V, it's an upsized car that has been made more rugged with the addition of AWD, larger wheels, more ground clearance, and a boxy body. Following the car's 2006 redesign, two engines are now offered: a 166-hp 4-cylinder and a 269-hp V6—RAV4's first V6. Both engines come only with an automatic transmission. ABS and traction/anti-skid control are standard. Front-drive RAV4s have a limited slip differential. Hill ascent/descent control is standard on V6 models and on seven-passenger 4-cylinder models. Sport models have a sport suspension. RAV4s have a side-hinged cargo door. Optional are front side airbags and side curtain airbags that cover the first two seating rows and include rollover deployment. The second-row seat is a split folding bench that moves fore and aft and has a reclining seatback. The optional third-row seat folds into a floorwell.

Although RAV4s have been around for a few years, you won't find many on the used-car market. Those that are for sale aren't cheap, either. However, the reworked 2001 and 2006 RAV4s are exerting some downward price pressure on the less refined, older used versions. Don't spend extra bucks opting for the 1999 or 2000 models; they're not much different from their predecessors except for a minor face-lift, the addition of a two-door softtop, and a full-sized spare tire. The two-door convertible was dropped from the year 2000 models. **2001**—Completely redesigned, growing in size and getting a more powerful engine, an upgraded suspension, a more rigid body, and new, aggressive styling. **2004**—The Highlander's 2.4L engine, rear disc brakes, vehicle skid control, a revised suspension and steering, a tire pressure monitor, and optional side curtain airbags. **2006**—A major redesign gives the 2006 new styling, a 17 cm (6.7 in.) longer wheelbase, 37 cm (14.5 in.) of additional length, 8.1 cm (3.2 in.) more width, a more powerful engine, and third-row seating to carry a total of seven passengers.

COST ANALYSIS: This year's larger RAV4 also carries a higher price, but it's well worth the difference when one considers the standard side airbags. The base 2007 starts at $29,300 (*2006: $28,700*), while the Limited sells for $33,195 (*2006: $32,595*). Base V6 models will go for $31,800 (*2006: $31,200*), the Sport will start at $33,590 (*2006: $32,990*), and the Limited V6 goes for $36,970 (*2006: $36,370*). **Best alternatives:** Ford Escape, Honda CR-V, Hyundai Tucson or Santa Fe, and Mazda Tribute.

When compared with the Honda CR-V, Honda has a slight edge from a performance perspective, up to the debut of the redesigned 2006 RAV4. Will quality suffer as was the case with the revamped 2004 and later Sienna, Camry, and Avalon? Undoubtedly it will, and that's why Toyota has delayed the arrival of some 2007 models this year. Other choices worth looking at are the Nissan Xterra or X-Trail, Subaru Forester, and Toyota Highlander. **Rebates:** There are few 2007s in stock, so don't expect any form of discount. Low-interest financing may kick in sometime in the spring of 2007. **Delivery/PDI:** $1,390. **Warranty:** Bumper-to-bumper 3 years/60,000 km; powertrain 5 years/100,000 km; rust perforation 5 years/unlimited km. **Supplementary warranty:** An extended warranty isn't needed. **Options:** Don't buy the V6 unless you are a power freak, or carry heavy cargo; the 4-banger has plenty of power for most driving chores. Take a test drive and see. **Depreciation:** Slow. **Insurance cost:** Above average. **Parts supply/cost:** Parts are moderately priced and fairly easy to find from independent suppliers. **Annual maintenance cost:** Below average, owing to the proven reliability of Camry and Corolla components used in the RAV4. **Highway/city fuel economy:** 8.1/10.7 L/100 km. *2006 and later models:* 7.8/10.1 L/100 km; V6 is estimated to be 7.7/11.1 L/100 km.

 QUALITY/RELIABILITY: Better-than-average quality control that almost always declines for several years when a vehicle is redesigned. **Owner-reported problems:** Many reports of frequent stalling or hesitation, brake noise, and throttle body whine between 2700 and 3000 rpm. Owners note that the brakes screech, squeal, or grind even after the pads have been replaced. Other noises: dash and cowl rattling (worse in low temperatures), rear suspension creaking when accelerating from a stop, and windshield cowling rattles (particularly in cold weather). To a lesser degree, owners tell of rear-view mirror and windshield cowling vibrations as well as minor electrical shorts. **Warranty performance:** Above average.

ROAD PERFORMANCE: Acceleration/torque: Brisk acceleration with the manual gearbox (found only on pre-2007 models), with an acceptable amount of low-end torque—this makes the RAV4 a competent performer for most daily chores, while giving it the power for traversing hilly terrain and doing some light off-roading. **Transmission:** Smooth shifting and particularly well suited for off-roading when mated to the AWD. With the 5-speed manual transmission, the 4×4 mode can be engaged by a push of a button on the dashboard. With the 4-speed automatic transmission, the standard centre differential is controlled by a hydraulic multi-plate clutch. Large 16-inch wheels provide stability. The high ground clearance, wide track, short overhangs, and four-wheel independent suspension make it more suitable for off-roading than some other "light" sport-utilities lacking these features. The automatic transmission, however, saps too much power. **Steering:** Power steering is now much more precise than with the pre-2004 versions. **Routine handling:** Good. Minimal body lean, a smooth ride, and less trucklike handling. **Emergency handling:** Despite the vehicle's high centre of gravity, its handling feels sure and responsive. **Braking:** Good.

SAFETY SUMMARY: Airbags: Dual front; optional side. **ABS:** Optional; disc/disc. **Safety belt pretensioners:** Standard. **Traction control:** Optional. **Head restraints F/R:** *1997:* ★★★; *1998:* ★★; *1999:* ★★★; *2001–03:* ★★★★★; *2003–06:* ★★. **Visibility F/R:** ★★★★★/★. **Maximum load capacity:** *1996:* 910 lb; *1997:* 895 lb.; *2001:* 760 lb.

SAFETY COMPLAINTS: 1990–2000—A new brake caliper grease will reduce front brake clicking when the brakes are applied. **1999**—Fire ignited in the engine compartment (electrical wires) and fuse box (insulation). • Spot welds broke away from frame, causing trailer hitch to separate. • Alternator short caused sudden loss of power. • Uneven pavement caused the vehicle to flip over. • Cruise control causes a power loss when it engages, or it won't disengage when the brakes are applied. • When driver applies the brakes gently, cruise control doesn't disengage; instead, it kicks in harshly when vehicle speeds up. • Fuel tank is easily punctured by rocks thrown up by the front wheels. • Premature failure of the rear shocks. • Frequent brake pad replacement. **2000**—Windshield is easily chipped. • Sudden tire blowout. **2001**—Airbag deployed when key was inserted into the ignition. • Sudden, unintended acceleration. • Vehicle suddenly accelerated when coming to a stop by applying ABS brakes. • Vehicle pulls to one side when accelerating; alignment and tires eliminated as cause. • Intermittent hesitation when accelerating. • Engine hesitates when making a slow turn or when accelerating from a stop. • Rear brake problems. • Brakes squeal or grind when braking. • Rear window suddenly shattered. • Excessive mirror vibration. • Front brake groan noise. **2002**—Fire ignited in the engine compartment. • Airbags failed to deploy. • Fuel throttle linkage failure causes abnormally high engine revs, sudden acceleration. • Excessive noise and vibration when driving with rear window lowered halfway. • Brake pedal is too small. **2003**—Airbags failed to deploy. • Bridgestone tire failure. **2004**—Fire ignited in the engine compartment. • Rear-door window shattered for no reason while vehicle was underway. • Sudden acceleration in Reverse accompanied by brake failure. • Stuck accelerator. **2005**—Engine rust protection (Cosmoline) heats up and emits a sickening odour into the cabin. • Fuel-hose leakage. • Sun visor is no longer padded.

Secret Warranties/Internal Bulletins/Service Tips

All years: Remedy for front brake clicking found in TSB #BR004-00. • Loose, poorly fitted trim panels. **1998–2000**—Delayed upshift to Overdrive with cruise control engaged. • Troubleshooting a lit MIL light. **2001**—Ticking noise at base of windshield. • Windshield creak noise. • Upgraded brake pads to reduce front brake noise. • Diagnosing noises in passenger-side dash and the A- and C-pillar areas. • Headlight retainer tab broken. • Improvement to the rear wiper washer nozzle. • Exhaust fumes enter into the interior. • Roof rack rattle or buzz. **2001–02**—Troubleshooting rear brake squeal; Toyota will replace the rear drums free of charge. • Backdoor rattles. • Noise from top of instrument panel. • Measures to remedy a MIL illumination. **2001–03**—Cowl noise troubleshooting tips. **2001–04**—Fix for an accessory drivebelt squeal and a rattling belt tensioner. **2002**—Service campaign to inspect or repair the cruise-control switch. • The MIL light stays lit because of a damaged fuel-tank vent. • Wind whistle from front edge of hood. • Steering wheel may be off-centre. • Speedometer fluctuations. **2002–06**—Correction for vehicles that pull to the right when accelerating. **2004**—Stinky exhaust countermeasure (see bulletin).

EXCESSIVE SULFUR DIOXIDE ODORS

BULLETIN NO.: EG010-04   DATE: MAY 7, 2004

2004 RAV4

Some customers may complain of excessive sulfur dioxide odor under the following conditions:

- Stop and go driving.
- Heavy acceleration.

In order to reduce the sulfur dioxide odor, a new catalytic converter has been developed.

RAV4 PROFILE

	1998	1999	2000	2001	2002	2003	2004	2005	2006
Cost Price ($) (firm)									
4X2	20,628	22,150	—	—	—	—	—	—	—
4X4 (22%)	22,048	22,500	24,185	23,260	24,420	24,485	24,485	24,585	28,700
Used Values ($)									
4X2 ▲	6,000	7,000	—	—	—	—	—	—	—
4X2 ▼	5,500	6,000	—	—	—	—	—	—	—
4X4 ▲	6,000	8,000	11,000	12,500	14,000	15,500	19,000	21,000	—
4X4 ▼	5,000	7,000	9,500	11,000	13,000	13,500	17,500	19,500	—

Reliability	5	5	5	5	5	5	5	5	—
Crash Safety (F)	4	4	4	4	4	4	4	4	5
Side	—	5	5	—	5	5	5	5	5
IIHS Side	—	—	—	1	1	1	1	1	5
Offset	2	2	2	3	3	3	3	5	5
Rollover	—	—	—	3	3	3	—	—	4

4RUNNER ★★★★

RATING: Above Average (1996–2007); Average (1986–95). Beefed up considerably for the 2003 model year, the newer version looks like an on- and off-road winner. Previous models had been yuppified so much that their off-roading capability was seriously compromised. **Strong points:** Part-time 4×4 system allows the driver to shift on the fly and can be used on dry pavement. Instrument panel features easy-to-read gauges and user-friendly controls. Plenty of legroom and headroom. Three can sit in the back as long as the road isn't rough. Seats are generally quite comfortable, though the rear seat feels too low; rear passengers especially may feel cramped. Good off-road performance, high ground clearance, top-quality mechanical components and body construction, legendary reliability, and incredibly slow depreciation. **Weak points:** This SUV stinks—the exhaust smells like rotten eggs. It vibrates excessively and assaults the ears when driven with a rear window or sunroof open. It's much less practical than the Highlander on-road; it's underpowered, especially when compared with Nissan's Pathfinder; it has no manual gearbox for a safer and more thrilling off-roading experience; it's hard-riding; its steering is somewhat numb; it has a cramped interior and a serious lack of headroom with the sunroof option; entry and exit are difficult because of the narrow doors and steep step-in height; the ventilation controls aren't easy to access; and it's a gas guzzler. The optional differential lock has been discontinued, a serious blow to hardcore off-roaders. **New for 2007:** Nothing important; a redesign is planned for the 2009 models.

MODEL HISTORY: One of the most rugged compact sport-utilities on the market, 1996–2002 4Runners are powered by a 3.4L V6—the same engine that powers Tacoma 4×4 pickups.

2007 TECHNICAL DATA

POWERTRAIN (REAR-DRIVE/4X4)
Engines: 4.0L V6 (236 hp) • 4.7L V8 (260 hp); Transmission: 5-speed auto.

DIMENSION/CAPACITY
Passengers: 2/3/2; Wheelbase: 110 in.; H: 68.5/L: 189/W: 75.2 in.; Headroom F/R: 3.0/4.5 in.; Legroom F/R: 41/29 in.; Cargo volume: 42.2 cu. ft.; Fuel tank: 87L/regular/regular; Tow limit: 5,000 lb.; Load capacity: 1,035 lb.; GVWR: 5,250 lb.; Turning circle: 40 ft.; Ground clearance: 9.1 in.; Weight: 4,345 lb.

All ratings on a numbered scale where 5 is good and 1 is bad. See page 220 for a more detailed description.

What can you expect after paying top dollar for a new or used 4Runner? Excellent off-road performance, better-than-average reliability, and incredibly slow depreciation. What you overspend in buying one, you'll likely recoup when you sell. Still, be wary of early 4Runner "bargains"—they're hard-riding, have mediocre highway handling, use biodegradable head gaskets up to 1997, and guzzle fuel. Whatever you do, don't try to save money by purchasing an underpowered, 4-cylinder-equipped version. Also ditch the Bridgestone, Firestone, or Goodyear tires (have them replaced with Michelin or Pirelli tires).

If the most recently redesigned 2003 and later models are too rich for your blood, consider a cheaper 1996–2001 version that underwent a previous revamping. They are lower, wider, and longer; have much more passenger room; are easier to enter and exit; use dual airbags and four-wheel ABS; and offer a user-friendly one-piece tailgate. Both the 4- and 6-cylinder engines were upgraded, and a fully independent suspension was added along with rack-and-pinion steering. Channel your savings into a model equipped with the more versatile 6-cylinder engine.

Handling wasn't the 4Runner's strong suit until the redesigned 1996 models came along. The slow steering response and excessive body roll on previous models didn't exactly inspire confidence. Although a bit harsh, the ride is relatively civilized for a truck-based sport-utility, but you should expect lots of cabin vibration. Despite the stronger V6, the 4Runner is no tire-burner. Transmission engagement isn't smooth or very precise, either, and the absence, until 1998, of full-time 4×4 in such a pricey vehicle is disappointing.

Interiors are acceptably appointed and finished, though one would expect a bit more luxury and some additional features, considering the 4Runner's cost. The body on pre-1996 4Runners is also fairly narrow, and rear-seat passengers especially may feel cramped. Entry and exit are also difficult for many who find the step-in height too steep when compared to the Ford Explorer or GM Blazer and Jimmy.

1999—Both the grille and bumper were restyled, along with the addition of a new 4×4 system that allows for full-time 4×4 as well as two-high, four-high, and four-low modes. Inside amenities include a new cupholder and centre console, along with an overhead console that houses a garage door opener. **2001**—Base models were killed, leaving only the Limited and SR5 versions, with all 4Runners coming with an automatic transmission. **2003**—Completely redesigned: It's larger than the outgoing model and features more powerful V6 and V8 engines borrowed from the Tundra pickup.

COST ANALYSIS: A 2007 SR5 V6 starts at $39,970, and the Limited V6 sells for $49,960. The top-of-the-line SR5 V8 with its new complement of standard equipment is $46,700, while the Limited V8 goes for $52,595. Off-roaders will want a second-series 2004 for the enhanced 4×4 capability and additional torque. Be wary of used models equipped with the 4-cylinder engine because it's only suitable for the lighter rear-drive versions. **Best alternatives:** Also look at the Lexus LX 470 or RX 300/330 and Toyota Sequoia. The Jeep Grand Cherokee is more agile but nowhere near as reliable. **Rebates:** $3,000, along with zero percent financing. **Delivery/PDI:** $1,390. **Warranty:** Bumper-to-bumper 3 years/60,000 km; powertrain 5 years/100,000 km; rust perforation 5 years/unlimited km. **Supplementary warranty:** Don't waste your money. **Options:** A good anti-theft system. **Depreciation:** A very slow rate of depreciation beats out most vehicles in its class. **Insurance cost:** Average. **Annual maintenance cost:** Average. **Parts supply/cost:** Good, owing to a strong dealer network. Expensive parts, though. **Highway/city fuel economy:** *V6:* 10.7/13.7 L/100 km; *V8:* 11.5/15.5 L/100 km.

QUALITY/RELIABILITY: Better than average, but why the heck does it take Toyota five years to clean up its exhaust? And how can they ignore the overpowering noise and vibration produced when their SUVs and pickups are driven with an open window? **Owner-reported problems:** Frequent owner complaints of stalling under all driving conditions, plus electrical shorts, premature brake wear, excessive driver-seat and seat-track creaking (covered by a TSB), driver-seat rattling, a foul-smelling exhaust, harmonic vibrations, engine ticking, and accessories and trim items that don't hold up. **Warranty performance:** Average.

SAFETY SUMMARY: Handling is steady at low speeds, but the rear end can swing out unexpectedly on slippery surfaces, or when cornering at high speeds. All versions have built-in roll bars and a removable roof. **Airbags:** There have been reports of airbags failing to deploy. **ABS:** Standard; some later models may have optional four-wheel ABS. **Safety belt pretensioners:** Standard. **Head restraints F/R:** *1996:* ★★/★; *1997:* ★★; *1999:* ★★/★; *2001–02:* ★★/★; *2003–06:* ★. **Visibility F/R:** ★★★★★. **Maximum load capacity:** *1996:* 1,320 lb.; *2001:* 1,115 lb.; *2003:* 1,035 lb.

SAFETY COMPLAINTS: All years: Sudden acceleration. • Intermittent stalling, especially when braking or decelerating. • Fuel, ammonia, or rotten-egg exhaust smell. • Brake failures. • Warped front rotors. • Tire sidewall blowouts. • Excessive engine/drivetrain vibration and harmonic humming, felt initially through the gas pedal between 1400 and 2000 rpm (worst in Fifth gear). • Painful noise produced when vehicle is driven with the rear window down or the sunroof opened. **1999—** Fuel line leak sprayed gasoline all over the engine. • Incorrect fuel gauge readings; Low Fuel warning light comes on way too early. **2000—**Wheel came off, and vehicle rolled over. • Gas gauge reads empty when the tank is half full. • Driver's door-mounted rear-view mirror is warped. **2001—**When applying brakes, driver has to turn foot sideways. • Emergency braking causes vehicle to slide or skid. **2003—**172 safety-related incidents reported. • Exhaust fumes leak into cabin:

> The exhaust smell from the truck has a horrific and sickening smell. I have not been driving the vehicle due to this issue. It has made me sick to my stomach at times and my wife and kids cannot stand the continuous smell either. I am very upset with

this and would like a refund of my purchase price. Toyota sent out a TSB regarding the smell, saying it was the gasoline (poor) that people use. Wrong! I use Amoco and Texaco only.

• Shifter pops out of Fourth gear while underway. • Insufficient heating, defrosting. • Faulty Dunlop Grand Trek tire. • Wheel caps fly off. **2004**—Sudden, unintended acceleration when braking. • Excessive steering-wheel and gas pedal vibration. • Loose driver's seat. • Instrument panel is washed out in daylight. • Tire pressure sensors malfunction. **2005**—Engine surging, especially when the AC compressor kicks on. • Shifter knocked from Drive into Reverse. • Excessive steering vibration at highway speeds. • Vehicle pulls sharply to the right at cruising speed. • No brakes, believed to be caused by a malfunctioning brake master cylinder. • Driver's seat moves and rattles. • Driver-side rear window suddenly shattered.

Secret Warranties/Internal Bulletins/Service Tips

All years: Loose, poorly fitting trim panels. **1999–2000**—An inaccurate fuel gauge may require a new fuel sender. **1999–2001**—Power windows activate on their own. **2000**—On vehicles equipped with a supercharger, a squeaking or rattling noise coming from the idler pulley is likely caused by an out-of-tolerance idler pulley shaft. **2002–06**—Tips on troubleshooting and fixing vehicles that pull to the right when accelerating. **2003**—Sunroof and headliner rattles. • Front-seat squeaks covered by TSB #00403, issued April 2003. • Free replacement of the fuel pulsation damper. **2003–04**—Replace deformed, warped windshield mouldings with a free, new service part to correct the condition (TSB #BO005-04). • Second-row passenger-side seat noise. • Moonroof rattle correction. **2003–05**—No-start in cold temperatures. **2004**—Free replacement of the engine crankshaft pulley and seal until May 31, 2007. **2005**—Free installation of an upgraded catalytic converter to curtail a rotten-egg exhaust smell.

4RUNNER PROFILE

	1998	1999	2000	2001	2002	2003	2004	2005	2006
Cost Price ($) (firm)									
4Runner 4X4 (24%)	29,828	30,800	30,800	36,670	36,250	39,100	39,220	39,620	39,960
Used Values ($)									
4Runner 4X4 ▲	9,500	11,500	13,500	16,500	19,500	23,000	28,000	32,000	—
4Runner 4X4 ▼	8,500	10,000	12,000	15,000	18,000	22,000	26,000	30,000	—
Reliability	④	④	④	⑤	⑤	④	⑤	⑤	—
Crash Safety (F)	③	④	④	④	④	④	④	④	④
Side	—	⑤	⑤	⑤	⑤	⑤	⑤	⑤	⑤
Offset	③	③	③	③	③	⑤	⑤	⑤	⑤
Rollover	—	—	—	②	②	③	③	③	③

2007 TECHNICAL DATA

POWERTRAIN

Engines: 2.4L 4-cyl. (155 hp) • 3.3L V6 (215 hp); Transmissions: CVT • 4-speed auto. • 5-speed auto.

DIMENSION/CAPACITY

Passengers: 2/3, 2/3/2; Wheelbase: 107 in.; H: 68.7/L: 184/W: 72 in.; Headroom F/R1/R2: 4.0/4.0/1.5 in.; Legroom F/R1/R2: 41/29.5/23 in.; Cargo volume: 38 cu. ft.; Fuel tank: 75L/regular/premium; Tow limit: 3,500 lb.; Load capacity: 1,160 lb.; GVWR: 4,985 lb.; Turning circle: 40 ft.; Ground clearance: 7.0 in.; Weight: 4,035 lb.; Ground clearance: 7.0 in.; Weight: 4,500 lb.

2007 HYBRID TECHNICAL DATA

POWERTRAIN

Engine: 3.3L V6 (268 hp); Transmission: CVT

DIMENSION/CAPACITY

Passengers: 2/3, 2/3/2; Wheelbase: 107 in.; H: 68.3/L: 185.4/W: 72 in.; Headroom F/R: 40/39.8 in.; Legroom F/R: 40.7/36.4 in.; Cargo volume: 10.5 cu. ft.; Fuel tank: 65L/regular/premium; Tow limit: 3,500 lb.; Load capacity: 1,605 lb.; GVWR: 5,675 lb.; Turning circle: 37.4 ft.; Ground clearance: 6.9 in.; Weight: 4,245 lb.

PART FOUR • SPORT-UTILITY VEHICLES

RATING: Above Average (2001–07). *Hybrid:* Above Average (2006–07). **Strong points:** Good acceleration with the V6; impressive manoeuvrability; comfortable, though firm, ride; well equipped; plenty of passenger space and cargo room; well laid-out and easy-to-read instruments and controls; little engine or road noise; offset crashworthiness and head restraint protection rated "Good" by IIHS; reasonably priced; slow depreciation; base engine uses regular fuel; and high-quality components and fit and finish. *Hybrid:* More powerful than the gasoline-powered version, a bit less fuel-thirsty, and fairly reliable during its first year on the market. **Weak points:** The 4-cylinder engine is adequate but has little reserve power; audio and climate system graphics aren't intuitive; high step-in; unbelievably high freight and PDI charges; poor fuel economy; and no low-speed transfer case. *Hybrid:* Way overpriced; over-hyped fuel economy; its stiff suspension makes it cumbersome around tight turns; the AC condenser easily damaged by road debris; and not designed for off-roading. **New for 2007:** Standard side and side curtain airbags; a redesign is scheduled for the 2008 model year.

MODEL HISTORY: The Highlander is a Camry-based sport-utility that's similar to the Lexus RX 330, though roomier and cheaper. It comes with either a 4-cylinder engine or optional V6 mated to a 4- or 5-speed automatic. A vulnerable undercarriage and the absence of a transfer case for low-range gearing compromises serious off-road performance.

Although not as powerful as the Sequoia, the Highlander runs quietly and comfortably accommodates five passengers, though it claims to carry seven. With its responsive handling, user-friendly controls, full-time 4×4, smooth powertrain, and folding third-row seat (for kids only), this is the ideal SUV for folks who want to step up from a 2005 or earlier RAV4 but don't want to shell out about $20,000 more for an RX.

2004—A 5-hp boost for the 4-banger, and a new 3.3L V6 used by the 2004 Sienna and Lexus RX 330.

Highlander Hybrid

Priced at $44,850 for the five-passenger base model, Toyota's 2007 Highlander Hybrid doesn't cost much more than last year's model. Its combined 268-hp rating is nearly 40 more ponies than a standard V6 gasoline-powered Highlander that sells for $38,470. A seven-passenger Limited Hybrid will cost $53,670 (about $500 more than a 2006, versus $39,520 for the equivalent non-hybrid version).

That's a big price difference, but most people wouldn't mind spending the cash if the Highlander delivered the 8.3 L/100 km highway and 7.7 L/100 km city fuel economy ratings touted by Toyota. It doesn't. Owners complain they barely get 11.7 L/100 km (20 mpg), and independent journalists have pegged the real fuel consumption at an average of 10.2 L/100 km (23 mpg). They estimate that it would take about five years for a buyer to break even with the Highlander Hybrid and about six years with the Lexus RX 400h.

COST ANALYSIS: **Best alternatives:** If you must get the Hybrid, buy a 2007 version and pay a few hundred dollars more to get better airbag protection and fewer factory-related glitches. Conventional models are better used-car buys. A used 2004 model offers the most quality and standard features at the lowest price. Other good buys are the Honda CR-V, Hyundai Santa Fe, Subaru Forester, and Toyota RAV4. If you really want to go green, consider buying a 2006 Jeep Liberty diesel now—soon there won't be any more. **Rebates:** Not likely; these cars are way too popular. **Delivery/PDI:** $1,390. **Warranty:** Bumper-to-bumper 3 years/60,000 km; powertrain 5 years/100,000 km; rust perforation 5 years/unlimited km. **Supplementary warranty:** Not necessary. **Options:** The V6 is essential for passing and merging with traffic; the sunroof, however, eats up valuable headroom. **Depreciation:** Below average. Hybrids lose their value just as quickly as conventional versions. **Insurance cost:** Higher than average. **Parts supply/cost:** Generic parts also used by the RX series are easy to find and moderately priced. **Annual maintenance cost:** Much lower than average; however, if you choose the Hybrid, get ready to pay $4,000–$7,000 for a battery pack after the warranty expires. **Highway/city fuel economy:** *2.4L:* 7.9/10.6 L/100 km; *3.3:* 9.0/12.7 L/100 km; *Hybrid:* 8.3/7.7 L/100 km. Remember, hybrids save the most fuel in city traffic.

QUALITY/RELIABILITY: Owner-reported problems: Excessive vibrations; painful pulsating pressure felt in the ears caused by wind noise when vehicle is driven with the rear windows down; poor acceleration; hard gear shifts; faulty automatic transmission and computer control unit; erratic speedometer; AC and door lock glitches; a musty interior odour; and paint peeling or chipping. **Warranty performance:** Better than average. Toyota has confirmed that it has let quality slip; some 2007 models may be delayed while the automaker tightens up its quality control.

SAFETY SUMMARY: Cupholders are positioned too close to the gearshift lever, making it easy to inadvertently bump the lever into Neutral when reaching for a drink (the Lexus RX 300 has the same problem). **Airbags:** Front; optional/standard side. **ABS:** Standard; disc/disc. **Safety belt pretensioners:** Front. **Traction control:** Optional limited slip differential. **Head restraints F/R:** 2004–06: ★★.**Visibility F/R:** ★★★★★.

SAFETY COMPLAINTS: All years: Brakes applied, and pedal went to the floor without braking. • If the back window is opened while underway, the vehicle vibrates wildly and creates a vacuum that's painful to the ears; rolling down the front window or opening the moonroof eliminates the problem:

> Extreme air pressure when driving above 35 mph [56 km/h] and either rear window is open. It feels [like] riding in an airplane.

2001—Airbags failed to deploy. • Automatic transmission failure. • Transmission bangs into gear. • Speedometer is unreadable with sunglasses and tinted windows. • Plastic fuel-tank shield is ineffective. • Centre cupholders are poorly designed; when you remove a drink, it's easy to knock gearshift lever, taking vehicle out of gear. **2002**—ABS failure. • The top of the dash panel reflects sunlight, blinding the driver. **2003**—Brake and gas pedal are mounted too close to each other. • Brakes provide inadequate stopping power. • Brake failures, overheating, defective master cylinder. • Inoperative door locks. **2004**—Side airbags failed to deploy when car was T-boned. • Sudden, unintended acceleration. • Delayed transmission response. • Faulty stability-control system. • Steering wheel suddenly locked up because of a faulty steering sensor. • Brake fluid cylinder-pin failure. • Jack is inadequate, particularly with 16-inch wheels. • Daytime running lights blind oncoming drivers (the 2004 Sienna has the same problem). • Doors locked themselves following a collision. • Prematurely worn Toyo tires. **2005**—Vehicle rolled over three times, and airbags didn't deploy. • Seat belt failed to restrain driver who was rear-ended. • Sudden stalling. • Gas pedal stuck. • Accelerator was applied, and vehicle hesitated and then surged forward. • Transmission takes a few seconds to respond to the throttle:

> While traveling approximately 30 mph [48 km/h] (or cruising speed), attempted to pass another vehicle. The accelerator was pressed to the floor and the vehicle refused to accelerate for a period of approximately 2 seconds. Acceleration resumed

All ratings on a numbered scale where ⑤ is good and ❶ is bad. See page 220 for a more detailed description.

after this period. Contacted Toyota. Toyota said this is a normal phenomenon in their drive-by-wire systems.

• Impossible to read instrument cluster while wearing sunglasses or in direct sunlight. • Wheel studs are easily broken. • Vehicle shudders excessively if driven on the highway with the side window down.

Secret Warranties/Internal Bulletins/Service Tips

All years: Poorly fitted trim panels. • Sulfur smell (Toyota will change the catalytic converter). **2001**—"Goodwill" extended warranty to correct engine oil sludge problem. • Check Engine light troubleshooting. • Wind noise at the A-pillar. **2002**—Excessive brake noise and increased pedal stroke when applying brakes. • Malfunctioning MIL light. • Moonroof moulding creak. • Squeak and rattle remedies. • Reducing front seatback noise. **2001–03**—Drive axle squeak (see bulletin). **2001–04**—Hood protector wind-noise countermeasures. **2001–05**—Engine fuel-injector ticking. **2002–06**—Diagnosing and correcting vehicle's tendency to pull to the right when accelerating. **2004**—Install improved catalytic converter to clean up smelly exhaust (TSB #EG009-04). **2004–05**—No-start in cold temperatures.

SQUEAK FROM RIGHT REAR OF VEHICLE
BULLETIN NO.: DL001-03   DATE: MAY 23, 2003
2001–03 Highlander (4WD) The right rear inner oil seal has been improved to correct this condition.

HIGHLANDER PROFILE

	2001	2002	2003	2004	2005	2006
Cost Price ($) (firm)						
Highlander FWD (18%)	33,000	31,990	32,330	32,900	32,900	37,855
Highlander AWD (19%)	36,100	36,190	34,530	36,900	36,900	
Used Values ($)						
Highlander FWD ▲	13,500	16,500	19,000	23,000	25,000	—
Highlander FWD ▼	12,500	15,000	17,500	21,000	24,000	—
Highlander AWD ▲	16,500	18,500	21,000	26,000	30,000	—
Highlander AWD ▼	15,500	17,500	19,000	24,000	28,000	—
Reliability	④	④	④	④	④	—
Crash Safety (F)	—	④	④	⑤	⑤	⑤
Side	—	④	⑤	⑤	⑤	⑤
Offset	⑤	⑤	⑤	⑤	⑤	⑤
Rollover	—	③	③	—	④	④

RATING: Recommended (2005–07); Above Average (2001–04). A refined, well-equipped, and fairly reliable SUV that's way overpriced at $65,000. **Strong points:** Potent V8 performance on the 2005, though the earlier V8 was a decent performer. Plenty of torque and low-end grunt; acceptable big-truck manoeuvrability; comfortable ride; lots of passenger space and cargo room; well appointed, with a nice array of easy-to-understand-and-access instruments and controls; high-quality mechanical components and body construction; and it runs on regular fuel. **Weak points:** High-priced; Sequoia's heft compromises acceleration needed for passing and merging; chronic engine and transmission hesitation/surging since 2001; large turning radius; right rear-quarter vision is obstructed by the second-row head restraint; tough to parallel park; step-in may be difficult for some; rear-seat access a bit awkward; vehicle shakes when driven with the rear window open; high freight and PDI charges; and poor fuel economy. **New for 2007:** Nothing significant. The redesigned 2008 Sequoia is expected to be the size of the Chevrolet Tahoe and use the new Tundra platform with a choice of V8 engines.

MODEL HISTORY: A Tundra-pickup-based sport-utility introduced in 2001, the Sequoia is a full-sized SUV competing with GM's Tahoe, Yukon, and Suburban and Ford's Expedition. A bit narrower than the above-mentioned vehicles, the Sequoia nevertheless offers eight-passenger, third-row seating and generous

2007 TECHNICAL DATA

POWERTRAIN
Engine: 4.7L V8 (273 hp); Transmission: 5-speed auto.

DIMENSION/CAPACITY
Passengers: 2/3/3; Wheelbase: 118 in.; H: 75.8/L: 203.9/W: 78.9 in.; Headroom F/R1/R2: 5.0/4.0/3.0 in.; Legroom F/R1/R2: 41/32/26 in.; Cargo volume: 73.6 cu. ft.; Fuel tank: 100L/regular; Tow limit: 6,200 lb.; Load capacity: 1,320 lb.; GVWR: 6,500 lb.; Turning circle: 43 ft.; Ground clearance: 10.6 in.; Weight: 5,280 lb.

interior dimensions. A high ground clearance allows for some off-roading; however, the rear suspension has been modified to prioritize comfortable cruising. Safety features include Vehicle Stability Control, standard four-wheel disc brakes with ABS, side curtain-shield airbags, and three-way seat belts for all passenger positions.

2003—A rear load-levelling suspension, a centre differential lock button, Brake Assist, a seven-pin towing connect, and larger wheels and tires. **2005**—A more powerful engine (42 more horses); a new 5-speed, electronically controlled automatic transmission (ECT) with lock-up torque converter; Overdrive cancel switch and cooler; and a tire pressure monitoring system.

COST ANALYSIS: Best alternatives: $65,100 will get you a new 2007; the Luxury Package costs $1,000 more. An upgraded 2005 is an excellent buy at $20,000 less. For more brawn than reliability, you'll want the GM Tahoe or Yukon. Ford's reworked and less tippy 2002 or later Explorer 4×4 is no bargain when its poor reliability is taken into account. **Rebates:** $3,500 rebates plus other discounts and zero percent financing. **Delivery/PDI:** $1,390. **Warranty:** Bumper-to-bumper 3 years/60,000 km; powertrain 5 years/100,000 km; rust perforation 5 years/ unlimited km. **Supplementary warranty:** Not needed. **Options:** Nothing worth the extra money. **Depreciation:** Much slower than average. **Insurance cost:** Higher than average. **Parts supply/cost:** Tundra-sourced parts aren't expensive and are easily found. **Annual maintenance cost:** Much lower than average. **Highway/city fuel economy:** 12.1/15.7 L/100 km.

QUALITY/RELIABILITY: Better than average. **Owner-reported problems:** Premature brake wear and vibration; excessive engine noise; rotten-egg exhaust smell (Toyota service bulletins recommend replacing the catalytic converter under warranty); pungent ammonia smell. **Warranty performance:** Better than average.

ROAD PERFORMANCE: Acceleration/torque: Acceleration is quick, smooth, and quiet. **Transmission:** Flawless performance. The Multi-Mode 4×4 features shift-on-the-fly from rear-drive to four-wheel drive. Multi-Mode's Automatic Disconnecting Differential (ADD) provides part-time 4×4 but adds the capability of running in 4×4 mode on dry pavement, similar to a full-time 4×4 system. **Steering:** Precise and responsive; less trucklike than the Tahoe or Expedition. **Routine handling:** Pleasant ride quality and handling except in tight spots and twisty roads, where the Sequoia's size and large turning radius compromise handling. Nevertheless, the standard Torsen limited-slip centre differential improves traction on challenging terrain. Very effective Vehicle Stability Control, and an automatic anti-skid system that regulates the throttle and selectively applies the brakes to individual wheels to correct under-steer or over-steer. **Braking:** Braking is exceptional, when the system isn't breaking down (see "Safety Complaints").

SAFETY SUMMARY: Airbags: Front; optional side and side curtain. **ABS:** Standard; disc/disc. **Safety belt pretensioners:** Front. **Traction control:** Yes. **Head restraints F/R:** N/A. **Visibility F/R:** ★★★★★/★★.

SAFETY COMPLAINTS: All years: Inconsistent braking; Brake light constantly lit. • If the back window is opened while underway, the vehicle vibrates wildly and creates a vacuum that's painful to the ears; rolling down the front window or opening the moonroof eliminates the problem. • Loose or poorly fitted trim panels. **2001—** Airbags failed to deploy. • Sudden stalling. • Chronic hesitation when accelerating. • Windshield is easily cracked by road debris. • Anti-skid system activates when it's not needed. • Passengers slip on running board's "non-slip" strip. **2001–02—** Excessive vibration when braking. **2002—**Vehicle will suddenly drift across the highway. • Faulty automatic stability-control system. • Defective drive shaft. **2003—**Transmission may slip from Park to Drive or from Park to Reverse. • Anti-skid control engaged when it shouldn't. • Vehicle surges from a stop or when accelerating out of a turn. • Engine drops to idle for about 6–10 seconds when completing a turn. • Rear-view mirror is too small. • Noxious gas fumes enter the cabin. • Door latch failure allowed door to open when turning. **2004—**Separation of passenger-side front wheel. • Excessive vibration; vehicle doesn't track well. **2005—**Excessive idle speed:

> Very excessive fast idle speed in my 2005 Sequoia. I too owned a previous Sequoia (2000) model and there is no comparison. It can take anywhere from 4 or more minutes to warm up the engine before there is any noticeable change in its idle. In fact, I can idle out of my subdivision without hitting the accelerator. This should not be. You can also hear an increase in its idle if you turn on the vehicle's heater. The engine revs even more. You can't start it, and let it warm up 2 or 3 minutes and put it in drive or reverse. Getting in a cold vehicle after a Packers game, you must sit there and wait…and wait…and wait while all of the other parked (and cold) vehicles have left the parking lot. If you do not let the vehicle warm up a good 5 mins. you also have problems getting it to shift gears. You can be giving it gas and it is not going anywhere. It gives you the feeling like your transmission is slipping and/or not engaging.

• When vehicle is first started, engine surging causes rear wheels to spin, and the vehicle slides sideways, out of control. • Transmission hesitates and then jerks forward. • When going down an incline with foot off the gas pedal, vehicle won't coast for the first 5 or 6 seconds. • Sudden stalling during highway travel. • Rotten-egg exhaust smell.

Secret Warranties/Internal Bulletins/Service Tips

2001—Inoperative high-beam indicator light. • Foglight moisture. • Front seat cover damage. **2001–02—**Hard starts or no-starts. • Vibrating front brakes can be corrected by installing improved front brake caliper assemblies. • Upgraded back-door pull strap. **2001–03—**AC compressor durability improvement:

BULLETIN NO.: AC001-04   DATE: FEBRUARY 11, 2004

2001–03 Sequoia

To improve the durability and integrity of repairs on 2001–03 model year Sequoia vehicles with rear AC, a new suction tube and in-line filter system is now available. Please follow the procedures in this bulletin if the compressor is being replaced because of a noise concern and/or has seized.

2001–04—If the AC doesn't sufficiently cool the cabin, TSB #AC004-04 says that the water control valve is the likely culprit. • Faulty oil pressure gauge. **2002–06**—Diagnosing and correcting vehicles that pull to one side. **2004–05**—AC blower motor noise. **2005**—No-start in cold temperatures. • An upgraded catalytic converter has been developed to reduce sulfur dioxide exhaust odour.

SEQUOIA PROFILE

	2001	2002	2003	2004	2005	2006
Cost Price ($) (firm)						
SR-5 (25%)	45,400	45,670	48,100	53,650	59,530	58,210
Limited (25%)	57,900	58,205	52,150	63,500	65,855	66,100
Used Values ($)						
SR-5 ▲	21,000	25,000	29,000	38,000	48,000	—
SR-5 ▼	19,000	23,000	27,000	36,000	46,000	—
Limited ▲	24,000	28,000	34,000	44,000	51,000	—
Limited ▼	22,000	27,000	32,000	41,000	49,000	—
Reliability	⑤	⑤	⑤	⑤	⑤	—
Crash Safety (F)	—	④	⑤	⑤	—	—
Rollover	—	③	③	—	—	—

MINIVANS AND VANS

Faulty Minivan Doors

Justice Shepard awarded the owner of a 2000 Windstar $7,500 for mental distress resulting from the breach of the implied warranty of fitness, plus $7,207 for breach of contract and breach of warranty. Problems: Like many minivan doors made by U.S. and Asian automakers, the Windstar's sliding door wasn't secure and leaked air and water. Plaintiff and wife were afraid children would fall out.

SHARMAN V. FORMULA FORD SALES LIMITED AND FORD MOTOR COMPANY OF CANADA
ONTARIO SUPERIOR COURT; NO: 17419/02SR, 2003/10/07; JUNE 4, 2002

Stay Away from Redesigns

"I really shouldn't say this because people aren't going to buy a new [redesigned] car in its first year," says Koki Hirashima, Honda's manufacturing chief in North America. After introduction, each new model makes a gradual improvement, he says, and "the car's quality is at its best toward the end of its model lifecycle."

THE WALL STREET JOURNAL
JUNE 4, 2002

Two Choices

Like sport-utilities, minivans fall into two categories: upsized cars and down-sized trucks. The upsized cars are people-movers. They're mostly front-drives, they handle like cars, and they get much better fuel economy than truck-based rear-drives. The Honda Odyssey, Toyota Sienna, and Hyundai Entourage/Kia Sedona are the best examples of this kind of minivan, with Chrysler's Caravan-sourced lineup running fourth.

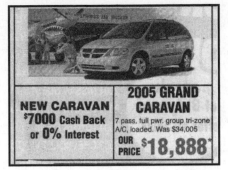

NEW CARAVAN
$7000 Cash Back
or 0% Interest

2005 GRAND CARAVAN
7 pass, full pwr. group tri-zone A/C, loaded. Was $34,005
OUR PRICE $18,888*

Detroit automakers combat their poor quality reputations by cutting prices instead of improving their products.

GM's Astro and Safari and Ford's Aerostar are downsized trucks that are dirt-cheap, particularly now that they are no longer manufactured. Using rear-drive, 6-cylinder engines and heavier mechanical components, these minivans handle cargo as well as passengers. On the negative side, their fuel economy is no match for the front-drives', and highway handling is ponderous at best. Interestingly, most rear-drive GM and Ford minivans are also somewhat more reliable and less costly to maintain than the front-drive Chrysler Caravan, Ford Windstar/Freestar, or GM's products (Montana, Montana SV6, Relay, Silhouette, Terraza, Trans Sport, Venture, and Uplander). This is due mainly to their use of sturdy mechanicals that are easily diagnosed and repaired by independent mechanics everywhere. As AWDs, though, all of these Detroit minivans will keep you in the repair bay for weeks and can easily cost up to $3,000 to repair.

Nevertheless, rear-drive vans are better suited for towing trailers in the 1,600–2,950 kg (3,500–6,500 lb.) range. Most automakers say their front-drive minivans can pull up to 1,600 kg (3,500 lb.) with an optional towing package (often costing almost $1,000 extra), but don't you believe it. Owners report white-knuckle driving and premature powertrain failures caused by the extra load. It just stands to reason that front-drives equipped with engines and transmissions that blow out at 60,000–100,000 km under normal driving conditions are going to meet their demise much earlier under a full load.

Quality—"Garbage In, Garbage Out"

Quality control has always been a more serious problem with minivans than vans, trucks, or SUVs because owners want a vehicle that provides both transportation and housing in a relatively small, "garageable" vehicle. This design makes mini-vans more complex and difficult to service. Plus, supplier cost-cutting and the addition of many new convenience, performance, and safety features have resulted in a steep decline in minivan reliability among the Detroit Big Three.

You know a vehicle has a serious reliability problem when its camping features are hyped more than horsepower in its ads.

Even VW, with the market all to itself in the '60s, couldn't build a minivan that was both reliable and an adequate highway performer. Despite a temporary hippie cult following, VW minivans quickly became known for constant breakdowns, glacial acceleration, and a heating system to match. And to this day, the VW Eurovan is more of a curiosity than a credible transporter.

Chrysler

But Chrysler minivans did catch on from their debut in 1984, when they were seen as fairly reliable and efficient people-haulers. Since they were backed by Chrysler's 7-year bumper-to-bumper warranty, much of the sting was taken out of repair costs. Since then, these minivans have dominated the market, despite their shorter warranty and biodegradable engines, automatic transmissions, brakes, air conditioners, and suspension strut towers. In fact, it's amazing how little Chrysler's defect patterns have changed during the past two decades.

The company's warranty has changed dramatically over the years. Initially, it was the industry's longest and most comprehensive powertrain warranty available. Now, Chrysler (or DaimlerChrysler, if you prefer) has once again dropped its 7-year powertrain warranty (resurrected from 2002 through 2004), leaving new minivan owners without coverage. Buyers are urged to forgo the purchase of any Chrysler minivan unless the discounted purchase price covers the cost of an extended powertrain warranty.

Hmmm...let's see, a $40,000 Dodge Sprinter, or a $23,000 Chevrolet Express? I'd buy the Chevy and vacation in Vegas with the savings.

When it comes to full-sized vans, the Detroit joke ("How do you pronounce DaimlerChrysler? Daimler...the Chrysler is silent.") becomes true. For the 2004 model year, Daimler-Benz decided to replace the Dodge Tradesman and Ram B-series vans with the Sprinter, a $40,000 diesel-powered, 5-cylinder Mercedes van that was previously sold and serviced by Freightliner. Not surprisingly, the Sprinter has been a marketing disaster due to its heft, mediocre fuel economy (yes, despite being diesel-powered), problematic servicing, and rapid depreciation.

Ford

Ford's minivans have gone from bad to worse. Its first minivan, the 1985–97 Aerostar, was fairly dependable, although it did have some recurring tranny, brake, and coil spring problems. Collapsing coil springs may cause tire blowouts on all model years, although 1988–90 models are covered by a regional recall. Other model years fall under a "goodwill" program, as this *Lemon-Aid* reader reports:

> On vacation in Washington, our 1995 Aerostar blew a tire that was worn right through from the left rear coil spring (broken in two places). The right rear coil spring is broken, as well. I showed Dams Ford in Surrey, B.C., the broken spring and they have "graciously" offered to replace the tire or repair the right side at no cost to us.

Ford's quality decline continued with the Mercury Villager, a co-venture that also produced the Nissan Quest. The Villager/Quest duo lasted through the 2000 model year. Quest continued on its own with minimal changes to its 2001 through 2003 models; the 2004 Quest was totally redesigned. First-year models were so glitch-prone that Nissan sent over 200 engineers to the States to correct the factory-related deficiencies.

Then Ford brought out the 1995 Windstar—one of the poorest quality, most dangerous minivans ever built. Renamed the Freestar in 2004, its failure-prone powertrain, suspension (broken coil springs), electrical, fuel, and braking systems can put both your wallet and your life at risk.

Ford has compounded the Windstar/Freestar's failings by copping a hard-nosed attitude toward customers with complaints and by refusing warranty coverage for what are clearly factory-induced defects. Fortunately, there's been a flood of Canadian small claims court decisions that have come to Ford owners' aid when Ford wouldn't. These Canadian courts say Ford and its dealers must pay for engine and transmission repairs, even if the original warranty has expired (see page 171).

Like the Dodge Sprinter, Freestar sales have hit rock bottom, and both vehicles are prime candidates for the chopping block.

General Motors

The second-best of a bad lot, GM's minivans are the most disappointing of all—not because of poor quality, but because of missed opportunities. Despite frequent redesigns and billions of dollars thrown at a series of five-year plans, most all of its minivans (except for the little-changed rear-drive Astro and Safari) are poor performers. Take, for example, GM's latest quartet of front-drive minivans: the Buick Terraza, Chevy Uplander, Saturn Relay, and Pontiac SV6. These identical models are slightly restyled versions of the decade-old Venture and Montana—spin-offs of GM's equally disappointing front-drive cars—known for their high maintenance costs, poor handling, lack of power, and fit and finish that's characterized by roof rust holes and paint blistering.

Okay, I know GM has a secret warranty to plug roof holes free of charge (see page 487), but why have holes in the first place?

Surprisingly, one would think that models like these that haven't changed much over the years would have quality built into them incrementally.

Think again. Each time General Motors tackled a generic defect—like failure-prone engine intake manifolds, blown-out automatic transmissions, and defective brake and fuel systems—the problems got worse, and GM's market share continued to plummet. Realizing that it cannot survive by building minivans that few people buy, GM plans to ditch all of its minivans by 2008 in favour of crossover-style large wagons.

Asian automakers

Asian competitors don't build perfect machines, either, as a quick perusal of NHTSA–registered safety complaints, service bulletins, and online complaint forums will quickly confirm. Asian companies, looking to keep costs down, have also been bedevilled by chronic engine and automatic transmission failures, sliding door malfunctions, catastrophic tire blowouts, and electrical malfunctions.

There is one big difference, though—Asian companies usually admit to their mistakes. The Big Three cover them up.

Some words of warning about Kia, Nissan, and Toyota: All of Kia's model lineup has been seriously failure-prone through the 2004 model year. Thereafter, Hyundai turned its attention to improving Kia quality with redesigned 2005 models that addressed most of the vehicles' shortcomings.

Nissan and Toyota have had the opposite problem. They made fairly dependable vehicles, including minivans, for over three decades. However, when the companies redesigned the 2004 Nissan Quest and Toyota Sienna minivans and Nissan launched the Titan and Armada trucks, reliability plummeted with these models. Even two years after the redesigns, overall quality is still nowhere near the pre-2004 levels.

European automakers

And, finally, we come back to where we started—Volkswagen. Its Vanagon (1979) and Eurovan/Camper (1993) have never been taken seriously since they came to North America in 1950 as a Transporter cargo van or a nine-seat, 21-window Microbus. A reputation for poor overall quality, puny engines, and insufficient parts and servicing support continues to drive buyers away.

The solution? VW has made a pact with Chrysler to sell 2007 Caravans under the VW logo.

Getting More for Less

Most minivans are overpriced for what are essentially upgraded cars or downsized trucks, and motorists needing vehicles with large cargo- and passenger-carrying capacities should consider Chrysler, Ford, or GM full-sized vans, even if it means sacrificing some fuel economy. You just can't beat their excellent forward vision and easy-to-customize interiors. Furthermore, parts are easily found and competitively priced because of the large number of independent suppliers.

Please remember that the following minivan ratings may differ somewhat from those in *Lemon-Aid Used Cars and Minivans 2006–07* because they use more current data and an additional author review of the ratings. Some minivans that are no longer built or are new on the market, like the Ford Aerostar and Mazda5, are given mini-ratings in Appendix II.

Full-Sized Vans

The North American full-sized van is a venerable institution. Contractors, electricians, and plumbers have turned these vans into portable toolboxes. Campers have customized full-sized vans to travel the country in comfort—canoe on top and trailer in tow. And retirees are cruising our nation's highways with large vans chock-full of every safety and convenience feature imaginable, turning their vehicles into mobile condos. Extended family? Hockey mom? No problem—an extended van can seat up to 15. Whatever the need, the full-sized van can accommodate it, if you can afford the gas.

Cheaper than an RV

Sure, they may not be sleek, fuel efficient, or sexy, plus their styling is likely decades old and their popularity has certainly waned, but large vans are relatively cheap, versatile carriers that have more grunt than front-drives and are much more reliable, as well. Okay, they *are* fuel-thirsty. But I'll bet that'll be the last thought on your mind when you pass more fuel-efficient front-drive minivans stuck on the side of the road with cooked engines or burned-out transmissions. There are also some safety reasons for choosing a large van, including superb forward visibility and plenty of room to sit away from the airbag housing. SUVs and other vehicles are also less likely to run up over the van's frame and crash into the passenger compartment.

Handling, though, is definitely not carlike (regardless of any hype to the contrary); expensive suspension modifications may be needed to produce a reasonable ride and manoeuvrability. Rear visibility is also problematic. Vans are susceptible to crosswinds, they wander at highway speeds, and they demand greater driving skills simply to corner safely and to park in the city. They are also not cheap, and in base form, all you get is a steel box on four wheels.

Fifteen-passenger vans are particularly hazardous. Often used to shuttle sports teams, church groups, and airport passengers, they are prone to roll over when fully loaded. In fact, they are three times more likely to roll over when carrying 10 or more passengers, according to NHTSA. This is because the van's centre of gravity shifts up and to the back unexpectedly, and excess baggage adds to this instability. Ford paid $37.5 million in a 2004 Kentucky van crash case after a Scott County jury found the automaker's 15-passenger van to be responsible for two deaths.

GM and Chrysler have substantially redesigned their full-sized vans within the past few years to improve both the handling and the ride, and to add important safety features like stability control, ABS, and additional airbags. Following this redesign, GM has led the Detroit pack with better-handling and smoother-riding models than those available from Ford or Chrysler.

Because Chrysler has been moving considerably upscale with the Mercedes-bred rear-drive Dodge Sprinter, Ford and GM should do quite well as long as fuel prices don't spike again, as they did during the first three quarters of 2006. GM has hedged its bets, however, by shoehorning the Duramax 6600 diesel engine into its large vans. This switchover should make the vans less fuel-thirsty and more attractive to frugal buyers. However, overall dependability is expected to drop and servicing costs are expected to increase substantially due to the Duramax's poor past performance combined with the government-mandated reformulation of diesel fuel planned for early next year (see "More Dirt on Diesels," page 75).

Chrysler's full-sized, American-built rear-drive vans are more reliable than its front-drive minivans. On one hand, this isn't saying much when you consider the expensive repair bills generated by blown transmissions and collapsed ball joints. On the other hand, the problems are well known and easily fixed.

Ford's Econoline joins GM in the rear of the pack from a warranty performance standpoint. Both companies are sticking with 5-year guarantees through 2006, even though they are in serious need of a 7-year powertrain warranty to restore confidence in their lineups.

GM's full-sized-van quality hasn't improved much over the years (though it isn't as bad as the company's front-drive minivans), and it's about equal to what Ford and Chrysler offer (except the Sprinter). Some of the more common problems shared by all three automakers are engine and drivetrain breakdowns, brake failures, premature brake and suspension/steering wearout, AC failures, electrical and computer module glitches, and both manual- and sliding-door defects.

The reason why there's such similarity in defect trends among Asian and Detroit van builders is that they all get their key components from a small band of suppliers. And, as they cut supplier profits, quality goes down the drain. Hence, as Toyota and Honda become more skinflint in their supplier payouts, they also see a corresponding quality decline, evidenced by engine and transmission defects and sliding-door failures.

The important difference lies in how each automaker responds to these quality problems. Chrysler brought back its 7-year base powertrain warranty in 2001 and then dropped it again on 2005 models; Toyota and Honda set up publicly disclosed 7- and 8-year "goodwill" extended warranties after owners blasted the companies for blaming engine and transmission defects on "poor maintenance"; and Ford and GM hide their faults, paying repair costs on a case-by-case basis, depending on how much the customer yells. And by the time Ford or GM finally admits there is a factory-related problem and extends their corresponding warranty retroactively, public confidence has already been shattered.

Full-Sized Van Advantages

- Lots of reasonably priced converted used models available
- Gasoline and diesel versions available
- Easy to repair, with excellent parts availability at reasonable prices
- Huge network of independent converters
- Versatile people- and cargo-haulers
- Easily converted to carry physically challenged occupants
- Commanding view of the road
- Excellent front and side crash protection
- Much lower-than-average collision repair costs

Full-Sized Van Disadvantages

- Quintessential gas hogs
- Depreciated prices are still higher than what many people can afford
- Homeowners' associations may prohibit vans parked outdoors
- Base models require costly options for comfortable performance
- Inadequate standard suspension needs expensive modifications
- Lack of power with base engines
- Uncomfortable seats in base models
- Expensive interior upgrades are necessary
- Poorly performing standard-issue tires (try replacing them with Michelin or Yokohama, instead)
- Poor handling at highway speeds and in winter conditions
- Difficult to access the engine
- Excessive road and tire noise resonates in cabin
- Large interior volume requires an extra AC and defroster
- Washing and waxing can be an all-day affair

- Clunky transmission noise amplified by "echo chamber" styling
- Sliding side doors usually rust out at the bottom and top runners; body panels rust out at the left and right upper-front welds, just above the windshield; and water pours off the roof into the power-window housing or onto front-seat passengers when they exit (add extra waterproofing to the window motor assembly, or expect to replace the motors every few years)

Safety-Related Problems

- Inadequate acceleration
- Lateral winds affect driveability
- Unforgiving, risky handling
- Trucklike manoeuvrability
- Uneven braking and loss of directional stability
- High-speed instability
- Poor rearward visibility
- Poor heating, defrosting, and ventilation systems
- Poor frontal crash protection (improved with airbag technology)
- Hazardous sliding doors

Full-Sized Van Tips

- Car washes spray directly into door-panel window channels, which plays havoc with the electrically operated windows and requires at least $400 per door to correct.
- Side mirrors are extremely hazardous. Objects are much closer than they appear in the side-view mirrors. Smart owners soon learn to rely on the rear windshield mirror instead, pulling back into traffic only when they can see a full profile of the following car.
- Built-in ice coolers are of minimal value; they're hard to clean and don't carry much.
- Heavy doors frequently need oiling and adjusting.
- Large front windshields tend to leak water through the top moulding, and the surrounding metal panels rust out early. Roof leaks are legion and are best plugged by adding a "hi-top" roof.
- It's a good idea to buy a light-coloured van: Dirt won't show as much, they're cooler in the summer (reflecting rather than absorbing the sun's rays), and the colour is easier to match when repainting.

Conversion Vans

A conversion van feels good. With dual captain's chairs (large plush seats with arm supports), lots of power accessories, a TV, a sofa/bed, and window shades…hey, it meets all our fantasies (or at least mine).

GM has one-half of a dying conversion van market, Ford has about one-third, and Dodge has the rest. Generating from $3,500 to $5,500 in profits, these vans are under fire from more fuel-efficient SUVs and minivans. GM bought most of the conversion van companies in 2004, following a dismal decade of poor conversion sales. Since 1988, conversions declined by more than 90 percent and have yet to recover. In fact, during the first half of 2004, consumers bought only about 15,000 conversion vans—compared with 204,000 units sold in 1988.

MINIVAN AND VAN RATINGS

RECOMMENDED
Honda Odyssey (2006–07)

ABOVE AVERAGE
Honda Odyssey (2003–05)
Kia Sedona (2006–07)

Toyota Sienna (2005–07)

AVERAGE
Chrysler Caravan, Voyager,
    Grand Caravan, Grand Voyager,
    Town & Country (2002–07)
Chrysler Ram Van, Ram Wagon
    (1980–2003)
Ford Econoline Cargo Van, Club
    Wagon (2004–07)
Ford Villager/Nissan Quest
    (1997–2003)
General Motors Astro, Safari
    (1996–2005)

General Motors Cargo Van,
    Chevy Van, Express, Savana,
    Vandura (1980–2007)
Honda Odyssey (1996–2002)
Hyundai Entourage (2007)
Kia Sedona (2002–05)
Mazda MPV (2002–06)
Toyota Previa (1991–97)
Toyota Sienna (1998–2004)

BELOW AVERAGE
Chrysler Caravan, Voyager,
    Grand Caravan, Grand Voyager,
    Town & Country (1998–2001)
Ford Econoline Cargo Van, Club Wagon
    (1980–2003)
Ford Freestar (2004–07)
Ford Villager/Nissan Quest (1995–96)

General Motors Astro, Safari (1985–95)
General Motors Montana, Montana SV6, Relay,
    Silhouette, Terraza, Trans Sport, Uplander
    Venture (1990–2004)
Mazda MPV (1988–2001)
Nissan Quest (2004–07)

NOT RECOMMENDED
Chrysler Caravan, Voyager,
    Grand Caravan, Grand Voyager,
    Town & Country (1984–97)
Chrysler Sprinter (2004–07)

Ford Villager/Nissan Quest (1993–94)
Ford Windstar (1995–2003)
General Motors Trans Sport, Venture (1990–96)

DaimlerChrysler

CARAVAN, VOYAGER, GRAND CARAVAN, GRAND VOYAGER, TOWN & COUNTRY ★ ★ ★

2007 TECHNICAL DATA

POWERTRAIN (FRONT-DRIVE)
Engines: 2.4L 4-cyl. (150 hp) • 3.3L
V6 (180 hp) • 3.8L V6 (205 hp);
Transmission: 4-speed auto.

DIMENSION/CAPACITY
Passengers: 2/2/3; Wheelbase: 119 in.;
H: 68.5/L: 201/W: 79 in.; Headroom
F/R1/R2: 4.5/3.5/2.5 in.; Legroom F/R1/
R2: 38.5/31/26.5 in.; Cargo volume: 60
cu. ft.; Fuel tank: 76L/regular; Tow limit:
1,800–3,800 lb.; Load capacity: 1,185
lb.; GVWR: 5,800 lb.; Turning circle: 41
ft.; Ground clearance: 5.0 in.; Weight:
4,515 lb.

RATING: Average (2002–07); Below Average (1998–2001); Not Recommended (1984–97). These minivans are for skinflint buyers willing to sacrifice some quality and refinement for a vehicle made in Canada and a low negotiated price (remember, the manufacturers' suggested retail price is just that—a *suggestion*). Nevertheless, everybody knows Chrysler, Ford, and GM minivans are at the bottom of the heap as far as quality and dependability are concerned. Chrysler, however, has had the best warranty for engines and transmissions, and only its transmissions are seriously defective. Ford and GM have serious transmission *and* engine problems. The Chrysler 2002–04 lineup with some of the original powertrain warranty remaining is your best choice. If the warranty has expired, or was never offered, ask the dealer to throw it into the deal. **Strong points:** Discounting can easily take $6,000 off of the suggested list prices, and rapid depreciation brings down ownership costs considerably on used models; a comprehensive powertrain warranty on some models; engines are fairly reliable; excellent braking; lots of innovative convenience features; user-friendly instruments and controls; driver-side sliding door; and plenty of interior room. **Weak points:** Neither as feature-laden nor refined as the Japanese and South Korean competition; the 7-year powertrain warranty isn't available on pre-2002 and post-2004 models; and the chintzy base warranty is inadequate to deal with automatic transmission, ABS, and body defects. Resale value plummets because of discounting on new minivans. Poor acceleration with the coarse 4-cylinder engine; the 3.8L V6 is a loud gas hog that's not as smooth or polished as the Honda or Toyota competition. Both automatic transmissions perform poorly in different ways, but the 3-speed (dropped after the 2003 model year) is decidedly the worse of the two. Mediocre handling with the extended versions. Headlight illumination may be inadequate. Skimpy storage compartments. Get used to a cacophony of rattles, squeals, moans, and groans caused by the vehicle's poor construction and subpar components. Optional side airbags. Crashworthiness has declined. **New for 2007:** Nothing important; a redesign is scheduled for the 2008 model year.

MODEL HISTORY: These versatile minivans offer a wide array of standard and optional features that include anti-lock brakes, seatback-integrated child safety seats, flush-design door handles, and front windshield wiper/washer controls that are located on the steering-column lever for easier use. Childproof locks are standard, and the front bucket seats incorporate vertically adjustable head restraints. The Town & Country, a luxury version of the Caravan, comes equipped with a 3.8L V6 and standard luxury features that make the vehicle more fashionable for upscale buyers.

Chrysler's minivans continue to dominate the new- and used-minivan market, though they're quickly losing steam because of market cooling and better product quality from Japanese and South Korean automakers. Nevertheless, they offer pleasing styling and lots of convenience features at used prices that can be very attractive. They can carry up to seven passengers in relative comfort, and they ride and handle better than most truck-based minivans. The shorter-wheelbase minivans also offer better rear visibility and good ride quality, and they're more nimble and easier to park than truck-based minivans and larger front-drive versions. Cargo-hauling capability is more than adequate. Caravans also give you excellent braking, lots of innovative convenience features, user-friendly instruments and controls, a driver-side sliding door, and plenty of interior room. Depreciation, though, is much faster than with pickups, SUVs, or Japanese minivans.

Don't make the mistake of believing that Chrysler's Mercedes connection means you'll get a top-quality minivan. You won't. In fact, owner complaints and service bulletins show that these vehicles continue to have automatic transmission, electrical system, brake, suspension, and body deficiencies similar to previous versions produced before the Mercedes-Benz buyout in 1998. The following *Lemon-Aid* reader's email is rather typical:

> My 2003 Dodge Caravan is a piece of garbage. My new Caravan had a recall for a part in the transmission. It's noisy, rough running, and it doesn't get the 21–27 mpg [8.7–11.2 L/100 km] as advertised. 12 mpg [19.6 L/100 km] is more realistic.

These minivans pose maximum safety risks because of their chronic electronic, mechanical, and body component failures. Owners report bizarre happenings with their minivans, like seat belts that may strangle children, airbags that deploy when the ignition is turned on, transmissions that jump out of gear, and sudden stalling and electrical short circuits when within radar range of airports or military installations.

Astoundingly, recently launched minivans continue to exhibit an array of serious mechanical deficiencies that belie Chrysler's so-called commitment to quality improvement. Some of the more serious and most common problems include steering-column glitches and the premature wearout of the engine tensioner pulley, automatic transmission speed sensors, engine head gaskets, motor mounts, starter motors, front brake discs and pads (the brake pad material crumbles in your hands), front rotors and rear drums, brake master cylinders, suspension components, exhaust system components, ball joints, wheel bearings, water pumps, fuel pumps and pump wiring harnesses, radiators, heater cores, and AC units. Fuel injectors on all engines have been troublesome; the differential pin breaks through the automatic transmission casing; sliding doors malfunction; engine supports may be missing or not connected; tie-rods may suddenly break; oil pans may crack; and the power-steering pump frequently leaks. Factory-installed Goodyear tires frequently fail prematurely at 40,000–65,000 km.

Since 1996, Chrysler's V6 engines have been far more dependable than similar engines equipping Ford and GM minivans. There have been some owner reports of engine oil sludging and head gasket failures, hard starts, stalling, serpentine belt failures, and power-steering pump hose blowouts (causing loss of power steering).

Automatic transmissions: Chrysler's Achilles' heel

Chrysler's A604, 41TE, and 42LE automatic transmissions, phased in throughout the company's 1991 product lineup, are a reliability nightmare that can have serious safety consequences (see "Safety Complaints"). Imagine having to count to three in traffic before Drive or Reverse will engage, limping home in Second gear at 50 km/h, or suddenly losing all forward motion. Catastrophic transmission failures are commonplace because of poor engineering, as the following reader discovered:

> My '99 Grand Voyager had a complete differential failure at 104,000 km. The retaining pin sheared off, which allowed the main differential pin to work its way out and smash the casing and torque converter.

> In our case this is what happened. The gear bit, the pin spun, shearing the retaining pin off. With the centrifugal force the main pin worked its way out of the housing and smashed a 2" x 4" [4 x 10 cm] hole through the bell housing and nearly punctured the torque converter. In my opinion this is a design flaw that should have been corrected 10 years ago. From my research I have determined that the transaxle identification number matches the original A604 transaxle. I was shocked that they would still use these in 1999.

Fit and finish has worsened over the past two decades. Body hardware and interior trim are fragile and tend to break, warp, or fall off (door handles are an example). The premature rust-out of major suspension and steering components is a major safety and performance concern. Paint delamination often turns these solid-coloured minivans into two-tone models with chalky white stripes on the hood and roof. Chrysler knows about this problem and often tries to get claimants to pay half the cost of repainting (about $1,500 on a $3,000 job) but will eventually agree to pay the total cost if the owner stands fast or threatens small claims court action.

And as the minivan takes on its albino appearance, you can listen to a self-contained orchestra of clicks, clunks, rattles, squeaks, and squeals as you drive. Giving new meaning to the phrase "surround sound," this noise usually emanates from the brakes, suspension and steering assemblies, poorly anchored bench seats, and misaligned body panels.

1991—Restyled second-generation models offered all-wheel drive, ABS, and a driver-side airbag (all optional); body was rounder and the glass area was increased. **1992**—Standard driver-side airbag. **1993**—Upgraded front shoulder belts; bucket seat tilts forward to ease entry and exit. **1994**—Passenger-side airbag, side-door guard beams, a redesigned dash, new bumpers, and moulding. **1996**—Third-generation models have more aerodynamic styling, a driver-side sliding door, roll-out centre and rear seats, a longer wheelbase, standard dual airbags and ABS (ABS later became optional on base models), and a more powerful 150-hp 2.4L 4-cylinder engine. **1998**—The 3.0L V6 engine was paired with a better-performing 4-speed automatic transmission, and the 3.8L V6 got 14 additional horses (180 hp). **2000**—A new AWD Sport model (it was a sales flop), and standard cassette player and AC. **2001**—A small horsepower boost for the V6s, front side airbags, adjustable pedals, upgraded headlights, and a power-operated rear liftgate. **2002**—Fuel-tank assembly redesigned to prevent post-collision fuel leakage; a tire air pressure monitor and a DVD entertainment system were added. **2003**—AutoStick transmission dropped; standard power liftgate on the Grand EX and ES models. **2005**—Side curtain airbags (optional in Canada), and second- and third-row seats that fold flush with the floor; AWD dropped.

COST ANALYSIS: A 2006 base Caravan costs $28,880 before substantial fall and winter rebates kick in, and a 2007 version will cost about $800 more. If you can get a discounted (15 percent) 2006 Caravan, do so; they are no different than the 2007 models. Better yet, hold out for a much cheaper, used 2005 that has some of its original warranty left. The same advice applies to the 2006 and 2007 Grand Caravan and Town & Country (2006: $31,500 and $44,750, respectively). **Best alternatives:** The 2005–07 Honda Odyssey should be your first choice, but earlier versions will do quite nicely. Toyota's 2004 Sienna should be avoided; however, 2005–07 and 2003 or earlier models are acceptable alternatives. GM and Ford front-drive minivans aren't acceptable because of their failure-prone powertrains; brake, suspension, and steering problems; electrical short circuits; and subpar bodywork. GM's Astro or Safari and Ford's Aerostar are cheap rear-drive minivans that are no longer made, but they are easily found and not particularly troublesome. Full-sized Ford, GM, and Chrysler rear-drive cargo vans, though, are more affordable and practical buys if you intend to haul a full passenger load, do some regular heavy hauling, are physically challenged, use lots of accessories, or take frequent motoring excursions. Don't splurge on a new luxury Chrysler minivan:

The upscale Town & Country may cost up to $15,000 more than a base Caravan yet be worth only a few thousand dollars more after six years on the market. **Options:** As you increase body length, you lose manoeuvrability. Don't even consider the 4-cylinder engine—it has no place in a minivan, especially when hooked to the inadequate 3-speed automatic transmission. It lacks an Overdrive and will shift back and forth as speed varies, and it's slower and noisier than the other choices. The 3.3L V6 is a better choice for most city-driving situations, but don't hesitate to get the 3.8L if you're planning lots of highway travel or carrying four or more passengers. Since its introduction, the 3.8L has been relatively trouble-free, and it's more economical on the highway than the 3.3L, which strains to maintain speed. None of the three engines listed above are as fuel-frugal, smooth-running, or quiet as what's offered by Honda or Toyota. As with all minivan manufacturers, sliding side doors have been trouble since they were first introduced. Child safety seats integrated into the rear seatbacks are convenient and reasonably priced, but Chrysler's versions have had a history of tightening up excessively or not tightening enough, allowing the child to slip out. Try the seat with your child before buying it. Power-adjustable pedals are an important upgrade, especially for short drivers. Other important features to consider are the optional defroster, power mirrors, power door locks, and power driver's seat (if you're shorter than 5′9″ or expect to have different drivers using the minivan). You may wish to pass on the tinted windshields; they seriously reduce visibility. Town & Country buyers should pass on the optional all-wheel drive coupled with four-wheel disc brakes (instead of the standard rear drums). Although the disc brakes have been improved, Chrysler's large number of ABS failures is worrisome. Ditch the failure-prone Goodyear original-equipment tires, and remember that a night drive is a prerequisite to check out headlight illumination, called inadequate by many. **Rebates:** $2,500–$3,000 rebates; 15-percent discounts and zero percent financing on the 2006 leftovers. **Delivery/PDI:** $1,200. **Warranty:** Bumper-to-bumper 3 years/60,000 km; rust perforation 5 years/100,000 km. **Supplementary warranty:** An extended powertrain warranty is a must-have. If buying the warranty separately, bargain it down to about one-third of the $2,000 asking price. Forget the bumper-to-bumper extended warranty—it's simply too expensive. **Depreciation:** Average; faster than average with the Town & Country. **Insurance cost:** Higher than average. **Parts supply/cost:** Easy-to-find, reasonably priced parts. **Annual maintenance cost:** Repair costs are average during the warranty period. **Highway/city fuel economy:** *Caravan:* 9.0/13.0 L/100 km; *Grand Caravan AWD:* 10.0/14.0 L/100 km; *Town & Country:* 9.0/14.0 L/100 km; *Town & Country AWD:* 10.0/15.0 L/100 km.

QUALITY/RELIABILITY: Below average. The 2005 Grand Caravan (91) and Town & Country (183) have elicited far more safety-related complaints that the Caravan/Voyager (43); apparently, the more luxurious models weren't better built. The 2004s, with their longer factory warranty, produced very few owner complaints. **Owner-reported problems:** These minivans are a hoot (and a howl, moan, squeal, chirp, and thunk) as they age. Powertrain failures are increasingly found to be caused by defective or poorly calibrated computer modules rather than by the hardware deficiencies seen a decade ago. Owner complaints focus on electrical glitches, erratic AC performance (compressor clutch burnout), rapid brake wear, and the accumulation of brake dust.

The following parts wear out quickly and are expensive to repair or replace: cooling system, clutches, front suspension components, wheel bearings, AC, and body parts (such as the trim, weather stripping that becomes loose and falls off, and plastic pieces that rattle and break easily):

> The entire light cover panel fell off of my 2005 Dodge Caravan while driving on the interstate. It was glued on, and the heat melted the glue. There are no screws holding this onto the car. I have met two other people with the same problem in the last 2 weeks.

A word about brakes: The front brakes need constant attention, if not to replace the prematurely worn or rusted pads or calipers, then to silence the excessive squeaks. Early wearout and warping of the front brake rotors within two years or 30,000 km is common and has serious safety implications. **Warranty performance:** Quite good through 2004; below average on the 2005 model year Grand Caravan and Town & Country.

 SAFETY SUMMARY: The 2006 and 2007 model year Caravans have similar NHTSA crash scores to the 2005 version, except for the addition of a four-star rollover rating. The 2006 Town & Country posted NHTSA crashworthiness scores that are identical to the 2005's ratings. IIHS concluded that side occupant protection on the 2006 Grand Caravan and Town & Country was "Poor" without side curtain airbags and "Average" with them.

Chrysler downplays the implications of its minivan safety defects, whether in the case of ABS failures or sudden transmission breakdowns. Seat belts are another recurring problem: They may become unhooked from the floor anchor, their buckles jam or suddenly release, and the child safety seat harness easily pulls out or over-retracts, trapping children. **Airbags:** Side airbags are optional. NHTSA has recorded numerous complaints of airbags failing to deploy in an accident or deploying unexpectedly—when passing over a bump in the road, or simply when starting the vehicle. **ABS:** Optional/standard. **Traction control:** Standard. **Head restraints F/R:** *Caravan: ★; Grand Caravan 1995: ★; 1996: ★★/★; 1997: ★; 1999: ★★/★; 2001–03: ★★★★/★★★; 2004–06 without adjustable lumbar support: ★; with adjustable support: ★★★. Voyager 2001–03: ★★/★; Town & Country 1995: ★; 1997: ★; 1999: ★; 2001–03: ★★★/★★/★; 2004–06 without adjustable lumbar support: ★; with adjustable support: ★★★.* **Visibility F/R:** *★★★/★★★★★.* **Maximum load capacity:** *2001 Grand Caravan Sport: 1,150 lb.*

SAFETY COMPLAINTS: All years: Sudden, unintended acceleration; owners report that cruise-control units often malfunction, accelerating or decelerating the vehicle without any warning. • Airbag malfunctions. • Get used to the term "clock spring": It's an expensive little component that controls some parts within the steering wheel and, when defective, can lead the Airbag warning light to come on or cause the airbag, cruise control, or horn to fail. It has been a pain in the butt for Chrysler minivan owners since the 1996 model year. Chrysler has extended its warranty for 1996–2000 model year minivans in two separate recalls and has replaced the clock spring at no charge. Apparently, the automaker has found that the part fails because it was wound too tightly or has short-circuited from corrosion. • Defective engine head gaskets, rocker arm gaskets, and engine mounts. • Engine sag, hesitation, stumble, hard starts, or stalling. • No steering, or steering lock-up. • Carbon monoxide comes through air vents. • Brakes wear out prematurely or fail completely. • Transmission fails, suddenly drops into low gear, won't go into Reverse, delays engagement, or jumps out of gear when running or parked. • One can move automatic transmission shift lever without applying brakes. • Several incidents where ignition was turned and then vehicle went into Reverse at full throttle, although transmission was set in Park. • ABS failure caused an accident. • Front suspension strut towers rust and then crack at the weld seams; jig-positioning hole wasn't sealed at the factory. • Brakes activated by themselves while driving. • Prematurely warped rotors and worn-out pads cause excessive vibrations when stopping. • Seatbacks fall backward. • Rear windows fall out or shatter. • Power window and door lock failures. • Sliding door often opens while vehicle is underway or jams, trapping occupants. • Weak headlights. • Horn often doesn't work. • Several incidents where side windows exploded for no apparent reason. • Adults cannot sit in third-row seat without their heads smashing into the roof as the vehicle passes over bumps. **1996–2002**—Steering may emit a popping or ticking noise. **1999**—Instrument panel fire. • Faulty speed sensors cause the automatic transmission to shift erratically and harshly. • Five-year-old child was able to pull shift lever out of Park and into Drive without engaging brakes. • Sudden tie-rod breakage, causing loss of vehicle control. • Chronic steering pump and rack failures. • Poor braking performance; brake pedal depressed to the floor with little or no effect; excessive vibrations or shuddering when braking. • Rusted-through front brake rotors and rear brake drums. • Power side windows fail to roll up. • Dash gauges all go dead intermittently. **2000**—Gas tank rupture. • Engine camshaft failure. • Although the owner's manual says vehicle should have a transmission/brake interlock, the feature may be lacking. • Cruise-control malfunctions. **2000–01**—Sudden loss of engine power accompanied by fuel leakage from the engine compartment. • Emergency parking brake may not release because of premature corrosion. • Right front brake locked up while driving, causing the vehicle to suddenly turn 90 degrees to the right; same phenomenon when braking. • Transmission shift lever blocks the driver's right knee when braking. • Fifth-wheel assembly fell off while vehicle was underway. • Instruments are recessed too deep into the dash, making it hard to read the fuel gauge and speedometer, especially at night. **2001–02**—Engine camshafts may have an improperly machined oil groove.

• Snow and water ingestion into rear brake drum. • Inaccurate fuel-tank gauge drops one-quarter to one-half while driving. • Faulty power seat adjuster. **2002**— Airbags deployed for no reason. • Airbag light comes on randomly, and clock spring defect disabled the airbag. • Middle seat belt unbuckles on its own. • Headlights come on and off on their own. **2003**—Exposed electrical wires under the front seats. • Excessive steering vibration. • Seat belts unlatch themselves. • Missing suspension bolt caused the right side to collapse. • Wiper blades stick together. **2004**—Chronic stalling. • Airbag clock spring failed, causing cruise control to also malfunction. • Seat belts don't latch properly. **2005**—Stuck accelerator and loss of brakes. • Engine stalling and surging. • Chronic stalling caused by defective fuel-pump module. • Transmission won't go into Reverse; intermittently jumps out of gear. • Van loses all power and steering while on the road. • Cold rain froze the rear brake drum rock solid. • Chemical used in the preparation of the vehicle (Hexane) causes allergy flare-ups and respiratory distress for some. • Back window exploded while parking vehicle. • Rear sliding doors cannot open from the inside; passengers could be trapped. • Rusty airbag sensors activate the Airbag warning light. **2006**—Improperly torqued power-steering hose came loose and sprayed steering fluid throughout the engine compartment. • Turn signals function erratically, and headlights flicker and dim.

Secret Warranties/Internal Bulletins/Service Tips

All years: If pressed, Chrysler will replace the AC evaporator for free for up to seven years. Other AC component costs are negotiable. **1993–2002**—Paint delamination, peeling, or fading. • A rotten-egg odour coming from the exhaust may be the result of a malfunctioning catalytic converter, probably covered under the emissions warranty. **1996–99**—A serpentine belt that slips off the idler pulley requires an upgraded bracket. • Upgraded engine head gasket. • Oil seepage from the cam-position sensor. **1996–2000**—Strut tower corrosion is a common structural defect. Chrysler has come up with a fix that will be partially compensated through a "goodwill" policy applied on a case-by-case basis. This defect is definitely caused by poor design and should have been targeted by a recall campaign. Stand your ground, and threaten to use the small claims court to get a full refund for the repair if Chrysler doesn't accept its responsibility for the correction of the problem. • Cruise control that won't hold the vehicle's speed when going uphill may have a faulty check valve. • Countermeasures detailed to correct a steering-column click or rattle. • Airbag warning light stays lit. **1996–2001**—AWD models *must* be equipped with identical tires; otherwise, the power transfer unit may self-destruct. • A suspension squawk or knock probably means the sway-bar link needs replacing under Chrysler's "goodwill" policy (5 years/100,000 km). **1996–2006**— Rusted, frozen rear brake drums:

REAR DRUM WATER/SNOW INGESTION/FREEZING

BULLETIN NO.: 05-002-04   DATE: FEBRUARY 17, 2004

SNOW/WATER INGESTION INTO REAR BRAKE DRUM
This bulletin involves installing a revised rear drum brake support (backing) plate and possible replacement of the rear brake shoes and drums.
2001–06 Town & Country/Voyager/Caravan
1996–2000 Town & Country/Caravan/Voyager
1996–2000 Chrysler Voyager (International Markets)
SYMPTOM/CONDITION: While driving through deep or blowing snow/water, the snow/water may enter the rear brake drums causing rust to develop on the rear brake drum and shoe friction surfaces. This condition can lead to temporary freezing of the rear brake linings to the drums. This symptom is experienced after the vehicle has been parked in below freezing temperatures long enough for the snow/water to freeze inside of the rear brake drums. When the parking brake has been applied the symptom is more likely to occur.

•Roof panel is wavy or has depressions. **1997–98**—Engines that run poorly or stall may need the PCM reprogrammed under the emissions warranty. **1997–2000**—If the ignition key can't be turned or cannot be removed, TSB #23-23-00 proposes four possible corrections. **1997–2001**—Rear brake noise. 1998—A faulty radiator fan relay may cause the engine to overheat; replace it with a new relay and reprogram the powertrain control module under Customer Satisfaction Notice #771. **1998–99**—Front brakes continue to wear out quickly on front-drive minivans. Owners report that Chrysler will pay half the cost of brake repairs for up to 2 years/40,000 km. • Silence a chronic squeaking noise coming from underneath the vehicle by installing a new strut pivot bearing. **1998–2000**—Troubleshooting AC compressor failure (see bulletin):

AC COMPRESSOR—LOCKS UP AT LOW MILEAGE

BULLETIN NO.: 24-15-99   DATE: JULY 9, 1999

OVERVIEW: This bulletin involves determining the extent of AC compressor lock-up and either working the compressor loose or replacing it.
1998– **2000** (NS) Town & Country/Caravan/Voyager
1998– **2000** (GS) Chrysler Voyager (International Market)
1998– **2000** (PL) Neon
SYMPTOM/CONDITION: The AC compressor may lock up, causing the drive belt to slip in the AC clutch pulley, producing a squealing noise at initial start-up.

1999–2000—Measures to prevent the right side sliding-door trim panel from hitting the quarter panel when the door is opened. **2000**—Delayed shifts. **2000–01**—Poor starting. • Rear disc brake squeal. • AC compressor failure, loss of engine power when switching on the AC, serpentine belt chirping, and spark knock can all be traced to a miscalibrated PCM. • No heat on front right side because of a defective blend air door. • AC compressor squeal. • Rear bench seat rattle or groan. • Hood hinge rattle. • Inoperative overhead reading lamp and rear wiper. • Noisy roof rack and power-sliding door. **2001–02**—Engine surging at highway speeds. • Engine knocking. • Engine sag and hesitation caused by a faulty throttle position sensor (TPS). • Engine mount grinding or clicking. • Steering-wheel shudder; steering-column popping or ticking. • Poor rear AC performance. • Wind or water leaks at the rear quarter window. • High-pitched, belt-like squeal at high engine rpm. • Sliding door reverses direction. • Incorrect fuel gauge indicator. • Loose tail light. • Flickering digital display. • Difficult to remove fuel cap (install a new seal); this free repair applies to the entire 2002 vehicle lineup. **2001–03**—Rear brake rubbing sound. • Oil filter leaks with 3.3L and 3.8L engines (confirmed in TSB # 09-001-03):

> On February 25, 2003, my 2002 Grand Caravan lost almost all of its engine oil, which resulted in engine failure. At no time did the vehicle's warning sensors indicate any problem with the engine. The failure was the result of a leak in the filter gasket of the FE292 Mopar oil filter. Documentation from the oil filter manufacturer indicates that the oil filter gasket overhangs the inside diameter of the adapter head.

2001–06—AC water condensate under the passenger-side carpet can be eliminated by installing an HVAC drain tube O-ring, says TSB #24-001-06, published February 23, 2006. • Troubleshooting a musty interior odour emanating from the AC. **2002**—Transmission slips in First or Reverse gear. • Airbags deployed for no reason. • Airbag light comes on randomly, and clock spring defect disabled the airbag. • Power-steering fluid leakage. • Middle seat belt unbuckles on its own. • Rear side vent window exploded while driving. • Erratically operating power sliding door or liftgate. • Headlights come on and off on their own. • Noisy engine and transmission. **2002–03**—Sliding door or liftgate malfunctions. **2003**—Steering-column pop, tick, or creak. Troubleshooting water leaks. • Three bulletins relating to automatic transmission malfunctions: delayed gear engagement; harsh 4–3 downshift; and excessive vibration and transfer gear whine. **2004**—Rough idle, hesitation, and hard starts. • Accessory drivebelt chirping. • Front suspension rattling. **2004–05**—Warm engine rough idle. • Transmission ticking. • Electrical locks inoperative; liftgate triggers the alarm. **2005**—Steering moan. • Rear quarter-panel speaker buzzing. • Third-row front seat leg won't retract. **2005–06**—Whistle sound from rear quarter glass area. • Steering-wheel rattle. • AC condenser road debris damage can be avoided by installing a condenser guard supplied by Chrysler (under warranty, of course).

CARAVAN, VOYAGER, GRAND CARAVAN, GRAND VOYAGER, TOWN & COUNTRY PROFILE

	1998	1999	2000	2001	2002	2003	2004	2005	2006
Cost Price ($) (very negotiable)									
Caravan (20%)	20,255	24,230	24,970	24,885	25,430	25,430	27,620	28,330	28,880
Grand Caravan (22%)	23,160	25,890	26,665	29,505	28,875	29,295	30,190	30,865	31,500
Town & Country (23%)	41,040	41,260	41,815	41,150	40,815	42,705	44,095	44,595	44,750
Used Values ($)									
Caravan ▲	4,500	5,500	6,500	8,000	10,000	12,000	14,500	17,000	—
Caravan ▼	4,000	5,000	5,500	7,000	9,000	10,500	13,500	15,500	—
Grand Caravan ▲	5,000	6,000	7,000	8,500	11,000	13,500	15,500	19,000	—
Grand Caravan ▼	4,500	5,500	6,500	7,500	10,000	12,500	14,500	18,000	—
Town & Country ▲	6,000	7,000	8,000	12,000	15,000	19,500	25,000	29,000	—
Town & Country ▼	5,500	6,500	7,500	10,500	13,500	18,500	23,500	27,500	—
Reliability	❷	❷	❷	❷	❸	❸	❸	❸	—
Grand Caravan, T & C	❷	❷	❷	❷	❸	❸	❸	❷	—
Crash Safety (F)									
Caravan	③	—	④	④	④	④	④	④	⑤
Grand Caravan	③	④	④	④	④	④	④	④	⑤
Town & Country	③	—	—	—	—	④	④	⑤	⑤
Town & Country LX	③	④	④	④	④	④	④	—	—
Side									
Caravan	—	⑤	⑤	④	④	④	④	④	④
Grand Caravan	—	⑤	⑤	④	⑤	⑤	⑤	⑤	⑤
Town & Country LX	—	⑤	⑤	④	⑤	⑤	⑤	⑤	—
Offset (G. Caravan)	❷	❷	❷	❶	❸	❸	❸	❸	❸
Town & Country	❷	❷	❷	❶	❸	❸	❸	❸	❸
Rollover (Caravan)	—	—	—	❸	❸	❸	—	—	④
Grand Caravan	—	—	—	❸	❸	❸	—	④	④
Town & Country	—	—	—	❸	❸	❸	—	④	④

Note: Voyager and Grand Voyager prices and ratings are almost identical to the Caravan and Grand Caravan. The Town & Country's rapid depreciation makes it almost as cheap as a Grand Caravan up to the year 2000 models, despite a $15,1500 premium when new.

RAM VAN, RAM WAGON, SPRINTER ★

RATING: *Sprinter:* Not Recommended (2004–07); *Ram Van, Ram Wagon:* Average (1980–2003). Fuel economy and cargo capacity trumps performance, and dealer support is questionable. **Strong points:** *Sprinter:* Fuel-efficient diesel engine, and lots of passenger and cargo space. *2003 and earlier models:* Powerful engines, lots of passenger and cargo space, airbag cut-off switch, and quiet running. **Weak points:** *Sprinter:* For starters, try a $1,990 freight charge. Additionally, it's overweight, underpowered, hard to service, and loses its value quickly. *2003 and earlier models:*

All ratings on a numbered scale where ⑤ is good and ❶ is bad. See page 220 for a more detailed description.

2006 TECHNICAL DATA

POWERTRAIN (REAR-DRIVE)
Engine: 2.7L 5-cyl. (154 hp);
Transmission: 5-speed auto.

DIMENSION/CAPACITY
Passengers: 10; Wheelbase: 118/158 in.;
H: 93.1/L: 197/W: 76.1 in.; Headroom:
N/A; Legroom: 37.9/33 in.; Cargo volume:
112–473 cu. ft.; Fuel tank: 98L/regular;
Tow limit: 5,000 lb.; Load capacity: 4,142
lb.; GVWR: 8,550–9,990 lb.; Ground
clearance: 7.4 in.; Turning circle: 36.7 ft.;
Weight: 4,408 lb.

Old technology, sparsely equipped, ponderous manoeuvring, excessive fuel consumption, and rear-wheel ABS have a history of failures. **New for 2007:** Dodge will give the Sprinter a taller hoodline and a modest horsepower boost with an inline 4-cylinder engine or a V6 diesel. New vertical headlights and a crosshair grille will further differentiate the Sprinter from its Freightliner twin.

MODEL HISTORY: This B-series ("Tradesman") van is one of the oldest van designs around. The full-sized van shares the same strengths and weaknesses as all of Chrysler's rear-drive trucks. Chrysler says they are used commercially 97 percent of the time, mostly as small school buses, car-rental shuttles at airports, and delivery vehicles. The Ram Van is the commercial truck; the Ram Wagon is the people-hauler. Base 1500s are about the size of a short GM Astro van. Both versions aren't hard to find and are generally reasonably priced. Its last model year was 2003, when it was replaced by the 2004 Sprinter.

It's hard to get excited about the basic Chrysler van; its seats are uncomfortable, and the lack of interior trimmings makes it essentially a shipping container on wheels. The sturdy 175-hp 3.9L V6 engine first appeared in the Dakota truck series and is adequate for most uses, but one of the optional V8s would be a better all-around choice, without much more of a fuel penalty. If you do get a used van with the V6, keep in mind that multi-point fuel injection, added in 1992 on both the V6 and V8 powerplants, makes for smoother engine performance (and more expensive troubleshooting). For 1993, the 5.9L V8 received the same upgrades as its 3.9L and 5.2L cousins—revised cylinder heads and fuel injection—boosting horsepower from 205 to 230.

Putting all of its cash into minivans, Chrysler didn't make any major improvements to these rear-drive trucks-disguised-as-vans until the spring of 1993; even then, the changes weren't all that dramatic. Five years later, Chrysler redesigned the 1998 version by restyling the interior and exterior, de-powering the airbags, adding a passenger-side airbag, and providing more front legroom and footroom. The 1999 models returned unchanged except for a larger fuel tank on vehicles equipped with 5.2L and 5.9L natural gas V8 engines. Since then, these vans were carried over without any major changes.

Dodge Sprinter

The $39,525 Sprinter is actually an old rear-drive Mercedes-Benz model that's been tooting around Europe and foreign markets since 1995. Freightliner first sold it in the States as a 2001 commercial hauler. Since 2004, DaimlerChrysler and Freightliner dealers throughout Canada and the United States have sold Sprinter as a passenger/cargo van.

The Sprinter offers a large load capacity and a fuel-sipping, 154-hp Mercedes-Benz 5-cylinder turbo diesel engine hooked to a 5-speed automatic transmission. Three wheelbase models are available: 118-inch, 140-inch, and 158-inch. Cargo area ranges from 7 cubic metres (247 cubic feet) to 13 cubic metres (473 cubic feet), and GVWR is between 3,878 kg (8,550 lb.) and 4,531 kg (9,990 lb.).

In its favour, the Sprinter offers impressive refinement, many body configurations, slightly better fuel economy than other vans, and class-leading passenger and cargo capacity. On the minus side: It's much more expensive than the competition; it's overweight and underpowered for everyday tasks; it's not easily repaired (yes, there is a right way, a wrong way, and a German way); it lacks a V8 for towing, hauling, and high-speed cruising; and it has never been crash-tested by NHTSA.

In summary, it's a loser.

COST ANALYSIS: Look for an off-lease 2003 traditional Chrysler van selling for about one-third of its original retail price. Wait for the improved 2007 Sprinter selling for about what the 2004–06 models originally cost. **Best alternatives:** Ford and GM full-sized vans are good choices. **Rebates:** Expect zero percent financing, rebates, and dealer incentives for the Sprinter. **Delivery/PDI:** $1,990. Yikes! **Warranty:** 3 years/60,000 km; powertrain 5 years/100,000 km; rust perforation 5 years/160,000 km. **Supplementary warranty:** Yes, on the powertrain, if it has expired. There is insufficient owner feedback regarding the Sprinter's long-term reliability. **Options:** None. The Sprinter comes well equipped. **Depreciation:** Faster than average with the Sprinter and the B-series wagon and van. **Insurance cost:** Above average; higher than average with the Sprinter. **Annual maintenance cost:** Higher than average with the Sprinter. Maintenance is a breeze on the traditional B-series vans, as is the case with most rear-drives. However, ABS, transmission, or AC repairs can easily wipe out your maintenance savings. **Parts supply/cost:** Good supply. Parts are a little less expensive than the competition's. *Sprinter:* Rare and costly. **Highway/city fuel economy:** *Sprinter:* 12.0 L/100 km.

QUALITY/RELIABILITY: *Sprinter:* Quirky and highly dealer-dependent for parts and servicing. The electronics, fuel system, and brakes are common trouble spots. *2003 and earlier models:* Competent servicing by dealers or independent garages is easy to find, and troubleshooting most problems is easy. Quality control is below average, however, and each redesign seems to carry over the same problem components. Sloppy assembly and poor-quality parts, in addition to fragile hardware, make the bodies rattletraps and allow for lots of air and water leaks. Paint peeling and delamination isn't as bad as on Ford and GM vans, but rusting is a problem. Be sure to inspect a potential purchase for premature rust, especially around the front suspension attachment points, doors, and exhaust/catalytic converter (stainless-steel exhaust systems excepted). **Owner-reported problems:** *2003 and earlier models:* Owners complain of AC, electrical system, fuel system, brake, and transmission failures. Paint delamination is also a common gripe, which Chrysler will often remedy for free up to six years of ownership. Owners also cite excessive brake pulsation (caused by premature front disc wear around 40,000 km). Corroded parking brake cables may also cause the brakes to seize. *Sprinter:* Premature wearout or warping of the brake rotors. The lack of a tailpipe allows diesel soot to enter the cabin. **Warranty performance:** Average.

 SAFETY SUMMARY: Complaints about airbags, brakes, door locks, seat belt failures, and chronic stalling when turning are quite common throughout the past decade of the B-series' production. **Airbags:** No side airbags. Severe injuries have been caused by airbag deployment, and there have been reports of airbags that deployed when the key was put into the ignition and of airbags that did not deploy. **ABS:** Two-wheel ABS is standard. **Head restraints F/R:** *1997 Van:* ★. **Visibility F/R:** ★★★/★★. Some owners report annoying dash reflection onto the front windshield (corrected by placing a dark drop sheet onto the dash).

SAFETY COMPLAINTS: 1999—Several wire harness fires under the dash. • Passenger-side wheel locked up and sheared off. • Tire studs frequently shear off. • Excessive road wander. • Cracked trailer hitch. • Cruise control self-activates. • Vehicle pulls unexpectedly to one side when braking. • Brakes lock up with light pressure. **2000**—Many complaints of excessive wandering over the highway. • When brakes were applied, pedal went to floor, extending stopping distance. • Transmission seal leaks continuously because of previous drive shaft failures. • Transmission popped out of gear while pulling a load uphill. **2001**—Faulty latch can cause seatback to collapse. • Child can put vehicle in gear without depressing brake pedal. **2002**—Not enough seat belts for the number of passengers that can be seated. *Sprinter:* **2005**—Chronic stalling while underway (disconnected fuel hose). • Transmission torque converter failures (see *autos.groups.yahoo.com/group/sprintervan*). • Tire valve stem failure. • Michelin tire failure. • Tires constantly lose air. • Electrical short circuit causes excessive battery drain. • Driver's side mirror doesn't adjust enough to see cars behind the vehicle.

ꟷecret Warranties/Internal Bulletins/Service Tips

1993–2000—Paint delamination, peeling, or fading. **1994–99**—TSB #23-43-90 gives lots of tips on locating water leaks through the dual cargo doors. **1994–2000**—Noisy rear leaf springs can be silenced by replacing the spring tip liners and installing new spring clinch clip isolators. **1996–99**—If the MIL light comes on, you may have to reprogram the JTEC powertrain control module (PCM).

1998–99—A knocking noise in the front suspension signals the need to install an upgraded stabilizer bar. • Measures to eliminate wind noise at the upper A-pillar area. 1998–2000—If the side or rear doors open beyond their normal travel, replace the check arm pin and bumper. • In cases where the sliding door won't open or close, consider installing a revised sliding-door rear latch assembly and latch rods and modifying the rear latch opening. 1998–2001—Hard starts, no-starts, and stalling may be caused by a malfunctioning central timer module. 2000—Excessive engine knock upon acceleration may be silenced by reprogramming the PCM. • Harsh transmission engagement can be fixed by replacing the transmission valve-body upper-housing separator plate and the valve-body check ball. You may also need to reprogram the JTEC PCM. 2000–01—If the MIL light comes on with a TCC/OD alert, consider replacing the transmission-pressure boost-valve cover plate. • A likely cause for sudden, widespread electrical failures may be a locked-up central timer module. • If the engine won't start or crank, you may have a blown starter relay; install a starter solenoid and circuit fuse. 2000–03—Doors lock and unlock on their own. 2001—Remedies for hard starts, no-starts, and stalling. • Radiators may leak between the filler neck and the cap. 2002—Indicated 9.25-axle vehicle speed may be inaccurate. 2004–05—Lack of power can be corrected by replacing the intake air temperature sensor. • Tips for fixing a chattering automatic transmission that is slow to engage.

RAM VAN, RAM WAGON, SPRINTER PROFILE

	1998	1999	2000	2001	2002	2003	2004	2005	2006
Cost Price ($) (very negotiable)									
Ram Van	24,480	25,120	25,695	26,250	26,008	26,100	—	—	—
Ram Wagon	28,000	28,845	29,080	29,720	31,000	31,300	—	—	—
Sprinter (22%)	—	—	—	—	—	—	40,290	40,290	39,525
Used Values ($)									
Ram Van ▲	4,500	5,500	6,500	8,000	10,000	12,500	—	—	—
Ram Van ▼	4,000	5,000	6,000	6,500	9,000	11,000	—	—	—
Ram Wagon ▲	5,500	6,500	7,500	9,000	12,000	15,000	—	—	—
Ram Wagon ▼	5,000	6,000	7,000	7,500	11,000	14,000	—	—	—
Sprinter ▲	—	—	—	—	—	—	25,000	28,000	—
Sprinter ▼	—	—	—	—	—	—	23,500	26,000	—
Reliability	❷	❷	❸	❸	❸	❸	❸	❸	—
Crash Safety (F)	—	—	—	❹	❹	❹	—	—	—
Rollover	—	—	—	❸	❸	❸	—	—	—

All ratings on a numbered scale where ❺ is good and ❶ is bad. See page 220 for a more detailed description.

Ford

2007 TECHNICAL DATA

POWERTRAIN (FRONT-DRIVE)

Engines: 3.9L V6 (193 hp) • 4.2L V6 (201 hp); Transmission: 4-speed auto.

DIMENSION/CAPACITY

Passengers: 2/2/3; Wheelbase: 120.8 in.; H: 68.8/L: 201/W: 76.4 in.; Headroom F/R1/R2: 5.5/6.0/5.0 in.; Legroom F/R1/R2: 40/29/27.5 in.; Cargo volume: 61.5 in.; Fuel tank: 75–94L/regular; Tow limit: 2,000–3,500 lb.; Load capacity: 1,315 lb.; GVWR: 5,880 lb.; Turning circle: 40 ft.; Ground clearance: 6.5 in.; Weight: 4,295 lb.

RATING: *Freestar:* Below Average (2004–07). Freestar is a warmed over Windstar, with its own serious quality control problems. Ford's planned changeover next year from the CVT automatic transmission to a new GM–designed 6-speed gearbox means Freestar's servicing and reliability problems will likely get much worse. *Windstar:* Not Recommended (1995–2003). Infamous for atrocious quality control, stonewalled complaints, and life-threatening defects. Windstars have similar transmission, brake, and AC failures to their Chrysler and GM competition, and their engines aren't very reliable. Unfortunately, Ford doesn't protect its owners with a 7-year powertrain warranty as Chrysler does, hence the lower rating for the Ford vehicles. **Strong points:** *Freestar:* The 4.2L V6 engine, new cabin appointments, optional side curtain airbags, easier rear access, flat-folding third-row seats, and larger four-wheel disc brakes. *Windstar:* Comfortable and well-appointed interior; comfortable ride; good instrument/controls layout; plenty of passenger space; lots of small storage spaces, in addition to the large amount of space for larger items; a low floor that improves cargo handling; and a five-star crashworthiness rating. **Weak points:** *Windstar:* Mediocre handling and restricted side and rear visibility. Driver's seat isn't comfortable for big, tall drivers, who complain of the lack of legroom, seat contouring, and lower back support. An abundance of clunks, rattles, and wind and road noise. These minivans have major failures that include faulty engines, transmissions, brakes, electrical systems, and suspension components. Sure, the Windstar combines an impressive five-star safety rating, plenty of raw power, an exceptional ride, and impressive cargo capacity. But self-destructing automatic transmissions, defective engine head gaskets and bearings, and "Do you feel lucky today?" brakes and front coil springs can quickly transform your dream minivan into a nightmare. And, as a counterpoint to Ford's well-earned Windstar crashworthiness boasting, take a look at the summary of safety-related complaints recorded by the U.S. Department of Transportation: coil spring breakage that blew the front tire, sudden acceleration, stalling, steering loss, windows exploding, wheels falling off, horn failures, sliding doors that open and close on their own, and vehicles rolling away while parked. **New for 2007:** Ford is dropping the continuously variable transmission (CVT) at the end of the 2007 model year in favour of a new GM–sourced 6-speed automatic, saving Ford about $1,000 per transmission. (Omigod!)

MODEL HISTORY: Ford can call it the Windstar or the Freestar; the fact remains, car shoppers want no part of it. In 2003, it competed as the Windstar and posted 70,404 sales in the first half of the year. In 2004, it was reincarnated under the Freestar name. Sales fell off by about 22 percent and have never recovered.

Freestar does feature upgrades in safety, interior design, steering, ride, and performance, but it still lags far behind the Japanese competition for performance and dependability. An optional "safety canopy" side curtain airbag system offers protection in side-impact collisions and rollovers for all three rows of seating. There's also better access to the third-row seat, which now folds flat into the floor. Entry-level LX models came with a 193-hp 3.9L V6, based on the Windstar's 3.8L engine. Up-level SE and top-line Limited models got a new 201-hp 4.2L V6, also derived from the 3.8L.

1996—45 more horses added to the 3.8L engine; a smaller 3.0L V6 powers the GL; upgraded seat belts; and a tilt-slide driver-side seat to improve rear-seat access. **1998**—A wider driver's door, easier rear-seat access, and new front styling. **1999**— A bit more interior space; the third-row bench got built-in rollers; improved steering and brakes (compromised by rear drums, though); ABS; an anti-theft system; new side panels; a new liftgate; larger headlights and tail lights; and a revised instrument panel. **2001**—No more 3.0L V6; an upgraded automatic transmission; a low-tire-pressure warning system; "smart" airbags; new airbag sensors; and a slight restyling. **2002**—Dual sliding doors. **2003**—Freestar debuts as a 2004 model; in the States, Mercury sells an upscale Freestar called Monterey to replace that brand's defunct Nissan-based Villager.

Engine and transmission failures

Engine and transmission failures are commonplace. The 3.0L engine is overwhelmed by the Windstar's heft and struggles to keep up, but opting for the 3.8L V6 may get you into worse trouble. Even when it's running properly, the 3.8L knocks loudly when under load and pings at other times. Far more serious is the high failure rate of 3.8L engine head gaskets shortly after the 60,000-km mark. Ford's 7-year/160,000 km Owner Notification Program only covers '95s, so owners are asked to pay $1,000–$3,000 for an engine repair, depending on how much the engine has overheated. Transmission repairs seldom cost less than $3,000.

Early warning signs are few and benign: The engine may lose some power or overheat, or the transmission pauses before downshifting or shifts roughly into a higher gear. Owners may also hear a transmission whining or groaning sound accompanied by driveline vibrations. There is no other prior warning before the transmission breaks down completely and the minivan comes to a sudden, banging, clanging halt:

> Phil, I just want to thank you for saving us at least $1,500. The transmission in our '98 Windstar went *bang* with only 47,300 miles [75,700 km]. After reading about Ford's goodwill adjustment, we were told by our local Ford dealer that owner participation would be $495. We received a new rebuilt Ford unit installed. Believe it or not, I am a fairly good mechanic myself and this came with no warning! We even serviced the transmission at 42,000 miles [67,200 km] and found no debris or evidence of a problem.

Ford admits automatic transmission glitches may afflict its 2001 Taurus, Sable, Windstar, and Continental. In a March 2001 Special Service Instruction (SSI) #01T01, Ford authorized its dealers to replace all defective transaxles listed in its TSB, which describes the defect in the following manner:

> The driver may initially experience a transaxle "slip" or "Neutral" condition during a 2–3 shift event. Extended driving may result in loss of Third gear function and ultimately loss of Second gear function. The driver will still be able to operate the vehicle, but at a reduced level of performance.

Ford's memo states that owners weren't to be notified of the potential problem (they obviously didn't count on *Lemon-Aid* getting a copy of their memo).

Brakes are another Windstar worry. They aren't reliable, and calipers, rotors, and the master cylinder often need replacing. Other frequent Windstar problems concern no-starts and chronic stalling, believed to be caused by a faulty fuel pump or powertrain control module (PCM); electrical system power-steering failures; hard steering at slow speeds; excessive steering-wheel vibrations; sudden tire-tread separation and premature tread wear; advanced coil spring corrosion, leading to spring collapse and the puncturing of the front tire (only 1997–98 models were recalled); rear shock failures at 110 km/h; left-side axle breakage while underway; exploding rear windshields; power-sliding door malfunctions; and failure-prone digital speedometers that are horrendously expensive to replace. There have also been many complaints concerning faulty computer modules, engine oil leaks, AC failures, and early replacement of engine camshafts, tie-rods, and brake rotors and calipers.

Getting compensation

Since 1997, I've lobbied Ford to stop playing *Let's Make a Deal* with its customers and to set up a formal 7-year/160,000 km engine and transmission warranty similar to its 3.8L engine's extended warranty and emission warranty guidelines (see bulletin on page 466). I warned the company that its failure to protect owners would result in huge sales losses as word spread that Ford's vehicles were lemons.

In the ensuing three years, under the capable leadership of Bobbie Gaunt, President of Ford Canada, hundreds of engine and transmissions claims were amiably settled using my suggested benchmark. But it didn't last. Ford U.S. got wind of it and then squashed the Canadian initiative. Interestingly, the three top Ford Canada executives who pleaded the Canadian case have since left the company. And Jac Nasser, the Ford U.S. CEO who rejected additional protection for owners, was fired shortly thereafter when he tried a similar move with Firestone claimants. No, Nasser isn't one of my favourite auto executives.

And as I predicted, Ford sales have plummeted, small claims court judgments are pummelling the company, and owners are vowing to never again buy any Ford product.

> Hi Phil: I just wanted to let you know that I did have to go to small claims court to nudge Ford into action. In pretrial settlement proceedings, the Ford representative at first gave me an offer of $980 for my troubles. I countered with the actual cost of $2,190 to replace my '96 Windstar's transmission. He did not like that idea, and we went back into the court setting. After instruction from the judge, I began to copy my 200+ pages (for the judge as evidence) of documentation for why this is a recurring problem with Ford transmissions (thank you, by the way, for all the great info).
>
> I think it made him a little scared, so I asked if he would settle for $1,600 (a middle ground of our original proposals) to which he accepted. My transmission costs were $2,190, so I basically paid about $600 for a new transmission (*not* a Ford replacement, either).
>
> Anyway, I figured a guaranteed $1,600 was better than not knowing what would happen in court. Thanks for your help!

Ford's denial of owners' claims has been blasted in small claims court judgments across Canada during the past few years. Judges have ruled that engines and transmissions (and power-sliding doors) must be reasonably durable long after the warranty expires, whether the vehicle was bought new or used, notwithstanding that it was repaired by an independent or had the same problem repaired earlier for free. (See the *Dufour, Schaffler,* and *Reid* engine judgments in Part Three.)

Automatic transmission lawsuits have also been quite successful. They are often settled out of court because Ford frequently offers 50–75 percent refunds if the lawsuit is dropped. See pages 194–196 for *Lemon-Aid* reader Alan MacDonald's tips on successfully beating Ford.

Dangerous doors

The courts have slammed Ford for allowing dangerously defective sliding doors to go uncorrected year after year. Here are some rather typical scenarios reported by owners and concerned parents: A sliding door slammed shut on a child's head while the vehicle was parked on an incline; passengers are often pinned by the door; the door reopens as it is closing; the door often pops open while the vehicle is underway; a driver's finger was broken while closing a manual sliding door; and the door's handle is too close to the door jamb, a hazard that has been reported on the Internet since 1999 (see *www.cartrackers.com/Forums/live/Ford*):

> I am writing about our 2003 Ford Windstar. Our passenger automatic sliding door frequently pops open after it appears to have latched shut. It has opened by itself on three occasions while the van was in Drive. Recently my three-year-old daughter almost fell out of the van headfirst onto concrete because the door popped back open as soon as it "latched" shut. The van has been in to repair this problem seven times without success. We first started having problems with both doors within the first two weeks of purchase. The times the door has popped back open are way too numerous to count.

> •

> The 2003 Windstar automatic sliding door opens by itself—no command; door will not power open; door lock assembly freezes. The door has opened itself while the vehicle is in motion—very scary and dangerous for my children. This is a problem Ford has known about but has not been proactive about fixing (see Ford TSB article 03-6-8).

Mental distress (door failures)

In *Sharman v. Formula Ford Sales Limited, Ford Credit Limited, and Ford Motor Company of Canada Limited* (Ontario Superior Court of Justice; No. 17419/02SR, 2003/10/07), Justice Shepard awarded the owner of a 2000 Windstar $7,500 for mental distress, resulting from the breach of the implied warranty of fitness, plus $7,207 for breach of contract and breach of warranty. The problem: The Windstar's sliding door wasn't secure and leaked air and water even after many attempts to repair it. Interestingly, the judge cited the *Wharton* decision (see page 159), among other decisions, as support for his award for mental distress:

> The plaintiff and his family have had three years of aggravation, inconvenience, worry, and concern about their safety and that of their children. Generally speaking, our contract law did not allow for compensation for what may be mental distress, but that may be changing. I am indebted to counsel for providing me with the decision of the British Columbia Court of Appeal in *Wharton v. Tom Harris Chevrolet Oldsmobile Cadillac Ltd.*, [2002] B.C.J. No. 233, 2002 BCCA 78. This decision was recently followed in *T'avra v. Victoria Ford Alliance Ltd.*, [2003] B, CJ No. 1957.

In *Wharton,* the purchaser of a Cadillac Eldorado claimed damages against the dealer because the car's sound system emitted an annoying buzzing noise and the purchaser had to return the car to the dealer for repair numerous times over two-and-a-half years. The trial court awarded damages of $2,257.17 for breach of warranty with respect to the sound system, and $5,000 in non-pecuniary damages for loss of enjoyment of their luxury vehicle and for inconvenience, for a total award of $7,257.17....

In the *Wharton* case, the respondent contracted for a "luxury" vehicle for pleasure use. It included a sound system that the appellant's service manager described as "high end." The respondent's husband described the purchase of the car in this way: "[W]e bought a luxury car that was supposed to give us a luxury ride and be a quiet vehicle, and we had nothing but difficulty with it from the very day it was delivered with this problem that nobody seemed to be able to fix....So basically we had a luxury product that gave us no luxury for the whole time that we had it."

It is clear that an important object of the contract was to obtain a vehicle that was luxurious and a pleasure to operate. Furthermore, the buzzing noise was the cause of physical, in the sense of sensory, discomfort to the respondent and her husband. The trial judge found it inhibited listening to the sound system and was irritating in normal conversation. The respondent and her husband also bore the physical inconvenience of taking the vehicle to the appellant on numerous occasions for repairs....

In my view, a defect in manufacture that goes to the safety of the vehicle deserves a modest increase. I would assess the plaintiff's damage for mental distress resulting from the breach of the implied warranty of fitness at $7,500.

Judgment to issue in favour of the plaintiff against the defendants, except Ford Credit, on a joint and several basis for $14,707, plus interest and costs.

COST ANALYSIS: Buyers should steer away from both the Windstar and Freestar; however, if you must make a choice, get a 2006 Freestar for $22,999 and haggle for a reduction of at least $5,000. **Best alternatives:** The Honda Odyssey and pre-2004 Toyota Sienna are recommended alternatives. Other, more reliable used minivans you may wish to consider: late-model Ford or GM rear-drives and the pre-2004 Quest. **Rebates:** $3,000 rebates, $2,000 discounts, and zero percent financing on 2006 and 2007 Freestars. **Delivery/PDI:** $1,200. **Depreciation:** Much faster than average. **Warranty:** Bumper-to-bumper 3 years/60,000 km; rust perforation 5 years/unlimited km. **Supplementary warranty:** An extended bumper-to-bumper warranty is a good idea. **Options:** Dual-integrated child safety seats for the middle bench seat and adjustable pedals are worthwhile options. Sliding side doors are an overpriced convenience feature and are failure-prone, as well. The Parking Assist beeper's false warnings will drive you crazy. **Insurance cost:** Above average. **Parts supply/cost:** Reasonably priced parts are easy to find, mainly because of the entry of independent suppliers. Digital speedometers are often defective and can cost almost $1,000 to repair. **Annual maintenance cost:** Average while under warranty; outrageously higher than average thereafter, primarily because of powertrain breakdowns either not covered by warranty or insufficiently covered by parsimonious "goodwill" gestures. **Highway/city fuel economy:** *Windstar:* 9.5/13.3 L/100 km.

QUALITY/RELIABILITY: Worst quality control among all minivans, including the much-maligned Kia. "Goodwill" payouts, where owners pay over one-third of the cost, have been used as a substitute for better quality control. **Owner-reported problems:** Engine, transmission, suspension (coil springs), and power-sliding door malfunctions lead the list of factory-related problems, but there have also been many complaints concerning computer modules, engine oil leaks, the timing cover gasket leaking coolant, early engine camshaft replacement, AC failures, premature brake rotor and caliper wear, and excessive brake noise. Poor body seam sealing causes excessive interior wind noise and allows water to leak into the cabin. Owners also report a smattering of paint delamination complaints and a windshield glare from the dash. **Warranty performance:** Incredibly bad. Customer reps read a script that says there's no more warranty protection and that requested repairs are the owner's responsibility. This is particularly sad because Ford had been improving customer service progressively over the past couple of years. Now, owners are once again complaining that Ford is unusually tight-fisted and duplicitous in giving out refunds for the correction of factory-related deficiencies.

SAFETY SUMMARY: The 2006 models earned a "Good" rating from IIHS for protecting occupants in frontal offset collisions. Head-restraint protection on vehicles with curtain head restraints was designated "Average," but the rating was "Poor" on models without side airbags. Base models may not have head restraints for all seats. The digital dash can be confusing. Optional adjustable pedals help protect drivers from airbag injuries. Be careful, though—some drivers have found that they are set too close together and say they often feel loose. Other nice safety features are a Sliding-Door warning light and airbags that adjust their deployment speed according to occupant weight. **Airbags:** Standard. **ABS:** Standard. **Traction control:** Optional. **Head restraints F/R:** *1995–97:* ★; *1999:* ★★★/★; *2001–03:* ★★★★/★★★/★★; *Freestar 2004:* ★★★★★; *2006:* ★★★. **Visibility F/R:** ★★★★★/★★. **Maximum load capacity:** *2001 SE Sport:* 1,360 lb.

SAFETY COMPLAINTS: All years: These are the most dangerous minivans on the market. Owners of the 1998 Windstar, for example, have logged over 1,549 safety-related complaints in the NHTSA database, compared to 708 incidents registered against Chrysler's 1998 Caravan, which had more than double the sales. And it gets worse the further back you go. The good news is that the 2004 Freestar, a revamped Windstar, has only generated 70 reports of safety-related failures. **1999**—The following is a summary of the several hundred complaints in the NHTSA database. Many of these defects have been found in previous model year Windstars, too: Airbag failed to deploy. • While parked, cruising, turning on the ignition, or applying brakes, vehicle suddenly accelerates. • Stuck accelerator causes unintended acceleration. • Chronic stalling caused by fuel vapour lock or faulty fuel pump. • Check Engine light constantly comes on because of a faulty gas cap or over-sensitive warning system. • Front passenger-side wheel fell off when turning at a traffic light; in another reported incident, dealer found the five lug nuts had broken in half. • Vehicle pops out of gear while parked and then rolls away. • Frequent transmission failures, including noisy engagement, won't engage Forward or Reverse, and slips or jerks into gear. • Transmission jumped from Park to Reverse and pinned driver against tree (this is a common problem affecting Ford vehicles for almost three decades). • Sudden loss of power steering, chronic leakage of fluid, and early replacement of steering components such as the pump and hoses. • Excessive brake fade after successive stops. • When brake pedal is depressed, it sinks below the accelerator pedal level, causing the accelerator to be pressed as well—particularly annoying for drivers with large feet. • ABS module wire burned out. • Complete electrical failure during rainstorm. • Horn button "sweet spot" is too small and takes too much pressure to activate; one owner says, "Horn doesn't work unless you hit it with a sledgehammer." • Windshield suddenly exploded when car was slowly accelerating. • Sliding door opens and closes on its own, sticks open or closed, or suddenly slams shut on a downgrade. • Sliding door closed on child's arm. • Door locks don't stay locked; passenger-side door opened when turning, causing passenger to fall out. • Many complaints that the side or rear windows suddenly exploded. • Rear defogger isn't operable (lower part of windshield isn't clear) in inclement weather when windshield wipers are activated. • Windshield wipers fail to clear windshield. • Water pours from dash onto front passenger floor. • Floor cupholder trips passengers. • Continental General tires lose air and crack between the treads. • Unspecified original-equipment tires have sudden tread separation. • Large A-pillar (where windshield attaches to door) seriously impairs forward visibility, hiding pedestrians. • Seat belts aren't as described in owner's manual (supposed to be automatically retractable). • Two incidents where flames shot up out of fuel-tank filler spout when gassing up. **2000**—Vehicle caught on fire while parked. • Sudden, unintended acceleration from a stop. • Chronic stalling; engine shuts down when turning. • Sometimes cruise control won't engage or engages on its own. • Lug nut failure caused right passenger-side wheel to come off. • One Ingersoll, Ontario, owner of a year 2000 Windstar recounts the following harrowing experience:

> Last week, as my wife was running errands, the support arm that goes from the rear crossmember (not an axle anymore) up under the floor, broke in half. The dealer replaced the whole rear end as it is one welded assembly. If she had been on the highway going 80 km/h she would probably have been in a bad accident.

• Check Engine light constantly comes on for no reason. • Driver heard a banging noise and then the Windstar suddenly went into a tailspin; dealer blamed pins that "fell out of spindle." • Transmission jumped out of gear while on highway. • Many reports of premature transmission replacements. • Transmission lever can be shifted without depressing brake pedal (unsafe for children). • After several dealer visits, brakes still spongy, pedal goes to floor without braking, and emergency brake has almost no effect. • When braking, foot also contacts the accelerator pedal. • Emergency brake is inadequate to hold the vehicle. • Dealers acknowledge that brake master cylinders are problematic. • Joints aren't connected under quarter wheel weld; one weld is missing, and three aren't properly connected. • Passenger door opened when vehicle hit a pothole. • While underway, right-side sliding door opens on its own and won't close (see *Sharman* judgment on page 461). • When parked on an incline, sliding door released and came crashing down on child. • Hood suddenly flew up on the freeway. • Steering failed three times. • Power-steering pump whines and lurches. • Steering wheel is noisy and hard to turn. • Rear side windows, liftgate window, and windshield often explode suddenly. • When the interior rear-view mirror is set for Night Vision, images become distorted and hard to see. • Windshield wipers are unreliable. • Second-row driver-side seat belt buckle wouldn't latch. • Original-equipment tire blowouts and sidewall bulging. • Driver must hunt for right place to push for horn to work. **2000–01**—Harsh 3–2 shifting when coasting and then accelerating. • Transmission fluid leakage. • 3.8L engine hum, moan, drone, spark knock, and vibration. • Power-steering grunts or shudders during slow turns; fluid leaks. • Faulty self-activating wipers and door, trunk, and ignition locks. **2001**—Airbag may suddenly deploy when the engine is started. • Transmission shudder during 3–4 shifts. • Transmission fluid leaks from the main control cover area. • Power-steering grunt or notchy feel when turning; leaks. • Drifting or pulling while driving. • Rear drum brakes drag or fail to release properly. • Fogging of the front and side windows. • Twisted seatback frame. **2002**—Airbags failed to deploy. • Sudden automatic transmission failure. • Gas and brake pedal are set too close. • Back door won't open or close properly. • Both sliding doors won't retract. • Child can shift transmission without touching brake pedal. **2003**—Wheel suddenly broke away. • Airbags failed to deploy. • Sudden, unintended acceleration when braking. • Engine surging. • Chronic stalling from blown fuel-pump fuses. • Coolant leaks from the timing cover gasket. • Advanced tracking system engages on its own, causing vehicle to shake violently. • Automatic transmission suddenly seized. • Steering wheel locked up. • Interior windows always fogged up because of inadequate defrosting. • Brake and gas pedals are mounted too close together. • Gas-pedal arm pivot causes the pedal to flip almost horizontally, exaggerating any pedal pressure. • Body seams not sealed; water intrudes into floor seat anchors. • Driver's seat poorly anchored. • Dashboard glare onto the windshield. • Check Tire warning light comes on for no reason. • Tire jack collapsed. *Freestar:* **2004**—Sudden loss of steering. • Airbag light stays on, may not deploy. • Driver heard a bang and then felt as if vehicle was running on a flat tire; A-frame had dropped out of the tie-rod collar. • Front axle suddenly broke while underway. • Left inner brake pad fell apart and locked up brake. • Dealer had to change pads and rotor. • Sliding door closed on a child, causing slight injuries. • Plastic running board broke, blocking sliding door operation and locking occupants inside the vehicle. • Headliner-mounted DVD screen blocks rear-view mirror. **2005**—Fuel tank leaks. • Brake failure; brakes are like sponges. • Brake pad sticks to the rotors. • Vehicle vibrates and shakes when going over bumps, and almost goes out of control. •

Excessive force needed to make power-sliding door retract. • Headlight beam pattern is inadequate. • Windshield wiper motor suddenly quits. • Use of a cell phone charger could make the airbags deploy. • Vehicle will not start if the fuel tank is one-quarter full and the van is parked on a steep incline.

 Secret Warranties/Internal Bulletins/Service Tips

All years: Engine intake manifolds: When engine oil mixes with coolant or the engine is losing coolant, this signals the need for revised engine lower intake manifold side gaskets and/or front cover gaskets. The following internal bulletin can go a long way toward getting a repair refund for any Ford model up to 7 years/ 160,000 km, since it shows that the defect is factory-related, an upgraded part has been devised, and the problem is covered by the much-longer emissions warranty and a U.S. class action settlement:

ENGINE COOLANT LOSS/OIL CONTAMINATION

BULLETIN NO.: 99-20-7   DATE: OCTOBER 4, 1999

3.8L AND 4.2L ENGINE—LOSS OF COOLANT; ENGINE OIL CONTAMINATED WITH COOLANT
1996–97 THUNDERBIRD
1996–98 MUSTANG, WINDSTAR
1997–98 E-150, E-250, F-150
1996–97 COUGAR
This may be caused by the lower intake manifold side gaskets and/or front cover gaskets allowing coolant to pass into the cylinders and/or the crankcase.
ACTION: Revised lower intake manifold side and front cover gaskets have been released for service.
WARRANTY STATUS: Eligible under the provisions of bumper to bumper warranty coverage and emissions warranty coverage

---

• An exhaust buzz or rattle may be caused by a loose catalyst or heat shield. • Sliding door malfunctions. • Buzzing noise in speakers caused by fuel pump. • A MIL lit for no reason may simply show that the gas cap is loose. • If the power-sliding door won't close, replace the door controller; if it pops or disengages when fully closed, adjust the door and rear striker to reduce closing resistance. • Front wipers that operate when switched off need a revised multi-function switch (service program and recall). **1995–99**—Tips for correcting excessive noise, vibration, and harshness while driving; side door wind noise; and windshield water leaks. **1995–2000**—A harsh 3–2 downshift/shudder when accelerating or turning may simply mean the transmission is low on fluid. • Diagnostic tips on brake vibration, inspection, and friction material replacement. **1995–2002**—Silencing suspension noise. **1995–2003**—Engines that have been repaired may have an incorrectly installed gear-driven camshaft-position sensor synchronizer assembly. This could cause poor fuel economy, loss of power, and engine surge, hesitation, and rough running. **1996–2003**—Tips on troubleshooting automatic transmission faulty torque converters. **1997–98**—A rattling or clunking noise coming from the front of the vehicle may be caused by a loose front tension-strut bushing retainer. **1998–99**—Tips on spotting abnormal ABS braking noise, although Ford says some noise is inevitable. **1999**—No Reverse engagement may be caused by torn Reverse clutch lip seals. • To improve the defogging of the driver-side door glass, install a revised window de-mister vent. **1999–2003**—Water may enter into the power control module or transaxle vent and cause delayed or harsh shifting, no reverse engagement, an engine misfire, or a rough idle. • Things that go beep in the night:

PARKING ASSIST—FALSE ACTIVATION

BULLETIN NO.: 04-7-1   DATE: APRIL 19, 2004

FALSE ACTIVATION OF WARNING TONE

1999–2003 WINDSTAR	2000–04 NAVIGATOR
1999–2004 EXPLORER	2002–03 BLACKWOOD
2000–04 EXCURSION, EXPEDITION	2003–04 AVIATOR
2001–04 F SUPER DUTY	1999–2004 MOUNTAINEER
2003–05 ESCAPE	2004 MONTEREY
2004 F-150; FREESTAR	

Various 1999–2005 vehicles equipped with the Parking Aid reverse sensing system (RSS) may sound a warning tone when the vehicle is in Reverse, even though there are no objects behind the vehicle. This condition may also occur on vehicles equipped with the forward sensing system (FSS) when vehicle is in Reverse or Drive.

ACTION: The condition MAY NOT be due to proximity sensor(s) malfunction but may be a normal operation characteristic, or due to sensor contamination (sensor being covered with dirt).

• Bulletin No. 04-2-3, published February 9, 2004, goes into excruciating detail about finding and fixing the sliding door's many failures. • Inoperative rear window defroster. **2001**—Ford admits automatic transmission defects (slippage, delayed shifts) in Special Service Instruction #01T01. **2001–02**—Service tips for reports of premature engine failures. • Vacuum or air leaks in the intake manifold or engine system causing lit warning lights. • Concerns about oil in the cooling system. • Engine cylinder heads that have been repaired may still leak coolant or oil from the gasket area. • Hard starts; rough-running engines. • Shudder while in Reverse or during 3–4 shifts. • Transmission fluid leakage. • Power-steering fluid leaks. • Brake roughness and pulsation. • Rear brake drum drag in cold weather. • Fogging of the front and side windows. • False Low Tire warning. • Repeated heater core failures. • Troubleshooting MIL warning light. **2001–03**—Remedy for a slow-to-fill fuel tank. **2002**—Automatic transmission fluid leaking at the quick connect for the transmission cooler lines. • MIL light comes on, vehicle shifts poorly, or vehicle won't start. • Instrument panel beeping. • Buzz, groan, or vibration when gear selector lever is in Park. • Some vehicles may run roughly on the highway or just after stopping. • Defective ignition switch lock cylinders. • Anti-theft system operates on its own. • Battery may go dead after extended parking time. • Sliding doors rattle and squeak. • Steering system whistle/whine. • Loose rear wiper arm. **2003**—Front-end grinding or popping noise when passing over bumps or making turns. • Airbag warning light stays lit. • Faulty rear window defroster. • Inoperative AC; compressor leakage. *Freestar*: **2004**—False activation of parking assist. (Remember, I said earlier that this optional safety device would drive you nuts with false warnings.) • Bulletin No. 04-2-3, published February 9, 2004, lists ways to find and fix sliding door's many failures. • Loose rear door trim. **2004–05**—Transmission has no 1–2 upshift (TSB #04-15-12). • Seat belt is slow to retract. • Inoperative power-sliding door and liftgate. • Remedy for front brake squeal or squeak. • Faulty 16-inch Goodyear Integrity tires may be the source of excessive vibration at high speeds. All four tires will be replaced free of charge on a case-by-case basis. **2004–06**—Same water contamination of the power control module as detailed in the Windstar 1999–2003 section. • Inoperative AC; compressor leakage. **2005**—A short circuit may cause the ABS warning light to remain constantly lit. **2005–06**—Tips to silence AC whistling.

FREESTAR, WINDSTAR PROFILE

	1998	1999	2000	2001	2002	2003	2004	2005	2006
Cost Price ($) (very negotiable)									
Freestar (23%)	—	—	—	—	—	—	27,295	27,995	22,999
Windstar (base)	24,495	24,295	—	—	—	—	—	—	—
LX	28,995	28,195	25,995	26,750	25,995	26,195	—	—	—
SEL	—	36,195	36,195	33,190	33,685	37,015	—	—	—
Used Values ($)									
Freestar ▲	—	—	—	—	—	—	13,000	15,000	—
Freestar ▼	—	—	—	—	—	—	12,000	13,500	—
Windstar (base) ▲	4,000	5,000	—	—	—	—	—	—	—
Windstar (base) ▼	3,000	4,500	—	—	—	—	—	—	—
LX ▲	4,500	5,000	6,000	7,500	10,000	11,500	—	—	—
LX ▼	3,500	4,500	5,500	6,500	8,500	10,500	—	—	—
SEL ▲	—	5,500	7,000	8,500	11,500	13,500	—	—	—
SEL ▼	—	5,000	6,000	6,500	10,500	12,000	—	—	—
Reliability	❶	❶	❶	❷	❷	❷	❸	❸	—
Crash Safety (F)	⑤	⑤	⑤	⑤	⑤	⑤	⑤	⑤	⑤
Side	—	⑤	④	④	④	④	④	④	④
Offset	⑤	❸	❸	❸	❸	❸	⑤	⑤	⑤
Rollover	—	—	—	④	④	④	④	④	④

Note: 2005 through 2007 models posted identical crashworthiness scores.

All ratings on a numbered scale where ⑤ is good and ❶ is bad. See page 220 for a more detailed description.

2007 TECHNICAL DATA

POWERTRAIN (REAR-DRIVE)
Engines: 4.6L V8 (225 hp) • 5.4L V8 (255 hp) • 6.8L V10 (305 hp) • 6.0L turbo diesel (325 hp); Transmissions: 4-speed auto. • 5-speed auto.

DIMENSION/CAPACITY
Passengers: 7–15; Wheelbase: 138 in.; H: 80.7/L: 211.8/W: 79.3 in.; Headroom F/R/: N/A; Legroom F/R: 40.0/36.9 in.; Cargo volume: 257 cu. ft.; Fuel tank: 132L/regular/diesel; Tow limit: 3,500–10,000 lb.; Load capacity: 1,995 lb.; GVWR: 10,000–20,000 lb.; Turning circle: 23.4 ft.; Ground clearance: 7.6 in.; Weight: 4,773 lb.

RATING: Average (2004–07); Below Average (1980–2003). **Strong points:** Good base warranty, and more reliable than any Detroit front-drive. Reasonably well equipped; more-refined powertrain and brakes phased in on the 2004s; good control and instrument layout; adequate interior room; and an acceptable ride. **Weak points:** Huge and heavy with sloppy handling, similar to the Ram lineup. With earlier vehicles, excessive braking distance and harsh transmission shifting and hunting. Limited second-row legroom and excessive engine, wind, and road noise. Quality control isn't the best, especially in regard to the failure-prone 6.0L diesel engine, the alternators, and the AC compressor. **New for 2007:** Shorter wheelbase models get standard stability-control.

MODEL HISTORY: First launched in 1961 on the Falcon platform, the rear-drive Econoline has long been a fixture in the commercial delivery market, primarily because of its 4,536 kg (10,000 lb.) carrying capacity. Like Chrysler, Ford has made few changes over the last several decades, figuring that a good thing is best left alone. The Ford Club Wagon, which is an Econoline dressed up for passenger duty, offers lots of room with capacity to spare for luggage. Nevertheless, full-sized vans have a very high floor, long panelled windows, and seats that are bolted to the floor—unlike most minivans, which feature powered middle windows and seats that stow into the floor or fold to the side.

Easily found at reasonable prices, Econolines don't possess any glaring virtues or vices; they all perform in a manner similar to that of Chrysler's and GM's large vans, and overall reliability is on par with the companies' comparable full-sized vans.

The 2004 models got a 4.6L V8 base engine; the 7.3L diesel was ditched for a problematic 6.0L turbocharged variant; and a new 5-speed automatic transmission was added (turbo models only) along with rear disc brakes on larger wheels. Much-needed standard electronic stability-control was added to the 2006 model lineup.

Econolines have had fewer quality-control deficiencies than Chrysler or GM, but they are merely the best of an old-tech, bad lot. Admittedly, Ford engine defects are legion. Electrical, fuel, and ignition systems are constantly on the fritz. The

3- and 4-speed automatic transmissions, steering and suspension components (lower steering shaft/tie-rods), and brakes (calipers, pads, rotors, and torn rear caliper boots) have also come under considerable criticism.

Econolines equipped with the 4.9L inline-six engine were offered with a 3- or 4-speed manual, or a 3-speed automatic transmission. All recent V8-equipped vans come with a 4-speed automatic. It would be best to find an Econoline or Club Wagon with the more refined and reliable 4-speed automatic and 5.0L V8, until we see how the base 4.6L handles long-term use. If heavy-duty hauling is your métier, then you'll be interested in getting an Econoline equipped with the optional 7.5L V8, capable of moving a gross combined weight rated at 8,392 kg (18,500 lb.).

Body fit and finish are typically below average and have been that way for the past several decades. Still, squeaks and rattles have been notably reduced on the more recent models. Premature rusting hasn't been a serious problem, either, since the mid-1980s (except for rusted-out oil pans), but water leaks through the windshield and doors and paint delamination and peeling are quite common.

COST ANALYSIS: $29,199 is the base cost for a 2007 E-Series full-sized van, but a second-series 2005 with some of the original warranty remaining will give you similar features for thousands of dollars less. However, stay away from any '05 equipped with the 6.0L diesel powerplant; opt instead for an '04 equipped with a 7.3L diesel engine. 2006 extended wheelbase models feature standard stability-control. **Best alternatives:** Earlier Dodge B-series vans are also worthwhile choices. The GM competition is a warmed-over 1990s design, while Chrysler has embraced the Sprinter, a narrow Mercedes-Benz van with a 152-hp turbodiesel engine, used mainly for commercial deliveries. **Rebates:** $3,000–$5,000 rebates and discounts on the 2006 and 2007 models. **Delivery/PDI:** $1,200. **Warranty:** Bumper-to-bumper 3 years/60,000 km; rust perforation 5 years/unlimited km. **Supplementary warranty:** An extended warranty is a must. **Options:** Running boards, upgraded sound system, heavy-duty alternator, remote keyless entry, power windows and door locks, and rear air conditioning. Look into a transmission oil cooler for the Overdrive transmission, particularly if you plan to do some trailering. **Depreciation:** Faster than average. **Insurance cost:** Higher than average. **Parts supply/cost:** There's a good supply of cheap parts. **Annual maintenance cost:** Higher than average. **Highway/city fuel economy:** *E-150 4.2L:* 11.7 /16.6 L/100 km; *4.6L:* 12.2/17.6 L/100 km; *5.4L:* 12.3/17.4 L/100 km.

QUALITY/RELIABILITY: Mediocre quality control and average reliability. With Ford's constant management reorganizations, the deck chairs get shuffled around, but the ship is still sinking. Many "goodwill" programs cover some of the owner problems listed below. However, this approach is mostly hit or miss, and it's no solution for Ford's poor quality control. **Owner-reported problems:** Poor engine performance characterized by constant stalling; turbocharger, high-pressure pump, and injector malfunctions; automatic transmission breakdowns; and chronic failures of key suspension or steering components, AC compressors, the engine oil pump alternator, and the EGR valve ("coking"):

> "Coking" (un-combustion) deposits form on the EGR valve causing drivability issues such as lack of power, surges, and stalling. This condition is especially dangerous when the bus develops this condition when crossing intersections, railroad tracks etc. and is transporting passengers both mobile and handicapped. Drivers have voiced their concern over this condition as they believe it is unsafe for them and their passengers. Ford motor company has replaced EGR valves (approx. 36–40) or recommends a fuel additive to try to take care of the problem.... Previously we had similar Ford vehicles with 7.3L diesel engines operating under identical conditions with no problems. These problems occurred when the 6.0L diesel was introduced.

Additionally, there are frequent electrical glitches, the brakes are noisy and wear out prematurely, and the body is invaded by omnipresent creaks, squeaks, rattles, buzzing, and whining. **Warranty performance:** Quite poor; that's why a getting a used model and taking it to a competent independent mechanic is your best bet.

 SAFETY SUMMARY: Insurance industry statistics show that Ford vans have had a lower-than-average frequency of accident injury claims when compared to all vehicles on North American roads. Many Econolines don't have front-seat head restraints; Club Wagons may have head restraints for the two front seats, depending on the trim level. **Airbags:** There have been reports of airbags failing to deploy. **ABS:** Four-wheel; standard. **Safety belt pretensioners:** Standard. **Head restraints F/R:** 2004: ★. **Visibility F/R:** ★★★★★/★★.

SAFETY COMPLAINTS: All years: Airbag malfunctions. • Chronic stalling. • Exhaust fumes enter into the vehicle. • Film covers inside of windshield, causing poor visibility. • Steering tie-rod end failures. • Tire-tread separation. **1998**—Windshield stress crack at base of wiper arm. • Fuel fumes permeate the interior. • Horn doesn't work. • Wheel rubs against the torsion bar when turning left. • Driver's seat moves forward when stopping. **1998–99**—Still lots of complaints of road wander, vibration, and premature brake rotor warpage and pad wearout, leading to extended stopping distances and front brake lock-up. **1998–2002**—Sticking or binding ignition lock cylinder. **1999**—Sudden acceleration when idling or when cruise control is activated. • Van rolled away while parked with emergency brake engaged. • Electrical shorts cause fuses to blow and make brakes, turn signals, and transmissions malfunction. • Vehicle tends to pull to one side when cruising. **2000**—Vehicle is equipped with non-adjustable camber bushings, causing premature outer tire wear in both front tires. • Child trapped between sofa bed and captain's chair. **2001**—Flat mirrors create a large blind spot. **2002**—Engine damaged because water entered through the intake. • Engine surges at idle. • Brake failure caused by brake pads sticking to the rotor. • Vehicle pulls to the right when brakes are hot. • Fuel tank won't fill up completely. • Jammed rear seat belt.

2002–03—Loss of power steering. **2003**—Engine stalled and then exploded. •
Transmission slipped out of Park into Reverse. • Excessive on-road shake. **2004**—
5.4L slow throttle response. • Loss of power steering; steering gearbox failure. •
Excessive highway wander; loose steering. • Fuel-pump failure caused by misrouted
electrical harness. • Seat belts may be too short. *E-150:* **2005**—When the vehicle
stalls going uphill, there are no brakes or steering to maintain control as it backs
down. *E-350:* **2005**—Assorted electrical wiring and alternator problems affect
powertrain performance and dash warning lights. • Ambulance firm complained
that their diesel-equipped ambulance was constantly stalling when sent out on
emergency calls:

> 2005 Ford E-350 ambulance had a total engine failure while driving to a 911 call.
> The Ford dealership service center diagnosed an oil pump failure as the cause and
> replaced it under warranty. This is complaint #2 of 6. All of the 2005 Ford ambulances
> we purchased have suffered total engine failures from either the oil pumps or the
> wiring harness systems, and several have had AC problems as well. Ford is unwilling
> to replace these parts on the other units until they fail. They are placing numerous
> lives in extreme jeopardy and refuse to admit there are major problems with the 6.0L
> diesel engine in the 2005 series ambulance chassis.

• Brake vacuum-pump failure caused loss of brakes. *E-450:* **2005**—Engine surging
when foot is taken off of the accelerator pedal. • Sticking throttle. • Chronic
stalling. • Faulty transmission torque converter.

Secret Warranties/Internal Bulletins/Service Tips

1993–2000—Paint delamination, peeling, or fading. **1996–2000**—A rear axle
whine on E-450 Super Duty with a Dana 80 can be silenced by putting in a damp-
ened rear driveshaft. **1997–2005**—Tips for correcting a rough idle. **1997–2006**—A
driveline clunk may signal that the slip yoke needs lubrication. Check this out
first, before spending big bucks on more involved tests or repairs. **1998–2003**—
7.3L diesel engine turbocharger pedestal may leak oil around the exhaust
back-pressure actuator; high-pressure oil pump may leak. **1999–2000**—To prevent the lower rear brake caliper boots from being damaged from driving over
gravel roads, Ford will install a brake caliper shield kit. **1999–2001**—Ford admits
to faulty 5.4L engines with defective head gaskets. The April 1, 2002, edition of
Automotive News says the automaker budgeted up to $4,500 (U.S.) to replace
affected engines and $800 (U.S.) to replace the cylinder heads and head gasket.
1999–2003—Models with the 7.3L diesel engine may have premature oil pan corrosion or a high-pressure oil pump leak (TSB #04-4-4).
1999–2005—Troubleshooting broken intake manifold studs. **2000**—Replace the
intake manifold gasket if leakage is evident. **2000–03**—Poor engine performance
(see bulletin). **2001**—Owner Notification Program says automatic transmission
could have internal damage, may lose Second gear, or be unable to engage any
gear. • Front shaft seal leakage. • An automatic transmission ticking or clicking

ENGINE CONTROLS—ROUGH IDLE/HESITATION

BULLETIN NO.: 03-9-11   DATE: MAY 12, 2003

2000–03 E-350, E-450, EXCURSION, SUPER DUTY F-SERIES

ISSUE: Some F250-F550 Super Duty and Excursion vehicles equipped with a 5.4L or 6.8L engine, and some E350/450 vehicles equipped with a 6.8L engine may exhibit a rough idle and/or hesitation when accelerating. This may occur intermittently within the first 2–3 minutes after start when engine is not warmed up (i.e., conditions other than hot restart). The condition is more likely to occur at ambient temperatures of approximately 60°F (160°C) and higher, and may be aggravated by an unmetered air leak or exhaust leak.

may be heard when First gear is engaged. • Water pump shaft seal leakage. **2002**—Repeat heater core leaks. **2003**—Incorrectly machined engine crankshaft. • Exhaust air rush noise, and reduced power. **2003–04**—6.0L diesel engine runs rough, loses power, or has fuel in the oil (Bulletin #04-9-3, published May 11, 2004). **2004–06**—TSB #06-9-7, issued May 15, 2006, gives more diagnostic and repair tips for poorly performing diesel engines. • Reasons why the AC may not cool properly. **2005**—Engine stalls when shifting into Drive or Reverse, or when coming to a stop. **2005–06**—Inadvertent transmission lock-up during 1–2 shifts.

ECONOLINE CARGO VAN, CLUB WAGON PROFILE

	1998	1999	2000	2001	2002	2003	2004	2005	2006
Cost Price ($) (very negotiable)									
Cargo Van (29%)	23,695	24,295	26,295	25,970	27,200	28,960	28,480	28,995	29,199
Club Wagon (24%)	27,795	28,195	29,295	28,615	29,000	30,050	31,120	31,375	31,899
Used Values ($)									
Cargo Van ▲	4,000	5,000	7,500	9,000	11,500	14,500	17,000	20,000	—
Cargo Van ▼	3,500	4,500	7,000	8,000	10,000	13,000	16,000	18,000	—
Club Wagon ▲	4,500	6,000	8,500	10,000	13,000	16,500	20,500	22,000	—
Club Wagon ▼	4,000	5,500	8,000	9,000	12,000	15,000	18,500	20,500	—
Reliability	②	②	③	③	③	③	③	③	—
Crash Safety (F)	—	④	④	④	④	④	—	④	④
Rollover	—	—	—	②	②	②	—	③	③

Ford/Nissan

RATING: *Quest:* Below Average (2004–07). Like driving an aquarium. Factory defects are legion. *Villager and Quest:* Average (1997–2003); Below Average (1995–96); Not Recommended (1993–94). Best used for city commuting rather than for fully loaded, long highway journeys. **Strong points:** Wide side sliding doors; third-row seats fold into the floor; small handgrips easily accessed by children; hefty discounts. *2003 and earlier models:* Impressive highway performance (as long as you're not carrying a full load) and easy, no-surprise, carlike handling; highway stability is above reproach; occupants get a comfortable ride with lots of seating choices; the 4-speed automatic transmission is particularly smooth and quiet; braking performance is quite good (when the brakes are working properly); plenty of passenger and cargo room (these vans are nearly 30 cm (12 in.) longer and 5 cm (2 in.) wider and higher than Chrysler's short-wheelbase minivans); and mechanical components have been tested for years on the Maxima. *Quest:* Carlike handling, lots of interior room, and well appointed. **Weak points:** Unreliable, and quirky dash and interior styling. *2003 and earlier models:* These fuel-thirsty minivans are quite heavy, and the 3.0L and 3.3L engines have to go all out to carry the extra weight. Surprisingly, GM's 2.8L engines produce more torque than what the Villager and Quest can deliver. Powertrain set-up trails the Odyssey in acceleration and passing. Other minuses: a cheap-looking interior; the control layout can be a bit confusing; suspension is too soft; and rear-seat access can be difficult. Some wind and road noise, and excessive engine noise under heavy throttle. *Quest:* High priced, suspension bottoms out on rough roads, and instrument panel

2002 TECHNICAL DATA

POWERTRAIN (FRONT-DRIVE)
Engine: 3.3L V6 (170 hp); Transmission: 4-speed auto.

DIMENSION/CAPACITY
Passengers: 2/2/3; Wheelbase: 112.2 in.; H: 64.2 /L: 194.8/W: 74.9 in.; Headroom F/R1/R2: N/A; Legroom F/R1/R2: 39.9/36.4/36.3 in.; Cargo volume: 127 cu. ft.; Fuel tank: 75L/regular; Tow limit: 2,000–3,500 lb.; Load capacity: 1,450 lb.; GVWR: 5,445 lb.; Turning circle: 39.9 ft.; Ground clearance: 5.8 in.; Weight: 3,850 lb.

2007 QUEST TECHNICAL DATA

POWERTRAIN (FRONT-DRIVE)
Engine: 3.5L V6 (240 hp); Transmissions:
• 5-speed auto.

DIMENSION/CAPACITY
Passengers: 2/2/3; Wheelbase: 124 in.; H: 70/L: 204/W: 78 in.; Headroom F/R1/R2: 6.5/7.5/3.0 in.; Legroom F/R1/R2: 40/28/32 in.; Cargo volume: 60 cu. ft.; Fuel tank: N/A; Tow limit: 3,500 lb.; Load capacity: 1,205 lb.; GVWR: 5,732 lb.; Turning circle: 44 ft.; Ground clearance: 4.0 in.; Weight: 4,410 lb.

produces windshield glare. **New for 2007:** More than $60 million was spent to rework the interior and to relocate the gauges from the centre of the instrument cluster to the area in front of the driver. The Quest will undergo a complete redesign for the 2010 model year.

MODEL HISTORY: Smaller and more carlike than most minivans, the pre-2004 Villager and Quest are sized comfortably between the regular and extended Chrysler minivans. These minivans' strongest assets are a 170-hp 3.3L V6 engine that gives them carlike handling, ride, and cornering; modular seating; and reliable mechanical components. Nissan borrowed the powertrain, suspension, and steering assembly from the Maxima, mixed in some creative sheet metal, and then left the job of outfitting the sound system, climate control, dashboard, steering column, and wheels to Ford. This resulted in an attractive, not overly aero-styled minivan.

1996—Motorized shoulder belts are dropped, a passenger-side airbag is added, and the dash and exterior are slightly restyled. **1997**—Buyers of the entry-level GS model may order captain's chairs. **1998**—Carried over unchanged in preparation for the redesigned '99 version. **1999**—The Pathfinder's 3.3L V6 replaced the 3.0L V6, giving the Villager and Quest an additional 19 horses. *Villager:* **1999**—A fourth door; more interior room; a revised instrument panel that's easier to reach; restyled front and rear ends; and improved shifting, acceleration, and braking (ABS takes less effort and is supposedly more durable). The suspension was retuned to give a more carlike ride and handling, the old climate control system was ditched for a more sophisticated version with air filtration, and optional ABS was made available with all models. Mercury's top-of-the-line model, the Nautica, was dropped. *Quest:* **1999**—An additional 11.6 cm (4.6 in.) in length and 3.0 cm (1.2 in.) in width, standard ABS brakes, and a driver-side sliding rear door. The second row of seats can now be removed, and the third row is set on tracks. Upgraded headlights and rear leaf springs. A cargo shelf added behind the rear seats gives owners an extra 0.28 cubic metres (10 cubic feet) of storage space. **2001–02**—An improved child safety seat anchoring system; performance, suspension, and comfort upgrades; a stabilizer bar on the GLE; freshened exterior styling; and a standard entertainment centre with a larger screen.

2004–07 Quest

A totally different minivan than its predecessor, the $31,698 Quest 3.5 S is one of the largest and priciest minivans on the road. Based on the Altima/Murano platform, it offers a more powerful engine and all the standard high-tech safety, performance, and convenience features one could want. Its long wheelbase allows for the widest opening sliding doors among front-drive minivans, rear seating access is a breeze, and a capacious interior allows for flexible cargo and passenger configurations that can easily accommodate 4′ × 8′ objects with the liftgate closed. Standard fold-flat third-row seats and fold-to-the-floor centre-row seats allow owners to increase storage space without worrying about where to store the extra seats, although third-row headrests must be removed before the seats can be folded away.

Although it feels a bit heavy in the city, the Quest is very carlike when driven on the highway. Ride and handling are enhanced by a new four-wheel independent suspension, along with front and rear stabilizer bars and upgraded anti-lock brakes. Safety features include standard head curtain supplemental airbags for outboard passengers in all three rows, supplemental front-seat side-impact airbags, standard traction control, and ABS brakes with brake assist.

COST ANALYSIS: Unless you require all the newest bells and whistles, you can save yourself thousands by getting a fully loaded 1999–2003 Quest. Stay away from the 2004 and later glitch-ridden models. **Best alternatives:** Other minivans worth considering are the Honda Odyssey and Toyota Sienna. **Options:** Nothing really worthwhile. **Rebates:** $3,000–$5,000 rebates early in the new year. **Delivery/PDI:** $1,297. **Depreciation:** Much faster than average due to the huge stockpile of unsold units. **Insurance cost:** Should be higher than average. **Parts supply/cost:** Good supply and reasonably priced, although the post-2004 models continue to experience long delays for some slow-moving body parts, and they're a bit costly. **Annual maintenance cost:** Less than average on 1997 through 2003 versions; higher than average on later models. **Warranty:** Bumper-to-bumper 3 years/80,000 km; powertrain 5 years/100,000 km; rust perforation 5 years/unlimited km. **Supplementary warranty:** Essential for all model years. **Highway/city fuel economy:** *Villager/ Quest:* 8.9/13.8 L/100 km; *2004 Quest:* 8.2/12.4 L/100 km.

QUALITY/RELIABILITY: Body integrity has always been subpar, with doors opening and closing on their own and poor fit and finish allowing lots of wind noise and water to enter the interior:

> Water has leaked into the car from the area of the sunglass holder on two occasions. The sunglass holder is located in the middle right at the top edge of the windshield. On one occasion it leaked after washing the car. On the second occasion it happened during a heavy rainstorm. The dealer would not fix or investigate the problem further because their glass contractor could not duplicate the problem using a hose.

There have also been some reports of panel and paint defects and premature rusting on the inside sliding door track. **Owner-reported problems:** Most owner-reported problems involve excessive brake noise and premature brake wear, door lock malfunctions, interior noise, and driveline vibrations. There have also been many reports of engine exhaust manifold and crankshaft failures, costing up to $7,000 to repair, and automatic transmission slippage. Other problems include electrical shorts; brake failures caused by vibration, binding, or overheating; premature wear of the front discs, rotors, and pads; chronic stalling, possibly caused by faulty fuel pumps or a shorted electrical system; and loose steering and veering at highway speeds. Owners also complain of film buildup on windshield and interior glass; a sulfur smell from the exhaust system; poor AC performance or compressor failures accompanied by musty, mildew-type AC odours; and a recurring fuel-pump buzzing heard through the radio speakers.

The 2005 and later models have many of the same problems, along with a few new ones, as this owner details:

> Ongoing problems which include: the windows failing to roll up when button is pushed, the gas gauge failing to register gas after filling it up, the gas meter after a half a tank never registers correctly (when light indicates no gas and tank is filled the van will only take 16 gallons [4.2L] and owners manual indicates a 20 gallon [5.3L] tank), the transmission slips, the sliding doors squeak and rattle, rear interior clamps on floor of car are rusting, idiot lights come on intermittently, the gaskets on the doors are coming off, the heated seats haven't worked in high and low, the entertainment system doesn't respond to rear AV, and the air conditioner is not cool enough and it stinks. The automatic slide doors will not stop for small objects but this product was designed for families. These doors will remove a child's finger and the switch to initiate the auto slide is low, where one child can push it while another is getting in, or has their hand in the way and didn't realize their brother pushed the button. I did my own little research test, I got pencils and everywhere I placed a pencil the door closed with the pencil being snapped into many pieces and crunched up in the door. Then I tried the same thing on my friend's Honda, but the Honda's auto slide doors bounced off every time.

Add these troubles to the above list: The fuel gauge doesn't give accurate readings with a half-full tank; doors rattle and are hard to open or close; the windows won't roll up; and there are water leaks and windshield cracks. **Warranty performance:** Below average.

 SAFETY SUMMARY: ABS: Standard. **Safety belt pretensioners:** Standard. **Head restraints F/R:** *1995:* ★★★; *1997:* ★★; *1999–2002:* ★. *Quest 2004–06:* ★. **Visibility F/R:** ★★★★★/★★.

SAFETY COMPLAINTS: 1993–2003—Airbags fail to deploy. • Inadvertent airbag deployment. • Vehicle suddenly accelerated forward. • Sudden stalling caused by faulty fuel pump. • Steering wander and excessive vibration. • Chronic ABS failures; brake pads and rotors need replacing every 5,000 km. • Brake failures (extended stopping distance, noisy when applied). • Brake and accelerator pedals are the same height, so driver's foot can easily slip and step on both at the same time. • Cycling or self-activating front door locks; occupants have been trapped in their vehicles. **1997–99**—Gas fumes leak into the interior. • Gas pedal sticks. **2000**—Vehicle tends to lurch forward when the AC is first engaged. • Weak tailgate hydraulic cylinders. • Instrument panel's white face hard to read in daylight hours. **2000–01**—Missing seat belt latch plate stopper button. • Broken shift-lock cable plate causes shift indicator to be misaligned. • 22-month-old child was able to pull the clasp apart on integrated child safety seat. • Seat belts don't retract properly. • Rear window on liftgate door shattered for unknown reason (replaced under warranty). • Power-steering fluid leakage caused by a split O-ring at rack gear. **2002**—Stuck accelerator pedal. • Excessive vibration at highway speeds. • Leaking front and rear struts degrade handling. • Steering wheel is off-centre to the left. • Continental tire-tread separation. **2004**—Airbag went off for no reason. • Sudden, unintended acceleration. • Sliding door trapped child; adults also trapped; door continually pops open. • Bad reflection of dash on windshield. • Automatic transmission won't downshift. • Dome light fuse blows continually. • Ineffective windshield washers. **2005**—Vehicle continued to accelerate even though brakes were applied. • Driver's seat belt won't stay latched. • Seat belt clasp gets stuck in the web stitching. • Vehicle rolls backward when stopped on a hill and foot is taken off the brake. • Dashboard continues to reflect onto the windshield, impairing the view forward. • Children's fingers can get caught in the sliding door, which doesn't stop for objects in its path. • Goodyear tires wear out prematurely ("feathered"). • Seat recall could not go ahead due to a lack of replacement parts.

Secret Warranties/Internal Bulletins/Service Tips

1993–2002—Paint delamination, peeling, or fading. • Repeat heater core failure. **1995–99**—Tips for correcting windshield water leaks and excessive noise, vibration, and harshness. **1996–2002**—Power door locks that intermittently self-activate are covered in TSB #98-22-5. **1997–98**—Tips on silencing rattles and creaks. • Hard starts, no-starts, stalling, or an exhaust rotten-egg smell can all be corrected by replacing the PCM under the emissions warranty. **1997–99**—An exhaust buzz or rattle may be caused by a loose catalyst or muffler heat shield. **1999–2004**—Troubleshooting abnormal shifting. • Side windows pop open. **2004**—No-start, hard start remedies. • Silencing a ticking engine/exhaust noise. • Tips on correcting an abnormal shifting of the automatic transmission. • AC blows out warm air from floor vents. • Leaks, overheating cooling system. • Guidelines on troubleshooting brake complaints. **2004–05**—Lack of power; automatic transmission sticks in Third gear. • Troubleshooting sliding door rattles and difficult opening/closing. • Water leaks in the cargo area. • Exhaust system rattles when accelerating. • Insufficient AC cooling. • Front power seat won't move. **2004–06**—Pop-out window rattling. • "Skyview" roof water leaks.

	1998	1999	2000	2001	2002	2004	2005	2006
Cost Price ($) (negotiable)								
Villager GS	24,595	24,595	24,595	—	—	—	—	—
Villager LS	29,495	29,495	29,495	—	—	—	—	—
Quest GXE/S (20%)	30,898	27,798	30,498	30,498	30,698	32,900	31,698	32,048
Used Values ($)								
Villager GS ▲	4,500	5,500	7,500	—	—	—	—	—
Villager GS ▼	4,000	4,500	6,000	—	—	—	—	—
Villager LS ▲	5,500	6,500	8,000	—	—	—	—	—
Villager LS ▼	5,000	5,500	7,000	—	—	—	—	—
Quest GXE/S ▲	6,000	7,000	9,000	11,000	13,500	21,000	24,000	—
Quest GXE/S ▼	5,500	6,000	7,500	9,500	12,500	19,500	22,000	—
Reliability	③	③	③	③	③	②	②	—
Crash Safety (F)	—	—	④	⑤	⑤	⑤	⑤	⑤
Side	—	—	⑤	⑤	⑤	⑤	⑤	⑤
Offset	②	❶	❶	❶	❶	⑤	⑤	⑤
Rollover	—	—	—	④	④	④	④	④

Note: 2007 crashworthiness scores match those of the 2005 and 2006 models. There was no 2003 model year Quest. Nissan dropped the 2005 Quest's price to counter slow sales.

General Motors

ASTRO, SAFARI ★★★

RATING: Average (1996–2005); Below Average (1985–95). Dropped at the end of 2005, these rear-drives are more mini-truck than minivan. Yet they're much more reliable and cheaper to buy and run than the problem-plagued Detroit front-drive minivans and the overpriced Asian competition. Stay away from the unreliable AWD models, though; they're expensive to repair and not very durable. **Strong points:** Brisk acceleration, trailer-towing capability, lots of passenger room and cargo space, and a well-laid-out instrument panel with easy-to-read gauges. Very low ground clearance enhances this minivan's handling but precludes most off-roading. Good brakes. Rock-bottom used prices, and average reliability and quality control. **Weak points:** Driving position is awkward for many; some drivers will find the pedals too close; obtrusive engine makes for very narrow front footwells that give little room for the driver's left foot to rest. Difficult entry and exit because of the high step-up and the intruding wheelwell. Harsh ride, limited front seatroom, interior noise levels rise sharply at highway speeds, and excessive fuel consumption is made worse by the AWD option.

MODEL HISTORY: More of a utility truck than a comfortable minivan, these boxy, rear-drive minivans are built on a reworked S-10 pickup chassis. As such, they offer uninspiring handling, average-quality mechanical and body components, and relatively high fuel consumption. Both the Astro and Safari come in a choice of either cargo or passenger van. The cargo van is used either commercially or as an inexpensive starting point for a fully customized vehicle.

1991—A more powerful V6; lap/shoulder belts. **1993**—Base engine gained 15 horses. **1994**—Driver-side airbag and side-door guard beams, plus a centre-mounted rear stop lamp was installed in the roof. **1995**—Lightly restyled front end, extended bodies, and a 190-hp engine. **1996**—Passenger-side airbag, a new dash, engine torque cut a bit, and more front footroom. **1997**—Upgraded power steering. **1998**—An improved automatic transmission. **1999**—A reworked AWD system. **2000**—Only seven- and eight-passenger models available; engine made quieter and smoother, while the automatic transmission was toughened up to shift more efficiently when pulling heavy loads; and a larger fuel tank was installed. **2001**—A tilt steering wheel; cruise control; CD player; remote keyless entry; and power windows, mirrors, and locks. **2002**—A rear heater on cargo models. **2003**—Upgraded four-wheel disc brakes.

The 1985–95 versions suffer from failure-prone automatic transmissions, poor braking systems, malfunctioning AC compressors, and fragile steering components. The early base V6 provides ample power, but it also produces lots of noise, consumes excessive amounts of fuel, and tends to have leaking head gaskets and failure-prone oxygen sensors. These computer-related problems often rob the engine of sufficient power to keep up in traffic. While the 5-speed manual transmission shifts fairly easily, the automatic takes forever to downshift on the highway. Handling isn't particularly agile on these minivans, and the power steering doesn't provide the driver with enough road feel. Unloaded, the Astro provides very poor traction, the ride isn't comfortable on poor road surfaces, and interior noise is rampant. Many drivers find the driving position awkward (there's no left legroom) and the heating/defrosting system inadequate. Many engine components are hidden under the dashboard, making repair or maintenance awkward. Even on more recent

---

2005 TECHNICAL DATA

POWERTRAIN (REAR-DRIVE)
Engine: 4.3L V6 (190 hp); Transmission: 4-speed auto.
DIMENSION/CAPACITY
Passengers: 2/3/3; Wheelbase: 111.2 in.; H: 74.9/L: 190/W: 78 in.; Headroom F/R1/R2: N/A; Legroom F/R1/R2: 41.6/36.5/38.5 in.; Cargo volume: 170.4 cu. ft.; Fuel tank: 95L/regular; Tow limit: 5,400 lb.; Load capacity: 1,764 lb.; GVWR: 5,900–6,100 lb.; Turning circle: 40.5 ft.; Ground clearance: 6.8 in.; Weight: 4,321 lb.

models, highway performance and overall reliability aren't impressive. Through the 2000 model year, the 4-speed automatic transmissions are clunky and hard shifting, though they're much more reliable than Ford or Chrysler gearboxes.

Other owners report that the front suspension, steering components, computer modules, and catalytic converter can wear out within as little as 60,000 km. There have also been lots of complaints about electrical, exhaust, cooling, and fuel system bugs; inadequate heating/defrosting; failure-prone wiper motors; and axle seals that wear out every 12–18 months.

Body hardware is fragile, and fit and finish is the pits. Water leaks from windows and doors are common yet hard to diagnose. Squeaks and rattles are legion and hard to locate. Sliding-door handles often break off, and the sliding door frequently jams in cold temperatures. The hatch release for the Dutch doors occasionally doesn't work, and the driver-side vinyl seat lining tears apart. Premature paint peeling, delamination, and surface rust are fairly common.

The 1995–99 models are a bit improved, but they still have problems carried over from earlier years, with stalling, hard starts, and expensive and frequent automatic transmission, power steering, wheel bearing, brake pad, caliper, and rotor repairs heading the list.

Year 2000–05 models are a bit more reliable and better performing, inasmuch as they underwent considerable upgrading by GM. Nevertheless, buyers should be aware that extra attention is merited in the following areas: excessive vibration transmitted through the AWD; automatic transmission clunk; poor braking performance (brake pedal hardens, and brakes don't work after going over bumps or rough roads), and expensive brake maintenance; electronic computer modules and fuel system glitches that cause the Check Engine light to remain lit; hard starts, no-starts, or chronic stalling, especially when going downhill; heating and AC performance hampered by poor air distribution; electrical system shorts; and sliding door misalignment and broken hinges.

COST ANALYSIS: Get a discounted 2003 for the latest upgrades and best performance. The 5- and 6-year-old models are also cheap and fairly reliable. **Best alternatives:** Most front-drive minivans made by Honda and Toyota have better handling and are more reliable and economical people-carriers; unfortunately, they lack the Astro's considerable grunt, essential for cargo-hauling and trailer-towing. **Warranty:** Bumper-to-bumper 3 years/60,000 km; rust perforation 6 years/160,000 km. **Supplementary warranty:** A toss-up. Individual repairs won't cost a lot, but those nickels and dimes can add up. A powertrain-only warranty is a wise choice. **Options:** Integrated child safety seats and rear AC. Be wary of models that were ordered with AWD; it exacts a high fuel penalty and isn't very dependable. **Depreciation:** Slightly faster than average. **Insurance cost:** A bit higher than average. **Parts supply/cost:** Good supply of cheap parts. A large contingent of independent parts suppliers keeps repair costs down. **Annual maintenance cost:** Average. Any garage can repair these rear-drive minivans. **Highway/city fuel economy:** *Rear-drive:* 10.6/14.6 L/100 km; *AWD:* 11.3/15.3 L/100 km.

QUALITY/RELIABILITY: Average; most of Astro's and Safari's defects are easy to diagnose and repair, leading to a minimum of downtime. Early rear axle failures. **Owner-reported problems:** Some problems with the automatic transmission, steering, electrical system, and heating and defrosting system as well as rear axle whine, premature brake wear, faulty suspension components, and glitch-prone sliding doors. **Warranty performance:** Average.

SAFETY SUMMARY: NHTSA has recorded numerous complaints of dashboard fires. Power steering locks up or fails unexpectedly, components wear out quickly, and steering may bind when turning. Seat belt complaints are also common—seat belts tighten up unexpectedly, cannot be adjusted, or have nowhere to latch. **Airbags:** Standard front. Reports of drivers' airbags failing to deploy in a collision. **Anti-lock brakes:** Standard; disc/disc. Reports of ABS failures, brakes hesitating when applied, brakes engaging for no reason, and premature brake wear. **Traction control (AWD):** Optional. **Head restraints F/R:** *1995:* ★; *1996–97:* ★★/★; *1999:* ★★; *2001–02:* ★★; *2003–05:* ★. **Visibility F/R:** ★★★★★/★★.

SAFETY COMPLAINTS: 1999—Very few safety-related complaints, compared with most other minivans. Many of the 1999 model problems have also been reported by owners of earlier model years. • Hard shifting between First and Second gear; transmission slippage. • Delayed shifting or stalling when passing from Drive to Reverse. • Leaking axle seals. • Rear cargo door hinge and latch slipped off, and door opened 180 degrees. • Floor mat moves under brake and accelerator pedals. • Fuel gauge failure caused by faulty sending unit. **1999–2000**—Brake and gas pedals are too close together. **2000**—When brakes are applied, rear wheels tend to lock up, while front wheels continue to turn. • Vehicle stalls when accelerating or turning. • Astro rolls back when stopped on an incline in Drive. • Sliding door slams shut on an incline, or hinges break. • Extensive damage caused to bumper and undercarriage by driving over gravel roads. **2001**—Sudden acceleration. • Chronic stalling. • Sudden total electrical failure, especially when going into Reverse. • Brake pedal set too high. • Differential in transfer case locked up while driving; defective axle seals. • Vehicle rolls backward on an incline while in Drive (dealer adjusted transfer case to no avail). • Fuel gauge failure. • Faulty AC vents. • Water can be trapped inside the wheels and freeze, causing the wheels to be out of balance. **2002**—Airbag failed to deploy. • Sticking gas pedal. • Brake pedal goes to floor without braking. • Seat belts in rear are too long; don't fit children or child safety seats. • Driver-side window failures. • Sliding-door window blew out. • Uniroyal spare-tire sidewall cracks. **2003**—Harsh, delayed shifting. • On a slight incline, sliding door will unlatch and then slam shut. • Intermittent windshield wiper failure. **2004**—Rear driver-side window exploded. **2005**—Driver's side airbag failed to fully deploy in an accident.

Secret Warranties/Internal Bulletins/Service Tips

1993–99—Tips on getting rid of AC odours. • Defective catalytic converters may cause a rotten-egg smell eligible for an emissions warranty refund. **1993–2005**—GM says that a chronic driveline clunk can't be silenced and is a normal characteristic of its vehicles. • Paint delamination, peeling, or fading. **1995–2000**—Dealer guidelines for brake servicing under warranty. **1995–2004**—Booming interior noise at highway speeds. **1996–98**—Rough engine performance may be caused by a water-contaminated oxygen sensor, and a rough idle shortly after starting may be caused by sticking poppet valves. **1996–2000**—Hard start, no-start, backfire, and kickback when starting may be corrected by replacing the crankshaft-position sensor. • A rough idle after start and/or a Service Engine light that stays lit may mean you have a stuck injector poppet valve ball that needs cleaning. **1996–2001**—Poor heat distribution in driver's area of vehicle (install new heat ducts). • Exhaust rattle noise. **1996–2003**—Engine noise remedy:

ENGINE RATTLE

BULLETIN NO.: 03-06-01-024B   **DATE: MARCH 4, 2004**

RATTLE NOISE IN ENGINE (INSTALL TIMING TENSIONER KIT)

1996–2003 Chevrolet Astro, Blazer, Express, S-10, Silverado

1996–2003 GMC Jimmy, Safari, Savana, Sierra, Sonoma

1996–2001 Oldsmobile Bravada with 4.3L V6 Engine

CONDITION: Some customers may comment on a rattle-type noise coming from the engine at approximately 1800 to 2200 RPMs.

CAUSE: The spark, rattle-type noise may be caused by torsional vibration of the balance shaft.

CORRECTION: Install a new tensioner assembly kit.

1996–2004—Silence a boom-type noise heard during engine warm-up by installing an exhaust dampener assembly (TSB #00-06-05-001A). **1997–98**—An engine ticking noise that sounds when the temperature falls may require an EVAP purge solenoid valve. **1997–99**—A hard start, no-start, and rough idle can be fixed by replacing the fuel-tank fill pipe assembly and cleaning the SCPI poppet valves. **1999**—Steering-column squeaking can be silenced by replacing the steering-wheel SIR module coil assembly. **1999–2000**—If the engine runs hot, overheats, or loses coolant, try polishing the radiator filler neck or replacing the radiator cap before letting any mechanic convince you that more expensive repairs are needed. • A popping or snapping sound may emanate from the right front door window area. **1999–2004**—Automatic transmission malfunctions may be caused by debris in the transmission (Bulletin No.: 01-07-30-038B). **2001**—Harsh automatic transmission shifts. • 2–4 band and 3–4 clutch damage. • Steering shudder felt when making low-speed turns. • Excessive brake squeal. • Wet carpet/odour in passenger footwell area (repair evaporator case drain to cowl seal/open evaporator case drain). • Delayed shifts, slips, flares, or extended shifts during cold operation (replace shift solenoid valve assembly). **2002**—Automatic transmission slips, incorrect shifts, and poor engine performance. • Service Engine light comes on, no Third or Fourth gear, and loss of Drive. • Slipping or missing Second, Third, or Fourth gear. • Inadequate heating. • Roof panel has a wavy or rippled appearance. • Water leak in the windshield area. **2002–03**—Engine runs rough, or Engine warning light comes on. • Sliding door difficult to open. **2003**—Hard starts, rough idle, and intermittent misfiring. • Transfer-case shudder. • Right rear door handle breakage. **2003–05**—Vehicle lacks power at high ambient temperatures. **2004**—Silencing a suspension pop.

ASTRO, SAFARI PROFILE

	1997	1998	1999	2000	2001	2002	2003	2004	2005
Cost Price ($) (very negotiable)									
Cargo	25,110	25,110	23,290	24,015	24,465	—	—	26,390	27,015
CS/base	26,920	23,839	25,675	25,675	26,440	27,255	27,600	27,615	29,035
Used Values ($)									
Cargo ▲	3,000	3,500	4,000	5,000	7,500	—	—	15,000	17,000
Cargo ▼	2,500	3,000	3,500	4,000	6,500	—	—	13,500	16,000
CS/base ▲	3,500	4,000	4,500	6,000	8,500	11,000	13,000	16,000	18,000
CS/base ▼	3,000	3,500	4,000	5,000	7,500	10,000	12,000	15,500	17,000
Reliability	②	③	③	③	④	④	④	④	④
Crash Safety (F)	③	③	③	③	③	③	③	③	③
Side	—	—	—	—	—	—	⑤	⑤	⑤
Offset	❶	❶	❶	❶	❶	❶	❶	❶	❶
Rollover	—	—	—	—	③	③	③	—	—

MONTANA, MONTANA SV6, RELAY, SILHOUETTE, TERRAZA, TRANS SPORT, UPLANDER, VENTURE ★★

RATING: Below Average (1997–2007); Not Recommended (1990–96). These minivans are bad choices for four reasons: They have serious automatic transmission and engine intake manifold gasket defects; quality control has gotten worse over the past fifteen years; GM's warranty is no match for the many factory-related deficiencies; and there's an over-abundance of safety defects that include sliding doors that crush and injure children. These minivans are worse performers than Ford's Windstar/Freestar, and they actually make Chrysler's minivans look good. *Montana SV6, Uplander, Terraza, and Relay:* While Honda, Toyota, and Nissan push the envelope in engineering and styling, these restyled GM minivans join the Ford Freestar as also-ran, pseudo-nouveau entries. **Strong points:** Dual sliding doors; plenty of comfort and convenience features; flexible seating arrangements; good visibility

2004 MONTANA, SILHOUETTE, VENTURE TECHNICAL DATA

POWERTRAIN (FRONT-DRIVE/AWD)

Engine: 3.4L V6 (185 hp); Transmission: 4-speed auto.

DIMENSION/CAPACITY

Passengers: 2/2/3, 2/3/3; Wheelbase: 120 in.; H: 67.4/L: 201/W: 72 in.; Headroom F/R1/R2: 5.5/4.5/4.0 in.; Legroom F/R1/R2: 41/30/30 in.; Cargo volume: 75.5 cu. ft.; Fuel tank: 94.6L/regular; Tow limit: 3,500 lb.; Load capacity: 1,365 lb.; GVWR: 5,357 lb.; Turning circle: 43 ft.; Ground clearance: 4.5 in.; Weight: 3,990 lb.

2007 MONTANA SV6, RELAY, TERRAZA, UPLANDER TECHNICAL DATA

POWERTRAIN (FRONT-DRIVE/AWD)

Engine: 3.9L V6 (240 hp); Transmission: 4-speed auto.

DIMENSION/CAPACITY

Passengers: 2/2/3; Wheelbase: 121 in.; H: 68/L: 205/W: 72 in.; Headroom F/R1/R2: 5.0/4.0/3.5 in.; Legroom F/R1/R2: 40.5/26/28 in.; Cargo volume: 75.5 cu. ft.; Fuel tank: 94.6/regular; Tow limit: 3,500 lb.; Load capacity: 1,290 lb.; GVWR: 5,357 lb.; Turning circle: 43 ft.; Ground clearance: 6.0 in.; Weight: 4,380 lb.

fore and aft; lots of storage bins and compartments. **Weak points:** Clumsy handling; harsh, noisy ride; average acceleration with a light load; unproven AWD that's no longer available; less effective rear drum brakes, and excessive brake fading; tall drivers will find insufficient headroom, and short drivers may find it hard to see where the front of the vehicle ends; low rear seats force passengers into an uncomfortable knees-up position; narrow cabin makes front-to-rear access a bit difficult; seat cushions on the centre and rear bench seats are hard, flat, and too short, and the seatbacks lack sufficient lower back support; cargo may not slide out easily because the rear sill sticks up a few inches; a high number of safety-related failures and engine exhaust manifold defects; and disappointing fuel economy. **New for 2007:** Montana will be axed by the end of 2006. *Uplander*: A 240-hp 3.9L V6 replaces the 201-hp 3.5L V6.; all-wheel drive and the load-levelling suspension option are gone.

MODEL HISTORY: These minivans have always had more carlike handling than GM's Astro and Safari, making them competent highway performers, although their engine and transmission are a bit rough. They also provide lots of seating and cargo room. The 2005 model year transformation into the Montana, Relay, Terraza, and Uplander gave these minivans more of an SUV look, along with a bit more length, height, and wheelbase. Seats may accommodate eight and can be folded down flat, creating additional storage space.

The Montana SV6, Relay, Terraza, and Uplander are essentially GM's old minivans dressed up to look new. Powered by 15 more horses than previous versions, there's still ample cargo room thanks to removable second- and third-row seats and flat-folding third-row seats. Early models were equipped with a 201-hp 3.5L V6 engine, an electronically controlled 4-speed automatic transmission, and many standard features such as 17-inch wheels, ABS, strut-type front suspension/non-independent rear suspension, an OnStar security system, and dual-stage driver and passenger front airbags. Important options up through the 2006 model year included AWD (not a good idea), a vehicle stability enhancement system (a good idea), side-impact airbags, and "smart" front airbags. Unfortunately, these new-styled minivans don't have side curtain airbags or flip-and-fold rear seats that merge with the cargo floor.

As with most minivans, be wary of vehicles equipped with a power-assisted passenger-side sliding door. It's both convenient and dangerous—despite an override circuit that should prevent the door from closing when it is blocked, a number of injuries have been reported. Furthermore, the doors frequently open when they shouldn't and can be difficult to close securely.

All model years have had serious reliability problems—notably, engine head gasket and intake manifold defects; electronic module (PROM) and starter failures; premature front brake component wear, brake fluid leakage, and noisy braking; short circuits that burn out alternators, batteries, power door lock activators, and the blower motor; AC evaporator core failures; premature wearout of the inner and outer tie-rods; automatic transmission breakdowns; abysmal fit and finish; chronic sliding door malfunctions; and faulty rear-seat latches. Other problems include a fuel-thirsty and poorly performing 3-speed automatic transmission; a poorly mounted sliding door; side-door glass that pops open; squeaks, rattles, and clunks in the instrument panel cluster area and suspension; and a wind buffeting noise around the front doors.

1994—A shortened nose; APV designation is dropped; driver-side airbag arrives. **1996**—3.4L V6 debuts, and the Lumina was replaced by the Venture at the end of the model year. **1997**—Dual airbags and ABS. **1998**—The sliding driver-side door is available on more models. **1999**—A 5-hp boost to the base V6 engine (185), de-powered airbags, an upgraded automatic transmission, a rear-window defogger, and heated rear-view mirrors. **2000**—Dual sliding rear side doors. **2001**—Slightly restyled, with a fold-flat third-row seat, driver-side power door, and a six-disc CD player added; cargo version dropped. **2002**—Optional AWD. **2003**—Optional ABS and front side airbags. **2005**—Venture drops the regular length model and AWD in a shortened model year run; 2005 Uplander arrives. **2006**—Optional second-row side airbags; introduction of a shorter-length model and an upgraded automatic transmission.

By the way, don't trust the towing limit listed in GM's owner's manual. Automakers publish tow ratings that are on the optimistic side—and sometimes they even lie. Also, don't be surprised to find that the base 3.1L engine (replaced in 1997) doesn't handle a full load of passengers and cargo, especially when mated to the 3-speed automatic transmission. The ideal powertrain combo would be the 4-speed automatic coupled to the optional "3800" V6 (first used on the 1996 versions). These minivans use a quiet-running V6 powerplant similar to Chrysler's top-of-the-line

3.8L 6-cylinder engine, providing good mid-range and top-end power. The GM engine is hampered by less torque, however, making for less grunt when accelerating and frequent downshifting out of Overdrive when climbing moderate grades. The electronically controlled 4-speed automatic transmission usually shifts smoothly—one advantage over Chrysler and Ford.

FRONT/REAR ROOF RUST PERFORATION

BULLETIN NO.: 02-08-67-006B   DATE: MARCH 2003

ROOF PERFORATION (REPLACE ROOF)

1997–2003 Chevrolet Venture

1997–2003 Oldsmobile Silhouette

1997–2003 Pontiac TranSport/Montana

IMPORTANT: Implementation of this service bulletin by "GM of Canada" dealers requires prior District Service Manager approval.

CONDITION: Some customers may comment that there is rust forming around the front or rear portion of the roof.

CAUSE: During production, the E-coating (ELPO primer) may have been missed in concealed areas of the front or rear portions of the outer roof panel.

The 1997 and later models are less rattle-prone because their body structure is more rigid than that of their predecessors. However, fit and finish quality is still wanting. The front windshield is particularly prone to water leaks from the top portion into the dash instrument cluster (a problem also affecting rear-drive vans and covered by a secret warranty). Owner-reported problems on post-'97s include chronic plastic intake manifold/head gasket failures (covered by a 6-year/100,000 km secret warranty), EGR valve failures, transmission fluid leaks, electrical glitches shorting out dash gauges and causing difficult starting, excessive front brake noise and frequent repairs (rotors and pads), and assorted body deficiencies, including water leaks in the jack well, premature rusting, and extensive paint peeling:

> Our 2002 Venture has a poorly fitted windshield and a misaligned dash and hood, as well as quarter panels, front doors, and the sliding rear door on the passenger side. I have inspected other 2002 and 2003 Chevrolet Ventures and have seen the same windshield fit errors.

> Here are the pics I told you I would send in regards to the 2000 (piece of crap) Montana [see example on page 436]. Some are of the hole in the roof which GM says that a rock could have caused...(my husband's thumb went through it). Also the paint is peeling to the bare metal underneath the wipers and the back hatch. The paint has now cracked on the driver's door coming right up the paneling, and there's a big blister on the hood.

> I asked GM about the service bulletin [see above] I had read about the perforated roof and she said that it was covered under warranty up till 160,000 km and since I

was hitting almost 200,000 km it was no longer valid to me. So today I called again after getting the *Lemon-Aid* book to again ask about the bulletin and they gave me the same response, so I asked them about the call I made back when it was 140,000 km, and their response was that at that time it was only peeling, flaking, and blistering...no rust had started.

COST ANALYSIS: Since there is very little difference between the 2006 and 2007 models, go for the cheaper 2006 versions, or the 2007 Uplander if you want a slightly more powerful engine. They should have many of the 2005's bugs worked out (TSB #06-07-030-011 says the automatic transmission got a major upgrade) and sell for much less than their original $23,240 and $23,915 base prices. But if you need the additional engine power, it's better to opt for a 2007 version. Most Saturn dealers refuse to haggle down their $26,995 suggested retail price, which is already $1,000 less than the 2005 price. Above all, stay away from the 2005 or earlier Venture, Montana, and Silhouette offerings. Yes, they are incredibly cheap, but what you save, you will likely pay out in powertrain repairs. **Best alternatives:** The 1999 or later Honda Odyssey, 1998–2003 Nissan Quest, and 1998–2003 Toyota Sienna. Full-sized Chrysler (not the Sprinter), GM, and Ford vans are also good choices. **Rebates:** $3,500 rebates and zero percent financing. **Delivery/PDI:** $1,250. **Warranty:** Bumper-to-bumper 3 years/60,000 km; rust perforation 6 years/160,000 km. **Supplementary warranty:** A powertrain-only warranty will do. **Options:** $5,000 (U.S.) "Sit-N-Lift" electrically powered seats for the physically challenged have performed well. Be wary of the AWD option because it's unreliable. Many of these vans are equipped with Firestone and Bridgestone tires—have them removed by the dealer, or ask for a $400 rebate. Integrated child safety seats are generally a good idea, but make sure they can be easily installed and your child can't slip out or get tangled in the straps. Be wary of the power-assisted passenger-side sliding door; it has a reputation as a wrist-breaker and child-crusher. The load-levelling feature is no longer offered, so look for a used model that has it equipped—it's a must-have for front-drive minivans. Weight is kept on the front wheels, giving you better steering, traction, and braking. Other options that are worth buying are the extended wheelbase version (provides a smoother ride), traction control, power side windows, a firmer suspension, self-sealing tires, and a rear air conditioner, defroster, and heater. **Depreciation:** Average. **Insurance cost:** Faster than average. **Parts supply/cost:** Powertrain and body parts are generic to GM's other models, so they are reasonably priced and not hard to find. **Annual maintenance cost:** Average during the warranty period, but much higher than average afterwards. Engine, transmission, ABS, and electrical malfunctions will likely cause maintenance costs to rise after the third year of ownership. **Highway/city fuel economy:** 9.3/13.5 L/100 km.

 QUALITY/RELIABILITY: The 1996–2004 models have chronic powertrain problems highlighted by engine manifold, head gasket, and camshaft failures along with frequent automatic transmission breakdowns and clunky shifting (which GM, with a straight face, says is a "normal" condition). **Owner-reported problems:** EGR valve and starter failures; electrical glitches; excessive front brake noise and frequent repairs (rotors and pads); early wheel bearing failures; blurry front windshields; failure-prone AC condensers; and assorted body deficiencies, including chronic windshield chipping, defective power-sliding doors, poor fit and finish, paint peeling and blistering, and roof perforations caused by extensive corrosion (covered by a secret warranty). **Warranty performance:** Very bad. The company still denies it has serious engine problems and often makes payouts only on the courthouse steps. Fed up by GM's stonewalling, Canadians have lodged a $1.2-billion class action that applies to all 1996–2004 models sold in Canada. A copy of the Canadian class action can be found in Appendix IV.

 SAFETY SUMMARY: Sudden steering loss in rainy weather or when passing over a puddle (serpentine belt slippage); ABS brake failures; ABS light stays on for no reason; airbags fail to deploy; sliding doors suddenly open, close, come off their tracks, jam shut, stick open, injure children, or rattle (1997–2001 models were recalled); fire may ignite around the fuel-filler nozzle or within the ignition switch; tie-rod failures may cause loss of control; during highway driving, transmission slips from Drive into Neutral; some front-door-mounted seat belts cross uncomfortably at the neck; and there's a nasty blind spot on the driver's side that requires a small stick-on convex mirror to correct. The 2006 and 2007 minivans all scored a five-star rating for frontal crash protection, four stars for side protection, and three stars for rollover prevention. IIHS rated the 2005 and 2006 Uplander "Good" for offset crash protection. However, the group's side crash rating for the 2006 and 2007 minivans equipped with standard head and torso side airbags was only "Marginal," and their rating dropped to "Poor" on vehicles manufactured after February 2006 that weren't similarly equipped. **Anti-lock brakes:** Standard; disc/drum. **Seat belt pretensioners:** Standard. **Airbags:** Side airbags are standard. **Traction control:** Optional. **Head restraints F/R:** *1997:* ★; *1999:* ★★★/★; *2001–04:* ★★★; *2005–06:* ★. **Visibility F/R:** ★★★★★. **Maximum load capacity:** *2001 Chevrolet Venture LS and similarly equipped Montana and Silhouette:* 1,365 lb.

SAFETY COMPLAINTS: All years: Chronic brake failures, or excessive brake fade. • Airbag malfunctions. • Transmission fails or won't hold gear on a grade. • Power-sliding doors constantly open, close, or jam on their own, plus they may crush anything that gets in their way. **1995–99**—Headlight assembly collects moisture, burns bulb, or falls out. • Seatback suddenly collapses. • Windshield wipers fail intermittently. • Accelerator and brake pedals are too close together • Fuel slosh or clunk when vehicle stops or accelerates (a new tank is useless). • Self-activating door locks trap occupants outside or inside. • Door handles break inside the door assembly. • Horn is hard to access. • Window latch failures. **2000–2001**—Fire ignited under driver's seat. • Windshield suddenly exploded outward while driving with wipers activated. • Firestone tire blowout. • Faulty fuel pump causes chronic stalling, no-starts, surging, and sudden acceleration. • Snapped rear control arm (described by this Montana owner from Kitchener, Ontario):

> In May we were driving our 2002 Pontiac Montana with six adults inside (luckily), on a small two-lane road, doing about 50 or 60 km/h. Suddenly, the right rear control arm snapped and the rear axle rattled and shook.
>
> Our mechanic said in 28 years he had never seen such a thing happen. If we'd been going 120 km/h on a 400 highway we'd be dead.
>
> The dealer we bought it from paid all the costs for a used part to be installed, even though there was no warranty, but our mechanic suggested we photograph the parts he had removed. He was surprised at the thinness of the metal of the control arm. Also that the control arm is welded to the axle, so it can't be replaced without replacing the entire component. New, they are $2,000!

• Steering idler arm fell off because of missing bolt. • Brakes activate on their own, making it appear as if the van is pulling a load. • Fuel tank is loose because of loose bolts/bracket. • Fuel tank cracked when passing over a tree branch. • Plastic tube within heating system fell off and wedged behind the accelerator pedal. • Bracket weld pin that secures the rear split seat sheared off. • Centre rear lapbelt isn't long enough to secure a rear-facing child safety seat. • Children can slide out of the integrated child safety seat. • Electrical harness failures result in complete electrical shutdown. • Headlights, interior lights, gauges, and instruments fail intermittently (electrical cluster module is the prime suspect). • Excess padding around horn makes it difficult to depress horn button in an emergency. • Weak-sounding horn. • Frequent windshield wiper motor failures. • Heater doesn't warm up vehicle sufficiently. • Antifreeze smell intrudes into interior. • Premature failure of the transmission's Fourth clutch. • Delayed shifts, slips, flares, or extended shifts in cold weather. • Poorly performing rear AC. • Flickering interior and exterior lights. • Airbag warning lamp stays lit. • Windshield glass distortion. **2002**—Rear hatch handle broke, cutting driver's hand. • Vehicle jumped out of Park and rolled downhill. • Vehicle suddenly shuts off in traffic. • Windshield water leaks short out dash gauges. **2003**—Rear seat belts failed to release. • Weld holding the lift wheel pin is not adequate to support weight of trailer. **2004**—Engine surging, stalling. • Loss of coolant, engine overheating. • Two incidents where a child's wrist was fractured after elbow and hand were caught between the seat and handle. • Tail lights fail intermittently. • Door opens and closes on its own while vehicle is underway. • Door doesn't lock into position; slides shut and crushes anything in its path:

> We are very concerned that another child, or adult, is going to be injured in this van's automatic sliding door. We were curious just how far the 2004 Venture's door would

go before it would bounce back open so we put a stuffed animal in the door and hit the auto door close button. I have to say, the stuffed animal did not fare well. We also put a large carrot and a banana in the door, in an attempt to simulate a small child's arm. The carrot was sliced right in half, and the banana was smashed and oozing out of its peel. I will never purchase a Chevrolet Venture after our experience with the van.

Uplander: 2005—Vehicle will stall if it has only half a tank of fuel and is on a hill. • Excessive swaying and poor handling. • Power-sliding door jammed; Door Ajar warning bell sounds constantly. • Power-sliding door opens and closes on its own:

They may open while going down the road. They will also open when not prompted in the middle of the night, when everyone is asleep. They also will not close on some occasions. They start to close, then give a warning bell & re-open. We bought this vehicle because I have a 24 yr. old son with cerebral palsy. I cannot, in good conscience, put him in this vehicle...due to the major safety issues. Would you put your child in this vehicle and wonder whether the doors would decide to come open while going 75 [mph] [120 km/h] down the interstate?

• Flickering/dimming headlights and interior lights. • Actuating bar for windshield wipers cuts into wiring harness. • Brakes applied to all four wheels without driver pressing the brake pedal. • Horn is hard to activate (covered by a service bulletin).

Secret Warranties/Internal Bulletins/Service Tips

1986–2006—V6 engine oil leaks at the crankshaft rear main oil seal. 1990–98—An oil odour coming from the engine compartment may be eliminated by changing the crankshaft rear main oil seal. 1993–2000—GM says that a chronic driveline clunk can't be silenced and is a "normal" characteristic of its vehicles. • Paint delamination, peeling, or fading. 1995–2000—Dealer guidelines for brake servicing under warranty. 1996–2001—Poor heat distribution in driver's area of vehicle (install new heat ducts). 1996–2004—Engine intake manifold/head gasket failures. Here is how the problem is described by editor and publisher Andrew Ross in his article "A Fate Sealed: How Factors Conspired to Create GM's Intake Manifold Gasket Troubles," found in the July 2006 edition of *Jobber News*, a Canadian automotive publication (*www.autoserviceworld.com*):

First, it should be noted that the construction of the original gasket was a plastic carrier with a silicone sealing bead system.

According to information from engineering sources that wished not to be named for fear of reprisals, at least part of the problem exists with the original material. While plastic carriers aren't bad, the particular plastic chosen was not quite right for life alongside the Organic Acid Technology (OAT) of Dex-Cool. This plastic, part of the nylon family, has a tendency to become hard and crack in an acidic environment.

But that's not the end of it.

In addition, the silicone used as the sealing bead is not quite right for the job, either. Sources say that it is not compatible with the fuel-air mixture or OAT coolant, particularly when that coolant has itself become degraded and more aggressive than the original chemistry might have been.

The cracking that is so prevalent on the failed gaskets is a result of the embrittling of the carrier combined with the swelling of the silicone bead in the presence of the coolant and/or the fuel-air mixture. The swelling puts pressure on the carrier and, because it has been weakened, it fails.

General Motors can't easily stonewall owners' claims when they come armed with engineering facts, like those above. Instead, the automaker is settling claims on a case-by-case-basis while denying the problem exists:

I just wanted to let you know that after contacting you back in January regarding our 2001 Chevy Venture head gasket problem, I have just received my judgment through the Canadian Arbitration Program.

I used the sample complaint letter as well as the judgment you have posted in the *Ford Canada vs. Dufour* court case. This combined with an avalanche of similar Chevy Venture complaints that are posted on the Internet helped us to win a $1,700 reimbursement of the $2,200 we were looking for.

The reason for us not receiving the full amount is that the arbitrator stated that GM Canada would have only replaced one head gasket instead of replacing both as we had done, and that a dealer would have supplied us with a car free of charge and therefore did not allow us the car rental expense we incurred.

We are still extremely happy with the results and thank you for your books and web-site, you have a fan for life.

1997–99—Upgraded front disc pads will reduce brake squeal. **1997–2000**—Front door windows that are inoperative, slow, or noisy may need the window run channel adjusted or replaced in addition to new weather stripping. **1997–2001**—Psst! GM minivans may show premature hood corrosion and blistering (no surprise, after seeing readers' comments). A dealer whistle-blower tells me that dealers have been authorized to repair the hoods free of charge (refinish and repaint) up to six years under a GM "goodwill" program. Here's the confidential service bulletin that was handed to me:

BLISTERING, BUBBLING PAINT

BULLETIN NO.: 01-08-51-004   DATE: OCTOBER, 2001

PREMATURE ALUMINUM HOOD CORROSION/BLISTERING (REFINISH)

1997–2001 Trans Sport (export only)

1997–2001 Venture

1997–2001 Silhouette

1997–98 Trans Sport

1999–2001 Pontiac Montana

Some vehicles may have the appearance of blistering or bubbling paint on the top of the hood or under the hood.

1997–2002—Mildew odour; water leaks. • Wind noise at base of windshield. **1997–2004**—Defective catalytic converters that cause a rotten-egg smell in the interior may be replaced free of charge under the emissions warranty. • Second-row seat belt won't release. • Windshield wind noise. **1998**—No-start, engine misfire, and rough idle may indicate that melted slush has contaminated the fuel system. **1998–99**—An inoperative sliding door may have a defective control module. **1998–2000**—Poor AC performance in humid weather may be caused by an undercharged AC system. **1999**—Diagnostic tips for an automatic transmission that slips, produces a harsh upshift and garage shifts, or causes acceleration shudders. **1999–2000**—If the engine runs hot, overheats, or loses coolant, try polishing the radiator-filler neck or replacing the radiator cap before considering more expensive repairs. • Before taking on more expensive repairs to correct hard starts or no-starts, check the fuel pump. • An automatic transmission that whines in Park or Neutral, or a Service Engine light that stays on, may signal the need for a new drive sprocket support bearing. **1999–2002**—Transmission noise/ no movement:

TRANSMISSION NOISE/NO MOVEMENT IN "D" OR "R"

BULLETIN NO.: 03-07-30-017   DATE: MAY, 2003

GRIND NOISE OR NO VEHICLE MOVEMENT WHEN SHIFTING INTO DRIVE OR REVERSE (INSPECT TRANSAXLE, REPLACE VARIOUS TRANSAXLE COMPONENTS)

1999–2002 Century, LeSabre, Park Avenue

2002 Rendezvous

1999–2002 Monte Carlo, Venture

2000–02 Impala

1999–2002 Intrigue, Silhouette

1999–2002 Bonneville, Grand Prix, Montana

2001–02 Aztek

IMPORTANT: If the vehicle DOES NOT exhibit a grinding condition but DOES exhibit shifting concerns, refer to Corporate Bulletin #00-07-30-002

1999–2003—Incorrect fuel gauge readings caused by a contaminated fuel-tank sensor/sender. If a fuel "cleaner" doesn't work, GM says it will adjust or replace the sensor/sender for free on a case-by-case basis (*Toronto Star*, June 13 and 14, 2003, and December 20, 2003). This failure afflicts GM's entire lineup and could cost up to $800 to repair. 2000–02—Service Engine light comes on, and automatic transmission is harsh shifting. • Hard start, no-start, stall, and fuel gauge inoperative. 2000–04—Tail light/brake light and circuit board burns out from water intrusion. Repair cost covered by a "goodwill" policy (TSB #03-08-42-007A). 2000–06—Hard starts, stalling, inoperative gauges, and lit warning lights can all be traced to water leaking onto the C305 connector, says TSB #01-08-45-005D. 2001—Customer Satisfaction Program (read: secret warranty) to correct the rear HVAC control switch. 2001–02—Poor engine and automatic transmission operation. 2001–03—Water in jack compartment. 2001–04—Inability to shift out of Park after installation of Sit-N-Lift device. • Slipping automatic transmission. 2001–06—Automatic transmission upgrade kit developed to improve durability. This is an excellent "smoking gun" TSB that shows these model year transmissions have quality control problems. 2003—Shudder, chuggle, hard shifting, and transmission won't downshift. 2003–04—Power-sliding door binding. • Windshield whistle. 2004–06—Noisy steering can be silenced by replacing the inner tie-rod boot, says TSB #06-02-32-005. 2005—Inoperative turn signals and tail lights. • Lumpy seats may require a new cushion. 2005–06—A defective harmonic balancer may cause severe engine damage. GM will retorque the balancer bolt free of charge. • Hard/no start, stalling, inoperative gauges. • High effort to sound horn. • Silencing sliding door rattles. • Steering may need to be fixed by replacing the inner tie-rod boot. • Poor AC performance:

A/C TEMPERATURE WON'T CHANGE/POOR PERFORMANCE

BULLETIN NO.: 06-01-39-004A   DATE: APRIL 25, 2006

2005–2006 Montana SV6, Relay, Terraza and Uplander

ATTENTION: THIS IS NOT A RECALL. "GM of Canada" dealers are not authorized to use this bulletin. This bulletin ONLY applies to vehicles in which the customer has commented about this concern AND the EI number shows in GMVIS. All others should disregard this bulletin and proceed with diagnostics found in published service information.

CONDITION: IMPORTANT: If the customer did not bring their vehicle in for this issue, DO NOT proceed with this bulletin.

Some customers may comment that they are unable to change the HVAC mode and/or temperature. Customers may also comment that the A/C may be inoperative or have poor performance.

CORRECTION: GM Engineering is attempting to determine the root cause of this condition. GM has a need to obtain information first hand BEFORE any repairs are made.

WARRANTY INFORMATION:

Labor Operation	Description	Labor Time
D9719*	HVAC — Engineering Investigation	1.0 hr
Add	Recover and Recharge A/C System WITH Rear A/C	0.7 hr
Add	Recover and Recharge A/C System WITHOUT Rear A/C	0.5 hr

*This labor operation is for bulletin use only. It will not be published in the Labor Time Guide.

This is a strange bulletin that excludes Canadians, tells Americans the problem exists but the cause is unknown, and estimates it will take over two hours to investigate. Smart owners will go to the dealer and ask for a fix under warranty. If refused, get an independent repairer to replace the system and then use the above bulletin to get a refund. • Inaccurate temperature and fuel readings.

MONTANA, MONTANA SV6, RELAY, SILHOUETTE, TERRAZA, TRANS SPORT, UPLANDER, VENTURE PROFILE

	1998	1999	2000	2001	2002	2003	2004	2005	2006
Cost Price ($) (negotiable)									
Montana	—	25,130	26,625	26,755	27,870	28,520	29,380	29,380	—
Montana SV6 (23%)	—	—	—	—	—	—	—	26,620	23,915
Silhouette	29,410	29,955	30,630	31,105	33,060	35,695	36,290	—	—
Relay (22%)	—	—	—	—	—	—	—	27,995	26,995
Terraza (23%)	—	—	—	—	—	—	—	33,745	32,210
Trans Sport/SE	24,650	—	—	—	—	—	—	—	—
Venture	24,145	24,725	24,895	25,230	25,195	25,865	26,680	30,590	—
Uplander (22%)	—	—	—	—	—	—	—	25,405	23,240
Used Values ($)									
Montana ▲	—	4,500	6,500	8,500	10,500	12,500	16,000	19,500	—
Montana ▼	—	5,000	5,000	7,000	9,000	11,000	14,500	18,000	—
Montana SV6 ▲	—	—	—	—	—	—	—	18,000	—
Montana SV6 ▼	—	—	—	—	—	—	—	17,000	—
Silhouette ▲	4,500	5,500	7,000	9,000	11,000	14,500	18,000	—	—
Silhouette ▼	4,000	4,500	6,000	8,000	10,000	13,000	16,500	—	—
Relay ▲	—	—	—	—	—	—	—	18,000	—
Relay ▼	—	—	—	—	—	—	—	17,000	—
Terraza ▲	—	—	—	—	—	—	—	21,000	—
Terraza ▼	—	—	—	—	—	—	—	19,500	—
Trans Sport/SE ▲	3,500	—	—	—	—	—	—	—	—
Trans Sport/SE ▼	3,000	—	—	—	—	—	—	—	—
Venture ▲	4,000	5,000	6,000	8,000	10,500	12,500	15,500	18,500	—
Venture ▼	3,500	4,500	5,000	6,500	9,000	11,000	14,000	17,000	—
Uplander ▲	—	—	—	—	—	—	—	17,000	—
Uplander ▼	—	—	—	—	—	—	—	15,500	—
Reliability	❷	❷	❷	❷	❷	❷	❸	❸	—
Crash Safety (F)	④	④	④	④	④	④	④	④	⑤
Side	—	⑤	⑤	⑤	⑤	⑤	⑤	⑤	④
Offset	❶	❶	❶	❶	❶	❶	❶	❶	—
Uplander/Montana/Relay/Terraza	—	—	—	—	—	—	—	⑤	⑤
Rollover	—	—	—	❸	❸	❸	—	—	❸

Note: The higher-priced 2005 Montana is the extended version.

2007 TECHNICAL DATA

POWERTRAIN (REAR-DRIVE)
Engines: 4.3L V6 (200 hp) • 4.8L V8 (285 hp) • 5.3L V8 (295 hp) • 6.0L V8 (300 hp) • 6.6L V8 (250 hp); Transmissions: 4-speed auto. OD • 4-speed heavy-duty auto. OD

DIMENSION/CAPACITY (BASE)
Passengers: 8–15; Wheelbase: 135/155 in.; H: 81.6/L: 224/W: 79.4 in.; Headroom F/R: N/A; Legroom F/R: 41.3/34.8 in.; Cargo volume: 204–237 cu. ft.; Fuel tank: 117L/regular; Tow limit: 10,000 lb.; Load capacity: 1,355/1,942 lb.; GVWR: 7,200–9,600 lb.; Turning circle: 43.4–49 ft.; Ground clearance: 7.6 in.; Weight: 5,017–6,333 lb.

RATING: Average (1980–2007). These rear-drive full-sized vans are about as good as the Ford Econoline, and they're cheaper and more easily serviced than Chrysler's 2004 and later Sprinter. Nevertheless, Chrysler's 2003 and earlier Ram Vans have an edge over Ford and GM vans if the 7-year powertrain warranty is in effect. **Strong points:** A large array of powerful engines; improved ride and transmission and brake upgrades; multiple wheelbase configurations; plenty of interior room; dual side access doors; and more fuel efficient than its rivals, even with the larger engines. **Weak points:** Spartan base model; tacky interior garnishing; difficult to enter and exit; and serious powertrain, brake, and body fit and finish deficiencies. Handling is still ponderous despite improvements. Quite a bit heavier than the typical full-size van. No crashworthiness data. **New for 2007:** A 5.3L V8 engine may be standard on 1500 passenger van models.

MODEL HISTORY: These vans are easily found at reasonable prices that are getting even more reasonable as fuel costs chase insurance premiums into the stratosphere. Passenger versions are usually heavily customized and can mean great savings if you don't pay top dollar for accessories you're not likely to use, or if you get a used model.

The Chevy Van and GMC Vandura (both dropped for the '96 model year) are big steel cocoons—without a separate frame—to which a subframe is attached for the independent front suspension and leaf springs that support the live rear axle. The Chevy versions cost about the same as the GMC variants and have a similar rate of depreciation, which hovers around 75 percent after seven years. Extended warranty coverage is a toss-up, inasmuch as most of the quality deficiencies can be diagnosed and remedied inexpensively.

The 3- and 4-speed automatics and manual transmissions are on the pre-1993 equipment list, after which the recommended 4-speed automatic is standard. The 3-speeds are jerky, fuel-thirsty, and overwhelmed by the van's heft. Overall reliability is average, as owners report serious problems with early 5.7L diesels and V8s as well as with front suspensions, steering components, and cooling, electrical, and braking systems. Interior accommodations are primitive on cargo models. Body assembly quality and paint application are particularly bad, so watch out for premature rust, paint delamination, and peeling. Water/air leaks and rattles are also commonplace.

1996–2007 Express and Savana

The product of GM's 1996 redesign of the Chevy Van and GMC Vandura, these full-sized cargo-haulers and people-movers are only a bit better than the vans they replaced. Powered by Vortec engines and a turbocharged diesel, these vans are built on longer wheelbases and use a ladder-type frame, as opposed to the unibody construction of their predecessors. This has improved ride quality somewhat, but overall performance remains unchanged.

Both vans are a better choice than the average full-sized van as far as hauling capacity, especially if you often need to carry a lot of cargo or large animals. They also outpull the average full-sized van by a big margin.

1999—De-powered airbags, and an upgraded transmission. **2001**—A powerful 8.1L V8 replaced the 7.4L. **2003**—New features included optional all-wheel drive, four-wheel disc brakes, a stiffer box frame, enhanced ride and handling, dual side doors that open outward, and a minor face-lift. Engines and transmissions were revised and the suspension retuned. Although the engine-gasket-challenged 200-hp remained the base engine, GM added the GEN III V8 engines used in full-sized trucks since 1999. **2004**—Standard stability-control on 15-passenger models. **2005**—Upgraded automatic transmission components. **2006**—Addition of a Duramax 6.6L turbo diesel. The new optional engine supposedly has better fuel economy, less diesel engine clatter, and quicker starts. Standard AM/FM radio becomes optional.

COST ANALYSIS: Choose an identical 2006 Express or Savana Cargo version ($27,080), and haggle for a 20 percent discount (prices are easily bargained down). Stay away from the AWD; it has a high failure rate and is a fuel-waster. **Best alternatives:** The Ford Econoline is an okay second choice, but it also has chronic factory-related defects and doesn't handle as well as the GM vans. Your best Detroit choice is one of the Chrysler-warranteed 2003 or earlier models equipped with a Cummins diesel and a manual transmission. **Rebates:** Look for $4,000 rebates early in the new year. **Delivery/PDI:** $1,200. **Warranty:** Bumper-to-bumper 3 years/60,000 km; rust perforation 6 years/160,000 km. **Supplementary warranty:** A toss-up. **Options:** Running boards, rear air conditioning, power windows and door locks, and heavy-duty alternator. You'll find the SLE garnish creates a much cozier interior. Don't go for the base V6 engine; it's not that much more fuel-efficient than the 5.0L or 5.3L V8 (the most engine you will need for everyday driving). If you plan to load up on power-draining optional equipment or do some heavy hauling, choose a model equipped with the 5.7L or 6.0L V8. Be wary of the optional $7,000 6.6L diesel engine; it has yet to prove itself, and next year it will have to deal with reformulated fuel and stricter emissions requirements. **Depreciation:** Higher than average. **Insurance cost:** Much higher than average. **Parts supply/cost:** Average for generic mechanical and body parts. **Annual maintenance cost:** Less than average; any independent garage can repair these vans. **Highway/city fuel economy:** *Express 4.3L with an automatic transmission: 11.4/16.0 L/100 km; 5.0L and automatic: 12.5/16.9 L/100 km; 5.7L and automatic: 11.9/17.3 L/100 km.*

QUALITY/RELIABILITY: Quality control and overall reliability have declined since these vehicles were redesigned a decade ago. **Warranty performance:** Average. **Likely failures:** Engine, diesel injectors, turbocharger, and cracked head; automatic transmission 6.5L diesel oil cooler lines and other diesel maladies; electrical system, starter, EMC fuses, fuel pump (black and gray wires fused together inside the fuel tank), and fuel sending unit; catalytic converter, suspension, steering gearbox, and power-steering pump; brake pads and rotors; ABS sensors; AC; tire-tread separation and sidewall splitting; and fit and finish (such as broken door hinges and paint flaking off of mirror, bumpers, and trim). One report of severe rusting around the brake bearing spindles and knock head joints.

SAFETY SUMMARY: For 1993, four-wheel ABS was added as a standard feature along with variable-ratio power steering. **Airbags:** Standard front and side. **ABS:** Standard; disc/disc. **Head restraints F/R:** N/A. **Visibility F/R:** ★★★★★/★.

SAFETY COMPLAINTS: All years: Front wheel flew off. • PCM/VCM computer module shorts from water intrusion. • Vehicle won't decelerate when gas pedal is released. • Power-steering and ABS brake failures. • Premature brake pad/rotor wear • Broken power seat anchor/brackets; seats come off their tracks, costing $900 to repair. • Broken or weak side-door hinges. • Fuel gauge failure. • Excessive side-mirror vibration. • Tire-tread separation. **1999**—Airbags deployed for no reason. • Gas pedal sticks when accelerating. • Differential failure. • Loose power-steering line leaks steering fluid. • Nut on steering column fell off, causing loss of steering. • Excessive brake fade after successive stops, and pedal will sometimes go to the floor without stopping the vehicle. • Rear-wheel seal leaks coat rear brakes with oil. • Sticking speedometer needle. • Positive post pulled out of battery. **2000**—Dashboard fire. • Unnecessary 4–3 downshifts. • Upper ball joint suddenly collapsed. • Chronic stalling. • Loose steering wheel. • Braking malfunctions and brake lock-up. • ABS performs erratically. • Rear shoulder belts cross too high on the torso. • Seat belt retractor doesn't lock properly. • Broken or stiff door hinges. **2001**—Under-hood fire caused by electrical short under dash on passenger side. • Chronic stalling caused by moisture in the distributor. • Delayed 2–3 transmission shifts. • Windshield tinted strip cuts visibility for tall drivers. • Brake pedal goes to floor without stopping vehicle. • Vehicle wanders all over the road at 100 km/h. • Firestone tread separation. • Faulty tire valve stems leak air. **2002**—Fire ignited at the bottom of driver's door. • Fuel leak. • 5.7L engine loses power when AC is engaged. • Cruise control won't decelerate vehicle when going downhill. • Leaking axle tube seals. • Leaking front grease seals contaminate the front inner disc brake pads, causing loss of braking effectiveness. • Front wheel speed sensor melted. • Tail lights blow when headlights are turned on. • AC Delco battery acid leaked out from broken positive cable post. • Door opened while vehicle was underway. 2003—Extended stopping distance when brakes are applied; sometimes they fail to hold. • Fire ignited from a short in the right rear door-lock motor. • Tailpipe exhaust leaks where it fits into converter. • Horn and wiper failure. 2005—Seat belt on a 15-passenger van malfunctioned, and passenger had to be cut free. • Original-equipment Bridgestone tires don't give adequate traction, and they degrade steering and braking performance. • Unsafe mirror design:

> I am concerned about the field of vision provided by the mirrors on my van. I have owned three full sized vans since 1995, and have never had this problem before. My concern is with the style and size of the exterior mirrors. Most full size van manufacturers have horizontal mirrors, but Chevy opted for a vertical that has cut down on the peripheral vision field of the driver. This concerns me greatly as I perceive it to be a safety hazard especially when trying to merge onto a freeway, and keeping abreast of approaching traffic from the rear of the van. The reduced peripheral vision has caused a number of near miss collisions.

Secret Warranties/Internal Bulletins/Service Tips

All years: GM bulletins say automatic transmission clunks are "normal." • Many diesel engine failures. **1992–96**—If the engine won't start or is hard to start, check the fuel pump pulsator. **1993–2002**—Paint delamination, peeling, or fading. **1994–99**—Hard starts on vehicles equipped with a 6.5L diesel engine may signal the need to replace the shut-off solenoid. **1996–99**—Engine bearing knocking on vehicles equipped with a 5.0L or 5.7L V8 may be silenced by using select-fit undersized connecting rod bearings and a special GM countermeasure kit to service the crankshaft. **1996–2000**—Poor starts, no-starts, and backfire on starting all point to the need to replace the crankshaft position sensor. • A rough idle or constantly lit Service Engine light may require that a cleaner be used to unstick and clean the central sequential fuel injection poppet valves. **1996–2002**—Cargo door binding requires new hinge pins and bushings (covered by a "goodwill" policy on a case-by-case basis). **1997–98**—Vehicles equipped with a 6.5L diesel engine with hard upshifts may need to reprogram the PCM/VCM. **1997–2001**—Diagnostic procedures to fix AC performance problems and leaks. **1998**—Engine stalling or surging and a slipping transmission may signal the need to repair the auxiliary oil cooler or replace the transmission torque converter. **1998–2000**—Stalling or surging can be corrected by installing updated transmission software. **1999–2000**—List of procedures to follow in correcting door wind noise. • An inexpensive cure for an overheated engine or coolant loss may be as simple as replacing the radiator cap or polishing the radiator-filler neck. **2001**—Automatic transmission harsh shifting. • Reports of automatic transmission 2–4 band or 3–4 clutch damage. • Inaccurate fuel gauge. **2002**—Check Engine light comes on, followed by poor engine and automatic transmission performance; transmission feels like it has slipped into Neutral. • Leaking engine oil cooler lines. **2003**—Hard starts, rough idle, and intermittent engine misfiring. • Drive shaft may fracture; a free repair under Customer Satisfaction #03040. • Thumping noise/feel in brake pedal • Voluntary emission recall to replace spark plugs. • Vehicle difficult to fill with fuel. **2003–04**—Suspension clunk and slap. GM will replace the spring insert and insulator for free (see Silverado "Secret Warranties/Internal Bulletins/Service Tips"). **2003–05**—Lack of power when the 4.3L engine is hot. **2003–06**—ABS activation at 3 km/h. • Ignition key cylinder won't turn. **2004**—Overdrive gear may fail because of a lack of lubrication at the factory; a free Customer Satisfaction repair (#04019).

EXPRESS, SAVANA PROFILE

	1998	1999	2000	2001	2002	2003	2004	2005	2006
Cost Price ($) (very negotiable)									
Savana Cargo (21%)	25,315	25,330	25,495	24,905	25,025	25,125	26,465	26,835	27,080
Express (21%)	29,140	29,155	29,330	30,885	29,105	29,215	30,000	26,785	27,080
Used Values ($)									
Savana Cargo ▲	4,500	5,500	7,000	8,500	11,500	14,000	17,000	19,000	—
Savana Cargo ▼	4,000	5,000	6,000	7,500	10,000	12,500	15,500	17,500	—
Express ▲	6,000	7,000	9,000	11,000	14,500	15,000	17,500	19,500	—
Express ▼	5,000	6,000	8,000	10,000	13,500	14,000	16,000	18,000	—
Reliability	③	③	④	④	④	④	④	④	—
Crash Safety (F)	—	—	—	—	—	—	—	⑤	⑤

Honda

All ratings on a numbered scale where ⑤ is good and ❶ is bad. See page 220 for a more detailed description.

2007 TECHNICAL DATA

POWERTRAIN (FRONT-DRIVE)
Engine: 3.5L V6 (255 hp); Transmission: 5-speed auto.
DIMENSION/CAPACITY
Passengers: 2/3/3; Wheelbase: 118 in.; H: 68.8/L: 201/W: 77 in.; Headroom F/R1/R2: 4.5/5.5/2.0 in.; Legroom F/R1/R2: 41.5/31/28 in.; Cargo volume: 66.5 cu. ft.; Fuel tank: 65L/regular; Tow limit: 3,500 lb.; Load capacity: 1,320 lb.; GVWR: 5,567 lb.; Turning circle: 40 ft.; Ground clearance: 5.0 in.; Weight: 4,615 lb.

RATING: Recommended (2006–07); Above Average (2003–05); Average (1996–2002). The upgraded 2005 model passes the Toyota Sienna in safety, performance, and convenience features. Nevertheless, there are some reports of safety- and performance-related failures on year-2005 and earlier Odysseys; hence the downgrade despite the 2005's overall improvements. Of particular concern are airbag malfunctions, automatic-sliding-door failures, engine failures, transmission breakdowns and erratic shifting, and sudden brake loss. Early Odysseys get only an Average rating because of their small engine and interior—identical shortcomings to those of Mazda's early MPV minivan. **Strong points:** *2005 and later models:* More power, room, and safety and convenience features. Additional mid-range torque means less shifting when the engine is under load; uses regular gas (the Sienna can burn regular but needs pricier high-octane to get the advertised horsepower and torque). *Pre-2005 models:* Strong engine performance; carlike ride and handling; easy entry and exit because of low step-up; second driver-side door; quiet interior; most controls and displays are easy to reach and read; lots of passenger and cargo room; an extensive list of standard equipment; and Honda's willingness to compensate owners for production snafus. **Weak points:** *2005 and later models:* Unlike with the Sienna, all-wheel drive isn't available; middle-row seats don't fold flat like other minivans, so they need to be stowed somewhere else; second-row head restraints block visibility. *Pre-2005 models:* Front-seat passenger legroom is marginal because of the restricted seat travel; you can't slide your legs comfortably under the dash; some passengers bump their shins on the glove box; the third-row seat is suitable only for children; the narrow back bench seat provides little legroom, unless the middle seats are pushed far forward, inconveniencing others; radio control access is blocked by the shift lever, and it's difficult to calibrate the radio without taking your eyes off the road; power-sliding doors are slow to retract; some tire rumble, rattles, and body drumming at highway speeds; premium fuel is required for optimum performance; poorer quality compared to later models; a high resale price, making bargains rare; poor head-restraint crashworthiness rating; and rear-seat head restraints impede side and rear visibility. The storage well won't take any tire larger than a "space saver"—meaning you'll carry your flat in the back. **New for 2007:** No significant changes.

MODEL HISTORY: When it was first launched in 1995, the Odyssey was a sales dud—Canadians and *Lemon-Aid* saw through Honda's attempt to pass off an underpowered, mid-sized, four-door station wagon with a raised roof as a minivan.

However, in 1999 and again in 2005, the Odyssey was redesigned, and it's now one of the better minivans on the Canadian market.

One can sum up the strengths and weaknesses of the 1996–98 Odyssey in three words: Performance, performance, performance. You get carlike performance and handling, responsive steering, and a comfortable ride, offset by slow-as-molasses-in-January acceleration with a full load, a raucous engine, and limited passenger and cargo space because of the narrow body.

1997—Small improvements. **1998**—A new 2.3L engine adds 10 horses (not enough!), and a restyled grille and instrument panel debut. **1999**—A new, more powerful engine and increased size make this second-generation Odyssey a more versatile highway performer; still, steering requires fully extended arms, and power-sliding doors operate slowly. **2001**—User-friendly child safety seat tether anchors, upgraded stereo speakers, and an intermittent rear window wiper. **2002**—A slight restyling, 30 additional horses, disc brakes on all four wheels, standard side airbags, and additional support for front seats. **2005**—A bigger Odyssey with a torquier 255-hp 3.5L V6, which has 15 more horses than last year's version and more horsepower than any other minivan. The new engine uses variable cylinder de-activation to increase fuel economy by up to 10 percent by automatically switching between 6-cylinder and 3-cylinder activation, depending on engine load. Other features are as follows: eight-passenger seating (EX); less road noise; upgraded rear shocks; an upgraded driver's seat; easier access to the back seats; a new power tailgate; more interior volume than the Sienna (interior lengthened by 5 cm/2 in.); second-row middle seats can be folded down to use as an armrest or can be removed completely, much like the middle-row captain's chairs, which can slide fore or aft by 25 cm (10 in.) in unison or separately; second-row power windows; and floor-stowable, 60/40 split third-row seats with 8 cm (3 in.) more of legroom. Convenience upgrades include climate, radio, and optional navigation controls that are easier to reach (and navigation voice recognition is bilingual, yippee!); air conditioning toggles with raised lips for easy flipping; and a more accessible dash-mounted gearshift. Safety has been enhanced with a more crash-worthy body, vehicle stability assist to prevent rollovers, side curtain airbags with rollover sensors for all rows, and adjustable brake and accelerator pedals. Run-flat tires may be used in Canada at a later date.

COST ANALYSIS: A 2006 Odyssey LX sells for $33,200, or $500 more than the 2005's original price, and is not much different than this year's version. There's some room for price-haggling; whereas Toyota dealers, spoiled by their ACCESS pricing gimmick, seldom budge from the MSRP. **Best alternatives:** Nissan's 1999–2003 Quest, or any Toyota Sienna except for the 2004 revamped model. If you're looking for lots of towing grunt, the rear-drive GM Astro, Safari, or full-sized vans are best. **Rebates:** Don't expect any substantial incentives before early 2007, if at all. **Delivery/PDI:** $1,455. **Warranty:** Bumper-to-bumper 3 years/60,000 km; power-train 5 years/100,000 km; rust perforation 5 years/unlimited km. **Supplementary**

warranty: Not needed. **Options:** Traction control is a good idea. Remember, if you want the gimmicky video entertainment and DVD navigation system, you also have to spring for the expensive (and not-for-everyone) leather seats. Ditch the original-equipment Firestone or Bridgestone tires: You don't need the extra risk or early wearout. **Depreciation:** Slower than average. **Insurance cost:** Higher than average. **Parts supply/cost:** Moderately priced parts; availability is better than average because the Odyssey uses many generic Accord parts. **Annual maintenance cost:** Average; any garage can repair these minivans. **Highway/city fuel economy:** *2005:* 8.6/12.3 L/100 km; *2004:* 8.5/13.2 L/100 km. The vehicle burns gas at a horrendous rate if the rear AC is switched on.

QUALITY/RELIABILITY: Reliability is much better than average, but like Toyota, one gets the impression that Honda is coasting on past laurels, at least through the 2005 models. Failure-prone sliding doors continue to be a hazard to children. They open when they shouldn't, won't close when they should, catch fingers and arms, get stuck open or closed, are noisy, and frequently require expensive servicing. The Check Engine light may stay lit because of a defective fuel-filler neck. There's a fuel sloshing noise when accelerating or coming to a stop, and the transmission clunks or bangs when backing uphill or when shifted into Reverse. There are also reports of rattling and chattering when put into Forward gear. Owners note a loud wind noise and vibration from the left side of the front windshield, along with a constant vibration felt through the steering assembly and front wheels. Passenger doors may also require excessive force to open. And owners have complained of severe static electricity shocks when exiting. Other potential problem areas are frequent and high-cost front-brake maintenance, and trim and accessory items that come loose, break away, or malfunction. **Owner-reported problems:** Transmission breakdowns—when shifting into Fourth gear, engine almost stalls out and produces a noise like valve clattering; transmission gear whine at 90 km/h or when in Fourth gear (transmission replaced under new "goodwill" warranty). Front-end clunking caused by welding breaks in the front subframe; exhaust rattling or buzzing; severe steering vibrations when underway, thought to be caused by faulty wheel bearings; vehicle pulls to the right when underway; premature front brake wear; excessive brake grinding noise; noisy AC blower motor; and the AC condenser is easily damaged by road debris:

> Poor design of 2005 Honda Odyssey. I have had to replace air conditioner twice in 18 months due to flying rock punctures. Honda dealership knows of exact repair (chicken wire) but won't do it. Hundreds of people on the Internet are experiencing [the] same problem.

Owners also note frequent sliding side-door malfunctions; electrical glitches; defective remote audio controls; leather seats that split, crack, or discolour; and accessory items that come loose, break away, or won't work. Plastic interior panels have rough edges and are often misaligned; paint peels from the bumpers and chips off the hood; and door weather stripping often falls away, allowing excessive wind and road noise to invade the cabin. **Warranty performance:** The comprehensive base warranty is usually applied fairly, with lots of wiggle room that the service manager can use to apply "goodwill" adjustments for post-warranty problems. However, after-warranty assistance and dealer servicing have come in for a great deal of criticism from *Lemon-Aid* readers, though the complaints aren't as serious, and owners aren't as angry, as with problems regarding Toyota Siennas. Owners complain that "goodwill" refunds aren't extended to all model years with the same defect, recall repairs take an eternity to perform, and dealers exhibit an arrogant, uncaring, "take it or leave it" attitude.

SAFETY SUMMARY: Power-sliding doors are a constant danger. NHTSA front, side, and rollover crash safety scores for the 2006 and 2007 Odyssey mirror the 2005 model rankings. IIHS rates the 2006s "Good" for offset and side crash protection. **Airbags:** Standard side airbags. **ABS:** Standard 4W; disc/disc. **Head restraints F/R:** *1995–97:* ★★; *1999:* ★★/★; *2001–06:* ★★. **Visibility F/R:** ★★★★★/★.

SAFETY COMPLAINTS: All years: Passenger seatbacks collapsed when vehicle was rear-ended. • Airbag malfunctions. • Sudden, unintended acceleration when slowing for a stop sign. • When minivan was put in Drive and AC was turned on, vehicle suddenly accelerated, brakes failed, and the minivan hit a brick wall. • Stuck accelerator. • Automatic transmission failures. • Transmission doesn't hold when stopped on a hill; gas or brakes have to be constantly applied. **1999**—Fire erupted in the electrical harness. • Another fire erupted as vehicle was getting fuel. • Plastic gas tank cracks, leaks fuel. • Gasoline smell when transmission is put into Reverse. • Side window exploded while driving. • Check Engine light comes on, and vehicle loses all power. • When driving, all the instrument panel lights will suddenly go out (faulty multiplex controller suspected). • When parked on a hill, vehicle may roll backward; transmission doesn't hold vehicle when stopped at a light on a hill and foot is taken off accelerator or brake. • Complete loss of power steering caused by a pinhole in the power-steering return hose. • Poor power-steering performance in cold weather. • Power door locks and unlocks on its own. • Design of the gear shifter interferes with the radio controls. • Child unable to get out of seat belt because buckle locked up. • Faulty fuel gauge. • Inconvenient cell phone jack location. **2000**—Almost 400 safety complaints recorded by NHTSA; 100 would be normal. • During fuelling, fuel tank burst into flames. • Many incidents where driver-side sliding door opened onto fuel hose while fuelling, damaging gas flap hinge and tank. • On cold days, accelerator pedal is hard to depress. • Catastrophic failure of the right-side suspension, causing wheel to buckle. • Vehicle continually pulls to the right; dealers unable to correct problem. • Excessive steering-wheel vibration at 105 km/h and over. • Electric doors often inoperative. • As child slept in safety seat, seat belt tightened progressively to the point where fire department had to be called; other similar incidents. • Chronic automatic transmission problems: Won't shift into lower gears, suddenly loses power, torque converter fails, and makes a loud popping sound when put into Reverse. • Two incidents where vehicle was rear-ended because of a transmission malfunction. • Power seatback moves on its own. • Dash lights don't adequately illuminate the dash panel. • Driver's seatback suddenly reclines, hitting rear passenger's legs, even though power switch is off. • Protruding bolts in the door assembly are hazardous. • Seat belt buckle fails to latch. • Driver-side mirror breaks away; mirror glass fell out because of poor design. • Easily broken sliding door handles. 2001—While fuelling, fuel tank exploded. • In a frontal collision, van caught fire because of a cracked brake fluid reservoir. • Chronic stalling (transmission replaced). • Many reports of sudden transmission and torque converter failure. • When Reverse is engaged, car makes a popping or clunking sound. • Cracked wheel rim. • Check Engine light constantly on (suspect faulty gasoline-filler neck). • Entire vehicle shakes excessively at highway speeds, and van pulls to the right (dealer said bar adjustment was needed). • Passenger-side door window suddenly exploded while driving on the highway. • Driver's seatback collapsed from rear-end collision. • Driver's power seat will suddenly recline on its own, squeezing the rear occupant's legs or falling on a child. • Rear seat belt tightened up so much that a child had to be cut free. • Too much play in rear lapbelts, which won't tighten adequately, making it difficult to install a child safety seat securely. • Inoperative driver's seat belt buckle. • Faulty speedometer and tachometer. • Remote wouldn't open or lock vehicle. • Placement of the gearshift lever interferes with the radio's controls. • Unable to depress accelerator pedal on cold days. • Can hear gasoline sloshing in tank while driving. • Frequent static electricity shocks. • Many owners report that the rear head restraints seriously hamper rear and forward visibility and that it's difficult to see vehicles coming from the right side. 2002—Over 232 complaints registered where normally 50 would be expected. Only 66 complaints recorded against the 2002 Toyota Sienna. • Owners say many engines have faulty timing chains. • Loose strut bolt almost caused wheel to fall off. • Axle bearing wheel failure caused driver-side wheel to fall off. • Left-to-right veering and excessive drivetrain vibration. • Loud popping sound heard when brakes are applied. • Many complaints that the brake pedal went to floor with no braking capability. • Sticking sliding door. • Head restraints are set too low for tall occupants. • Rear windshield shattered from area where wiper is mounted. • Rear seat belt unlatched during emergency braking. • Brake line freezes up in cold weather. • Abrupt downshift on deceleration. • Driver-side door came off while using remote control. • Dashboard lights come on and off intermittently. • Passenger window exploded. • Airbag light comes on for no reason. 2003—Fire ignited in the CD player. • Child injured from a side collision; the second-row seat belt failed to hold her in because of gap caused by door attachment. • Rear seat belts lock for no reason. • Seat belt extenders aren't offered. • Defective speed sensor caused vehicle to suddenly lose power when merging into traffic. • Vehicle suddenly shut down in traffic. • Hard starts and engine misfiring. • Faulty steering causes wander. • Sudden brake failure. • Driver often shocked when touching door handle. • Fuel spits out when refuelling. • Inaccurate fuel gauge readings. • Sliding door closed on driver's hand; child trapped by the door closing on him. 2004— Stuck gas pedal. • Fuel smell in the interior. • Front airbags failed to deploy. •

Passenger airbag often turns itself off. • Chronic stalling even after recall repairs to the fuel-pump relay to correct the problem. • Automatic transmission slippage:

> At 20,000 miles [32,000 km], the transmission has started to slip. Also, it rolls backwards when it is in Drive in our driveway. Our driveway is not steep. It did not do that when we first got it. The dealer said that was normal. We almost slammed into a car that was parked in front of us on a hill. We were facing downward. I put the van in reverse, then I took my foot off the brake to make some room so I could get around the car parked in front of us. The van rolled forward and I had just enough time to avoid causing major damage. I had to find the owner of the car in front so he could move out of the way so I could get out of there.

• Interior lights flicker on and off. • Jammed rear seat belt; passenger had to be cut free. • Problems with automatic doors:

> Problems with door on 2004 Honda Odyssey. The door was ajar 6 inches [15 cm] and would not open nor close all the way. The close button was pressed but nothing happened. The door handle was pulled and the door started to close and crushed the tip of the consumer's finger, fracturing it. The vehicle was inspected but no problems were found.

> •

> One month ago, I opened the passenger side automatic door on my 2004 Honda Odyssey and it pinned a Publix bagger and shopping cart between my vehicle and another vehicle. The door did not stop and continued to ram itself open. Thankfully, the bagger was not injured.

• Back hatch struts collapsed. • Front doors don't have enough tension to stay open; they close on occupants' legs. • Self-locking feature often locks driver out of the van after a delay of about 10 seconds. • Child safety seats are quite difficult to latch securely in the second-row seats. **2005**—Seat belt unlatches, or sometimes won't unlatch. • Hatch struts continue to fail at an alarming rate. • Entire electrical system goes dead. • Faulty VSA control unit disables ABS and braking assist. • Vehicle won't accelerate when foot is on the gas pedal, but it begins to accelerate when the brakes are applied. • Constant steering shimmy. • Driver's seat isn't level; it's lower on left side. • Windshield leaks; replacements are on back-order nationwide. • Painful noise in the cabin when rear windows are opened:

> Very loud pulsating sound when rear windows open. It vibrates and is so loud I thought I had a flat tire. My ears and my children's ears hurt. It occurs when we are driving 35–40 mph [56–64 km/h].

• Power-sliding door opened completely while vehicle was in motion; fails to close and latch. • Automatic sliding door almost crushed child's hand. • Rear windshield wiper self-activates. • Michelin PAX tires wear out prematurely and can only be replaced by authorized dealers at great cost:

> The PAX tire system by Michelin gives marginal tire wear. The tires wore out at 25,000 miles [40,000 km]. The tires can only be changed by PAX authorized dealers making them nearly impossible to find convenient[ly or] inexpensive[ly]. What is meant to make us safer has only made us poorer.

• Poor headlight illumination.

Secret Warranties/Internal Bulletin/Service Tips

All years: Most of Honda's TSBs allow for special warranty consideration on a "goodwill" basis by the company's District Service Manager or Zone Office, even after the warranty has expired or the vehicle has changed hands. Referring to this euphemism will increase your chances of getting some kind of refund for repairs that are needed to correct obvious factory defects. • There's an incredibly large number of sliding door problems covered by a recall and a plethora of service bulletins too numerous to print here. Ask Honda politely for the bulletins or "goodwill" assistance. If refused, subpoena the documents through small claims court, using NHTSA's summary as your shopping list. • V6 engine oil leaks. **1999**— Poor engine performance may fall under a free service campaign whereby the company will replace, at no charge, the rear intake manifold end plate and gasket, the PCV hose, and the intake manifold cover. • Problems with the fuel-tank pressure sensor are covered in TSB #99-056 and could call for the installation of an in-line orifice in the two-way valve vacuum hose. • AC knocking may require the installation of a new compressor clutch set. • Front windows that bind or are noisy. • An inaccurate fuel gauge is likely caused by a faulty sending unit. **1999– 2001**—Extended warranty coverage on Odysseys with defective 4- and 5-speed automatic transmissions to 7 years/160,000 km (100,000 miles) to fix erratic or slow shifting. **2000–01**—Third-row seat won't unlatch. • Clunk or bang when engaging Reverse. • Bulletin confirms Honda U.S. is currently investigating complaints of pulling or drifting (Service Bulletin #99165; Bulletin Sequence #802; 99/09; NHTSA Item #SB608030). • Excessive front brake noise. • Dash ticking or clicking. **1999–2003**—Engine oil leaks will be corrected under a "goodwill" policy. • Deformed windshield moulding. **2002**—Hesitation when accelerating. • Diagnosing automatic transmission problems. • No-starts; hard starts in cold weather. • Driver's seat heater may not work. • Thump at cold start. • Loose rear wiper arm. • AC can't be turned off while in defog setting. **2002–03**—Free replacement of the engine timing belt auto-tensioner and water pump under both a recall and "product update" campaign (see bulletin). **2002–04**—Free tranny repair or replacement for insufficient lubrication that can lead to heat buildup and broken gears. Transmission noise will signal if there is gear breakage; transmission may also lock up. • Rear brake noise (see bulletin). **2003**—Engine cranks but won't start. • ABS problems. • Power-steering pump noise. • Warning lights blink on and

RECALL—ENGINE TIMING BELT AUTO-TENSIONER AND WATER PUMP

BULLETIN NO.: 03-081   DATE: OCTOBER 27, 2003

DEFECT: On certain minivans, sedans, coupes, and sport utility vehicles equipped with V6 engines, a timing belt tensioner pulley on the water pump is misaligned and could cause the timing belt to contact a bolt on the cylinder head. Eventually the belt could be damaged and fail. If the timing belt breaks, the engine will stall, increasing the risk of a crash.

REMEDY: Dealers will inspect the water pump, and if it is one of the defective pumps, the water pump and timing belt will be replaced.

PRODUCT UPDATE

BACKGROUND: The timing belt tensioner is filled with oil to dampen oscillation. Due to a manufacturing problem, the tensioner oil can leak. If enough oil is lost, the timing belt loosens and causes engine noise.

MODELS: 2002–03 Odyssey and 2003 Pilot

CORRECTIVE ACTION: Replace the timing belt auto-tensioner.

REAR BRAKE CLUNK

BULLETIN NO.: 04-019   DATE: MARCH 23, 2004

2002–04 Odyssey

2003–04 Pilot

The rear brake calipers clunk when you first apply the brakes after changing the direction of the vehicle. The outer shims on the rear brake pads do not allow the pads to slide easily when you press the brake pedal. This causes the outer pad to hit hard during a change of direction, resulting in a clunk.

CORRECTIVE ACTION: Replace the rear brake pad shims.

off. • Exhaust rattling. • Remote audio-control troubleshooting. • Leather seat defects. • HomeLink range is too short; hard to program. • Factory security system won't arm. • Faulty charging system; electrical shorts. • Front door howls in strong crosswind. • Squealing from rear quarter windows and motors. • Fuel-tank leak. • Front damper noise. • Steering wheel bent off-centre. • Manual sliding door is difficult to open. **2005**—Free electronic computer module replacement on the EX-L and Touring models. • Excessive steering-wheel vibration. • Windshield cowl noise remedy. • Front and rear AC temperature varies. • Correction for middle-row seat that won't unlatch. **2005–06**—Free tire valve stem cap replacement.

ODYSSEY PROFILE

	1998	1999	2000	2001	2002	2003	2004	2005	2006
Cost Price ($) (negotiable)									
LX (18%)	29,800	30,600	30,600	30,800	31,900	32,200	32,400	32,700	33,200
EX (18%)	—	33,600	33,600	33,800	34,900	35,200	35,400	35,900	36,400

All ratings on a numbered scale where ⑤ is good and ❶ is bad. See page 220 for a more detailed description.

Used Values ($)									
LX ▲	8,000	9,500	12,000	14,000	17,000	19,500	23,000	27,000	—
LX ▼	6,500	8,000	10,500	12,500	15,500	18,000	21,500	25,000	—
EX ▲	—	10,500	13,500	15,500	18,500	21,500	25,000	29,000	—
EX ▼	—	9,500	12,000	14,000	17,000	20,000	23,500	27,500	—
Reliability	③	③	②	②	②	③	④	③	—
Crash Safety (F)	—	⑤	⑤	⑤	⑤	⑤	⑤	⑤	⑤
Side	—	—	—	⑤	⑤	⑤	⑤	⑤	⑤
Offset	②	⑤	⑤	⑤	⑤	⑤	⑤	⑤	⑤
Rollover	—	—	—	④	④	④	—	④	④

Kia/Hyundai

SEDONA/ENTOURAGE ★★★★/★★★

2007 TECHNICAL DATA

POWERTRAIN

Engine: 3.8L V6 (242 hp); Transmission: 5-speed manumatic

DIMENSION/CAPACITY

Passengers: 2/2/3; Wheelbase: 118.8 in.; H: 69.2/L: 202/W: 78.1 in.; Headroom F/R: 5.0/2.0 in.; Legroom F/R: 41.7/40.9/34 in.; Cargo volume: 65 cu. ft.; Fuel tank: 80L/regular; Tow limit: 3,500 lb.; Load capacity: 1,186 lbs.; GVWR: 5,898 lbs.; Turning circle: 41 ft.; Ground clearance: 6.6 in.; Weight: 4,400 lbs.

RATING: *Sedona:* Above Average (2006–07); Average (2002–05). *Entourage:* Average during its first year on the market (2007). The 2006–07 Kias have all of the makings of winners, if Kia has improved its quality control as much as it has improved the performance of these feature-laden minivans. The 2005 Sedona is a very user-friendly, roomy, practical, versatile, and comfortable mid-sized minivan. It simply lacks refinement and isn't very reliable. **Strong points:** *2006–07:* Reasonably priced; well appointed; competent engine accelerates well from a stop and merges into traffic reasonably well; transmission shifts smoothly and quietly; low ground clearance adds to stability and helps access; low step-in; comfortable ride; convenient "walk-through" space between front seats; well laid-out, user-friendly instruments and controls; lots of storage areas; good visibility; fairly well built; minimal engine and road noise; good braking; quality control seems to be better than average; and a comprehensive base warranty. *2005 and earlier models:* Quite cheap. **Weak points:** *2006–07:* The Entourage's base price and freight charges are inflated. The automatic transmission has a superfluous manual mode, which seems out of place in a minivan. There's still some road and wind noise (mirrors?) when cruising. A weak dealer network. *2005 and earlier models:* Engine power is drained by the Sedona's heft; 10–20 percent higher fuel consumption than V6-equipped Dodge Caravan or Toyota Sienna; subpar, vague steering and handling; and excessive engine and wind noise. Quality control is the Sedona's weakest link through the 2005 model. **New for 2007:** Arrival of Sedona's Hyundai twin, the Entourage.

MODEL HISTORY: Forget about previous models—the 2006 and carried-over 2007 Kias are safer, larger, and better performing than previous Sedonas. Almost everything is new or upgraded, like 15 percent more interior room, thanks to a larger wheelbase and a wider, longer platform; a more powerful 3.8L engine; four-wheel ABS; power-adjustable pedals; six airbags (side curtain); optional electronic stability-control; an upgraded transmission; larger brakes; four-wheel independent suspension; and fold-flat third-row seats.

The 2005 and earlier models are hardly worth considering, even though they do come with many standard features, including a 195-hp 3.5L V6 engine hooked to an automatic 5-speed transmission, a low step-in height, and a good view of the road. For convenience, there are two sliding rear side doors (automatic doors aren't available); folding, removable second- and third-row seats; a flip-up hatchback; standard front/rear air conditioning; and a large cargo bay.

Hyundai Entourage

A Kia Sedona clone (don't forget, Hyundai owns Kia and wants a little minivan action of its own), the 2007 Entourage is Hyundai's first-ever minivan, so Hyundai is desperate to make it appear more upscale than it really is. The seven-passenger, entry-level GL sells for about $29,995, and a GL with the Comfort package, at $31,995, gives you the usually troublesome power-sliding doors, non-essential electric rear quarter windows, pretty alloy wheels, and fuel-wasting roof rails. Auto critics report that the Sedona outpulls the Entourage by a large margin, even though both minivans have the same engine and transmission layout.

So, is the Entourage worth the extra cost? Well, no.

COST ANALYSIS: 2006 Sedonas range in price from $29,495 (LX) to $31,895 (EX). The 2005 version is much cheaper, but it isn't as well equipped or as refined as the 2006 or 2007. The upgraded Sedona is a better buy than its Entourage twin this year during the Entourage's first year on the market. Having been launched a year earlier, the reworked Sedona has had time to correct the usual first-year glitches that all redesigns engender. Also, a second-series 2006 Sedona will cost thousands of dollars less than a 2007 Entourage, and Kia dealers will be more eager to haggle over the 2007 price—$29,495 for a Sedona versus the Entourage's MSRP of $29,995— and throw in some extra goodies like a more extensive warranty and the backup sensor, sold as an option on the higher-end Entourage. Test-drive both vehicles, and try to choose the dealer who is the most convenient and who doesn't split their inventory among a handful of different automakers. **Best alternatives:**

The Honda Odyssey and pre-2004 Toyota Sienna are two other good choices. **Rebates:** Look for $3,000 rebates and low-financing rates on the Kias in early 2007; Entourage's $2,000 rebates won't kick in until the summer of 2007. **Delivery/PDI:** *Sedona:* $1,395; *Entourage:* $1,545 (why pay more?). **Warranty:** Bumper-to-bumper 5 years/100,000 km; powertrain 5 years/100,000 km; rust perforation 5 years/unlimited km. **Supplementary warranty:** A wise buy for both vehicles, considering Kia's previous transmission troubles and the likelihood of some first-series factory-related defects afflicting the Entourage. **Options:** Seriously consider the electronic stability-control. **Depreciation:** Average on the pre-2006; unknown for the 2006 and 2007 versions. **Insurance cost:** Average for an entry-level minivan. **Parts supply/cost:** Average cost, but expect long delays for parts. **Annual maintenance cost:** Expected to be higher than average once first-year models lose their base warranty protection. **Highway/city fuel economy:** 10.9/15.6 L/100 km.

QUALITY/RELIABILITY: Reliability is average. **Owner-reported problems:** Seat belts, fuel and electrical systems, prematurely worn brake pads and warped rotors, AC compressors, windows, and fit and finish. **Warranty performance:** Average.

SAFETY SUMMARY: No side airbags on early models. These vehicles come with anti-lock brakes, four-wheel discs, front-seat active head restraints, front-seat side airbags, and side curtain airbags for all three rows. (The Entourage and its Kia Sedona sibling have earned the highest "Gold" rating in U.S. crash tests from the IIHS, the only minivans to do so, which indicates top performances in frontal offset, side, and rear protection.) The 2006 and 2007 Sedonas and the 2007 Entourage posted the identical impressive crashworthiness ratings to the 2005 Sedona. The 2006 Sedona was given a "Good" ranking for offset crash protection. Some owners report that the airbags may fail to deploy. **ABS:** Optional/standard; disc/drum and disc/disc. **Head restraints F/R:** 2002–04: ★★★★; 2006: ★★★★★. **Visibility F/R:** ★★★★★. **Maximum load capacity:** *Pre-2006 models:* 1,160 lb.

SAFETY COMPLAINTS: 2002—Fuel tank design could cause fuel to spray on hot muffler in a collision. • Oil leaks onto the hot catalytic converter. • Fuel leaks from the bottom of the vehicle. • Loose fuel line to fuel-pump clamp. • Fuel-tank filler hose vulnerable to road debris. • Fuel spits back out when refuelling. • Vehicle continues to accelerate when brakes are applied. • Intermittent stalling. • Brake failure; pedal simply sinks to the floor. • Excessive brake shudder when slowing going downhill. • ABS brake light comes on randomly. • Power-steering pulley broke. • Windshield may suddenly shatter for no apparent reason. • Windshields have distortion at eye level. • Second- and third-row seats don't latch as easily as touted. • Oil leaks onto the catalytic converter. • Electrical shorts cause lights, windows, and door locks to fail. • Sliding doors won't retract if object is in their way. • Stuck rear hatch door. • Child safety seat can't be belted in securely. • Child door safety lock failure. • Inoperative back-seat seat belts. • Seat belt holding child in booster seat tightened progressively, trapping child. • Kumho tire-tread separation. **2003**—Under-hood fire ignited while car was underway. • Airbags failed to deploy. • Sudden, unintended acceleration. • Stuck accelerator pedal. • Brakes fail because of air in the brake lines. • Fuel odour in cabin. • Broken window regulator. • Following the rear-seat removal instructions can throw your back out. • Tires peeled off the rim. • When reclined, passenger seatback was released upright and slammed a young child forward. • AC condenser vulnerable to puncture from road debris. • Electrical shorts cause door lock malfunctions. **2004**—Frequent stalling. • Excessive brake rotor wear. • Parking brake didn't hold vehicle on an incline. • Chronic stalling. • Windshield has a cloudy haze. **2005**—Sudden acceleration without steering assist. • Delayed recall repairs. • Chronic brake failures. • Gas tank leaks.

Secret Warranties/Internal Bulletins/Service Tips

2002—Correction for engine hesitation after cold starts. • Free replacement of seat belt buckle anchor bolts. **2002–03**—Changes to improve alternator output to prevent hard starts or battery drain. **2004**—Engine head gasket leak. **2005**—Shift flare, harsh engagement, late shifts.

SEDONA PROFILE

	2002	2003	2004	2005	2006
Cost Price ($) (negotiable)					
LX (20%)	24,595	24,995	25,595	26,995	29,495
EX (22%)	27,595	28,295	28,995	29,495	31,895
Used Values ($)					
LX ▲	9,500	11.500	14,500	17,500	—
LX ▼	8,000	10.500	13,000	16,000	—
EX ▲	10,500	13,500	16,000	18,500	—
EX ▼	9,000	12,500	15.000	17,500	—
Reliability	❸	❸	❸	❹	—
Crash Safety (F)	❺	❺	❺	❺	❺
Side	❺	❺	❺	❺	❺
Offset	❸	❸	❸	❸	❺
Rollover	❹	❹	—	❹	❹

Mazda

MPV	★★★

RATING: Average (2002–06); Below Average (1988–2001). There was no 1999 model. Mazda has accomplished an amazing turnaround with the revamped 2002

All ratings on a numbered scale where ❺ is good and ❶ is bad. See page 220 for a more detailed description.

2006 TECHNICAL DATA

POWERTRAIN (FRONT-DRIVE)

Engine: 3.0L V6 (200 hp); Transmission: 5-speed auto.

DIMENSION/CAPACITY

Passengers: 2/2/3; Wheelbase: 112 in.; H: 68.7/L: 188/W: 72 in.; Headroom F/R1/R2: 6.5/5.0/3.0 in.; Legroom F/R1/R2: 41/27.5/27.5 in.; Cargo volume: 56 cu. ft.; Fuel tank: 75L/regular; Tow limit: 3,000 lb.; Load capacity: 1,305 lb.; GVWR: 5,229 lb.; Turning circle: 41 ft.; Ground clearance: 7.1 in.; Weight: 3,925 lb.

and later MPV during the past few years; the MPV is now smaller, sportier, and more nimble than its more space- and comfort-oriented counterparts. Early models were underpowered, lumbering, undersized, and overpriced. **Strong points:** Well appointed (lots of gadgets), an adequate engine, smooth-shifting 5-speed automatic transmission, comfortable ride and easy handling, good driver's position, responsive steering, and innovative storage spots. Without a doubt, the MPV manages its limited interior space far better than the competition does. Remarkably few factory-related defects reported at NHTSA or in the service bulletin database. **Weak points:** Smaller than most of the competition; don't believe for a minute that the MPV will hold seven passengers in comfort—six is more like it. Elbow room is at a premium, and it takes a lithe figure to move down the front- and middle-seat aisle. Excessive engine and road noise. Transport and preparation fee is excessive. Dealer servicing and head office support have been problematic in the past. Early door-bottom rusting. **New for 2007:** Nothing—there won't be a 2007 model.

MODEL HISTORY: Manufactured in Hiroshima, Japan, this small minivan offers a number of innovative features, like theatre seating (the rear passenger seat is slightly higher) and a third seat that pivots rearward to become a rear-facing bench seat or folds into the floor for picnics or tailgate parties. Another feature unique among minivans is Mazda's Side-by-Slide removable second-row seats, which move fore and aft as well as side-to-side while a passenger is seated. Sliding door crank windows are standard on the entry model. Windows are power-assisted on the LS and ES versions.

Mazda's only minivan quickly became a bestseller when it first came on the market in 1989, but its popularity fell just as quickly when larger, more powerful competitors arrived. Mazda sales have bounced back recently as a result of price-cutting and the popularity of the automaker's small cars and pickups. This infusion of cash has allowed the company (34 percent of which is owned by Ford) to put additional money into its 2002 redesign. Early MPVs embodied many of the mistakes made by Honda's first Odyssey—its 170 horses weren't adequate for people-hauling, and it was expensive for what was essentially a smaller van than buyers expected— 30 cm (12 in.) shorter than the Ford Windstar and 15 cm (6 cm.) shorter than the Toyota Sienna or Nissan Quest.

1992—5-speed manual transmission deleted, and the 3.0L V6 got a 5-hp boost. 1993—A driver-side airbag. 1994—A centre brake light and side-door impact beams. 1995—Seven-passenger seating and a 155-hp 3.0L engine. 1996—A passenger-side airbag, four-wheel ABS, and four doors. 2000—A new model with front-drive and sliding side doors. 2002—A 200-hp V6 and 5-speed automatic transmission, power-sliding side doors, revised suspension settings, and 17-inch wheels. 2003—More standard features (LX) that include power-sliding rear side doors, 16-inch wheels, a flip-up side table, and a doormat. 2004—Refreshed interior and exterior styling of no real consequence, except the additional lumbar support for the driver's seat.

Presently, the MPV uses the Taurus 200-hp 3.0L Duratec V6. Some refinements produce a lower torque peak—3000 rpm versus 4400 rpm—giving the Mazda engine better pulling power at a lower speed. Making good use of that power is a smooth-shifting 5-speed automatic transmission, which should cut fuel consumption a bit. One immediate benefit: The 3.0L is able to climb hills without continually downshifting, and Mazda's "slope control" system automatically shifts to a lower gear when the hills get very steep. Torque is still less than the Odyssey's 3.5L or the 3.8L engine in top-of-the-line Chryslers, though it's comparable with lesser Chrysler products and GM's Venture or Montana. The suspension has been firmed up to decrease body roll, enhancing cornering ability and producing a sportier ride than other minivans. This firmness may be too much for some.

I've been tougher on the MPV than have *Consumer Reports* and others because of Mazda's price-gouging and poor servicing and the vehicle's small size, underpowered drivetrain, and reliability problems (all too common on pre-2000 models). Presently, it looks like most of these concerns have been met, although I'm still worried that the 3.0 Duratec may not hold up.

COST ANALYSIS: There won't be a 2007 model, and Mazda dealers have a large inventory of unsold MPVs. Consequently, a 2006 GX which lists for $27,895 can be purchased at a 25-percent discount through sustained haggling. An identical, cheaper used 2005 would also save you a lot, but servicing and parts supply and costs will become increasingly problematic the longer these minivans are off the market. Better yet, seriously consider the more fuel-efficient and sleeker 2006 Mazda5 wagon/minivan. When the MPV is compared with Honda's latest Odyssey or the revamped pre-2004 Toyota Sienna, there's not enough savings and quality to make up for the MPV's smaller size and less powerful engine.

Also, be wary of unwarranted extra charges, says one *Lemon-Aid* reader:

> There are far too many "extra" charges for things (like $70 for getting Scotiabank financing) that should be included in the price of the MPV. All these extra charges add up and create friction with the dealer that doesn't need to exist.... Wheel lock bolts should be standard when buying alloy wheels. It seems very petty to add $31.50

for wheel locks to the price of the $3,000 Sport Package. How can Mazda charge an extra $105 for certain paint colours on a $30,000 vehicle? This is no way to make friends.

Best alternatives: The MPV is still best suited to those owners who don't want the biggest family-hauler on the block, those who prefer sporty handling, and those who don't mind spending less to get less. When the MPV is compared with Honda's Odyssey, the value equation gets a little murkier. With the price reduction, the base MPV LX gains a competitive advantage over the base Odyssey. When compared with the more expensive Odysseys, there's not enough savings to make up for the MPV's smaller size and less powerful engine. And the Odyssey is already available with a DVD entertainment system. If good servicing is assured, consider a 2003 MPV for about $15,000, or almost half what the minivan sold for originally. Other models to consider are GM's Astro or Safari, Honda's Odyssey, Nissan's early Quest, and Toyota's pre-2004 Sienna. **Rebates:** Expect $4,000 rebates and zero percent financing. **Delivery/PDI:** $1,390. **Warranty:** Bumper-to-bumper 3 years/80,000 km; powertrain 5 years/100,000 km; rust perforation 5 years/ unlimited km. **Supplementary warranty:** An extended warranty is worth having, particularly since powertrain problems have plagued these vehicles after their first three years of use. **Options:** Rear AC and seat height adjustment mechanisms are recommended convenience features. The higher trim levels don't offer much of value, except for power windows and door locks and an ignition immobilizer/ alarm/keyless entry system. **Depreciation:** Worse than average. **Insurance cost:** Higher than average. **Parts supply/cost:** Often back-ordered and costly; dealers will not add to their MPV parts inventory knowing they're serving a diminishing clientele. **Annual maintenance cost:** Average now, but costs are expected to become quite expensive as service managers turn their attention and parts budget to the latest models. Any garage can repair these minivans; however, trouble-shooting common failures may be time-consuming. Invest $25 (U.S.) in an ALLDATA bulletin printout to quickly get to the source of the problem (see Appendix I). **Highway/city fuel economy:** 7.1/11.0 L/100 km. Owners report fuel consumption may overshoot this estimate by at least 15 percent.

QUALITY/RELIABILITY: Below-average reliability of early models; a "take it or leave it" attitude when handling warranty claims; mediocre, expensive scheduled mainte-nance; and high fuel and parts costs make ownership costs higher than normal. Overheating and head gasket failures are commonplace with the 4-banger, and the temperature gauge warns you only when it's too late.

Redesigned 2003 MPVs have improved workmanship, a stronger powertrain, and more rugged construction. Nevertheless, choose a second-series 2003 or later model to avoid the early redesign glitches.

Despite the upgrades, more recent models have their own subset of serious defi-ciencies; for example, stalling and surging, oil leakage, and valve lifter problems are common. Some cases of chronic engine knocking in cold weather with the 3.0L have been fixed by installing tighter-fitting, Teflon-coated pistons. Winter driving is compromised by the MPV's light rear end and mediocre traction, and low ground clearance means that off-road excursions shouldn't be too adventurous.

Owner-reported problems: Owners report that the electronic computer module (ECU), automatic transmission, upper shock mounts, front 4×4 drive axles and lash adjusters, AC core, and radiator fail within the first three years.

> Transmission failure in a 2002 Mazda MPV van. There was always erratic shifting especially when engine was cold. After it warmed up it seemed ok but during highway driving if having to suddenly accelerate it would feel like the transmission would for lack of a better description "slip" between gear shifts and bog down and then catch again.

Premature brake caliper and rotor wear and excessive vibration/pulsation are chronic problem areas (repairs are needed about every 12,000 km). Cold temperatures tend to fry the automatic window motor, and the power-sliding door is often jammed open or shut. Paint is easily chipped and flakes off early, especially around the hood, tailgate, and front fenders, and apparently this problem afflicts white MPVs the most. Reports of early rusting of the door bottoms (rocker panels) through the 2005 model year. **Warranty performance:** Inadequate base warranty; mediocre servicing that's bound to get worse now that the MPV will be dropped from the lineup.

 SAFETY SUMMARY: The 2006 and 2007 models have crash scores that are identical to the 2005's. IIHS rates the 2006 models "Good" for side crashworthiness and head-restraint protection. **Airbags:** Side airbags are optional on the LX and standard on the ES model. NHTSA has recorded several complaints of airbags failing to deploy in a collision. **ABS:** 2W; 4W: Standard; disc/drum. **Head restraints F/R:** 1995–96: ★★; 1997: ★; 2000: ★★★; 2001–03: ★★/★; 2004–06: ★. **Visibility F/R:** ★★★★★/★★★.

SAFETY COMPLAINTS: 1998—Rear anti-sway bar brackets snapped off from rear axle housing. • ABS brake failure. • Defective gas cap causes the false activation of the Check Engine light. **2000**—Fixed seat belt anchors and buckle placement prevent the safe installation of child safety seats. • Vehicle windshield and side glass suddenly shattered while parked. • Excessive vibrations while cruising. • Rear hatch door flew open when rear-ended. **2000–01**—Engine valve failure. • Cupholders will spill drinks when making a sharp turn; holders were redesigned in 2002. **2000–03**—Airbags failed to deploy. **2001**—Engine surging. • Malfunctioning #1 spark plug causes chronic engine hesitation. • Tranny lever can be shifted out of Park without key in ignition; sometimes it won't shift out of Park when you want it to. • Brake failure. • Brake caliper bolt fell off, causing vehicle to skid. • Sliding doors don't lock in place. • Rear visibility obstructed by high seatbacks. **2002–**

All ratings on a numbered scale where ⑤ is good and ❶ is bad. See page 220 for a more detailed description.

03—Engine oil leakage. • Sudden stalling. • Shifter obscures dash and is easily knocked about. **2003**—Child's neck tangled in seat belt. **2004**—Engine seized when connecting rod failed. • Engine quit due to a faulty ECU computer module. • Transmission failure caused by worn shaft solenoid. • Jammed power-sliding door. • Blown tire sidewall. • Tread separation on Dunlop tires. **2005**—Transmission slippage, failure.

Secret Warranties/Internal Bulletins/Service Tips

All years: TSB #006-94 looks into all the causes and remedies for excessive brake vibrations, and TSB #11-14-95 gives an excellent diagnostic flow chart for troubleshooting excessive engine noise. • Serious paint peeling and delaminating will be fully covered for up to six years under a Mazda secret warranty, say owners. • Troubleshooting tips for correcting wind noise around doors. • Tips for eliminating a musty, mildew-type AC odour. **2000–01**—Hard starts caused by inadequate fuel system pressure because a fuel pressure regulator is stuck open. • Front brake clunking can be silenced by replacing the eight brake-guide plates under warranty (TSB #04-003/00). • Insufficient airflow at bi-level setting. • Door key difficult to insert or rotate. **2000–03**—Rotten-egg exhaust smell. • Remedy for a musty, mildew-type odour from the AC. • A corroded rear heater pipe may leak coolant; Mazda will fix it for free (see TSB #07-004/03). **2000–05**—AC temperature varies between dash vents. **2001**—Rear brake popping, squealing, or clicking. **2002**—Engine tappet noise. **2002–03**—Cargo net hooks detach. **2002–04**—Remedies for shift shock (transmission slams into gear). **2002–05**—Engine camshaft ticking.

MPV PROFILE

	1998	2000	2001	2002	2003	2004	2005	2006
Cost Price ($) (negotiable)								
DX/GX (23%)	—	25,505	25,095	25,975	26,090	26,600	27,595	27,895
LX/GS (23%)	25,200	29,450	29,450	29,150	29,090	29,995	30,295	30,595
Used Values ($)								
DX/GX ▲	—	8,500	9,500	12,500	14,500	17,000	20,000	—
DX/GX ▼	—	7,500	8,000	11,000	13,000	15,500	18,500	—
LX/GS ▲	6,000	8,000	10,500	13,000	15,500	19,000	21,000	—
LX/GS ▼	5,000	7,000	9,000	11,500	14,000	18,000	19,500	—
Reliability	3	4	4	4	4	4	4	—
Crash Safety (F)	4	4	4	5	5	5	5	5
Side	—	5	5	5	5	5	5	5
Offset	—	3	3	3	3	3	3	3
Rollover	—	—	3	3	3	—	—	—

Note: 4×4 models cost about $500 more. There were no 1999 models.

Toyota

2007 TECHNICAL DATA

POWERTRAIN (FRONT)

Engine: 3.3L V6 (215 hp); Transmission: 5-speed auto.

DIMENSION/CAPACITY (LE)

Passengers: 2/2/3, 2/3/3; Wheelbase: 119 in.; H: 69/L: 201/W: 77 in.; Headroom F/R1/R2: 3.5/4.0/2.5 in.; Legroom F/R1/R2: 40.5/31.5/25 in.; Cargo volume: 70.5 cu. ft.; Fuel tank: 79L/regular; Tow limit: 3,500 lb.; Load capacity: 1,325–1,570 lb.; GVWR: 5,690 lb.; Turning circle: 39 ft.; Ground clearance: 5.5 in.; Weight: 4,365 lb.

RATING: *Sienna:* Above Average (2005–07); Average (1998–2004). Has the Sienna been over-rated over the past three years? You bet it has. Buyers have been demanded to pay a ransom of exorbitant extra charges, without the benefit of no-haggle pricing; quality control has slipped markedly; and there has been a resurgence of safety-related defects reported since the 2004 Sienna was redesigned. Run-flat tires and collapsing liftgate struts, for example, can be killers if you aren't careful. Hopefully, strong price competition from much-improved feature-laden Hyundai and Kia minivans (actually the same company) will give both Honda and Toyota a reality check. *Previa:* Average (1991–97). The Previa offers reasonable reliability, mediocre road performance, and limited interior amenities. Nevertheless, it's far better than any of Toyota's earlier LE minivans. **Strong points:** *2005–07:* A smooth-running V6 engine and transmission; standard ABS and side airbags (LE, XLE); available AWD; a comfortable, stable ride; a tighter turning circle; plenty of standard safety, performance, and convenience features; a fourth door; easy entry and exit; better-than-average fit and finish and reliability; enhanced seating versatility and storage capacity; and a quieter interior. **Weak points:** Unacceptably high freight and PDI charges; V6 performance compromised by AC and automatic transmission power drain; and it lacks the trailer-towing brawn of rear-drive minivans. Less-efficient rear drum brakes; rear visibility is obstructed by middle roof pillars and rear head restraints; low head-restraint crashworthiness rating; the wide centre pillars make for difficult access to the middle seats; removing middle- and third-row seats is a two-person chore; radio speakers are set too low for acceptable acoustics; and an unusually large number of body rattles and safety-related complaints (158 safety complaints, or three times what is considered normal). Suspect towing capability; mediocre braking; third-row head restraints are mounted too low; and expensive options. **New for 2007:** Nothing major; the 2010 model may be a gas-electric hybrid.

MODEL HISTORY: Completely redesigned in 2004, the Sienna provides plenty of interior room to accommodate up to eight passengers, handles fairly well for its size, rides comfortably, and is powered by a competent, fuel-efficient engine. A new 3.3L 230-hp V6 turns in respectable acceleration times under 9 seconds, almost as good as the Odyssey. Handling is completely carlike, with less vulnerability to wind buffeting and minimal road noise.

The entry-level front-drive is the CE, in seven- or eight-passenger seating; followed by the LE, in seven- or eight-passenger; and the XLE, in seven-passenger only, as are the AWD models. Important recommended features such as traction and stability-control are standard only on the front-drive XLE and the AWD models. The Sienna's interior and exterior have been gently restyled over the years. Its third-row seats split and fold away (unlike Chrysler's uber-convenient Stow 'n Go seating configuration), head restraints don't have to be removed when the seats are stored, and the second-row bucket seats are easily converted to bench seats.

Honda's Odyssey has similar quality and features, except for all-wheel drive. Although GM's extended minivans are slightly longer, there's not as much usable room, and interior trim and amenities look and feel tacky. Ford's Freestar feels cramped inside and doesn't provide comparable performance.

The Sienna is Toyota's Camry-based front-drive minivan. It replaced the Previa for the 1998 model year and abandoned the Previa's futuristic look in favour of a more conservative Chevrolet Venture styling. The Sienna seats seven and offers dual power-sliding doors with optional remote controls and a V6 powerplant. It's built in the same Kentucky assembly plant as the Camry and comes with lots of safety and convenience features, including side airbags, anti-lock brakes, and a low-tire-pressure warning system. Its trailer-towing brawn, however, leaves something to be desired:

> Imagine our surprise when we discovered within the owner's manual a "Caution" stating that one must not exceed 72 km/hr [45 mph] while towing a trailer.... This limit is not stated in the promotional literature we were provided, or on the *Toyota.ca* website, or in any trailer-towing rating guide. This limit was also not mentioned at any time during our purchase negotiations. Alarmingly, Toyota defines a "Caution" as a "warning against anything which may cause injury to people if the warning is ignored." As it turns out, the dealer was not aware of this speed limit.

Although the rear seats fold flat to accommodate the width of a 4′ × 8′ board, the tailgate won't close, the heavy seats are difficult to reinstall (a two-person job, and the centre seat barely fits through the door), and the middle roof pillars and rear head restraints obstruct rear visibility. There's also no stability- and traction-control for all versions, less-efficient rear drum brakes are used on some versions, the vehicle provides mediocre fuel economy, the low-mounted radio is hard to reach, and third-row seats lack a fore/aft adjustment to increase cargo space.

Reliability is still problematic on 1997–2004 models. Although mechanical and body components are generally reliable except for the sliding doors, there's been a disturbing increase in factory-related powertrain defects reported by owners during the past few years. The most serious reliability problems concern self-destructing, sludge-prone engines on 1997–2002 models and defective automatic transmissions on 1998–2004 Siennas.

Toyota Canada advises owners who notice the telltale signs of engine sludge formation to take their vehicle to their local dealer to have the engine inspected. These signs may include the emission of blue smoke from the tailpipe and/or excessive oil consumption, which may cause overheating, rough running, or the Check Engine light to come on. Take Toyota's advice, but if the dealer tries to blame the problem on "poor maintenance" or refuses to fix the engine unless you prove the oil was changed regularly, threaten small claims court action.

Other recent model problems reported by owners include a clunk or banging in the driveline; the car jolting or creeping forward when at a stop, forcing you to keep your foot firmly on the brake; premature brake wear and excessive brake noise (mostly screeching); a chronic rotten-egg smell; distracting windshield reflections and distorted windshields; sliding door defects; windows suddenly shattering; and various other body glitches, including a hard-to-pull-out rear seat, water leaks, and excessive creaks and rattles (seat belt, sun visor).

Previa

The redesigned 1991 Previa's performance and reliability were so much improved over its LE predecessor that it almost seemed like a different vehicle. Roomier and rendered more stable thanks to its longer wheelbase, equipped with a new 2.4L engine (supercharged as of the 1994 model year), and loaded with standard safety and convenience features, 1991–97 Previas are almost as driver-friendly as the Chrysler and Mazda competition. Still, they can't match Ford, GM, or Chrysler front-drive minivans for responsive handling and a comfortable ride, and Toyota's small engine is overworked and doesn't hesitate to tell you so. Previa owners have learned to live with engine noise, poor fuel economy, premature front brake wear, excessive brake vibration and pulsation, electrical glitches, AC malfunctions, and fit and finish blemishes. The 4×4 models with automatic transmissions steal lots of power from the 4-cylinder powerplant, though they have fewer reliability problems than similar drivetrains found on competitors, especially Chryslers.

1995—DX models get a supercharged engine. 1996—Supercharged engine is the only powerplant offered. 1997—Extra soundproofing. 1998—Introduction of the Sienna; no more Previa. 2001—A rear defroster, some additional horsepower and torque, and a driver-side sliding door added to the Sienna. 2004—Sienna completely redesigned. 2006—Standard front and side airbags, and side curtain airbags in all three rows; new bumper, grille, headlights, rear lights, and body side moulding; a standard roof rack for the base CE; new power-folding mirrors with memory; and front and rear wipers clean more windshield area. Top-line model gets a power-folding third-row seat.

COST ANALYSIS: Crafty Toyota is keeping most prices near last year's levels, which isn't surprising, since the 2007s are essentially identical, warmed-over 2006s (models that didn't differ much from the 2005s). Base models start at $30,800 for the seven-passenger CE; an eight-passenger version costs $1,200 more. The CE AWD sells for $36,700. Prices for the LE start at $36,255, and the AWD version fetches $40,655. The top-of-the-line XLE all-wheel drive will set you back $50,875 (for a minivan?). **Best alternatives:** Consider a Honda Odyssey for its peppier engine and rear disc brakes. The small Mazda5 and the pre-2004 Nissan Quest are also acceptable. Bargain hunters take note: Used cargo Siennas (year 2000 or earlier) cost thousands less than the base CE. **Rebates:** $2,000 on the '07s in early 2007, but only if you pay the full retail price. **Delivery/PDI:** $1,390. **Warranty:** Bumper-to-bumper 3 years/60,000 km; powertrain 5 years/100,000 km; rust perforation 5 years/unlimited km. **Supplementary warranty:** Not needed. **Options:** Power windows and door locks, rear heater, and AC unit. Be wary of the power-sliding door. As with the Odyssey and GM minivans, these doors can injure children and pose unnecessary risks to other occupants. Go for Michelin or Pirelli original-equipment tires. **Depreciation:** Much slower than average. **Insurance cost:** A bit higher than average. **Parts supply/cost:** Excellent supply of reasonably priced Sienna parts taken from the Camry parts bin. The only exception has been fuel-tank components needed for recall repairs. Automatic transmission torque converters are frequently back-ordered because of their poor reliability. Previa parts are in limited supply. **Annual maintenance cost:** *Sienna:* Like the Camry, much lower than average. *Previa:* Maintenance costs are higher than average, and only Toyota dealers can repair these older minivans, particularly when it comes to troubleshooting the supercharged 2.4L engine and All Trac. **Highway/city fuel economy:** *3.3L V6:* 8.1/12.2 L/100 km; *3.0L V6:* 8.8/12.4 L/100 km.

 QUALITY/RELIABILITY: Reliability concerns include stalling when the AC engages, electrical shorts, excessive brake noise, sliding door defects, and various other body glitches, including excessive creaks and rattles and paint that's easily chipped. **Owner-reported problems:** Premature brake wear and noisy brakes, engine replacement because of sludge buildup, automatic transmission failures, fuel-tank leaks, tires lose air pressure, rear wiper doesn't work, blower motor and damper wear out quickly, distracting windshield reflections and distorted windshields, power-sliding door malfunctions, interior squeaks and rattles, and rusting of the AC lines:

> The Sienna's front to back AC lines rust out because they are made of aluminum and are connected to the body frame with another type of metal fastener. This combination causes extensive leakage. Toyota says it will cost $500 to correct this design defect.

Warranty performance: Average, but you have to stand your ground and ignore head office bullcrap to the effect that "goodwill" repair reimbursements only apply if you show maintenance receipts or if repairs were done by the dealer.

SAFETY SUMMARY: Many complaints that the steering wheel locks up when making a turn, won't return to the centre without extreme effort, or simply no longer responds. Owners have also complained that the vehicle pulls sharply to one side or another when driving at moderate speeds. The 2006 and 2007 models posted identical NHTSA crashworthiness scores to the 2005 Sienna. **Airbags:** Reports of airbags failing to deploy in a collision. **ABS:** Standard; disc/drum. Numerous reports of ABS failures, loud grinding or groaning noises when braking, and the brake pedal going to the floor without any braking effect. **Seat belt pretensioners:** Standard. **Head restraints F/R:** *1998–99:* ★; *2001–03:* ★★; *2004:* ★★★★/★★★; *2005–06:* ★. **Visibility F/R:** ★★★★★/★★. Owners report windshield problems, which have been corrected in the 2007 models:

> The right windshield wiper leaves much water directly in front of me before the left wiper removes it. Every wipe, while the water is in my line of sight, I struggle to see the road. This is definitely a hazard to my family's safety, and should be easily repaired with a simple improvement in the design of the wiper cycle.

SAFETY COMPLAINTS: All years: A multiplicity of sliding door defects covered by internal bulletins. • Windshield distortion. • Reflection of the dashboard on the windshield impairs visibility. **1999**—Wheel lug nuts broke and allowed wheel to fall off. • Window exploded at stoplight. • Rear brake drums may overheat and warp. • Faulty fuel cap causes the Check Engine light to come on. **2000**—Sudden acceleration during rainstorm. • Check Engine light continues to come on because of a defective transmission torque converter. • Chronic transmission failure because of faulty torque converter. • Wheel lug nuts sheared off. • Driver's seat belt anchor bolt on door pillar unscrewed and fell to the floor. • Premature tire blowouts (Dunlop and Firestone). • Right rear passenger window suddenly exploded. • Annoying dash/windshield reflection also impairs visibility (very bad with black and beige colours). **2001**—Sudden stalling when the AC is turned on. • Automatic transmission suddenly went into Neutral while on the highway. • Defective transmission torque converter causes the Check Engine light to come on. • Sudden, unintended acceleration. • Vehicle rolled away with shifter in Park, on a hill, and ignition shut off. • Rear seat belts can't be adjusted. • Centre rear seat belt doesn't tighten sufficiently when children are restrained. • Slope of the windshield makes it hard to gauge where the front end stops. • Rear window exploded as front door was closed. • Sunroof flew off when opened while Sienna was underway. **2002**—Several electrical fires in the engine compartment. • Neither front nor side airbag deployed in a collision. • Defective power steering. • Loss of steering. **2003**—Unsafe transmission Overdrive design. • Child safety seat second-row tethering is poorly designed. • Vehicle jerks to one side when accelerating or stopping. **2004**—Engine surging with minimal pedal pressure. •

When proceeding from a rolling stop, acceleration is delayed for about two seconds.

> While parking, accelerating no more than 5 mph [8 km/h] vehicle surged forward. Although I was applying the brake, the car would not stop until it ran into a tree trunk.

• Child knocked gearshift lever into Drive from Park, without key in the ignition. • Difficulty shifting into a higher gear. • Sluggish transmission downshift; vehicle sometimes seems to slip out of gear when decelerating. • Skid control system lock-up. • Fuel tank leakage after recall repairs; leaking fuel line. • Complete loss of brakes. • Rapid brake degradation (glazed and warped rotors). • Sliding door caught passenger's arm and child's leg; manual door doesn't latch properly (particularly when windows are open); door opens when turning, jams, or closes when vehicle is parked on an incline:

> Our two-year-old son pulled on the sliding door handle, and the door began to open (we thought the child locks were on, but this was not the case). He was surprised and was afraid of falling out of the van, so he just held onto the handle. As the door was opening, his head then was dragged between the sliding door and the side of the van. But the van door did not stop opening. It just continued opening, exerting even more force on our son's head. Fortunately we were able to grab the door and forcefully pull it back closed before our son was horribly injured.

• Second-row seat belt locks up; faulty seat belt bracket in rear passenger seat. • Seat belts won't retract. • Battery-saver device doesn't work, particularly if interior lights are left on (they don't turn off as advertised). • Small brake lights inadequate. • Foot gets stuck between pedals. • Rotten-egg smell. • Daytime running lights blind oncoming drivers (2004 Highlander has the same problem). • Long delay for fuel-tank recall campaign parts. **2005**—Sudden acceleration when parking or shifting to Reverse. • Many reports that the front and side airbags failed to deploy. • Airbag deployed for no reason while vehicle was underway. • Hesitation when accelerating and then sudden acceleration. • Laser-controlled cruise control jerks back to former speed when the way seems clear; doesn't hold the speed when going downhill. • Automatic transmission shifts erratically. • Gearshift lever can be accidentally knocked from Fourth gear to Reverse. • Brake pedal stiffens intermittently. • Run-flat tires don't signal driver when they are damaged; may catch fire:

> 2005 Toyota Sienna has Bridgestone run flat tires and the back right passenger tire went flat, then smoked and caught fire.

•

Catastrophic tire failure on a 2005 Toyota Sienna AWD van with run flat tires. Fortunately, no major injuries or damage this time. The tire pressure monitoring system failed to sense the lack of pressure in one of the tires. Driving on the tire with no air pressure caused catastrophic tire failure.

• Dunlop run-flat tires won't hold more than 25 psi of air, and warning light doesn't illuminate. • When the rear windows are down, the door will not stay open. • Liftgate hydraulic strut failures allow the liftgate to suddenly fall:

I went to put boxes in the rear of my 2005 Toyota Sienna LE and as soon as I lifted the door, it fell on my head. After looking at the door, I noticed what appeared to be oil on my bumper and the ground right below where the struts holding the door were. It worked perfectly fine the previous day, but I am concerned that this really could have injured my children if it were them opening the door. The door will no longer stay up by itself and it is a very heavy door. There was absolutely no indication that there was a problem with the door prior to this. I called the dealership and since I am out of warranty, I will have to pay for the replacement. On top of that, they have replaced the strut so I also will have to pay for new brackets. The 2004 have a TSB on that very part, why not the 2005??

• Sliding doors fail to latch when they are opened. • Sliding door continues closing even if a child or pet is in its way (similar to complaints on previous model year Siennas). • Automatic interior light shut-off fails intermittently, draining the battery. • Rear heater core leaks coolant.

Secret Warranties/Internal Bulletins/Service Tips

All years: Sliding door hazards, malfunctions, and noise are a veritable plague affecting all model years and generating a ton of service bulletins. • Owner feedback confirms that front brake pads and discs will be replaced under Toyota's "goodwill" policy if they wear out before 2 years/40,000 km. • Loose, poorly fitted trim panels (TSB # BO017-03, revised September 9, 2003). • Rusting at the base of the two front doors. Will be repaired at no cost, usually with a courtesy car included. According to *www.siennaclub.org*, the proper fix is as follows: Repaint the insides of doors (presumably after removing paint and rust), cover with 3M film, and then replace and coat inside seals with silicone grease. **1997–2002**—Free engine overhaul or replacement because of engine sludge buildup. The program includes 1997 through 2002 Toyota and Lexus vehicles with 3.0L V6 or 2.2L 4-cylinder engines. There is no mileage limitation. Tell Toyota to shove it if they give you a song and dance about proof of oil changes. **1998**—Upgraded brake pads and rotors should reduce brake groan and squeak noises. **1998–2000**—An 8-year/160,000 km warranty extension for automatic transmission failure. Says Toyota:

We have recently become aware that a small number of Sienna owners have experienced a mechanical failure in the automatic transaxle, drive pinion bearing. This failure could result in slippage, noise, or a complete lack of movement.

To ensure the continued satisfaction and reliability of your Sienna, Toyota has decided to implement a Special Policy Adjustment affecting certain 1998–2000 Sienna models.... This Special Policy will extend the warranty coverage of the automatic transaxle to 8 years or 160,000 km, whichever occurs first, from the original warranty registration date.

• Outline of various diagnostic procedures and fixes to correct vehicle pulling to one side. • Power-steering squeaks can be silenced by installing a countermeasure steering-rack end under warranty. • Power-steering feel can be improved by replacing the steering-rack guide. • False activation of the security alarm can be fixed by modifying the hood latch switch.
• Power-window rattles can be corrected by installing a revised lower window frame mounting bracket. **1998–2003**—A new rear brake drum has been developed to reduce rear brake noise (see bulletin).
• An upgraded alternator will improve charging (see TSB #EL013-03) and is also subject to "goodwill" treatment. **1999–2001**—Tips on fixing power-seat motor

REAR BRAKE SQUEALING
BULLETIN NO.: BR003-04   DATE: MARCH 16, 2004
1998–2003 Sienna A new rear brake drum has been developed to reduce rear brake squeal noise.

cable to prevent a loose seat or inoperative seat adjustment. • Power-sliding door transmitter improvements. **2000**—Toyota has field fixes to correct washer fluid leakage from the rear washer nozzle and to eliminate moisture and odours permeating the vehicle interior. • Correction for an inoperative spare-tire lift. **2000–01**—Speedometer or tachometer troubleshooting. **2001**—False activation of the security alarm. • Power-window rattling. • Entertainment system hum. • Inoperative third-row sliding seat. • Special service campaign to inspect or replace the front subframe assembly on 2001 models. • Water leaking into the trunk area. • Troubleshooting interior moisture or odours. • Loose sun visor. • Front wheel bearing ticking. **2002**—Troubleshooting complaints that vehicle pulls to one side. **2002–03**—Steering angle sensor calibration. • Loose sun visor remedy. **2004**—Vehicle stability-control activates intermittently when it is not needed. • New ECM calibration for a poorly shifting transmission (TSB #TC007-03). • Premature front brake pad wear is corrected with upgraded brake pads. • Rear disc brake groan (TSB #BR002-04). • Intermediate steering-shaft noise on turns. • Steering-column pop, squeak, and click. • Front-door area wind noise (TSB #NV009-03). • Power-sliding door inoperative, rattles (the saga continues). • Backdoor shudder and water leaks. • Charging improvement at idle (TSB #RL013-03). • Seat heaters only operate on high. **2004–05**—No-start in cold temperatures. • Correction for the AWD transmission shifter that may become progressively harder to move. • AC blower motor noise. **2004–06**—Sliding door rattles. • Power back door leaks and shudders. • Slow-speed front suspension ticking. • Temperature may vary between the front and rear heaters.

SIENNA PROFILE

	1998	1999	2000	2001	2002	2003	2004	2005	2006
Cost Price ($) (negotiable)									
Sienna Cargo 3d	24,438	24,570	24,570	—	—	—	—	—	—
Sienna CE 4d (16%)	26,808	26,940	27,770	29,535	29,335	29,060	30,000	30,000	30,800
Sienna LE 4d (17%)	29,558	29,980	30,705	31,900	32,985	31,925	35,000	35,420	36,255
Used Values ($)									
Sienna Cargo 3d ▲	5,500	7,500	9,500	—	—	—	—	—	—
Sienna Cargo 3d ▼	4,500	6,000	8,000	—	—	—	—	—	—
Sienna CE 4d ▲	6,500	8,500	10,500	13,000	14,500	17,500	21,500	24,000	—
Sienna CE 4d ▼	5,000	7,000	9,000	11,500	13,500	16,000	20,000	22,000	—
Sienna LE 4d ▲	8,000	10,000	11,500	14,000	15,500	18,500	23,500	26,500	—
Sienna LE 4d ▼	6,500	8,500	10,500	13,000	14,500	17,000	22,000	25,000	—
Reliability	4	4	4	4	4	4	3	4	—
Crash Safety (F)	5	5	5	5	5	5	5	4	4
Side	—	4	4	4	4	4	5	5	5
Offset	5	5	5	5	5	5	5	5	5
Rollover	—	—	—	4	4	4	4	4	4

All ratings on a numbered scale where ⑤ is good and ❶ is bad. See page 220 for a more detailed description.

PICKUP TRUCKS

Diesel Urea Fill-Ups

Mercedes wants drivers to have the urea tank filled at the dealership at each scheduled oil change. But Meissner said the company also is working to set up a hot line for drivers to call so they can get urea sent to them overnight if the tank should run out in an area of the country where there is none available.

AUTOMOTIVE NEWS
SEPTEMBER 25, 2006

Ford Power Stroke: A "Power Joke?"

The 6-liter Power Stroke diesel V8, built by a unit of Navistar for Ford, commands nearly half the U.S. market for diesel pickups. But a raft of problems and repeat trips to dealerships for repairs has left some owners upset, threatening Ford's efforts to rebuild a reputation for quality vehicles.

Soon after the new engines went on sale in November in heavy-duty Ford pickups and the Ford Excursion sport-utility vehicle, owners started reporting problems. Among the costliest is diesel fuel seeping into the engine's oil supply in amounts large enough to ruin the engine. Other complaints included engines that ran roughly or stalled, lack of power at low speeds and harsh shifts.

JUSTIN HYDE, *REUTERS*
AUGUST 20, 2003

Nissan's very own *Titanic*, the failure-prone Titan pickup proves that Asian automakers can screw up, too.

Trucks Still Rule

No, I am not a fan of big trucks. However, many Canadians are, because of their jobs, their geographic locations, or just "because." So it's not surprising that despite the spike in fuel prices last summer, when a litre of regular gasoline topped $1.10, only the largest pickups showed a sales decline, while mid-sized and small pickup sales grew. Now that fuel prices have stabilized to about 90 cents per litre, auto industry analysts expect a resurgence in the popularity of some larger pickups, but the days of the *Exxon Valdez* models are long gone. Buyers are downsizing their choices and purchasing more fuel-efficient hybrids and diesels.

Now there would be nothing wrong with creating smaller, cleaner, and more economical pickups, if such a thing would come to pass. But it won't.

American automakers won't stand for it. They want to keep churning out fuel-wasting, fully loaded large pickups because that's what generates the most profits. Sure, there will be small steps taken to burn less fuel—but these will be baby steps. Ford is losing money with hybrids, and it has just cut back its ambitious plans to expand hybrids across its model lineup. General Motors is touting hydrogen- and fuel-cell-powered vehicles for the future—but that future has no definite date. And Chrysler, stuck with a huge truck inventory, won't bring back the Liberty diesel SUV and is instead looking to China's Chery Automobile Co., Ltd., to supply cheap-running vehicles other than trucks.

"Gentrified" pickups

Cheap Chinese imports aside, consumers want trucks with as much cachet as cargo-hauling capacity, and female truckers are demanding practical features never imagined by the male-dominated, hay-hauling "Hulkamaniacs." Trucks now represent about half of North America's vehicle production, and they're continuing to make inroads into the passenger-car niche by offering larger interiors and more carlike styling, handling, comfort, and convenience features. Safety features have also been added to give pickups greater stability, better braking, and improved crashworthiness.

In general, entry-level models are cheaper than cars with comparable features, but prices for full-sized pickups can easily top $50,000 for fully equipped versions with extended or crew cabs, 4×4, and a full list of amenities. Extended cabs have a small rear seat and doors, while crew cabs generally have large interiors that can sit up to six passengers, four full-sized doors, a full-sized back seat, and windows that roll down.

So who are the major players in this lucrative league?

Ford, to begin with. Its F-Series pickup has been North America's best-selling vehicle for almost three decades. Its strength is particularly evident in western Canada, where it has ruled the top vehicle sales spot from British Columbia to Manitoba, usually with other full-sized pickups just a tad behind. The F-Series was temporarily dethroned in June 2005 by GM's heavily discounted pickups, but it's now more competitively priced. In fact, for 2005, the three top-selling vehicles in the United States were the F-Series, General Motors' Chevrolet Silverado/Sierra, and the Dodge Ram, in that order.

CANADA'S TOP-SELLING LIGHT TRUCKS

		2005	2004	% CHANGE
1.	Ford F-Series	69,549	71,791	–3.1%
2.	Dodge Caravan	65,002	63,559	2.3%
3.	GMC Sierra	38,657	39,391	–1.9%
4.	Dodge Ram Pickup	37,483	37,709	–0.6%
5.	Chevrolet Silverado	37,012	38,005	–2.6%
6.	Ford Escape/Hybrid	23,495	20,360	15.4%
7.	Chevrolet Uplander	21,271	1,193	1,683.0%
8.	Pontiac Montana SV6	20,755	1,343	1,445.4%
9.	Honda CR-V	15,976	15,388	3.8%
10.	Ford Freestar	15,608	21,733	–28.2%

Source: DesRosiers Automotive Consultants

General Motors sells a balanced mixture of trucks and cars, while Ford and Chrysler are practically kept on life-support by truck sales, augmented by a few car purchases. Honda, Nissan, and Toyota are the major Asian players in the full-sized truck segment.

This year, more pickups will be powered by smaller, all-aluminum engines with fuel-efficient variable-valve timing instead of the decades-old iron-block designs. Innovative power management, such as a 4-6-8-cylinder engine, and hybrid electrical/gasoline setups are also in the works. Never mind that aluminum engines in the past have encountered serious sealing and durability problems, or that GM's first (and last) 4-6-8-cylinder engine used in its early '80s Cadillacs was a fiasco, providing 8-cylinder power in the city and 4-cylinder power just as you were merging onto the highway. The GM trucks' electric motor engages on acceleration and has a stop/start system that shuts off the gasoline engine at traffic lights. A built-in generator is also standard.

Ford had practically cornered the market on hybrid pickups with its widely popular Escape pickup. However, consumers looking for hybrid pickups at dealerships selling Detroit Big Three brands will have a hard time finding them this year. Chrysler, Ford, and GM have put their hearts into diesels, not hybrids. Ford says it has changed its mind and won't offer hybrid variants throughout its 2007 model lineup, GM builds only a few thousand gasoline-electric Silverados and Sierras per year and sells them only in the States, and Dodge has built just a few hundred diesel-electric Rams that are mostly used by fleets.

Asian automakers

The major truck players here are Honda, Mazda, Nissan, and Toyota.

Nissan Motor Co. secured a foothold in the pickup market with its small Frontier pickups and then leapfrogged a few years ago into the full-sized category with the Titan. Its sales of light commercial trucks have been impressive: In the fiscal year that ended March 31, 2006, Nissan sold 400,267, up from 182,000 in the fiscal year to March 31, 2003. Nissan now wants to sell light commercial trucks, ambulances, and other vehicles built for "extreme customer usage."

This is Nissan's direct attack on Ford's decades-long dominance of the rescue and emergency vehicle market with its E-Series vans and modified F-Series pickups.

Depreciation

High fuel prices are driving down resale values for full-sized trucks as buyers opt for cheaper-running alternatives. As with cars, imports hold their value better than domestics. For example, a Ford Ranger will be worth less than 30 percent of its initial value after three years, yet a Toyota Tacoma PreRunner Double Cab will retain almost half of its value during the same period. Toyota's Double Cab Tundras depreciate the slowest, keeping almost 60 percent of their value after three years.

Pickup quality decline

Over the past decade, American automakers have churned out millions of new pickups equipped with more complicated and hard-to-service safety, performance, and convenience features. At the same time, they have squeezed equipment suppliers to give them more for less as they constantly change part specifications, confounding suppliers even more.

Industry insiders agree that the above actions have contributed largely to a dramatic decline in pickup quality over the past decade—a conclusion also reached by J.D. Power and Associates and *Consumer Reports*. *CR* says that their poll results show that American trucks become less reliable as they age and don't match the Asian automakers' trucks for overall quality. They gave top marks to the Toyota Tundra and Nissan Titan (one of *CR*'s few mistakes), and they picked Ford's F-150 as the "least reliable" pickup. J.D. Power, however, insists that the American automakers are closing the quality gap with their latest models.

The Dark Side of Diesels

The pickup-truck category is the only vehicle segment in which diesel engines are used extensively. In recent years, General Motors and the Chrysler Group have upgraded their diesel lineup to better compete against Ford, the sales leader in diesel-equipped vehicles. Incidentally, Nissan is also considering a diesel version of its Titan, perhaps for the 2008 model year.

Although diesel engines are promoted by automakers for their fuel-efficient and dependable performance, recent studies and owner complaints indicate that diesels burn more fuel than advertised, are more likely to break down than gasoline-powered engines, and produce emissions that exacerbate the rates of emphysema and may be responsible for 125,000 cases of pulmonary cancer in the States.

www.problematicpowerstroke.com is an excellent resource site for Canadian owners sickened by Ford's toxic diesel fumes.

Cancer dangers

Diesel exhaust contains more than 40 chemicals that are listed by the U.S. Environmental Protection Agency as toxic air contaminants, known or probable human carcinogens, or reproductive toxins or endocrine disrupters. In the United States, the national associations of state and local air-quality control officers estimate that after a lifetime of exposure to diesel fumes, an estimated 119,570 people in metropolitan areas and an additional 5,540 in suburban and rural areas will develop cancer. There are also hundreds of different chemical compounds that wreak havoc on air quality, playing a role in generating ozone formation, particulate matter, regional haze, and acid rain.

Normally, diesel emissions could be "cleaned" by the exhaust system's catalytic converter. However, the diesel fuel that's used in North America is so high in sulfur content that it disables the converter. Sulfur is like a poison to diesel pollution-control devices, much as lead was a poison to catalytic converters in the 1970s. Although cleaner fuel is expected by the end of 2006, there is no guarantee it will be clean enough to work with present-day emissions-control devices. Owners claim that their diesel exhaust makes them ill. Sean Fortier has this to say on his *www.problematicpowerstroke.com* website:

I purchased a new 2005 E-350 Super Duty Cargo Van outfitted for a 24-hour locksmithing company, which I've been operating from a fully equipped van for the last 17 years. At 300 km, the engine light came on, so I drove the van to the dealer to get it repaired. They said the #8 injector was defective and needed to be replaced, but needed to be ordered. I drove the van for the next three weeks and experienced an offensive smelling odour inside and outside the passenger compartment. My customers were asking me to turn the van off or move it from the area. When I took the van in for service four weeks later when the part arrived, I asked to have the van checked for an exhaust leak. When I came to pick up the vehicle I asked if they found the leak, I was told there was none. I drove the van home and called the dealership to inform them that the problem still existed.... Over the weeks I had become increasingly ill and went to my doctor. He started me on a course of anti-inflammatory drugs to reduce the inflammation of my central nervous system. After a few more weeks my workers and I experienced numerous headaches while inside the vehicle. We had to drive all day in the cold with the windows down and the heater on high but it didn't appear to be helping.

Unreliable performance

All three Detroit manufacturers are having injector problems with their newer diesel engines. Ford is covering repair costs through a variety of "goodwill" programs, Chrysler is using its 7-year warranty to authorize repair refunds on 2002 through 2004 models, and General Motors has extended fuel injector warranty coverage for owners of all 2001 and 2002 model-year Chevrolet and GMC pickup trucks equipped with Duramax 6600 engines. GM's Special Policy #04039 was set up in June 2004, giving additional warranty protection for 7 years from the date the vehicle was placed into service or 330,000 km (200,000 mi.)—whichever comes first.

Trucking companies are scouring dealer lots for 2002 and earlier diesel-equipped heavy trucks in an effort to avoid getting cleaner but problem-prone 2003 and later diesels. Mandated by the U.S. Environmental Protection Agency and seconded by Canadian regulators, these new diesels cost $3,000 to $5,000 more than previous versions, are 3–5 percent less fuel efficient, and use new technology to re-circulate exhaust gases through the engine. Oil changes are more frequent and repair costs have been much higher than before because few mechanics and dealers have the diagnostic tools and experience to correct factory-related defects that are commonplace with new designs.

For example, J.D. Power's 2004 Vehicle Dependability Study found that the most fuel-efficient vehicles—diesels and gas-electric hybrids—have more engine problems than similar gasoline-powered vehicles—a conclusion backed by automaker service bulletins and complaints sent to NHTSA. The discrepancies are an eye-opener:

- Ford and Chevrolet diesel pickups were worse than similar gas models, while Dodge and GMC trucks were better overall.
- Owners of 2001-model Toyota and Honda hybrids reported twice as many engine problems as did owners of gas-engine Toyotas and Hondas.
- Owners of Volkswagen diesels reported up to twice as many engine problems as did owners of VWs burning gas.

Chrysler

Although Chrysler's Cummins engine is now the most reliable diesel sold by American automakers, it also has a number of serious manufacturing flaws, one of which is the lift pump. Here's how independent mechanic Chuck Arnold (*chuck@thepowershop.com*) describes the problem:

> The Cummins 24-valve injector pumps will not live without an adequate lift pump fuel supply. These pumps are totally fuel-lubricated and cooled. Without excess fuel flow for cooling and lubrication, these injector pumps die if asked to pull heavy loads. Four out of the last ten lift pumps purchased by the PowerShop have been bad. Two brand new pumps would not pump enough to prime the system and start the truck. Two others would not supply enough fuel to maintain pressure under load conditions. Cummins needs to improve quality control on their lift pumps and Dodge should investigate moving the lift pump to inside the fuel tank where cavitation and engine heat can't lead to failure over time. [Unfortunately], the Dodge-recommended lift pump tests do not find marginal performing pumps.

Arnold ends with these comments:

> Low fuel pressure is very dangerous because it is possible for the engine to run very well right up to the moment of failure. There may be no symptom of a problem at all before you are walking. If you notice extended cranking before startup of your Cummins 24-Valve engine you should get your lift pump checked out fast. Addition of fuel lubricant enhancing additives to every tank of fuel may minimize pump damage and extend pump life. Finally, Cummins and Bosch should re-engineer their injector pump to make it less sensitive to low-fuel-pressure-induced failure. Existing safety systems designed to limit performance or signal engine trouble need to be redesigned to work when fuel pressure is inadequate so that very expensive injector pumps are not destroyed without warning.

Incidentally, DaimlerChrysler's Customer Satisfaction Notification No. 878 authorizes the replacement of the lift pumps in some 2000 and 2001 Dodge pickups.

Ford

F-Series 2003 and 2004 model-year trucks equipped with the 6.0L Power Stroke diesel engine were so badly flawed that they couldn't be fixed, forcing Ford to buy back over 500 units. Wary customers are snapping up Ford's earlier 7.3L diesels, which are apparently more reliable, though less powerful (275 hp versus 325 hp). Power Strokes have a history of fuel injectors that leak into the crankcase, and on the 7.3L diesel water can leak into the fuel tank, causing the engine to seize. Other glitches affect the turbocharger, the fuel injection control pressure sensor, and the engine control software.

FORD:

1999–2005 F-350, F-450

ISSUE: Some 1999–2005 vehicles equipped with the 6.0L or 7.3L diesel engine and a 40-gallon (151.4L) fuel tank behind the rear axle, may exhibit water in the fuel tank. This is due to snow and ice accumulating around the mushroom vent cap, melting, and being pulled into the tank through the mushroom cap.

ACTION: Replace the mushroom cap with a vent line assembly kit.

One Ford dealer mechanic has seen it all:

> You name it, we've seen it. Oil "blowing" into the cooling system (fortunately, not the other way around), numerous running problems, tubes blowing off the turbos, and oil leaks. We had one truck with 8 miles [13 km] on it that we had to pull the engine on. It was a truck going to Hertz, so it wasn't a big deal to the customer, Ford owned [it] anyway, but still, it was a new truck coming off the autohauler sounding like it had a 5-hp air compressor running under the hood and a dead skip. We're pulling heads off of a 6.0 now with 4,000 miles [6,400 km] on it. All these problems I've mentioned are on trucks with less than 20,000 miles [32,000 km]. My diesel tech constantly wishes that since they had worked all the kinks out of the 7.3, Ford would have kept it. So far, we've had six buybacks. The one we're pulling the heads off of now will be the next. Before this, I only had one buyback, in four years.

Before you buy a new Ford truck equipped with a Power Stroke diesel, remember this: Owners say you probably won't smell the offensive emissions or encounter any performance problems until the vehicle has been driven for a few weeks, so don't base your decision on the test-drive alone.

General Motors

GM's diesel engine failures primarily affect the 6.6L Duramax engine, which has been plagued by persistent oil leaks and excessive oil burning, defective turbochargers, fuel-injection pumps, and injectors causing seized engines, chronic stalling, loss of power, hard starts, and excessive gas consumption. To its credit, GM has a Special Policy that extends the warranty to 11 years/193,000 km (120,000 mi.) on injection pumps installed in 1994–2002 models (see bulletin on page 4).

Future Diesel Problems: How's Your Urea?

As stated earlier, U.S. and Canadian emissions regulations are being tightened so that diesel engines will be cleaner-burning by 2007. This will require reformulated, low-sulfur fuel as well as new diesel engines. The fuel will be more expensive and won't be found everywhere, while the engines will be completely redesigned and, consequently, more expensive. In fact, industry insiders say the newer urea-based exhaust treatment systems (Selective Catalytic Reduction, or SCR) can add as much as $50,000 to the cost of large diesel engines. Plus they say SCR isn't the best technology:

> "The innovations in the design of the Scuderi engine reduces the cost of diesel systems by eliminating or dramatically reducing three of the most expensive and complex parts of a diesel system—turbocharging, injectors and exhaust treatment," said Sal Scuderi, president of The Scuderi Group. "Because of the inherent design advantages of the Scuderi Air-Hybrid diesel engine, we estimate that this engine can lower the cost of diesel engines by as much as 40–50%."

> ...The two biggest emission problems for diesel engines (NO_x and soot) are eliminated or drastically reduced. Emission reduction has been the greatest challenge for today's diesel engine manufacturers, with the sophistication and cost of the exhaust treatment systems growing rapidly. The newer urea-based Selective Catalytic Reduction (SCR) exhaust treatment systems can add from $11,000 to over $50,000 to the cost of large diesel engines. In addition, the extra weight and complexity increases the cost of maintenance and repairs.

> Because of the built-in supercharging capabilities of the Scuderi Engine, the need for turbochargers is eliminated. The cost of turbochargers alone can save thousands of dollars per system.

> Because the Scuderi Engine fires only on half of its cylinders, only half of the fuel injectors are required. The cost of today's high pressure injectors can amount to over 30% of the base engine cost. In addition, because of the high turbulence created by the air transferring into the power cylinder from the transfer passage, the Scuderi Diesel Engine will be able to use low pressure, low cost injectors instead of expensive high-pressure injectors.

> "SCUDERI DEBUTS AIR-HYBRID DIESEL ENGINE IN HANOVER"
> *EVWORLD.COM*, SEPTEMBER 15, 2006

Honda claims to have developed a diesel engine that cuts emissions to gasoline-engine levels without using urea. Environmentalists have greeted the news as a groundbreaking achievement, similar to Honda's innovative 1974 CVCC engine—the first gasoline engine to meet American 1970s' emissions rules without using a catalytic converter.

Unfortunately, my fellow tree-huggers are probably too young to remember that the CVCC engine frequently self-destructed, leaving owners with $5,000 repair bills.

Honda's CVCC engine was no exception to the rule: As Leonard Cohen says, "Everybody knows the deal is rotten," and everybody also knows that new designs make for poor reliability and expensive servicing. New SCR technology means that dealers will have to invest millions as they split their parts inventory in two, parts will be in short supply for both conventional and clean-burning engines, service technicians will have to go back to school, and auto owners will find maintenance costs skyrocketing as they search in vain for a urea fill-up—an essential fluid for the new engines. Here's how the U.S. government's Department of Energy lays out the problems (*www.eia.doe.gov/oiaf/servicerpt/ulsd/chapter2.html*):

> There is currently no infrastructure in place for the distribution of urea, however, and other issues remain to be addressed, including freezing of the urea solution in extreme weather conditions as well as operator compliance. Several engine manufacturers are working on infrastructure development plans for liquid urea. Although the EPA agrees that the technology is promising, it has serious concerns about compliance issues, because truck drivers may forgo refilling the urea tanks in an effort to save on operating costs.

> ...Currently, the EPA expects NO_x adsorbers to be the most likely emission control technology applied by the industry. Using current catalyst technology, the fuel-rich cycle reduces fuel efficiency by 4 percent. The majority of the reduction in fuel efficiency comes from the reduction of sulfur in the exhaust stream. The sulfur accumulates on the NO_x adsorber catalyst, and eventually adsorber storage capability is completely lost. Even at ultra-low-sulfur levels, further desulfurization must occur to ensure that the NO_x adsorber is not "poisoned."

> To date, no NO_x adsorber system has proven feasible. Although NO_x adsorbers have demonstrated compliance using ULSD (7 ppm), the systems show losses in conversion efficiency after 2,000 miles [3,200 km] of operation. Concerns have also been raised about the ability of the technology to perform over a range of operating temperatures and loads.

The SCR feature reduces oxides of nitrogen (smog) by injecting urea into the exhaust system. The cost of the new engines and the urea needed to run them, the availability of urea, urea's effects on other vehicle components, and the environmental side effects are still being discussed. Here's what *Diesel Fuel News* predicted in an August 5, 2002, report by Jack Peckham:

If every retail diesel station in the U.S. had to install urea tanks and co-fueling nozzles/dispensers for selective catalytic reduction (SCR) for vehicle nitrogen oxides (NO_x) control, then the urea cost could soar to a "prohibitive" $35/gallon [approximately $132 per litre].

So finds a now-final study...by Arthur D. Little [Global Management Consulting] (ADL) for National Renewable Energy Laboratory (NREL) and U.S. Department of Energy (DOE).

The "Selective Catalytic Reduction Urea Infrastructure Study" indicates that urea throughput at most retail fuel stations would be too low to justify hefty tank/nozzle investments, whereas a relatively few high-volume truckstops could enjoy much better economies-of-scale.

...The NREL/DOE study finds that about 1 gallon [3.8L] of urea would be consumed for each 18 gallons [68L] of diesel fuel, in order to hit U.S. EPA's ultra-low NO_x targets starting in 2007.

The Arthur D. Little study (see *www.nrel.gov/vehiclesandfuels/apbf/pdfs/adl_urea.pdf*) also points out the following problems:

- A new grade of urea may be needed in order to avoid the contamination of SCR systems.
- High-grade urea will have to be shipped separately in specially lined tanks.
- If temperatures dip below 14°F (−11°C), urea heating systems will be required on vehicles and in retail storage tanks.
- Increased demand for cleaning up other environmental polluters, like large plants and refineries, would make North America highly dependent on world urea production; notably, the Arab Gulf states, former Soviet Union, and Venezuela, areas with huge natural gas surpluses (the feedstock for urea/ammonia).
- There would be more urea leaks or spills. The U.S. Occupational Safety & Health Administration (OSHA) considers urea spills to be potentially hazardous.
- Urea spilled into a water aquifer converts to ammonia, then to ammonium, and then to nitrate, which is regulated under EPA's drinking water standards (10 mg/L limit). Consuming drinking water with elevated concentrations of nitrate can cause a blood disorder known as methenoglobinemia in infants.
- Urea overexposure can cause irritation, erythema, nausea, vomiting, and increased urination.

Pros and Cons of Pickup Ownership

Part of the pickup's popularity is by default. The station wagons that used to haul families to the beach and the cottage are practically extinct, though Chrysler's Dodge Magnum may revive the wagon's popularity. And minivans don't have the awesome towing capacity and big-engine grunt (torque) that some motorhome owners, boaters, and off-roaders require.

Just as the minivan saved Chrysler over two decades ago, Detroit automakers hope that increased pickup and SUV sales via heavy discounting will rescue them from what has been a dismal year for profits. As with sport-utilities, even though it's unlikely you'll need the 4×4 versatility or a brawny V8, for many, it's reassuring to know it's there—just in case. Consequently, despite rising fuel costs and a fragile economy, small and mid-sized pickups will be the last vehicles to be sacrificed on the altar of fuel efficiency and rising ownership costs. Full-sized pickups, however, will remain popular with commercial users, who will undoubtedly pass on the increased costs to their customers.

Pickup Advantages
- Relatively low base price for the smaller pickups
- Fuel efficient (4- and 6-cylinder engines)
- Both gasoline and diesel used versions available
- Good support network for parts and servicing
- Numerous body, engine, and suspension choices
- Available in 4×2, part-time 4×4, or full-time 4×4
- Versatile cargo- and RV-haulers
- Easy to customize or convert into a recreational vehicle
- Easy to repair, with excellent parts availability at reasonable prices
- Rear ABS is now standard (but you really need four-wheel ABS)
- Commanding view of the road
- Much lower-than-average collision repair costs

Pickup Disadvantages
- Many have full-strength airbags and are often equipped with dealer-installed, failure-prone Bridgestone, Firestone, Goodyear, or Continental tires
- Diesel reliability and fuel-economy claims may not be true
- New diesel engines and diesel fuel will cost more and be less reliable
- Accelerated depreciation on feature-laden medium- and large-sized models
- Homeowners' associations may prohibit trucks parked outside
- Trucks used commercially are the quickest to lose value
- Chassis may be rust-cankered; box is rust-prone without a liner
- Truck, tools, and cargo are easily stolen
- Small pickups don't offer much cab room and are underpowered
- Centre front-seat passenger lacks legroom
- Three adults can't sit comfortably in the rear seat on base models
- A bone-jarring ride unless the suspension is modified
- Can't be driven with rear windows down because of deafening, painful boom
- Tire upgrade needed on base models to improve handling
- Entry and exit may be difficult without running boards or an extra door

- Some compacts can't haul a 4´ × 8´ sheet of plywood flat on the cargo bed
- Long box makes in-town parking a problem
- Fuel-thirsty V6s and V8s
- Hybrids' fuel economy may be illusory
- Base models are relatively bare
- Loading up on options can greatly escalate base price
- Rear bench seat usually comes with an uncomfortably upright seatback
- Rear doors don't always operate independently of the front doors
- The 4×4 can't always be engaged while running on dry pavement
- Rear wheels spin on slippery roads
- Four-wheel ABS isn't always available
- Rear end tends to swing out
- Heaters are slow to heat the cabin
- Taller, narrower trucks are more prone to rollovers
- High-mounted headlights blind other drivers

Full-sized pickups have changed considerably over the past decade, beginning with Ford's 1996 model redesign, continuing with GM's 1999 and 2004 model revamping, and highlighted by Ford's upgraded F-150, the bold and powerful new Nissan Titan, and the innovative Honda Ridgeline. Pickups have been re-engineered to become more carlike, with better handling characteristics and more convenience features (like extra doors, interior space, padding, and carpeting) that enlarge their appeal from farmer and tradesperson trucks to vehicles for everyday transportation. Still, the half-ton full-sized pickups haven't abandoned their base clientele—they just come in a larger variety of sizes and powertrains to suit more diverse driving needs.

Nevertheless, no matter how carlike these trucks become, you'll be constantly reminded that these are trucks (especially with Dodge Rams) whenever you brake, corner, stop for fuel (which will be often), or climb on board—literally.

When choosing a pickup, consider cost, reliability, size, and style, in that order. Start small with reliable entry-level Mazda, Nissan, or Toyota light-duty trucks. If you need more brawn and performance and must buy something Detroit-made, go for Chrysler's Ram series. And then consider Ford or GM. But be prepared for high maintenance costs and rapid depreciation on all Detroit Big Three models.

Getting the best for less

Full-sized used-truck prices are decreasing this year because of high-priced fuel and an unprecedented number of used trucks coming off lease. Coopers and Lybrand's Autofacts division predicts that over the next few years the capacity for building light trucks will be far beyond what the market can absorb, leading to much lower MSRPs, more substantial dealer incentives and customer rebates, and fierce price competition for both new and used pickups.

What do you do if all the *Lemon-Aid*–recommended full- or medium-sized pickups are either too expensive or not what you require? Downsize your needs if you can, go down a notch, and buy a cheaper, Japanese-made used compact pickup. Or better yet, wait another year for the market to be saturated with pickups and for prices to level out.

PICKUP TRUCK RATINGS

RECOMMENDED
Honda Ridgeline (2007)   Toyota Tacoma (2005–07)
Nissan Frontier (2006–07)

ABOVE AVERAGE
Chrysler Ram (2002–04)   Nissan Frontier (1985–2005)
Ford Ranger/Mazda B-series   Toyota Tacoma (1987–2004)
   (2003–07)   Toyota Tundra (2006–07)
Honda Ridgeline (2006)

AVERAGE
Chrysler Dakota (2005–07)   General Motors C/K, Sierra, Silverado
Chrysler Ram (2005–07)   (2007; 1988–98)
Ford F-Series (2007)   General Motors S-10, Sonoma,
Ford Ranger/Mazda B-series (1984–2002)   T-10 (2000–04)
General Motors Avalanche (2007)   Toyota Tundra (2004–05)

BELOW AVERAGE
Chrysler Dakota (1987–2004)   General Motors S-10, Sonoma,
Chrysler Ram (1986–2001)   T-10 (1996–99)
Ford F-Series (1990–2006)   Isuzu Space Cab, Hombre (1989–2002)
General Motors Avalanche (2002–06)   Subaru Baja (2003–07)
General Motors Canyon,   Toyota Tundra (2001–03)
   Colorado (2004–07)
General Motors C/K, Sierra,
   Silverado (1999–2006)

NOT RECOMMENDED
General Motors S-10, Sonoma,   Nissan Titan (2004–07)
   T-10 (1986–95)

DaimlerChrysler/Mitsubishi

DAKOTA/RAIDER ★★★

2007 TECHNICAL DATA

POWERTRAIN (REAR-DRIVE/4X4)

Engines: 3.7L V6 (210 hp) • 4.7L V8 (230 hp) • 4.7L V8 (260 hp); Transmissions: 6-speed man. • 4-speed auto. OD • 5-speed auto. OD

DIMENSION/CAPACITY

Passengers: 3/3; Wheelbase: 131 in.; H: 63.6/L: 219/W: 74 in.; Headroom F/R: 4.5/3.5 in.; Legroom F/R: 41.5/28 in.; Cargo volume: 26.7 cu. ft.; Fuel tank: 57L/68L/regular; Tow limit: 6,500 lb.; Load capacity: 1,700 lb.; GVWR: 4,390–6,150/5,100–5,650 lb.; Turning circle: 46 ft.; Box length: 6.5–8/6.5 ft.; Ground clearance: 7.9 in.; Weight: 4,790 lb.

RATING: *Dakota:* Average (2005–07); Below Average (1987–2004). *Raider:* Presently not available in Canada; may be sold in 2007. Chrysler's agreement with Mitsubishi Canada prevents Mitsubishi from selling any vehicle for less than the Chrysler equivalent or offering a longer warranty (Raider carries a 10-year guarantee). **Strong points:** Brisk acceleration; available 4×4; lots of low-end torque; well-appointed, carlike interior; lots of front headroom and legroom; and attractively styled. It features a competent base V6 that's said to be more fuel-frugal; the 2005–06 V8 also has a bit more power; either engine can be hooked to a new 6-speed manual transmission; and the interior has been upgraded. **Weak points:** Quad Cab uses a shortened 1.6 m (5´3″) bed. *2004 and earlier models:* Poor acceleration with the 4-cylinder engine; underpowered with the entry-level V6; watch out for false tow ratings on the R/T version; automatic transmission shifts erratically; awkward entry and exit from the rear seat (Club Cab); uncomfortable rear seats; folding rear bench seat is inadequate for three passengers, mainly because of the limited room for legs and knees; Quad truck cannot be driven with rear window down because of a deafening, painful noise created by the vacuum; poor front, rear, and side visibility; steering wheel blocks driver's view of key instruments and gauges; sunlight glare off the gauges is distracting; inadequate headlight illumination on some versions; interior controls are from the Pleistocene era; lousy fuel economy; poor results in offset crash tests; and an unacceptably large number of performance- and safety-related defects reported to NHTSA and other agencies. **New for 2007:** Nothing significant; a restyled, upgraded version is scheduled for the 2010 model year.

MODEL HISTORY: The 2006 mid-sized Dakota and Raider are carryovers from last year's much-improved and well-equipped Dakota, which incorporated many of the redesigned Durango's features, including a more powerful base engine; a roomier, more refined interior; and less noise, vibration, and ride harshness. Unfortunately, for a model launched in 1987, it's too little, too late. Owners still must contend with mediocre handling; a jittery, wandering ride; marginal braking; and subpar quality control.

The 2004 and earlier models are seriously underpowered when equipped with the standard 4- or 6-cylinder engine. With an optional, more powerful engine, the Dakota outclasses the compact competition for sheer towing power. As if they needed it, both optional motors—the V6 and V8—got substantial horsepower increases in 1992.

There are plenty of used Dakotas around, but they aren't cheap, especially the 2002–04 models that came with a 7-year powertrain warranty. If you buy outside of these years, plan on spending part of your savings on a $1,500–$2,000 extended warranty, preferably one sold by Chrysler rather than an independent. You'll need the extended protection because of the many engine, transmission, and electrical glitches and other mechanical and body failings that can inflate upkeep costs considerably.

1991—A V8 engine became available, 4-cylinder engines got 17 more horses, and the front end was restyled. **1992**—V6 and V8 engines gained 55 and 65 horses, respectively. **1993**—A de-powered 4-cylinder engine, optional four-wheel ABS, stainless steel exhaust, and upgraded seat cushions. **1994**—A driver-side airbag and padded knee bolster, side-door guard beams, and centre-mounted brake lights. **1995**—A shift interlock and a 4×2 Sport Club Cab debuts. **1996**—A Magnum 4-cylinder base engine and an upgraded automatic transmission (no real improvement). **1997**—A slight restyling, dual airbags, a stiffer frame, and a tighter turning radius for slightly better handling (though the ride remains choppy). **1998**—An optional 5.9L V8, de-powered airbags, and airbag off-switches. **2000**—Four full-sized doors (called the Quad Cab) and a new 4.7L V8; the 2.4 m (8 ft.) bed is gone. **2002**—Arrival of the SXT version, sporting 16-inch wheels and bucket seats. **2003**—Larger tires and an upgraded automatic transmission coupled with the 4.7L V8 and standard four-wheel disc brakes; the puny 4-cylinder engine was dropped. **2004**—Base V6 gets 35 extra horses, while the 4.7L V8 loses 5 horses. R/T model and its 5.9L V8 are gone.

COST ANALYSIS: The 2007 Dakota carries an MSRP of $25,210, only about $300 more than the 2006 model. **Best alternatives:** Considering its many upgrades, the second-series 2005 Dakota is the better buy. Other choices include the Chevrolet Colorado, Ford Ranger, GMC Canyon, Honda Ridgeline, Mazda B-series, Nissan Frontier, and Toyota Tacoma. **Rebates:** $3,000 rebates and zero percent financing. **Delivery/PDI:** $1,050. **Warranty:** Bumper-to-bumper 3 years/60,000 km; powertrain 5 years/100,000 km; rust perforation 5 years/160,000 km. **Supplementary warranty:** A good idea; try to get a 7-year powertrain warranty thrown in with the deal. **Options:** Although the V6 is adequate for most light-duty chores, invest in the smaller V8 powerplant for best performance and resale value. Four-wheel ABS is a must-have, given the poor braking performance with standard brakes. The remote keyless entry system is also a good idea—it turns on your dome light when pressed, cutting down search time in crowded parking lots. **Depreciation:** A bit slower than average. **Insurance cost:** Above average. **Annual maintenance cost:** Average; easily repaired by independent garages. **Parts supply/cost:** Good parts supply and reasonable costs; easy servicing (Dodge). **Highway/city fuel economy:** *4×2 and 3.9L:* 10.4/14.8 L/100 km; *4×4 and 3.9L:* 11.9/16.3 L/100 km; *4×4 and 4.7L:* 11.4/16.5 L/100 km; *4×4 and 5.2L:* 13.5/18.5 L/100 km.

QUALITY/RELIABILITY: Very poor quality control. Transmission, axle, ball joint, and fuel system problems are covered by secret warranties; however, they can take the truck out of service for considerable periods of time. Fit and finish is embarrassingly bad. **Owner-reported problems:** Fuel and emissions control systems, transmission, chronic upper ball joint/control arm failures, brakes (premature wear and pulsation), clunks and rattles, and body defects. Other complaints include chronic stalling; excessive engine valve knocking and ticking; a noisy rear end; brake shudder; thunking, erratic-shifting transmission; squeaking ball joints; front wheelwells that have a large gap between where the inner fender ends and the frame starts, allowing water and snow to enter the engine compartment; window fogging; excessive interior noise and a violent cabin shake whenever the rear window is opened; fuel-tank thud when stopping; noisy front CV joint boots; and a thumping noise from the left rear axle. **Warranty performance:** Below average. "Goodwill" after-warranty assistance is spotty at best.

SAFETY SUMMARY: The 2007 models posted identical crashworthiness scores to the 2006s. The 1998–99 Dakotas have a towing capacity of only 907 kg (2,000 lb.), despite the fact that Chrysler's sales literature says they can tow over three times as much—2,903 kg (6,400 lb.). Chrysler Canada officials tell me that the higher towing rating was a misprint and that all owners who have complained have been compensated. **Airbags:** Many reports of airbags failing to deploy or deploying when they shouldn't. **ABS:** Standard 2W; optional 4W. **Traction control:** Optional. **Head restraints F/R:** *1997:* ★★★; *1998:* ★★★/★★; *1999:* ★★★; *2001–04:* ★★★/★; *2005–06 models without adjustable lumbar seats:* ★★★; *2005–06 with adjustable lumbar seats:* ★. **Visibility F/R:** ★★/★.

SAFETY COMPLAINTS: All years: Vehicle fires. • Airbag failures. • Sudden acceleration with cruise control engaged or because of a sticking accelerator pedal. • Sudden failure and premature wearout of the upper ball joints. • Vehicle wanders all over the road. • Left in Park, vehicle rolls away on an incline. • Frequent transmission failures and noisy operation (grinds and clunks); it sticks in a lower gear. • ABS failures; pedal went to the floor without stopping vehicle. • Frequent replacement of front brake pads and rotors. **1999**—Reports of several engine fires of unknown origin. • Poor brake performance. • Front-brake lock-up on wet roads. **1999–2000**—Intermittent harsh shifting into Reverse. **2000**—Under-hood fire at stoplight believed to be caused by faulty wire. • Another fire, this time started when transmission fluid was pumped out of filler tube onto hot exhaust pipe. •

Airbags failed to deploy. • Broken axle caused vehicle to go out of control. • Rear brakes lock up intermittently. • Cruise control failed to disengage. • Chronic stalling. • Transmission fluid leaks onto engine. • Transmission jumped into Neutral while vehicle was underway. • Heater core fell off and slipped underneath brake pedal. • Exterior mirrors block visibility. • Seatback collapsed because weld gave way. **2001**—Vehicle caught on fire while parked. • Several cases of sudden axle failure while vehicle was underway. • Transmission jumps out of gear while cruising. • Windows fog up because of inadequate heater and defroster. • No outside air flows in through the vents. • Poor braking. • Excessive brake pulsation. • Lug nut failure caused wheel to fly off vehicle. • Transmission can be shifted without applying brakes. • Brake release handle is easily broken. **2002**—Wheel bearing failures. • Automatic transmission jumped to Reverse when vehicle was put in Park with the engine running. • Shift lever indicator doesn't always show the correct gear. • Without any warning, transmission will shift from Overdrive to Second gear. • Sometimes driver must step on the brakes to get vehicle to shift. • Vehicle stalls on acceleration. • Excessive steering-wheel play, and steering randomly goes from heavy to light turning assist. • Instrument-cluster light fuse blows repeatedly. **2003**—Gearshift lever can be inadvertently knocked out of gear. **2004**—Vehicle rolled over, and driver was suffocated by airbag/seat belt. • Front wheel fell off because of the lack of an upper ball joint bolt. • Defective upper and lower ball joints replaced at owner's expense. • Steering lock-up. • Hesitates when accelerating, and pops out of gear. **2005**—Vehicle won't go into Reverse on a slight incline; dealer said all V6-equipped models have the same problem. • Steering shaft failure caused loss of all steering. • Rear-seat head restraints obscure the view through the rear window. • Seat disassembly is a real knuckle-buster. • Steering wheel blocks the view of the speedometer and other instruments. • Severe rear vibration while underway (vehicle's rear end will hop about); said to be caused by faulty Goodyear Eagle LS tires. • Equally bad vibration when braking. • Excessive stress on the front brake hoses when turning all the way to the left or right. • Right door mirror obstructs front view of traffic.

Secret Warranties/Internal Bulletins/Service Tips

1993–2002—Paint delamination, peeling, or fading. **1997–2000**—A squeaking noise coming from the rear leaf springs can be silenced by replacing the spring tip liners and installing spring cinch clips and isolators. **1997–2003**—Upper and lower ball joints, control arm, and bushing failures covered by a secret warranty. **1998–99**—Poor AC performance may require the adjustment of the temperature control cable or the replacement of the evaporator under warranty. **2000**—If the central timer module locks up, many of your power-assisted features and lights will malfunction and vehicle may not start. **2001**—Water leaks around the rear window. • Drivetrain noise or vibration. • Service 4×4 light comes on for no reason. • Vehicle may surge with cruise control engaged. • Steering-column popping noise. **2000–03**—Doors lock and unlock on their own. **2001–04**—Water leaks on passenger-side floor (see bulletin). **2002**—Automatic transmission filler-tube rattle. **2002–03**—Reprogram the JTEC PCM if the truck won't shift out of Second gear when climbing a grade. **2003**—An erratically shifting automatic transmission may require a re-calibrated PCM or transmission control module (TCM). • Customer satisfaction notification regarding the torque converter drain-back valve. • Harsh shifts because of a sticking pressure-sensor transducer. • Transmission shift/speed control improvements. • Transmission may overheat. **2005**—Steering column snaps or ticks. • Chrysler will replace the front glass run channels free of charge to fix windows that operate erratically.

PASSENGER SIDE FLOOR WATER LEAKAGE

BULLETIN NO.: 23-010-04 **DATE: APRIL 29, 2004**

This bulletin involves sealing the opening for the evaporator hose/drain tube with RTV sealer.
2001–04 Dakota
2000–03 Durango
2001–04 Caravan, Voyager, Town & Country.

DAKOTA/RAIDER PROFILE

	1998	1999	2000	2001	2002	2003	2004	2005	2006
Cost Price ($) (firm)									
4X2 (14%)	16,795	17,585	18,380	18,780	21,815	21,960	22,675	24,605	24,925
4X4	21,490	22,295	22,375	27,915	25,670	30,250	—	—	—
Used Values ($)									
4X2 ▲	3,500	4,500	5,500	6,500	9,000	10,500	13,000	16,000	—
4X2 ▼	3,000	4,000	5,000	5,000	8,000	9,500	11,500	15,000	—
4X4 ▲	5,500	6,000	7,000	8,500	11,000	15,500	—	—	—
4X4 ▼	4,500	5,500	6,500	7,500	10,000	14,000	—	—	—
Reliability	❷	❷	❷	❸	❸	❸	❸	❸	—
Crash Safety (F)	—	—	—	④	④	❸	❸	⑤	⑤
Ext. 4X2	④	—	—	—	❸	❸	—	⑤	⑤
Quad 4X2	—	—	—	—	—	④	—	—	—
Side (Ext. 4X2)	—	⑤	⑤	⑤	⑤	⑤	⑤	⑤	⑤
Quad 4X2	—	—	—	—	—	⑤	—	—	—
Offset	❶	❶	❶	❶	❶	❶	❶	❸	❸
Rollover (Ext. 4X2)	—	—	—	④	④	④	—	④	④
Ext. 4X4	❸	❸	—	—	—	—	—	—	—
Quad 4X2	—	—	—	—	❸	❸	—	④	—

DaimlerChrysler

2007 TECHNICAL DATA

POWERTRAIN (4X2/PART-TIME 4X4)
Engines: 3.7L V6 (215 hp) • 4.7L V8 (235 hp) • 5.7L V8 (345 hp) • 6.7L inline-six (350 hp) • 8.3L V10 (500 hp); Transmissions: 6-speed man. • 4-speed auto. OD • 5-speed auto. OD
DIMENSION/CAPACITY (1500 4X2/4X4 REGULAR)
Passengers: 3/3; Wheelbase: 138.7/154.7 in.; H: 70.0/L: 228/W: 80 in.; Headroom F/R: 6.0/3.5 in.; Legroom F/R: 42/27 in.; Cargo volume: N/A; Fuel tank: 98/132L/ regular/diesel; Tow limit: 8,600 lb.; Load capacity: 1,270 lb.; GVWR: 6,010–6,400 lb.; Turning circle: 49 ft.; Box length: 5.0/6.5/8 ft.; Ground clearance: 9.5 in.; Weight: 5,380 lb.

2007 MEGA CAB TECHNICAL DATA

POWERTRAIN (FULL-TIME 4X4)
Engines: 5.7L Hemi V8 (345 hp) • 8.0L V10 Turbo (325 hp); Transmissions: 5-speed man. • 6-speed man. OD • 4-speed auto. OD • 5-speed auto. OD
DIMENSION/CAPACITY (1500 4X2/4X4 REGULAR)
Passengers: 3/3; Wheelbase: 160.5 in.; H: 74.5/L: 247.7/W: 79.5 in.; Headroom F/R: N/A; Legroom F/R: 41/44.2 in.; Cargo volume: 7.6 cu. ft.; Fuel tank: N/A; Tow limit: 15,800 lb.; Load capacity: 2,840 lb.; GVWR: 9,900 lb.; Turning circle: N/A; Box length: 6.3 ft.; Ground clearance: N/A; Weight: N/A

RATING: Average (2005–07); Above Average (2002–04) with the extended warranty; Below Average (1986–2001). **Strong points:** *2006–07:* Cylinder deactivation for better fuel economy; and more power, interior room, and convenience features. *Pre-2006 models:* Average quality buttressed by a better-than-average warranty (2002–04) combined with assertive styling, a high-tech engine, full-time 4×4, adequately sized cabs with good stowage utility, one of the longest and roomiest cargo boxes available, and a comfortable and well-designed interior with easily accessed and understood instruments and controls. The 1500-series models have better handling, improved steering, and fewer rattles. Other pluses: powerful Hemi, V8, and V10 engines; a bit more reliable Cummins diesel; good trailering capability; a smooth-shifting automatic transmission; and four-door versatility. **Weak points:** *2006–07:* The Mexican plant where these vehicles are made isn't one of Chrysler's best facilities, cylinder deactivation may be glitch-prone, and initial Mega prices could be exorbitant. *Pre-2006 models:* The 1500-series engines may be outclassed by Ford and GM powerplants, although some Dodge trucks carry a stronger warranty. The Hemi V8 is quite fuel-thirsty and has had a few quality problems during the few years it has been on the road. Considering Chrysler's inability to make reliable and safe ball joints, ABS brakes, and automatic transmissions, the 2005's engine "cylinder deactivation" feature appears ominous. The 2500 and 3500 models were left in the Jurassic Age until the 2006 redesigned models came on board; 4×4 must be disengaged on dry pavement; outdated mechanical components, like an inconvenient transfer case and a solid front axle, make for a jittery ride (on 2500s and 3500s only); poor V6 acceleration; rear entry and exit are problematic (Club Cab); back seat is rather tight, hard, and too upright; slow steering response; still bouncy over rough spots; controls aren't easy to calibrate; 1.8 m (6 ft.) bed looks stubby; truck sits very high, meaning shorter drivers and passengers will definitely have problems getting into this pickup; high hood hides obstacles from view; and very poor fuel economy that ties Ford pickups at a "real-world" average of about 21.0 L/100 km (11 mpg). As with Ford and GM trucks, Rams also have a disturbingly large number of safety- and performance-related defects reported to NHTSA. **New for 2007:** Nothing much worth mentioning, except for the new 350-hp 6.7L inline-six Cummins turbodiesel (25 more horses than the 2006 version) and the debut of the Class 3 Chassis Cab, equipped with either a 330-hp 5.7L Hemi V8, or a torquier Cummins turbodiesel V8.

MODEL HISTORY: Not a spectacular performer with its standard powertrain hookup, the Dodge Ram is a full-sized pickup that mirrors Ford's and GM's truck lineups, but with a bit more reliability and warranty protection thrown in. It's sold in 1500, 2500, and 3500 chassis designations (approximate load capacities: half ton, three-quarter ton, one ton) with Regular Cab, Club Cab, Chassis Cab, and Mega Cab configurations. Drivetrains include 4×2 and part-time 4×4 modes coupled to various engine offerings. Ram 3500 models have dual rear wheels.

The 2004 and later 1500-series models come with a 3.7L V6 base engine and optional 4.7L and 5.7L V8s. The latter is called the Hemi, and it's sold only with a 5-speed automatic transmission. The V6 and 4.7L V8 offer a manual transmission or a 4- or 5-speed automatic, respectively. Automatics include a tow/haul mode for heavy loads.

Chrysler plays the nostalgia card with its 345-hp 5.7L Hemi high-performance engine, last seen as an allegedly 425-hp powerhouse offered from 1965 to 1971. At the time, it was offered as a $500–$1,100 option in Dodge Coronets and Chargers and Plymouth Belvederes and Satellites. Now the Hemi is an optional engine sold with the 1500 series, heavy-duty Ram pickups, and the Dodge 300C/Magnum wagon. Drivers can expect to shave about 3 seconds off the 1500's 0–100km/h in 10.5 seconds time, all the while praying that the engine doesn't kill the tranny.

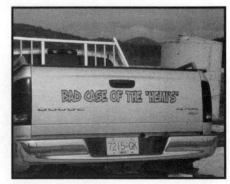

1995—Debut of the Club Cab, equipped with a folding three-place rear bench seat. 1996—An optional suspension package delivers extra towing and hauling capacity; increased power for the Cummins turbodiesel. 1997—The 5.9L V8 got a 5-hp boost. 1998—Launch of the Quad Cab full-sized four-door pickup and a passenger-side airbag with an On-Off switch. 2001—Improved steering and an upgraded rear-suspension system. 2002—Revamped handling and ride comfort. The 1500 models (2500/3500 versions were upgraded in 2003) got more aggressive styling, two new engines, roomier cabs, and optional side airbags. The two-door extended Club Cab was axed, Quad Cabs were given four front-hinged doors, and short-box models gained 7.6 cm (3 in.) of cabin length and lost 7.6 cm (3 in.) of bed length. The 4×4-equipped Rams got an independent front suspension. 2003—2500 and 3500 series were revised and given the Hemi 345-hp 5.7L V8 and rack-and-pinion steering. The 1500 series got new wheels. 2004—An expanded model lineup that includes a Hemi-powered Power Wagon off-roader and the SRT-10 Quad Cab, equipped with the Dodge Viper's 8.3L 500-hp V10 engine. 2005—More models available with 6-speed manual transmissions (hmmm…word must be spreading that the automatics are pure fecal matter). 2006—The 1500 Ram gets a stiffer frame, a softer front suspension, reduced-drag brake calipers, higher-intensity headlights, an electrically operated front-axle disconnect system, a revised interior and body style (Mega Cab), weather seals, and constrained layer (quiet steel) technology in the dash panel area—improvements that should reduce clunks, rattles, and wind noise. It's also the first pickup with a cylinder cut-off system, which also should boost fuel economy if it functions properly (do you feel lucky?). The Mega Cab option is available on the Ram 1500, 2500, and 3500. Chrysler claims the Mega Cab has the largest pickup interior on the market, providing 0.2 cubic metres (7.6 cubic feet) of cargo space behind the rear seats and capable of seating six passengers in comfort—not possible with earlier models. The new cab is about 30 cm (1 ft.) longer than Ford's four-door version of the F-150, and comfort is enhanced through reclining rear seats that split, fold down, and move forward. Hauling capacity is more than adequate with the truck's standard 1.9 m (6′3″) box. Power is supplied by the 345-hp Hemi 5.7L V8 mated to a heavy-duty 5-speed automatic transmission.

COST ANALYSIS: These pickups aren't hard to find, though new prices tend to be on the high side because truck buyers are lured to anything with a large cab, a bed,

The 2006 Dodge Ram Mega Cab.

and an attitude. Chrysler has boosted the 2007 base 1500's price by $275 to make it $26,395. **Best alternatives:** A second-series Honda Ridgeline, Nissan Frontier, or Toyota Tundra. **Rebates:** $5,000 rebates, plus zero percent financing in the new year. Expect mega prices for the Mega Cab to soften by winter, followed by rebates later in 2007. **Delivery/PDI:** $1,175. **Warranty:** Bumper-to-bumper 3 years/60,000 km; powertrain

5 years/100,000 km; rust perforation 5 years/160,000 km. **Supplementary warranty:** Buy extended coverage if Chrysler's base warranty has expired, particularly after the fourth year, when quality-control problems multiply. **Options:** Some options worth considering are power windows and locks, a transmission/oil cooler, and running boards. The Hemi engine, bought by about half Ram's shoppers, is a gas-guzzler and hasn't proven itself yet. The 20- and 22-inch wheels degrade ride comfort. **Depreciation:** Slower than average. **Insurance cost:** Higher than average. **Annual maintenance cost:** Average. The powertrain warranty has kept repair costs down. **Parts supply/cost:** With the exception of some Cummins diesels, parts are easily available and reasonably priced. **Highway/city fuel economy:** *4×2 and 3.9L:* 11.0/15.9 L/100 km; *4×4 and 5.2L:* 13.1/18.9 L/100 km. With the Multi-Displacement System, the Hemi V8 is rated 8.8 L/100 km on the highway and 13.9 L/100 km in the city. The latest V6 engine is estimated at 8.1/12.2 L/100 km. As stated earlier, pre-2006 models' real-world fuel consumption has been reported at 21.0 L/100 km.

QUALITY/RELIABILITY: Below average quality and reliability. Keep in mind that the Ram 2500, 2500 Heavy Duty, SRT10, and Mega Cab are all built in Saltillo, Mexico. That plant placed tenth for efficiency among all of Chrysler's full-sized pickup factories, well behind plants in Michigan and Missouri. Fit and finish and powertrain, suspension, steering, brake, electrical, and fuel-system components are still not top quality. Hemi engines have had problems with broken valve springs and rear main seal leaks. The Cummins diesel engine has performed exceptionally well, but some serious problems remain, as confirmed by this Albertan Ram owner:

> I have a 2003 Dodge Ram 2500 4X4 equipped with a Cummins diesel engine. At 7,000 km, I began to experience stalling problems with the engine, specifically at stop signs and lights. The problem came and went until a major failure at 18,500 km. This problem was compounded by poor fuel economy (5–7 mpg [34–47 L/100 km]). The Edmonton dealer took eight days to overhaul the fuel system.
>
> After I left the dealership, my injection pump started leaking fuel (60,500 km). I was told the Toronto "Tech Line" only operated on EST time and I would have to wait until the next day as the mechanics cannot make repairs without consulting the "Tech Line." The next day I was told the injection pump needed to be replaced and I would have to wait another five to eight days for it to arrive from Toronto.
>
> This is my second injection pump, as well as one "transfer" or "lift" pump. The dealer service manager told me, "about two weeks ago we had over eight trucks sitting out there waiting for 'lift' pumps."

Considerable downtime because of automatic transmission malfunctions and breakdowns. The problem isn't as severe as those of the Dakota or Ford F-Series, though. **Owner-reported problems:** Owners report chronic automatic transmission, electrical, ignition, engine cooling system, steering, suspension, fuel, brake, and body problems for all years. Cold or wet weather doesn't agree with these trucks, either—generating lots of reports of chronic hard starting and stalling, even when the engine is warm. Chrysler has done little to deal with this basic flaw, which has been a generic Chrysler problem for decades. The ignition system on 1993–96 models earns low reliability marks, as well. There have been some reports of misaligned drivelines leading to excessive vibration and prematurely worn clutches. The body is squeak- and rattle-prone, and water and air leaks are common:

> The rear window leaks during rainstorms. Mold began to grow in the vehicle because the problem was discovered two months after the incident occurred.

The exhaust system leaks and overheats, and rust tends to start fairly early. Other owner-reported problems: Electrical fire at the power disbursement box under the hood; accelerator pedal jams while backing up; and sudden transmission and differential failures. Be wary of front differential damage caused by road debris striking the unprotected housing.

Owners also report poorly performing brakes that must be adjusted at almost every oil change; premature (5,000 km) wearout of the rear brake hubs and front brake pads; complete ABS brake failure; the weak stabilizer bar is easily bent when passing over potholes; the lack of an anti-sway bar on the rear axle in the trailer towing package means excessive swaying, causing steering instability; some trailer hitches are cracked; transmission seal leakage and excessive noise through the 2006 models; obstructive rear door latching mechanism prevents easy access to the rear seat; fragile front ball joints; excessive vibration when approaching 100 km/h; very loose steering allows vehicle to wander all over the roadway; faulty steering gearbox; defective steering pump causes loss of steering control; truck changes lanes even though steering wheel isn't turned; constant pulling to the right on the highway; inadequate cooling because of AC freeze-up; odour coming from the AC ducts; oil-filter adapter plate and speed-sensor oil seepage; clunk or rattle felt in steering wheel after running over a rough surface; front disc brake noise on the 3500 series; clunking or rattling noise from the front suspension; ringing noise from the rear of the vehicle; excessive shimmy after hitting a bump or pothole; shudder when pulling away from a stop when near maximum GVWR; absence of a baffle in the fuel tank allows gas to slam forward and back in the tank, subjecting connections to stress and causing early failure; ignition fuse link blows intermittently, shutting down the vehicle; and the lapbelt rides too high on the abdomen and shoulder belt lies too close to neck and jaw. **Warranty performance:** Below average. "Goodwill" payouts have neither rhyme nor reason but track in the 50-percent range. A threat of small claims action can raise the offer to 75 percent just prior to mediation or trial.

 ROAD PERFORMANCE: Acceleration/torque: Owners report the Hemi has trouble getting up to speed, requiring a lot of throttle. Hill climbing is poor until the engine hits the higher rpm at nearly full throttle. Once the Hemi finds its sweet spot, it does well, but towing at high rpm cuts considerably into fuel economy. The Cummins Turbo Diesel won't break any speed records, either, but it will haul just about anything when hooked to the 5-speed manual transmission. The 3.7L V6 is smooth and acceptable for light chores, but the 4.7L V8 gives you the reserve power needed for heavier work. The 5.9L V8 is the engine of choice for hauling or towing anything weighing more than 1,800 kg (4,000 lb.). Shifting into 4×4 is done via a hard-to-reach floor lever; however, the 2002 and later 1500s offer an optional dashboard-mounted switch. **Transmission:** The 4-speed automatic transmission shifts smoothly when it's working right. **Steering:** Vague and slow to respond. Excessive steering wander on Quad Cabs and extended cabs. **Routine handling:** The Ram's performance, ride, and handling are more trucklike than with its Ford or GM rivals. The ride can be especially rough without a full load in back. **Emergency handling:** Although the 2002 1500 series rides well, other Rams are quite jittery on the highway (thanks to an antiquated solid front axle) and ponderous in their handling. They also have a lower ground clearance than their rivals. Rapid cornering isn't advisable because of the excessive rear-end sway. **Braking:** Not impressive, in spite of rear-wheel ABS (100–0 km/h: 45 m). Some fading after repeated application.

 SAFETY SUMMARY: 2007 Rams posted crashworthiness scores identical to the 2006s. Child safety seat can fit in the rear centre seat if an extended belt is used. Most early Dodge trucks won't have head restraints. **Airbags:** Many complaints of airbags failing to deploy or deploying when they shouldn't. **ABS:** Standard 2W; optional 4W; disc/drum. **Head restraints F/R:** *1997:* ★; *1999:* ★★/★; *2001:* ★; *2003–05 without adjustable lumbar seats:* ★; *2003–05 with adjustable lumbar seats:* ★★★; *2006:* ★. **Visibility F/R:** ★★★★★. **Maximum load capacity:** *1999 SLT 5.2L:* 1,265 lb.

SAFETY COMPLAINTS: All years: Sudden acceleration. • Chronic stalling. • Repeated ABS failures; pedal goes to floor without any braking effect. • Severe pull to the side when braking. • Warped rotors and worn-out brake pads. • When parked, vehicle rolls down an incline. • Frequent transmission failures and fluid leaks. • Overdrive engages poorly in cold weather. • Vehicle wanders excessively at highway speeds; loose steering makes for imprecise corrections. • Steering wander is especially severe with diesel-equipped vehicles. • Vehicle sways and tilts when underway. **1999**—Transmission suddenly jumps into Neutral (transmission shift sensor suspected). • Power-steering binding or lock-up. • Seat belt buckle won't latch. **2000**—The speed control fails to keep an even speed, and the automatic transmission is always gear hunting. • Brakes don't stop the vehicle, require constant and expensive maintenance. • When braking, vehicle pulls violently to the side. • Power-steering and rear-wheel brake drum failures. • Michelin LTX tread separation. **2001**—Many reports of electrical shorts causing under-hood fires. • Fuse box caught fire because battery cable wasn't properly installed at the factory. • Evaporator canister, power-steering box and hose, and seat belt retractor failures. • Power-steering line blew out. • Brake-pad rivets come loose, and rear brake light fuses keep blowing. • Excessive crankcase oil vapours enter the passenger compartment. • Front suspension bottoms out on speed bumps. • Excessive vibration of side mirrors. • Rear window shattered. • Hood flew up and shattered windshield. **2002**—Front end jumps from side to side when vehicle passes over uneven pavement, or it easily hydroplanes when passing over wet roads. • Bed may damage the cab. • Premature brake master cylinder failure. • Differential and rear axle bearing failed prematurely. • Automatic transmission stuck in Reverse. • Loose side-mounted rear-view mirrors. **2003**—Accelerator pedal fell off. • Stalling and hard starting. • Front suspension collapse. • Automatic transmission won't shift into Reverse. • Lowered tailgate falls onto the roadway when vehicle goes over a bump. **2003–04**—Ram 2500 and Ram 3500 pickups with automatic transmissions might roll backward when shifted into the Park position. NHTSA says 42 crashes and three injuries have been linked to the problem. **2004**—Fire ignited in the driver-side rear wheelwell. • Brake lock-up. • Sudden stalling while cruising. • Stalling Hemi engine (EGR valve on national back-order). • Excessive on-road vibration. • Erratic reading on odometer and speedometer after water gets into the wiring harness. • Wheel bearing failure. • Rear axle broke. • Coolant cap leaks. • Horn failure. • Headlight high beams aren't bright enough. **2005**—Electrical fire ignited in the engine compartment. • Chronic stalling, especially when turning. • Vehicle speeds up when going downhill. • Sudden automatic transmission failure. • Transmission slipped from Park to Reverse while it was parked and idling. • Early ball joint failure. • Exhaust pipe leak; catalytic converter shows signs of overheating. • Premature tire wear (scalloping).

Secret Warranties/Internal Bulletins/Service Tips

1993–2002—Paint delamination, peeling, or fading. **1994–99**—Engine knocking and high oil consumption may be caused by an intake manifold pan gasket oil leak. Stand fast for a refund of repair costs up to 7 years/160,000 km:

ENGINE—SPARK KNOCK/OIL CONSUMPTION		
BULLETIN NO.: 09-05-00		**DATE: FEBRUARY 25, 2000**
1994–99	(AB)	Ram Van
1994–99	(AN)	Dakota
1994–99	(BR/BE)	Ram Truck
1998–99	(DN)	Durango
1994–98	(ZJ)	Grand Cherokee
1996–98	(ZG)	Grand Cherokee

SUBJECT: Spark Knock and Engine Oil Consumption due to Intake Manifold Pan Gasket Oil Leak
OVERVIEW: This bulletin involves the replacement of the engine intake manifold plenum pan gasket.

• Accelerated front and rear brake lining wear can be controlled by installing countermeasure linings developed to prevent early wearout. • A squeaking noise coming from the rear leaf springs can be silenced by replacing the spring-tip liners and installing spring-cinch clips and isolators. **1994–2000**—A rattle from the door area may be corrected by installing a revised window channel. **1994–2001**—If a higher-than-normal steering-wheel movement is required to keep the vehicle from wandering (vehicle slow to respond to normal steering-wheel input), perform the Over-Centre Adjustment Repair Procedure. • Many 4×4 Rams with several years of hard use are developing steering wander because of worn track bars. To check a track bar, start the engine and observe the ends of the track bar while someone saws the wheel from side to side. Any movement at either end of the track bar indicates that the track bar is bad. If play is observed, replace the track bar. **1997–2000**—A squeaking, creaking steering column likely needs a new lock housing and attaching screws. **1997–2002**—A power-steering hissing may only require replacing the power-steering hoses. **1998–99**—A knocking or tapping noise coming from the engine compartment may be corrected by replacing the duty-cycle purge-valve bracket. **1999–2001**—Erratic engine operation:

SURGE/LACK OF POWER IN THIRD GEAR/ERRATIC SHIFTS

BULLETIN NO.: 18-006-02 REV. C   DATE: JUNE 3, 2002

OVERVIEW: This bulletin involves selectively erasing and reprogramming the JTEC Powertrain Control Module (PCM) with new software.

MODELS: 1999–2001 (BE/BR) Ram Trucks equipped with a 5.2L, 5.9L, or 8.0L engine.

SYMPTOM/CONDITION: Some vehicles may exhibit one or more of the following performance conditions:

1. Perceived lack of power in Third gear due to converter lock-up in Third gear. This reprogramming eliminates Third gear lock-up.

2. Surge after lock-up (40–45 mph [64–72 km/h]) in Fourth gear. This reprogramming raises torque converter lock-up speed to 52 mph [84 km.h].

3. Transmission does not upshift from Third gear after a 4–3 downshift. (Most often noticed when cruise control is engaged.)

POLICY: Reimbursable within the provisions of the warranty.

2000–02—Doors lock and unlock on their own. **2001**—Engine may not crank because of a blown starter-relay circuit fuse. • Engine cranks but won't start, or starts and stalls. • Low fuel output from the transfer pump may be the cause of hard starts or no-starts. • Vehicles used for extended heavy trailering may experience a loss of exhaust manifold bolt torque. • Troubleshooting tips for complaints of poor diesel engine performance. • Low engine power when transmission is in Overdrive. • Harsh transmission engagement when the torque converter clutch is applied. • Remedy for steering wander (1500 series). • Rear may sit too high to attach a fifth wheel. • Spark knock when accelerating. • Rear leaf spring clicking, squeaking noise. • Tie-rod adjusting sleeve slot may be the source of a high-pitched whistle. • Tapping or knocking during idle. **2001–04**—Water leaks on passenger-side floor (see Dakota "Secret Warranties/Internal Bulletins/Service Tips").

2002—Hard starts and idle speed fluctuation in cold weather. • Inoperative tachometer. • Faulty oil pressure gauge. • Oil pan gasket leaks. • Hood distortion and low spots. • Seat rocking movement when accelerating. 2002–04—Water leaks at grab handle. 2003—Low start-up oil pressure with the Hemi engine requires the replacement of the oil pump pick-up tube. • Brake vibration or shudder requires the replacement of many major brake components, says Bulletin #05-008-03, published November 28, 2003. • An erratically shifting automatic transmission may require a re-calibrated PCM or TCM. • Instrument panel whistle. • Poor idle and coasting. • Lack of air from floor vents. • Buzzing, vibration from front of vehicle. 2003–04—Loose, rattling bug deflector. • Dirt accumulates in door opening area (Chrysler will install an improved secondary door seal). 2003–05—Steering snaps or ticks. 2004—Brake kit will be installed to eliminate brake shudder, vibration. • Power-window binding or slow operation. • Torn drip-rail door seam. • Poor sound quality from Infinity speakers.

RAM PROFILE

	1998	1999	2000	2001	2002	2003	2004	2005	2006
Cost Price ($) (negotiable)									
D-150, 1500 (20%)	18,890	20,345	20,630	18,750	23,255	23,865	24,910	26,975	26,020
Quad Cab	—	—	—	—	27,280	26,900	—	—	—
SRT-10 (30%)	—	—	—	—	—	—	61,000	58,465	61,555
Used Values ($)									
D-150, 1500 ▲	4,500	5,500	6,000	8,000	10,000	13,500	16,000	18,500	—
D-150, 1500 ▼	4,000	4,500	5,500	7,000	8,500	12,000	14,500	17,000	—
Quad Cab ▲	—	—	—	—	13,500	16,500	—	—	—
Quad Cab ▼	—	—	—	—	12,000	15,000	—	—	—
SRT-10 ▲	—	—	—	—	—	—	39,000	45,000	—
SRT-10 ▼	—	—	—	—	—	—	37,000	43,000	—
Reliability	➋	➋	➋	➋	➌	➌	➌	➌	—
Crash Safety (F)	—	—	—	➎	➍	➍	➎	➎	➎
Ext. cab	➍	➍	➍	➍	—	—	—	➎	➎
Quad cab	➍	➌	➌	➍	—	—	—	➎	➎
Side	—	➎	➎	—	—	—	➌	—	—
Quad Cab	—	—	—	—	➍	➎	➌	—	—
Offset	➊	➊	➊	➊	➎	➎	➎	➎	—
Rollover	➊	➊	➊	➌	➌	➌	—	➍	➍

All ratings on a numbered scale where ➎ is good and ➊ is bad. See page 220 for a more detailed description.

Ford

RATING: *F-150:* Average (2007); Below Average (1990–2006). The F-Series trucks are versatile and brawny haulers, with much-improved handling, a quieter ride, and a more comfortable interior incorporated into the 2005 model's redesign. Quality control, however, remains abysmally poor. Over the past decade, I've seen a dramatic increase in owner complaints relating to poor-quality powertrain components and serious safety-related defects that include sudden tie-rod separation, torsion bar failures, unintended acceleration, and the complete loss of braking. Service bulletins reinforce the fact that these trucks aren't well made, and they won't likely improve until their 2009 model-year redesign. **Strong points:** Good choice of powerful V8 engines; easy and predictable handling; pleasant ride on bad roads; well-thought-out ergonomics, instruments, and controls; and fourth-door access. With a few exceptions (like tacky cloth seats), base models are nicely appointed, with lots of handy convenience features and a classy interior. The F-Series offers a commanding view of the road, lots of cab space, and excellent interior ergonomics. The front bench holds three in relative comfort, though there's insufficient footroom for the front centre passenger. One of the quietest pickups available. **Weak points:** Needs to lose weight. Underpowered base V6 engine and 4.6L V8 don't have sufficient passing power; questionable engine, transmission, suspension/steering, and brake performance and reliability; poor braking performance with four-wheel ABS; and an uncomfortable rear seat. Climate-control system is a bit slow in warming up the cabin. There's no left foot-rest on some models, and the cramped and upright rear seats can't match GM's for comfort. Cargo flexibility is compromised by second-row layout. An inordinate number of serious safety-related complaints have been collected by NHTSA, with cruise-control switch fires, tie-rod end and front torsion bar failures, and steering vibration and drivetrain shudder heading the list. Warranty payouts have been unacceptably Scrooge-like in the past, and fuel economy is astoundingly poor. **New for 2007:** Nothing much. There will be no major F-150 changes until the redesigned

CRUISE CONTROL DEACTIVATION SWITCH

BRAKE FLUID PLASTIC RESERVOIR

2007 TECHNICAL DATA

POWERTRAIN (REAR-DRIVE OR 4X4)

Engines: F-150: 4.2L V6 (202 hp) •
4.6L V8 (231 hp) • 5.4L V8 (300 hp);
F-250, F-350, etc.: 5.4L V8 (300 hp) •
6.8L V10 (355) • 6.0L V8 diesel (325);
Transmissions: 5-speed man. • 4-speed
auto. OD

DIMENSION/CAPACITY (F-150)

Passengers: 3/3; Wheelbase: 138.5/157.1
in.; H: 72.8/L: 220.8/W: 78.4 in.;
Headroom F/R: 5.0/4.0 in.; Legroom F/R:
40/32 in.; Cargo volume: N/A; Fuel tank:
131L/regular/diesel; Tow limit: 2,000–
21,800 lb.; Load capacity: 1,510 lb.;
GVWR: 6,050–10,000 lb.; Turning circle:
47 ft.; Box length: 6.5/8.0 ft.; Ground
clearance: 8 in.; Weight: 5,690 lb.

2009 model arrives. F-250 and F-350 pickups, however, have been redesigned for the 2007 model year, and they'll offer a new 6.4L 350-hp V8 diesel engine for 2008 to replace the quality-plagued 6.0L diesel used presently.

MODEL HISTORY: In Ford's glory days, it and GM were the only pickup games in town, and relations with parts suppliers were cordial. Now, Chrysler, Honda, Nissan, and Toyota are gobbling up Ford's market share, and supplier relations are testy at best. Buyers are clamouring for more versatile and reliable trucks that mix hi-tech with dependability and are covered by stronger warranties. Unfortunately, Ford's latest F-Series 2005 model-year revamp is too little, too late.

The most obvious changes on the 2005s are the F-Series' new angular styling; four-door configuration (a first for entry-level trucks); a bigger, quieter cab; a bed box that is 6 cm (2.5 in.) deeper; and an upgraded interior. Ride comfort is improved by a roomier interior and new rear suspension. SuperCab models gained 15 cm (6 in.) in cab length plus larger rear doors and entry and exit handles. Other nice touches include a power-sliding rear window controlled by a button on the overhead console, power rear side windows, and an easier-to-lift tailgate that houses a torsion-bar-assist mechanism built in.

Adding to the truck's performance are a stiffer frame, better shock absorber placement, rack-and-pinion steering, and a double-wishbone designed front suspension with coil-over shocks. Drivers will notice there's less skipping on washboard roads, less bounce, and great cornering thanks to the 17-inch tires and larger leaf springs that reduce sway and enhance towing stability.

The Ford 4.2L V6 is rated better in fuel mileage than the 4.6L V8, but the V8 gets better mileage in the real world. The V6 also was known for oil pump problems and has been dropped from the reworked F-150. An engine Ford should have dropped, but didn't, the 300-hp 5.4L V8, known for early production glitches, was added a few years ago. It features three valves per cylinder, variable-cam timing, and an electronic throttle control that dealer mechanics are still trying to master.

The 2005 F-150 allows you to ease down the steepest inclines in First gear without the need to ride the brakes, though overall braking has been improved, as well.

Fully vented four-wheel disc brakes with ABS and Electronic Brake Force Distribution (a system that varies braking according to perceived load) provides extremely smooth and predictable braking with little fade and no sudden jolts like we've felt with GM's trucks. Their complexity, however, could mean costly repairs later on.

Safety features on the 2005s have been augmented to include multi-stage front airbags; a sensor to determine if the front passenger seat is empty; five three-point seat belts, with the front shoulder belts integrated into the seats; and a LATCH (lower anchors and tethers for children) system to facilitate the installation of child safety seats.

2004 and earlier models

The F-150 is Ford's base model, followed by the 250, 250 Heavy Duty, 350, and F-Super Duty. For 2001, the Super Duty F-650 Super CrewZer debuted as Ford's medium-duty pickup, aimed at the horse-trailering crowd. All versions are available with rear-drive or 4×4. A wide variety of wheelbase and box lengths is available.

There's a wide range of engines, making the F-Series a very versatile truck. The standard engine is a 4.2L V6 powerplant, borrowed from the Windstar; two Triton V8s, based on a Lincoln engine; and a 7.3L diesel engine. A 5-speed manual transmission, a 6.8L V10, and a 4-speed electronically controlled automatic transmission are also likely to be found on these carried-over models.

For light-duty use, stick to the F-150 for the best combination of a tolerable ride, decent handling, and good load capacity. Various combinations of extended cabs and longer cargo boxes are available in all years, including the more heavy-duty F-250 and F-350 models. Keep in mind, however, that ride and handling suffer as size and weight increase.

Most of the engines have not changed radically for over 15 years. The basic 4.9L 6-cylinder engine, used through the 1996 model year, is a good, economical light-duty powerplant, understood by most dealers and independent mechanics. If you need more power, go directly to the small V8. Transmission choices for these vehicles run the gamut from a primitive but sturdy 3-speed manual to the trouble-prone 4-speed automatic and the 4- and 5-speed manuals. The 4×4 versions have been available since 1986.

1995—Arrival of the 7.3L diesel engine. 1997—The truck-buying public wasn't enthralled with the 1997 model's new design; buyers complain that there's nothing really distinctive about the restyling and that quality deficiencies weren't seriously addressed. 1999—A restyled front end, upgraded front seats, and the arrival of a four-door SuperCab. 2001—The F-150 Crew Cab debuted with four full-sized doors and a full rear-passenger compartment; the 4.6L V8 gained 20 additional horses; the F-250 and F-350 got a horsepower upgrade for the 7.3L Power Stroke turbodiesel engine; the Trailer Tow package became standard on all models, as did four-wheel ABS; and the Lightning got a slight increase in power and a shorter final drive ratio. **2002**—The mid-year return of the Harley-Davidson Edition; SuperCrew models came with 20-inch wheels and special trim; and the 260-hp 5.4L V8 was joined by a 340-hp supercharged variant. **2003**—Lightning models received a stiffer rear suspension to support a 635 kg (1,400 lb.) payload. **2004**—The entry-level Heritage debuts. **2005**—Redesigned.

Hauling capacity, interior comfort, and handling vary greatly depending on the model chosen. Although a bit rough-riding, the half-ton suspension should serve well for most purposes. Early models had poor front/rear brake balance when carrying a light load, so when rear ABS was added in 1987, it was hailed as a much-needed improvement. The euphoria was short-lived, however—owners soon complained that the ABS locked up on wet roads and was failure-prone. These same braking problems have continued with the 2004 models and some of the 2005s.

COST ANALYSIS: High fuel prices have hit F-Series sales particularly hard, forcing Ford to cut 2007 production by one-third and to reduce their MSRP over the past few years by several thousand dollars. For example, a 2007 F-150 XL sells for $22,499—$1,341 *less* than what a 2005 model cost. A second-series 2005 would be the best used F-Series choice, if you must buy a Ford. **Best alternatives:** Mazda, Nissan, and Toyota pickups are a lot safer and more reliable. Incidentally, the base Toyota pickups' used prices are very competitive after a few years on the market (see the Tacoma section). **Rebates:** Look for the resumption of a "take no prisoners" discount war as GM fights to maintain its pickup gains. Chrysler and Ford will likely counter with their own discounts, $3,000 rebates, and zero percent financing. **Delivery/PDI:** $1,200. **Warranty:** Bumper-to-bumper 3 years/60,000 km; rust perforation 5 years/unlimited km. **Supplementary warranty:** An extended powertrain warranty figured into the base price is a must to counter Ford's poor quality control. **Options:** Get the small 4.6L 231-hp V8 engine, or you'll be kicking yourself for getting stuck with the anemic V6. Other options you should consider are four-wheel ABS (standard with most 2004 F-150s), remote keyless entry, and a heavy-duty battery. Short drivers may require running boards and, to get away from the airbag's explosive deployment, the optional power seat with height adjustment and the extended pedals. Parking-distance beeper is a waste of money. **Depreciation:** Average. **Insurance cost:** Higher than average. **Parts supply/cost:** With the exception of Power Stroke diesels, parts are generally widely available from independent suppliers and of average cost. **Annual maintenance cost:** Higher than average, but easily repaired by independent garages. **Highway/city fuel economy:** Very poor; average real-world fuel economy hovers around 21.0 L/100 km (11 mpg)—equal to the Dodge Ram. *4×2 and 4.2L:* 11.1/15.1 L/100 km; *4×2 and 4.6L:* 11.3/16.2 L/100 km; *4×2 and 5.4L:* 12.3/17.4 L/100 km; *4×4* *and 4.2L: 12.2/15.9 L/100 km; 4×4 and 4.6L: 12.9/17.4 L/100 km; 4×4 and 5.4L: 13.6/18.6 L/100 km.*

QUALITY/RELIABILITY: Terrible. It's interesting how Chrysler, Ford, and GM trucks have similar patterns of powertrain, suspension, and brake failures. Could it be because they use the same suppliers and pirate cost-cutting techniques from each other? Interestingly, many owners report that dealer service managers routinely downplay the seriousness of major failures by responding that they're "normal," or that they can't be duplicated or fixed. Apparently, Ford's '96 and '04 redesigns created more bugs than they fixed. In fact, the company's flagship 6.0L diesel engines, introduced in December 2003, were so badly flawed that Ford had to initiate a service program to fix them and buy back over 500 trucks. Their problems included a rough idle, loss of power, stalling, excessive exhaust smoke, leaky fuel injectors, high fuel consumption, and engine seizures. Ford says the engines are fine now, but there are many skeptics. Non-diesel engines aren't very durable, either, and they have severe engine knock through the 2005s. Another serious defect afflicting 1996–2004 models that's likely to gain national attention soon is the collapsing tie-rods/torsion bars in the steering/suspension system that throw the truck out of control when they fail. Ford has sent a letter to owners asking them to *please* have their vehicles inspected and repaired—at their own cost, of course. That's just another example of Ford's crappy customer relations attitude. **Owner-reported problems:** Engine and automatic transmission breakdowns top the list. Owners report failure-prone engine gaskets (covered by a number of special warranty extensions—see "Secret Warranties/Internal Bulletins/Service Tips"), timing belt tensioners, oil pumps, fuel and ignition systems, and drivelines (principally clutches); poor-quality front and rear brake components that include premature pad and caliper replacement and chronic rotor warping (also covered by a secret warranty—see page 168); faulty powertrain control modules that cause sudden stalling at full throttle; excessive vibration felt throughout the vehicle; a lack of sufficient support in the driver's seat; and front suspension and steering problems. There are also body defects, including door cracks on 1997–2000 models covered in Ford SSM 12071 (see "Not What It's Cracked Up to Be," *www. F150online.com/articles/cracks.html*) and confirmed by internal bulletins supplied by ALLDATA. Ford may replace the door or install a reinforced plate. Careful checking of frame rails and underbody panels is a must on older trucks. Both dealers and owners report that late-model Ford trucks and sport-utilities are equipped with defective torsion bars, which usually fail while the vehicles are being driven, resulting in loss of vehicle control. Additionally, owner complaints target FX-15 air conditioner compressors, fuel and electrical systems, brakes, premature catalytic converter failure, and poor-quality fit and finish:

> My father purchased a 2003 model F-350 dually last fall for his new ranch truck. This spring when the frost came out of the roads (35 km of gravel) the dirt/mud stuck to the inner plastic fenders and both of them were damaged.... There are a lot of these

dually trucks in that area (Fort St. John, B.C.) and the body shop has said many that drive on the dirt roads have this problem.

Other complaints include excessive vibration and shaking at idle and at cruising speed; noisy steering and suspension; rear-end rattles; exhaust system leaks; loose manifold air intake hoses; transmission rear seal and bushing leaks, squealing, and humming; drive shaft clunks when accelerating or decelerating; excessive brake pedal pulsation when brakes are applied; and front shocks that leak oil. The 2001 models are particularly plagued by engine and rear-end failures. **Warranty performance:** Way below average. While reports of safety- and performance-related defects have soared, Ford's customer relations performance has soured.

 SAFETY SUMMARY: 2007 F-Series trucks posted the same crashworthiness scores as the 2006s. 1997–2000 model-year F-150, F-250, Blackwood pickups, and Expeditions are part of ongoing class actions filed in Canada (see *www.willbarristers. com*) and in the States alleging they have faulty door latches. Ford has settled one lawsuit out of court (see *www.defectivedoor.com*). Earlier Ford pickups don't have head restraints. **Airbags:** A number of incidents where the airbags deployed without cause. **ABS:** Standard 2W; optional 4W. **Head restraints F/R:** *1997:* ★; *1999:* ★★/★; *2001:* ★★★/★★; *2002–03:* ★★/★; *2004–06 without integrated seat belts:* ★★; *with integrated seat belts:* ★. *1999 and 2001 F-250:* ★★; *2002–04 F-250:* ★★★/★; *2002–04. F-350:* ★★★. Lack of rear-seat head restraints on early production 2001 models. **Visibility F/R:** ★★★★★. **Maximum load capacity:** *1999 F-150 XLT 5.4L:* 1,290 lb.

SAFETY COMPLAINTS: All years: Tie-rod and front torsion-bar failures send the truck out of control. • Sudden acceleration. • Sticking accelerator pedal. • Chronic stalling. • Airbag malfunctions. • Wheel lug nut failures. • Firestone and Goodrich tire tread separation. **1999**—Cruise control fails to disengage. • Brakes fail. • Engine gasket failures. • Broken spare tire cable lets tire fall on highway. • Driver-side door cracks just above window line (dealer replaced door). • Horn difficult to activate because of the small area that must be depressed. • Rear side window leaks. **2000**—Other incidents of sudden, unintended acceleration in a variety of situations. • Chronic stalling. • Driver's face was burned when airbags deployed and gases caught on fire. • Steering loss because of shearing of the sector shaft. • Loss of brakes caused by prematurely worn calipers and pads. • Truck parked with emergency brake set rolled down incline. • Transmission torque converter may lock up without warning. • Halogen lights look like high beams to other drivers. • Metal cable broke, allowing spare tire to fall on the highway. • Left rear tire flew off truck. • Radio heats up to the point where tapes can melt. • Windows suddenly shatter for no reason. **2001**—An incredible number of complaints have been registered by NHTSA. Owners cite most of the aforementioned defects plus a host of new safety-related failures. • A golf cart bumped the truck while it was parked, and the truck rolled about 4.5 metres. • Suspension is not strong enough for the rated towing capacity. • On early production 2001s, the rear seat doesn't have head restraints, allowing passenger's head to hit the back window. • Frequent automatic transmission failures. • Driver's seat belt buckle won't fasten. • Sudden brake loss. • While parked on an incline, truck rolled away. **2001–02**—High seats positioned so that driver stares into the coloured top part of the windshield, and inside rearview mirror blocks forward visibility. **2002**—Fire ignited under the power-adjusted seat mechanism. • Automatic transmission slips in Reverse or downshifts; jerks when vehicle accelerates. • Headlights and dash lights fail intermittently. • Small wheel hubs cause vehicle to vibrate excessively. • Water leaks into the interior. • Speedometer often falls to zero. • Side window suddenly shattered while underway. **2003**—Faulty EGR valve causes throttle to stick wide open and brakes to fail. • Automatic transmission slippage and leakage. • Rear axle failure; wheel came off. • Left front wheel separated, and truck ran into a wall. • Sudden tire-tread separation. • Brake failure as pedal went to the floor. • Harley Truck Club (*www.nhtoc.com*) owners report that rubber strips on stainless steel gas pedals peel off, making the pedal too slippery. • Fuel-tank leakage. • Driver's seat belt fails to lock up. **2004**—133 complaints have been logged by NHTSA; normally, one would find a couple of dozen. • Transmission slips. • Driving with rear window open makes the cabin vibrate violently. • Steering vibration (shimmy, "nibble") and rear end shudder at highway speeds:

> 2004 Ford F-150 has extremely high amount of vibration. Vibration is felt throughout the entire operating range in the cab of the vehicle from the floorboard to the roof. The vibration is so bad that it will literally put your feet to sleep after about fifteen minutes and your hands begin to go numb after about thirty minutes. The truck has been in the dealership on four occasions for repairs and nothing they have done has helped the problem in the least amount.

• Painful, high-pitched noise comes from the dash area. • Tire chains cannot be used. • Tailgate fell off. • Wiper leaves a 15 cm (6 in.) blind spot near the driver's side pillar. **2005**—Many complaints of sudden, unintended acceleration with complete loss of braking capability. • Airbags continue to fail when needed:

> In auto accident at a high rate of speed, around 45 mph [70 km/h]. Hit truck and the airbags failed to deploy. The impact was so hard I split the other truck in half. I broke my neck in two places.

• When parked, vehicle slipped out of gear and went into Reverse. • Excessive vibration at moderate speeds:

> Excessive frame/tire "wobble" with my 2005 Ford F150 4X4. Vibration at 50–70 mph [80–110 km/h]. Brake pads and rotors overheating, causing warped rotors then increasing vibration with possible "death wobble." Tested three 2005 F150 trucks with service manager who confirmed and later backtracked with: "Ford 2005 F150 trucks wobble, and it's normal..."

• Brake pedal went to the floor without braking; master cylinder was found to be defective. • Tailgate fell off. • Tire-tread separation. • Tire jack won't raise truck high enough to allow the mounting of a fully inflated spare. • Faulty ignition keys. • Leaking sunroof. *F-250:* Sudden, unintended acceleration. • Faulty diesel engine fuel injectors and exhaust system cause sickening exhaust fumes to enter the cabin:

> Diesel fumes came out of passenger air vents making myself nauseous and sick from CO_2 poisoning. Brought it in to the Ford dealer and service manager smelled the problem, said that there might be a problem with the Y-flange on exhaust manifold. Called back and pulled manifold and didn't see a problem was going to order a new one. Says not an uncommon problem.

• When the diesel engine is turned off for refuelling, it cannot be restarted. • Engine blew because of a faulty camshaft fuse. • Frequent fuel-pump failures. • Truck will not shift down automatically when carrying a load. • On the highway, the truck vibrates excessively and sways uncontrollably. • Tire-tread separation. *F-350:* Diesel exhaust fumes still enter into the cabin, making occupants sick, dizzy, and light-headed. • Long delay when accelerating. • Converter/transmission snap ring and solenoid failures. • Multiple brake failures. • When towing a trailer, the brakes don't work at low speeds (10–15 km/h). • Defective brake booster and engine oil pump. • Weak coil springs won't support a plow. • Side windows are easily scratched.

Secret Warranties/Internal Bulletins/Service Tips

1980–97—Bulletin #97-3-10 is an extensive guide to troubleshooting popping or creaking noises coming from the front frame or suspension brackets. **1993–2002**—Paint delamination, peeling, or fading. **1995–99**—Countermeasures to correct vibration, noise, and a harsh ride are all listed in TSB #99-11-1. **1997–99**—If you have a hard time removing the key from the ignition, you may have a misaligned shift-column shaft bushing. • A moaning noise coming from the front differential while in 4×2 mode may be fixed by replacing the front differential side and pinion gears with revised gears. • The source of an annoying whistle from the dash may be an air leak at an instrument panel grommet. • If the rear brake drum grabs when cold, install Ford's revised rear brake drum shoe kit. **1997–2000**—Ford will provide a free inner fender shield to protect the fender from rocks thrown up by the tires. • Free "goodwill" repairs for door cracks (TSB #01-18-2; Date: September 17, 2001). **1997–2002**—High idle speeds; throttle sticks in cold weather (see bulletin). **1997–2004**—Tips for correcting a rough idle. **1997–2005**—Ford will install a special axle kit to stop rear axle noise. Ford's bulletin admission of this defect is actionable in small claims court if Ford won't pay for the 6-hour repair (see bulletin). **1997–2006**—A driveline clunk may signal that the slip yoke needs lubrication. Check this out first, before spending big bucks for more involved tests

IDLE—HIGH IDLE SPEEDS—THROTTLE STICKS AFTER STEADY STATE DRIVING IN EXTREME COLD AMBIENT TEMPERATURES—VEHICLES BUILT THROUGH 11/01/01 EQUIPPED WITH 5.4L ENGINE

ENGINE—5.4L—PCV SYSTEM ICING—VEHICLES BUILT THROUGH 11/01/01

FORD: 1997–98 EXPEDITION, F-150, F-250 LD

2000–02 EXPEDITION, F-150

LINCOLN: 1998 NAVIGATOR

This article is being republished in its entirety to update the Model Year and vehicle applications and the Service Kit part number.

ISSUE: In rare instances, throttle sticking may occur on a few vehicles in very cold ambient temperatures after operating at steady speed or extended idle for a period of time. This may be due to ice build-up in the PCV gas on the throttle plate or throttle body.

or repairs. **1998**—An automatic transmission ticking noise on initial start-up may be caused by the Overdrive clutch steel separator plates rubbing against the case internal spline. **1999**—Door locks that lock and unlock on their own need to have the GEM module serviced. **1999–2000** Install a new clutch pack kit if the rear axle chatters when turning or cornering. **1999–2001**—Ford will repair or replace 5.4L engines with faulty head gaskets. The April 1, 2002, edition of *Automotive News* says that the automaker allocated about $5,300 (U.S.) to replace the engine and cylinder heads/head gasket on each afflicted vehicle. **1999–2004**—Troubleshooting broken intake manifold studs. **1999–2005**—Water leaks from the roof flange area and accumulates in the headliner, or the leak may occur at the cab floor pan area. • Drivetrain drive-away shudder or vibration. **1999–2006**—Vehicle sags to one side. **2000**—Replace the intake manifold gasket and ask that "goodwill" cover the cost. **2001**—Automatic

REAR AXLE WHINE OR HUM

BULLETIN NO.: 05-6-18   DATE: APRIL 4, 2005

1997–2005 Expedition, F-150

2002–2005 Explorer

1998–2005 Navigator

2003–2005 Aviator

2002–2005 Mountaineer

ISSUE: Some vehicles may exhibit an axle whine or hum during acceleration, deceleration, and/or cruise.

ACTION: An axle repair kit has been developed, which incorporates most parts required for a comprehensive axle repair. The kit should be used instead of installing a complete axle assembly to repair an axle whine/hum.

transmission clunk when shifting from Second to First gear. • Erratic 4×4 shifting; vehicle sticks in Fourth gear. • High-speed driveline vibration may damage drivetrain. • No-starts. • Tie-rod end squeaking. **2000–05**—Seat belts slow to retract. **2002**—Throttle may stick in cold weather. • Engine power loss in hot weather. • 4.6L engines may have a higher-than-normal idle speed. • Repaired aluminum engine heads may continue to leak coolant or oil. • Vacuum or air leaks in the intake manifold and engine. • Heater core leaks. • Faulty ignition switch lock cylinder. • Excessive front suspension noise when turning or shifting into Reverse. • A clunk may be heard when parking. **2003–05**—Remedy for false parking-aid warnings. **2003–06**—Inoperative AC; compressor leakage. **2004**—Faulty handle cables could make it impossible to open the doors from the inside. • Steering-wheel vibration at 97 km/h (60 mph) or higher may require replacing the steering gear. **2004–05**—Remedy for warm engine knocking or ticking. • Correction of axle chatter, shudder, or vibration during low-speed turning manoeuvres. • Remedies for steering-wheel and body vibrations. • Upgraded brake rotors will be installed to stop brake shudder and vibration. • Cooling fan noise on trucks equipped with 4.6L and 5.4L engines. • Free butyl bed pad removal to prevent corrosion. **2005**—Engine won't crank, hard starts, or runs rough. • Cooling system overheats when using a snowplow; an extra-cost clutch fan must be purchased from Ford (offer to pay only half the cost). • Ford will replace for free faulty transmission snap rings and CD players. • Excessive steering-wheel shimmy after passing over bumps. • Steering moan, groan • Loose roof ditch moldings. *Diesels:* **2003–04**—Remedies for 6.0L diesel engines that have fuel in oil, lose power, or run roughly are covered in TSB #03-14-6 and the following bulletin:

DIESEL ENGINE DRIVEABILITY CONCERNS

BULLETIN NO.: 03-20-12   DATE: OCTOBER 13, 2003

2003–04 EXCURSION, F SUPER DUTY

Some vehicles may exhibit various driveability conditions listed below:

- Rough/Rolling Idle When The Engine Is Warm
- Rough/Rolling Idle And White Smoke After Hot Restart
- Lacks Power After Initial Start-Up
- Cold Idle kicker Performance At Warm Ambient Temps
- U0306 Codes After Reprogramming
- P2263 Code Set During Extended Idle
- False P0196 Codes

ACTION: Reprogram the PCM/TCM/FICM modules to the latest calibration level (B27.9) or later. This calibration should only be installed on customer vehicles that exhibit one of the conditions addressed above.

2003–05—Troubleshooting tips for misfire, lack of power, excessive smoke, and excessive cranking to start. Keep in mind that Ford *must* pay for this troubleshooting and repair under the much longer Emissions Warranty. Don't take no for an answer (see bulletin). **2003–06**—TSB #06-9-7, issued May 15, 2006, gives more diagnostic and repair tips for poorly performing diesel engines. **2005**—Engine stalls when shifting into Drive or Reverse, or when coming to a stop. **2005–06**—Inadvertent transmission lock-up during 1–2 shifts.

2003–2005 Excursion, F-Super Duty; 2004–2005 E-Series, F-650, F-750

ISSUE: Some 6.0L vehicles may exhibit a misfire, lack of power, buck/jerk, excessive smoke, or crank/no-start. There are several potential causes for these symptoms, including injector concerns.

ACTION: If normal diagnostics lead to an injector concern, use the following diagnostics to confirm the cause of injector failure and/or to rule out other conditions which may cause the same symptoms as a failed injector.

LOW OR NEGATIVE FUEL PRESSURE

Internal injector damage can be caused by lack of fuel system supply pressure. Restricted fuel filters and/or fuel line(s), or an inoperative fuel pump can create a low or negative fuel supply pressure. Low or negative pressures may hinder the return stroke of the injector intensifier plunger to its rest position, leading to internal injector damage. To diagnose for low or negative fuel pressure and to confirm if any injectors have been damaged:

1. Perform standard diagnostic procedures, including verification of supply fuel pressure while the symptom is evident.
2. Repair causes for low pressure on the supply side of the fuel system.
3. Diagnose for failed injector(s) only after rectifying fuel supply pressure.

COMBUSTION GAS ENTERING THE FUEL SYSTEM

1. Remove outlet fuel lines from the fuel filter housing on top of engine.
2. Install a balloon over each fuel line with a zip tie.
3. Disable the fuel pump and FICM relays.
4. Crank engine and watch for compression pulses in the balloon.
5. For each line where compression pulses are evident, remove all but one of the glow plugs from the affected cylinder head(s).
6. Crank engine and watch again for compression pulses.
7. Remove the glow plug and transfer it to the next cylinder in the head and repeat Step 6.
8. For each cylinder where compression pulses are evident remove injector(s) and inspect copper gasket and lower O-ring, replace if necessary. If gasket(s) and O-ring(s) are OK, replace injector(s). Retest to confirm repair.

ERRATIC HIGH PRESSURE OIL SUPPLY

Erratic supply of high pressure oil to injectors may cause a rough running engine. High pressure oil flow can be disrupted by faulty check valve(s) or a faulty IPR valve.

To diagnose, first perform a slow neutral run up in park/neutral. If the engine runs rough between 1200 and 1900 RPM proceed to Check Valve Diagnosis; if the engine runs rough between 3000 and 4000 RPM replace the IPR valve.

CHECK VALVE DIAGNOSIS

1. To isolate the bank with the faulty check valve, disconnect all of the injector electrical connectors on one bank.
2. Perform a Power Balance test. Engine misfires should be constant on the four disconnected cylinders and the operational cylinders should be contributing evenly.
3. Repeat steps 1 and 2 on the opposite bank.
4. If the operating contribution is erratic on one bank, replace the check valve on that bank.

WARRANTY STATUS: Eligible under provisions of New Vehicle Limited Warranty Coverage and Emissions Warranty Coverage

F-SERIES PROFILE

	1998	1999	2000	2001	2002	2003	2004	2005	2006
Cost Price ($) (negotiable)									
XL (20%)	23,195	22,995	22,295	22,710	23,310	23,380	22,850	23,840	22,499
Used Values ($)									
XL ▲	5,000	5,500	7,000	9,500	11,500	13,500	16,500	18,000	—
XL ▼	4,500	5,000	6,000	8,500	10,000	12,500	15,000	16,500	—
Reliability	2	2	2	2	2	2	2	3	—
Crash Safety (F)	5	4	4	5	5	—	5	5	5
Side	—	5	5	5	5	5	—	—	—
Ext. cab	—	—	—	4	4	4	—	—	—
Side	—	—	5	5	5	5	—	—	—
SuperCrew	—	—	—	—	5	5	—	—	—
Offset	1	1	1	1	1	1	5	5	5
Rollover	—	—	—	—	—	3	4	4	4
4X4	—	—	—	—	—	2	—	—	—

Ford/Mazda

RANGER/B-SERIES ★★★★

2007 TECHNICAL DATA

POWERTRAIN (4X2/PART-TIME 4X4)
Engines: 2.3L 4-cyl. (143 hp) • 3.0L V6 (154 hp) • 4.0L V6 (207 hp);
Transmissions: 5-speed man. • 5-speed auto. OD

DIMENSION/CAPACITY (REG. CAB 4X2/4X4)
Passengers: 3/2; Wheelbase: 126 in.; H: 64.1/L: 202/W: 70 in.; Headroom F/R: N/A; Legroom F/R: 42.4/35.1 in.; Cargo volume: N/A; Fuel tank: 64L/79L/regular; Tow limit: 3,180–6,070 lb.; Load capacity: 1,250–1,650 lb.; GVWR: 4,700/5,100 lb.; Turning circle: 45 ft.; Box length: 6/7 ft.; Ground clearance: 6.1/7.2 in.; Weight: 3,870 lb.

RATING: Above Average (2003–07); Average (1984–2002). Mazda pickups are generally the least expensive of the "gang of three" small Japanese pickups (Mazda, Nissan, and Toyota). Actually, from the 1994 model onward, your Mazda is really a Ford Ranger. Overall, they're acceptable, but performance-wise they are only mediocre. Powertrain defects are worrisome. **Strong points:** Good engine performance (4.0L V6), well-designed interior, comfortable seating, classy interior trim, user-friendly control layout, four-door extended cab, good off-road handling, and good resale value. **Weak points:** Weak 4-cylinder engine (carried over into early 2001), barely adequate 3.0L V6, harsh ride, excessive braking distance, 4×4's

All ratings on a numbered scale where 5 is good and 1 is bad. See page 220 for a more detailed description.

extra height hinders easy entry and exit, rear doors are hinged at the back and won't open independently of the front doors, spare tire is difficult to remove, and many safety-related complaints reported to NHTSA. **New for 2007:** Nothing important until the arrival of redesigned 2010 models.

MODEL HISTORY: Base Rangers come with a SuperCab option, there is 4×2 and part-time 4×4 versatility, and flare-side models are available with XL and XLT models. Mazdas follow the same program, shared among three badges, the B2500, B3000, and B4000, which are indicative of each model's engine size.

Properly equipped, these vehicles almost match the versatility of a full-sized pickup. Since the 4-cylinder engine is unsuitable for anything but the lightest chores, the larger V6 is the preferred engine choice. Its additional torque can better handle serious towing and off-roading, and fuel economy is practically the same as with the smaller V6. An electric shift transfer case and shift-on-the-fly controls are standard on 4×4 models. The upscale trim level should appeal to buyers who want to combine reliability with a more sedan-like interior.

Since 1994, the Ranger and its Mazda B-series twin have changed little. The 1995 models got a standard driver's airbag, a small horsepower boost, and four-wheel anti-lock brakes. The following year's models were the first in the industry to install an optional passenger-side airbag with a shut-off switch. The 1997 models were given an optional upgraded 5-speed automatic transmission.

Extensively redesigned for the '98 model year, these small pickups got more powerful, torquier engines, an upgraded standard 5-speed automatic, shift-on-the-fly 4×4, and 4×2s with standard power steering. Other '98 improvements included a stiffer frame, an upgraded front suspension, more precise power steering, 8 cm (3 in.) more of cab space, and a mild exterior restyling with a lower hood line, new grille and headlights, a larger rear window, and 16-inch wheels.

1999—Ranger and B-series returned unchanged, except for the SuperCab's fourth door, while the following year's models got torsion bar suspension and a larger wheel/tire package for the 4×2. **2001**—Models got the Explorer's 207-hp 4.0L SOHC V6; the flexible-fuel feature on the 3.0L V6 was dropped; and a new base 2.3L 4-cylinder replaced the 2.5L. ABS became a standard feature. **2002**—Models were joined by an XLT FX4 off-road 4×4 model, heavy-duty suspension, 31-inch tires, a heftier skid plate, and tow hooks. **2003**—The extension of Quadrasteer to other models and an improved electrical system and passenger-side airbag sensors.

COST ANALYSIS: The base 2007 Ranger sells for $18,499, or $200 more than last year's model; an equivalent Mazda is priced at $18,195, also $200 more than the 2006 model. **Best alternatives:** The Nissan Frontier and Toyota Tacoma are two other pickups worth considering. **Options:** The 4.0L V6, four-wheel ABS, running boards, transmission/oil cooler, remote keyless entry/anti-theft system, upgraded sound system, and power windows and door locks. Dealers are using Firestone space-saver tires as spares; ask for regular-sized tires from a different manufacturer. Stay away from the weak 2.5L 4-cylinder engine. **Rebates:** $2,000 rebates and low financing rates on all model years. **Delivery/PDI:** *Ford:* $1,150; *Mazda:* $1,390. **Depreciation:** Much slower than average. **Insurance cost:** Average. **Annual maintenance cost:** Below average. **Parts supply/cost:** Excellent supply and relatively inexpensive from independent suppliers. **Warranty:** Bumper-to-bumper 3 years/60,000 km; rust perforation 5 years/unlimited km. **Supplementary warranty:** A good idea, judging by recent owner complaints. **Highway/city fuel economy:** *4×2 and 2.5L:* 8.8/11.7 L/100 km; *4×2 and 3.0L:* 9.4/14.0 L/100 km; *4×2 and 4.0L:* 9.7/13.9 L/100 km; *4×4 and 3.0L:* 10.6/14.8 L/100 km; *4×4 and 4.0L:* 10.9/14.7 L/100 km. Owners report fuel consumption is often way higher than these averages.

QUALITY/RELIABILITY: Assembly and component quality are below average. Reliability isn't impressive. Owners note serious engine problems (poor idle, surge, and stalling), erratic transmission performance and failure, brake and fuel system issues, and breakdowns. **Warranty performance:** Below average with Ford; average with Mazda staffers. **Owner-reported problems:** Extremely poor gas mileage; 3.0L engines may have a spark knock (ping) under acceleration; the camshaft may have been incorrectly heat-treated; Flex-Fuel engines may experience a hard start or no-start; 4.0L engines may have excessive oil consumption and surging, clogged, or plugged fuel injectors; transmission fluid leak from the transmission extension housing; oil leak from the rear seal of the transmission extension housing; no 4×4 Low range, or gets stuck in Low range; oil leak from the front-axle pinion oil seal area; manual transmission clutch squawks on takeoff; manual-transmission-equipped 3.0L vehicles may maintain a too-high engine idle when decelerating; automatic transmission fluid leaks at radiator; manual transmission buzzing, grinding noise during 2–3 upshift; steering vibration at idle or at low speeds; wind noise from the windshield cowl, top-of-door glass seal, or the weather stripping moulding area; water leaks through rear window, likely caused by the seat pushing up against the glass; poor AC performance; faulty dome and Door Ajar lights; front wipers operate when switch is set to Off; clutch squawking noise; chucking, squeaking noise from rear doors; rear-end sag; side mirrors flutter or shake at highway speeds; and premature paint peeling and delamination.

SAFETY SUMMARY: The 2007 Ranger and B-series scored five stars for both frontal and side crash protection, three stars for front-drive rollover protection, and two stars for 4×4 rollover protection. ABS is standard on rear wheels only, making for less-than-impressive braking with the 1997 version. **Airbags:** There have been reports of airbags failing to deploy, or deploying when they shouldn't, resulting in severe injuries. **ABS:** Standard 2W; disc/drum. **Safety belt pretensioners:** Standard. **Head restraints F/R:** *Ranger 1997–98:* ★★/★; *1999:* ★★; *2001–03:* ★★/★;

2004–5: ★★★★★; *2006:* ★. *B-series: 1997:* ★★/★; *1999–2003:* ★; *2004–5:* ★★★★★; *2006:* ★.

> Rear passenger safety restraints are not adequate to prevent injury of passengers. Passengers bump their heads on rear window if driver must brake quickly or accelerate rapidly.

Visibility F/R: ★★★★★; *2004–05:* ★★★★★/★. **Maximum load capacity:** *1998 Ranger XLT 4.0L:* 1,210 lb.

SAFETY COMPLAINTS: All years: Ford Ranger and Mazda B-series passengers slam their heads into the back glass during sudden stops or in rear-end collisions. • Steering-wheel lock-up. • Excessive shaking when cruising. • Malfunctioning airbags and burns caused by airbag deployment. • Defective tie-rod. • When parked on an incline with shifter lever in Park, vehicle jumps into Neutral and rolls away. • Transmission failures:

> I suffered a complete transmission failure and was forced to limp into a local Ford truck sales place. The failure occurred without any advance warning and left me limping along at 35–40 mph [55–65 km/h] on the I-90 thruway during rush hour, with heavy traffic travelling 65–70 mph [105–115 km/h]. I had totally lost Reverse gear and had substantial slippage occurring in forward gears.

> Ford tech consultants revealed that this is happening to many Ford Rangers, but no recall has been issued. Apparently, the torque on the transmission was increased without redesigning the transmission or seals to be able to withstand the higher torque.

• Drive shaft sheared off while driving at high speed. • Fuel leaks (tank and fuel lines). • Sudden acceleration, often when braking. • A faulty idle air control valve may be responsible for the vehicle not decelerating properly. • Stalling. • Complete loss of ABS. • Gas and brake pedals are too close together. • Brakes don't work properly, with stuck brake calipers, overheating, and excessive pad and rotor wear. • Windshield wiper comes on by itself, or won't come on at all. • Tire-tread separation. *Ranger:* **1999**—Airbag-induced injuries. • Jerks to the side when braking or accelerating. • Chronic window fogging. **2000**—Left front wheel flew off vehicle. **2001**—Excessive wander on the highway, especially bad when passing over uneven terrain or after hitting potholes. • Inaccurate fuel-tank level indicator and fuel gauge. • Fuel tank overflows when refuelling. • Faulty engine computer causes hard starts. • Brake line abraded by rubbing against leaf spring. • Excessive vibration called "harmonic imbalance" by dealer. • Passenger-side seat belt unbuckles at random. **2002**—A large number of serious safety-related incidents have been reported. • Sudden acceleration after vehicle jumps from Park into gear. • Premature replacement of clutch slave cylinder. • Complete brake failure because of a defective idle control, among other causes. • Rear shock absorbers quickly wear out. • Front tire fell off because of defective carter pin. • Interior and exterior lights go out intermittently. **2003**—Throttle sticks as pedal sinks to the floor. • Misaligned driver-side door allows wind and water entry. **2004**—Chronic stalling, loss of power. • Stuck accelerator. • Airbags failed to deploy. • Vehicle left in Park with the engine idling shifted into Reverse. • Transmission slippage; slams into gear. • Frequent brake lock-up when brakes are applied. • Premature front tire wear and tread separation on front and rear tires. • Front seat pushed rearward and window popped out. • High rear head restraints block side and rear visibility. • Odometer can't be seen in daylight. **2005**—Vehicle stalls on the highway repeatedly because of a defective inertia switch. • Ford assembly-line worker says the Ranger rear axle sway bar is mounted incorrectly and designed poorly. • Seatbacks hamper rear visibility.

Secret Warranties/Internal Bulletins/Service Tips

Keep in mind that Ford service bulletins will likely also apply to Mazda. *Ranger:* **1988–97**—Repeat heater core failures. **1989–99**—Poor radio reception, including whining and buzzing, may be caused by a faulty fuel pump. Install an RFI filter on the in-tank pump. **1993–99**—A buzzing or rattling noise coming from underneath the vehicle indicates the need to secure the heat shield. • A pinging or creaking driveline noise on 4×4-equipped vehicles may be silenced by replacing the transfer case rear output flange, says TSB #99-16-1. **1993–2002**—Paint delamination, peeling, or fading. • Loud AC clutch cycling. **1995–2000**—Temperature gauge fluctuation or a knocking or thumping noise coming from the engine compartment may be fixed by installing a coolant bypass kit. **1995–2002**—Automatic transmission slips or has a delayed engagement. **1997–2003**—Front-drive axle vent tube leaks. **1998–99**—An acceleration or deceleration thump or bump may be corrected by installing a revised drive shaft. • Hard starts and poor engine performance can both be traced to a chafed wire harness, says Ford TSB #00-5-4. **1999**—If the automatic transmission slips, is slow to shift, or won't shift, replace the EPC solenoid and bracket. • Water leaks through doors on four-door models. **1998–2000**—Excessive clutch noise on vehicles equipped with manual transmissions may require a new clutch disc and revised pressure plate assembly. *B-series:* **All years:** TSB #006/94 outlines all the possible causes and remedies for brake vibration or pulsation. **1994–99**—Heat shield rattling can be prevented by installing four worm clamps. **1995–98**—A chattering noise heard when lowering the power windows can be silenced by installing a redesigned glass guide bracket assembly. **1995–2003**—Incorrectly installed camshaft position (CMP) sensor synchronizer assemblies may cause loss of power, engine surge, hesitation, and rough acceleration. **1997–2005**—Front axle leaks (see bulletin). **1998–99**—Hard starts and poor engine performance can both be traced to a chafed wire harness, a problem shared with Ford Rangers. **1998–2000**—Noisy manual transmission shifting is addressed in TSB #003/00. **1998–2003**—Wind noise around doors. • Seat track rattling. **1998–2005**—Driveline clunk remedy. **2000–03**—Persistent rotten-egg sulfur smell invades the cabin. **2001**—Unable to reach wide open

FRONT DRIVE AXLE VENT TUBE LEAKS

BULLETIN NO.: 03-5-8

DATE: MARCH 17, 2003

1995–2001 EXPLORER
1997–2003 RANGER
2001–03 EXPLORER SPORT TRAC; EXPLORER SPORT
1997–2001 MOUNTAINEER

Article 02-4-2 is being republished in its entirety to update the model year applications.

ISSUE: Fluid may leak out of the front axle vent tube after being thrown toward the axle vent by the gears during vehicle operation.

ACTION: Replace the axle cover and install the Axle Cover kit (F6TZ-4033-BA).

throttle, lack of power. • 3.0L engine leaks oil at the oil filter mounting surface. • Vacuum or air leaks in the intake manifold. • 4.0L engine may lose power or have a low idle when first started. • Clutch may be hard to disengage. • Front axle squeal or whistle. • 4×4 SuperCab models may have a drive shaft thump and vibration when accelerating or stopping. • Inaccurate fuel gauge. • Front end may produce a squeal or whistle. • Delayed Reverse engagement. • Condensation leads to early fog lamp failure. • Heater core leaks. • Faulty speedometer. **2001–03—** Transmission whine on vehicles with the 4.0L engine:

1ST/2ND GEAR WHINING NOISE

BULLETIN NO.: 02-22-2

DATE: NOVEMBER 11, 2002

2001–03 EXPLORER SPORT TRAC, EXPLORER SPORT, RANGER

ISSUE: Some vehicles may exhibit a gear whine type of noise in 1st and 2nd gear ONLY. This may be caused by the Reverse and Forward Planetary assemblies and/or the driveshaft.

2002—Check Engine light troubleshooting. • 4.0L engine may produce a spark knock or fluttering noise, or leak oil. • 2.3L engine may idle poorly and surge or hesitate when accelerating. • Automatic transmission fluid leaks. • Manual-transmission-equipped vehicles may lose power when decelerating. • Damaged fuel-return line. • Fluid leaks from the front axle vent tube. • Heater core leaks. • Air leaks or vacuum in the intake manifold or engine. • Faulty ignition switch lock cylinder. • Inaccurate temperature gauge. **2002–03**—Noisy manual transfer-case shifter. **2002–05**—Rear brake "grabbing." **2003–06**—Inoperative AC; compressor leakage. **2004–05**—No Third gear. • Wrong transmission fluid put in originally by Ford may cause harsh, delayed shifts.

	1998	1999	2000	2001	2002	2003	2004	2005	2006
Cost Price ($)									
Base/XL 4X2 (20%)	15,945	15,995	16,395	16,995	18,595	17,395	16,775	17,810	18,299
Base/XL 4X4	20,245	20,295	21,395	24,675	23,715	24,495	—	—	—
Used Values ($)									
Base/XL 4X2 ▲	3,500	4,000	5,000	6,000	7,500	8,500	10,000	12,000	—
Base/XL 4X2 ▼	3,000	3,500	4,500	5,500	6,500	8,000	9,000	10,500	—
Base/XL 4X4 ▲	5,000	6,000	7,500	8,500	9,500	11,000	—	—	—
Base/XL 4X4 ▼	4,500	5,500	6,500	8,000	9,000	10,000	—	—	—
Reliability	③	③	③	③	③	③	③	④	—
Crash Safety (F)	④	④	④	—	④	④	④	④	④
Ext. cab	—	—	④	④	④	④	④	④	④
Side	—	⑤	⑤	⑤	⑤	⑤	⑤	⑤	⑤
Ext. cab	—	—	④	④	④	④	④	④	④
Offset	③	③	③	③	③	③	③	③	③
Rollover (4X2)	—	—	—	—	—	③	—	③	③
4X4	—	—	—	—	—	②	—	—	—
Ext. cab (4X2)	—	—	—	—	—	③	—	③	③
Ext. cab (4X4)	—	—	—	—	—	③	—	—	—

General Motors

AVALANCHE ★★★

RATING: Average (2007); Below Average (2002–06). **Strong points:** A Suburban clone; drives much like the similarly equipped Suburban and Silverado/Sierra; plenty of passenger and cargo room; a relatively high towing limit achieved through a variety of V8 engines; a smooth powertrain (with some exceptions); and plenty of standard amenities. The 2004 and later models' hydroboost brake feature enhances brake feel, but no word as to whether the poor durability problem has been addressed. Four doors provide easy access for six occupants who are given plenty of headroom and legroom. "Midgate" panel adds to the pickup's practicality. Angular styling similar to the Cadillac Escalade and Pontiac Aztek gives the Avalanche an aggressive stance. Other positives are a high ground clearance and a comfortable, quiet ride. **Weak points:** Excess weight cripples performance and fuel economy, premature brake wear, suspension and steering vibrations, numb steering even after the 2007 redesign, and powertrain deficiencies similar to those afflicting the Suburban and Silverado. The cabin, although improved this year, still has thinly padded armrests and an abundance of hard plastic interior trim. Front

All ratings on a numbered scale where ⑤ is good and ❶ is bad. See page 220 for a more detailed description.

2007 TECHNICAL DATA

POWERTRAIN (4X2/4X4)

Engines: 5.3L V8 (310 hp) • 5.3L V8 (320 hp) • 6.0L V8 (355 hp); Transmission: 4-speed auto.

DIMENSION/CAPACITY

Passengers: 3/3; Wheelbase: 130 in.; H: 77/L: 221/W: 79 in.; Headroom F/R: 4.0/4.0 in.; Legroom F/R: 41.5/29 in.; Cargo volume: 53.9 in; Fuel tank: 117–142L/regular; Tow limit: 7,800–8,000 lb.; Load capacity: 1,355 lb.; GVWR: 6,800–8,600 lb.; Turning circle: 43 ft.; Box length: 5.3–8.1 ft.; Ground clearance: 9.1 in.; Weight: 5,810 lb.

and rear visibility is not reassuring for parking or merging with traffic. The 4-speed automatic transmission is inadequate; it kicks in as early as 70 km/h, and you have to stomp on the accelerator to get it to kick down when passing other vehicles. Noisy Bridgestone tires. **New for 2007:** Still a Suburban with a cargo bed, this year's redesigned model gets an all-new platform, interior, and look also found on GM's 2007 Tahoe and Suburban. A fuel-saving Active Fuel Management feature is standard, and a 6.0L V8 with variable valve timing and the same Active Fuel Management joins the lineup early in 2007. Both engines run on regular fuel; however, the 5.3L can also run on E85 (85 percent ethanol and 15 percent gasoline). GM's stability-control system with new anti-rollover technology is standard, while head-protection side curtain airbags are optional. The bed is 5 cm (2 in.) longer.

MODEL HISTORY: Sharing 85 percent of its parts with the Suburban, the Avalanche is a full-sized crew-cab pickup with a unique bed and cab design and performance features that make it one of the most versatile and powerful sport-utility/truck crossovers you can find. But it looks like a gimmicky "what's that?" kind of vehicle not seen since the El Camino sedan-*cum*-pickup or the weirdly styled Aztek. Carrying a base 5.3L V8 engine mated to a rear-drive/4×4 4-speed automatic powertrain, the Avalanche nevertheless comes loaded with potential. For example, its Convert-a-Cab feature allows you to fold the rear passenger seat/midgate and extend the standard bed by about 86 cm (34 in.), giving the bed an impressive 2.5 m (8′1″) length. Or you can remove the rear window, fold the midgate, and get an open-air feel. The Avalanche won't win any fuel economy or retained-value prizes, and its price and factory-related deficiencies will discourage all but the most daring. Best advice: Don't look for a Swiss Army knife SUV; determine your most basic requirements and buy a simpler, less costly, and less gimmicky pickup. **2003**—A redesigned dash; optional power-adjustable brake and accelerator pedals; and standard front side airbags become optional. **2004**—Optional anti-skid control. **2005**—Standard OnStar assistance.

COST ANALYSIS: The base 2007 Avalanche sells for $38,985, or about $1,400 less than last year's model, and is the best choice, considering its many improvements. **Best alternatives:** The Dodge Ram Quad Cab, Honda Ridgeline, Nissan Frontier, and Toyota Tacoma are other pickups worth considering. **Options:** Consider head-protecting side-impact curtain airbags, electric adjustable pedals, AC, and an engine block heater. Ditch the Bridgestone AL2 all-season tires—they lack sufficient grip and are noisy, as well. **Rebates:** $5,000 rebates and low financing rates on all model years. **Delivery/PDI:** $1,250. **Depreciation:** Faster than average. **Insurance cost:** Higher than average. **Annual maintenance cost:** Average. **Parts supply/cost:** Excellent supply, and relatively inexpensive from independent suppliers. **Warranty:** Bumper-to-bumper 3 years/60,000 km; powertrain 5 years/160,000 km; rust perforation 5 years/unlimited km. **Supplementary warranty:** A good idea, judging by owner complaints relative to powertrain failures. **Highway/city fuel economy:** 12.0/16.2 L/100 km. Owners say they get much worse fuel economy than what the government's and automaker's figures predict.

QUALITY/RELIABILITY: Poor quality mechanical and body components impair the Avalanche's overall reliability. Major problem areas are engine malfunctions, automatic transmission failures and subpar performance, and brake/fuel system breakdowns. **Owner-reported problems:** Faulty engine, transmission (clunky, grinding noise when accelerating, and glitch-prone), steering, seat belts, and airbags; early brake pad and rotor replacement. Constant AC humming and vibration, and the steering assembly produces a "popping" noise when turning. Premature paint peeling and delamination. Water leaks into the bed area and through the midgate:

> Water enters the cab through the mid gate, causing the carpet and matting to become soaked with water to the point that water pools on top of the carpet. This more than likely will result in the immediate rusting of the floor and possible growing of mold in the constantly wet carpet and matting.... Dealership has replaced...seals on several location[s as] well as added additional silicone, although no attempt at repair[s] have been successful in slowing down or stopping the water leak.

Owners also mention that pad/rotor problems cause excessive vibration when braking and that components frequently overheat. Extremely poor real-world gas mileage. **Warranty performance:** Unsatisfactory.

SAFETY SUMMARY: The 2007 models earned a three-star rollover rating; no other crash tests have been undertaken. **Airbags:** Standard front airbags; optional side curtain airbags. **ABS:** Standard 4W; disc/disc. The redesigned 2007 ABS brakes work flawlessly. **Safety belt pretensioners:** Standard. **Head restraints F/R:** N/A. Rear head restraints appear to be useless; no restraint for the rear middle seat. **Visibility F/R:** ★★/★. **Maximum load capacity:** 1,230 lb.

SAFETY COMPLAINTS: All years: Braking is dangerously poor on wet pavement in pre-2007 models. **2004**—Chronic warm-weather stalling. • Exterior light lenses have excessive condensation, which reduces their effectiveness. • Electrical charge passing through cabin may be a health hazard:

The electricity from the automatic control monitor that controls the air conditioning and temperature control on the roof of the truck was causing the consumer to experience severe headaches and she was no longer able to drive the vehicle with the heat or air on. She had to pull the fuse that controlled the monitor because [after] turning it off the wave of electricity was still flowing. The gauss meter that checked the wave of electricity was flashing red when she held it up to her head. It was not supposed to be like that. The symptoms were: her scalp was real tender and swollen, her left side of shoulder and neck was hurting a lot, and she had to use contacts in her left eye because of vision problems. All of these symptoms were from the automatic control monitor. She has never had any of these symptoms prior to this. Since she unplugged the fuse these symptoms disappeared, and she felt better. Her concern was that other people driving this vehicle may never be able to figure out what caused these problems.

• Too much tire sidewall flex, and an under-sprung suspension cause the back end to kick out dangerously when passing over bumps or expansion joints. • Brakes come on by themselves. • Clunks when turning; GM bought vehicle back after many repairs proved futile. • Tailgate falls down when truck accelerates. • Cracked wheel rims. 2005—Airbags didn't deploy when needed. • Fuel spews out when refuelling. • Truck stalls when turning. • Automatic transmission failed. • Vehicle wanders into oncoming traffic. • Instrument panel "blows out" and shuts down; cost: $600+. • Headlight fell out. • Tires rub on the front fenders. • The GM Passlock anti-theft system can easily be bypassed through a pin hole in the driver-side key tumbler; an aftermarket anti-theft system must be added. • Sudden blowout of a Firestone Wilderness tire.

Secret Warranties/Internal Bulletins/Service Tips

2002–04—Suspension clunk, slap. GM will replace the spring insert and insulator for free (see Silverado "Secret Warranties/Internal Bulletins/Service Tips"). 2002–06—Discoloured cargo covers or body cladding (seen as a chalky colour) will be corrected under a secret warranty. 2003–04—Remedies for an inoperative front power-window and steering-wheel clunk. 2004–06—Automatic transmission shudder due to water intrusion (see Tahoe section).

AVALANCHE PROFILE

	2002	2003	2004	2005	2006
Cost Price ($) (negotiable)					
Avalanche (21%)	37,372	38,135	39,155	39,910	40,400
Used Values ($)					
Avalanche ▲	18,000	20,000	25,000	29,000	—
Avalanche ▼	16,500	18,500	23,500	27,000	—
Reliability	③	③	③	③	—
Crash Safety (F)	③	③	③	③	③
Rollover	②	②	—	③	③

2007 TECHNICAL DATA

POWERTRAIN (REAR-DRIVE/4X4)

Engines: 4.3L V6 (195 hp) • 4.8L V8 (295 hp) • 5.3L V8 (295 hp) • 5.3L V8 (310 hp) • 6.0L V8 (300 hp) • 6.0L V8 (367 hp) • 6.4L TD V8 (320 hp) • 6.6L V8 TD (360 hp) Transmissions: 5-speed man. • 6-speed man. • 4-speed auto. OD • 5-speed auto. OD • 6-speed auto.

DIMENSION/CAPACITY (1500/2500)

Passengers: 3/3; Wheelbase: 144 in.; H: 68/L: 230.7/W: 79 in.; Headroom F/R: 6.5/4.5 in.; Legroom F/R: 42/30 in.; Cargo volume: N/A; Fuel tank: 95–129L/regular/diesel; Tow limit: 7,500–15,900 lb.; Load capacity: 1,655–1,965 lb./2,614–3,334 lb.; GVWR: 6,200 lb./9,200 lb.; Box length: 6.5/8 ft.; Ground clearance: 9.0 in.; Weight: 5,300 lb. (est.)

RATING: Average (2007; 1988–98); Below Average (1999–2006). GM's last redesign in 1998–99 produced mediocre, unreliable haulers. Hopefully it won't make the same mistake with its 2007 models. The new 6.4L diesel engines are expected to have serious performance and quality failings during their first few years on the market, judging by the Duramax's prior performance. **Strong points:** *2007 and later models:* A cylinder deactivation feature that *may* actually cut fuel usage, better handling and a more comfortable ride, and a stylish interior. *All models:* A well appointed, competent optional powertrain for towing and hauling; user-friendly controls for full-time 4×4 system; effective brakes and responsive steering; well laid-out instruments and controls; seats are roomy and supportive; lots of leg clearance; a contoured cushion and a reclined seatback to further enhance comfort; doors open wide and feature useful pull-lever handles; a large cabin; a high ground clearance; good noise insulation; and a rattle-resistant body. **Weak points:** *2007 and later models:* Cylinder deactivation hasn't produced promised fuel savings when used on the 2007 Avalanche and Tahoe. *2006 and earlier models:* The 6.0L Duramax diesel has serious reliability and performance problems. The base 4.3L V6 needs more grunt, transmission hunts for the right gear and produces an incessant whine, base suspension provides a too-compliant ride, there's insufficient room for the driver to reach between the door panel and seat to access the seat-adjusting mechanism, some engine noise intrudes into the cabin, serious reliability problems, and an incredibly high number of performance- and safety-related complaints reported to NHTSA and confirmed through confidential bulletins and whistle-blowers. **New for 2007:** The adoption of many of the 2007 Avalanche and Tahoe upgrades like Active Fuel Management cylinder deactivation with the 5.3L V8; more powerful engines (the 4.8L V8 gets 10 more horses, the 5.3L has five more, and the 6.0L is given 22 more); a 980 kg (2,160 lb.) payload rating; towing capability boosted to 4,763 kg (10,500 lb.); and an E85 (ethanol) compatible fuel system. GMC and Chevy trucks get a new Duramax 6.4L diesel with at least 360 horsepower. Other improvements include a reinforced chassis, upgraded suspension and steering systems, a larger cabin and bed, and new exterior and interior styling to dramatically distinguish the Chevrolet Silverado from the GMC Sierra, despite the fact that they are mechanical twins. StabiliTrak stability-control is a standard feature on Crew Cab versions.

MODEL HISTORY: Similar to Detroit's other pickups, these models are classed as 1500 half-ton, 2500 three-quarter-ton, and 3500 one-ton models. They come with a wide range of engine options, body styles, and bed sizes. The "C" designation refers to 4×2, and the "K" designation to 4×4. The 3500 series offers a four-door cab with a full rear seat. The variety of cab and cargo bed combinations, along with a choice of suspensions, makes these pickups adaptable to just about any use. Standard features include one of the biggest cabs among pickups, a fourth door, a three-piece modular truck frame, rack-and-pinion steering, and four-wheel disc brakes with larger pads and rotors.

An AutoTrac AWD drivetrain allows the driver to select an automatic mode that delivers full-time 4×4 (particularly useful if you live in a snowbelt area), while a 4-speed automatic features an innovative "tow/haul" mode that stretches out the upshifts to tap the engine's power at its maximum. There's also a potent family of four Vortec V8s in addition to a 6.6L turbodiesel (360 hp), 16-inch tires and wheels, and the highest minimum ground clearance among the Big Three pickups.

Chevy and GMC full-sized pickups are good domestic workhorses—when they're running. Of course, that's the problem—they're not dependable. On the one hand, these large pickups have a large, quiet cabin and give relatively easy access to the interior. On the other hand, their size and heft make for lousy fuel economy, a mediocre ride, and subpar handling and braking. Nevertheless, these are GM's most popular and highest-priced pickups. Although reasonably priced on the used market, new models will cost you the equivalent of a down payment on a home.

Early full-sized GM trucks may look like bargains, but they have as many or more serious factory-related deficiencies as their smaller S-10 cousins. Consequently, be sure to get extended warranty coverage. Keep in mind that engine and automatic transmission failures are quite common, and together they can give you a $7,000 headache. Also, try to find a pickup with running boards already installed. You'll save a few hundred dollars and make entry and exit a lot easier. Check out towing claims carefully as well. One owner reports that his truck was advertised as able to pull 3,856 kg (8,500 lb.), but the owner's manual says the towing limit is 3,402 kg (7,500 lb.).

From 1994 through 1998, GM's full-sized pickups were better built than its own smaller pickups and front-drive cars and more reliable than the Ford and Chrysler competition. Unfortunately, that's no longer the case, up through the 2006 models.

Earlier versions will have a 4-speed manual or 3-speed automatic transmission; later ones come with a 5-speed manual or a 4-speed automatic. Three-quarter-ton pickups offer more cargo capacity, but their harder suspension makes for an uncomfortable ride when lightly loaded and also affects handling. The 1999–2006 models got many new features that make them more powerful, versatile, and accommodating, and they're safer than previous models. However, these changes also made them less reliable than the pickups they replaced. Major powertrain, brake, suspension, electrical system, and body deficiencies have turned these "dream machines" into motoring nightmares.

The 1998 and later Sierras and Silverados have been plagued with severe vibrations that GM has routinely ignored. Owners have nicknamed their trucks "Shakerados," and they say that the new frame braces added to the 2001s to stop the shakes haven't worked (see *agmlemon.freeservers.com/index.html*).

Another generic failing is engine knocking or "piston slap," a term used to describe knocking engines. Owners claim the problem affects GM's 3.1L, 3.4L, 4.3L, 4.6L (Northstar), 4.8L, 5.3L, 5.7L (LS1), 6.0L, and 8.1L engines, which were poorly designed and not given adequate quality control. We're not talking about a small amount of light tapping upon start-up that disappears completely once the engine has warmed up—this is a loud, embarrassing, and damaging internal engine knock. There are currently six technical service bulletins that are relevant to piston slap: Engine Knock #01-06-01-022; Engine Knock #01-06-01-028; Engine Knock #01-06-01-028A; Cold Engine Tick #01-06-01-005; Engine Oil Consumption #01-06-01-011; and Engine Oil Consumption #01-06-01-011A. For more details, check out *www.pistonslap.com* or type "GM piston slap" into a search engine like Google.

2000—The 2000 Sierra and Silverado came up with an optional fourth door on extended-cab models, and a small power boost for the Vortec 4800 and 5300 V8 engines. **2001**—Debut of three-quarter-ton and one-ton versions of the Silverado. They offered two engines: the 6.6L Isuzu-built Duramax V8 diesel and GM's home-grown 8.1L Vortec V8. A traction-assist feature became available on rear-drive V8 automatics. The Sierra C3 luxury truck offered a number of new features, including a 325-hp 6.0L Vortec V8; full-time all-wheel drive (no two-speed transfer case for serious off-roading, though); upgraded four-wheel disc anti-lock brakes; an increased-capacity suspension system; and a luxuriously appointed interior. The Sierra HD truck lineup came with stronger frames; beefed-up suspensions, axles, brakes, and cooling systems; new sheet metal; bigger interiors; and three new V8s—a 6.6L Duramax turbodiesel and two gas engines, a hefty 8.1L and an improved 6.0L. One of the four transmissions, a new Allison 5-speed automatic, was designed especially for towing and hauling with GM's tow/haul mode and a new grade-braking feature. **2003**—Quadrasteer expanded to other models, improved electrical system and passenger-side airbag sensor, a new centre console, and dual-zone temperature and steering-wheel controls. **2004**—Standard cruise control, power door locks, and a CD player. **2006**—A new 360 hp 6.6L V8 turbo-diesel engine late in the model year; Quadrasteer option dropped.

COST ANALYSIS: Buy an upgraded, second-series 2007, and hope that GM doesn't screw up this redesign like it did in 1998. Remember, anything but a bare-bones version will be quite expensive. **Best alternatives:** A used Dodge Ram (mainly for the warranty and less troublesome, but not perfect, Cummins diesel); Mazda B-series; Nissan Frontier V6 or 2006 Titan; and Toyota T100, Tacoma, or Tundra. **Rebates:** $3,000 rebates on leftover fully-loaded 2006s; This year's models will be discounted about 15 percent by mid-2007. **Delivery/PDI:** $1,200. **Warranty:** Bumper-to-bumper 3 years/60,000 km; powertrain 5 years/160,000 km; rust perforation 6 years/160,000 km. **Supplementary warranty:** A good idea for the powertrain, judging by last year's high number of consumer complaints, the high incidence of diesel engine deficiencies, and the usual prevalence of redesign errors. **Options:** This is where GM really sticks it to you. Consider the remote keyless entry, upgraded sound system, heavy-duty battery, and transmission fluid and oil coolers. **Depreciation:** Faster than average. **Parts supply/cost:** Mechanical parts are widely available and reasonably priced due to the proliferation of independent suppliers. The 2007 model's body parts may be costly and in short supply. **Insurance cost:** Higher than average. **Annual maintenance cost:** Upkeep costs for these trucks are high; use independent garages to keep costs down. **Highway/city fuel economy:** *4.3L V6 and manual: 9.5/14.1 L/100 km; 4.3L V6 and automatic: 10.6/14.6 L/100 km; 4.8L V8 and automatic: 10.5/14.6 L/100 km; 5.3L V8 and automatic: 12.0/16.2 L/100 km; 5.3L V8 hybrid and automatic: 13.2/10.4 L/100 km.*

 QUALITY/RELIABILITY: Below average. Powertrain and brake repairs and troubleshooting complaints of excessive vibration often sideline the vehicle for days at a time, and repair suggestions don't make any sense:

> Then after the shimmy vibration continued, GM Technical Assistance to the dealership stated that all the 2004 Chevrolet Silverado 1500 Series have this vibration and it is classified as "beam shake." Their solution was to put 200 pounds [90 kg] of weight over the axle in the bed of the truck, stating, "It will ride like a Cadillac." The weight did not change the vibration and now they have a GM field engineer coming to look at the truck.

GM plant workers claim that the porous frame on both Sierras and Silverados cracks behind the cabin and near the tow hook. Original-equipment springs are also failing en masse:

> The front springs on 2003 Chevrolet 1500 [Silverado] Quad Cab trucks are collapsing and GMC/Chevrolet knows about problem and says...the owners [are] responsible to fix their mistake in designing and engineering the truck. They sent out a technical service bulletin to all dealers about [the] problem and [it] says...the owners need to pay $18.00...for rubber bushing to push up spring and $380.00 in labor. It's not

the company's fault. I think they need a recall and [need to] replace the springs with heavy duty springs at their cost not the owner's cost.

Owner-reported problems: Vehicle lacks power at high ambient temperatures. Excessive engine knock (faulty engine-connecting rod bolts, confirmed by internal bulletins) and exhaust system noise; diesel engine ticking noise; Check Engine light often comes on and requires replacement of many emissions components before it goes out; rough idle; and excessive oil consumption. Many complaints of rear differential pinion seal oil leaks; transmission failures; shifts for no reason from 4×4 to 4×2 or from 4×2 to 4×4 Low; delayed transmission shifting; failures to upshift; slipping in Overdrive; and shuddering in Drive or Reverse. Other problems include AC blower motor failure and wipers that don't shut off unless you replace the motor cover and controller module for $100+:

> While driving home during a rain storm my windshield wipers started to malfunction. I had them on an intermittent speed and they all of sudden went to high. Once I was home, I attempted to turn my wipers off and they only went to low. I am unable to turn my wipers off. I had to remove the fuse. If I need my wipers I must put the fuse back in. I am working now to determine if it is the multiple function switch that has gone bad. Upon looking up data about my vehicle online I found trucks dating back to the mid 90s with the same issue.

There are also excessive steering gear box failures; front-end vibrations felt throughout the chassis, steering, and floorboards at 100 km/h (dealers blame vibrations on Goodyear tires, but the problem persists after tires are replaced); defective lower control arm and steering bushings, suspected as the cause of excessive vibrations; premature wheel bearing wear on 2003 and 2004 models; and frequent and costly brake repairs involving rotor and pad replacement:

> I have a '99 GMC Sierra 1500 4WD (purchased new in Sept 2000) that went off the base warranty in October 2002. The vehicle currently has 37,000 km on [its] clock.

> As I have found stopping distances to be increasing of late, I recently took the vehicle in for servicing. GM advised that it is "normal" for pads to be replaced every 15–20,000 km. I said I disagreed very strongly with this estimate, and that pads alone should last at least 25,000 km under any conditions. The GM rep also said brake rotors on these vehicles cannot be reconditioned (turning) as they are "too thin," and generally require replacement in the 50–60,000 km range. I asked if there were "known problems" with the brake system on these vehicles that contribute to these early failures. The representative said there were no known problems, just normal wear.

> After taking the vehicle to a third party for inspection, I was told that the pads are finished and that all four rotors must be replaced as they are rusted through. I

inspected the vehicle myself in the shop and found that the third party was completely correct in this. The net cost for this work is expected to be in the $1,600–$2,000 range. I find the thought of a $2,000 bill every three years for replacement brakes unacceptable.

And there are even more complaints that include excessive brake noise and steering-column squeaks, an inadequate front defroster, a front-end popping noise, hubcaps that often fly off the vehicle, tires that won't stay balanced, and poorly fitted trim and body panels. **Warranty performance:** Average. GM has a number of extended warranties in place to compensate owners for defects, but getting information on which "secret" warranties apply and obtaining compensation isn't easy.

SAFETY SUMMARY: The 2007 models scored four stars for frontal and rollover crash protection. Very few early versions were sold with front-seat head restraints, and the driver's head is very close to the rear window on regular-cab versions. **Airbags:** Reports of airbags failing to deploy. **ABS:** Standard 4W; disc/drum. **Traction control:** Optional. **Head restraints F/R:** *C/K:* 1997: ★; *Silverado 1500 1999:* ★; *2001–06:* ★. **Visibility F/R:** ★★★★★. **Maximum load capacity:** 1,655 lb.

SAFETY COMPLAINTS: All years: Sudden, unintended acceleration. • Airbag failed to deploy. • Intermittent loss of power steering. • Brake failures (pedal goes to the metal with no braking effect) with ABS light lit constantly. • Brake pad failure and warped rotor. • Parking brake doesn't hold. • ABS doesn't engage; results in extended stopping distances and wheel lock-up. • Chronic stalling. **1999**—Inability to shut off headlights without shutting down vehicle. • Delayed transmission shifting in cold weather. • Broken spare-tire cable allows spare to fly off. **2000**—A very common problem appears to be that the rear frame breaks from the bottom up to about 5 cm (2 in.) in front of the tow hook attachment. • Transmission jumped from Park into Reverse. • Fuel line leakage. • Several cases relating to a broken power-steering pump shaft. • Rear left emergency brake shoe and drum allow for salt and debris to get into drum and drum elbow. • Dash light failures, and headlight switch burns out. • Many incidents of tire-tread separation. • Excessive vibration felt throughout vehicle. **2001**—Loose lug nuts caused left rear wheel to fall off. • Spongy brakes lead to extended stopping distances. • After driving in snow and parking vehicle, brakes wouldn't work. • Emergency brake gave way on flat ground. • When accelerating from a stop, vehicle momentarily goes into Neutral. • Sometimes, transmission suddenly shifts from Fifth to Third gear, or down to Second gear while cruising on the highway. • Defective transmission valve body results in transmission jumping out of gear. • Truck drifts all over the highway. • Driver's seat belt causes pain in the shoulder. • Upper ball joint and right sway bar ends may be missing nuts and cotter keys. • Fuel line leak allows fuel to spray out rear. **2002**—Fire ignited in the dash. • Throttle sticks. • Chronic engine surging when braking. • Automatic transmission suddenly downshifts when accelerating, as engine surges then clunks into gear. • Steering wheel locks up while driving. • Passenger-side front end suddenly collapsed (replaced outer tie-rod end). • Steel wheel collects water that freezes and throws wheel out of balance. • Steering-column bolt came apart. • Interior rear-view mirror distortion. • Dimmer switch overheats. • Driver's seatback will suddenly fall backwards. • Head restraint blocks vision to right side of vehicle. **2003**—Fire ignited in engine compartment. • Cracked transmission transfer case. • Automatic transmission slips when shifting from First to Second gear. • 4×4 shifts erratically, causing serious highway instability. • Seat belt and steering lock-ups. • Tailgate pops open. **2004**—Collapsed front axle assembly. • Sway bar mounting bracket broke, causing the frame and mounting bar to come off. • Brake failures when coasting downhill or when decelerating. • Brakes are too soft and set too close to the accelerator pedal. • Cruise control surges when going downhill. • Transmission suddenly jumped from Second gear to Reverse. • Steering lock-up. • Tailgate came apart in owner's hands. • Doors won't unlock in cold weather. • Driver's door window shattered for no reason. • Hood coil spring failed, injuring owner. • Jack slipped off the vehicle. • Side mirrors constantly vibrate and are easily scratched when wiped off. **2005**—Dual airbags failed to deploy. • Airbag warning light comes on, even when seat is occupied by an adult. • Sudden acceleration and chronic stalling.

> Diesel system has a problem transferring fuel into the truck for use. It runs out while the front fuel tank is still full of fuel. The fuel tank never reads over half full.

• Transmission slips when accelerating, making the truck an easy target when turning into an intersection. • Sudden drive shaft failure:

> GMC Sierra 1500 Crew Cab; while driving at interstate speed, the drive shaft fell off the vehicle and shattered. There was substantial damage to the underside of the vehicle, including muffler, yoke, heat shield, and driveshaft.

• The 4.3L engine and 4-speed automatic transmission work poorly together, constantly downshifting and gear hunting when going up an incline. • On diesels, fuel gauge and transfer pump fail repeatedly. • Rear diesel tank sprays fuel on the highway. • Vehicle is hard to move from a stopped position; feels like the rear brakes are locked up (master cylinder was changed). • Front brakes seemed to stick and then overheated and ignited a fire. • Leaf springs aren't very durable. • Wheel hubcap nuts overheat, and the hubcaps fly off. • Interior door handles easily snag clothes or purse straps when opening the door. • Front doors won't close properly. • Inoperative power-seat keyless fob. • Outside rear-view mirrors don't show the rear bumper area when backing up and are useless when hauling a trailer. • GM bug shield causes the outside mirror to shake. • Jack bent under weight of vehicle and collapsed. • Tire-tread separation.

Secret Warranties/Internal Bulletins/Service Tips

1996–99—Engine bearing knocking on vehicles equipped with a 5.0L or 5.7L V8 may be silenced by using a special GM countermeasure kit to service the crankshaft and select-fit undersized connecting rod bearings. • No-starts, hard starts, and poor engine performance can all be traced to a faulty crankshaft position sensor. **1998–99**—If the 4×4 won't engage, you may need to install a new transfercase actuator and shift detent plunger. • Before you spend big bucks overhauling the transfer case, remember that a bump or clunk heard on acceleration may be silenced by simply changing the transfer-case fluid. **1999**—If the front wheels slip while in 4×4, consider replacing the transfer-case clutch plates and front-drive axle lubricant. • A steering-column squeak noise may be silenced by replacing the steering-wheel SIR module coil assembly. **1999–2000**—Wind noise coming from the side may be silenced by replacing the quarter window assembly under warranty. **1999–2003**—An exhaust moan or vibration can be corrected by installing an exhaust-system flex pipe kit. **1999–2004**—Chronic engine knock or piston slap. • Prematurely worn and noisy brake rotors and pads may be replaced with higher-quality aftermarket parts for about half the price. • GM says in TSB #00-05-23-005B that owners should invest in a GM mud flap kit (#15765007) to make their rear brakes last longer. Again, save money by shopping at independent retailers. • Inoperative power windows. • Remedy for steering-wheel clunk. • Suspension clunk, slap. GM will do this repair for free as "goodwill" up to 3 years/60,000 km and will offer a 50 percent refund thereafter:

SUSPENSION—REAR LEAF SPRING SLAP OR CLUNK NOISE

BULLETIN NO.: 03-03-09-002A   DATE: APRIL 29, 2004

REAR LEAF SPRING SLAP OR CLUNK NOISE (REPLACE SPRING INSERT AND INSULATOR)

1999–2004 Chevrolet Silverado 1500/2500 Series Pickups

2000–04 Chevrolet Suburban 2500 Series

2002–04 Chevrolet Avalanche 2500 Series

2003–04 Chevrolet Express 2500/3500 Vans with 8500 GVWR (RPO C5F), 8600 GVWR (RPO C6P) or 9600 GVWR (RPO C6Y)

1999–2004 GMC Sierra 1500/2500 Series Pickups

2000–04 GMC Yukon XL 2500 Series

2003–04 GMC Savana 2500/3500 Vans with 8500 GVWR (RPO C5F), 8600 GVWR (RPO C6P) or 9600 GVWR (RPO C6Y)

Some customers may comment on a rear leaf spring slap or clunk noise. This noise is most apparent when the vehicle is operated over irregular road surfaces.

1999–2005—Install an exhaust system flex pipe kit to stop an exhaust moan, vibration. **2000–04**—Troubleshooting delayed gear engagement. **2000–05**—Rattle, squeak from front of vehicle. **2001**—Loose engine connecting-rod bolts may cause engine knock and complete engine failure. • Loss of turbo boost accompanied by thick black smoke. • No-starts or hard starts. • Harsh shift remedies. •

When in 4×4 and in Reverse gear, engine won't go over 1000–1300 rpm. • Transmission slips when placed in 4×4. • 6-speed manual transmission clutch fluid may be contaminated by water entering through the reservoir cap. • Automatic transmission 2–4 band or 3–4 clutch damage. • Inoperative wiper motor; fuse blows repeatedly. • Windows are slow to defrost. • Steering-column lock shaft doesn't lock. **2001–02**—Troubleshooting tips to correct slow or no automatic transmission engagement, no-starts, or a blank PRNDL. **2001–03**—The torque converter relief spring and lube regulator spring may need to be changed to correct automatic transmission delayed shifts or loss of power. GM service bulletins TSB #01-07-30-043 and 03-07-30-031 explain why the automatic transmission may slip or leak. **2001–05**—Fuel gauge reads empty on trucks with a spare tank. **2002**—Check Engine light comes on as automatic transmission begins shifting erratically. • 1–2 shift shudder. • Diagnostic tips for a slipping automatic transmission. • Clunk noise from under the hood. • Clunk, bump, or squawk heard when accelerating or coming to a stop. • Shudder or vibration when accelerating from a stop. • Driveline growl or prop shaft ring noise. • Steering shaft clunk. • Noisy brakes. • Water leak at the roof centre clearance light. • Inability to control temperature setting. • Intermittent failing of the tail lights, backup lights, or trailer harness. **2003**—Harsh automatic transmission 1–2 shifting; slipping caused by a faulty pressure control solenoid (Bulletin #03-07-30-020, May 2003). **2003–04**—Remedies for buzz noise or vibration felt in floor or throttle pedal. Inoperative front power window. **2003–05**—AC blower motor won't shut off. **2004–05**—Front end pop or snap. **2004**—Cold engine rattling. **2004–06**—Automatic transmission shudder due to water intrusion (see Tahoe section). **2005**—Poor automatic transmission performance troubleshooting tips (2005 and earlier models). • Free replacement of the powertrain/engine control module; courtesy transportation available. • Loose, rattling hubcaps. **2005–06**—Troubleshooting a steering-column shaft clunk. *Diesel engines:* **1994–2002**—Special Policy covers fuel injection pump failure up to 11 years/193,000 km. **1997–98**—Hard upshifts may be corrected by reprogramming the PCM/VCM. **2001**—Excessive vibration and surging. **2001–02**—"Goodwill" warranty will pay for faulty fuel injectors:

SPECIAL POLICY ADJUSTMENT (REPLACE INJECTOR)

BULLETIN NO.: 04039   **DATE: JUNE 2004**

2001–02 Silverado/Sierra (6.6L Duramax Diesel)

CONDITION: Some customers of 2001–02 model year Chevrolet Silverado and GMC Sierra vehicles, equipped with a 6.6L Duramax Diesel (RPO LB7 – VIN Code 1) engine, may experience vehicle service engine soon (SES) light illumination, low engine power, hard start, and/or fuel in crankcase, requiring injector replacement, as a result of high fuel return rates due to fuel injector body cracks or ball seat erosion.

SPECIAL POLICY ADJUSTMENT: This special policy covers the condition described above for a period of 7 years or 200,000 miles (320,000 km), whichever occurs first, from the date the vehicle was originally placed in service, regardless of ownership. The repairs will be made at no charge to the customer.

All ratings on a numbered scale where ⑤ is good and ❶ is bad. See page 220 for a more detailed description.

2001–04—Troubleshooting a turbocharger failure. 2001–04—Free O-ring replacement.

DIESEL ENGINE OIL LEAK

BULLETIN NO.: 02-06-01-023C   DATE: JULY 20, 2004

OIL LEAK AT OIL COOLER TO 6.6L DIESEL ENGINE BLOCK MATING SURFACE (REPLACE O-RINGS, APPLY SEALANT)

2001–04 Chevrolet Silverado 2500/3500
2001–04 GMC Sierra 2500/3500
2003–04 Chevrolet Kodiak C4500/5500
2003–04 GMC Topkick C4500/5500

CAUSE: Minor imperfections in the engine block machined surfaces at the oil cooler interface may allow oil seepage past the oil cooler O-rings.

C/K, SIERRA, SILVERADO PROFILE

	1998	1999	2000	2001	2002	2003	2004	2005	2006
Cost Price ($)									
C/K	20,995	21,735	—	—	—	—	—	—	—
Sierra, Silverado (18%)	20,955	21,895	22,100	22,060	22,410	23,240	24,070	24,925	24,900
Used Values ($)									
C/K ▲	4,000	5,500	—	—	—	—	—	—	—
C/K ▼	3,500	4,500	—	—	—	—	—	—	—
Sierra, Silverado ▲	5,000	6,000	7,500	9,500	11,500	14,000	15,500	18,500	—
Sierra, Silverado ▼	4,500	5,500	6,500	8,500	10,000	12,500	14,500	17,000	—
Reliability	3	2	2	2	2	2	3	3	—
Crash Safety (F)	—	—	—	—	—	—	4	4	4
Ext. cab	4	—	3	3	3	4	4	4	—
Offset	—	2	2	2	2	2	2	2	2
Rollover	—	—	—	—	—	—	4	4	4
Ext. cab	—	—	3	3	3	4	4	4	4
Ext. cab 4X4	—	—	3	3	3	3	4	4	4

General Motors/Isuzu

S-10, SONOMA, T-10/SPACE CAB, HOMBRE, CANYON, COLORADO ★★

2003 TECHNICAL DATA

POWERTRAIN (4X2/PART-TIME 4X4)
Engines: 2.2L 4-cyl. (120 hp) • 4.3L V6
(175–190 hp); Transmissions: 5-speed
man. • 4-speed auto.
**DIMENSION/CAPACITY (REGULAR CAB/
EXTENDED CAB)**
Passengers: 3/2; Wheelbase:
108.3/117.9–122.9 in.; H: 63.3/L:
189/W: 67.9 in.; Headroom F/R: 5.0/3.0
in.; Legroom F/R: 42.4/42.4 in.; Cargo
volume: 48.1 cu. ft.; Fuel tank: 76L/
regular; Tow limit: 2,100–5,200 lb.;
Load capacity: 1,150–1,633 lb.; GVWR:
4,200–5,150 lb.; Turning circle: 51 ft.;
Box length: 6/7.5 ft.; Ground clearance:
6.8–10.3 in.; Weight: 3,350 lb.

2007 CANYON, COLORADO TECHNICAL DATA

POWERTRAIN (4X2/PART-TIME 4X4)
Engines: 2.9L 4-cyl. (185 hp) • 3.7L
5-cyl. (242 hp); Transmissions: 5-speed
man. • 4-speed auto.
**DIMENSION/CAPACITY (REGULAR CAB/
EXTENDED CAB)**
Passengers: 3/3; Wheelbase: 126 in.;
H: 62/L: 207/W: 69 in.; Headroom F/R:
5.0/3.0 in.; Legroom F/R: 42/26 in.;
Cargo volume: 26.8 cu. ft.; Fuel tank:
74L/regular; Tow limit: 4,000 lb.; Load
capacity: 1,125 lb.; GVWR: 4,700–5,300
lb.; Turning circle: 48 ft.; Box length:
6.0/7.5 ft.; Ground clearance: 8.0 in.;
Weight: 4,270 lb.

RATING: *Canyon, Colorado:* Below Average (2004–07). *S-10, Sonoma, T-10:* Average (2000–04); Below Average (1996–99); Not Recommended (1986–95). *Space Cab, Hombre:* Below Average (1989–2002). These pickups are no match for the Japanese competition in almost every category. Like GM's full-sized pickups, the Sonoma hasn't shown much improvement during its 15-year run. The Space Cab was re-designated the Hombre for the 1997 model year. **Strong points:** A well-appointed pickup, good V6 acceleration, reliable and smooth-shifting automatic transmission, user-friendly controls and instruments, extended cab offers a spacious interior and storage space, airbag cut-off switch, easy loading and unloading, and one of the quietest interiors you'll find. **Weak points:** Wimpy 4-cylinder engine, harsh ride, poor handling, plastic door panels make for a tacky-looking cabin, difficult entry and exit on the 4×4 version, awkward rear access almost makes the optional third door a necessity, limited rear-seat room, jump seats in the extended cab are tiny and uncomfortable, and an extraordinary number of safety-related defects reported to NHTSA. *Colorado:* No outside key door lock. **New for 2007:** *Canyon/Colorado:* Nothing significant; a redesign is planned for the 2009 model year.

MODEL HISTORY: These mostly identical pickups (they vary somewhat in trim and equipment) are compact, light-duty vehicles that are available in regular and extended-cab versions. For easier entry and exit, a driver-side third door is available on the extended-cab pickups.

The trucks are available in 4×2 and part-time 4×4. A 2.2L 4-cylinder or 4.3L V6 powerplant may be hooked to a 5-speed manual or 4-speed automatic transmission. The 4×4 is engaged with InstaTrac shift-on-the-fly, and there's low-range gearing for off-road excursions.

These attractively styled S-series pickups do have some good points, like a powerful V6 and user-friendly controls. But these advantages have to be weighed against some rather serious shortcomings: a wimpy 4-cylinder engine (also a Canyon and Colorado problem), a clunky and quirky automatic transmission, difficult entry and exit, a harsh ride, and excessive gas consumption. S-10s don't offer any space or load capacity advantages over their Japanese counterparts.

1996—Performance was enhanced through the addition of improved V6 engines, a smoother 4-speed manual transmission, a sportier suspension, four-wheel ABS, and a third-door access panel on the driver's side of extended cabs. **1997**—GM strengthened the frame on the rear-drives and added a smoother-shifting automatic throughout the lineup. **1998**—De-powered airbags, four-wheel disc brakes, and a more refined transfer case on vehicles equipped with an automatic transmission. **1999**—Extreme Sport package replaced the SS, more automatic transmission enhancements were carried out to improve sealing and durability, and a new AutoTrac electronic push-button transfer case was added. Again the following year, GM felt compelled to upgrade the engine (same horsepower, though), manual transmission, ABS, and exhaust system. **2000**—Trucks carrying the ZR2 package were given a new axle ratio for better acceleration. **2001**—A new four-door crew-cab 4×4 version was offered, with enough room for five (small) passengers, plus an InstaTrac 4×4 system and SLS trim. Powertrain upgrades included an advanced control module for the V6 and Flex-Fuel capability for the 4-cylinder. There were also new aluminum wheels with the sport suspension, and programmable power door locks. **2002**—Standard air conditioning and a long cargo bed option (initially dropped, then reinstated). **2003**—A new fuel injection system and a minor face-lift. **2004**—Canyon and Colorado arrive.

Space Cab, Hombre

This Isuzu-built pickup, once sold through GM's short-lived Passport division, is barely acceptable basic transportation in small-truck guise. Its main drawbacks are underperforming engines, weak brakes, spotty reliability, and hard-to-find parts.

The standard engines are weak 2.2L and 2.3L 4-cylinders; if you intend to do hauling or light towing, look for a version equipped with the optional 2.6L

4-banger mated to a 5-speed manual or 4-speed automatic transmission. For off-roading, the 4×4 is the best choice, with its GM-built V6 coupled to a 5-speed manual gearbox.

The 1997–2000 Hombre is essentially a Chevrolet S pickup with Isuzu sheet metal; quality-control is only marginally better than what you'd find with GM's homegrown counterpart. Initially, the only engine choice was GM's anemic 4-banger. **1997**—Included an optional extended-cab housing and a better-performing 4.3L V6. **1998**—4×4 capability, dual airbags, and a passenger-side airbag cut-off switch. The next two model years saw few changes, as these vehicles remained near mirror images of GM's S-10, lacking some configurations such as V6-equipped regular cabs and manual-transmission-equipped 4×2 V6 extended cabs.

Canyon, Colorado

Replacing the S-10, these small light-duty pickups sacrifice hauling capacity for good fuel economy and a softer, quieter ride. They are slightly larger than the S-10 and come with 4×2 or 4×4 and in regular-cab, extended-cab, and crew-cab configurations. Three suspension packages are available: standard, sport, and off-road.

The 3.5L inline 5-cylinder is derived from GM's 4.2L inline-six, first used in the 2002 Chevrolet TrailBlazer. Dual balance shafts within each engine help eliminate vibrations, while variable valve timing improves idle smoothness, reduces emissions, and increases gas mileage. Other features include a shift-on-the-fly 4×4 system, an optional locking differential, and traction control. Both mid-sized pickups include federally mandated child seat anchors, four-door child locks, front-seat airbag Off switches for regular cab models, and the same three-point safety belts found in automobiles. On the minus side, no V6 is available, towing capacity is limited, and the 5-cylinder engine is unproven.

COST ANALYSIS: The 2007 Colorado LS costs $20,760, versus $19,320 for a 2006 LS. A stripped-down 2006 commercial variant costs a couple thousand dollars less, but it's hard to find because dealers often load these pickups with thousands of dollars' worth of non-essential options. **Best alternatives:** Remember, there are many overlapping features between GMC, Chevrolet, and Isuzu pickups. You may be able to find a better-equipped GM or Isuzu version of the Sonoma carrying a different nameplate. Also take a gander at the Mazda B-series, Nissan Frontier, and Toyota Tacoma. **Rebates:** Generous discounts, $1,500 rebates, plus zero percent financing on the 2006 and 2007 models. **Delivery/PDI:** $1,100. **Warranty:** Bumper-to-bumper 3 years/60,000 km; powertrain 5 years/160,000 km; rust perforation 6 years/160,000 km. **Supplementary warranty:** An extended powertrain warranty would be a good idea. **Options:** The V6 is a prerequisite if the vehicle is equipped with an automatic transmission—a choice not available with the Canyon and Colorado. **Depreciation:** Average. The 2003 and earlier models have a higher depreciation rate than that of most pickups in this class. **Insurance cost:** Average. **Annual maintenance cost:** Average. **Parts supply/cost:** Japanese-sourced parts can be hard to find and are fairly costly. **Highway/city fuel economy:** *4×2 and 2.2L: 8.5/12.4 L/100 km; 4×2 and 4.3L: 10.1/14.2 L/100 km; 4×4 and 4.3L: 10.6/14.7 L/100 km.* There are many complaints that actual fuel consumption on the Canyon and Colorado is far more than the above figures show.

QUALITY/RELIABILITY: Average. *Canyon and Colorado:* General Tire sidewall blowouts, water leaks, and a bad odour from the AC. On 2003 and earlier models, owners complain of engine knock, automatic transmission malfunctions, wire harness melting, expensive oxygen sensor replacements, electrical shorts, upper control-arm bushings that rapidly wear out, worn brake rotors and pads, power-window failures, and inaccurate fuel gauges. Fit and finish isn't as good as with most other pickups; there's excessive wind noise, especially with the Colorado; the thickness of the paint coat varies considerably, and paint will chip easily (the worst is Midnight Blue). Watch out for Colorado and Canyon engine failures, writes one *Lemon-Aid* reader from North Bay, Ontario:

> I purchased a 2004 GMC Canyon SLE Crew Cab on August 14, 2004. In October, I noticed the engine light come on flashing, indicating an engine misfire. After hooking a recorder to it, the dealer was able to see what was happening. GM advised them to replace the valve springs. This took one month to complete between Dec. 15 and Jan. 15.
>
> Problem was not solved and it took a replaced O_2 sensor and a new intake manifold. Still the light came on. This time I called the customer care at GM, it helped in that the next solution was "reprogramming the computer," since I complained that I was tired of seeing the engine taken apart and [the repairs] not solving anything.
>
> This repair lasted a month, and then the light came back with conviction. I turned the truck over on May 28 to have a new cylinder head installed, and also all new valves.

Colorado: Fuel lines are easily cracked; right and left side-door water leaks; and the lumbar support may be too high for some people. **Warranty performance:** Below average.

SAFETY SUMMARY: The lack of head restraints on early models is a safety hazard. U.S. federal government researchers have opened investigations into reports of ABS failures (1991–94), the spare tire falling off the vehicle (1991–96), and post-crash fuel leakage (1994–99). There are over 1,000 reports of safety-related failures registered by NHTSA for the 1995 model year alone. The most frequent failures are sudden, unintended acceleration; head restraints that can't be adjusted and are too low to be effective; airbags that fail to deploy; blown engine head gaskets; an ABS that doesn't brake but does break; intermittent windshield wiper failures (they also often stop in the middle of the windshield); tires that rub the front wheelwell when turning; and spare tires that fall off on the highway. Most 2007 models earned four-star crashworthiness scores in front, side, and rollover crash tests; however, the 2007 four-door Canyon and Colorado earned five stars for occupant protection in a frontal collision. **Airbags:** The airbag cut-off switch permits the use of a child safety seat up front. **ABS:** Standard 4W; disc/drum. **Safety belt pretensioners:** Front. **Head restraints F/R:** *S10: 1997:* ★; *1998:* ★★★★; *1999:* ★★★★; *2001–03:* ★★★★/★; *2004–06:* ★★. **Visibility F/R:** ★★★★★/★★★. **Maximum load capacity:** *2001 S-10 LS V6:* 1,000 lb.; *2007 Canyon/Colorado V6:* 1,125 lb.

SAFETY COMPLAINTS: All years: No airbag deployment. • Chronic stalling. • Transmission and differential failures. • ABS failures. • Premature front pad wear and rotor warping. • Plastic gas tank is easily punctured. • Driver's seat slides back and forth while driving. *S-10, Sonoma, T-10:* **1999**—Transmission lock-up, poor braking performance, and headlight failures. **1999–2000**—461 complaints recorded by NHTSA. • AC froze, causing the serpentine belt to catch fire. • Oil lines and oil pan gaskets frequently fail. • Wiring harness caught fire while vehicle was parked. • Stuck gas pedal. • Transfer case gets stuck in 4×4 High and Low. • Vehicle jumps out of First gear when accelerating. • Reverse band slips and spreads fibres throughout transmission and converter. • Drive shaft broke while vehicle underway. • Rear-end pinion seal failed. • No-starts and hard starts. • Cruise control doesn't shut off when brakes are applied. • Battery leaked acid onto brake line, resulting in complete loss of braking. • Brake lock-up caused vehicle to go out of control. • Broken driver- and passenger-seat recliners. • AC wires burned out clutch fan. • Bad relay causes sudden dash light and headlight failure. • Wipers don't operate properly. • Horn sounds by itself. • Exhaust fumes leak through ventilation system. • Right and left side wheels fell off because of a missing cotter pin. • Spare-tire cable broke, allowing tire to fly off. • Goodyear Wrangler tire-tread separation. • Loose ball joints cause excessive tire wear. • Doors have fallen off because of hinge weld failure. • Third-door handle breaks easily. • Rear-view side mirror falls off. • Side window shattered as door was closed. • Loose front seats and headlight failures. • Payload label may be incorrect. **2001**—Over 150 complaints recorded by NHTSA. • ABS engages when vehicle passes over a bump. • Engine surging. • During a collision, airbags deployed and ignited a fire. • Vehicle rolled down driveway even though engine was shut off and parking brake was applied. • Undercarriage fires. • Tire-tread separation. • Steering stiffens. • Loose passenger seat. • Wipers stop in middle of windshield. **2002**—Stuck gas pedal (not carpet related). • Axle suddenly snapped. • Harsh-shifting automatic transmission. • Door water and air leaks. **2003**—Long hesitation when accelerating and then suddenly drops into First gear. • Airbags didn't deploy. • Quirky steering; suddenly pulls to one side. • Goodyear sidewall defect; and Uniroyal tires wobble. • Faulty fuel gauge. • Fuel tank always overflows when refuelling. • Excessive on-road vibration. • Tailgate fell off. • Drive shaft fell out. • Primary hood latch releases while driving. • Headlights dim without warning. *Hombre:* **1997**—Tall drivers not protected by head restraints. • Cracked rear axle caused transmission lock-up. • Electrical shorts cause lights to go out. • Poor brake performance. • Engine ingested water in sufficient quantity to cause hydraulic lock-up of the engine pistons. **1998**—Brake failure. • Sudden breakage of the front axle. **2000**—Sudden steering-rod failure while underway. **2003**—Manual transmission pops out of gear. *Canyon and Colorado:* **2004**—Engine surging. • Brake pedal went to floor without effect. • Tailgate fell down while driving. • Transmission failures. • Excessive on-road vibration. *Canyon:* **2005**—Front wheels suddenly locked up while vehicle was going about 80 km/h. • Excessive vehicle shaking when underway. • Windshield cracks easily. *Colorado:* **2005**—Complete brake failure. • Rear drum brakes failed at 10,000 km; pistons blew out of cylinders. • Rear drive shaft broke off at universal joint while truck was driving 100 km/h. • Many rear main seal leaks. • ABS doesn't work properly. • Poor headlight illumination.

Secret Warranties/Internal Bulletins/Service Tips

S-10, Sonoma, T-10: **1993–99**—Cure AC odours by installing GM's cooling coil coating kit. **1993–2002**—Paint delamination, peeling, or fading. **1995–2001**—Hood hinge rattling. **1995–2002**—A rough idle or Check Engine light warning may only signal the need to clean the fuel injection system. **1997–2001**—Transmission stuck in Third gear, MIL light comes on, and instrument cluster is inoperative. **1998–99**—Incorrect fuel gauge readings can be corrected by reprogramming the VCM module. **1998–2002**—AWD malfunctions:

DRIVETRAIN—NOISE/VIBRATION/LEAKS/SLIPPING IN 4X4

BULLETIN NO.: 02-04-21-005A   **DATE: FEBRUARY 2003**

SUBJECT: Slips in 4X4, noise, vibration, leaks, hot odour (diagnose and repair front differential and/or transfer case)

1999–2000 Cadillac Escalade

1998–2002 Chevrolet S-10, Silverado, Blazer, Suburban, Tahoe

2002 Chevrolet Avalanche

1998–2002 GMC Sierra, Sonoma, Jimmy, Suburban, Yukon, Yukon XL

with Autotrak transfer case (RPO NP8) (selector pad on instrument panel must have auto 4X4, 4HI, 4LO, and 2HI selections)

CAUSE: The front axle may have excessive preload in the pinion or carrier bearings or may be locked up, not allowing the pinion to rotate freely.

1999–2004—Vehicle stalling; won't restart. • Vehicle appears to be out of fuel, but the fuel gauge reads above Empty. **2000–03**—Hard starts, poor idle, and misfires. **2001**—Engine-oil cooler hose is incorrectly oriented. • Harsh shifts. • Automatic transmission 2–4 band or 3–4 clutch damage. • Security light flashes • Engine stalls or won't start. • Rear suspension popping noise when going over a bump or when turning. • Lights flicker while driving at night. *Space Cab, Hombre:*

All years: Replace the distributor seal to stop engine oil from leaking into the distributor. • Knocking from the steering column when the wheel is turned from side to side can be fixed with a steering shaft repair kit (#8-97077-575-0) and rubber boot (#8-97079-655-0). • TSB #SB96-11-L002 suggests the front fender inner liners be replaced to prevent ice buildup around the lower door-to-fender area, which can damage the door and fender. *Canyon and Colorado:* **2004**—Automatic transmission slipping. • GM says it's "normal" to hear a shift clunk. (Sigh…) **2004–05**—Popping, snapping noise coming from the exhaust system. • AC hum, whistle, hiss. • Premature front tire wear. **2005**—Harsh 1–2 upshifts.

S-10, SONOMA, T-10, HOMBRE, CANYON, COLORADO PROFILE

	1998	1999	2000	2001	2002	2003	2004	2005	2006
Cost Price ($) (negotiable)									
S-10, S-14	16,190	16,410	16,495	18,217	17,060	17,870	—	—	—
T-10 4X4	21,150	21,370	21,170	26,097	—	—	—	—	—
Sonoma	16,190	16,410	16,495	17,025	17,060	17,870	—	—	—
Hombre	14,825	13,995	14,095	—	—	—	—	—	—
Hombre 4X4	—	22,961	26,995	—	—	—	—	—	—
Canyon/Colorado (17%)	—	—	—	—	—	—	16,995	17,195	17,195
Used Values ($)									
S-10, S-14 ▲	3,500	4,500	5,500	6,500	8,000	11,000	—	—	—
S-10, S-14 ▼	3,000	4,000	5,000	6,000	7,500	10,000	—	—	—
T-10 4X4 ▲	5,500	6,500	7,000	8,500	—	—	—	—	—
T-10 4X4 ▼	5,000	6,000	6,000	7,500	—	—	—	—	—
Sonoma ▲	3,000	4,000	5,000	6,000	8,500	11500	—	—	—
Sonoma ▼	2,500	3,500	4,500	5,500	8,000	10,500	—	—	—
Hombre ▲	2,500	3,500	4,000	—	—	—	—	—	—
Hombre ▼	2,000	3,000	3,500	—	—	—	—	—	—
Hombre 4X4 ▲	—	5,500	7,500	—	—	—	—	—	—
Hombre 4X4 ▼	—	4,500	6,000	—	—	—	—	—	—
Canyon/Colorado ▲	—	—	—	—	—	—	11,000	12,000	—
Canyon/Colorado ▼	—	—	—	—	—	—	9,500	11,000	—
Reliability									
S-10, Sonoma, T-10	❶	❶	❶	❷	❷	❷	—	—	—
Hombre	❸	❹	❹	❹	❹	❹	—	—	—
Canyon/Colorado	—	—	—	—	—	—	❸	❸	—

All ratings on a numbered scale where ⑤ is good and ❶ is bad. See page 220 for a more detailed description.

Crash Safety (F)

S-10 4X2	—	—	③	③	③	③	—	—	—
Ext.	④	②	②	②	②	②	—	—	—
S-10 4X4	—	—	—	②	—	—	—	—	—
Sonoma	④	②	③	③	—	—	—	—	—
Sonoma Ext.	—	—	②	②	—	—	—	—	—
Hombre	—	—	③	—	—	—	—	—	—
Canyon/Colorado	—	—	—	—	—	—	④	④	⑤
Side									
S-10 4X2	—	—	④	④	④	④	—	—	—
Ext.	—	③	③	③	③	③	—	—	—
S-10 4X4	—	—	—	③	—	—	—	—	—
Sonoma	—	—	④	—	—	—	—	—	—
Sonoma Ext.	—	—	③	—	—	—	—	—	—
Hombre	—	—	④	—	—	—	—	—	—
Canyon/Colorado	—	—	—	—	—	—	④	⑤	⑤
Offset	②	②	②	②	②	②	⑤	⑤	⑤
Rollover	—	—	—	③	③	③	—	④	④

Honda

best buy

RIDGELINE ★★★★★

RATING: Recommended (2007); Above Average (2006). Honda's first-year vehicles and redesigns haven't been as glitch-prone as Detroit's new products, Toyota's redesigned 2004 Sienna, or Nissan's revamped Quest. **Strong points:** Very smooth engine performance with exceptionally quick, carlike throttle response; uses a smooth and reliable 5-speed automatic transmission borrowed from the Pilot; extra traction can be obtained by using a dash-mounted button to lock in power to the rear wheels; unibody construction reduces body flexing and creaking, keeping road noise to a minimum; agile handling and enhanced ride comfort, thanks to a front and rear independent suspension; good braking; well-appointed, with plenty of innovative and easily accessed cabin storage compartments; versatile box with a trunk built into the floor, accessed through a tailgate that swings out as well as down; the bed surface has a strong plastic protective layer with tie-down hooks and tire indents to carry motorcycles or an ATV; no rear wheelwell intrusion into the bed area; large, user-friendly cabin instruments and controls; plenty of rear legroom; rear seats can be stowed vertically, creating extra storage space; a five-star safety rating for both front- and side-impact occupant protection, and a four-star score for rollover protection; excellent fit and finish; and good quality control. **Weak points:** Way overpriced for a compact truck; acceleration is a bit slower than with competitive V6-equipped pickups; not built for heavy-duty hauling or serious off-roading; lacks low-range gearing; low-speed steering is a bit slow; excessive body lean when cornering; rear visibility is hampered by the sloping sides and small rear window; thin rear-seat padding, and seatback is too upright; and door openings are a bit narrow. **New for 2007:** Nothing important; a hybrid may be offered for the 2009 model year.

MODEL HISTORY: The Ridgeline, built in Alliston, Ontario, is Honda's first truck—a crew-cab cloned from the company's Pilot sport-utility. It's about as long as the Explorer Sport Trac and comes with lots of standard features like all-wheel drive, a 5-speed automatic, Vehicle Stability Assist (electronic stability-control) with traction control, ABS brakes, front side airbags and full-length side curtain airbags with a rollover sensor, and power locks, windows, and mirrors.

COST ANALYSIS: Dealers have complained privately to Honda that the 2006 Ridgeline was overpriced (*LX:* $35,200; *EX-L:* $39,700; *EX-L SR:* $40,900; *EX-L NAVI:* $44,400). As a result, Honda has increased the 2007 prices less than $500 and has given dealers sales incentives to cut the actual transaction price by about

2007 TECHNICAL DATA

POWERTRAIN (4X2/PART-TIME 4X4)
Engine: 3.5L V6 (255 hp); Transmission: 5-speed auto.
DIMENSION/CAPACITY
Passengers: 2/3; Wheelbase: 122 in.; H: 71/L: 207/W: 76 in.; Headroom F/R: 6.5/4.5 in.; Legroom F/R: 42/28 in.; Cargo volume: 26.2 cu. ft.; Fuel tank: 83L/regular; Tow limit: 5,000 lb.; Load capacity: 1,530 lb.; GVWR: 6,050 lb.; Turning circle: 45 ft.; Box length: 5 ft.; Ground clearance: 7.5 in.; Weight: 4,550 lb.

10 percent. **Best alternatives:** Consider the Mazda B-series, Nissan Frontier, and Toyota Tacoma or Tundra. **Rebates:** $3,000 discounts, $1,500 rebates, plus zero percent financing. **Delivery/PDI:** $1,455. **Warranty:** Bumper-to-bumper 3 years/60,000 km; powertrain 5 years/100,000 km, and rust perforation 3 years/ unlimited km. **Supplementary warranty:** Not needed. **Options:** This well-appointed truck doesn't require anything extra. Honda's extra-cost bed extender needs to be flipped out whenever the trunk lid is opened. **Depreciation:** Predicted to be higher than average because of the Ridgeline's high MSRP. **Insurance cost:** Higher than average. **Annual maintenance cost:** Predicted to be lower than average. **Parts supply/cost:** Parts are in short supply; costs not yet determined. **Highway/city fuel economy:** 10.1/14.4 L/100 km.

Secret Warranties/Internal Bulletins/Service Tips

2006–07—Automatic transmission is hard to shift into Fourth gear.

Nissan

FRONTIER ★★★★★

RATING: Recommended (2006–07); Above Average (1985–2005). Nissan has hit a home run with its Frontier. Year after year, this "Baby Titan" pickup performs well without any serious complications, bypassing the serious design glitches found with Nissan's 2004 Titan. It's as good as the Mazda and Toyota competition and better than Chrysler's over-hyped and fuel-guzzling semi-Hemi, Ford's quality-challenged Ranger, and GM's puny, Isuzu-bred Canyon/Colorado munchkins and Silverado/Sierra hulks. Let's face it, the pre-2005 models are mediocre performers;

nevertheless, they are reliable, relatively inexpensive, competent for light chores, easy to maintain, and fun to drive. **Strong points:** *2005–07:* Better-performing, more powerful engines (especially with the V6 and vehicles equipped with a manual transmission); the new 5-speed automatic transmission shifts more smoothly than the previous 4-speed, and it conserves fuel; nice handling; very comfortable ride up front; fairly reliable; and a high resale value. *2004 and earlier models:* Standard four-wheel ABS on some models; a user-friendly interior layout; an acceptable ride over smooth roads, and reasonably good handling; and extremely reliable. **Weak points:** The 4.0L will run on regular fuel (wink, wink, nudge, nudge), but 91-octane is recommended.

2007 TECHNICAL DATA

POWERTRAIN (REAR-DRIVE/PART-TIME 4X4)
Engines: 2.5L 4-cyl. (154 hp) • 4.0L V6 (265 hp); Transmissions: 5-speed man. • 6-speed man. • 5-speed auto. OD

DIMENSION/CAPACITY
Passengers: 2/3; Wheelbase: 126 in.; H: 68/L: 206/W: 73 in.; Headroom F/R: 3.0/3.5 in.; Legroom F/R: 40/27 in.; Cargo volume: 27 cu. ft.; Fuel tank: 60L/regular; Tow limit: 6,100 lb.; Load capacity: 1,160 lb.; GVWR: 4,701–5,202 lb.; Turning circle: 46 ft.; Box length: 4.6 ft./6.2 ft.; Ground clearance: 8.5 in.; Weight: 4,650 lb.

Test-drive your choice for engine performance—Nissan has been notorious for overrating their engines. *2005–07:* Poor steering feedback, a cheap-looking interior, and limited rear seating. *2004 and earlier models:* Poor acceleration (4-cylinder); choppy ride over uneven terrain ("rear-end hop") is accentuated with an empty load; lots of body lean when cornering; slow, vague steering offers little feedback; mediocre braking; drive shaft carrier bearing failures on earlier models; automatic transmission shifter obstructs view of the climate controls and blocks access to the wiper switch; difficult rear entry and exit (King Cab); low seats make the height-adjustment feature essential for many drivers, and the King Cab's rear jump seat is laughably small; limited rear legroom on the hard rear bench seat; small cargo bed on the Crew Cab; few standard features; the cabin looks like plastic central; and many gauges are too recessed to be easily read. Lots of engine, wind, and tire noise. Mediocre fuel economy on 2001–04 models. Triple-whammy safety complaints: sudden acceleration, brake failures, and Firestone tire defects. **New for 2007:** Nothing; a light freshening is planned for the 2008 models.

MODEL HISTORY: The 2005–07 Frontier is a significantly improved pickup that's larger, more powerful, easier to handle, and safer than previous models. Its wheelbase is a whopping 25 cm (9.8 in.) longer, its width went up by 4.0 cm (1.6 in.), its height increased by 7.6–8.9 cm (3.0–3.5 in.), and its overall length was stretched by 25 cm (9.8 in.). Did somebody mention power? The entry-level King Cab now carries a 2.5L 4-cylinder engine, while most other models use a 265-hp 4.0L V6. A 5-speed automatic replaced the 4-speed. A new dual-range 4×4 setup with shift-on-the-fly electronic control, rack-and-pinion steering, and a slew of handling improvements was also carried over this year. Occupant crash protection is improved on the 2005–07 models through the use of new front side airbags and optional side curtain airbags triggered by rollover sensors.

Frontier pickups have always been reliable and versatile haulers. Most models initially used a lethargic 143-hp 2.4L 4-cylinder, supplemented by a better-performing 180-hp 3.3L V6 and a barely-worth-the-trouble, premium-fueled, and temperamental supercharged 210-hp V6 variant. The King Cab V6 addition gave these pickups the power boost they lacked in the past. ABS is standard on the rear wheels and optional on all four wheels. It's standard, however, on all recent 4×4s and Crew Cabs and on the Desert Runner.

Introduced in 1985, these pickups are more comfortable, perform better, and aren't as rust-prone as their Datsun predecessors. The different 4-cylinder engines offered through the years have all provided adequate power and reasonable reliability. Engine choices through the '90s include the 2.4L 4-cylinder or the more powerful 3.0L V6 borrowed from Nissan's 240SX. Although the powerful 6-cylinder is more fuel thirsty, it's the engine of choice for maximum hauling and off-roading versatility.

You won't have to look far to find a reasonably priced used Nissan pickup. These small pickups, like Mazda's trucks, didn't cost much when they were new and their used prices have drifted downward accordingly. On newer models, though, you'll find prices have firmed up considerably because of the general popularity of two- and three-year-old crew-cab pickups and downsized sport-utilities. Depending on the year, you'll find a standard 4- or 5-speed manual or an optional 3- or 4-speed automatic. Later 4-speed automatics have a fuel-saving lock-up torque converter, but a manual transmission will get the most power and economy out of these motors. The 4×4 option is available with either manual or automatic hubs. The manual version is a pain because you have to stop and turn the hubs. The automatic form isn't much better because it can't be engaged above 50 km/h, and to disengage it you have to stop and back up a metre or two. These pickups handle impressively well and have firm but reasonably comfortable rides, although some owners say the bucket seats only fit bucket bottoms. The King Cab is a must for tall drivers or those who require extra interior storage space. Don't look for a fourth door—Nissan didn't offer one until the 2000 model year.

1995—Rear wheel ABS added. 1998—A larger, roomier model debuted with more refined interior ergonomics. 1999—King Cabs got more powerful V6 engines and a host of other standard and optional features. 2000—A Crew Cab model was given a full-sized forward-hinged fourth door and a short bed. 2001—A supercharged 210-hp V6 on SE King Cabs and Crew Cabs along with a slight restyling and standard 17-inch wheels. Other additions: a new instrument cluster, interior upgrades, and a security system. 2002—The regular-cab model was dropped, Crew Cabs were offered with a long bed, and all pickups got a restyled interior. 2003— 6-cylinder engines for the 4×4s, Crew Cabs got 10 more horses, and more options were added, like a tire-pressure monitor and anti-skid/traction control. **2006—Redesigned.**

COST ANALYSIS: $24,298 is the price for the base 2006 front-drive Frontier, and it will be discounted by about 10 percent as winter approaches. The 2007 models will likely cost about $500 more. So, buying an identical 2006 Frontier will save you almost $3,000. A good used choice would be the much-improved second-series 2005 version. **Best alternatives:** Some other small pickups you might want to consider are the Mazda B-series and Toyota Tacoma. **Rebates:** $2,500 discounts or rebates plus zero percent financing. **Delivery/PDI:** $1,296. **Warranty:** Bumper-to-bumper 3 years/60,000 km; powertrain 5 years/100,000 km; rust perforation 5 years/unlimited km. **Supplementary warranty:** An extended warranty isn't needed. **Options:** Consider a limited slip differential, four-wheel ABS, and running boards. Don't go for the Off-Road Package unless you crave a bouncier ride. **Depreciation:** Slower than average. **Insurance cost:** Average. **Parts supply/cost:** These trucks have been around for decades with few design changes, so parts are widely available and relatively inexpensive. **Annual maintenance cost:** Below-average maintenance costs; the simple design makes for easy servicing by any independent garage. **Highway/city fuel economy:** *2.4L and auto.: 9.1/12.0 L/100 km; 3.3L V6 and 4×4: 11.5/15.3 L/100 km.*

 QUALITY/RELIABILITY: Assembly and component quality are above average. Fortunately, Nissan products are generally so well made that they don't need lots of warranty work. But when they do, owners report that the company's customer relations staff in Canada isn't all that sensitive to their needs. For example, in several instances, Nissan Canada and its Infiniti spin-off have refused to recognize "goodwill" programs detailed in the company's U.S. service bulletins. Their reasoning? Apparently, Nissan Canada isn't obligated to give the same treatment to Canadian owners. Hmmm…let's see Nissan put that in their TV ads! **Owner-reported problems:** Engine exhaust intake manifold failures have been common; drive shaft and ball joint defects cause excessive vibration; minor trim and accessory defects; premature front-brake wear; and electrical short circuits.

 ROAD PERFORMANCE: Acceleration/torque: The fuel-sipping 4-cylinder engine is adequate for light-duty use. However, add an automatic transmission, and you'll wish you had the V6. The supercharged V6 is an impressive performer that's less noisy than the 4-banger. **Transmission:** Easy-shifting manual transmission, and the electronically controlled automatic transaxle is both smooth and predictable. **Steering:** Acceptable, but not very responsive or precise; the 2005 model corrects this problem. **Routine handling:** Average for a truck; improved with the upgraded suspension added in 1998 and steering/suspension enhancements found on the 2005s. Firmer ride with long wheelbase and supercharged models. **Emergency handling:** Better than average, in spite of the pickup's heft and size. **Braking:** Mediocre (100–0 km/h: 44 m).

SAFETY SUMMARY: The 2007 models' crashworthiness scores were identical to the 2006s'. **Airbags:** There have been reports of airbags failing to deploy, or deploying when they shouldn't, resulting in severe injuries. **ABS:** Standard 2W, 4W. **Safety belt pretensioners:** Standard. **Traction control:** Optional. **Head restraints F/R:** *1997:* ★; *1998:* ★★★/★★; *1999:* ★★★; *2001:* ★★★; *2002–04:* ★★; *2005–06:* ★. **Visibility F/R:** ★★★★★.

SAFETY COMPLAINTS: 1999—Rattles inside steering column. • Exhaust leak under driver's seat. • Drive shaft failure. • Driveline vibration on acceleration. • Tires lose traction on wet roads. **1999–2000**—Brake pedal goes to floor without braking. • Stalling at full throttle. **2000**—Under-hood fire. • Sudden acceleration. • Severe vibration during acceleration or while pulling a load. • Front-end bushing bolt sheared. • Loss of brakes. • Brake master cylinder failure. • Faulty drive-shaft carrier bearing; Nissan's "fix" is inadequate. • When parked on an incline, emergency brake failed and truck rolled into garage door. • Too-soft suspension causes serious swaying. **2001**—Airbags failed to deploy. • Front passenger seat belt can't be pulled out for usage (on national back-order). • High idle at low speeds with clutch depressed. • Fuel overflows from filler neck. • Brakes lack sufficient hydraulic pressure to stop vehicle. • Blocked cowl vent restricts fresh air flow. **2002**—No airbag deployment. • Automatic transmission jumped out of Park into Reverse. • Leaking fuel tank. • Brake failure. • ABS light comes on for no reason. • Sudden loss of power caused by defective oxygen sensor or kicking in of Nissan speed limiter. • Controller fuse blows repeatedly, shutting vehicle down. • Gas and brake pedal set too close together. • Tail light fills with water. • Defective sidewalls on General Grabber tires. **2003**—Sudden, unintended acceleration when brakes are applied. • Engine has to be shut down to turn off AC if defroster is engaged. **2004**—Slipped out of Park and rolled downhill. • Excessive vibration caused by corroded upper and lower ball joints. **2005**—Truck won't start because of a corroded fuel-sending unit. • Power-assisted driver-side mirror can't be adjusted to eliminate a blind spot. • Original-equipment tires wear out prematurely (tread peels away). • Tailgate fell off due to its poor design. • Tailgate gap allows sand or other fine material to spew out. • Water leaking into the tail light can cause the truck to shut down:

> What they are basically saying is that driving this vehicle in the rain could cause a breakdown, and all they did was fix my tail light.

Secret Warranties/Internal Bulletins/Service Tips

1996–2002—Troubleshooting tips for noisy, hard transfer-case shifting. **1998–99**—An easy fuel gauge fix is outlined in TSB #NTB99-064. **1999–2000**—A pop or clunking noise is addressed in TSB #NTB00-075. **1999–2001**—Repair tips for a cracked exhaust manifold set the stage for after-warranty assistance, since this bulletin shows that it's a recognized defect:

EXHAUST MANIFOLD (R/H)—TICKING/EXHAUST NOISE

BULLETIN: NTB01-038   **DATE: MAY 22, 2001**

1999–2001 Frontier (D22)

2000–01 Xterra (WD22)

If a cracked right-hand exhaust manifold is discovered during unrelated service when the exhaust heat shield is removed, a replacement right-hand exhaust manifold is available to correct the incident. If one of these symptoms should occur, use the service procedure provided in this bulletin to diagnose the condition, replacing the right-hand exhaust manifold and related parts as described.

1999–2004—A faulty radiator cap may be the cause of coolant loss or engine overheating. **2000**—Idle fluctuation when coasting to a stop with the clutch depressed. • Remedy for excessive body vibration at 100 km/h. • Water may enter the distributor assembly. • Rough idle or excessive engine vibration at idle. • Clunk or rattle heard when turning the steering wheel. • Front bumper rattling. • Troubleshooting squeaks and rattles. **2000–03**—ABS trouble light stays lit. **2001**—Cloudy, hazy appearance of plastic headlight. • Warm air from fresh air vents. • Speedometer may not work. **1999–2002**—Loss of supercharged engine power. • Surging, no automatic transmission upshifts. • Steering pull during braking. • MIL light may malfunction. • Silencing bearing noise from the transfer-case area. • Knocking noise above idle. **2003**—Remedy for AC that won't turn off. **2003–04**—Cold engine start-up rattle. **2004–05**—Troubleshooting spray-in bed liner defects. **2005**—More engine rattles. • Free body control module sub-harness to improve electrical connection for trailering. **2005–06**—Rear leaf spring squeaks • Right front seatback rattles and moves sideways.

FRONTIER PROFILE

	1998	1999	2000	2001	2002	2003	2004	2005	2006
Cost Price ($) (negotiable)									
4X2 (15%)	14,498	14,498	14,498	20,998	22,890	23,498	23,450	22,998	24,298
4X4 (16%)	20,999	21,498	21,498	26,498	27,553	27,398	27,400	28,998	29,598
Used Values ($)									
4X2 ▲	4,500	5,500	6,000	7,500	9,500	11,500	14,000	16,500	—
4X2 ▼	4,000	5,000	5,500	6,500	8,000	10,000	12,500	15,000	—
4X4 ▲	6,500	7,500	8,500	9,500	12,000	15,000	17,000	22,000	—
4X4 ▼	6,000	7,000	8,000	9,000	11,000	13,500	15,500	20,500	—
Reliability	④	④	④	⑤	⑤	⑤	⑤	⑤	—
Crash Safety (F)	❷	❸	❸	—	④	④	④	④	④
Ext.	—	—	—	—	—	—	—	—	❸
Side	—	—	④	④	⑤	⑤	④	⑤	⑤
Offset	❷	❷	❷	❷	❷	❷	❷	⑤	⑤
Rollover	—	—	—	❸	❸	❸	—	—	❸

All ratings on a numbered scale where ⑤ is good and ❶ is bad. See page 220 for a more detailed description.

2007 TECHNICAL DATA

POWERTRAIN (4X2/PART-TIME 4X4)

Engine: 5.6L V8 (305 hp); Transmission: 5-speed auto.

DIMENSION/CAPACITY

Passengers: 3/3; Wheelbase: 140 in.; H: 70/L: 224/W: 79 in.; Headroom F/R: 5.5/5.0 in.; Legroom F/R: 41.5/32 in.; Cargo volume: N/A; Fuel tank: 76L/regular; Tow limit: 9,400 lb.; Load capacity: 1,105 lb.; GVWR: 16,200 lb.; Turning circle: 49 ft.; Box length: 6.7 ft.; Ground clearance: 10 in.; Weight: 5,380 lb.

RATING: Not Recommended (2004–07). One of the worst Japanese pickups on the market. This year, *Lemon-Aid* has downgraded the Titan's rating as evidence of its faults has come in from government agencies, owner forums, and owner emails. Owner complaints will likely intensify as the base warranty expires. Safety-related defects are legion, and Nissan's customer relations staff has been totally incapable of providing fair and adequate warranty support:

Rear end in my new (2,500 miles [4,000 km]) Nissan Titan was on its way out (humming). Complained to dealer they said that the hum and metal shavings in the diff[erential] were normal. Had to threaten to park truck in their showroom through the window to get them to even look at it. When they did they kept the truck for 5 days to replace rear end that was "normal" according to their tech.

Strong points: Poor sales mean major discounting; the powerful V8 engine has slightly more torque than does the Chrysler Hemi and notably more than the Ford, Chevrolet, or GMC V8s in standard-duty trucks; good off-road performance; a roomy interior; the King Cab's rear doors swing back almost flat against the side of the cargo box; high utility-bed option is a hauler's dream; a security system with an immobilizer is standard; high-quality, factory-applied spray-on bed liner; optional adjustable pedals. **Weak points:** A plethora of factory-related deficiencies; insensitive Nissan staffers; the only engine available is a fuel-thirsty 5.6L gasoline V8; a jumpy throttle causes jerky acceleration; one wheelbase must fit all; if you want more passenger space with the Crew Cab, you give up 30 cm (1 ft.) of bed length; no standard regular-cab or heavy-duty versions; part-time 4×4 must be shifted out of 4×4 on dry or hard surfaces, while Chevy and GMC trucks have a full-time system; excessive on-road vibration and a

TERRIBLE RADIO RECEPTION

AIRBAG SENSOR DEFECTS

FREIGHT AND PDI FEE PRICE GOUGING

JERKY ACCELERATION

EXCESSIVE ON-ROAD VIBRATION

SERIOUS PREMATURE BRAKE WEAR

hopping ride; nonstop exhaust roar; premature brake wear and airbag sensor defects; and a plastic-laden interior. **New for 2007:** Nothing much; a diesel may come on board in the 2008 model year.

MODEL HISTORY: Introduced as a 2004 model, the Titan's bold, rugged look harkens back to the macho, in-your-face styling of the Dodge Ram when it starred in the movie *Twister*. This large pickup has lots of engine torque, headroom, rear-seat legroom, and 4×4 ground clearance—and horrendous problems. The Titan also offers a lighted tailgate, a cargo access area in the rear quarter panel, King Cab rear doors that swing open 168 degrees, and an optional locking rear differential (a major problem area).

COST ANALYSIS: Recent owner complaints reinforced by service bulletins confirm the Titan's status as a very risky buy. If you must buy a Titan, get the 2007 version and hope that some of the ongoing safety- and performance-related defects have been corrected. The base price for a 2007 4×2 is estimated to be $32,398 ($38,998 for the 4×4 version). **Best alternatives:** Honda's Ridgeline and Chrysler pickups equipped with a manual transmission. The Ford F-150, Chevrolet Silverado/GMC Sierra, and automatic transmission–equipped Dodge Ram come up way short for reliability. Toyota's early Tundras are smaller and a bit more problem-prone. **Rebates:** Poor sales have led to fairly generous rebates and dealer incentives in the $5,000–$7,000 range, along with some financing incentives likely to kick in early next year.

QUALITY/RELIABILITY: Way below average quality-control makes these trucks both dangerous and unreliable. These noisy, failure-prone powertrains have been used in Jeeps for years. It's not surprising that early rear axle seal failures are showing up in alarming numbers on 2004 through 2006 model-year Titans:

> The rear axle seals on the Nissan Titan years 2004–current have a severe and persistent problem with leaking. I have had my 2006 Nissan Titan in the shop once to replace the right rear axle seal at 18,000 miles [28,880 km] and now at 20,000 miles [32,000 km] it is leaking again. The location of the leak is what worries me. When the axle seal fails, it sprays gear oil on the brake components (rotors, calipers, pads) and I am worried that the pads will become contaminated and not work.

Owners report brake rotors warping within a few months and pads wearing out early; terrible radio reception, which fades out of stereo and FM mode; the $1,800 premium Fosgate radio uses cheap Clarion components; power-window and driver's power-seat malfunctions; driver's seat may be crooked; rear axle leakage; dash rattles and steering wheel clicks; easily chipped paint; and water leaks from the AC evaporator drain tube and between the headliner and rear window:

> Water leaks inside of truck through the fire wall. A/C drain hose fix was done but it still leaks water. Dealership is unable to repair. Water inside of truck caused mold to grow

in the carpet and spores into the HVAC system. This caused two people to have to go to the doctor for difficulty breathing. This is an ongoing problem for 1 1/2 years.

SAFETY SUMMARY: The 2007 models posted crashworthiness scores identical to the 2006 versions. The much-needed electronic stability-control is an optional feature, whereas the competition offers it as a standard item. **Airbags:** Side curtain airbags are optional. Some reports of airbags failing to deploy, or deploying when they shouldn't, resulting in severe injuries. **ABS:** Standard 4W. **Safety belt pretensioners:** Standard. **Traction control:** Optional. **Head restraints F/R:** 2005–06: ★★★. **Visibility F/R: ★★★★★.**

SAFETY COMPLAINTS: All years: Serious design and manufacturing deficiencies jeopardize both your life and your wallet. **2004**—Over 331 safety-related defects recorded by NHTSA; 50 or so would be normal. • Rear axle seal blowouts are legion. • Fuel spews out when refuelling. • Transmission overheats towing 3,630 kg (8,000 lbs.), despite rating of 4,345 kg (9,600 lbs). • Vehicle jumped out of Park into Reverse while parked (also a Frontier problem). • Complete steering loss. • Airbag is disabled even though a 170-pound passenger is seated. • Headlight switch easily bumped to On or Off—not enough resistance to rotation. • Brake rotors are too small, warp easily:

> The vehicle is now in the shop with 12,113 miles [19,500 km], having the rotor replaced again. I believe that there is a defective part manufactured for this vehicle. My driving habits are not such that they would cause this much excessive brake rotor warping. These brakes are not cheap to replace, I think it is unrealistic to advertise [that] a vehicle can tow 9,400 lbs [4,264 kg] and cannot even stop with its own body weight, [let alone do] any towing. The brake system in my opinion is undersized or there is a manufacture spec that is not being met. God forbid I actually used this vehicle to tow, as advertised.

• Defective Bridgestone Dueler A/T 110S tires. • Faulty seat belt retractors:

> The seat belt retractors in the rear are defective. They do not allow for movement, and get tighter and tighter until you have to unbuckle (defeating the purpose of a seat belt) and readjust. See the other identical complaints on this site [NHTSA] for details. My problem is just as they describe. In dealing with the Nissan dealer, they first said they could not duplicate the problem. I took the service writer to the vehicle, and demonstrated the problem for him. He then replied, "Oh that problem (I had made the problem perfectly clear when I took it in), well, they all do that. We had another customer complain, and we checked an 06 model, and they work the same way." All that means is that the 2004s and 2006s are defective, and probably the 2005s as well.

2005—119 safety-related failures recorded by NHTSA; many relate to rear axle seals. • Right front wheel spindle fractured. • Vehicle shakes violently when brakes are applied because of warped rotors and worn-out pads. • Brake failures caused by faulty ABS sensors. • Many of the brake components and an upgraded brake kit are on nationwide back-order. • Transmission failures. Writes one Kamloops, B.C., 2005 Titan owner:

> The complete wiring harness in the engine compartment has to be replaced due to corrosion issues. There was only one available in Canada, and it was flown in. While it was being installed, something else went wrong, and the last one left in North America was flown in.
>
> I finally I got a phone call: They're still having electrical issues with my truck. Prognosis unknown. It's now into week 3.
>
> The initial diagnosis into the corrosion issue was made because of a factory bulletin detailing the same problem on 2004 models of the Titan and since my Titan was built in Aug. 2004 (a 2005 model) the mechanic had a hint of where to look. I spoke to a Nissan rep in Mississauga about getting the warranty extended to cover wiring issues, and was stonewalled.

• Seat belt would not release; child was cut free. **2006**—Already 31 safety-related failures have been recorded by NHTSA. • Airbags didn't deploy as the vehicle rolled over. • Frequent rear differential failures preceded by excessive vibration, a humming noise, and metal shavings in the transmission fluid:

> The differential failed when turning right onto a busy street. There was a loud bang then a grinding sound. The truck would not drive after that. Every time I tried to accelerate the truck would just grind and not move.

• Excessive steering shudder when braking. • Driver's window only rolls up halfway. • Fuel gauge doesn't work after refuelling. • Broken rear door latch. • Poorly performing Goodyear Wrangler tires:

> I have a 2006 Nissan Titan King Cab. It has Goodyear Wrangler tires SRA 265 70 R18 on it. In the first two times I have had it in light rain on good highways it hydroplanes horribly at medium speeds (45 to 55 mph [72–88 km/h]). I have nearly lost control of this vehicle several times in light rain. The tires on this vehicle do nothing to channel away water in my opinion. I went into a slight curve in the rain and the vehicle just wanted to go straight. The match of this tire with this truck is going to kill someone. The tire option[s] listed later in this complaint [NHTSA] do not give Goodyear Wrangler as an option.

Secret Warranties/Internal Bulletins/Service Tips

2004—Warranty payout guidelines and troubleshooting tips for brake shudder and vibration are detailed in TSB #BR00-004a and NTB00-033a, dated June 11,

2003. • Slow tire leak. • Inoperative DVD. • Coolant leaks and engine overheating blamed on faulty radiator cap. **2004–05**—No start; engine doesn't crank. • Too-high idle speed. • Transmission fluid leaks from the air cooler line. • Tips for correcting brake vibration. • Water leaks from the rear sliding window track. • Poor AC cooling in hot weather. • AC condenser fan rattling. • Tips on trouble-shooting spray-in bed liner defects. • Discolouration of sprayed-on bed liner. • Free body control module sub-harness to improve electrical connection for trailering. • Fuel gauge stays on Full. • Front door creaking or ticking. • Back-glass water leaks. **2004–06**—Right front seatback rattles and moves sideways. • Damaged bed liner spray. • Tips on fixing sprayed-in bed liner damage.

TITAN PROFILE

	2004	2005	2006
Cost Price ($) (negotiable)			
4X2 (22%)	31,900	31,900	32,398
4X4 (23%)	38,200	38,500	38,998
Used Values ($)			
4X2 ▲	22,500	25,500	—
4X2 ▼	21,000	24,000	—
4X4 ▲	26,000	28,500	—
4X4 ▼	24,500	27,500	—
Reliability	❷	❷	—
Crash Safety (F)	④	⑤	⑤
Offset	⑤	⑤	⑤
Rollover	—	—	④

Subaru

BAJA ★★

RATING: Below Average (2003–07). A Legacy spin-off going into its fifth year, Baja is touted as a crossover that's part wagon and part pickup, but it winds up offering little that is useful or fun. **Strong points:** Poor sales mean deeply discounted prices; uniquely styled like a mini-Avalanche; uses a shortened Legacy platform. **Weak points:** Way overpriced; uncomfortable upright rear seating; bed is too short to carry a bike without extending the tailgate into part of the bed; no 5-speed automatic transmission; absence of a folding midgate means the flip-and-fold versatility isn't as practical as Subaru pretends; essentially a resurrected Subaru Brat (1977–87). Head restraints ranked Marginal by IIHS. **New for 2007:** The Baja will be dropped at the end of 2006.

MODEL HISTORY: The 2007 Baja costs $35,595 and is basically a Legacy Outback with its rear roof chopped off and 15 cm (6 in.) added to the rear floor to make a mini pickup bed. Like the Chevy Avalanche, the Baja has a "switchback" door similar to the trunk pass-through door in a sedan, creating a 2.5 m (7.6 ft.) cargo bed. The car/truck comes with standard four-wheel disc ABS, AC, sunroof, anti-theft device, front passenger-side airbag, a 5-speed manual or 4-speed automatic transmission, and upgraded child restraint anchors.

Baja projects a rugged, utilitarian look with its large fender flares, 16-inch alloy wheels, and sport bars, but its 165-hp flat-four engine fails to deliver the driving performance its styling promises. A turbocharged variant of the same 4-banger provides more power, but it exacts a 10-percent fuel penalty. Nevertheless, if you're not in a hurry to go anywhere and value fuel economy (7.6/10.3 L/100 km) over driving thrills, the all-wheel-drive Baja equipped with the non-turbo engine will fill the bill.

2007 TECHNICAL DATA

POWERTRAIN (FULL-TIME 4X4)
Engines: 2.5L 4-cyl. (165 hp) • 2.5L 4-cyl. Turbo (210 hp); Transmission: 5-speed man. • 4-speed auto.

DIMENSION/CAPACITY
Passengers: 2/2; Wheelbase: 104 in.; H: 61/L: 193/W: 70 in.; Headroom F/R: 2.5/1.5 in.; Legroom F/R: 41.0/27 in.; Cargo volume: N/A; Fuel tank: 64L/regular; Tow limit: 2,400 lb.; Load capacity: 800 lb.; GVWR: 4,555 lb.; Turning circle: 41 ft.; Box length: 7.5 ft.; Ground clearance: 6.0 in.; Weight: 3,575 lb.

SAFETY COMPLAINTS: 2004—Headliner caved in when the driver pulled on the seat belt. • Hard to see lit brake lights because sunlight reflects from the light coverings. **2005**—Handbrake doesn't keep vehicle from rolling backward. • Bridgestone Potenza RE92 tire tread peels away.

Secret Warranties/Internal Bulletins/Service Tips

2004—Transfer clutch binding on turns. • Wind noise from door mirror. **2005**—A loose baffle inside the muffler may be the source of a rear-end pinging sound.

BAJA PROFILE

	2003	2004	2005	2006
Cost Price ($) (negotiable)				
AWD (15%)	35,695	29,995	29,995	29,995
Used Values ($)				
AWD ▲	15,000	18,000	21,000	—
AWD ▼	13,500	17,500	19,500	—
Reliability		⑤	⑤	⑤	—

All ratings on a numbered scale where ⑤ is good and ❶ is bad. See page 220 for a more detailed description.

Toyota

TACOMA ★★★★★

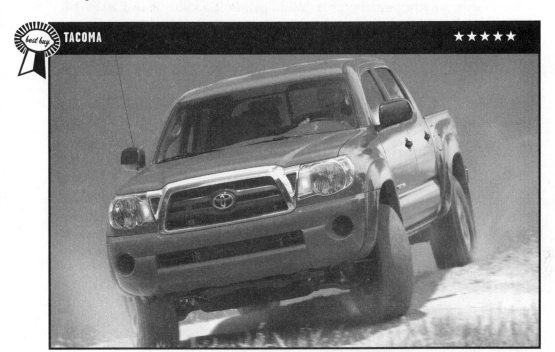

RATING: Recommended (2005–07); Above Average (1987–2004). This is a low-tech, relatively reliable, unadorned pickup. The 2005 improvements make Tacoma a big pickup player. **Strong points:** *2005–07:* Incredibly powerful 4- and 6-cylinder engines give smooth performance without guzzling fuel; ride and handling are improved with firmer, shorter springs, gas shocks, a limited slip differential, and larger tires; towing capability increased by 680 kg (1,500 lb.); upgraded interior, and a new composite cargo bed with extra storage compartments and adjustable tie-down anchors; additional interior room makes back seats acceptable for adult passengers. Additional safety features, like side curtain airbags. *2004 and earlier models:* Competent V6 engine performance; rugged, impressive off-road

2007 TECHNICAL DATA

POWERTRAIN (4X4 OR 4X2/PART-TIME 4X4)

Engines: 2.7L 4-cyl. (159 hp) • 4.0L V6 (236 hp); Transmissions: 5-speed man. • 6-speed man. • 4-speed auto. • 5-speed auto.

DIMENSION/CAPACITY

Passengers: 2/3; Wheelbase: 128 in.; H: 64/L: 208/W: 75 in.; Headroom F/R: 4.0/3.0 in.; Legroom F/R: 42.5/28 in.; Cargo volume: 25.9 cu. ft.; Fuel tank: 57L/regular; Tow limit: 6,500 lb. (4X4); Load capacity: 1,200 lb.; GVWR: 4,244–5,104 lb. Turning circle: 43 ft.; Box length: 6.2 ft.; Ground clearance: 8.5 in.; Weight: 4,115 lb.

capability; good braking; roomy interior; and good build quality. The high resale value, above-average reliability, slow depreciation, and good fuel economy somewhat offset the stiff purchase price. **Weak points:** Handling is still somewhat trucklike; 6-speed manual transmission is a bit clunky; rear drum brakes (Toyota says they perform better in wet conditions); and a small, 1.5 m (5 ft.) bed. *2004 and earlier:* Mediocre ride and wet-weather handling; bereft of many standard features offered by competitors; front seat is set too low and far back; cushions are too small in the rear seat, where legroom is limited; climate controls are obstructed by the cupholders; smaller bed than many competitors; StepSide bed is quite narrow; difficult entry and exit require a higher step-up than with other 4×4 pickups; less towing capability than domestic competitors; and may not achieve stated towing capacity (be very wary). Lots of engine and road noise. **New for 2007:** Nothing significant.

MODEL HISTORY: Redesigned for the first time in 10 years, the 2005 Tacoma targeted the Dodge Dakota crowd with a powerful V6 and a 6-speed manual/5-speed automatic transmission to counter Dodge's less sophisticated powertrain setup at the time. Set on the same platform as the 4Runner and Lexus GX 470, recent Tacomas are about 15 cm (6 in.) longer, 10 cm (4 in.) wider, and 5 cm (2 in.) taller than 2004 and earlier versions.

This compact pickup is available as a Regular Cab, Xtracab, or Double Cab (a four-door crew cab) in 4×2 or 4×4. There's no denying the added convenience of four doors, but the Double Cab also provides a 60/40 folding rear bench seat for more versatility. The 245-hp V6 beats Dodge's 3.7L 215-hp V6, Ford's 4.2L 202-hp V6, and GM's 4.3L 200-hp V6. Available engines on 2004 and earlier models are a 2.4L and 2.7L 4-cylinder and a 3.4L V6. A dealer-installed supercharger package will give the V6 50 additional horses (295 hp). The shift-on-the-fly 4×4 system is optional on 4×4 trucks and standard on the 4×4 SR5 V6.

Toyota has been building good cars for quite a while, but its pickups have always missed the quality and performance mark by a little bit because they were undersized, underpowered, or both. Their mechanical reliability is better than that of American pickups, but that's not saying much. Tacomas don't offer a lot of razzle-dazzle or carlike handling, but they aren't dangerous to life, limb, or your pocketbook.

1990—SR5 V6s got standard rear-wheel ABS. **1991**—A wider distribution of shift-on-the-fly 4×4 and ABS, and no more manual transmission. **1993**—Introduction of the full-sized T100, a one-ton model carrying a 150-hp V6 capable of handling 1,168 kg (2,575 lb.). **1994**—Dropped the long-bed option and added side door beams. **1998**—Fresh styling and a passenger-side airbag and cut-off switch. **1999**—Seat belt pretensioners and force limiters. **2000**—4×4 improved gearing. **2001**—Debut of the Double Cab and a new StepSide version, revised front styling and new alloy wheels, a differential locking system, 31-inch tires on alloy wheels, and a tachometer. **2003**—Standard ABS and upgraded child restraint anchors. **2005**—Larger, more powerful, and equipped for the first time with side curtain airbags.

Reliability has been compromised during the past several decades by lapses in quality-control leading to expensive V6 engine head gasket failures through 2004. Automatic transmission and brake problems have carried over to the latest models.

COST ANALYSIS: Tacoma has been coasting since its 2005 model redesign, so neither the 2006 nor the 2007 models give you much more for the extra money. If you get a new Tacoma, understand that it will cost you at least $22,535; an AWD version costs about $7,000 more and really isn't worth the extra money. If AWD is really needed, get a used second-series Tacoma with that option. In fact, the 2005s are your best buys from a price and quality perspective. In 2002–04 models, the 2,250 kg (5,000 lb.) towing capability may not be possible. **Best alternatives:** The Mazda B-series and Nissan Frontier are credible alternatives. Watch out: As with Mazda's B-series, you'll pay way over the base price for a loaded Tacoma. It's interesting that the new 4×4 sells for about $7,000 more than the 4×2 and then depreciates almost to the 4×2's level after five years. **Rebates:** Look for $2,000–$3,000 rebates and zero percent financing. **Delivery/PDI:** $1,390. **Warranty:** Bumper-to-bumper 3 years/60,000 km; powertrain 5 years/100,000 km; rust perforation 5 years/unlimited km. **Supplementary warranty:** An extended powertrain warranty would be wise on the pre-2005 models. **Options:** Try to get a model equipped with electronic stability-control. Ditch the Firestone and Bridgestone tires. **Depreciation:** Slower than average. **Insurance cost:** Average. **Parts supply/cost:** Parts are easily found at dealerships and independent suppliers, and costs are very reasonable. **Annual maintenance cost:** Far below average when compared with the American competition and most other Japanese automakers. Good dealer network and service. **Highway/city fuel economy:** *4×2, 2.4L, and automatic: 8.8/11.1 L/100 km; 4×4 and 2.7L: 10.4/13.1 L/100 km; 4×4 and 3.4L: 10.9/13.6 L/100 km; 4×4 and 4.0L: 10.9/15.0 L/100 km.*

QUALITY/RELIABILITY: *2004–07:* Better than average. Not as good as it once was, and the 2005's changes have brought their own set of problems, including the following: oil leaks between the transmission and crankshaft; assorted short-circuits; water leaks onto the floorboard from the A-pillar; cabin mount bolts and bushings contract and loosen in cold weather, resulting in a loud banging noise in the cabin area; paint is easily chipped (rocker panels, lower doors, and front of the bed sides); tailgate failed when truck was on the highway; Delphi battery sprayed acid around the engine compartment. **Owner-reported problems:** *2004 and earlier models:* Powertrain, brake (especially 2000–03 models), and AC failures; engine seized after ingesting water when vehicle passed through a puddle; electrical shorts; premature front brake wear; and subpar fit and finish (excessive paint chipping). Some reports that the truck is hard to start, and the driver's seat's inadequate lumbar support is painful on long drives. **Warranty performance:** Average. Owners allege that speedometer readings are inflated by 8 percent, robbing owners of the same percentage of warranty coverage:

> My 2005 Tacoma's speedometer has been reading approximately 7 miles per hour [11 km/h] faster than actual. I couldn't figure out why so many cars were passing me on the highway when I was doing around 65 [105 km/h]! I checked it by following my wife in her car and also compared against mile markers. I took [the vehicle] to the dealer and they hooked it up to the diagnostic computer and found nothing wrong.

SAFETY SUMMARY: The 2007s' crashworthiness scores are identical to the 2006 model ratings. Xtracab's right rear seat will accommodate a child safety seat. Owners report that the truck's suspension can barely handle a 227 kg (500 lb.) payload, despite Toyota's assertion that it has a 544 kg (1,200 lb.) rating. **Airbags:** Front. There have been reports of airbags failing to deploy. **ABS:** Optional 2W and 4W. **Safety belt pretensioners:** Standard. **Head restraints F/R:** *1997:* ★★★/★★; *1998:* ★★★/★★; *1999:* ★; *2001–04:* ★; *2005–06:* ★★; *1999 Extended Cab:* ★★. **Visibility F/R:** ★★★★★.

SAFETY COMPLAINTS: All years: Airbag malfunctions. • Sudden acceleration. • Brake failures, overheating, extended stopping distance, and prematurely worn calipers and rotors. • Vehicle wanders all over the road after hitting a bump. • Firestone, Goodyear, and Dunlop tire-tread separation. • Loose or poorly fitted trip panels. **1999**—Stuck accelerator. • When airbag deployed, it melted a hole in the dash. • ABS brakes locked up. • Truck accelerates when heater motor comes on. • Shift lever jumped out of First and into Second gear. • Transfer-case seizure. • Left front axle assembly failure caused by defective front ball joint nut. • Rear differential failed. • Check Engine and Airbag warning lights stay on constantly. • Rear leaf spring and overload spring break easily when passing over rough terrain. **1999–2000**—Under-hood fires. • Excessive vibration when underway. • Turn signals don't work. **2000**—Parking brake failed. • Side mirror is hard to focus. • Nothing in place to prevent rear-seat passengers' heads from striking the rear window in a collision. **2001**—Incorrectly installed ABS sensor led to brake failure. • Vehicle is prone to hydroplane over wet roads at relatively slow speeds. • Intermittently, alarm system fails to unlock vehicle. • Loose front-drive shaft bolts. • Rear wheel fell off. **2001–04**—Dash pad rattle repair tips. **2002**—Brake and gas pedal mounted too closely together. • Brake master cylinder leaks. • Automatic transmission shudders, clunks, surges, shifts erratically, and jumps from gear to gear • Transmission line blew out. • Defective front and rear shock absorbers. • Water enters the cabin through the driver-side support handle. • Defective wheel rims and tires. • Poorly designed jack handle makes for risky tire-changing. **2003**— Sudden rollover. • Sudden engine surging caused by a defective throttle actuator control. • Loss of power caused by a faulty throttle body sensor:

You can only open the throttle body butterfly the first 25% with the pedal, then the computer opens it the rest of the way. These throttle by wire [or highly-responsive accelerators] are crapping out left and right and Toyota is...claiming [they are covered under the less-generous 3 year/60,000 km bumper-to-bumper warranty and not the 5 year/100,000 km powertrain warranty].

• Truck sways and pitches excessively. • Shifter can be accidentally bumped and will shift into Neutral. • Front seats rock back and forth. • Water leaks onto the driver-side floor and through the passenger door. • Doors don't close fully and lock. • Broken wheel lug nuts:

While the inspector was placing the tires back onto the truck, two of the wheel studs broke on the front hub. He stated that this happens on almost every 2000–2003 Toyota pickup they work on. He even showed me that the stud wasn't cross-threaded and removed the stud from the lug nut using a pair of pliers. The stud came right out with little pressure.

• Defective Firestone and Goodyear Wrangler tires. **2004**—Several incidents of fire igniting while vehicle was being driven. • Front airbags didn't deploy as required. • Transmission jerks when going into gear. • Both rear springs failed when cornering. • Side rear-view mirrors fog up badly. • Goodyear Wrangler sidewall blowout. • Loss of braking ability in inclement weather. • Parking brake hits driver's knee. • Seat lumbar supports cause lower back pain. **2005**—Sudden, unintended acceleration. • 6-speed manual transmission has serious judder and shifts only with considerable difficulty:

The judder problem was particularly bad and was evident with every start in First gear and sometimes in Second gear. It became more violent with each start and at one point, after the clutch pedal was fully released, there was a sudden slip of the clutch disc followed by sudden friction. This resulted in loss of traction of the drive wheels and subsequent total loss of control of the vehicle. Control was regained relatively quickly by depressing the clutch pedal to remove drive power from the wheels and a catastrophic event was narrowly avoided.

• Total brake failure. • Skid plate catches air and causes the vehicle to shake violently at highway speeds. • Exhaust crossover pipe hangs below the transfer-case mount and can be easily crushed when off-roading. This would allow carbon monoxide to enter into the cabin. • Left turn signal quits intermittently. • Right-side rear-view mirror vibrates excessively (especially on windy days) and also creates a large blind spot in the right front quarter of the vehicle. • Defective Firestone and Bridgestone Potenza RE050A tires crack and split. • Tailgate is dangerously weak, unable to support normal weight without bending out of shape.

Secret Warranties/Internal Bulletins/Service Tips

All years: If there is a delay when shifting from Park or Neutral to Reverse, Toyota will install an upgraded B3 return spring, B3 Brake piston O-rings, and a low-coast modulator spring to correct the problem. Toyota doesn't say if the repair will be covered by its base warranty or "goodwill"; however, a good rule of thumb is that any transmission malfunction, like a delay in this case, would be the automaker's responsibility for at least the first 7 years/160,000 km. • To minimize noise when shifting 4×4 automatic transmissions, Toyota will change various transmission components under the base warranty. A Toyota insider tells me that the work will also be done for free up to 5 years/80,000 km under a "goodwill" special policy. • Consult TSB #AC002-97, issued May 9, 1997, to eliminate musty odours emanating from the AC. Usually, the problem is caused by a blocked evaporator-housing drain pipe. • Countermeasures for rotten-egg smell from exhaust. • TSB #BR95-003 says Toyota has a new brake pad kit that reduces brake noise and increases brake durability. • Consult TSB #BR94-002 and #BR95-001, where the company outlines all the possible ways brake pulsation/vibration can be further reduced. Incidentally, this problem has affected almost all of Toyota's cars and trucks over the past decade. • Toyota has also developed a new grease to prevent brake pad clicking. **1995–2000**—That undercarriage noise you hear may be caused by a loose exhaust manifold heat shield. **1997–2004**—Tips on plugging body water leaks. **1999**—Install an upgraded clutch pedal kit to silence pedal squeaking. **2000**—Fix to prevent paint chipping on the rear quarter panels. • Dirt builds up on shoulder belt. • Squeak and rattle noises from the idler pulley. **2001**—Faulty power door locks. **2001–02**—Tube step knocking, squeaking, and rattling fix. • Dash pad rattles. • Loose fender flare pad. • Tearing of the seat material on Double Cabs. **2002**—Vehicle pulls to one side. • Off-centre steering wheel. • MIL light stays lit. **2001–03**—Special Campaign relative to the fuel inlet protector. **2002–06**—Correction for vehicles that pull to the side. **2003–07**—Tips for silencing an upper or lower windshield ticking noise. **2005**—No-start in cold temperatures. • Front cowl water leaks. • Suspension slap, squeak noise. **2005–06**—Deformed window runs.

TACOMA PROFILE

	1998	1999	2000	2001	2002	2003	2004	2005	2006
Cost Price ($) (negotiable)									
Base (15%)	15,548	16,390	16,765	21,630	21,920	22,370	22,570	22,125	22,535
4X4 (17%)	24,868	25,705	26,150	27,045	27,335	28,065	29,400	29,240	29,560
Used Values ($)									
Base ▲	4,500	5,000	6,000	8,000	10,500	12,000	14,500	16,500	—
Base ▼	4,000	4,500	5,000	7,000	9,500	11,000	13,000	15,000	—
4X4 ▲	6,500	7,000	8,000	10,000	13,000	14,500	16,500	22,000	—
4X4 ▼	6,000	6,500	7,000	9,000	12,000	13,500	15,000	20,500	—

All ratings on a numbered scale where ⑤ is good and ❶ is bad. See page 220 for a more detailed description.

Reliability	④	④	④	④	④	③	③	④	—
Crash Safety (F)									
4X2	—	—	—	—	④	—	—	⑤	⑤
Ext. Cab.	④	—	③	③	③	③	③	⑤	⑤
Double	—	—	—	—	—	④	④	—	—
Side									
4X2	—	—	—	—	⑤	—	—	⑤	⑤
Ext. Cab	❶	❶	③	③	③	③	③	⑤	⑤
Double	—	—	—	—	—	⑤	⑤	—	—
Offset	③	③	③	③	③	③	③	⑤	⑤
Rollover	—	—	❷	❷	❷	④	④	—	④
Ext. Cab	—	—	—	—	❷	—	—	④

TUNDRA ★★★★

2007 TECHNICAL DATA

POWERTRAIN (4X2/4X4)

Engines: 4.0L V6 (236 hp) • 4.7L V8 (271 hp) • 5.7L V8 (350 hp); Transmissions: 6-speed man. • 5-speed auto.

DIMENSION/CAPACITY

Passengers: 3/3; Wheelbase: 145.7 in.; H: 76.4/L: 228.7/W: 79.9 in.; Headroom F/R: N/A; Legroom F/R: N/A; Cargo volume: N/A; Fuel tank: 100L/regular; Tow limit: 10,000 lb.; Load capacity: 1,505 lb.; GVWR: 3,795–5,700 lb.; Turning circle: N/A; Box length: 78.7 in.; Ground clearance: N/A; Weight: N/A

RATING: Above Average (2006–07); Average (2004–05); Below Average (2001–03). The rating for early versions has been downgraded because the competition has better-performing models, higher levels of quality control, and cheaper prices. The high number of brake and transmission failure complaints is also a factor. **Strong points:** *2006 and earlier:* Twin-cam V8 acceleration; low-range gearing for off-roading; smooth, quiet ride; a roomier Double Cab (2004); passenger-side airbag can be switched off with a key; well appointed; easy front access; good fit and finish; standard transmission and engine oil coolers; slow depreciation; better-than-average predicted reliability. **Weak points:** *2006 and earlier:* Less engine torque than the competition; difficult rear exit and entry; 4×4 can't be used on dry pavement (unlike the GM Silverado and Sierra); excessive body sway, and tends to be a bit bouncy; poorly performing rear brake drums; rear-hinged back doors on the Access Cab don't open independently of the front doors; no four-door Crew Cab model available, and the V8 requires premium fuel. The 2003 and earlier models aren't as roomy in the rear half of the extended cab as other extended full-sized trucks—you feel like you're entering a Dodge Dakota or Ford Ranger; paint is not up to Toyota standards; weak door indents; dash LCDs are unreadable with sunglasses; bland styling; and incredibly high rate of safety-related defects involving brake, airbag, and seat belt failures. **New for 2007:** Arriving in early 2007, the redesigned Tundra is larger, more powerful, and better appointed, and it provides many new body and engine configurations. It's 25 cm (10 in.) longer, 13 cm (5 in.) taller, and 10 cm (4 in.) wider, and it's powered by a new 5.7L i-Force V8 mated to an also new heavy-duty 6-speed automatic transmission. Other new features: a lockable tailgate with safety hinges, extra-large side mirrors, a centre console big enough to hold a file folder, and a trailer hitch integrated into the frame. In a bid to attract more commercial users, the new cabin has large door handles and controls that can be operated with gloves on and headroom has been increased to accommodate occupants wearing hardhats. Braking is improved via heavy-duty front disc brakes with four-piston calipers and vented rotors increased by nearly 4 cm (1.5 in.) as well as standard rear disc brakes. High capacity cooling and electrical systems have been added to enhance towing capability. Finally, Tundra will ride on a reinforced chassis platform with 30-percent higher tensile strength steel.

MODEL HISTORY: Larger, stronger, safer, and roomier than its T100 predecessor, the 2001 Tundra was Toyota's first serious foray into the lucrative, though crowded, full-sized pickup market. Unfortunately, Toyota's new truck wasn't quite full-sized, and sales suffered.

Toyota corrected that shortcoming with its 2004 models by stretching the Dana-built frame to make the Tundra more competitive with Detroit's Big Three pickups. This improvement was accompanied by a slight decline in quality, which was addressed in subsequent years. Two engines, a 190-hp 3.4L V6 and a 240-hp 4.7L V8, are offered up to the 2005 model year, when the 4.0L came on board. A 5.7L 350-hp V8 is expected to be available on the 2007 models near the beginning of the year.

2002—The Limited gets a standard in-dash CD changer, anti-lock braking, and keyless remote entry. **2003**—A new V8-equipped Access CAB StepSide model; ABS, grille, bumper, power-sliding rear window (Limited), 17-inch wheels (optional on the SR5), new centre console, and vinyl flooring. **2004**—A more powerful, brawnier Double Cab that gains 30 cm (12 in.) in wheelbase and length and 7 cm (3 in.) in width. **2005**—More power, new transmissions, and optional side curtain airbags; a 4.0L 245-hp V6 replaced the 190-hp 3.4L; a 6-speed manual transmission replaced the 5-speed, and a 5-speed automatic replaced the 4-speed; the 4.7L V8 got 42 more horses.

COST ANALYSIS: The upgraded 2007 Tundra will likely sell for about $1,000 more than last year's version, and it's worth it. However, a year's wait will ensure you get a better-quality truck at a more competitive price. A 2005, with its extra cabin space and four-door convenience, is the best used choice. **Best alternatives:** Consider the Honda Ridgeline, Mazda B-series, and Nissan Frontier. **Rebates:** Look for $3,000 rebates and low financing on the 2006s; 2007s will likely sell for the full list price. **Delivery/PDI:** $1,390. **Options:** Choose optional equipment judiciously—you could pay almost $40,000 for a loaded version. Recommended are running boards and the All Weather Guard package that includes a heavy-duty starter and heater. **Depreciation:** Much slower than average. **Insurance cost:** Higher than average. **Parts supply/cost:** Most parts are widely available and of average cost. Some drivers wait as long as two months for powertrain components, though. **Annual maintenance cost:** Maintenance and repair costs have been much less than average; however, the 2007 Tundra could turn out to be more difficult to service and, hence, more costly to maintain. The service bays at many Toyota dealerships cannot handle these behemoths, so they'll have to be retrofitted to accommodate the new Tundra: The bays are too small and too close together, lifts can't raise the truck high enough to work on, and the alignment racks are too short. **Warranty:** Bumper-to-bumper 3 years/60,000 km; powertrain 5 years/100,000 km; rust perforation 5 years/unlimited km. **Supplementary warranty:** An extended warranty is a waste of money. **Highway/city fuel economy:** *4×2, 3.4L, and man.:* 11.1/14.3 L/100 km; *4×2, 3.4L, and auto.:* 10.9/14.1 L/100 km; *4×4, 3.4L, and man.:* 12.1/15.4 L/100 km; *4×4, 3.4L, and auto.:* 12.3/14.4 L/100 km; *4×2, 4.0L, and auto.:* 9.7/12.7 L/100 km; *4.7L and auto.:* 11.9/15.6 L/100 km; and *4×4, 4.7L, and auto.:* 12.6/15.4 L/100 km.

QUALITY/RELIABILITY: Varies from below average on early models to above average for the latest versions. Most of the serious defects are clustered around the 2000 model year and relate to brake failures and excessive vibration, premature transmission failures, engine manifold rust-outs, paint peeling, and poor quality Dunlop tires. The 2001s have garnered barely one-third of the complaints, and most of those relate to the brake calipers and rotors. **Owner-reported problems:** Excessive front-brake vibration or pulsation makes the truck almost uncontrollable and causes the Tundra to shake violently when brakes are applied; brake drums and rotors warp within 7,000 km; steel wheels rust prematurely; chronic rear axle noise and suspension knocking; ABS brakes make a loud banging sound upon engagement; V8 engine knocking when started in cold weather; excessive drive-train vibration at 100 km/h; automatic transmission binding; 4×4 system grinds and pops out of gear; poor transmission performance:

> I have a 2005 Toyota Tundra. At times, it doesn't shift up properly and the engine revs up very high, but the truck doesn't accelerate. At times, when I am coasting down a hill, it will shift down, causing the truck to slow down. I took it to the dealer and was told that the transmission is completely electronic and that happens sometimes. I feel that this is a factory defect. Last week, I was trying to make a left turn at an intersection. I pressed the pedal but the truck didn't accelerate. I could have been hit by an oncoming car.

Paint is easily chipped; oil dipstick is incorrectly calibrated or too short, leading to incorrect readings; loose windows rattle constantly; exhaust smells like rotten eggs. **Warranty performance:** Average, but Toyota must stop blaming its customers for its own manufacturing errors and stonewalling legitimate claims.

SAFETY SUMMARY: The 2007 models haven't yet been crash-tested. **Airbags:** Front and side curtain; there have been reports of airbags failing to deploy. **ABS:** 4W standard; disc/disc. **Safety belt pretensioners:** Front; seat belt failures are also common. **Head restraints:** *2001–02:* ★★★★; *2003–04:* ★★★★/★★★; *2005–06 models without adjustable lumbar seats:* ★★★; *2005–06 models with adjustable lumbar seats:* ★★. **Visibility F/R:** ★★★★★. **Maximum load capacity:** *2000 SR5 4.7L:* 1,340 lb.

SAFETY COMPLAINTS: All years: Airbags failed to deploy. • Seat belt/retractor failures. • Vehicle rolled away after it was put in Park and the emergency brake was applied. • An incredibly high number of brake complaints relative to brake failures, rotor and drum warping, and excessive vibration/shudder. • Brakes overheat and fade after successive application; extended braking distance. • Ball joint failure caused wheel to separate. • Loose, poorly fitted trim panels. **2001**—Sudden, unintended acceleration caused by faulty oxygen sensors, which are frequently back-ordered. • Exhaust manifold cracking. • With a full fuel tank and when riding uphill, gas fumes enter the cabin. • Gear selector fails to engage the proper gear. • When applying lube to the drive-shaft bearings, the grease just squirts around the fitting, not in. • Broken weld in tow hitch caused accident. **2002**—Cab separated from chassis. • Automatic transmission goes into the wrong gear or slams into gear. • Sudden brake lock-up. • Lug nuts are easily broken when tightened. • Bent wheel rims. • Bridgestone tread cracking. • Tires hydroplane easily. **2003**—Airbags failed to deploy. • Vehicle stalls out. • Engine oil leaks. • Sudden tie-rod failure caused Tundra to flip. • Accident caused by right lower ball joint separation. • Transfer-case malfunction leads to reduced power and excessive vibration. • Faulty transmission Overdrive causes engine surge. • Vehicle rolled back while in Park. **2004**—Sudden, unintended acceleration. • Many reports of the ball joint or lower control arm suddenly failing on vehicles not included in the recall to fix the problem. • Driver-side front wheel sheared off (caused by failure of right front ball joint). • Broken wheel lug nuts. • Defroster brings in carbon monoxide. • Goodrich Rugged Trail tire cracks. • Rear window popped out, and sunroof exploded. **2005**—Front wheel detached:

> While I was driving 55 mph [88.5 km/h] on a two lane highway, my 2005 Toyota Tundra 4WD driver side front wheel detached, folding under the front left side frame behind the wheel well with the truck landing on the flat side of the wheel. I was then in a controlled skid on a straight part of the highway and held the steering wheel in that position. I did not apply the brakes as I did not want to alter the direction of the skid. The vehicle drifted slightly to the right after about a 150 foot [45 metre] skid. The wheel hub had separated from the upper and lower control arm, the ball joint had detached from the A-frame.... I contacted my Toyota dealer who didn't seem too interested since there were no injuries. This incident occurred with 72,000 miles [115,900 km] on the truck meaning that the 36 month, 36,000 mile [57,940 km]

warranty would not cover the damage. In researching the ball joint complaint I found that there was a recall on the 2004 Tundra.

• Automatic transmission failure (won't go into gear, or jumps out of Drive into Neutral). • Cruise control downshifts two gears on slight upgrades. • Extreme pulling to the left and right. • Driver's captain chair rocks back and forth. • Faulty tire-pressure monitoring system.

Secret Warranties/Internal Bulletins/Service Tips

2000–02—Hard starts/no-starts (see bulletin). • Damaged front-seat cover. **2000–04**—If the AC doesn't sufficiently cool the cabin, TSB #AC004-04 says the water control valve is the likely culprit. **2000–05**—Troubleshooting front and rear brake vibrations. • Engine squealing noise on cold start-up. • Front-door window rattles. **2001**—New parking struts developed to reduce rear brake vibration. • Inaccurate temperature gauge. • Inadequate application of seam sealer in driver's footwell area. • Loose antenna mast. • Improved durability of the quarter-window lock. **2001–03**—Oil pressure gauge reads abnormally low. • Front-brake repair tips. • Rotten-egg exhaust smell (a replacement catalytic converter has been devised). **2002**—Vehicle pulls to one side. • Off-centre steering wheel. **2002–06**—Remedy for vehicle pulling hard to the left or right. **2003–07**—Tips for silencing an upper or lower windshield ticking noise. **2004–05**—Rear shock squeaking. • No-start in cold temperatures. • AC blower noise. **2004–06**—Ticking noise from lower A-pillar when passing over rough terrain. **2005**—No-start in cold weather.

> ### ENGINE NO START CONDITION
> **BULLETIN NO.: EG016-02**   **DATE: AUGUST 30, 2002**
>
> 2000–02 Tundra (2UZ-FE)
> 2001–02 Sequoia
> This may be caused by an inoperative fuel pump and/or blown EFI fuse. The Fuel Pump Assembly and Pick-up Sock have been improved to correct this condition.

TUNDRA PROFILE

	2000	2001	2002	2003	2004	2005	2006
Cost Price ($) (negotiable)							
Base (18%)	23,915	23,110	23,520	23,520	24,565	25,580	26,100
4X4 V6/V8 (20%)	28,380	28,600	29,270	29,270	30,320	30,650	31,080
Used Values ($)							
Base ▲	8,000	10,000	13,000	14,500	16,500	19,000	—
Base ▼	7,000	9,500	11,500	13,500	15,500	17,500	—
4X4 V6/V8 ▲	11,000	13,000	15,500	17,500	21,000	23,000	—
4X4 V6/V8 ▼	9,500	11,500	14,500	16,000	19,500	21,500	—

Reliability	❷	❸	❹	❹	❺	❺	—
Crash Safety (F)	❹	❸	❹	❹	❹	❹	❹
Side	—	—	❺	❺	❺	❺	—
Offset	❺	❺	❺	❺	❺	❺	❺
Rollover	—	—	—	—	—	—	❸
Ext.	—	❸	❸	—	—	—	❸

All ratings on a numbered scale where ❺ is good and ❶ is bad. See page 220 for a more detailed description.

Appendix I
INTERNET HOT SPOTS

Finding Out What You Aren't Supposed to Know

Recent surveys show that close to 80 percent of car buyers get reliability and pricing information from the Internet, *before* visiting a dealer or private seller. This trend has resulted in easier access to confidential price margins and secret warranties—if you know where to look.

Here's what to do: First, compare a new vehicle's "discounted" MSRP prices published on different automakers' websites with invoices downloaded from sites such as *CarCostCanada.com*, *OnTheHoist.com*, the Automobile Protection Association (*apa.ca*), the Canadian Automobile Association (CAA, *www.caa.ca*), and a host of other agencies. Second, check the prices you find against the ones listed in this book.

Unearthing reliability information from independent sources on the Net takes a bit more patience. You should first wade through the thousands of consumer complaints logged in the NHTSA database. Next, use the NHTSA and ALLDATA service bulletin databases to confirm a specific problem's existence, to find out if it's caused by a manufacturing defect, and to learn how to correct it. Augment this information with tips found on car forums and protest/information sites. *Lemon-Aid* does this for you in its guides, but you can stay current about your vehicle's problems or research a particular failure in greater depth on your own by using the above search methods.

Automobile companies have helpful—though self-serving—websites, most of which feature detailed sections on their vehicles' histories and research and development as well as all sorts of information of interest to auto enthusiasts. Some automakers, such as Toyota, will even give you an online appraisal of your trade-in. Manufacturers can easily be accessed through a search engine like Google or by typing the automaker's name into your Internet browser's address bar followed by *.com* or *.ca*. Or for extra fun and a more balanced presentation, type in the vehicle model or manufacturer's name into a search engine, followed by "lemon."

Nationally known auto consumer advocates, like Alan Gelman (L), host of CFRB radio's *Car Talk*, and Mohamed Bouchama (R), head of Car Help Canada (*info@carhelpcanada.com*), give Ontario car owners practical tips they won't find elsewhere. Allan has 25 years' experience, both as a mechanic and as owner of Glennalan Motors in North York. For many years, Mohamed has been the host of the *Auto Shop* show on City TV.

Auto Safety, Costs, Servicing, and Reviews

Alberta Vehicle Cost Calculator (*www1.agric. gov.ab.ca/app24/costcalculators/vehicle/ getvechimpls.jsp*)
Estimate and compare the ownership and operating costs of vehicles with variations in purchase price, options, fuel type, interest rates, or length of ownership.

ALLDATA Service Bulletins (*www.alldata.com/ consumer/TSB/yr.html*)
Free summaries of automotive recalls and technical service bulletins. Detailed summaries will cost only $25 U.S. for hundreds of bulletins applicable to your vehicle, dating back over 30 years.

Automobile Protection Association (*apa.ca*)
APA is a membership-based, non-profit, national association dedicated to promoting consumer interests in the marketplace. It is the oldest and toughest of Canada's Nader-associated consumer groups.

BBA-reman.com (*www.bba-reman.com*)
BBA-reman specializes in automotive remanufacturing, providing a quality alternative to buying expensive new parts. All of their remanufactured products are covered by a 2-year warranty. The website also catalogues automakers' parts with high failure rates and identifies the symptoms pointing to each part's failure.

BBC TV's *Top Gear* Car Reviews (*www.topgear.com*)
Hated by European automakers, *Top Gear* gives raw, independent reviews of the best and worst European-sold vehicles, auto products, and industry practices. When they tested South Korean cars, the hosts put paper bags over their heads.

Canadian Automobile Association (*www.caa.ca*)
The CAA provides good general-interest automobile articles, despite its fear of riling automakers. There's a nice checklist for "Keeping Track of Your Own Vehicle Costs" in their *Driving Costs* pamphlet, available at *www.caa.ca/pdf/ 3708-en-2005.pdf*.

CanadianDriver (*www.canadiandriver.com*)
A homegrown, exceptionally well-structured, and current website for new- and used-vehicle reviews, MSRPs, and consumer reports. Other auto magazines' websites you should take a look at are as follows:

- *Automotive News (www.autonews.com)*—engine "sludge," GM "piston slap," etc.
- *Car and Driver (www.caranddriver.com)*—good hybrid reports
- *Motor Trend (www.motortrend.com)*
- *Road & Track (www.roadandtrack.com)*
- *Trailer Life (www.trailerlife.com)*—check out the trailering forum

CarProof (*www.carproof.com*)
Operating out of London, Ontario, this service starts at $29.95 plus GST per report. It lists liens, the past history of the vehicle and its owners, accident claims, and much more (Tel: 1-519-675-1415). Information requests can be processed online. In most provinces, you can do a lien and registration search yourself, but it's hardly worth the effort, considering the low cost of this service.

CarTrackers (*www.cartrackers.com*)
Used vehicles, consumer advice, and environmental issues are all well covered on this site. It features a terrific auto image gallery and an excellent automotive glossary.

CBC TV's Marketplace (*www.cbc.ca/consumers/market/files/cars/index.html*)
An impressive array of auto consumer info gathered from investigative reports and other sources. Well-researched, useful Canadian information.

Center for Auto Safety (*www.autosafety.org*)
A Ralph Nader–founded agency that provides free online info on safety- and performance-related defects on each vehicle model. Free vehicle reports based on owner complaints and service bulletins are sometimes dated, but it's a good site nonetheless.

Chrysler Products' Problem Web Page (*www.wam.umd.edu/~gluckman/Chrysler*)
This is a great site for finding technical info and tips on getting action from DaimlerChrysler.

Consumer Reports and **Consumers Union** (*www.consumerreports.org*)
It costs $4.95 (U.S.) monthly or $26.00 (U.S.) annually to subscribe online, but *CR*'s database is chock full of comparison tests and in-depth stories on products and services. Pay the monthly rate once and then download all the info you need during the first month of your subscription.

Crashtest.com (*www.crashtest.com/netindex.htm*)
A website where crash tests from around the world can be analyzed and compared.

Edmunds and ***Kelley Blue Book*** (*www.edmunds.com, www.kbb.com*)
In-depth reviews and owner critiques of almost every vehicle sold in North America, plus an informative readers' forum. Ignore the zip code request.

Ford insider info (*www.blueovalnews.com*)
This website is the place to go for all the latest insider info on Ford's quality problems and future models.

Fuel prices (*www.gastips.com* and *www.gasbuddy.com*)
Hourly listings of the cheapest gas stations in most major North American cities.

Lemon-Aid (*www.lemonaidcars.com*)
The official website of the *Lemon-Aid* annual consumer car guides. It is frequently updated with follow-up stories and comments from regional correspondents. And, like Tim Hortons doughnuts and Buckley's mixture, it's made for Canadians but good for Americans, too.

Metric conversions online (*www.sciencemadesimple.net/conversions.html*)
A great place to instantly convert gallons to litres, miles to kilometres, etc. Also, an excellent website for converting fuel economy figures is *www.pege.org/fuel/convert.htm* (Planetary Engineering Group). When considering fuel economy, keep in mind that North American figures are generally quoted in miles per U.S. gallon (mpg), which measures about five-sixths of the larger British gallon.

National Highway Traffic Safety Administration (*www.nhtsa.dot.gov/cars/problems*)
This American site has a comprehensive, free database covering owner complaints, recall campaigns, crashworthiness and rollover ratings, defect investigations, service bulletin summaries, and safety research papers.

OnTheHoist (*onthehoist.com*)
Kurt Binnie is a freelance auto expert who hails from Toronto. His site is both comprehensive and current, and he doesn't play any favourites. If he doesn't know the answer, he knows who does.

Finally, here are a number of other websites that may be helpful:

General Auto Sites:

canadianautopress.auto123.com/en
forum.freeadvice.com
www.all-lemons.com
www.autoblog.com
www.autowarrantyreviews.org

www.baileycar.com
www.canadianwarrantycorp.com/news_tips.htm
www.carcostcanada.com
www.carforums.com/forums
www.cartrackers.com/Forums
www.everythingfordrivers.com/carforums.html
www.mycarsucks.com
www.samarins.com
www.straight-six.com
www.which.net and www.60millions-mag.com/page/common.accueil. (British and
    French car ratings)
www.womanmotorist.com
www.worktruck.com

Automakers

AUDI: www.audiworld.com

BMW: www.bmwboard.com
www.mwerks.com

CHRYSLER: dodgestories.blogspot.com
www.angelfire.com/pa5/mspaul/autohome.html
www.cs.cornell.edu/Info/People/kreitz/Jeep/main.html
www.daimlerchryslervehicleproblems.com
www.datatown.com/chrysler
www.donotbuydodge.ca
www.dontbuyone.org
www.flinksnorph.com/chrysler.html
www.minerich.com/dodge_ram.htm
www.mydodgesucks.org

FORD: www.consumeraffairs.com/automotive/ford_spark.html (Ford cars and trucks
    spitting out spark plugs)
www.consumeraffairs.com/automotive/ford_transmissions.htm (Ford's faulty trans
    missions)
www.ford-trucks.com/forums
www.v8sho.com/SHO/autoweek_online_cam_story.htm
www.v8sho.com/SHO/BlueOvalNewsCoverageofCamSprocketLawsuit.htm
www.v8sho.com/SHO/CamFailureClassActionSuitFiled.htm

GM: agmlemon.freeservers.com/index.html
experts.about.com/q/GM-GMC-781/6-5-lt-diesel.htm (Lots of diesel dirt)
forums.gminsidenews.com
www.mygmlink.com

LAND ROVER: *www.freelanderliving.com/default.asp*

LEXUS: *us.lexusownersclub.com*

MAZDA: *www.finishlineperformance.com/mazda3/bulletins_index.html* (Service bulletins for all Mazdas)

MERCEDES-BENZ: *forums.mbnz.org*
www.mercedesproblems.com
www.nagele.co.uk/ml320.htm
www.troublebenz.com/my_opinion/actions/links.htm

MITSUBISHI: *www.mitsubishisucks.com*

SAAB: *www.saabclub.co.uk*

TOYOTA: *www.siennaclub.org*

VW: *www.myvwlemon.com*
www.tdiclub.com
www.thesamba.com/vw
www.vwvortex.com

Help for Consumers

ARTICLES AND CONSUMER INFO: *www.autosafety.org/article.php?did=312&scid=93* (Why regional recalls are a scam)
www.consumersearch.com/www/automotive/tires (Lots about tires)
www.dieseldoctor.com/messageboard/data/31.html (Can you handle the truth?)

www.driveandstayalive.com/info%20section/research/road%20safety%20research%20 papers%20and%20publications%20--%20index.htm (Highway safety research papers from around the world; impress and worry your friends)

GOVERNMENT AND NON-GOVERNMENT ASSOCIATIONS: *www.carhelpcanada.com*
www.consumeraffairs.com/index.html
www.epa.gov/otaq/consumer/warr95fs.txt

INSURANCE: *www.autoinsurancetips.com*
www.insurance-canada.ca/consquotes/onlineauto.php
www.insurancehotline.com

JUDGMENTS AND CAMPAIGNS: *www.bettersuv.org*
www.ontariocourts.on.ca/decisions/2004/june/barrickC39837.htm
www.sshwlaw.com
www.law.fsu.edu/journals/lawreview/downloads/282/Rearden.pdf (The replacement part rip-off—why pay $101,000 for a $23,000 Camry?)

www.law-lib.utoronto.ca/resguide/chapt4a.htm (A good place to look for supporting court decisions)

www.vehicle-injuries.com/suv-safety-news.htm

OLD BARGAINS AND NEW "LEMONS"

There are lots of cheap used SUVs, vans, and trucks out there that are good buys—and there are a number of new 2007 models you should avoid. The trick is knowing which vehicles are the cheapest, safest, most reliable, and most fuel-efficient.

First, consider the following 10 rules:

1. Looks don't matter. GM's Astro and Safari minivans are boxy and bland, fairly reliable, cheap, and easy to find.
2. Used is always a better buy than new. There's less depreciation and no bogus administrative or freight charges.
3. American front-drives are usually poor buys. They are less reliable than rear-drives and cost more to repair.
4. Be wary of "orphans" like the Ford Windstar, Jeep Cherokee, and Toyota Previa. Parts will be hard to find, and no one will want to service them.
5. Stay away from European luxury "lemon" SUVs like the Mercedes M-Class and the BMW X3 and X5. They are way overrated and overpriced. Parts and servicing can be a problem, and quality control is declining. Heck, recent polls show that Europeans don't trust their own automakers and tend to prefer Japanese makes. *Mais, oui!*
6. Look for 5-year-old Asian vehicles (unless they're Kias). Stay away from Mitsubishi until they become financially viable and their key executives get out of jail.
7. Buy small, entry-level Japanese pickups from Mazda, Nissan, or Toyota. Don't worry about paying too much; you'll get the extra dollars back when you sell.
8. Shop for rear-drive, full-sized vans instead of American minivans; high gas prices have sent vans' resale values somewhere south of Patagonia. A few thousand dollars more off the selling price will buy lots of fuel.
9. Don't buy for fuel economy alone: A 4-cylinder minivan or SUV *is* cheap to run, but highway merging will scare the heck out of you. Nor should you believe the hybrid- and diesel-savings hype; your hybrid fuel economy may be 40 percent *less* than what is advertised, and Chrysler, Ford, and GM diesels have become as temperamental and failure-prone as gasoline-fed engines.

10. Finally, if a vehicle's alphanumeric name doesn't make sense or can't be pronounced, get something else—forget the Cadillac SRX, Lincoln MKS/MKX/MKZ, Saab 9-7X, and VW Touareg.

Decade-Old Models?

It's getting pretty hard to find a vehicle that's 10 years old or more and is safe and reliable. Personally, I'd be reluctant to buy any decade-old vehicle from someone I didn't know, or one that has been brought in from another province. All of that accumulated salt is a real body killer, and it's just too easy to fall prey to scam artists who cover up major mechanical or body problems resulting from accidents or environmental damage.

Nevertheless, if you know the seller and an independent mechanic gives you the green light, you might seriously consider a 10-year-old, beat-up-looking pickup or van. Look for one of those listed below, or if you have a bit more money to spend and want to take less of a risk, look up the 1998 and later Recommended or Above Average models found in Part Four.

Model Choices

The following new and used choices will help you hunker down and choose reliable, safe, fuel-efficient, and inexpensive wheels that will tide you over until you can get that more expensive dream machine you've always wanted.

Warning: No matter what you buy or how much you spend later on, you will remember your first "beater" as one of the best cars you ever owned. Furthermore, you'll quickly learn to drive with the windows and sunroof closed to avoid the painful, deafening boom so common to most SUVs, vans, and trucks.

Sport-Utilities

Anyone buying a sport-utility that's a decade old or more is asking for trouble because many SUVs are worked hard off-road. The danger of rollovers is also quite high (particularly with Ford, Isuzu, and Suzuki versions); safety features are rudimentary, dangerous, and unreliable (airbags and ABS, especially); overall quality-control is very poor; and performance and handling cannot match today's models.

It's no wonder that many buyers are opting for new or almost-new SUVs manufactured during the past three years. During that time, prices have come down considerably because more products are in the supply line, electronic stability-control and full-torso side airbags are more widely available as standard features, and crashworthiness scores have climbed higher.

Nevertheless, new models need at least a year to prove their overall reliability, real-world performance, and degree of factory and dealer support. For these reasons, many of the following recommendations counsel buyers to either put off their purchases until the aforementioned data can be studied or choose one of *Lemon-Aid*'s suggested alternatives.

Audi Q7—This replacement for the Allroad is Audi's first real SUV. A Not Recommended buy during its first year on the market, the Q7 is, essentially, a stretched (an additional 30 cm/12 in. in length) Porsche Cayenne and VW Touareg masquerading as an Audi. The large seven-seat AWD crossover was launched in June 2006, and it targets BMW X5, Mercedes GL Class, Porsche Cayenne, Volvo XC90, and VW Touareg buyers. Q7 sells for just over $55,000 U.S. and comes with a standard VW-designed 280-hp 3.6L V6 or an optional 350-hp 4.2L V8 hooked to a 6-speed Tiptronic automatic transmission. Owners benefit from Q7's carlike ride and handling in addition to luxury features and a large interior.

Volkswagen and Audi have a history of engine, transmission, brake, and electrical problems that are particularly evident in new models or in those vehicles that have been redesigned. In this case, Audi presents a new design based on a quality-challenged old VW Touareg platform, which means double trouble.

Owners are dissatisfied with Audi's MMI system, a standard feature that forces them to scroll through multiple menus on the centre console while also trying to watch the road. BMW's iDrive feature has met with similar owner disdain. Other minuses: The controls for the AC are too complicated and there's insufficient air for the two furthest back seats, storage space is at a premium, sunglasses don't fit into the sunglass holder (Hyundai's Elantra has a far better design), and the sunshade covering the panorama sunroof does little to keep the sun and heat out.

NHTSA crash test results give the Q7 five stars for occupant protection in frontal crashes and four stars for protection from rollovers.

Chrysler Aspen—Not Recommended. A Dodge Durango with a different front grille. This name was used once before in the '70s as the nameplate for the unreliable and rust-prone Dodge Aspen compact sedan.

Ford Edge and **Lincoln MKX**—Not Recommended during their first year on the market. These are two small car-based SUVs that use the Mazda6 platform, share Volvo CX-7 parts, and take their styling cues from the Ford Fusion. Lincoln's MKX is a luxury variant of the Edge. In the past, an infusion of Mazda parts has always helped bring up the quality of Ford's cars and trucks, including the Escort/Tracer, Probe/MX6, and Escape/Tribute. However, mixing in Volvo components as well presents too many additional risks that quality and servicing will go down the tubes. Third-row seating is unavailable. Competitors worth considering: the Honda CR-V, Hyundai Tucson or Santa Fe, Nissan Murano, and Toyota RAV4.

GM Acadia, **Enclave**, and **Outlook**—Priced in the $30,000 range, these practically identical mid-sized front-drive/all-wheel-drive SUVs use a car-based Lambda platform that incorporates a third-row seat that allows for a maximum of eight passengers. Power is provided by a 3.6L V6 mated to a newly designed 6-speed automatic transmission. GM says the upgraded powertrain set-up gives 8-percent improved performance and up to 4-percent improved fuel economy when compared with current front-drive 4-speed automatics. Both the GMC Acadia and the Saturn Outlook will be sold as 2007 models, while the Buick Enclave will arrive in mid-2007 as a 2008 model. Competing models worth considering are the Chrysler Pacifica, Honda Pilot, Nissan Murano, Mazda CX-9, and Toyota Highlander.

2007 FORD EDGE AND LINCOLN MKX TECHNICAL DATA

POWERTRAIN (FRONT-DRIVE/ALL-WHEEL DRIVE)
Engines: 3.5L V6 (265 hp); Transmission: 6-speed auto.

DIMENSION/CAPACITY (BASE)
Passengers: 5; Wheelbase: 111.2 in.; H: 68.7/L: 186.5/W: 75.8 in.; Headroom F/R: N/A; Legroom F/R: 40.7/38.1 in.; 40.7/39.3 in.; Cargo volume: 32 cu. ft.; Fuel tank: 117L/regular; Tow limit: 3,500 lb.; Load capacity: 1,011 lb.; GVWR: N/A; Turning circle: 37 ft.; Ground clearance: 8.0 in.; Weight: 4,086 lb./4,220 lb.

Saturn's Outlook, the first model to be released, is expected to eventually replace the Relay minivan. It rides on a unibody platform, which cuts weight by eliminating the usual hefty trucklike frame and other heavy-duty chassis components. The user-friendly interior resembles GM's new 2007 Yukon and Tahoe cabins, with relatively roomy and easily accessed seating. Furthermore, an innovative second-row seat can be pushed forward and folded against the front row, thereby enlarging the pathway to the third-row seating area. Low entry/exit height. The rear tail light design isn't to everyone's taste.

As with most of GM's recent SUVs, standard safety features abound. For example, there's electronic stability-control with rollover mitigation, front and side airbags plus two head-protecting side curtain airbags for all three rows, and four-wheel anti-lock brakes. A wide stance and low centre of gravity reduces the threat of a rollover; however, keep in mind that independent crashworthiness test data is still unavailable.

Some of the minuses inherent in GM's new crossover trio: Outlook prices are expected to be unacceptably high ($28,000–$35,000) until the first quarter of 2007, when they should drop by about 15 percent as the new Acadia and Enclave

2007 SATURN OUTLOOK TECHNICAL DATA

POWERTRAIN (FRONT-DRIVE, ALL-WHEEL DRIVE)

Engines: 3.6L V6 (265 hp); Transmission: 6-speed auto.

DIMENSION/CAPACITY (BASE)

Passengers: 8; Wheelbase: 118.9; H: 72.8; L: 200.7; W: 78.2 in.; Headroom F/R1/R2: 40.4/39.3/38.4 in. (based on GM-supplied figures); Legroom F/R1/R2: 41.3/39.3/38.4 in. (also based on GM-supplied figures); Cargo volume: 68.9 cu. ft., plus 19.7 cu. ft behind the third-row seat; Fuel tank: 83L/regular; Tow limit: 4,500 lb.; Load capacity: 1,355/1,942 lb.; GVWR: 6398 lb.; Turning circle: 40.4 ft.; Ground clearance: 7.4 in.; Weight: 4,722 lb.

2007 CADILLAC SRX TECHNICAL DATA

POWERTRAIN (REAR-DRIVE/ALL-WHEEL DRIVE)

Engines: 3.6L V6 (255 hp) • 4.6L V8 (320 hp); Transmissions: 5-speed auto. • 6-speed auto.

DIMENSION/CAPACITY (BASE)

Passengers: 7; Wheelbase: 116 in.; H: 67.8/L: 195/W: 72.6 in.; Headroom F/R: N/A; Legroom F/R1/R2: 42.1/41/24.2 in.; Cargo volume: 40 cu. ft.; Fuel tank: 76L/regular/premium; Tow limit: 4,250 lb.; Load capacity: 1,200 lb.; GVWR: 6,008 lb.; Turning circle: 39.7 ft.; Ground clearance: 8.2 in.; Weight: 4,229 lb.

cannibalize the market. Third-row seating is a bit cramped, the new 6-speed tranny has yet to prove itself, and the V6 powerplant is a mixed-breed design from Australia, Germany, Sweden, and North America that was first introduced on Cadillac's CTS sedan and SRX SUV crossover. SRX and CTS complaints logged by NHTSA and others frequently mention engine and transmission/differential failures. Furthermore, GM's touted fuel economy savings associated with its new powertrain (*Front-drive:* 9.4/13.8 L/100 km; *AWD:* 9.8/14.7 L/100 km) may be illusory when compared to real driving reports. Finally, mechanics will need at least a year to figure out how to troubleshoot these new designs, and GM dealers won't dump a lot of money into a huge parts inventory until they see if these vehicles sell.

Lemon-Aid believes these triplets won't sell in sufficient numbers to nourish three GM divisions, even though they will shortly replace the automaker's entire front-drive minivan lineup. Expected poor sales will result in huge price cuts in early 2007. Actually, a GMC version makes no sense when Buick and Saturn have the same territory covered. Add in the possible Chevy version to replace the TrailBlazer and a Saab version to replace the 9-7x, and you've got the same old GM brand name flim-flam trying to hide the fact that GM has too many products in the same market segment competing against one another.

Cadillac SRX—Below Average. A mid-sized rear-drive or all-wheel-drive crossover, the SRX has been on the market since 2004, when it originally sold for $52,250 as a front-drive SUV, $54,875 with a V6 added, and $63,965 for a V8 AWD. Today, the same vehicles are worth $32,000, $33,000, and $37,000, respectively. The 2007 SRXs have also been especially hard hit by cheaper competitors. They are now listed at $49,495, $52,120, and $63,710—less than their original selling prices three years ago.

SRX owners report frequent transmission and differential breakdowns in addition to brake and electrical failures and fit and finish deficiencies. The 2004 through 2007 models scored a five-star crashworthiness rating for frontal and side crash protection.

> **2007 MAZDA CX-7 TECHNICAL DATA**
> ***
> **POWERTRAIN (FRONT-DRIVE/AWD)**
> Engines: 2.3L Turbo 4-cyl. (244 hp)
> Transmission: 6-speed auto.
> **DIMENSION/CAPACITY (BASE)**
> Passengers: 5; Wheelbase: 108.3 in.; H: 64.8/L: 184.3/W: 73.7 in.; Headroom: N/A; Legroom F/R: 41.7/36.4 in.; Cargo volume: N/A; Fuel tank: 69L/regular; Tow limit: 3,000 lb.; Load capacity: 1,000 lb.; GVWR: N/A; Turning circle: N/A; Ground clearance N/A; Weight: 3,710 lb.

Mazda CX-7 and **CX-9**—Rated Above Average and retailing for about $35,000, the sporty five-passenger 2006 and 2007 CX-7 is a promising new unibody, four-door crossover SUV based on the Mazda5 and Mazda6. This is an SUV that's not suitable for off-roading, though it looks like it could go anywhere. The turbocharged 4-cylinder engine is taken from the MazdaSpeed6 and hasn't accumulated enough road time to determine its long-term durability. Electronic stability-control is a standard feature. A longer version, the CX-9, will be equipped with a V6 and a third-row seat. It arrives in early 2007 and will cost about $10,000 more than the CX-7. Because this is its first year on the market, the CX-9 is Not Recommended.

Porsche Cayenne—A bestseller since it was first launched as a 2003 model, the Cayenne is skipping the 2007 model year and will return as a 2008 model. It is a mid-sized luxury unibody SUV that shares many of the VW Touareg parts (remember, VW, Audi, and Porsche are all under the same corporate umbrella), hence, reliability has been subpar. Cayenne does have some limited off-road capability, thanks to its low gearing, sophisticated electronics, and Touareg-sourced V6 engine, plus Porsche V8 and twin-turbo variants—a 3.2L V6 (247 hp); 4.5L V8 (340 hp); 4.5L Twin-Turbo V8 (450 hp); and another, more powerful 4.5L Twin-Turbo V8 (520 hp). Transmissions consist of a 6-speed manual and a 6-speed automatic. On-road capability is a big disappointment, however, since the car lacks Porsche's handling prowess. Furthermore, many of the cabin controls are needlessly complex and confusing. Crashworthiness has not yet been rated.

Cayennes hold their value as well as luxury Japanese cars. For example, a $78,250 2003 model is now worth about $45,000. A new $60,100 2006 version will only be discounted by $5,000 if bought used.

2007 TOYOTA FJ CRUISER TECHNICAL DATA

POWERTRAIN (REAR-DRIVE/AWD)

Engine: 4.0L V6 (239 hp); Transmissions: 5-speed auto. • 6-speed man.

DIMENSION/CAPACITY (BASE)

Passengers: 5; Wheelbase: 106 in.; H: 72/L: 184/W: 75 in.; Headroom F/R: N/A; Legroom F/R: 41.9/31.3 in.; Cargo volume: 27.9 cu. ft.; Fuel tank: 72L/premium; Tow limit: 5,000 lb.; Load capacity: 1,325 lb.; GVWR: 5,330 lb.; Turning circle: 41.8 ft.; Ground clearance: 9.6 in.; Weight: 4,350 lb.

Toyota FJ Cruiser—Taking its inspiration from the Toyota FJ40 Land Cruiser built between 1956 and 1983, the $29,990 2007 FJ is an Above Average SUV that competes especially well off-road against the Ford Escape, Honda Element, Jeep Liberty and Wrangler, and Nissan Xterra. It is powered by a competent 4.0L 239-hp V6 that can be used for either two-wheel or four-wheel drive. A 5-speed automatic transmission comes with both versions, and a 6-speed manual gearbox is available with the all-wheel drive. Although the FJ's turning circle is about 1.5 m (5 ft.) larger than that of similar-sized SUVs, off-roading should be a breeze, thanks to standard electronic stability-control, short overhangs, and better-than-average ground clearance.

Interestingly, NHTSA crashworthiness scores for front and side impacts have been five stars; however, the rollover rating was only three stars, an Average rating. This is disappointing, and it's almost never seen with vehicles that are equipped with electronic stability-control.

The rear side doors are taken from the Honda Element, which means rear and side visibility is severely limited. There is also some side wind vulnerability, and annoying wind noises are generated by the large side mirrors. Although touted as a five-passenger conveyance, a normal-sized fifth passenger in the back seat won't be comfortable. Plus the rear seats are hard to access, forcing front occupants to unbuckle every time a rear occupant gets in or out. Front-seat headrests may be uncomfortably positioned for short occupants. Another minus is the requirement that premium fuel be used.

VW Touareg—Not Recommended. Slightly restyled this year, VW says its 2007 V10 turbodiesel will be modified to be cleaner-burning and more fuel efficient. This isn't good news, inasmuch as VW has had a high percentage of factory goof-ups each time it has modified its lineup. Furthermore, the Touareg has already earned a bad reputation for poor reliability and expensive servicing ever since it was first launched as a 2005 luxury SUV listed at $55,010. In the following year, poor sales forced VW to cut prices drastically: A new 2006 sold for almost 10 percent less at $50,790; and the 2007 retails for $51,525. The 2005 is now worth between $37,000 and $39,000; a used 2006 will fetch about $4,000 more.

Is there any good reason to buy a Touareg, apart from the nicely appointed interior? No.

Despite its sharing of some parts with the Porsche Cayenne, all you get as a trade-off are befuddled mechanics; long waits for parts; complicated controls; a modest cargo area; myriad electrical, powertrain, and brake problems; premature tire wear; and performance and handling that's abysmal. Softly sprung, this 2,360 kg (5,200 lb.) gorilla gulps premium fuel and struggles to get up to a decent speed with the 3.2L V6. A 276-hp 3.6L V6 became the standard engine in the summer of 2006; however, it is just as thirsty and only slightly less lethargic. An optional 4.2L V8 offers a bit better performance, but only the turbocharged V10 diesel manages to give this beast the grunt it requires, especially when used for off-roading.

Crashworthiness ratings are fairly impressive: The 2005 and 2006 models scored four stars for frontal collision occupant protection and five stars in side-impact tests. The 2007s were judged to give five-star protection in both tests. Rollover, offset, and head-restraint crashworthiness data is unavailable.

Don't assume that European luxury SUVs are more reliable. To the contrary, BMW, Land Rover, and Mercedes-Benz SUVs have garnered a reputation for being poor-quality vehicles with head-spinning depreciation.

Land Rover's **Discovery** was replaced by the 2005 and 2006 **LR3 SE/HSE** ($61,900/$67,900), a much more refined vehicle that was completely re-engineered by Ford and given a Jaguar-sourced 300-hp 4.4L V8 along with decent disc/disc brakes. It retains about a third of its value and is now worth between $22,000 and $24,000. A

2007 VW TOUAREG TECHNICAL DATA

POWERTRAIN (AWD)

Engines: 3.2L V6 (220 hp) • 3.6L V6 (276 hp) • 4.2L V8 (310 hp) • 5.0L V10 (310 hp); Transmission: 6-speed auto.

DIMENSION/CAPACITY (BASE)

Passengers: 5; Wheelbase: 112.4 in.; H: 68/L: 187.2/W: 75.9 in.; Headroom F/R: 4.0/4.5 in.; Legroom F/R: 41/27 in.; Cargo volume: 35.5 cu. ft.; Fuel tank: 100L/premium; Tow limit: 7,716 lb.; Load capacity: 1,280 lb.; GVWR: N/A; Turning circle: 38 ft.; Ground clearance: 11.8 in. (variable); Weight: 5,086 lb.

LAND ROVER QUALITY IS NOT "JOB 1"

Problems per 100 vehicles, compared with industry average

YEAR	LAND ROVER	INDUSTRY
2006	204	124
2005	149	118
2004	148	119
2003	190	133

Source: J.D. Power and Associates 2006 Initial Quality Study.

2007 LR2 has come on the scene as the Freelander's replacement. It shares most of its powertrain and other major components with Volvo's S80 and S40. Prices will be announced in the late fall.

According to J.D. Power's 2006 Initial Quality Study (IQS), Land Rover remains at the bottom of the quality heap with 204 problems per 100 vehicles—more than two problems per vehicle, and a far cry from the industry average of 124 problems. Nevertheless, the poor showing is no surprise for the British automaker now owned by Ford. It has been a bottom-feeder for three of the past four years. Industry watchers say the company's dead-last IQS finish was caused by electronic glitches that followed the replacement of Land Rover's BMW-sourced engines with Jaguar engines during the 2006 model year. For example, the 2006 Range Rover adopted the Jaguar engine but retained the original BMW electrical architecture—a sure-fire recipe for trouble and a constantly lit Check Engine light.

Range Rover launched a sportier-looking $77,800 **Sport** version last year. Equipped with the LR3's V8 engine (a $16,000 optional supercharger adds 25 horses) and loaded with performance features, the new Sport targets the FX45 and Porsche Cayenne crowd. Sport sales have been underwhelming, and used models go for $58,000 to $60,000.

Range Rover and **Discovery** versions don't hold their values well, either: A 1996 $42,000 Discovery is now worth about $6,500, and the same-year Range Rover, originally priced at $80,000, *may* fetch $10,000 on a good day.

The cheapest of the three is the **Freelander**, launched in 2002 (now worth about $13,000) and then dropped in 2006. The 2005 versions no longer include the HSE and are sold as the **SE** and **SE3** ($25,000/$27,000). They carry a wimpy 174-hp 2.5L V6 engine, feature a removable hardtop that takes a two-man crew to install, and use antediluvian disc/drum brakes.

More softly styled than its larger, squared-off Discovery brother, the Freelander is an underpowered, small, cramped truck with luxury SUV pretensions. Don't look for the seat height-adjustment control—there isn't one (posing a serious problem for tall drivers). Headroom is at a premium for tall drivers, and storage space behind the back seats is clearly inadequate. Ground clearance is also quite low when compared with the competition. When pushed, the 174-hp V6 engine whines and struggles to hold its own. A stick shift isn't available, so there's no way to improve the mediocre 15.0 L/100 km average fuel economy. This year Land Rover will resurrect the Freelander as the 2007 LR2, set on a Volvo platform and sharing many of the Volvo S40 components as well as the S80's 230-hp 6-cylinder engine.

On paper, the latest rendition of these models looks impressive, indeed, with a long list of standard safety, performance, and convenience features. But, as with other Land Rovers, when you buy one of these entry-level British imports, you are buying into a make that's unreliable, outclassed by most other automakers, and served by a limited, chaotic dealer network that is poorly administered by Ford.

Now we come to **Mercedes-Benz** and its problem-wracked foray into luxury sport-utilities in 1997. Known collectively as the **M-Class**, these SUVs are lousy buys from 1998 to 2005. **ML320, ML350, ML430,** and **ML500** models are a far cry from being cheap wheels, even though they, too, depreciate about 50 percent after five years (a $47,550 1999 ML320 is now worth about $13,500). The main drawbacks of these luxury lemons are poor quality-control; unreliable, limited servicing; and so-so parts availability. Owners report automatic transmission failures, frequent engine oil leaks and engine oil sludge, and electrical system shorts. Other problems afflict brake pads, rotors, master cylinders, fuel pumps, oxygen sensors, mass airflow sensors, and fit and finish.

Mercedes-Benz redesigned the 2006 M-Class to make it longer, lower, and wider. It handles and rides in a more carlike fashion because of the retuned suspension and the removal of its truck frame. Power is supplied by a new 3.5L 268-hp V6 or by last year's 5.0L 302-hp V8. Off-roaders can order a 2-speed 4×4 transfer case. A new entry-level ML350 sells for $55,750, and is worth about $10,000 less used. A used ML500 that originally sold for $72,500 is now worth approximately $58,000.

Is the redesigned M-Class more reliable and glitch-free?

No, nothing indicates that this is the case. In fact, consumer complaints are still highlighting electronic, brake, and powertrain problems as the cars' more common failings. Mercedes-Benz may need another year to work out their design and component quality problems.

The same caveat applies to Mercedes' just-launched 2006 and 2007 **R-Class**. It fills the gap between a wagon and the M-Class with a six-passenger crossover reminiscent of the Chrysler Pacifica. It's available with a 3.5L 268-hp V6, a 5.0L 302-hp V8, and an incredibly powerful and totally inappropriate 5.5L 360-hp V8 AMG engine. On- and off-road driving is aided by the electronically controlled 4ETS four-wheel-drive system used in the M-Class and G-Class, an Airmatic air suspension system, and a high-pressure brake system. A new 2006 **R350** costs $64,400 and loses about $15,000 if sold

2007 VOLVO XC90 TECHNICAL DATA

POWERTRAIN (FRONT-DRIVE/AWD)
Engines: 3.2L 6-cyl. (235 hp) • 4.4L V8 (311 hp); Transmission: 6-speed auto.

DIMENSION/CAPACITY (BASE)
Passengers: 5–7; Wheelbase: 112.6 in.; H: 70.2/L: 189.3/W: 74.7 in.; Headroom F/R1/R2: 4.0/4.5/N/A in.; Legroom F/ R1/R2: 40.5/27/23.5 in.; Cargo volume: 38 cu. ft.; Fuel tank: 79.9L/regular; Tow limit: 4,960 lb.; Load capacity: 1,210 lb.; GVWR: N/A; Turning circle: 42 ft.; Ground clearance: 7.5 in.; Weight: 4,464 lb.

used. A used 2006 **R500** takes less than half the hit: Sold originally for $75,950, it is now worth about $70,000.

Again, no matter what the price, these two new designs are both Not Recommended during their first year on the market.

The **Volvo XC90** mid-sized SUV is another poor performer from Europe that's Not Recommended. Available with either a 6-cylinder or Yamaha-sourced V8 engine, this four-door has a well-appointed interior and tons of standard safety and convenience features. Its major failings are an unjustifiably high price, mediocre acceleration with the 6-cylinder powerplant, excessive fuel consumption with the must-have V8, and a history of automatic transmission, electrical system, suspension, brake, AC, and body fit and finish deficiencies. Last time Yamaha built engines for Ford, thousands of Ford Taurus owners sued the company for selling them self-destructing engines that cost up to $10,000 to repair, before they would fail again.

Prices are to be announced in late fall.

Acura's first SUV wannabe (it's really more a large station wagon that's not intended for off-road use), the 2007 **RDX** is an all-wheel drive cobbled together from mostly Honda CR-V parts, with a few extra refinements like turbocharging thrown in. Rated Above Average, the vehicle is well appointed, with many standard features that would be optional with competing makes. Powered is supplied by a 2.3L 240-hp 4-cylinder engine mated to a 5-speed automatic transmission that drives all four wheels. RDX targets the premium SUV market presently served by vehicles like the BMW X3. It also copies BMW's confusing iDrive cockpit controls with its own 42 buttons and knobs mounted in the centre console area. It is expected to cost about $40,000, plus a few thousand more for technophiles who must have the optional DVD player, navigation system, and GPS capability.

RECOMMENDATIONS—The **Jeeps** are the best of a bad lot, particularly the **Wrangler** versions. Their tendency to roll over isn't as high as that of other small sport-utilities; parts are more easily obtainable; and servicing, if not given with a smile, at least isn't accompanied by a snarl or head-scratching. Nevertheless, the early **CJs** and **Wagoneers** have been known for their rattle-prone bodies, air and water leaks, electrical glitches, and high-cost brake maintenance. Expect to spend $2,000 tops for a decade-old entry-level CJ and a thousand more for an even older Wagoneer.

Selling for as little as $3,500–$10,000 for a 1996 **Rodeo S, Isuzu**'s 1993–2004 **Ascender, Axiom, Rodeo, Rodeo Sport**, and **Trooper** are ideal SUVs for light city commuting. Although they look tacky and feel outdated, these Isuzus are competent performers with powerful V6s, shift-on-the-fly capabilities, versatile transmissions, nice and predictable rear-drive handling, spacious interiors, and very few complaints of safety-related defects. Less attractive characteristics are a wimpy 4-cylinder engine, part-time 4×4 that can't be used on dry pavement, a harsh ride over bumpy terrain, excessive body lean when cornering, obstructed rear visibility, narrow rear doors, excessive road and engine noise, and poor fuel economy. Some of the safety-related failures tabulated by NHTSA include brake loss, sudden and unintended acceleration, and automatic transmission failures.

Of course, if you don't mind paying a little more, there's nothing wrong with a 1987–89 **Toyota Land Cruiser**, which sells for about $3,500. Just be sure to pull the wheels off to examine the brakes, check for undercarriage corrosion, and make sure the engine head gasket is okay.

AVOID—Ever heard of **American Motors**? Well, back in 1981, they came out with the first 4×4 passenger car/sport-utility, called the **Eagle** (others called it the Turkey), which was basically a Concord 4×4. It now sells for about $500. Be wary of its failure-prone drivetrain, ignition system, and clutch; master slave cylinder leaks; low rust resistance; and marginal crash protection. But at least it didn't roll over, something that can't be said for **Ford**'s **Bronco II**.

Speaking of the Bronco II, stay away from the 1981–90 models, even though their $500–$1,000 price may seem like a bargain. Broncos are unreliable, rollover-prone, rust-attracting 4×4s that are forever finding new ways to strand you. You can cut repair costs by using independent garages, but parts can be quite expensive (especially TFI ignition components and computer modules). Between 1985 and 1989, the Bronco II was the undisputed leader in rollover deaths in the U.S. According to internal memoranda, Ford released the Bronco II in 1981 with full knowledge of the stability dangers inherent in the design. Critics contend that the present-day Explorer's rollover problems can be traced back to its Bronco heritage.

This sport-utility suffers from worse-than-average reliability. The 4-speed automatic transmission has been the worst contributor to owners' woes. The complicated electronic fuel-injection system is a headache to diagnose and has a bad repair history. Brakes and 4×4 components are also often included on the list of potential problems. Overall, body assembly and paint quality are mediocre.

The 1987–94 **Suzuki Samurai** is another orphan you shouldn't buy, despite its low cost ($500–$750). Parts are almost impossible to find and are quite expensive. Crash test results of the 1986 model, which can be extrapolated to later versions, concluded that the driver and passenger would have sustained severe leg trauma. Unsteady road manners, coupled with a high centre of gravity, make the Samurai susceptible to sudden rollovers if the vehicle is not driven carefully, especially on rough terrain. This is particularly true of the 1987–88 models, where NHTSA records show the largest grouping of owner complaints and accident injury reports.

Minivans and Wagons

Assuming that you can't afford big bucks for a Honda Odyssey or Toyota Sienna, you have a number of cheaper old minivans to choose from: Chrysler's Colt/Summit/Vista wagons; Ford's Aerostar; GM's Astro and Safari; and Nissan's Axxess. There are also the 2006 and 2007 Mazda5 mini-minivans that show a lot of promise.

RECOMMENDATIONS—**Chrysler**'s **Colt**, **Summit**, and **Vista**. Priced from about $700 for an '88 version to about $1,000 for a '95, these are three fairly reliable, easy-to-repair, and fuel-efficient Mitsubishi imports. The only exceptions are the 1985–88 models, which were quite troublesome.

The Vista and the Summit wagon are small minivans with five- to seven-passenger seating. They have excellent crash ratings and are more reasonably priced, practical, and fuel efficient than many other small wagons. The five-passenger Colt wagon, like the Summit and Nissan Axxess, offers the extra versatility of a third seat in the back and a tall body. As such, it makes a great car for a small family with space to haul loads to the cottage. The wagon series is available in 4×4 (not recommended) and uses practically the same mechanical components as the other Colt models. The Summit wagon is essentially a wagon version of the Colt 200.

On post-1990 Colts and Summits, the 2.4L head gasket may fail prematurely. Shocks aren't very durable, braking isn't impressive, and the front brakes have a short lifespan. Be especially wary of the troublesome 4×4 powertrain on 1989–91 wagons and the 16-valve turbo, dropped in 1990.

The 1995–97 **Ford Aerostar** isn't a bad choice, though 1986–94 models are risky buys. A 1992 XL would cost about $2,000, while a fully equipped 1997 version (1997 was the Aerostar's last year) should cost between $3,500 and $4,000. These primitive rear-drives are brawnier and more reliable than Chrysler, Ford, and GM front-drive minivans, and they've posted impressive crashworthiness scores since 1992. Just make sure Ford pays for cracked coil springs up to 10 years of use.

The 1986–94 models are at the bottom of the evolutionary scale as far as quality control is concerned. However, the last three model years showed lots of improvement. Repair costs are reasonable (except for high automatic transmission, AC, and computer module costs), and many of the Aerostar's myriad mechanical and body defects can be fixed quite easily by independent garages.

Nissan's 1991–95 **Axxess** small minivan is a good choice. It is fairly reliable, easily serviced, and has posted respectable crash-safety ratings. Expect to pay from $2,000 to $2,500 for the top-of-the-line **SE**. You may have trouble finding one; word has gotten out that they are "beater" bargains.

The 2006–07 **Mazda5** is a modern version of the Nissan Axxess and Colt/Eagle/ Summit, which were dropped more than a decade ago. It is basically a compact MPV that's based broadly on the Mazda3 and carries six passengers in three rows of seats. Suited mostly for urban errands and light commuting, the "5" shares with the Mazda3 its peppy, fuel-frugal 2.3L 157-hp 4-cylinder engine hooked to a standard 5-speed manual transmission or a 4-speed automatic. So far, the engine has had few problems during the three years it has run in Canada. Its use of a timing chain instead of a belt also lowers maintenance costs.

This is a relatively tall and narrow car with a thick, obtrusive front A-pillar. Nevertheless, it handles well, despite some body roll and steering that's a bit vague. Drivers will find it a breeze to park, easy to manoeuvre, and fairly spacious inside. Two wide-opening sliding doors make for easy entry and exit; however, the lower door hinge can trap little feet. Headroom is adequate, legroom is limited, and the rear seat is for children only. Seats can't be removed, but they do fold forward to make a flat cargo floor.

Fuel consumption is impressively low. With a 5-speed manual transmission, you can expect 10.6 L/100 km in the city and 8.0 L/100 km on the highway; a 4-speed automatic should average 11.2 L/100 km in the city and 8.3 L/100 km on the highway.

Available in European and Asian markets since 1999, these small vans still have had some first-year production bugs that cause automatic transmission gear-hunting, rapid brake wear, and electrical system shorts. Nevertheless, their overall popularity means that most dealers will be selling them close to the listed MSRP. Still, buyers will score a decent small minivan for much less than the larger minivans sold by the competition. The **GS** will retail for $19,995, and the upscale **GT** for $22,795—thousands of dollars less than the Chevrolet Uplander and about $10,000 below Honda's Odyssey or the Toyota Sienna.

AVOID—Stay away from bargain-priced minivans that require frequent and costly repairs. Chief among these are $1,000–$7,000 **Chrysler minivans** (1984–2001) and $1,500–$2,000 **Mercury Villager/Nissan Quest** models (1993–96). Chrysler minivans had engine, drivetrain, suspension, electrical and fuel system, AC, brake, and body deficiencies galore. Villagers and Quests had chronic engine exhaust manifold stud failures. **VW Campers** are a good idea, but poorly executed. These minivans are nicely laid out, but they aren't reliable and servicing is practically non-existent. On top of that, they are relatively costly: $2,500–$3,000 for a 1985– 89 model.

Pickups

As a general rule, old trucks aren't very collectible, unless they were used for a specific purpose, like fire trucks, army vehicles, or commercial vehicles (milk trucks, etc.). For most decade-old small trucks made by the Detroit Big Three, you can expect to pay $2,000–$3,000. Asian imports may cost a few thousand more because of their reputation as being better made and more reliable. If you're looking for a larger pickup, the price may vary from $3,000 to $5,000, with no real Asian competition in sight.

Old trucks are bought for function, not appearance. Full-sized Chrysler, Ford, and GM pickups from the first half of the '70s are all practically equal in performance and reliability (although Ford vehicles were extremely rust-prone). After 1976, stringent emissions regulations mandated the use of failure-prone fuel injectors, computer modules, and catalytic converters. As leaded fuel was phased out, vehicles became much more complicated to troubleshoot, more expensive to repair, and less reliable.

Post-'76 GM trucks are afflicted with poor-quality computer modules that make for hard starts and poor engine performance, early catalytic converter failures, unreliable diesel engines, and poorly engineered braking systems where the rear brakes are vulnerable to premature backing-plate corrosion. GM's use of the "side-saddle" gas tank design also increased the risk of fire in a collision. From late 1998 to the present, GM's truck quality hasn't improved. Engines, transmissions, brakes, and fit and finish continue to be major trouble spots.

From the late '70s to the present, Ford's trucks have been gas hogs; their fuel and ignition systems often fail, causing fires and full-throttle stalling; and fuel pumps, AC, and electrical systems can be chronically dysfunctional. Automatic transmissions have become "bump and jump" affairs, and collapsed coil springs and steering/suspension tie-rod failures bring new meaning to the term "off-roading."

But Chrysler's trucks are no better, except for their fairly reliable Cummins diesel powerplants. And even these engines can get nasty with fuel injection problems. Chrysler's trucks have always been plagued by persistent brake, computer module, suspension, and automatic transmission failures. They have a tendency to wander all over the road and are often hard to troubleshoot.

RECOMMENDATIONS—Stick with the smallest Japanese-made truck you can find that will do the job. This means choosing a small pickup like the **Mazda B-series**, the **Nissan King Cab**, or **Toyota**'s **Pickup**, **Tacoma**, and **T100**.

AVOID—Steer clear of Japanese pickups sold under an American label.

LEMON-PROOFING BEFORE YOU BUY

Buyers' Rights

This section shows you how to check out what's offered without a lot of hassle. But if you are deceived by a seller despite your best efforts, don't despair. As discussed in Part Three, Canadian federal and provincial laws dish out harsh penalties to new- and used-car dealers who hide or embellish important facts. Ontario's recent *Consumer Protection Act* (*www.e-laws.gov.on.ca/DBLaws/Statutes/English/02c30_e.htm*), for example, lets consumers cancel a contract within one year of entering into an agreement if a seller makes a false, misleading, deceptive, or unconscionable representation. This includes using exaggeration, innuendo, or ambiguity about a material fact, or failing to state a material fact, if such use or failure deceives or tends to deceive.

Just keep in mind the following points:

- Dealers are *presumed* to know the history, quality, and true performance of what they sell.
- Even details like a vehicle's fuel economy can lead to a contract's cancellation if the dealer gave a higher-than-accurate figure. In *Sidney v. 1011067 Ontario Inc. (c.o.b. Southside Motors) 15*, the plaintiff was awarded $11,424.51 plus prejudgment interest. The plaintiff claimed the defendant advised him that the vehicle had a fuel efficiency of 800 to 900 kilometres per tank of fuel, when in fact, the maximum efficiency was only 500 kilometres per tank.

A Check-Up Checklist

Now, let's assume you are dealing with an honest seller and that you've chosen a vehicle that's priced right and seems to meet your needs. Take some time to assess its interior, its exterior, and its highway performance with the checklist below. If you're buying from a dealer, ask to take the vehicle home overnight in order to drive it over the same roads you use in your daily activities. Of course, if you're buying privately, it's doubtful that you'll get the vehicle for an overnight test—you may have to rent a similar one from a dealer or rental agency.

Safety Check

1. Is the vehicle equipped with electronic stability-control?
2. Do the side airbags protect both the head and torso?
3. Are the airbags de-powered?
4. Is outward visibility good in all directions?
5. Are there large blind spots impeding vision, such as side pillars?
6. Are the mirrors large enough for good side and rear views? Do they block your view?
7. Are all instrument displays clearly visible (not washed out in sunlight)? Is there daytime or nighttime dash glare upon the windshield? Are the controls easily reached?
8. Are the handbrake and hood release easy to reach and use?
9. Does the front seat have sufficient rearward travel to put you at a safe distance from the airbag's deployment (about 30 cm/12 in.) and still allow you to reach the brake and accelerator pedals? Are the brake and accelerator pedals adjustable and spaced far enough apart?
10. Are the head restraints adjustable or non-adjustable? (The latter is better if you often forget to set them.)
11. Are the head restraints designed to permit rear visibility? (Some are annoyingly obtrusive.)
12. Are there rear three-point shoulder belts similar to those on the front seats?
13. Is the seat belt latch plate easy to find and reach?
14. Does the seat belt fit comfortably across your chest?
15. Does the seat belt release easily, retract smoothly, and use pretensioners for maximum effectiveness?
16. Are there user-friendly child-seat anchor locations?
17. Are there automatic door locks controlled by the driver, or childproof rear door locks? Does the automatic side sliding door latch securely, and does it immediately stop when encountering an object as it opens or closes?
18. Do the rear windows roll only halfway down? When they are down, are your ears assailed by a booming wind noise or does the vehicle vibrate excessively?

Exterior Check

Rust

A serious problem with the roofs of GM vans for more than two decades, rust is a four-letter word that means trouble. Don't buy any used vehicle with extensive corrosion around the roof rails, rear hatch, wheelwells, door bottoms, or rocker panels. Getting body work in these areas is usually only a temporary solution.

Cosmetic rusting (rear hatch, exhaust system, front hood) is acceptable and can even help push the price way down, as long as the chassis and other major structural members aren't affected. Premature corrosion or repairs resulting from an accident may cause bumps, bubbles, or ripples under the paint. Don't dismiss this as a mere cosmetic problem—the entire vehicle will have to be stripped down, reprimed, and repainted. GM has a secret warranty covering these hood repairs that can be extrapolated to other models and different body panels (see GM Montana/Venture minivans in Part Four).

Knock gently on the front fenders, door bottoms, rear wheelwells, and rear doors—places where rust usually occurs first. Even if these areas have been repaired with plastic, lead, metal plates, or fibreglass, once rusting starts, it's difficult to stop. Use a small magnet to check which body panels have been repaired with non-metallic body fillers.

Use a flashlight to check for exhaust system and suspension component rust-out. Make sure the catalytic converter is present. In the past, many drivers removed this pollution-control device in the mistaken belief that it would improve fuel economy. The police can fine you for not having the converter, and you'll be forced to buy one ($400+) in order to certify your vehicle.

Tires

Be wary of tire brands that have poor durability records. Stay away from Firestone/Bridgestone. Don't be concerned if the tires are worn, since retreads are inexpensive and easy to find. Look at tire wear for clues that the vehicle is out of alignment, needs suspension repairs, or has serious chassis problems. Getting an alignment and new shocks and springs is part of routine maintenance, and it's relatively inexpensive to do with aftermarket parts. However, if your vehicle is a 4×4 or the MacPherson struts have to be replaced you're looking at a $1,000 repair bill.

Accident damage

Accident repairs require a further inspection by an independent body shop in order to determine if the frame is aligned and the vehicle is tracking correctly. Frameless minivans need extensive and expensive work to straighten them out, and proper frame and body repairs can often cost more than the vehicle is worth. In British Columbia, all accidents involving more than $2,000 in repairs must be reported to subsequent buyers.

Here are some tips on what you can do to avoid buying a damaged vehicle. First, ask the following questions about the vehicle's accident history:

- Has it ever been in an accident?
- If so, what was the damage and who fixed it?

- Is the auto body shop that repaired the vehicle registered with the provincial government? Is there any warranty outstanding? Can I have a copy of the work order?
- Has the vehicle's certificate of title been labelled "salvage"? ("Salvage" means that an expert has determined that the cost to properly repair the vehicle is more than its value. This usually happens after the vehicle has been in a serious accident.)

If it has been in an accident, you should either walk away from the sale or have the vehicle checked by a qualified auto body expert. Remember, not all "salvage" vehicles are bad—properly repaired ones can be a safe and sound investment if the price is low enough.

What to look for

1. If the vehicle has been repainted recently, check the quality of the job by inspecting the engine and trunk compartments and the inside door panels. Do it on a clear day so that you'll see any waves in the paint.
2. Check the paint—do all of the vehicle's panels match?
3. Inspect the paint for tiny bubbles. They may identify a poor priming job or premature rust.
4. Is there paint overspray or primer in the door jambs, wheelwells, or engine compartment? These are signs that the vehicle has had body repairs.
5. Check the gaps between body panels—are they equal? Unequal gaps may indicate improper panel alignment or a bent frame.
6. Do the doors, hood, and rear hatch open and shut properly?
7. Have the bumpers been damaged or recently repaired? Check the bumper support struts for corrosion damage.
8. Test the shock absorbers by pushing hard on a corner of the vehicle. If it bounces around like a ship at sea, the shocks need replacing.
9. Look for signs of premature rust or displacement from a collision on the muffler and exhaust pipe.
10. Make sure there's a readily accessible spare tire as well as a jack and tools for changing a flat. Also look for premature rusting in the side wheelwells and for water in the rear hatch channel.
11. Look at how the vehicle sits. If one side or end is higher than the other, it could mean that the suspension is defective.
12. Ask the seller to turn on the headlights (low and high beams), turn signals, parking lights, and emergency blinking lights and to blow the horn. From the rear, check that the brake lights, backup lights, turn indicators, tail lights, and licence plate light all work.

Interior Check

The number of kilometres on the odometer isn't as important as how well the vehicle was driven and maintained. Still, high-mileage vehicles depreciate rapidly because most people consider them to be risky buys. Calculate 20,000 kilometres per year as average and then subtract about $200 for each additional 10,000 kilometres above this average from your offer. Be suspicious of the odometer reading. Confirm it by checking the vehicle's maintenance records.

The condition of the interior will often give you an idea of how the vehicle was used and maintained. For example, sagging rear seats plus a front passenger seat in pristine condition indicate that your minivan may have been used as a minibus. Delivery vans will have the paint on the driver's doorsill rubbed down to the metal, while the passenger doorsill will look like new.

What to look for

1. Watch for excessive wear of the seats, dash, accelerator, brake pedal, armrests, and roof lining.
2. Check the dash and roof lining for radio or cellular phone mounting holes (as used in police cruisers, taxis, and delivery vans). Is the radio tuned to local stations?
3. Turn the steering wheel: Listen for unusual noises and watch for excessive play (more than 2.5 cm/1 in.).
4. Test the emergency brake with the vehicle parked on a hill.
5. Inspect the seat belts. Is the webbing in good condition? Do the belts retract easily?
6. Make sure that door latches and locks are in good working order. If rear doors have no handles or locks, or if they've just been installed, your minivan may have been used to transport prisoners.
7. Can the seats be moved into all the positions intended by the manufacturer? Look under them to make sure that the runners are functioning as they should.
8. Can head supports be adjusted easily?
9. Peel back the rugs and check the metal floor for signs of rust or dampness.

Road Test

1. Start the vehicle and listen for unusual noises. Shift automatics into Park and manuals into Neutral with the handbrake engaged. Open the hood to check for fluid leaks. Do this test with the engine running and then repeat it 10 minutes after the engine has been shut down following the completion of the test-drive.
2. With the motor running, check out all dashboard controls: windshield wipers, heater and defroster, and radio.
3. If the engine stalls or races at idle, a simple adjustment may fix the trouble. But loud clanks or low oil pressure could mean potentially expensive repairs.
4. Check all ventilation systems. Do the rear side windows roll down? Are there excessive air leaks around the door handles?
5. While in Neutral, push down on the accelerator abruptly. Black exhaust smoke may require only a minor engine adjustment; blue smoke may signal major engine repairs.

6. Shift an automatic into Drive with the motor still idling. The vehicle should creep forward slowly without stalling or speeding. Listen for unusual noises when the transmission is engaged. Manual transmissions should engage as soon as the clutch is released. Slipping or stalling could require a new clutch. While driving, make absolutely sure that a four-wheel drive can be engaged without unusual noises or hesitation.

7. Shift an automatic transmission into Drive. While the motor is idling, apply the emergency brake. If the motor isn't racing and the brake is in good condition, the vehicle should stop.

8. Accelerate to 50 km/h while slowly moving through all the gears. Listen for transmission noises. Step lightly on the brakes. The response should be immediate and equal for all wheels.

9. In a deserted parking lot, test the vehicle's steering and suspension by driving in figure eights at low speeds.

10. Make sure the road is clear of traffic and pedestrians. While driving at 30 km/h, take both hands off the steering wheel to see whether the vehicle veers from one side to the other. If it does, the alignment or suspension could be defective, or the vehicle could have been in an accident.

11. Test the suspension by driving over some rough terrain.

12. Stop at the foot of a small hill and then see if the vehicle can climb it without difficulty.

13. On an expressway, it should take no longer than 20 seconds for most cars and minivans to accelerate from a standing start to 100 km/h.

14. Drive through a tunnel with the windows open. Try to detect any unusual motor, exhaust, or suspension sounds.

15. After the test-drive, verify the performance of the automatic transmission by shifting from Drive to Neutral to Reverse. Listen for clunking sounds during transmission engagement.

Many of these tests will undoubtedly turn up some defects, which may be major or minor (even new vehicles have an average of a half-dozen major and minor defects). Ask an independent mechanic for an estimate, and try to convince the seller to pay part of the repair bill if you buy the vehicle. Keep in mind that many 3- to 5-year-old vehicles with 60,000–100,000 km on their odometers run the risk of having an engine timing belt or timing chain failure that can cause several thousand dollars' worth of repairs. If the timing belt or chain hasn't been replaced, plan to do it and deduct about $300 from the purchase price for the repair.

It's important to eliminate as many duds as possible through your own cursory check, since you'll later invest two hours and about $100 for a thorough mechanical inspection of your choice. Garages approved by the Automobile Protection Association (APA) or members of the Canadian Automobile Association (CAA) usually do a good job. CAA inspections run from $100 to $150 for non-members. Remember, if you get a bum steer from an independent testing agency, you can get the inspection fee refunded and hold the garage responsible for your subsequent repairs and consequential damages, like towing, missed work, or a ruined vacation.

Appendix IV

LEGAL TOOLS: FORD AND GM ENGINE GASKETS

The following recent Ford small claims court judgment and GM class action lawsuit contain information that can be quite helpful in framing your claim in a letter to an auto-maker's legal affairs department. Additionally, you may wish to use the jurisprudence and cited legal principles to argue your own case in court or to get a settlement without going to court.

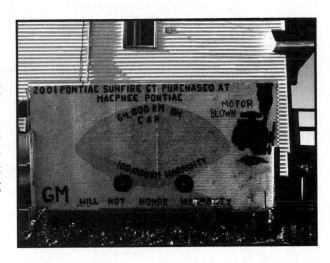

Ford Engine Head Gasket Judgment

Chams v. Ford Motor Company of Canada, Limited, and Courtesy Ford Lincoln Sales, Limited

[2004] O.J. No. 5868 Court File No. 103/04
Ontario Superior Court of Justice; Small Claims Court; London, Ontario
J.D. Searle Deputy J.
Heard: November 16, 2004
Judgment: November 22, 2004

REASONS FOR JUDGMENT

1 J.D. SEARLE DEPUTY J.:—The defendant Ford Motor Company of Canada, Limited, hereinafter referred to as "Ford" is a corporation based in Oakville, Ontario and is a manufacturer of motor vehicles. The defendant Courtesy Ford Lincoln Sales Limited, hereinafter referred to as "Courtesy" is a corporation which carries on the business of a Ford dealer in the city of London in the county of Middlesex.

2 Samir Chams resides in the city of London. In 1997 he purchased from Courtesy a low kilometerage 1995 Ford Windstar van with a 3.8 liter engine. By 1998 at the latest Ford was aware the head gaskets of such engines had a defect which could destroy the engine. In 2000 it offered to the plaintiff and other owners an "additional warranty" for this defect but limited the warranty to seven years from the date the vehicle first went into service or 160,000 kilometers, whichever came first. Upon receiving notice of the additional warranty in 2000 the plaintiff took his van to Courtesy but no problems were manifest. For the plaintiff the original warranty had expired by passage of time. The additional warranty expired on March 08, 2002 by passage of time.

3 On January 11, 2004, some 22 months after the additional warranty expired, the plaintiff's engine overheated and was destroyed within a matter of minutes. The van had only 80,000 kilometers on the odometer. In due course the engine was replaced at a cost of over $4,000.00 paid by the plaintiff. As the court understands the plaintiff's case he is suing outside the expired warranty. Against Ford he alleges manufacturing defect. Against Courtesy he alleges negligence in 2000 in not replacing the defective head gasket to avoid possible engine destruction or at least telling him that was an option at his own expense. He also invokes manufacturer's warranty.

4 Ford contends it has no responsibility beyond its warranty and the destruction of the engine was from a cause or causes other than the head gasket. The court finds the highly probable cause of destruction of the engine was failure of the head gasket. The allegation of alternate causes is speculation not supported by the evidence. Pure economic loss does not apply because there was damage to property. See also *Winnipeg Condominium Corporation No. 36 v. Bird Construction Co. Ltd* [1995] 1 S.C.R. 85.

5 Courtesy contends it was not negligent: the additional warranty issued by Ford only applied to cases with manifest problems and to merely replace a head gasket at a cost to the customer of $1,200.00 to $1,400.00 in the absence of manifest problems did not make economic sense.

6 In the Nova Scotia case of *Ford v. Kenney* (2003, unreported) Boudreau J. of the Nova Scotia Supreme Court was hearing an appeal from a decision of the Small Claims Court Adjudicator. At page 5 of the oral reasons His Lordship said:

> Ford Motor Company has the right to decide which vehicles they are going to provide repairs to and which vehicles they are not. That doesn't mean that they couldn't be successfully challenged by that on negligent—proper negligent manufacturing evidence, but there was not that evidence in this case.

7 *Campbell v. Ford* is a judgment of the Nova Scotia Small Claims Court rendered on January 31, 2002 and not reported. The plaintiff's 1995 Ford Windstar van was showing signs of head gasket problems and the head gasket was replaced at 168,000 [km] at the $1,600.00 expense of the plaintiff. At 207,000 kilometers the engine was destroyed. The engine was rebuilt or replaced at a much greater cost. In both instances the vehicle was beyond the kilometerage caps of both the original and additional warranties.

8 The Adjudicator dismissed the replacement of the head gasket as pure economic loss but said of the engine rebuilding or replacement:

> It is certainly arguable that if the head gasket failed and it was due to negligence of the designer/manufacturer and that failure in turn caused physical damage to the property of the Claimant, consequential damage to the engine itself, that may well be a recoverable head of damage and the basis for an action in negligence.

The Adjudicator found there was insufficient admissible and reliable evidence to establish a causal connection between the gasket failure sought to be corrected at 168,000 kilometers and the destruction of the engine at 207,000 kilometers. The important point is that the Adjudicator was discussing the potential liability of Ford quite apart from its original or additional warranties.

9 *Beshara v. Barry* is an Ontario Small Claims Court judgment of Tierney J. with reasons released a few days before trial in the case at bar and not yet reported. The unrepresented plaintiff sued the president of Ford for the estimated cost of replacing an engine similar to the one in the case at bar. The action was dismissed because the failure occurred after the expiry of Ford's original and additional warranties and the negligence alleged was that of the repairer and not Ford. The repairer was not a party.

10 The foregoing cases were furnished to the court by the agent for Ford. In each case involving Ford that company was successful. The court did additional research.

11 In *Kozoriz v. Chrysler Canada Ltd.* [1992] O.J. No. 3937 the problem was a transaxle seal which failed at 16,000 kilometers. Thereafter there was frequent leaking and repair work. As the van neared the 80,000 kilometer warranty expiry the 80,000 kilometer inspection was done at a Chrysler dealership and no problem was found with the trans-axle seal or the transmission. A few days later in Iowa there was an expensive failure of these apparently related parts. Tierney J. of the Ontario Small Claims Court found both parts failed due to a nearly continuous leak of the seal since 16,000 kilometers.

12 Chrysler pleaded the failure occurred after the expiry of the 80,000 kilometer warranty. In part the warranty described itself as "[a] guarantee of the quality and engineering excellence…". Judge Tierney found that to be equivalent to a warranty that the product was free of defect. He found the axle seal was defective almost immediately and failed after only 16,000 kilometers and the defect led to the transmission damage after the expiry of the warranty. At page 3:

> Those damages occurred as a direct result of the manufacturer's breach of warranty. For that reason, it is my view that the amounts are recoverable as damages for breach of contract, even though the actual breakdown occurred after the warranty period had expired.

13 A similar case is *Shields v. General Motors of Canada Ltd.* [1997] O.J. No. 5434 (Ont. Sm. C.C.). A 1991 Pontiac with a three year warranty began losing an extensive amount of its paint in 1995. Zochodne, D.J. found the problem was a failure to ensure proper bonding when the vehicle was being painted originally. At page 6:

> The defect, which I have found, that is the lack of primer surfacer, occurred at the time the vehicle was manufactured. At that point, however, the defect was latent. The defect became patent when the paint began to bubble, flake and then peel off the vehicle.

That being the case His Honour found the warranty must respond to the loss. Judgment was in favour of the plaintiff.

14 *Schaffler v. Ford Motor Co. of Canada and Embrum Ford Sales Ltd.* [2003] O.J. No. 3165 (Ont. Sm. C.C.) is yet another Ford Windstar case involving an engine identical to the one involved in the case at bar. On March 02 of 2000, August 06 of 2001 and October 16 of 2001 the plaintiff took the van to Embrum with problems involving coolant levels, one of the indicia of head gasket failure. On those dates the respective kilometerages were 59,850, 84,000 and 89,000. The additional warranty expired by passage of time on August 07, 2002. Two months later there was serious damage to the engine as a result of head gasket failure.

15 Deputy Judge Langlois found the dealer liable for failure to diagnose the head gasket problem and Ford liable on its additional warranty which had been invoked by the plaintiff within the additional warranty period although the major damage occurred after expiry of the warranty.

16 It is distressing to note that although Barry Holmes was able in the case at bar to produce cases from both Ontario and Nova Scotia when Ford was successful he produced none where Ford was not successful. That includes the *Schaffler* case of one year ago and in which he was Ford's representative. In the case at bar he was Ford's agent and only witness.

17 In the case at bar the plaintiff received notice in 2000 from Ford of a potential problem with the head gasket in his van. His response was to take the van to Courtesy and enquire what should he done about it. Although they are only estimates the van was 5.5 years from the original warranty start date and had traveled 49,000 kilometers. Courtesy took in the van and gave the plaintiff and his family a ride home. About one half hour later Courtesy called and said the van was ready to be picked up. There was no paperwork introduced at trial evidencing this occurrence and it is probable none exists. William Taylor was the service manager and a helpful and credible witness at trial. He was not surprised at the absence of paperwork and said by way of summary that "[w]e do not charge for conversation."

18 It is probable that what happened is this: the plaintiff took his van to Courtesy, did not have the Ford notice with him, told Courtesy he had received a notice about head gaskets, asked what should he done and got a ride home. Courtesy was readily able to identify the van by its vehicle identification number and pull up its file on the vehicle, including at least references to technical service bulletins and notices affecting the plaintiff's vehicle and others in its class.

19 Having received no report from the plaintiff nor made any observations themselves the Courtesy service people would not be aware of any of the mostly gross symptoms Ford said could trigger warranty work on the head gasket. According to Mr. Taylor Courtesy had done "a lot" of gasket-related work under the warranty program in 1999 and 2000. In the absence of reports or observations of at least one of the gross symptoms Courtesy would inspect the head gasket only if the customer paid. The court finds the absence of paperwork on this visit by the plaintiff makes it a near certainty there was no gasket inspection.

20 One of the four symptoms listed in the Ford notice received by the plaintiff in 2000 was "constant loss of coolant" and another was flashing of the "low coolant" sensor light. Neither the plaintiff nor his wife testified to the existence of either of these symptoms and Courtesy does not note, except perhaps informally on the back of a work order, whether coolant has been "topped up." The plaintiff's vehicle was well maintained and in otherwise good condition throughout with much of the servicing done at Courtesy and some oil changes at a large department store if Mrs. Chams was shopping there.

21 Based on what Courtesy knew at the time of this visit Mr. Taylor would not recommend changing the head gasket for two reasons: the cost would be $1,200.00 to $1,400.00 to head off a problem which was only potential and there is a risk of nonpayment and alienation if the work is done and the customer starts contending it is warranty work. The mechanic who owns and operates the independent vehicle repair

shop which eventually replaced the plaintiff's engine said that due to the problems which can arise from it he will not permit his shop to change a head gasket for the sole purpose of changing the head gasket.

22 Nothing more relevant to an engine problem happened until Sunday, January 11, 2004. The Chams family fueled the van and moved it a short distance to a car wash. While entering the wash the plaintiff noticed the engine temperature digital readout was climbing. It maximized after the wash when they were back on the street. Mr. Chams pulled into the next "Petro" or "petrol" station and looked under the hood but saw nothing awry. He drove about two blocks to his house where the engine would not restart.

23 He asked a friend knowledgeable about motor vehicles to come over. That person observed coolant coming from the exhaust and coolant mixed with oil under the hood. The van was towed to Courtesy that day or early the next.

24 The diagnosis was "coolant in cylinders, no start, no heat, intermittent hydraulic lock. No start due to coolant leak inside engine. Suspect head cracked." The recommendation was replacement of the engine with a rebuilt engine. The kilometerage was noted to be 80,671. The charge for the inspection was $79.00 plus tax, later voluntarily waived by Mr. Taylor in recognition of several members of the Chams family being good customers and, no doubt, because of the arising of a warranty issue. Further, according to Mr. Chams he had urged a friend with a similar vehicle to his to go to the dealer in 2000 and the result was the replacement of the head gasket.

25 Courtesy advised Mr. and Mrs. Chams the problem was not covered by warranty. The occurrence was 22 months after the expiry of the additional warranty. Mr. and Mrs. Chams spent time unsuccessfully trying to get Ford and Courtesy to take responsibility for the problem. Either directly or indirectly the Chams had the van towed to Automotive Solutions. That is a London vehicle repair shop owned and operated by Mohamed Omar who employs two class "A" automotive mechanics in the shop and who himself is in the final stage of his apprenticeship. Mr. Omar testified.

26 The van was stored at Automotive Solutions for about three months until a rebuilt engine and ancillary equipment was purchased by Mr. Chams and installed by Automotive Solutions on and about May 01.

27 When he studied the engine of the Chams van, seemingly in the company of one of his licensed mechanics, Mr. Omar observed the engine appeared not to have been apart before. The head gasket was found to [be] "blown." Coolant was mixed with oil. The coolant had leaked into the inner part of the engine through the No. 1 cylinder where it could mix with the oil. Oil mixing with coolant can cause the head gasket to "blow." One purpose of the head gasket is to prevent coolant getting into the interior of the engine.

28 In the opinion of Mr. Omar if the head gasket failed in 2000 the vehicle could not be driven until 2004. Head gaskets in most cars do not fail by 80,000 kilometers. He

was aware the 3.8 liter Ford engine had a head gasket problem and he has worked on "a few" with such a problem. He is not "100% sure" of the reason for the failure of the Chams engine.

29 William Taylor is the Courtesy service manager. Courtesy did "a lot" of head gasket related repairs to 3.8 liter engines in 1999 and 2000. He understands the problem is a head gasket wrongly configured or "too weak." He has not seen the Chams engine but testified that theoretically the damage could be caused by a defective head gasket, a cracked head or the timing cover.

30 Barry Holmes was Ford's agent and only witness. He is a licensed mechanic and is employed by Ford in its product liability department. His direct evidence was largely on the Ford warranty and there was little or no evidence by him on defect or otherwise the cause of the major engine damage. On cross examination he said he did not know the failure rate of the head gaskets in the affected 3.8 liter engines. On further examination he acknowledged it was possibly 85% but he was not sure and had not brought that information to court with him. The court does not accept that denial of knowledge. The court notes its comments above with respect to cherry picking of cases. Mr. Holmes is a Ford product liability employee. The figure of 85% figured in another case involving a Ford 3.8 liter engine. The case at bar is at least the third nearly identical case in which Mr. Holmes has been noted in the reasons for judgment as Ford's agent or witness or both. The court finds that Ford knows it has had a failure rate of at least 85% in this head gasket which is a component which can quickly destroy an engine if it fails. That makes it nearly a certainty that unless the offending gasket is replaced in time the engine will be destroyed by its failure.

31 As to warranty this court finds, as was found in the *Shields* case, (supra), the defect was in existence and known to the giver of the warranty not only during the period of the additional warranty but also during the period of the original warranty. Ford is therefore liable on its warranty.

32 As to negligence there can be no doubt the gasket has had a design or manufacturing defect which has existed since the time of design or manufacture. It is that defect which caused the destruction of the plaintiff's engine and made its replacement necessary.

33 Ford's warranty attempts to limit its liability to what it grants in the warranty. It is ancient law that one who attempts to limit his liability by, for example, excluding common law remedies, must clearly bring that limitation to the attention of the person who might lose those remedies. The evidence in this case is clear the buyer of even a new car does not get a warranty booklet until after purchasing the car although he "would be" told the highlights sooner.

34 Courtesy was not negligent nor in breach of any other obligation to the plaintiff. Ford would not entertain repairs under either of its warranties unless certain "symptoms" had become manifest before the work was done. The court has no doubt Mr. Chams would have declined if Courtesy had asked if he would pay $1,200.00 to

$1,400.00 to replace the head gasket in 2000 when his vehicle was manifesting no problem. The action is therefore dismissed against Courtesy with costs of $375.00 payable by Ford. This court will leave the fancy dancing of Bullock orders and the like to the higher courts.

35 At trial the focus was understandably on liability with damages consigned to the periphery. The rebuilt engine and ancillary parts were obtained from a NAPA dealer. The net NAPA bill is $2,375.67 but to that must be added a down payment of $250.00 and from it must be deducted a core deposit of $300.00. The old core is still available for credit. The radiator and water pump are valid expenses in that they are essential to obtaining a NAPA warranty on the rebuilt engine.

36 One legitimate Automotive Solutions bill is for $776.25 for towing and storage. The other is for $1,383.45 for labour, fluids, minor parts and an alternator. Storage is acceptable, particularly when one notes the absence of a substitute vehicle claim or loss of use. The alternator could not be proved as related to the engine failure and so $126.50 will be deducted.

37 Damages are assessed at $4,358.87 and there will be judgment in that amount against Ford. That sum will attract interest pursuant to the provisions of the *Courts of Justice Act* from January 12, 2004. The Clerk is requested to make that calculation.

38 As to costs a sealed document has now been opened and found to be an October 18, 2004 offer by Ford to settle by waiving allowable costs which stood at $25.00 or $75.00 at the time of the offer.

39 The trial was scheduled for two days but was completed in one. Mr. Ferguson was helpful to the court, particularly by creating document briefs for all parties, thus collecting dozens of potential exhibits into a handful. The court agrees with Mr. Ferguson's contention that many of the [I]nternet printouts collected by or on behalf of the plaintiff and included in one of the briefs were nevertheless inadmissible. Mr. Dupuis as agent for the plaintiff put in his client's case in a way that was economical in terms of trial time but nevertheless thorough and it underscores the need for reform of the law which does not currently permit the court to award a counsel fee with respect to agents even in substantial cases. The plaintiff shall have costs fixed at $200.00 against Ford.

General Motors Intake Manifold Gasket Class Action

The Canadian class action lawsuit cited below was launched on April 24, 2006, and seeks $1.2 billion (CDN) in damages to compensate owners of 1996–2004 GM vehicles with defective engine intake manifold gaskets.

The lawyers have carefully framed the legal arguments and material facts to give their clients the best chance of winning this suit. Look at the lawsuit's text to pick out those paragraphs that are relevant to your claim. Again, you are free to join this class action (see *www.classproceedings.ca*), or you could negotiate your own settlement with GM using the material facts and legal principles contained in this petition.

06-CV-310082 PD1
Court File No.

ONTARIO
SUPERIOR COURT OF JUSTICE

BETWEEN:

KENNETH DAVID STEWART

Plaintiff

- and -

GENERAL MOTORS OF CANADA LIMITED
and GENERAL MOTORS CORPORATION

Defendants

Proceedings commenced pursuant to the *Class Proceedings Act, 1992*, S.O. 1992, c. 6.

STATEMENT OF CLAIM

DUTIES OF CARE OWED BY THE DEFENDANTS TO THE PLAINTIFF AND THE CLASS (AS DEFINED BELOW)

11. The plaintiff pleads that the defendants owed to the plaintiff and the Class the following duties of care to avoid the acts and omissions described in paragraph 11 and more generally:

(a) to ensure that the IMG was designed, marketed, tested, and/or manufactured safely, properly and in a good and workmanlike manner so that it would not degrade prematurely;

(b) to warn the plaintiff and the Class of the IMG defect once it became aware (or through reasonable due diligence could have become aware) of its existence;

(c) to remedy the IMG defect upon discovering it through the recall and repair of the Class vehicles.

NEGLIGENCE OF THE DEFENDANTS

12. The defendants negligently designed, marketed, tested and manufactured the Class Vehicles. The particulars include the following:

(a) the IMG was designed in a manner which, under normal conditions, usage and applications causes it to degrade and fail, which in turn causes the engine to overheat and fail;

(b) the IMG was manufactured in a manner which, under normal conditions, usage and applications would overheat and fail;

(c) the IMG was not properly or adequately tested to avoid the IMG defect;

(d) the Class Vehicles were marketed in such a manner as not to reveal the IMG defect and its consequences;

(e) the Class Vehicles failed to perform at their optimal level because of premature degradation and the defendants' failure to rectify the IMG defect;

(f) the IMG design was not altered to avoid premature degradation;

(g) the IMG design was not changed promptly once the defendants knew the IMG was subject to premature degradation;

(h) inadequate testing was carried out to ensure a proper design and to ensure proper and prompt modifications to the IMG to eliminate the foreseeable risks;

(i) the defendants consciously accepted the risk of the IMG defect;

(j) the defendants failed to attach a warning or warning label to the IMG or the owners' manuals alerting users and mechanics to the risk of the premature failure;

(k) the defendants failed to develop any appropriate method for testing the IMG before they were manufactured, assembled, distributed and sold;

(l) the defendants failed to establish any adequate procedures to educate their distributors, sales and service representatives or ultimate users;

(m) the defendants failed to establish any adequate procedure to ensure that possible design defects in the IMG were discovered and users' complaints were transmitted from them to the customers, sales representatives or distributors;

(n) the defendants failed to establish any or any adequate procedure for evaluating customers' complaints with respect to the IMG;

(o) the defendants failed to recall and repair or to ensure the repair of Class Vehicles that Class members gave to the defendants or the defendants' agents for servicing;

(p) the defendants failed to accurately, candidly, promptly and truthfully disclose the defective nature of the IMG;

(q) the defendants failed to identify, implement and verify that procedures were in place to address design problems, complaint handling or timely notification of IMG failures or complaints;

(r) the defendants failed to implement adequate performance specifications for the IMG;

(s) the defendants failed to conduct in-process and finished device testing to ensure performance specifications for the IMG were met;

(t) the defendants failed to adequately define or control written manufacturing specifications, processes, procedures and controls for the IMG;

(u) the defendants failed to conform with good manufacturing and distribution practices;

(v) the defendants failed to introduce proper quality assurance programs to identify, recommend or provide adequate solutions for the IMG defect;

(w) the defendants failed to change their design, manufacturing and assembly process with respect to the IMG in a reasonable and timely manner;

(x) the defendants hired incompetent personnel and appointed incompetent officers and directors;

(y) the defendants failed to properly supervise their employees, their subsidiaries and associated and affiliated corporations;

(z) the defendants failed to advise the plaintiff and the Class that the IMG was defective and needed to be replaced;

(aa) the defendants knew or ought to have known of the abnormal wear and tear and risk of damage to vehicles if the IMG was not replaced;

(bb) the defendants failed to conduct adequate testing and research regarding the risk of using the IMG;

(cc) the defendants failed to engage in adequate pre-market and production testing of the vehicles in respect of the IMG;

(dd) the defendants continued to fail to fulfill their ongoing obligations to fully disclose the results of their testing and research regarding the damage to GM vehicles arising from the IMG; and

(ee) the defendants used and recommended the use of coolants which were too abrasive having regard to the design and manufacture of the IMG.

13. By virtue of the acts and omissions described above, the defendants were negligent and caused damage to the plaintiff and the Class.

14. The plaintiff pleads that by virtue of the acts and omissions described above, the defendants are liable in damages to him and to the Class members and that each defendant is responsible for the acts and omissions of the other defendants for the following reasons:

(a) each was the agent of the other;

(b) each companies' business was operated so that it was inextricably interwoven with the business of the other as set out above;

(c) each company entered into a common advertising and business plan to distribute and sell GM motor vehicles containing the IMG;

(d) each defendant owed a duty of care to the other and to each Class member by virtue of the common business plan to manufacture, distribute, market, test and sell GM motor vehicles with the IMG defect;

(e) the defendants intended that their businesses be run as one global business organization.

FAILURE TO DISCLOSE AND RECALL

15. The defendants have known about the IMG defect for years but have failed to take any adequate remedial steps. In 2001, in an internal service bulletin, the defendants wrote:

"Some owners may comment on excessive engine coolant consumption, or an engine coolant leak near or under the throttle body area of the upper intake manifold."

"Upper intake manifold composite material may degrade...and could result in an internal or external coolant leak."

16. Following the manufacture of the Class Vehicles, the defendants were aware that the Class vehicles were experiencing engine failure during operation due to the IMG defect and that such engine failures were occurring with unreasonable

frequency and were resulting in considerable expense to owners and lessees of said motor vehicles.

17. From 1995 through to the present, the defendants concealed the nature and scope of the IMG defect from the members of the Class and regulatory bodies in the United States and Canada. Particulars of this concealment include the fact that where any information was provided to such authorities or to the public generally, such information was incomplete or misleading in that it sought to attribute any problems to issues other than the IMG defect.

18. The defendants had a duty to recall the Class Vehicles and rectify the IMG defect. As pleaded above, the defendants became aware following the manufacture of the Class Vehicles of the existence of the IMG defect and its dangers and in breach of said duty failed to recall the Class Vehicles to correct the IMG defect.

STATUTORY REMEDIES

19. As used below "Representation" means the defendants' failure to state any or all of the following material facts:

(a) the IMG was not free of defects;
(b) the IMG was not fit for the purpose intended;
(c) the IMG was designed in a manner which under normal conditions, usage and applications would cause it to degrade prematurely; or
(d) the IMG was manufactured in a manner which under normal conditions, usage and applications would cause it to degrade prematurely.

20. The plaintiff states that the Representation deceived or tended to deceive the plaintiff and the Class and that the Representation constituted an unfair practice which induced the plaintiff and the Class to purchase the Class Vehicles as a result of which they are entitled to damages pursuant to the *Business Practices Act* (Ontario and its equivalent in other provinces).

21. The plaintiff and each other Class member relied on the Representation.

22. The reliance upon the Representation by the plaintiff and every other Class member is established by his/her purchase and/or use of the Class Vehicles. Had the plaintiff and each Class member known that the Representation was false and misleading he/she would not have purchased and/or used the Class Vehicle.

23. The defendants made the Representation to the public and in so doing breached s. 52 of the *Competition Act* because the Representation:

(a) was made for the purpose of promoting the business interest of the defendants;
(b) was made to the public;
(c) was false and misleading in a material respect; and
(d) stated a level of performance of the IMG that was not based on adequate and proper testing.

24. The plaintiff and every other Class member relied upon the Representation by buying or using the Class vehicles and suffered damages and loss.

25. Pursuant to s. 36 of the *Competition Act* the defendants are liable to pay the damages which resulted from the breach of s. 52.

26. Pursuant to s. 36 of the *Competition Act* the plaintiff and the other Class members are entitled to recover their full costs of investigation and substantial indemnity costs paid in accordance with the Act.

27. The plaintiff and the other Class members are also entitled to recover, as damages or costs, in accordance with the Act the costs of administering the plan to distribute the recovery in this action and the costs to determine the damages of each Class member, which administration costs probably will exceed $5,000,000.00.

28. The damages suffered by the plaintiff and members of the Class as a result of the breach of the *Business Practices Act* and *Competition Act* are those damages claimed in paragraph 1 above.

WAIVER OF TORT AND UNJUST ENRICHMENT

29. The plaintiff and Class plead the doctrine of waiver of tort and, due to the negligence and failure to warn of the defendants, is entitled to a restitutionary award of the benefits which accrued to the defendants as a result of their negligence and/or failure to warn.

30. The benefits which accrued to the defendants as a result of their negligence and/or failure to warn include:

(a) the saving of costs of recalling the Class Vehicles;
(b) the saving of costs of replacing the IMG in the Class Vehicles with a new IMG;
(c) the saving of costs of redesigning the IMG in the Class Vehicles to overcome the IMG defect; and
(d) revenues from the sale of replacement IMGs or the components thereof.

31. The benefits which accrued to the defendants as a result of their negligence and/or failure to warn were unjust in the circumstances and there is no juristic reason for them.

DAMAGES

32. In the alternative, as a result of the breach of the failure to warn, negligence, breach of statutory duties and failure to disclose and recall as pleaded above, the plaintiff and members of the Class have suffered loss and damage and have incurred damages, the particulars of which include:

(a) repair expenses in attempts to identify and/or rectify the IMG defect;
(b) resultant damage to persons or property other than the IMG or the Class vehicles;

(c) overpayment for Class vehicles, which contained a latent hazardous defect;

(d) diminution in the value of the Class Vehicles of the members of the Class and,

(e) future costs of repair of the TFI defects;

(f) damages for having been put at risk.

PUNITIVE, EXEMPLARY AND AGGRAVATED DAMAGES

33. The conduct of the defendants in deliberating concealing the IMG defect and deliberately exposing the Class members to considerable expense and inconvenience is highhanded and demonstrates an indifference to the consumers of their products such that it offends the moral standards of the community and warrants the condemnation of the court.

LEGISLATION

34. In addition to the *Competition Act* and the *Business Practices Act,* the plaintiff pleads and relies upon the *Class Proceedings Act* and the *Negligence Act* (and equivalent in every province).

REPRESENTATIVE PLAINTIFF

35. Stewart is the owner of a 1997 Pontiac Trans Sport and a 2002 Pontiac Montana in which the IMG has been subject to the IMG defect. Stewart has suffered damages as a result of the IMG defect. The damages include out-of-pocket expenses, repair and replacement costs and diminution of vehicle value.

36. The plaintiff states that this claim may be served, without a court order, on GM USA outside Ontario on the basis that:

(a) the damage was sustained in Ontario (Ontario Rule 17.02(h);

(b) GM USA is a necessary and/or proper party to a proceeding properly brought against GM Canada (Ontario Rule 17.2(o));

(c) the tort was committed in Ontario (Ontario Rule 17.02(g))

(d) GM USA carries on business in Ontario (Ontario Rule 17.02(p));

(e) the claim is authorized by statute, the *Competition Act* and the *Business Practices Act* (Ontario Rule 17.02(n)).

37. The plaintiff proposes that this action be tried at the City of Toronto, in the Province of Ontario.

APRIL 24, 2006